SELLING

Random House
Business Division New York

SELLING
PERSONALITY
PERSUASION
STRATEGY

Second Edition

Walter Gorman

Revised by
Richard Wendel

Second Edition

987654321

Library of Congress Cataloging in Publication Data

Gorman, Walter (Walter P.)
  Selling: personality, persuasion, strategy.

  Includes index.
  1. Selling. I. Wendel, Richard. II. Title.
HF5438.25.G67 1983   658.8′5   82-18592
Manufactured in the United States of America

ISBN 0-394-33003-X

PERMISSIONS ACKNOWLEDGMENTS

Fig. 10.3 Reprinted with permission from Jan. 16, 1978 issue of *Advertising Age.* Copyright 1978 by Crain Communications, Inc.

Fig. 11.2 Reprinted by permission from Sales & Marketing Management magazine. Copyright 1977.

Fig. 11.3A Reprinted by permission of the Xerox Corporation.

Fig. 11.3B Courtesy AT&T Long Lines

Fig. 11.5 Courtesy of the NCR Corporation.

Fig. 14.1 Reprinted by permission from Sales & Marketing Management magazine. Copyright 1976.

Incident 14.2 Selected excerpts from THE GRAPES OF WRATH by John Steinbeck. Copyright 1939 by John Steinbeck. Copyright renewed 1967 by John Steinbeck. Reprinted by permission of Viking Penguin Inc.

Table 15.1 Reprinted by permission of the publisher, from *Sales Personnel Report,* 24th Edition, 1979/80, *Executive Compensation Service,* by AMACOM, a division of American Management Associations, Inc. All rights reserved.

Fig. 15.1 Courtesy of The Procter & Gamble Company.

Photos

1.1 NCR Corporation

1.2 Courtesy, Xerox Corporation

1.3 Courtesy, Sales & Marketing Management

(fig.) 2.3 © Ed Hof/The Picture Cube

2.1 ©Jerry Berndt/Stock, Boston

3.1 (a–d) © Leonard Speier 1982

4.1 Courtesy of William H. Baker

8.1 Alex Webb/Magnum

8.2 Dan Brinzac/Peter Arnold, Inc.

9.1 ©Bohdan Hrynewych/Stock, Boston

10.1 ©Ken Robert Buck/The Picture Cube

10.2 Courtesy, 3M Corporation

13.1 ©Laimute Druskis/Taurus Photos

13.2 ©Eric Kroll/Taurus Photos

17.1 Burt Glinn/Magnum

ADVISOR'S FOREWORD

This second edition of Walter Gorman's *Selling Personality Persuasion Strategy* continues the excellent tradition established in the first edition—to portray selling at the personal level as a vital marketing tool, which requires a high level of competence from trained marketing professionals. The great success of the first edition underscores the validity of this approach to personal selling. Unquestionably, the late Professor Walter Gorman made an outstanding contribution to the literature of personal selling and to higher education in the field.

The legacy of Professor Gorman has been carried forward superbly by Professor Richard Wendel who was asked by Random House to revise the Walter Gorman text for the second edition. Professor Wendel has done a skillful and careful job of preserving the basic thrust, ideas, and themes of Gorman's original work while at the same time refining and updating the material to reflect new developments affecting personal selling education. Professor Wendel deserves high praise for the fine job he did in performing this difficult task. The second edition of *Selling Personality Persuasion Strategy* continues its unbroken leadership position in meeting the challenges of higher education in personal selling.

As the advisor in marketing for Random House, I am most proud to be associated with this outstanding text.

Bert Rosenbloom
Drexel University

To the memory of Walter Gorman, whose life gave credence to the idea that true success can only be achieved through kindness.

Paul S. Donnelly
Executive Editor
Random House
Business Division

PREFACE

In the midst of this revision, its author, Walter Gorman, died. His death came as a great shock to all of us here at Random House and to all those who knew him either personally or through his works.

Dr. Richard Wendel's involvement in this edition began early in its development. As a reviewer of the first draft material, he demonstrated an uncanny appreciation for the intended direction and tone of the text. His insights and recommendations during this stage complemented Dr. Gorman's material significantly and we were inspired to call on Dr. Wendel to assist in an authorial capacity subsequent to Dr. Gorman's death. As an author, Richard Wendel brought fresh ideas and examples to the material and worked diligently to bring the book up to date without sacrificing any of the strengths of the first edition. The emphasis remains on the fact that success in personal selling depends on the total personality and not just a knowledge of standard selling techniques. Competition is tough in today's world and while a thorough understanding of tested selling methods is a significant part of the persuasive profile, much more is needed to build sales professionals capable of projecting favorable corporate images and influencing sophisticated buyers. Accordingly, many practitioners have incorporated personality-building elements into their instructional programs—elements such as success and attitude training, self-image building, transactional analysis, and nonverbal communication training. This text was written to harmonize techniques and strategies with personality development, so that sales students might move toward their full potential in selling. In the tradition of persuasion, the first chapter uses selling techniques to interest and motivate students. Chapter sixteen explains important procedures for finding and getting the "right" selling job. Techniques for developing learning, listening, creative, and memory skills are included to help the persuasive personality mature. Chapter seventeen's discussion of special selling situations should help students match their qualifications with market opportunities. A chapter on selling environments is offered, in keeping with the "total preparation" theme of the text. Part I focuses on personal development; Part II emphasizes tested techniques and strategies, climaxing in the face-to-face meeting of the sales representative and the prospect; and Part III centers on the long-range career considerations of sales aspirants.

Retained and updated in the second edition are the many examples, illustrations, figures, cartoons, and special listings. Richard Wendel gave special attention to the incidents; the best from the first edition were retained and new ones were added, bringing to the book a wider scope of special selling challenges. The review and application questions were completely revised by Ronald Vogel and Bruce Seaton, both of Florida International University, and have been broadened as well as fine tuned to be exceedingly clear and thought provoking.

An updated glossary is included for better understanding of selling terminology, and an index is furnished for easy subject reference.

The text was written to provide a new and more realistic direction for the academic preparation of students for selling careers, but it also expands traditional techniques to form a more complete presales foundation. If it points students in the right direction for a successful career in sales, then its purpose will have been accomplished.

ACKNOWLEDGMENTS

There are many people to thank for the development of the second edition. Susie Lee Gorman was instrumental in helping us to organize the initial revision material. Ronald H. Vogel and Bruce Seaton, both of Florida International University, did an excellent job revising the review and application questions, as well as completely rewriting the test questions in the instructor's manual. Their work reflects a great deal of writing skill and hard work, and we are very grateful for their contribution.

We are also very grateful to our reviewers for their perception, opinions and useful advice during the development of the second edition. They are:

Margorie J. Caballero, The University of Texas at Arlington
John Clancy, Middlesex County College
Benjamin J. Cutler, Bronx Community College
G. Dean Kortge, Central Michigan University
Thomas R. Lang, St. Petersburg Junior College
Reza Pars, Montclair State College
Donald T. Sedik, William Rainey Harper College
Thomas E. Schillar, Fort Steilacoom Community College
Ronald H. Vogel, Florida International University

Paul Donnelly, Executive Editor, College Department, Business Division, provided the guidance for keeping the revision on the proper course. Anna Marie Muskelly used her talent and experience as a project editor to successfully manage the project from manuscript to textbook. Linda Goldfarb did an equally competent job managing the production side of the project. Cas Psujek handled the production of the instructor's manual with the perfect combination of calm and competence.

Valerie Raymond, Developmental Editor
Random House Business Division

CONTENTS

PART 3

Insuring Future Opportunities 403

DETAILED CONTENTS

Channels with Customers ■ Give Customers Attention ■ Give Good Service ■ Help Buyers by Offering Advice ■ Handle Customer Complaints Fairly

Competence ■ Fairness ■ Positiveness ■ Supervisory Style

Planning Organizational Relationships ■ Territorial Estimates and Sales Forecasting ■ Product Planning ■ Territorial Planning ■ Setting Quotas ■ Budgeting

Determining the Quantity and Kind of Personnel Needed ■ Sources of Applicants ■ Screening Applicants ■ Selecting the Right Person for the Selling Job

Goals of the Training Program ■ Content of the Training Program ■ Methods and Personnel to Be Used ■ Evaluation of the Program

The Motivational Problem ■ Usable Theory in Motivating Sales Personnel ■ Motivational Style ■ Compensation Plans ■ Sales Contests ■ Sales Meetings and Conferences

SELLING

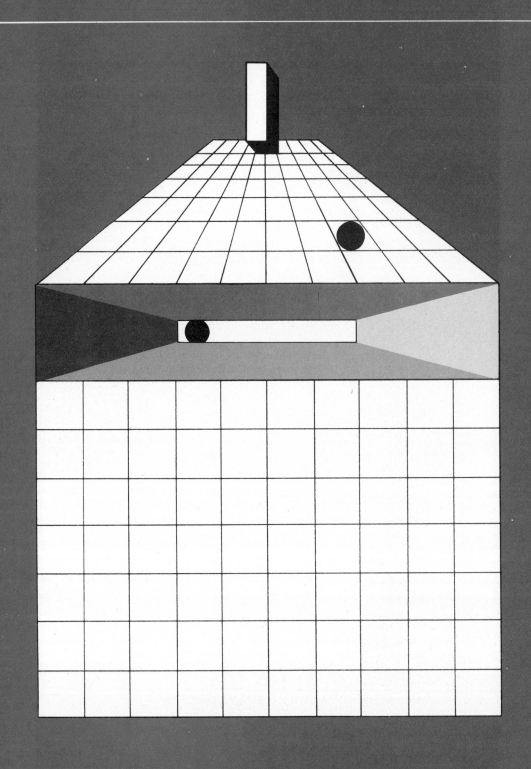

PERSONAL PREPARATION

The ability to persuade others is a vital attribute in an open-market economy, but to be persuasive requires more than just a knowledge of selling methods. The ability to communicate and a persuasive personality that projects a positive selling image are just as important. The chapters in this part are designed to help in evaluating career selling opportunities, exploring the informational and attitudinal requirements of sales success, building a persuasive personality, learning communications skills and theory, understanding buyers, and sharpening awareness of differences in selling environments. All these discussions focus on personal development for meeting persuasive opportunity.

Career Opportunities

A knowledge of persuasive techniques combined with a persuasive personality is power—especially in an open-market economy. Persuasive power can be used to:

- Sell products
- Win elections
- Free the accused
- Write more effective advertising
- Convert sinners
- Get ideas across
- Gain personal promotion
- Ease daily interpersonal conflicts

Ronald Reagan is a persuasive personality. For all his other virtues, Jimmy Carter is not. Billy Graham, Bob Hope, William Jennings Bryan, Golda Meir, Karl Marx, Patrick Henry, and Fidel Castro are other examples of persuasive personalities.

Reviewing the careers of outstanding persuasive personalities is in the best tradition of selling. It is through looking at their lives that the error of playwright Arthur Miller's scornful assertion that a salesman is the "distance between a smile and a shoeshine" can be seen (1). A persuasive personality is a major reason for success, whether that success is purely personal or is financial and seen by the world.

EXAMPLES OF SUCCESS THROUGH PERSUASION

Persuasive Men

John H. Patterson, a native of Dayton, Ohio, and a Dartmouth graduate, was the first modern supersalesperson. Patterson invented modern personal selling when he started building a business on an expensive article almost no one wanted or knew how to use. It sold for $50 and was known as a "thief catcher." Its purchase by business owners aroused fury among bartenders and café cashiers. Today, it's called a cash register. The company Patterson built upon it is NCR, the National Cash Register Company. Before Patterson, selling was glad handing, a matter of exploiting one's genial personality to attract a following in "the trade." After Patterson, selling was never the same.

Nearly a hundred years ago, Patterson pioneered sales contests, sales training in product and communication skills, guaranteed territories, open-ended commission payments against a guarantee, sales quotas based on equal selling opportunities, the first sales manual, and the sales convention. He epitomized the key to persuasive selling: Later expressed by Elmer Wheeler, who was billed as America's Number 1 salesman, *Don't sell the steak, sell the sizzle*! To his other inventions, Patterson added the assumptive close, showmanship in selling—"Visualize! Analyze! Dramatize! The optic nerve is twenty-two times stronger than the auditory nerve!" the trial-close,

Photo 1.1
John H. Patterson

Barry Rand took a selling job for Xerox while studying at Stanford University. Continuing his education to acquire an M.B.A., as well as a Masters of Management Science, he was promoted rapidly through Xerox from a sales manager, branch manager, region operations manager, Corporate Director, Major Accounts Planning, and currently Vice President, Major Account Marketing Operations.

and quite contemporary methods of handling objections. He even invented IBM's famed motto "Think." A star trainee named Thomas J. Watson, Sr., took it along when he converted the Computing-Tabulating-Recording Company into today's fabulous monolith and NCR rival, IBM.

At Patterson's death in 1922, the company that he had created—out of nothing more than a legal right to market a mechanism for which there was at first no demand—was selling $29 million worth of "thief catchers." His work is a link between that long-ago era of gaslight, Prince Albert coats, and high collars, and today (2).

One Big Deal

John A. (Jack) Bozzone was instrumental in selling $40 million worth of nuclear coolant pumps to Babcock & Wilcox Co. in 1978. Trained as a mechanical engineer, Bozzone could not deny the "salesmanship in his veins." His father sold office equipment in New York; his grandfather, an immigrant from Italy, sold ice from a horse-drawn wagon. Bozzone switched from engineering to sales in 1961. Bozzone works out of McLean, Virginia, for the Byron Jackson Division of Borg-Warner Corporation. Bozzone said of the $40 million sale, "It took more than Jack Bozzone being a supersalesman. It took marketing, management, the engineering department—all these people helped make the sale." Only 39 at the time of the big sale in 1978, Bozzone expected his income to exceed $50,000 that year. Bozzone's one big deal gave him the opportunity to be considered for management of six sales offices of the Byron Jackson Division (3).

Many Deals Add Up

Joe Girard sold 1,208 Chevrolets to individual customers in 1972. He was ranked the Number 1 automobile salesperson in the nation for seven straight years (4). He worked as a sales representative for Merollis Chevrolet in Detroit. His staff consisted of two assistants to scout prospects and one to handle the extensive paper work resulting from his sales. Although satisfied customers received $25 for referring new customers to him, the secret of his success was in his short, customer-oriented sales presentation. If he didn't make a sale in twenty minutes, he would go on to the next prospect. He tried to give his prospects the best deal in town. He relied on volume rather than on high mark-ups. He worked only six to eight hours a day, five days a week. In the early 1970s, he made about $160,000 a year.

Persuasive Women

Sara Breedlove Walker, daughter of poor farmers, born near Delta, Louisiana, discovered a formula for styling black women's hair. Sara Walker used persuasion to sell her "Walker method" door to door. She gained both customers and agents. She founded the Madame C. J. Walker Manufacturing Company. Distributing her products throughout the United States and the Caribbean, she became one of the first black millionaires. She died in 1919 (5).

Barry Cook, daughter of a Navy officer, moved often during her school years, learning to adjust to new people and to new environments. She graduated from the University of California in 1966. After a year as a systems support representative for another company, she joined Honeywell Information Systems as a technical sales representative. In 1974, she became the first woman to join Honeywell's President's Club, one of Honeywell's highest honors (6). In February 1978, Barry Cook was a National Account Manager, selling to important accounts from Honeywell's San Francisco branch (7). Barry Cook's story is no longer exceptional.

Until recently, most companies reserved sales jobs for men. But now businesses are recognizing that women are an untapped sales resource. Sales jobs give women the same opportunity to show proof of competence that they give men. Says Patricia M. Carr, a lumber sales representative for Boise-Cascade Corporation, who broke the million-board-feet level during 1978, "Selling is not a matter of male or female. It's personal chemistry." By 1979,

the base salaries, together with such fringe benefits as company cars, commissions, and/or bonuses gave some experienced saleswomen earnings of more than $45,000 a year. Rosemarie Sena, a senior vice president of Wall Street's Shearson Hayden Stone, Inc., consistently earns more than $300,000 a year. Her view? "If a woman is good at sales at all, she's apt to be better than a man" (8).

Kentucky's Persuasive Colonel

Harlan Sanders was prepared to retire on the income he earned from his small restaurant in Corbin, Kentucky. The restaurant was at one time valued at $164,000. His specialty was fried chicken, and Duncan Hines, a famed food and restaurant critic, had even recommended his restaurant. When the highway on which the restaurant was located was rerouted, Sanders went bankrupt. His only income at age sixty-five was his $105 monthly Social Security check. However, he had two important things—his chicken recipe and the determination to sell the idea. He traveled through Ohio and Indiana, sleeping in his ten-year-old Ford by night and demonstrating his chicken cooking process by day. After two years, he had sold only five franchises. He persisted in trying to sell his idea. Suddenly, his sales began to boom. Today, Kentucky Fried Chicken is one of the largest fast-food franchises in existence, with thousands of outlets worldwide. "Colonel" Sanders sold his business in 1964 to a Nashville businessman and a Louisville attorney for $2 million (9). Perhaps he sold too cheaply!

A Persuasive Lifetime

Arthur George Gaston learned about the power of persuasion early in life. As a child, he charged his playmates buttons for the privilege of using his backyard swing. He then sold the buttons to neighborhood women. When he needed capital during his days as a laborer, he sold peanuts and lent his earnings to fellow laborers at interest. Gaston founded the Smith and Gaston Burial Society and the Booker T. Washington Insurance Company. They were the beginnings of a network of businesses. By 1972, Gaston's holdings were estimated at $24 million (10).

CONTRIBUTING TO SOCIETY THROUGH PROFESSIONAL SELLING

Personal selling is of social worth only to the extent that it delivers social benefits. Few people can take satisfaction from an occupation if their efforts do not contribute to the prosperity of others. The emergence of national markets and the rise of the mass media of radio and television have obscured the critical role of sellers in introducing the new and desirable into society. It was the itinerant merchants of the ninth and tenth centuries who introduced the wonders of the more sophisticated East to medieval Europe (11). It would be their counterparts, called "drummers," who a thousand years later introduced the 1803 American invention of the icebox into nearly every urban American household by the start of the Civil War (12). It was a corps of drummers who brought the $123 Singer Sewing Machine to the American frontier in the 1850s (13). By creating ownership satisfaction through persuasion, salespeople contribute to society. Personal selling serves as an aid in contacts between those who would buy and those who would sell. As marketing scholar Reavis Cox has observed:

"Even in a relatively simple economy, where the 'surplus' most producers have available for exchange with others is quite small, an individual faces difficulties in finding what he can buy or sell, where it is available and on what terms. . . . So we need not find it particularly surprising that in our economy, where millions of people exchange among themselves a 'surplus' comprising a million or more products that are extracted, processed, and consumed at thousands of places, that the [task of making marketing contacts] . . . is expensive in terms of time or money expended." (14)

Although the making of marketing contacts through personal selling is expensive and has been identified with slick and unethical practices, how much poorer would everyday life be without the many goods introduced by those who, in the words of the train-borne drummers of the *Music Man,* "knew the territory"?

Although selling has been denigrated and disregarded by its critics, a new appreciation is emerging of that old sales adage: "Nothing happens until somebody sells something!" A sales representative is:

- A change agent for progress
- A promoter of mass-production economies
- A promoter of other economic activities
- A creator of customer satisfaction
- A professional in systems

A Change Agent for Progress

Anthropology (the study of people and their cultures) demonstrates that "change agents" are responsible for social progress. Change agents persuade other people to accept new cultural tools and better ways of doing things. The sales representative's role is that of change agent—to speed the acceptance of new products that offer advantages over existing products—thus raising the living standards of all culture members. Pioneers like Cyrus McCormick, who invented and sold the reaper, Gustavus Swift and P. D. Armour, who made it possible for city dwellers to replace salt pork with beef raised on the western prairie through introduction of the refrigerated railway car, and Henry Ford, who marketed motor cars for the average American, are very much responsible for the high standard of living enjoyed in the United States today. No matter how useful an invention, it is worthless to society if it is not "sold."

Today, good sales representatives contribute even more to the economy than pioneers contributed to their economies. Many pioneers lived at a time when the market would readily accept new manufactured goods, for all goods were in short supply. Today, competition is keener, and older products are more solidly established. Continued progress may depend on introducing better products to the market and selling them successfully. Many factories manufacture products that cannot be sold by advertising alone. If such plants were to go out of business, the economy would be affected negatively. Today, sales representatives are persuading buyers to use the new and more efficient products to run their factories and households. Without personal selling, many customers would buy less, leading to a reduction in the amount of available goods and services, which would lead to higher prices and higher unemployment.

A Promoter of Mass-Production Economies

At one time, shopkeepers made *and* sold their products at one location. As a result, they had firsthand contact with their markets. Later, the Industrial Revolution demonstrated that mass production could result in great economic savings, since assembly lines could turn out large quantities of uniform multiple units more cheaply. Large-capacity machinery furthered mass production. Big operations provided even greater savings for producers and lower prices for consumers. However, markets for the products had to be sought—sometimes far away—to keep factories in full operation. A separation between maker and buyer resulted. Sales forces had to be created to reach prospects—potential buyers—in distant markets.

Today, the separation between manufacturer and market is increasing rather than decreasing. There is a growing need for salespeople to communicate, to "fit" standardized products to individual customer needs. Without the help of salespeople, large operations would not have adequate markets for their goods. They would not be able to increase profits. Employing a sales force is a high-yield investment.

A Promoter of Other Economic Activities

Selling helps not only to introduce new products into the marketplace but also to promote innovation. By making product improvement profitable, it promotes innovation. Sales representatives constantly remind product researchers about market needs and the necessity for products that solve prospect problems in new ways. All of a firm's activities depend on sales. Levels of production, hiring, financing, and purchasing depend on how many units of a product can be sold in the market. Because selling focuses on persuading people rather than on producing products, companies using scientific calculations to figure production costs may be willing to pay a premium to highly successful salespeople, whose individual worth cannot be evaluated on a calculator.

A Creator of Customer Satisfaction

Personal selling adds to the enjoyment of goods and services by increasing the buyer satisfaction level. Salesperson knowledge and assurances add to buyer enjoyment of a purchase. Salespeople can tell buyers things about a product that help them to increase its useful life. A better informed and better assured consumer is a better satisfied customer. Thus the products bought are worth more. Sales representatives in estate planning (insurance) and accounting-systems selling, for example, act as consultants (advisers) to individuals and small businesses. The advice of sales professionals has saved many small businesses from bankruptcy.

A Professional in the System

With longer training periods, higher standards of conduct, and more exacting selection standards, the image of salespersons is changing. This is due in part to the increasing complexity of products and to the realization by managers of enterprise that sales representatives who meet buyers face-to-face influence customer images of a company. Consequently, highly qualified sales representatives are being hired to sell products such as investments and complex industrial machinery. Selling is acquiring a more professional image because more intelligent people are entering the field, training periods are longer, and standards of admission are higher. Today, corporations search for problem solvers who can think technically and strategically. The more complex the problem and the greater the amount of money involved, the higher the need for polished, professional, and intelligent sales representatives.

Certified life underwriters, licensed real-estate brokers, industrial equipmen salespeople, development personnel of not-for-profit enterprises, and sales engineers are helping to refurbish selling's image. Truly professional salespeople are no longer compared to hucksters attracting trade on the sidewalk or barkers at carnivals and circus sideshows. Because of the complexity of today's markets and the current emphasis on prospect cultivation, a new sales professional is developing. Today's new sales professional has higher ethical standards and more exacting service attitudes than yesterday's Willie Lomans. The public is beginning to recognize that men and women in sales can act as high-level consultants rather than as "peddlers."

KINDS OF SELLING OPPORTUNITIES
THE DIVERSITY OF SALES WORK

Everybody Sells

Persuading is a universal activity. It plays a role in everyone's daily life. Since the American free-enterprise system is not coercive, and since most people do not *have* to accommodate sales representatives or any one else, people find themselves constantly using persuasion to get what they want:

- Children try to persuade parents.
- Traffic offenders try to persuade judges.
- Teachers try to persuade students.

- Students try to persuade teachers.
- Buyers try to persuade sellers.
- Applicants try to persuade employers.
- Employees try to persuade supervisors.
- Supervisors try to persuade employees.

Even physicians, politicians, and accountants depend on selling talents to promote their ideas. Everyone must sell to advance.

Personal Selling Is Open to Everyone

The variety of selling opportunities offers a chance to nearly every type of positive personality. Even introverts capable of complex thinking are urgently required for certain sales jobs. While introverted personalities might benefit from more openness, the ability of introverts to think analytically and to resolve buyer problems is most important to many companies. Almost anyone with average intelligence who is willing to make minor personality adjustments where necessary can make an exceptionally good living in sales.

One of the reasons selling pays so well is that many young people have developed a false image of selling, leaving the field open to others. A ten-year-old boy might sell popular magazines door to door and conclude, incorrectly, that all selling is at that level. Many people have had unsuccessful experiences with low-level selling. Because of incomplete information about available opportunities in sales occupations, many search elsewhere for jobs. The number of persons seeking sales work is limited, increasing the rewards for those who do go into the field.

Types of Selling Situations by the Extent of Closing Effort Required

The special challenge of personal selling is to secure definite commitments from prospects—that is, to close sales. Support sales representatives, order-taking sales representatives, order-getting sales representatives, and order-making sales representatives are classified by the amount of closing effort required for them to succeed in their jobs.

Support Sales Representatives. Support sales representatives do not use persuasion as a main technique of their jobs. Their primary goal is to help buyers locate merchandise and to offer prospects advice on the use of goods. Repair personnel, for example, may sell repair and operating supplies only in conjunction with machinery maintenance. Technical representatives may accompany order-getting and innovative salespeople to explain the operation of equipment to prospective buyers. Only rarely do they solicit big orders alone.

Order-Taking Sales Representatives. Order-takers deal with prospective customers with previously established needs. Order-takers, such as milk and potato chip route drivers, serve customers on a predetermined route. Order-taking salespeople take care of stock, display products, and answer questions about merchandise. They also use suggestion selling to create wants for additional products. In other words, they suggest to customers that additional units or kinds of goods should be bought.

Order-Getting Sales Representatives. Order-getting sales representatives stimulate wants and directly or indirectly ask for orders. They systematically search out customer problems and needs and help prospects to make up their minds by offering solutions to problems through purchase of a product. They must find a prospect's real needs and translate these needs into wants. Order-getters usually go to prospects and initiate interviews. Order-getters must have self-confidence, a positive self-image, and a knowledge of persuasive techniques. Whereas order-takers primarily serve customers who know what they want, order-getters use standard persuasive techniques with prospects who are uncertain of their needs.

Order-Making Sales Representatives. The salesperson who uses imagination and creativity—interjecting new ideas into sales situations—is an order-maker. Order-makers develop new ways to use products and new approaches to prospects. Order-makers are distinguished by an ability to close accounts that order-getters cannot close using more conventional means. Order-makers approach each sales situation in an organized way. They examine all aspects of relationships and make adjustments easily. They work to build future sales opportunities by focusing on the long-range aspects of situations. To meet prospect needs, order-makers must have detailed product knowledge, know competitors' strategies and strengths, and possess highly developed selling skills. Order-makers use personal experience, competence, and intuition to achieve consistent and sustained high levels of sales. Order-makers are always in demand to solve complex selling problems and to handle difficult closes.

Types of Selling Situations by Employing Firms

Salespeople sell tangible and intangible products at every level of distribution. They can be classified as *retail, wholesale, manufacturer's,* and *intangible* sales representatives according to the nature of the employing enterprise. *Retail sales representatives* are expected to be patient, helpful, and friendly. They are sometimes thought of as order-takers and may not receive high salaries. However, managers of retail stores, successful store owners, and retail salespersons who work on a bonus or commission basis are creative closers and often command exceptional incomes. *Wholesale sales representatives* make sure that buyers are adequately supplied with needed items. They also see that stock is displayed attractively and that store managers are informed about new items. They must be friendly, dependable, and helpful. Personality is especially important in wholesale selling. *Manufacturer's sales representatives* range from order-takers who service a route to order-makers who sell complex industrial equipment and train other sales representatives. Sales engineers who sell technical products, detailers who call on doctors and other professionals, and missionary salespersons who train dealer sales personnel are examples of people with jobs with rigorous requirements and high rewards. *Intangible sales representatives* must create images (pictures) in the minds of prospects. They may sell life insurance, investments, or consulting services. They must be sincere, self-assured, and professional. (See Figure 1.1 for summary classifications of selling jobs.)

A new kind of intangible sales career opportunity is emerging among not-for-profit enterprises. Colleges, universities, hospitals, museums, art galleries, symphony orchestras, opera and dance companies have financial needs that normal revenues cannot meet. The marketing arm that raises the extra monies needed to sustain the existence of these organizations is called development. Forward-thinking development offices of these enterprises now employ the same kinds of selection criteria and training programs in choosing their "sales" representatives as do businesses. Increasingly, for example, college and university development officers conduct training sessions among volunteers for solicitation of key alumni who have the means to make major contributions to the schools they attended. Pulling together the appeals—to nostalgia, public recognition needs, and the satisfaction of contributing to the future—that a prospect will have a positive response to requires intangible selling skills of the highest order.

THE NATURE OF THE SALES JOB—
OTHER DUTIES BESIDES SELLING

Most sales representatives spend a majority of their time accomplishing vital marketing duties other than face-to-face selling. The time spent *traveling* varies with the nature of the product sold, the distance between prospects and markets, the salesperson's territory, and the work attitude of the individual sales representative. In most high-level selling, the sales representative goes to prospects. Even salespersons with city territories may have to travel hundreds of miles each week. Since prospects can seldom be seen as soon as sales representatives arrive, they must learn to *wait* patiently and productively. Time must be spent *routing and planning* to achieve maximum effectiveness and efficiency in territorial coverage. Industrial specialty salespersons may make *studies* of prospect problems, write detailed *proposal letters*

Figure 1.1   Classifications of Selling Jobs

Types by Employer Served	Description
Retail sales representative	Sells to the ultimate consumer and usually sells at an established place of business. Many jobs for salespeople are in this category.
Wholesale sales representative	Sells to customers in the field. Many are service salespeople who check stocks and set up displays.
Manufacturer's sales representative	An order-getting salesperson, usually with extensive training and knowledge. Job can involve complex problems and may result in sizable rewards.
Intangible sales representative	A salesperson who does not have a tangible product and therefore must create images in the minds of prospects.

Types by Extent of Closing	Description
Support sales representative	Provides technical and advisory assistance. Not usually involved in closing.
Order-taking sales representative	Serves customers who know what they want. Uses suggestion selling methods.
Order-getting sales representative	Serves customers who are uncertain about their needs. Uses persuasive selling methods.
Order-making sales representative	Uses imagination and creativity in addition to the standard selling methods.

outlining solutions to prospect problems, *install equipment,* or even *train operators* in equipment use. Some salespersons must *program* the machines they sell.

Sales representatives have *reporting* obligations. Since most sales representatives work independently, they must furnish accounts of their activities for feedback and analysis. They may be expected to attend *trade fairs* and to demonstrate equipment or services. Sometimes sales representatives *collect money from accounts* that have become delinquent. Salespersons are expected to *study and learn* about new applications and new company products. They must *attend sales meetings* to learn new strategies and to learn to work as a team in promoting company products. Senior sales representatives and supervisory sales representatives may be expected to *train other salespersons*. Manufacturers' missionary salespersons, for example, may act as sales managers for dealer sales representatives who sell their products at another channel level. Salespersons are expected to write letters, entertain prospects, send advertisements, and carry out many auxiliary functions in addition to making prospect presentations. Most good sales representatives, however, spend as much time as possible in direct contact with prospects. Quotas are reached by closing deals. Usually this occurs in the presence of prospects. (See Figure 1.2 for an example of job specifications and a training program for a salesperson.)

EVALUATING SELLING AS A CAREER

There will be a need for professional persuaders as long as the free-enterprise system exists. Fundamental questions are: Does a career in personal selling constitute a rewarding lifetime occupation? Do advantages outweigh disadvantages? While the answers depend somewhat on the individual, every student should at least consider selling as a possible career choice. The kinds of sales jobs available are shown in Figure 1.3. A career in personal selling offers:

- Personal development and growth
- Freedom
- Many high-paying openings
- Opportunities for financial success
- Opportunities for rapid advancement
- People-centered work
- Continual learning
- Opportunities for travel (15)

Figure 1.2

 THE UPJOHN COMPANY

MEDICINE...DESIGNED FOR HEALTH...PRODUCED WITH CARE

DOMESTIC PHARMACEUTICAL SALES   *An Equal Opportunity Employer*

8667—7/76

Job Specification – Pharmaceutical Representative

Nature of Work	Provide information on company products and policies, verbally and by use of literature to: physicians, pharmacists and other licensed practitioners in private practice, institutions and industrial concerns. The objective is to obtain product specification and sales where applicable, and at the same time develop and maintain good professional relations for the company.
Functions of Job	***Physicians*** Call on each physician in the territory to present products and literature, tailoring the presentation to fit the specialty or special interest of each physician. The objective: obtain product specification on prescriptions and product sales where feasible.
	Pharmacists Call on each pharmacy in the territory as often as necessary to provide product information, check stocks, encourage stocking new items, sell special product promotions, encourage the use of various merchandising aids such as window and counter displays, watch credit and encourage prompt payment of invoices; contact new stores opening in the territory to add to the customer list.
	Other Practitioners Call on dentists and other licensed practitioners as time permits, handling them in the same manner as the physician, with the product presentation tailored to fit the special interest of each individual.
	Hospitals Call on hospitals in the territory to present products and literature to staff physicians, residents and interns, again tailoring the presentation to fit special interests; acquaint staff nurses with products; contact the pharmacist. The objective: obtain product specification and maintain adequate product inventory in the pharmacy.
	Industrials Call on industrial firms which maintain an industrial health department with a physician in charge. The objective: sales of products which are used in such plants.
Requirements	***Academic Training*** Baccalaureate Degree desirable. A background in pharmacy or life science is beneficial. Continued study of company-provided product and medical information is required.
	Experience Qualifications None required (work in a pharmacy, other retail stores, or direct selling experience is helpful).
	Personal Requirements Good physical condition; neat and well groomed; good posture and bearing; ability to think and talk clearly and concisely; present own ideas; good natured and personable; energetic and enthusiastic.
	Initiative And Resourcefulness Must use initiative in planning calls, tailoring product presentation to practitioner's individual interest, locating new physicians and stores. Be resourceful in budgeting time, gaining audience with physicians and pharmacists, and handling problems which may arise.

(cont. on next page)

Figure 1.2 (cont.)

8952 11/77

Training Program–Pharmaceutical Representative

	The Upjohn training program begins the day new representatives are hired and comes to an end only when they relinquish their final assignment at retirement. This program is designed to help prepare the representatives to successfully accomplish whatever challenge or responsibility they are called upon to face. The major emphasis in both time and effort involves actual performance by the trainee in the physician's office, the hospital and the pharmacy. The program is essentially a four phase operation which is carried out in the sales area office, the national learning center, the field, and at the home office in Kalamazoo, Michigan. The following outline highlights the sequence of events and principal activities. Timing is flexible and the program is adjusted to the personal requirements of each individual.
Sales Area Office Training	Several weeks are devoted to this phase of the training program. Under the direction of the area sales manager and the distribution center manager, new representatives are enrolled, briefed on the mechanics of the job and the operations of the sales area office, receive initial disease and product information, and their territory supplies.
Initial Home Office Training	This portion of training takes place under the leadership of national sales trainers and consists of several weeks of intensive activity at The Upjohn Company's Learning Center in Kalamazoo, Michigan. Using the latest educational techniques, the new representative touches everything from product knowledge and application to role playing in sales situations. The trainee will use films, videotapes, programmed learning, listening training and small group sessions to help develop the problem-solving attitude required in professional selling. With the guidance of the sales trainers, the representative will embrace all phases of sales from retail merchandising of nonprescription products to hospital sales. Also included is a tour of the Company's research, production and office facilities.
Field Training	A minimum of three weeks is utilized for this phase of the training program, which is completed under the guidance of the district manager. The locale is the territory to which the new representative has been assigned. This is essentially a "laboratory" application of the subject matter presented in the sales area and national learning center. It involves both demonstration and actual practice–demonstration by the district manager with the new representative as observer and performance by the representative with the district manager as advisor.
Subsequent Home Office Training	After approximately 18-24 months in a sales territory, and at periodic intervals thereafter, representatives return to the Home Office in Kalamazoo, Michigan for one-week seminars and workshops under the leadership of the Sales Training Unit. A review of pharmacy, practical physiology and therapeutics, and additional product information occupy much of the time. Films, group discussions and question-and-answer sessions are an important part of these conferences.
	After returning to the territory, the representative is kept up to date on products, policies and the latest medical developments through regular sales area conferences. All training programs have been formulated with one purpose in mind: to help representatives accomplish whatever goals they set for themselves within the company structure.

20
Personal Preparation

Personal Development and Growth

Success in sales requires the development of an appealing and persuasive personality. Salespersons acquire and develop traits that promote acceptance by other people. They learn to put themselves second, to let prospects express their feelings and enjoy being the center of attention. Sales representatives learn to be sympathetic listeners and to sparkle with optimistic enthusiasm. By adjusting their personalities to the needs of others, sales representatives sell both themselves and their products. Personality develops

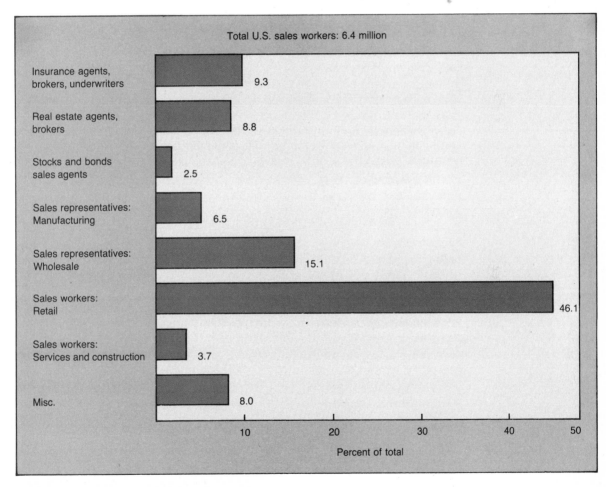

Total U.S. sales workers: 6.4 million

Insurance agents, brokers, underwriters	9.3
Real estate agents, brokers	8.8
Stocks and bonds sales agents	2.5
Sales representatives: Manufacturing	6.5
Sales representatives: Wholesale	15.1
Sales workers: Retail	46.1
Sales workers: Services and construction	3.7
Misc.	8.0

Percent of total

Figure 1.3   Distribution of Sales Occupations

Source: U.S. Department of Labor; Bureau of Labor Statistics, *Employment and Earnings,* March 1982.

consciously and unconsciously under the challenges of the needs and wants of the prospect and the salesperson.

Freedom

Some people are temperamentally suited to spending long hours doing detailed figure work behind a desk. Some even enjoy working with machines and numbers more than dealing with people. Others, while they may tolerate desk work, prefer to be outside company offices, free from confining routine. Sales representatives are usually free to do most of their own routing; to call on prospects of their own choosing; to plan their own strategies; and, within the confines of spending their time in marketing activities, to do what they feel is best to solicit business. A typical salesperson contacts dozens of people each day and faces situations that are anything but routine.

Many High-Paying Openings

The outlook for future openings in high-paying sales jobs is very good. The statistical data in Table 1.1 show the projected growth of selected sales occupations through 1990. The average-annual-increase figure includes the

TABLE 1.1   OUTLOOK FOR SELECTED SALES OCCUPATIONS

OCCUPATION	EMPLOYMENT 1978	PROJECTED EMPLOYMENT 1990	PERCENT GROWTH 1978–1990	AVERAGE ANNUAL INCREASE	GROWTH	REPLACE-MENTS
Insurance agents & Brokers	568,000	682,000	20.0	30,000	9.5	20,500
Manufacturer's salesworkers	402,000	499,000	24.0	21,700	8.0	13,700
Retail-trade salesworkers	2,851,000	3,785,000	32.8	226,000	78.0	148,000
Securities salesworkers	109,000	120,000	10.0	5,500	.9	4,600
Wholesale-trade salesworkers	840,000	958,000	14.0	40,000	10.0	30,000
Real-estate salesworkers	555,000	670,000	20.7	50,000	10.0	40,000

Source: Occupational Projections and Training Data, 1980, Bulletin No. 2052, U.S. Government Printing Office, U.S. Department of Labor, Bureau of Labor Statistics, pp. 45–47.

dual effects of growth (from an increase in total employment) and replacement (from retirements and other types of turnover).

Many yearly openings in each category result from both growth and turnover each year. While these classifications were selected to represent interests of college-trained sales aspirants, most wholesale salesworkers do not have college training. The majority of securities sales representatives, however, have had college educations. Many have MBAs. In 1981, beginning manufacturer's salesworkers could expect $15,200. Most experienced manufacturer's salesworkers earned between $30,140 and $33,724 (16).

Financial Opportunities

The financial rewards of selling vary greatly and depend on factors such as:

- The difficulty and complexity of the selling problems
- The sophistication of personality necessary
- Closing creativity required
- The risk or security present
- The compensation level and the payment method
- The future outlook of the employing enterprise
- The social status of the job
- The amount of travel and relocation involved

Persons interested in selling careers must realize that college training is not as necessary in jobs where there are fewer problems, more limited challenges, and easier closes. The greater the problems, the more complex or expensive the products, the greater the rewards. Jobs that require salespersons to project a corporate image and to meet with high officials demand exceptional intelligence and polish. Consequently, such jobs pay more. Salespersons who depend on commissions and bonus arrangements rather than on salaries generally make more money. Salespersons willing to travel, relocate, work longer hours, or sell products of questionable social value may also be able to command more money. Firms whose future outlook is highly dependent on business cycle fluctuations may have to promise more to attract competent sales representatives. With these reservations in mind, and realizing that compensation varies among sales jobs more than among jobs in most other fields, look at the following general data.

In 1977, college graduates selling consumer goods and services had an average income of $11,040, an increase of 6.9 percent over the previous year. Those selling industrial goods and services averaged $12,600, an increase of 3.8 percent. MBA graduates with nontechnical undergraduate degrees averaged $16,920, while graduates with other master's degrees and technical undergraduate degrees averaged $18,038. New graduates with bachelor's degrees in sales-marketing could expect to be hired at an average of $12,636 (17).

More important than starting salaries are salaries of sales representatives who have been in the field for several years. Table 1.2 summarizes sales representatives' annual compensation for consumer and industrial products. Note that sales representatives selling industrial products consistently average more than those selling consumer products. Those on incentive compensa-

TABLE 1.2   SALES REPRESENTATIVES' ANNUAL COMPENSATION BY TYPE OF REPRESENTATIVE

SALESPERSON LEVEL	CONSUMER PRODUCTS			INDUSTRIAL PRODUCTS		
	1981	1980	% CHANGE	1981	1980	% CHANGE
Sales trainee						
Straight salary	$15,200	$13,900	+ 9.4%	$16,650	$15,257	+ 9.1%
Salary plus incentive						
Salary	14,650	12,733	+15.1	17,375	15,367	+13.1
Incentive	1,250	1,333	− 6.2	2,825	2,933	− 3.7
Total	16,250	14,400	+12.8	20,600	18,222	+13.1
A&B salespeople*						
Straight salary	18,100	16,187*	+11.8	24,392	22,954	+ 6.3
Salary plus incentive						
Salary	19,060	17,040	+11.9	21,171	19,427	+ 9.0
Incentive	4,160	3,220	+29.2	5,753	5,093	+13.0
Total	24,320	21,840	+11.4	27,771	24,693	+12.5
Senior salespeople†						
Straight salary	28,200*	28,060	+ 0.5	30,357	27,682	+ 9.7
Salary plus incentive						
Salary	23,820	21,460	+11.0	25,765	24,160	+ 6.6
Incentive	4,560	4,840	− 5.8	7,835	6,407	+22.3
Total	30,140	27,000	+11.6	33,724	30,647	+10.0
Sales supervisor						
Straight salary	32,500	31,694*	+ 2.5	35,825	32,400	+10.6
Salary plus incentive						
Salary	30,080	27,460	+ 9.5	31,687	29,500	+ 7.4
Incentive	5,420	6,080	−10.9	9,120	7,857	+16.1
Total	35,420	33,480	+ 5.8	41,147	37,550	+ 9.6

Note: Some differences between years reflect changes in the organizations that reported data. It should also be noted that in the "salary plus incentive" category, the "total" compensation will not equal the sum of the "salary" and "incentive" components because not all respondents provided information for each of the components.

Source: American Management Association, *Executive Compensation Service.* Reported in *Sales and Marketing Management* (February 22, 1982):70.

Salespeople grade A: "regular" salespersons who have little or no selling experience except that which has been acquired in the company sales training program. *Salespeople grade B:* salespersons who have broad knowledge of the company's products and services and who sell in a specifically assigned territory. They develop new prospects.
†*Senior salespeople:* salespersons with the highest level of selling responsibility.

tion plans average more than those on straight salary. It is important to remember that this table includes many types of salespersons, with and without college training. Sales representatives in high-level selling jobs will obviously earn higher salaries.

Figure 1.4 shows how salespersons' compensation fared through the severe recession of 1973 and up to 1981. Figure 1.5 charts actual increases for salespersons on various rungs of the experience ladder. Students considering sales careers should compare these statistics with those for other occupations in the same time period. Salary differences that reflect both college and noncollege backgrounds should be allowed for.

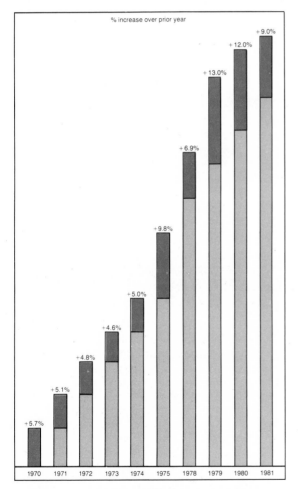

Figure 1.4 Compensation Gains Accelerate

Source: American Management Association, *Executive Compensation Service for 1973–1975*; 1976–81, in *Sales & Marketing Management* (February 22, 1982):75.

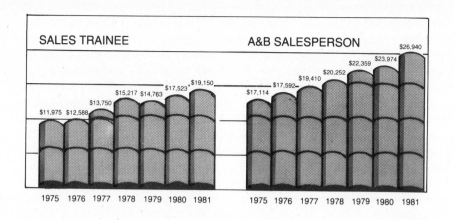

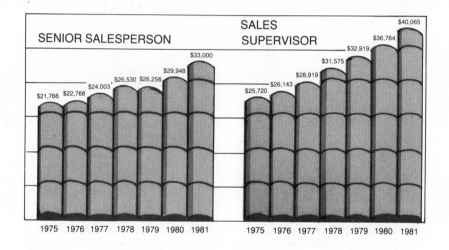

Figure 1.5 How Salespeople's Total Compensation Is Growing

Note: Salaries plus commission incentives. Figures apply to consumer goods, industrial goods, and "other," that is, insurance, services, transportation, and utilities. Source: American Management Association, *Executive Compensation Service*. In *Sales & Marketing Management* (February 22, 1982):69.

Opportunities For Rapid Advancement

A typical promotional route is junior sales representative, sales representative, senior sales representative, zone sales manager, sales manager, vice president in charge of sales and marketing, president. Junior sales representatives are generally considered on-the-job trainees. Most people in this apprentice category are not experienced or knowledgeable enough to justify their compensation through their contributions to profitability. After juniors are given a territory and work mostly on their own, they are usually considered fullfledged sales representatives. Senior sales representatives usually are those who have been with a company several years. They have proven their profitability and been entrusted with important accounts. When a significant part of their formal duties involves training and supervising junior salespersons, they may be formally recognized as assistant sales managers or zone managers. A sales manager or sales branch manager may be promoted to vice president, and perhaps to president. Often, field sales representatives doing well in their territories are reluctant to take desk jobs. Since desk jobs may require relocation or even a cut in compensation (which changes from commission to salary), many field sales representatives prefer better territories as a reward for exceeding quotas and not "promotion" to lower-paying desk jobs.

Within sales operations, a wide variety of career opportunities are available. Figure 1.6 shows the varied possibilities at one company. Many top executives have come up through the selling ranks. Many top corporate executives and board members believe that selling experience is a vital qualifying variable for top management. Most top corporate positions involve employee management and public relations, and sales experience is an excellent indication that a person has learned to adjust to and to accommodate the views and feelings of others. Success in sales also indicates an ability to listen to others.

People-Centered Work

There is great satisfaction in dealing with and learning from people. Many sales representatives find their work challenging and enjoy the variety of people they meet. Personal contacts made in selling often carry over into social life. It is helpful to have a wide range of friends and acquaintances, since they often add to representatives' selling potential by referring new prospects to them.

Opportunities for Travel and Learning

It is interesting to meet new people and to see what is going on in a sales territory each day. Sales professionals selling accounting systems, insurance sales representatives, and investment salespersons, to name a few, have opportunities to learn about the "inside" of major business operations. Nearly every sales representative benefits from the learning experience that comes from involvement in customer problems and personal contacts. Many sales

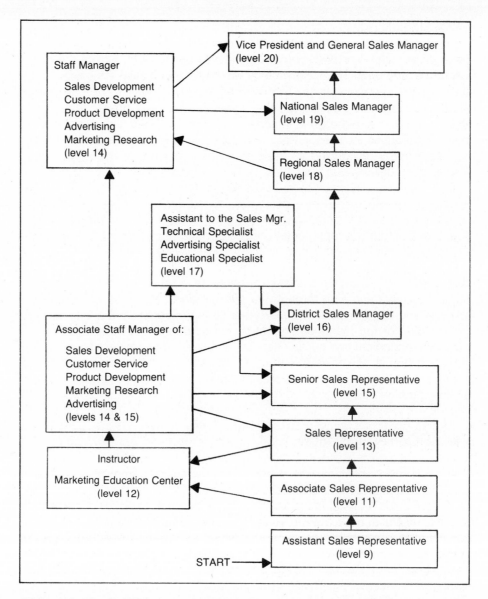

Figure 1.6 Career Options in Sales

representatives find the travel aspect of their jobs and the interaction with a variety of people exciting.

Although the advantages are significant, selling is not without its disadvantages:

- It is hard work.
- It is sometimes psychologically difficult.
- It may require time away from home or even relocation.
- It may not be sufficiently valued by the employing firm.

Hard Work

Sales recruiters often ask new sales applicants if they are looking for a "job" or a "position." If an applicant says position, the interview may end right there, with the explanation that no positions are being offered—just hard work. While sales work is varied, it requires physical and psychological stamina and persistent effort. It may require driving in traffic and lifting heavy products. It may require study, research, and concentration. It requires calling on a maximum number of prospects and taking adequate time to prepare for and interview each one. Other selling duties must also be done correctly. Sales representatives are usually free to work as long and as hard as necessary to sell as much as they want to sell.

Psychologically Difficult Work

Sales representatives may have to take a certain amount of abuse from prospects who are testing the salesperson's personality. In a sales situation, a prospect may bring up objections or may attempt to irritate a salesperson in order to determine the truth about the product offered and the salesperson. In fact, sales situations may be thought of as contests, with prospects increasing conflict and sales representatives attempting to minimize conflict. Salespersons must be able to take on an understanding role. They must restrain their inclinations to be argumentative, overbearing, or too self-assertive. Prospects, on the other hand, are under no such restraints. Prospects who wish to defer the displeasure and risk of decision making may avoid and discourage sales representatives. Consequently, they may not treat salespersons in a socially graceful manner. Persons particularly sensitive to criticism, who take the probing of prospects personally, may find that they are too "thin-skinned" to enjoy selling. Fortunately, most prospects are understanding and nice. The few who try to take advantage of their superior bargaining positions are exceptions and not the rule in high-level selling. Most prospects value the knowledge and professionalism of sales representatives. Just as surgeons must overcome an aversion to bad accident cases, so sales representatives must overcome aversion to occasional emotional confrontations, since emotions accompany decision pressures.

Time Away from Home and Relocation

Many sales jobs, such as real estate, insurance, and city territorial assignments do not involve extensive travel or relocation. The market for industrial goods, however, may be concentrated in one area, or it may be highly scattered, depending on the good. Usually, corporate selling entails some out-of-city travel. For certain items, like pollution control systems, extensive air travel may be required. Some people have deep roots in a community in terms of friends and family. Depending on the market, sales aspirants who are unwilling to travel or relocate may have to make money and promotion sacrifices in their careers. With many corporations, promotion means relocation. Corporations like their top personnel to have varied experience, and local openings often offer only limited experience.

The Non-Employee-Oriented Firm

Some corporations have been known to take advantage of salespersons by "milking" their best years and releasing them when they are middle-aged or older and can no longer relate to many prospects because of their age. Insurance firms have been known to hire agents, expecting them to become discouraged and quit the straight commission job after they have sold their friends and acquaintances. Other high-pressure companies will raise quotas impossibly high to pressure even successful sales agents out of the job. Certainly, most firms realize that trained, producing sales representatives are their most valuable asset. The more training a salesperson has, the more investment the company has in that person. The sales aspirant should therefore determine a potential employer's philosophy by finding out policies and talking to employees.

SUMMARY

Persuasive power, a vital force in a free-enterprise system, has been used by many in their climb to financial success. Personal selling (which is persuasive power directed toward moving products) contributes to society by helping to maintain the level of effective demand, allowing for economies of scale and specialization, encouraging innovation, and creating consumer satisfaction. Selling is becoming more of a professional activity because of the need for greater market cultivation and the desire to project a more favorable company image. Almost anyone wishing a selling career can find a place, since there is a wide variety of selling opportunities available. However, special rewards await creative thinkers with pleasing personalities who can solve prospect problems and move a firm's products. Sales careers offer freedom, personality development, a chance to work with people, and the growth afforded by continual learning. Selling, however, is hard work, and sometimes it is psychologically difficult. It may require relocation and extensive travel. Everyone should learn about selling, because persuading is a part of everyday life.

REVIEW QUESTIONS

1. John H. Patterson, Joe Girard, Sara Breedlove Walker, Barry Cook, Harlan Sanders, and Arthur George Gaston are cited as persuasive personalities. Highlight the elements that contributed to their success.

2. "Nothing happens until somebody sells something." Do you agree or disagree? Why?

3. Personal selling has often been associated with slick practices and unprofessional conduct. To counter this image, firms have given salespeople a variety of sanitized titles. Can you suggest any? Is this an effective strategy?

4. In what ways do sales representatives contribute to the economy?

5. Do you believe selling is gaining a more professional image? If yes, what are the factors contributing to this enhanced image? Is professionalism a factor in your evaluation of selling as a career?

6. An important distinction between selling situations is the degree of closing effort involved. Briefly distinguish between the four types of selling situations characterized on this dimension.

7. Sales representatives are primarily associated with face-to-face selling activities. However, there are many other activities that professional salespeople perform. List and review them.

8. Compare retail selling and the selling of intangibles such as life insurance or consulting services.

9. What are the advantages and disadvantages of selling as a career?

APPLICATION QUESTIONS

1. This chapter presented some stories about people who have been successful using persuasion and also gave you some idea about what personal selling is. The next chapter will include a definition of these and other terms. Before you read

what other people say persuasion and personal selling is, give some thought to the following:

a. Over the last couple of days did you try to "persuade" someone to do something? Were you successful? Do you think you could have done a better job of "persuasion"? How do you think you could have done it better? In what other situations do you think being very good at persuasion would help you? Based on this, what do you think persuasion is?

b. You have just met someone at a party and when you ask what her job is, she says that she is a salesperson. Are you impressed? When you think of personal selling, what do you think of?

c. When talking to some of your friends, tell them that you are thinking about getting a job selling life insurance. Tell some others that you're considering selling computers, and tell a third group that you're thinking about working for a short time selling television sets in a local retail store. What are their reactions? Why do you think they react this way?

Write down some brief notes about what happened and review them after you have finished the course to see if your thoughts and feelings have changed.

INCIDENT

1–1

At the age of 29, Kim Kelley is already something of a legend around Honeywell Inc. "He's the one who cried when he made his sale, isn't he?" a fellow Honeywell salesperson asks with a chuckle. Indeed he is. Kim stood there in his customer's office last June and bawled like a baby. And for good reason. Kim had just shaken hands on an $8.1 million computer sale to the state of Illinois. He had gambled his whole career on making that sale. He had spent three years laying the groundwork for it, and for three solid months he had been working six days a week, often 14 hours a day, competing against salespeople from four other computer companies.

It was a make-or-break situation for Kim Kelley, and, standing there with tears of joy and relief streaming down his cheeks, he knew he had made it. A bright future with Honeywell was assured, and he had just made an $80,000 commission—more money than he had earned in all four of his previous years with the company. Looking back on it now, Kim says: "I'd never want to go through it again." Such is the life of the "big-ticket" salesperson who pursues multimillion-dollar contracts while others sell in bits and drabs. Lured by fat commissions (1 percent of the equipment's total value in Honeywell's case), they devote months to delicate planning and months more to the heat of battle, all to make one big sale.

GAMBLING A PIECE OF YOUR LIFE

"You're playing for big stakes, and what you ante is your life," says Kick Kuszyk, a Honeywell computer salesperson in Pittsburgh. He just "gambled three years" of his life, he says, to sell a $4.5 million computer to Jones & Laughlin Steel Corp. Before he finally clinched the deal, his home life got so hectic that his wife packed up and went home to her mother for seven weeks. A Honeywell salesperson in Denver, Don Sather, was so wrapped up in trying to sell a $250,000 prototype computer system to Mountain States Telephone that he barely found time to slip away when his wife gave birth at 1:08 a.m. last August 15. "I stayed through labor and delivery, and then went back to the office," he says. He made the sale.

Kim Kelley thrives on such high-stakes action and always has, according to his mother in Davenport, Iowa, Dorothy Rynott. He was aggressive even as a paper boy; he pulled in $150 in Christmas tips one year. After a year at the University of Iowa he spent a year in California cooking pizza, selling shoes and hustling at pool. He returned to Iowa, married his high school sweetheart in 1965 and prepared to follow the career of his late father, who had been a tire salesman. For four years he wandered from one retail sales job to another. Finally, in 1969, he landed at a Honeywell sales office in Peoria, Illinois.

VISITING THE LEGION HALL

He was sent to Springfield in 1970 and told to keep four or five big sales simmering but to put only one at a time "on the front burner." Kim wasted little time picking his target, the state government, the biggest potential customer in his region. His long-range strategy was to devote at least half his time to pursuing the state, and to use the balance to scratch out small sales elsewhere to meet his annual quota of $500,000 worth of new equipment.

For three years, he patiently made daily rounds of key state offices, pausing a few minutes in each one to drop off technical documents or just to chat. He pursued the bureaucrats further at after-hours hangouts like the American Legion Hall.

"People don't buy products, they buy relationships," Kim believes. To that end, he even molded his personal life to suit his customer's preferences. He bought a big Buick and expensive suits, even though he could barely afford them. "People like to deal with a winner," Kim reasons. "They don't buy $8 million products from some guy who's worrying can he pay his rent." On the other hand, he says, it doesn't pay to appear too prosperous; for that reason, he quit his country club when he sensed that state employees resented his being able to afford it.

Thanks to a succession of nonstate sales, Kim's income was steadily, if unspectacularly, expanding, from $18,000 in 1970 to $22,000 in 1971 and $25,000 in 1972. The state bought hardly anything. In those three years, Kim made less than $3,000 in commissions on sales to the government.

THREE-MONTH SCRAMBLE

But when the break finally came, Kim was ready. Toward the end of 1972, the Illinois secretary of state asked for bids for a massive new computer system. Five manufacturers responded: Honeywell, Burroughs, Univac division of Sperry Rand, Control Data, and International Business Machines.

In the ensuing three-month scramble, Control Data was eliminated because of "high cost," according to Noel Sexton, head of a technical committee assigned by the state to evaluate the bids. IBM was never in strong contention, says Hank Malkus, who was then division administrator in the secretary's office. "IBM doesn't tailor its equipment to a customer's need. They just say, 'Here's our equipment, you make your system fit it,'" Malkus contends. That made the contest a three-horse race between Honeywell, Burroughs, and Univac. "The equipment was close," says Patrick Halperin, executive assistant to the secretary of state. "But the staff felt far more comfortable with Honeywell because they felt Kim had been more thorough in his marketing."

Indeed he was. Kim dealt solely with the committee. "Some of the other vendors put more emphasis on selling to the front office and tried to play on previous friendships," Sexton recalls. Kim fed the committee information, not persuasion. "When we asked to see customers," says Malkus, "Kim just gave us a list of Honeywell users and said, choose." Univac, on the other hand, annoyed committee members by discouraging them from interviewing users.

Kim flew in Honeywell experts and top marketing officials from Boston, Minneapolis, Phoenix and Chicago to answer technical questions on engineering, financing, installation, and service. "He showed the ability of his firm to cooperate," says Halperin. "Incredible attention to detail" helped, too, Kim thinks. The committee was asking for new bits of information daily—things like how much air conditioning his equipment would need. Kim answered every question within two days, always hand-delivering replies to each committee member. "That gave me five minutes more selling time with each one," he explains.

A SLOW PLANE RIDE

Kim hates to fly, but he flew the six committee members and their bosses to Atlanta to meet Honeywell users, to Phoenix twice to see performance tests at a Honeywell facility there, and to Houston to interview another user. When he could, he used Honeywell's "slow propeller plane," carefully chosen, Kim says to allow more selling time in the air. Kim and his secretary arranged everything—hotel and plane reservations, rental cars, meals, meetings, even the committee's spare time.

For the Houston trip Kim even made a dry run by himself beforehand, so he'd know the best flights, how to find the Hertz counter, good restaurants and ways to avoid rush-hour traffic. The committee had picked up a rumor that Tenneco Inc., in Houston, was dissatisfied with its Honeywell computer. Kim knew the rumor to be false, but wanted to let Tenneco itself tell that to the committee. He persuaded Tenneco to give the committee a bargain rate at a hotel it owns, and while scouting Houston, he learned that two companies there were having trouble with a competitor's equipment. He dropped hints about them to Pat Halperin, who took the bait and spent his time in Houston talking with a disgruntled customer of another vendor. "I left nothing to chance," Kim says. "Detail is what sells computers."

Kim's hot pursuit of the sale meanwhile, was taking a toll on his family. Sandy Kelley says the "tension" was dreadful. Kim "snapped" at their three-year-old daughter, Brook, and had only a few hours on Sundays to spend with her. "Every morning she asked if Daddy would be home tonight," Sandy says.

"I'd keep lists of things I wanted to talk to Kim about," Sandy says. She resented having to manage the family alone, even the new house they were building. "When Kim walked into the new house for the first time, he was like a stranger." Had this happened earlier in their marriage, she says, "it might have reached the point of breaking up." As it was, what she did most was worry. "I'd wake up in the middle of the night and wonder what I'd do if Kim didn't get the order. I knew he'd be crushed, and I didn't know how it would affect our lives."

A GRIN, A HUG AND TEARS

Kim was worried sick himself. When Hank Malkus gruffly ordered him down to the state capitol last June, Kim knew it was "decision day," but he didn't know who had won. He paused only long enough to vomit into a wastebasket before hurrying to Malkus's office. Minutes later, Malkus was grinning, his secretary was hugging Kim, and Kim was crying.

By now, Kim has recovered his poise and made his peace with Sandy and Brook. He's busy supervising installation of the equipment, a chore that will take him until next September to complete. How well he handles this job and how smoothly the equipment performs later are important in keeping his new customer happy and in paving the way for future sales to the state. And Kim is also stalking other big game. He put the finishing touches on a campaign with A. E. Staley Manufacturing Company in December and expects to close the $1.8 million deal in February. It was a relatively easy sale to a long-time Honeywell customer that Kim had worked diligently to provide with special services. Now the Illinois Department of Revenue is "going on the front burner," Kim says. His goal: an $8 million to $10 million sale of dual computers sometime in 1974.

Meanwhile, Kim is still a bit astonished when he thinks back on what he endured to make his first big sale and when he looks at his current bank balance. He got 40 percent of his commission, or about $32,000, when he signed the contract in August. He'll get the rest when it's all installed next September.

Kim traded in his 1972 Chrysler (which he bought after driving the Buick for a while) for a new $9,250 Lincoln Continental (paying the $5,430 balance in cash), turned Sandy's old Ford in for a $2,200 used Volkswagen and paid cash for a $2,000 dining room set. But the Kelleys have no plans to continue their spending spree. "A year from now our lives will be the same, except that I'll have $60,000 more in cash," Kim says.

And he likes that just fine. In fact, when Honeywell recently rewarded Kim by promoting him to sales manager, he requested "demotion" in order to avoid going on straight salary. Honeywell refused but did allow Kim a special status where he runs an 18-person sales office but stays on commission. His salary is $12,600 a year. Kim says he expects to move high in management eventually, but right now, "I can't afford the pay cut."

How does Kim Kelley's story resemble those of others mentioned in the text?
What do you see as the primary reason for Kim's success?
How might early success spoil Kim's future?

NOTES

1. Arthur Miller, *Death of a Salesman* (New York: Viking Press, 1949), p. 138.

2. Adapted from Gerald Carson, "The Machine That Kept Them Honest," *American Heritage,* August 1966, pp. 50–59.

3. "Company Man," *Forbes,* October 16, 1978, p. 158.

4. "Autos Joe," *Newsweek,* July 2, 1973, pp. 62–64.

5. Edward T. James, Janet Wilson James, and Paul S. Boyer, *Notable American Women 1607–1950: A Biographical Dictionary,* vol. III (Cambridge, Mass.: Belknap Press, 1971), pp. 533–534.

6. Sally Scanlon, "Manage Sales . . . Yes, she can," *Sales and Marketing Management,* vol. 118, no. 8 (June 13, 1977), pp. 33–39.

7. Barry Cook, telephone interview, February 8, 1978.

8. "Corporate Woman: The Industrial Salesman Becomes a Salesperson." *Business Week,* February 19, 1979, pp. 104–110.

9. "Chicken Colonel," *Newsweek,* July 25, 1966, p. 79.

10. Arthur George Gaston, Sr., *The Ebony Success Library,* vol. II (Chicago: Ebony Johnson, 1973), pp. 84–87.

11. Robert L. Heilbroner, *The Making of Economic Society,* 3rd ed. (Englewood Cliffs, N.J.: Prentice-Hall, 1970), p. 43.

12. Daniel Boorstin, *The Americans: The National Experience* (New York: Random House, 1965), p. 11.

13. Peter Lyon, "Isaac Singer and His Wonderful Sewing Machine," *American Heritage,* October 1958, p. 122.

14. Reavis Cox, in association with Charles S. Goodman and Thomas C. Fichandler, *Distribution in a High Level Economy* (Englewood Cliffs, N.J.: Prentice-Hall, 1965), pp. 98–99.

15. Charles M. Futrell, "Measurement of Salespeople's Job Satisfaction: Convergent and Discriminant Validity of Corresponding INDSCALES and Job Descriptive Index Scales," *Journal of Marketing Research,* vol. 16 (November 1979), pp. 594–597, presents research on job satisfaction among salespeople on these and other job satisfaction attributes.

16. *Occupational Outlook Handbook, 1974–1975 Edition,* Bulletin No. 1785, Washington, D.C., U.S. Government Printing Office, Department of Labor.

17. Abbot, Longer & Associates, college recruiting report, 1977. In "Salesmen's Annual Compensation," *Sales & Marketing Management,* vol. 120, no. 3 (February 27, 1978), p. 69.

Strategic Selling Knowledge

The opportunities discussed in Chapter 1 can be translated into success by those prepared to meet the challenge. The following chapters are designed to give you the knowledge and direction needed to take advantage of selling opportunities.

Effectiveness and poise in selling situations are promoted when a salesperson has: (1) a broad educational background that provides self-confidence in talking to people in areas of *their* interests, (2) specialized training in representing the company and selling its specific products, (3) a willingness to improve through self-development methods, (4) an understanding of persuasive techniques, and (5) the ability to recognize the strategic information needed to use persuasive techniques effectively. A broad educational background comes from taking courses in many academic areas, having good reading habits, and having a variety of work experiences. Companies usually provide training in specific selling principles needed for their product lines. The remaining three requisites will be examined in this text. Chapters 3 through 7 of Part I include ideas designed to help in achieving success, in developing a selling personality, in understanding the thinking of prospects, and in increasing awareness of selling environments. Part II contains descriptions of tested selling techniques that can be applied to any field of persuasion. Part III deals primarily with career advancement.

This chapter features a discussion of basic strategic information that every sales representative should know before calling on customers. Strategic planning requires a knowledge of strategy-guiding definitions and a recognition of what information should be acquired to perform the selling function competently. The following areas will be analyzed:

- Strategy-guiding definitions
- Knowledge of the company and its products
- Knowledge of pricing, discounts, and buying arrangement alternatives
- Knowledge sources

STRATEGY-GUIDING DEFINITIONS

Definitions are needed to guide a salesperson's general approach to and mental preparation for selling. *Strategy* is the overall or coordinated plan for achieving goals. *Planned strategy* can be formulated from definitions that suggest the best methods for reaching selling goals. Strategic plans can be compared to basic definitions. If there are any incompatibilities between plans and definitions, salespersons can replan or redefine. The definition of a market, for example, is people who have the ability and willingness to buy. By searching a territory for people with these qualifications, a sales representative can learn which products in a product line have the best chances for success and which products should be sold to particular prospects. Careful definition can be used to qualify or evaluate each potential prospect, because money and wants—the shapers of ability and willingness to buy—are the important elements in buying decisions.

Marketing

Marketing includes those activities that are necessary to assure that the right products and services are made available efficiently to prospects through the right routes, at the right prices, using the right promotional blend (see Figure 2.1). Personal selling strategy must be coordinated with other parts of the total marketing effort, such as pricing, delivery, and distribution. Selling strategies must be compatible with advertising and other promotional decisions. In formulating strategy, sales representatives must be conscious of other marketing efforts by the firm. Only in this way can all selling plans be integrated to achieve maximum marketing impact.

Customer Orientation

Customer orientation means focusing primary attention on satisfying the needs and wants of customers at a profit. If an enterprise is to survive and

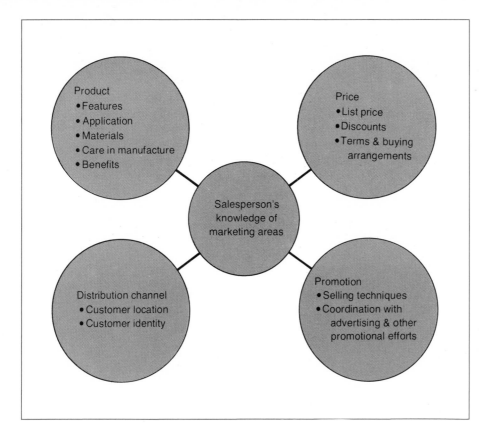

Figure 2.1 Salesperson's Knowledge of the Marketing Mix

grow, all employees and operations should reflect this philosophy. It is especially important for salespersons to remember that selling's primary function is to serve customers profitably. Every transaction should benefit both buyer and seller. Further, buyers must always sense that sellers have a genuine interest in their needs and wants.

Persuasion

Persuasion is an open appeal, either rational or emotional, to influence someone into action or belief (1). Particular attention should be paid to the word *emotional* in this definition. Expensive items usually cannot be sold to individuals without arousing some level of emotion. Parting with money or making a decision affecting one's position in a firm is an emotional experience for most people. Famed psychologist Ernest Dichter points out that even selling industrial goods requires recognition of emotional motivations in buyers (2). It is extremely hard to persuade someone to buy, unless there is at least a tinge of excitement stimulated in the sales interview. This is why enthusiasm is so vital in selling—it stirs prospect feelings.

Personal Selling

Personal selling has been defined by the Definitions Committee of the American Marketing Association as "the personal ... process of assisting and/or persuading a prospective customer to buy a commodity or a service or to act favorably upon an idea that has commercial significance to the seller" (3). This traditional definition, arrived at after considerable thought in the 1950s seems too limited to describe the role of personal selling for the 1980s.

To some, "Persuasion ... has no rightful place in modern selling" (4). To others, it is nothing else. "You cannot force a customer or prospect to do anything. You have to influence her or persuade him. *Selling is the art of persuasion,* the ability to influence someone to your way of thinking and to motivate him to buy your product or service" (5).

Even the "official" American Marketing Association definition includes persuasion as part of the personal selling process. Unfortunately, persuasion is a value-loaded term to some. There are those who would focus on persuasion's use of emotional appeals, forgetting that facts can be quite persuasive. Obviously, emotional browbeating of a prospect to force a sale is a repugnant practice. Moreover, it unlikely to be effective.

Facts rarely speak for themselves. To be an effective user of rational appeals for persuasion, a sales representative must select those facts that are relevant to a prospect and pertinent to a buy/no-buy decision. Contemporary standards of business behavior demand that sales provide satisfaction to buyers as well as sellers. An old-fashioned definition of selling that captures the flavor of this idea is selling is "moving out goods that don't come back to customers who do." It is upon the first part of the traditional definition—assisting prospective customers—that modern selling is based.

Modern personal selling guides people to buy through reducing their perceptions of risk by supplying information about the product or service and assurances on the wisdom of purchasing it. It creates an atmosphere of harmony. Professional sales representatives strive to avoid conflicts between themselves and their prospects. Guiding prospects to make choices that are beneficial to both buyers and sellers is today's selling approach. Most people do not like being sold. They prefer to choose to buy through making up their own minds on rational grounds. Sales representatives who guide customer choices establish a proper atmosphere for buying. Whether or not a customer accepts a sales representative's guidance on a particular call, the rapport a representative builds over time through obvious interest in solving customer problems means the welcome mat will be out for future calls.

Prospects hesitate to buy because of the inherent risks they perceive in making a choice. Few people make a commitment to spend without first feeling adequately informed. Industrial buyers who make purchases on behalf of their firms put their careers on the line when they buy. Prospects have a tendency to resist changes that involve risk. Few changes are perceived as being riskless. Positive information—information that informs prospects of buyer benefits—reduces the risk they perceive in making the purchase. Sales representatives must suggest buyer benefits to overbalance the perceived risks of buying. In other words, the benefits of saying yes must be presented in such a way that they outweigh the risks of saying no.

The benefits of saying yes are enhanced by communicating to prospects about a selling company's reputation for honesty, its available maintenance services, its policies on return of unsatisfactory products, its warranties, and other evidence that the seller's offer is made in good faith. Trials of products, where available, can do much to assure prospects that there is little or no risk in accepting a sales representative's offer. Information and assurances inspire confidence and create excitement about the benefits of saying yes to a sales representative's offer.

A sales call is a potential conflict-of-interest situation. Salespeople are interested in persuading prospects to buy. Prospects are interested in preserving their resources until assured of a good buy. A congenial atmosphere allows both sellers and buyers to communicate more effectively. Sales representatives must be good listeners—sensitive to the nuances of prospect needs and wants. Good listening builds harmony between those who would sell and those who would buy. It is an old sales representative's lament that prospects buy from their friends. Indeed, they do (6). Successful sales representatives are those who have become their prospects' friends. Winning an argument with a prospect may be the best way to lose a sale. Sales representatives do not make calls on customers to argue with them. Calls are made for the benefit of both buyer and seller.

Building harmony and establishing rapport with a prospect do not require salespeople to accept attacks on their personal honesty or against the companies they represent. To some prospects, a sales call is a kind of game. Such prospects see themselves as losers if salespeople win by getting an order easily. Subjugating personal preferences, retaining poise, and supplying prospect problem-solving information are the most effective ways of dealing with prospects who view sales presentations as winner-take-all games. The proper method for sales representatives in today's increasingly sophisticated markets is to gain sales through offering prospects greater service than can be obtained from competitors.

KNOWLEDGE OF COMPANY AND PRODUCTS

Company Knowledge

Prospects want to know how well a company stands behind its products. To customers, sales representatives *are* the companies they represent. Representatives without basic knowledge of their companies "can give outsiders the impression of incompetence on the part of the entire organization" (7). Facts about the company's history, its size, its place in the industry, and its policies furnish needed assurances. Any company is of particular interest to several types of customers: those who buy expensive industrial equipment that requires expert installation and servicing; those who buy products that may have to be returned; those who purchase intangibles such as life insurance or consulting services, where seller expertise is important in obtaining desired results. Bankruptcy of an industrial-equipment company could mean improper maintenance support and loss of trade-in value, while mismanagement of an investment portfolio could mean loss of capital investment.

Sales representatives' morale, confidence, efficiency, and persuasiveness are affected by their understanding of the system within which they work. Knowledge of a firm's history can inspire pride in sales representatives and give them a sense of identification with important corporate traditions. It is important for a Burroughs representative to know of Burroughs' role as devel-

All customers, particularly expert buyers, are interested in important details about the product.

"That price is for our stripped down model. With options including tinted nose cone, chrome finish, and our super Deluxe T-67 rocket engine, the price is $7,500,000.00 complete. Tax and license not included."

Burroughs had its beginning in St. Louis, Missouri, in 1886 with the first production of the adding machine by its predecessor, the American Arithmometer Company. Our worldwide operations began very shortly thereafter, with the formation of the first overseas subsidiary in England in 1896, and the first overseas manufacturing plant in Nottingham, England, in 1898.

In 1904, the Company moved its United States operations to Detroit, Michigan, which has been the location of its World Headquarters ever since.

Burroughs products have grown from the original adding machine to a broad range of data processing equipment and services. Our products include large, medium, and small-scale computer systems; business mini-computers; peripheral equipment; terminal products and systems; data preparation products; small application machines; program products; business forms and supplies; custom products, and electronic components.

Today, we are a major company in the data processing industry—an industry which some predict will be the largest in the world by the end of this century. We are a worldwide company employing over 48,000 people. We have engineering and manufacturing facilities in nine countries, and our products are supplied in more than 120 countries.

Burroughs growth has been particularly rapid in recent years, as illustrated by our financial progress. Since 1963, worldwide revenue has grown from $391 million to $1.284 billion. During the same period, net income has risen from $8.5 million to $115.9 million.

Burroughs World Headquarters in Detroit is located on a site that has been the Company's home since 1904.

Figure 2.2   A Brief History of the Burroughs Corporation

Source: *Burroughs in Brief,* a company publication to acquaint customers and other interested publics with the history and products of the Burroughs Corporation. Burroughs Corporation, Detroit.

oper of the adding machine and of the corporation's commitment to the data-processing industry (see Figure 2.2).

A sales representative should know company employees by name, particularly higher officials, people concerned with order processing, and supporting service personnel. Knowing the names of superiors can save embarrassment and promote the sales representative's advancement. Knowing the names of order processors can facilitate communication and expedite service and delivery to customers. Acquaintance with support personnel can foster a team spirit in serving customers.

The sales representative is an agent of the company and must understand its policies and rules. Many salespersons have the power to bind their companies legally, so they must be aware of corporate policies regarding offers to buyers. Most companies have policy manuals to assure integrity in dealing with "buyers." Prospects are especially interested in price and discount policies, credit policies, delivery policies, and rules about merchandise return. Such information is outlined in most company policy manuals.

Product Knowledge

A product is more than a physical object (hardware). It is a "total package" that includes the purchasing environment, delivery, credit, installation, training in use, warranties, advertising, maintenance, and other services. A product is the entire unit offered to a consumer—the sum total of buyer satisfactions delivered. The physical object, if one exists, is meaningful only in terms of the satisfactions it provides. A product plus all its attendant services is known as an *offering*.

Why Product Knowledge Is Important. The key ingredient to professionalism in selling is product knowledge. Expert buyers such as engineers and purchasing agents complain that vague knowledge of the product is a great weakness of many sales representatives. Buyers often have to justify purchase of particular products in detail. They are unable to do so if a salesperson lacks knowledge about the product. Physicians sell medical services. If they don't know their product, their patients are in mortal danger. Even a deficient selling personality may be overlooked if the salesperson has an expert understanding of how a product can be applied to prospect needs. When a sales representative projects confidence and enthusiasm based on product knowledge, prospects gain confidence in the offer made. Given full information about a product, the prospect can visualize its ideal use and overcome risk barriers. In addition, salespersons who confront the silent type of prospect never need to be at a loss for words. They can make smooth presentations based on product information and specifics instead of generalities. The mark of the unprofessional salesperson is a loss for words or constant use of meaningless adjectives like "wonderful," "outstanding," and "terrific." Sales representatives are asked the most searching questions about product offerings. Ignorance keeps salespersons from closing many sales. Selling a line of complex products requires diligent study. Gaining adequate product knowledge can be a sales representative's greatest challenge (see Figure 2.3). Some companies completely revamp their product lines every few years to keep up in the frantic technology race and to provide themselves with real competitive advantages.

The shift from hardware (equipment) to software (programs) in the computer

Figure 2.3
Computers are complex and require diligent study by the salesperson to understand their features, operations, and applications.

industry illustrates how market changes require sales representatives to keep updating their product knowledge. Other markets may not demonstrate the same degree of change, but the days when a newly trained salesperson could feel confident that the product knowledge gained in an initial training program would last through a career are over. Between 1980 and 1990, the composition of the computer industry's markets is expected to change significantly (see Figure 2.4). New markets with new customers working to solve new problems will place different demands on those salespeople who would sell them the means to solve these new problems. Maintaining a state-of-the-art level of product knowledge is a necessity in this and most other markets.

Manufacturing Facts. Prospective buyers may appreciate information about research, the quality of input materials, the care taken in manufacture, the skilled labor involved, tests the product can stand, quality control stand-

Where the Chips Will Fall

Microcomputer (computer-on-a-chip) sales will rocket from $4.0 billion in 1980 to $26.4 billion in 1990, according to Market Venture Consultants (MVC), a Newport Beach, CA, research firm. Industry changes will be as dramatic as the sales curve. While Apple, Atari, Commodore, and Tandy have dominated the market up to now, by 1982 Hewlett-Packard, IBM, and Xerox will also be contenders in the race for market leadership. The important shift, of course, will be from hardware to software, but the proliferation of retail outlets will be significant, too. "The industry will turn into a consumer marketing game," says MVC chief Gerry Guyod, "as vendors rely upon different types of stores to sell their products."

1980
$4.0 Bil.

1990
$26.4 Bil.

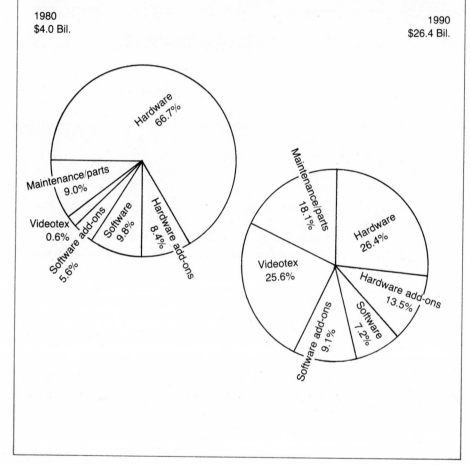

Figure 2.4

Source: *Sales and Marketing Management* (November 16, 1981):18.

ards, and other data implying product quality. Many products go into production only after careful research indicates they will have a relative marketing advantage over existing offerings. The results of research can be used to show potential customers the special benefits that add to its value to them.

Materials used in manufacturing processes are of interest to prospective customers because they affect the product's durability and performance and may indicate its resistance to rust, temperature changes, and other detrimental environmental elements. All the precautions taken to make and test a product should be explained to convey the idea of quality construction. For example prospects who might question the quality of less expensive screws made abroad might accept the results of breaking-strength tests as proof of the screws' durability as component parts. Quality control standards also affirm a manufacturer's commitment to excellence. Purchasing agents prefer to buy from sellers with formal quality control programs.

If companies can prove their manufacturing experience through evidence of government contracts or long-term pioneering in a field, buyers may be impressed. An office-equipment corporation gained much of its experience in computers by making units for the space missile program. It was able to use this experience to enter the highly competitive data-processing computer market. This type of background information helps give a salesperson confidence in the offering and in the company. Both are crucial to attitude.

Product Features. A product's or a service's benefits to a buyer are the focal point of a sales interview. Prospective buyers are interested in a product's characteristics and how these characteristics or features can benefit them.

The salesperson who goes into an interview with inadequate product knowledge may not be able to answer prospect questions. Few things can end an interview faster than loss of confidence in a salesperson. Both enthusiasm and confidence stem from product knowledge. While it is important to know all features and characteristics of a product, it is imperative to know those advantages that differentiate your product from those of competition. Competitors can actually help a salesperson sell by creating prospect interest in the product, in general. Superiority of a particular offering in terms of buyer benefits delivered creates potential for a sale. Statements like the following explain why a customer should choose your product: "This machine is 30 percent faster than any other machine on the market," or "You simply press this button to change the program on this machine, while other machines require a separate control unit for each separate application," or "Because this equipment has a special feature that allows you to print an original ledger and statement, you don't have to handle expensive and messy carbons. Your customers will be impressed with the clear copies of the invoice they receive."

All *performance* features of a product should be discussed, for it is difficult to determine in advance which ones will be important to a customer. Nearly every product has performance features:

- Paint sellers talk about coverability, durability, and spreadability.
- Fuel merchants speak in terms of power ingredients and additives.
- Do-it-yourself floor advertisers broadcast ease of application.
- Tissue commercials demonstrate softness.
- Insurance companies stress fast payments of claims.
- Food brokers promote shelf life and nutritional value.
- TV dealers push "lifelike" color.

Some performance features of machinery and equipment are capacity, speed of operation, ease of operation, flexibility in application, operating-materials costs, infrequency of repair, operator skill needed, safety features, and low maintenance requirements.

Other facts about the total offering can be equally important. Customers who take their time making up their minds still expect to get *delivery* as soon as possible. The salesperson should be very honest about how long delivery takes and should make every effort to get the purchased item to the buyer within the promised time limits. *Warranties* reduce buying risks and should always be mentioned in sales presentations. Many appliances and machines have a service warranty, and when the warranty expires, the customer usually may purchase a service contract on a yearly basis. In selling products to middlemen for resale, *consumer advertising* is often a significant feature in a sales representative's product offering. Merchants who are concerned with inventory turnover and profits want to know the extent and quality of advertising and promotional materials backing up product sales.

Often, *Consumer Reports* or findings from *independent research firms* may compare a product favorably to those of competitors. For selling purposes, this "unbiased" information can be regarded as a part of the product's total offering. The *price* is probably the most asked about part of an offering. Some sales representatives have so many products to sell that they have to refer to price lists, and prices of certain raw materials and industrial goods fluctuate frequently, requiring new lists nearly every day. Naturally, it is better to be able to make an offer and close a sale without having to refer to a price list. But for special orders, a salesperson must have a price list and use it without embarrassment (see Figure 2.5).

Buyers often want a selection, so a sales representative should be able to explain how the product offered fits into the total line of products sold and why alternative products offered by the company might also be needed by the customer. Prospects should be told of all the features of a product and not just of those features that solve particular problems indicated as important by the prospects. Buyers may want to trade in or sell the product later, or they may need the product for other applications in the future. The total capacities of a

Figure 2.5 Price List* The Jan-Chem Company
Price Schedule (Institutions): 1-1-79 through 3-31-79

Jan-Towels (paper towels) 12 rolls	$3.00 dozen

NONAEROSOL SPRAY CANS

Jan-Pure, Disinfectant and Deodorant	27.00 dozen
Jan-Oven-Baking Surface Cleaner	24.50 dozen
Jan-Surface Clean (all purpose)	21.00 dozen
Jan-Gleem, Glass Cleaner	20.00 dozen
Combo-Jan, Deodorant, Disinfectant, and Cleaner	22.00 dozen
Jan-Ceptic, Toilet Bowl Antiseptic	20.00 dozen
Jan-Sting Insecticide, Bees and Wasps	33.00 dozen
Jan-Kill, Insecticide	30.00 dozen
Jan-Cide, Ant and Roach Insecticide	33.00 dozen
Jan-Shine, Furniture Polish	28.00 dozen
Jan-Alum, Aluminum Polish	23.50 dozen
Jan-Panel, Paneling Renew	21.00 dozen
Jan-Elec, Electric Contact Cleaner	38.00 dozen
Jan-Strip, Paint Stripper	32.00 dozen
Jan-Degreaser	33.00 dozen
Jan-OGT, (oil, grease, and tar remover)	37.00 dozen
Jan-Back, Chalkboard Cleaner	24.50 dozen
Jan-Wax, Vinyl Wax	27.00 dozen
Jan-Vin, Vinyl Cleaner	23.00 dozen
Jan-Porce, Porcelain Cleaner	21.00 dozen

FLOOR FINISHES

Jan-Acril, Acrylic Finish (55-gallon drums†)	6.00 gallon
Jan-Gym (55-gallon drums†)	7.50 gallon

DRUM CONTAINER CLEANSER

Jan-Detergent (general) (55-gallon drums†)	5.00 gallon

HAND CLEANER

Jan-Moist Waterless (24–30 ounces)	42.00 case

SPECIAL DEALS

1 case of Jan-Moist with any $2,000 purchase
1 dozen Jan-Pure with any 5-drum–purchase floor finish

*Fictitious price list.
†Ask about our discount schedule for large purchases.

product reflect its maximum potential value and help tip the scales in favor of buying. Some equipment is so flexible and has so many possible applications that knowing about its total use is almost impossible. Computer capabilities, for example, are limited only by the human mind's ability to discover and program all jobs that the machines might accomplish. Every salesperson is expected to know the common applications and capacities of each unit in the entire iine.

Strategic Use of Features. Features should be used to show prospects *how* they can satisfy their wants and solve their specific problems. A key selling strategy is finding out what prospective buyers want and convincing them that the offered product can fill their needs. Knowing all the technical qualities and scientific virtues of an offering is not enough; buyers must be convinced that each product feature will benefit them. An air conditioner, for example, may have a 15,000 BTU capacity and a sealed motor. These may be meaningless features unless the buyer is convinced that it can cool a vacation cottage and does not have to be oiled. An outboard motor with 50 horsepower becomes meaningful if the potential customer learns that it can pull two skiers at 35 miles per hour. A removable printing element on a typewriter means the type can be changed easily and quickly and cleaning is much simpler.

Product features have value in making a sales presentation only as they can be translated into buyer benefits. A magic phrase in personal selling is "This product has . . . , which means to you . . . ." It is the bridge that connects product features to buyer benefits. Benefits that competitors cannot match make the most forceful selling points. Sometimes called U.S.P.s—unique selling propositions—they make clear the distinctions between one sales offering and another.

The good sales representative learns and uses magic phrases in such a way that prospects can visualize themselves using the product and deriving maximum satisfaction from it. Words are the tools of the selling trade. Every product has special words associated with it that cast it in a special light. Often, selling phrases can be found in advertising copy or in other company publications, but sometimes a salesperson must learn them from experience. Examples of magic selling phrases are:

- Air-cooled means you are ready to go and you don't need antifreeze.
- Sleeping on a Sealy is like sleeping on a cloud.
- Gives you finished pictures in sixty seconds.
- The kind of boots the real cowboys wear.
- Just turn the knob to change the job.
- Goes from 0 to 60 in six seconds.
- Lucite turns you loose.
- All you add is love.

- Finger-lickin' good.
- Shake and bake.
- Squeezably soft.

Notice that nearly every one of these phrases translates some feature into a benefit. Notice also that each suggests a picture of the buyer using the product under ideal circumstances.

Certain words other than those used in key phrases must also be learned. Above all, a salesperson does not want to hint, by using poorly selected words, that a product has certain weaknesses. Words like "cheap" and "substitute" should not be used in association with most products. Learning the right sequence of words and phrases to convince a prospect is also important. Finally, the salesperson should learn and use the vocabulary used in the business. This shows that the salesperson is a part of the industry and speaks the language of the trade.

To fit benefits to prospect problems, a representative must know how prospective buyers can use a product to best advantage. Salespersons selling minicomputers, for example, sell the "hardware" only in connection with accounting-system ideas that will improve a prospect's data processing. Systems sales representatives have to study good mechanized accounting operations and know more than their prospects to justify a recommended change of procedure. Because many buyers look to professional salespersons for consulting advice, salespersons have to know how their products will fit into the operations of each customer. It is impossible to know too much about a product, its benefits, and its applications.

Competitive Product Knowledge. Foreign and domestic competition have increased in nearly every industry over the last few years. It is now even more important for sales representatives to know what offers are being made to their prospects by other sales representatives. To sell effectively, a sales representative must know a great deal about competitors' offerings. It is necessary to know features, benefits, delivery times, warranties, maintenance requirements, services, competitive strategies, and prices. Product knowledge, market knowledge and a willingness to keep buyers posted, and knowledge of the buyer's product line were the second-, fourth-, and sixth-ranked qualities of outstanding salespersons as indicated by buyers in *Purchasing* magazine's 1981 Top Ten Salesmen *(sic)* Contest (8). These qualities outranked diplomacy, sales-call preparation and regularity, and technical education! Many large companies analyze competitive products. They collect information about strengths and weaknesses just as coaches send out scouts to find out about the plays of the other team before devising a game plan for that opponent. Competitive information is relayed to salespersons at sales meetings, conventions, and through special firm memorandums. Even if you work for a small company, you can learn much about your competition from customers, fellow sales representatives, and advertisements. Salespersons should be wary, however, of information given by prospects. In an effort to make a deal, prospects may stretch the truth, or they may be mistaken about competitive offers. In trying to get the best bargain, prospects may quote a price lower than a competitive salesperson actually offered, or they may compare the price of a competitive product of lower quality with the price quoted on an item of higher quality.

KNOWLEDGE OF PRICING, DISCOUNTS, AND BUYING ARRANGEMENT ALTERNATIVES

The basic attitude of a firm's executives toward price and price concessions will affect selling strategy. The following discussion of basic pricing, discounts, and buying arrangements is designed to show possible alternatives in prices and price offerings.

Basic Pricing

Mature products are sold on a market basis, an above-market basis, or a below-market basis. If the company's prices are above competition, sales reps have to prove a relative advantage in their offering—in other words, they have to sell quality. If the company's prices are below competition, price is emphasized in a presentation. With competitively priced products of similar quality and features, sales reps should emphasize their personality and their company's reputation in their presentation. New products are sold on either a skimming price strategy or a penetration price strategy. "Skimming" means selling at high prices to elite buyers and lowering the prices later to tap additional buyers. Plain plastic ball-point pens sold for $15 each when they were first introduced. Great care must be taken to select prospects and to sell an innovation's unique characteristics. Sometimes new, mass-produced products are priced to penetrate markets. This means the product is expected to be sold "en masse" and the innovating company's market share (portion of the market) is to be enlarged or maintained. In this case, volume can be gained by spreading the information by telephone or direct mail and by cultivating a broad range of prospects. Specific price policies and psychology are beyond the scope of this text, but persons contemplating going into business for themselves should know many pricing alternatives. Price is a central consideration in the minds of most buyers.

Discounts

Nearly every buyer expects a discount, since most firms give quantity, trade, or cash discounts. Quantity discounts are given to a buyer for purchasing in multiple units or bulk. They must be given strictly according to company schedules, or legal troubles may follow. The pattern of agencies, from producer to consumer, through which goods must move is termed the marketing channel. Trade discounts are given to wholesalers and retailers because of their positions in a marketing channel. Cash discounts are given for paying bills before certain dates, but to the buyer they are seen as reductions in list price. Discounts reduce risks by reducing the cost of products. Sometimes advertising allowances or special services are given with purchases. Again, it is important that company policy be strictly followed to avoid legal problems.

Buying Arrangements

Many buyers have a definite need for a product and can mentally justify buying it; however, they may not have the money. The buyer in bad financial condition obviously needs profits or cost-saving products more than the buyer with large cash reserves. Most large concerns can offer several options to pay for equipment. Sales representatives must know these options or be able to direct buyers to bank plans or financial concerns that lend money. Some corporations are stricter than others as to which customers will be extended credit. A salesperson must coordinate selling plans with credit management policies. Usually, durable goods can be purchased on an installment plan, or they can be rented. Buyers will want to know about interest charges. A representative must be able to figure out accurately what the monthly payments will be. If calculations of the monthly payments are accidentally too small, buyers may cancel their orders when they find out the price is higher. If calculations of the installment payments are too large, they may not buy in the first place. Some buyers would rather rent equipment, because rent can be deducted as a cost of doing business and may mean important tax savings, while total equipment costs can be deducted only in part—one year of depreciation at a time. In justifying a deal, monthly benefits may be directly compared to monthly costs. The amount of time in which cost-saving equipment can pay for itself (payback) may be an important consideration. Some sales representatives can control price by offering seconds or demonstrators, by allowing more or less for trade-ins, or by offering used products. Remember, your firm wants everyone in its sales force to be a profitable member of the sales team. Too many concessions too early should be avoided. The prospect sold a low-priced, "fighting brand" may have needed and wanted the first-line product, and price may well be forgotten long before a durable product needs to be replaced.

A salesperson should know all buying terms that make a product affordable to the prospect.

Reprinted by permission of the artist, Joseph Zeis.

THE SATURDAY EVENING POST

"And now I suppose you're wondering if you can afford it."

KNOWLEDGE SOURCES

To be effective, sales representatives need quick access to information sources. Knowing where to find needed information saves time, promotes learning, and frees the mind to store those important facts that must be recalled during an interview. A wealth of information can be obtained from company literature, sales meetings and conferences, outside material, personal sources, and careful observation.

Company Literature

Many companies, particularly large companies, publish policy manuals; sales-training texts; product-information manuals; visual-aids materials, such as charts and diagrams; newsletters; advertising copy; annual reports; research reports; and other matter that can supply a salesperson with fast information. Each company varies the format of these references, and smaller companies usually provide fewer publications than do large ones. Beginning salespersons should make a special point to locate everything the company has that will help them learn the business. This may not be easy, since most companies have sources in many different places and not in a centralized library.

Trainees should spend hours looking through the manuals to select information they might use and to become thoroughly familiar with each source. They should read about the firm's historical heritage, philosophies, and role in its industry. They should look into employee policies that affect them, such as retirement, vacations, sick leave, and compensation regulations. They should study the company's order-handling, price, discount, credit, returns, allowance, service, and complaint-handling policies. These policies represent the company's experience in dealing with its markets. They have been prepared to ensure that employees handle recurring situations uniformly and legally.

Some manuals or publications will also contain in-depth product information. Detailed chemical, mechanical, or descriptive product analyses may be available to give beginners insight into product composition and benefits. Salespersons should locate and study charts, diagrams, and other visual aids available for learning and selling. Competitive product information may also be found in current company newsletters. Annual reports contain trends, products, and the future direction of the company. Product and market research may be available on request, and advertisements such as the one shown in Figure 2.6 are often on display racks in the sales office.

Sales-training texts may be part of a formal training course. These materials embody the company's experiences in salesperson-customer relationships and contain product information, role-playing situations, sample sales presentations, cases, and ways to handle common problems. These can help a trainee adjust previous information and experience to the special problems of selling a specific company offering.

Sales Meetings and Conferences

Sales meetings are usually held when calling on prospects is least productive. This varies with particular sales situations. In the game of selling, sales meetings may be considered strategic "half-time" meetings designed to tie the sales force together, discuss selling strategy, and assess goal accomplishments. New information is often introduced about company and competitive products. Selling experiences are shared. Yearly sales conferences are usually more formal meetings, where company experts offer explanations of new corporate commitments, new product applications, new products, and revised selling strategies.

ALL FEET ARE NOT CREATED EQUAL.

Those little footprints on your birth certificate aren't there for decoration. They were the best way you had of saying — I'm an individual; I'm unique.

And the moment you start treating your feet like they belong to someone else, they're going to let you know about it. Via blisters, shin splints, stress fractures or any number of other ailments.

No one has done more to get on an intimate basis with feet than Nike. We built one of the most sophisticated sports research labs in the world — the only one in the shoe industry — and staffed it with researchers in biomechanics, anatomy and exercise physiology.

Feet, we've found, can be pretty articulate. But you have to know how to listen.

First, pay attention to their prints. There are three basic types, and you can spot yours the next time you step out of the shower.

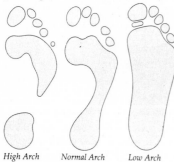

High Arch   Normal Arch   Low Arch

According to our ongoing anatomy study, nearly four runners

out of ten have something other than a normal arch.

Those with extremely low arches may take solace in the fact they share this trait with Henry Rono and Patti Catalano.

Unfortunately, some low arched feet overindulge. They're so flexible, they love to pronate. A little pronation is a good thing because it absorbs shock. Too much of a good thing, however, can lead to various knee and foot problems.

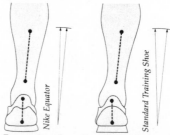

Two rear views of pronation, taken from high speed film. Although runner and speed are identical, angle between lower left leg and rearfoot is less in Nike Equator than standard training shoe.

To give them a bit of self-discipline, we designed the Equator. Through computer analysis of high speed film, our lab reports show this shoe reduces rearfoot motion up to five degrees, or slightly less than a hard orthotic.

The high arched foot has its own story to tell. And frequently, it's a shocker. If this foot is also rigid, as is often the case, it will do little to absorb impact.

That's why for the likes of Steve Ovett, Joan Benoit and Herb Lindsay, cushioning is everything.

We want shoes that do more than "feel" soft in the store. So we

check out materials with dynamic load displacement tests. And run prototypes across force platforms to judge their shock attenuation.

But don't think because you're blessed with a normal arch that you can give your feet just anything to wear.

After your next shower make two sets of footprints, one while sitting, one standing. If the second set is much flatter than the first, your feet are flexible. Look for a shoe with good motion control. If there's little difference, go for cushion.

Best of all, take your feet to an expert. A knowledgeable dealer can put you into the shoe your foot was created for. And if you have persistent health problems, don't mess around. See an orthopedist or podiatrist.

For our part, we're seeing runners. In the lab, at the schools, in meets and races all over the country.

We're compiling information. Modifying our lasts, creating new ones. We want to be certain we're making the proper shoe for the proper individual.

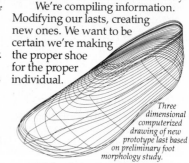

Three dimensional computerized drawing of new prototype last based on preliminary foot morphology study.

Of the thousands of runners we've seen so far, we've never met a foot we didn't like. Or couldn't help.

NIKE

Beaverton, Oregon

Figure 2.6

Outside Material

Useful noncompany materials can be found in libraries, trade association offices, magazine articles, media advertisements, competitive annual reports, and publications of other companies. Public and university libraries contain census data with details about territories and markets, books on selling, and current magazine articles concerning industries, products, trends, and selling in general. Reference librarians, periodical guides, and card catalogues will unlock the vast store of information in any library. Books on personal success, magazines for sales representatives, and sometimes even tapes, records, and films may be examined. Trade association offices collect information about industries that may include competitive comparisons and standings (market shares) of firms.

Sales & Marketing Management magazine and *Industrial Distribution* are designed for sales representatives. *Sales & Marketing Management* covers selling costs, comparative salaries, current selling methods, territorial potential indexes, and other important data. *Industrial Distribution* is of particular interest to industrial sales representatives. *Consumers Research Bulletins* and *Consumer Reports* give detailed comparisons of competing consumer products and make purchase-decision recommendations to customers. If a product is favorably compared and recommended by either of these supposedly unbiased sources, that recommendation can help sell prospects. Media advertisements show the selling benefits of competitive products, while competitive annual reports feature the progress and new offerings of competitors. The Bell Telephone Company furnishes booklets on telephone selling techniques. The Success Motivation Institute of Waco, Texas, sells tapes and records on success selling methods. For a fee, private research corporations like A. E. Nielsen, Inc., of Evanston, Illinois, will furnish company sales trends.

Personal Sources

Sales managers, fellow sales representatives, customers, repair personnel, competitors, and others can be good information sources. A good sales representative is always on the alert for marketing intelligence. Sales representatives are expected to know the answers or to know where to find them. Senior sales representatives can give junior sales representatives information and pointers on technique. There is no substitute for watching an innovative salesperson get an order from a prospect. Customers are the best source of information on customer problems and often on competitive selling techniques and offerings. Repair personnel know when an old product is wearing out and can tell representatives facts about a product that they should know. Competitive sales representatives can be a source of information about customers they can't serve. Careful, diligent questioning and listening by a representative is the key to more profitable prospecting. It is a recurring myth that effective salespeople must be good talkers. What they really must be is good listeners. Good listening together with careful observation can produce high payoffs.

Careful Observation

A vast amount of information can be obtained by watching other sales representatives sell, looking for changes in the territory that could lead to new prospects (see Photo 2.1), and observing prospects' environments and body movements for clues about interests and attitudes. Although each sales personality is different, a clearer concept of the sales interview interaction is gained from following the tactics of a senior salesperson observed in action. Machine sales representatives who do not watch their territories for new construction or fire damage are missing important sources of prospects. Insurance sales representatives who do not clip marriage and birth announcements may not be observing carefully enough to succeed. More will be said about observing prospect environments and body movements in later chapters.

SUMMARY

The aim of this chapter was to identify the areas of knowledge and self-development that are important to a successful selling career. More specifically, it was designed to show what basic information must be acquired before an effective selling strategy can be formulated. The earlier learning and development goals are set, the faster progress can be made. Once development goals are set, assimilation of information from texts, formal education, social experiences, and the company environment is accelerated.

The requisites for good selling are a broad educational background, specialized training in a company's products, a disposition toward self-improvement, a knowledge of selling techniques, and an awareness of what basic information is necessary for selling strategy. Definitions can help guide selling strategy. By knowing the definition of *marketing,* you can help coordinate your selling strategy with other parts of the marketing effort. By knowing the definition of *consumer orientation,* you can increase your awareness of the importance of both profits and consumer satisfaction. By knowing the definition of *persuasion,* you can remind yourself that both emotion and reason are important in selling appeals. And by knowing the definition of *selling,* you understand that *leading* (not driving) people to buy, by reducing their risks, in a harmonious atmosphere, is the desirable approach.

The aspiring salesperson should also know what specific facts must be learned about the company, the products, the competitors, the prices, and the

buying terms before interviewing prospects. Generally, prospects are quite interested in the financial strength, market position, technical experience, policies, and reputation of the company a salesperson represents. They are interested in the total product—the total of satisfactions that can be gained from using a product. While technical product features are important to expert buyers, all buyers want to know the details about what the product can do to satisfy specific needs. Buyers should always be told about the competitive advantages of a product. In this regard, the salesperson should study the product features, prices, services, and policies of competitors to be able to offer ethical comparisons and to devise strategy to win sales. All customers want to know about price, and many want to know about buying terms. Buying arrangements, discounts, and rental arrangements can help induce customers to buy your product.

Strategic information can be found in company literature, at sales meetings and conferences, in noncompany publications, by asking knowledgeable persons, and by careful observation. Policy manuals, product manuals, and advertising can reveal much product information. Libraries have a variety of sources of information about markets and competitive operations. Customers and competitive advertising can tell a representative much about competitive practice. If a representative knows what important strategic information is needed when first taking a job, the rep will be able to find it, learn it, and use it faster and more effectively.

1. Summarize the key requirements for effective and poised personal selling ability.

2. What is meant by each of the following terms? What is their significance for the salesperson?
   a. Persuasion
   b. Personal selling
   c. Offering

3. In what types of selling environment is a salesperson's knowledge of his/her company of particular importance?

4. What specific types of information and assurances reduce buyer risk?

5. Explain how the "total offering" is a more comprehensive concept than the "physical product."

6. "The key ingredient to professionalism in selling is product knowledge." Why?

7. From a salesperson's perspective, what is the relevance of product features?

8. Of what value is a "magic phrase" to a sales representative?

9. Why is competitive product knowledge important to a salesperson? What are some sources of such competitive product knowledge?

10. What are the basic price-level strategies for mature products?

11. New products may be introduced with either of two pricing strategies. Name them, and discuss the circumstances in which each is appropriate.

12. Describe the various types of discounts.

13. What types of company literature are available to the salesperson?

14. Where can the following information be obtained?
    a. Characteristics of company customers
    b. Company pricing policies
    c. Methods of solving selling problems
    d. Company history
    e. Product analysis
    f. Books on the theories of successful selling

APPLICATION QUESTIONS

1. The importance of product knowledge is stressed in this chapter. Remembering that the product is the entire unit offered to the consumer, including the purchasing environment, delivery, credit, and so on, do the following:

a. Picture yourself working in a retail store selling watches. List all the product knowledge that you should have.

b. Picture yourself selling new Corvettes for a local automobile dealer. What product knowledge would you want to have?

2. People involved in marketing realize that a product is purchased because of the benefits the purchaser will receive when using the product.

a. What benefits would you be looking for if you were buying a watch? A new Corvette?

b. How do these benefits match up with the product features that you listed above?

c. What product knowledge would you use to convince prospects that they would receive the desired benefits?

INCIDENTS

2–1

David Donelson is looking at a new car on the lot—here comes salesman James Longodds.

James:	That's a nice car, isn't it? It's our deluxe model.
Donelson:	It should be, at that sticker price.
James:	If you think that's high, we have one inside for about $500 more that has all the extras.
Donelson:	What does this little knob here on the dashboard do?
James:	I'm not sure. If you'll wait a minute, I'll go in and ask the sales manager.
Donelson:	That's O.K. It unlocks the trunk.
James:	If we gave you $400 off of list, would you buy it today?
Donelson:	I don't know what it has on it yet. What kind of city mileage does this one get?
James:	Oh, about sixteen miles per gallon, but it should do twenty on the road, I think.
Donelson:	What kind of engine does it have?
James:	Did you mean what cubic-inch displacement? That's in one of the manuals inside.
Donelson:	I see. It's here on the sticker.
James:	Pretty color, isn't it?
Donelson:	Does it come in a medium green?
James:	We only have two greens, forest and moss. But I don't think we have any on the lot.

Donelson: *(Starting the car)* It sounds good. How do you adjust the seat?

James: I'm not sure. Isn't there a little lever on the side? By the way, I'm James Longodds. I'm sorry I don't know more about this model, but I've just been working here a month.

Donelson: James, I'm David Donelson, co-owner of this dealership.

QUESTIONS

1. Evaluate James' knowledge of strategic facts that would have helped him sell the product.

2. What should he have known about the product before attempting to sell it?

3. Should he have made it a special point to meet the co-owner before now?

2–2

Willa Sargeant is just about to finish school and has been wondering about what kind of job she should look for. Willa has always wanted to have a job that would involve working with people. Ever since Girl Scouts, she has felt that she is a leader and could influence others. Now that the time has come to make a career decision, Willa is not quite so sure of what she wants to do. Willa has always heard that sales representatives who are successful are "born talkers." Despite her record as a student leader, Willa does not see herself as particularly talkative or extroverted. Indeed, her own view is that she is rather quiet. Rather than talk, Willa is inclined to listen to others and to rephrase their views before talking. She wonders if she might be too introspective to do the kinds of work—in selling, personnel, or advertising—that she has always wanted to do.

One day in her class in personal selling, her professor gave a test developed by Learning Dynamics, Inc., of Boston. After Willa had taken the test, she felt a lot more confident about herself and her abilities to succeed at a sales job.

Here is the test that Willa took:

YOUR PREDOMINANT SELLING STYLE

Circle the number of each item that would apply to you as a salesperson. If a statement does not apply to you, do not circle its number.

1. I believe in telling the prospect what's best for him or her.
2. I believe knowledge of human relationships is as important as product knowledge.
3. I think you have to appeal to whatever needs motivate the individual.
4. If you ask enough questions, you can usually manipulate the prospect into agreeing with you.
5. I enjoy formal sales meetings that have a prearranged agenda.

6. I think people buy from their friends.
7. I always relate the features to the benefits.
8. I always adhere to company policies.
9. I think a salesperson should always have a funny story ready.
10. I would rather call on a pleasant customer than an unpleasant one who has more to spend.
11. I think the only goal is to get a sale.
12. I believe that getting my paper work done on time is as important as any other part of my job.
13. I think objections are useful for getting more information and proving more benefits.
14. I like to memorize my sales pitch.
15. I dislike it when people don't stick to established procedures.
16. Shooting the breeze helps get more sales.
17. If your product is good enough, it sells itself.
18. I try to have a number of different closes available.
19. I don't give up trying to sell a prospect until the prospect is ready to kick me out.
20. Customers know what they want, you don't have to push them.
21. I plan and use my time efficiently.
22. I don't like anybody criticizing the way I do things.
23. I work smoothly with different managers in my company.
24. I don't like to pass on bad news.
25. There's no point looking for new business until you've put to bed your current business.
26. Keeping old customers happy is more important than finding new ones.
27. A good closing tactic is to point out to the prospect that *not* buying my product could result in the prospect's loss of prestige.
28. Keeping on friendly terms with competitors is good business.

How many differing selling styles do these views suggest to you?
Which responses would you place in each category?
How would you describe your personal selling style?
An interpretation of this exercise will be presented by your instructor.

2–3

Marjorie Jowers is a manufacturer's representative who specializes in selling women's apparel for clothing manufacturers on a commission basis. In the clothing industry, it is common to allow department stores and other buyers to purchase on credit up to a certain amount. The "line of credit" or credit limit depends on the merchants' financial condition and credit standing. Halperin's Department Store is one of Marjorie's best customers and has always enjoyed a good credit rating. Marjorie persuaded Sam Halperin to buy a line of ladies' coats on credit for $30,000, which was $5,000 over the store's credit limit with Claybaugh Manufacturing

Company. Claybaugh granted the extra $5,000 credit to Halperin's, after Halperin returned a fully answered, detailed questionnaire about the store's financial condition. Unfortunately, Halperin's had a very disappointing fall season, and the coats didn't sell too well. Sam Halperin didn't pay his bill to Claybaugh on the due date but planned to pay it five days late after Saturday's sales revenues came in. The new credit manager with Claybaugh sent a very short and tactless letter to Sam Halperin the day after the due date. The letter read:

Dear Mr. Halperin:

As you know, Claybaugh allowed you to exceed your credit limit on the purchase of the $30,000 worth of ladies' coats. We demand this sum forthwith. To delay further would jeopardize your credit rating, and if payment is not tendered within ten days from the date of this letter, legal proceedings will be instituted.

Sincerely,

Albert Whittle, Credit Manager
Claybaugh Manufacturing Company

Mr. Halperin called Marjorie long distance and explained the situation. He could not understand the attitude of Claybaugh's credit manager, since he had been just a little late before with another manufacturer but had been treated courteously by the other supplier. Marjorie is over 200 miles away and has a full schedule of prospects.

How should she handle the situation?

2–4

Brian Butler was a handsome polite young man who always showed proper respect to his professors and those in authority. He projected a good image and was quite popular with nearly everyone who knew him. Although he tried hard at the university, he passed descriptive courses with difficulty and accounting and statistics by the skin of his teeth. He finally graduated with just six quality points over the minimum. He successfully avoided chemistry, biology, and foreign languages. Brian interviewed a pharmaceutical house that was quite impressed with his respectfulness and personality. Although the interviewers saw that his transcript was marginal, they decided to base their final decision on his major professor's evaluation of his capabilities. Professor Dinwitty certainly did not wish to ruin one of his marketing major's chances for a lucrative job. Accordingly, he dwelt on Brian's personality and character attributes. He said that Brian was an acceptable student who could, he felt, acquire the technical knowledge necessary to discuss drugs and pharmaceuticals with physicians and other professionals.

Brian entered the three-month training program of the pharmaceutical company with great expectations. He found himself in competition with people who had in-depth backgrounds in biology, chemistry, and medical terminology. In spite of his diligence, he simply could not absorb the training, and after two months and a conference with his superiors, he decided that pharmaceuticals was not his line. He took a job selling candy to retailers instead and is at present doing quite well. The pharmaceutical house recruiter no longer stops at the university.

Did Brian's recruiter and professor do him a favor by recommending him for the pharmaceutical job even though each of them had reservations about his background?

Evaluate the experience from Brian's point of view in terms of the effect on his self-image and confidence. Was Brian hurt or strengthened by the experience?

What effect might the episode have on future students who might wish to enter pharmaceutical sales?

NOTES

1. *Webster's New World Dictionary* (New York: World, 1966), p. 1092.

2. Ernest Dichter, "Emotion, the Third Ear and Industrial Sales," *Industrial Marketing,* July 1980, pp. 80–81.

3. Ralph S. Alexander and the Committee on Definitions of the American Marketing Association, *Marketing Definitions: A Glossary of Marketing Terms* (Chicago: American Marketing Association, 1960), p. 21.

4. Carlton A. Pederson, Milburn D. Wright, and Barton A. Weitz, *Selling: Principles and Methods,* 7th ed. (Homewood, Ill.: Irwin, 1981), p. 5.

5. James F. Robeson, H. Lee Mathews, and Carl G. Stevens, *Selling* (Homewood, Ill.: Irwin, 1978), p. 5.

6. Arch G. Woodside and J. William Davenport, "The Effect of Salesman Similarity on Consumer Purchasing Behavior," *Journal of Marketing Research,* May 1974, pp. 198–202.

7. Robin T. Peterson, *Personal Selling: An Introduction* (New York: Wiley, 1978), p. 69.

8. Somerby Dowst, "How Top Industrial Salespeople Serve Customers," *Industrial Marketing,* November 18, 1981, p. 94.

Success in Selling

Success in selling takes more than just a knowledge of facts and of common selling practices. It depends heavily on attitude and other personality factors. The next few chapters present information that will help you become successful in selling instead of just salespeople with a mechanical knowledge of selling techniques. There is a need to relate to sales experience and to build on it. A significant part of sales experience is success in closing.

There is a collection of principles that has been built using the success ideas of outstanding men and women. The basic assumption is that anyone who follows advised techniques and philosophies with faith and self-discipline can achieve success, perhaps even wealth, fame, rank, or achievement of other personal goals. Books, records, and speeches on success ideas have been marketed to practicing salespeople for millions of dollars. Good ideas are often hidden in a forest of obvious and conflicting suggestions, vague statements, and repeated slogans. The discussion of success in this text is the result of sifting through the literature of success for dominant ideas. The core idea of success is *personality factors*. This chapter will treat major success elements, and the next chapter will focus on personality development. A review of success stories indicates ten key elements:

- Defining personal goals
- Planning methodically
- Forming appropriate attitudes
- Dynamic awareness

- Building motivation and self-image
- Questioning and listening
- Focusing on a dominant theme
- Evidencing enthusiasm
- Developing personality
- Learning persuasiveness

DEFINING PERSONAL GOALS

Goal definition, the expression of major purposes in concise guiding statements, is so fundamental that most success discussions emphasize it. Unfortunately, defining goals is widely violated in practice. Early determination of precise personal objectives provides both direction and motivation. Napoleon Hill, in his *Think and Grow Rich*, writes that purpose is the basis for getting anything done. Individuals can achieve whatever they conceive and believe (1). Hill suggests that after major goals have been defined and written down in detail, they should be repeated aloud each morning and night, and future success should be visualized (2). Writing and reviewing major goals focuses conscious and unconscious efforts on their achievement. Writing out yearly,

Ziggy

weekly, and even daily goals on index cards frees the mind for accomplishing those goals.

Although well-directed efforts result in the achievement of most goals, setting the *right* objectives and selecting the most important subobjectives can be difficult. A sales representative must spell out objectives in detail for sales, demonstrations, interviews, services, collections, and product knowledge. Fuller discussion of the setting of objectives follows in later chapters. Pursuing intermediate objectives and subobjectives alone is a narrow approach. Success-oriented sales representatives must interest themselves in a balanced physical, mental, and spiritual development. Strength and health are important assets. Sales representatives without stamina and vitality cannot be as effective as those who enter interviews with vibrancy based on a vigorous physical condition. Discussions of personal success emphasize mental outlook and positive thinking. Having definite learning goals helps to assure growth, optimism, and self-confidence. Spiritual growth is basic to high-level motivation and healthy personality development. Success theorists Norman Vincent Peale (3) and W. Clement Stone (4) note that the sense of guilt, frustration, worry, and destructive perceptions of self, which destroy so many in sales, can be overcome by a healthy spiritual life.

Success in achieving wrong goals can be a greater problem than failure to achieve right goals. Too many sales representatives have "succeeded," only to realize that their efforts have been wasted on unworthy objectives. Although early decisions on goals are important, it is essential for salespersons to have enough prior information and experience to set goals that are worthwhile and productive. People also fail because they set conflicting goals. Unwilling to decide which goals are important, they fail to focus their efforts on achievement of some basic purpose. It is important to realize from the beginning that accomplishing most goals requires sacrifices of time and effort. Reckoning the price to be paid for achievement of personally defined goals is part of the goal-defining process.

What makes a top salesperson? Figure 3.1 lists in order of importance qualities cited by industrial purchasing agents as those of outstanding sales reps that call on them. In order to achieve success in selling, you need to engender in your customers similar perceptions of your performance. The primary aim of this chapter is to define success and to discuss the ways that a salesperson can achieve ratings like those of top representatives.

What Is Success?

In his last speech, famed Green Bay Packer coach Vince Lombardi said:

You've got to pay the price for anything worthwhile and success is paying the price. You've got to pay the price to win, you've got to pay a price to

Figure 3.1 What Makes a Sales Winner?

Buyers cite these qualities of an outstanding salesperson in order of importance to them:

Thoroughness and follow-through

Knowledge of his or her product

Willingness to go to bat for the buyer within supplier firm

Market knowledge and willingness to keep the buyer posted

Imagination in applying his/her products to the buyer's needs

Knowledge of the buyer's product line

Diplomacy in dealing with operating departments

Preparation for sales calls

Regularity of sales calls

Technical education

Source: Somerby Dowst, "How Top Industrial Salespeople Serve Customers," *Industrial Marketing,* November 1981, p. 95.

Figure 3.1   What Makes a Sales Winner?

stay on top, and you've got to pay a price to get there. In other words, you don't do what is right once in a while but all the time. Success is a habit just like winning is a habit. Unfortunately, so is losing. (5)

Success is not measured by money, or education, or fame. Everyone knows successful people. Preachers, teachers, plumbers, carpenters. How is success recognized? Successful people exhibit a sense of commitment. They strive to do the best they can.

If success—getting to the "top"—is defined too narrowly—as say, being president and chief executive officer of General Motors—then only one person can be successful at any given time. In a study of the senior executives of America's thousand largest firms, Philadelphia psychiatrist Peter Brill found that more than half of "the 10,000 most successful people in their fields . . . considered themselves failures."

Is upward mobility the only definition of success? Mark Twain, looking back on his life, wrote, "The miracle or the true power that elevates the few is to be found in their industry, application, and perseverance, under the promptings of a brave and determined spirit." Brill put it another way: It is increasingly clear that psychological health "requires you to define your own terms of success" and not to accept without question those of others (6). To rephrase Twain's view, successful people are those who continually look for ways to do better.

Success in personal selling comes only to those who do their best. Calvin Coolidge once said, "Nothing in the world can take the place of persistence. Talent will not; nothing is more common than unsuccessful men with talent. Genius will not; unrewarded genius is almost a proverb. Education will not; the world is full of educated derelicts. Persistence and determination alone are omnipotent. The slogan 'Press on' has solved and always will solve the problems of the human race" (7).

It's been observed that hard work does not always lead to success, but it is equally true that nobody ever became a success without working hard. Successful people are those who seek constantly to improve themselves and their performance. Success, therefore, is relative. People are successful to the degree that what they are doing and what they will do in the future are better in some way than what they have done in the past. A successful person is someone who is making remarkable progress and has a need for continuing improvement.

PLANNING METHODICALLY

Mathematics, statistics, accounting, and other step-by-step methods are all designed to facilitate planning. In athletics, players who follow tested methods of procedure have better chances to excel. Many are attracted to the glamour of being "winners"; few are willing to endure the disciplinary rigor needed. In selling, study and practice of tested methods for prospecting, routing, approaching, answering objections, and closing sales increase chances for success. Planned efforts are more organized, more unified, and more successful than unplanned efforts.

Hard work may be superior to high intellect in goal achievement. Industrialist Charles Schwab is reported to have sent consultant Ivy Lee a $25,000 check for the following simple idea: "At the beginning of each day determine what are the really essential things you should do. You'll get more accomplished if you organize your tasks, doing them one at a time in the order of their importance" (8). While this type of goal organizing is an excellent way to plan, many people fail at the task because they do not consider a wide range of alternative goals before selecting the most satisfying ones and the best route to their objectives. The concept of expanding goal choices depends on both method and intelligence and might be called *breadth of consideration*. Going to other people who know and asking for information is one way of expanding choices. Committee discussions can expand a person's range of alternatives.

Traditionally, career planning has emphasized individual roles and ranks within an organization. Today, many look not for external rewards—those that are recognized by others—but rather for the rewards of self-esteem. Formerly, people measured their success primarily by the deference accorded them by others because of their position, salary, and power within a corporate hierarchy. Today, many consider work satisfaction, freedom, marketability of their skills, and opportunity for personal growth to be the elements of success. Table 3.1 compares the emerging view of careers as "protean"—in which individuals look inward to measure success—with the traditional view of careers—in which individuals look to others for confirmation of success.

The word *"protean"* comes from the name of the sea god of Greek mythology, Proteus, who could foretell the future and change his shape at will.

TABLE 3.1   AN EMERGING VIEW OF CAREERS:
THE PROTEAN CAREER

ISSUE	TRADITIONAL CAREER	PROTEAN CAREER
Who's in charge?	ORGANIZATION MANAGES	PERSON MANAGES
What do I value most?	ADVANCEMENT: POWER	FREEDOM: GROWTH MARKETABILITY
How do I measure success?	POSITION LEVEL; SALARY	PSYCHOLOGICAL SUCCESS (Let Jones shift for himself!)
What is my attitude toward work?	WORK SATISFACTION; LOYALTY TO ORGANIZATION (local)	WORK SATISFACTION, LOYALTY TO PROFESSION (cosmopolitan)
What is my basis for self-esteem?	ESTEEM FROM OTHERS—Am I respected in this organization?	SELF-ESTEEM— Do I respect myself?
What does my future success depend on?	ORGANIZATIONAL AWARENESS— What *should* I do? Expect?	SELF-AWARENESS —What do I *want* to do? (when I grow up)

Source: D.T. Hall, *Careers in Organizations* (Pacific Palisades, Calif.: Goodyear). As modified by John F. Veiga in "Plateaued Versus Nonplateaued Managers: Career Patterns, Attitudes, and Path Potential." *Academy of Management Journal,* vol. 24, no. 3 (September 1981), pp. 566–577.

Proteus's behavior was confusing to outsiders who sought his forecasts of the future. He kept his own counsel about what the shape of the future was and what form he would take to survive in it.

Similarly, protean career seekers look inward to see if job experiences are satisfactory, playing different roles to achieve individually defined measures of success. Protean career planners are more flexible and cosmopolitan than are their traditional counterparts. More able to move with rapidly changing times, protean career planners are more likely to experience goal achievement in each of the positions they occupy during their careers.

Protean career planners are not "plateauers" (9). When careers plateau, the individuals find themselves struggling to maintain the past level of achievement or are even allowed to stagnate. Career planning is a complex task and requires new tools and complex problem-solving methods, for all people are, indeed, complex and must decide for themselves what will be the most satisfying career plan. The following methods and ideas are designed to increase the number of your choices and to aid you in making the right choice:

- Complex problem solving
- Creativity
- Learning methods
- Systems thinking

Complex Problem Solving

Complex problem solving (10) encourages the use of maximum thought, concentration, and consideration of alternatives. Sales reps run into complex problems every day. A complex problem is a problem or group of problems requiring prediction of how differing choices will pay off in the future. It is a problem worthy of Proteus himself. Selecting a job, making a creative sales pitch with insufficient knowledge, and even deciding on weekly routing can be complex problems.

In the period since World War II, decision makers in business, government, the armed forces, and the arts have borrowed from mathematicians' techniques of modeling to improve the quality of their decisions. The word *model* has many different meanings. Sometimes it means an "exact" replica—say, a scale model of an aircraft, boat, or automobile. By scaling down, the exactness of the model is reduced because some detail is lost, but the most important characteristics of the original are retained.

Sometimes the word *model* refers to an ideal form of something. An ideal mother is a model mother. When cities are successful in rehabilitating and renewing their infrastructures, they obtain monies under a federal program known as model cities legislation.

Models are also used to demonstrate the items of a line of clothing, where each garment displayed is called a model. The persons who wear the clothes to display them to prospective buyers are referred to as models. The work they do is called modeling.

Modeling in complex problem solving uses all of these meanings of *model* and *modeling*. Builders of problem-solving models use simplified representations of reality, just as the makers of scale models do. These representations contain the essentials of a problem. Since the model builders choose those aspects of most interest to them for achieving a desired solution, the models built focus on finding a "best" or an "ideal" solution under the conditions that prevail. This means that more than one model can exist for any given complex problem. By showing what the payoffs are likely to be for several different courses of action, a model demonstrates a best choice.

Models rarely demonstrate all the complexities of reality. Many models are *symbolic*—that is, they use symbols or signs to simplify complex problems. It is in the increasing use of symbolic models that business decision makers have turned to mathematics. For example, a familiar symbolic, decision-making model for determining the area of a circle is:

$$A = \pi r^2$$

By altering the decision on radial length, a decision maker can change the area of the circle. It can be used by a decision maker, has more than one course of action, and has an outcome related to the decision made: The area of the circle varies with the decision maker's choice of the length of the radius. Finally, there is π. Even if the definition of π is expanded from its usual form of 3.14 to 3.1415926536, a decision maker using it can still only approximate either the area or the circumference of the circle chosen. Indeed, even if expanded to a hundred thousand places, π remains but an approximation of the relationship of r to A. Even the apparent certainty of these familiar models leaves a decision maker with only a close answer.

In most selling problems, the decision maker must settle for even more uncertain approximations than are present in deciding how big to make a circle. The inability to come to any degree of exactness in forecasting outcomes of choices made is called *uncertainty*. Since much cannot be known in many selling decisions and since making decisions alters conditions in which an alternative is exercised, salespersons and their managers must try to estimate what is most likely to result from their choice of appeals to use with a prospect or their choice of scheduling one set of calls on a particular day instead of another set. A general model of a "real world" problem situation is:

$$V = f (A_i, S_j)$$

where

> V = the value to a decision maker of taking a particular course of action—for example taking a job with XYZ Company (Table 3.2)

A_i = the choices available

S = factors affecting the outcomes of a particular choice not under the control of a decision maker

$f(\ )$ = the functional relationship between the choices available, $A_1, \ldots,$ $S_1, \ldots {}_j$, and the payoffs perceived by the decision-making rep or manager, $V_{11} \ldots {}_{i, j}$.

The functional relationship of this general problem model is like that of the model of the area of a circle, $A = \pi r^2$. Like π, f is only an approximation of the interaction between a decision maker's choices and the states of nature within which a decision maker exercises choice.

In complex problem solving, it is recommended that the most important problem or the easiest one be singled out of the problem cluster and ap-

TABLE 3.2 ANALYSIS OF ALTERNATIVE NUMBER 1—TAKE A JOB WITH XYZ COMPANY*

ITEM	Advantages CERTAINTY VALUE	CHANCE OF OCCURRENCE	ADJUSTED VALUE
Better-than-average salary	$10,000	0.8	$ 8,000
Good chance for advancement	8,000	0.7	5,600
Good management	4,000	0.9	3,600
Long training program	5,000	1.0	5,000
Executive customers	3,000	1.0	3,000
Good fringe benefits	2,000	1.0	2,000
Bonus arrangements	6,000	0.5	3,000
Value of advantages			30,200

ITEM	Disadvantages CERTAINTY VALUE	CHANCE OF OCCURRENCE	ADJUSTED VALUE
Much traveling	$ 8,000	0.9	$ 7,200
Product weak	15,000	0.7	10,500
Excessive pressure	10,000	0.8	8,000
Possible bad territory	10,000	0.4	4,000
Relocation	6,000	0.6	3,600
Value of disadvantages			33,300
Net disadvantage of alternative			(3,100)

*Based on discussions in Kenneth E. Schnelle, *Case Analysis in Business Problem Solving* (New York: McGraw-Hill, 1967).

proached separately. Perhaps the biggest difficulty is identifying the right problem to solve first. The following steps are recommended:

1. Statement of the problem
2. Statement of the facts
3. Statement of alternative courses of action
4. Advantages and disadvantages of alternative courses of action
5. Evaluation of advantages and disadvantages
6. Certainty of occurrence of advantages and disadvantages
7. Selection of the best alternative
8. Implementing the selected course of action
9. Comparing expected with actual results of the decision

Steps 5 and 6, assigning values and chance of occurrence, almost always involve educated guessing. Making assignments of the likelihoods of events is not difficult. Assigning a monetary value means expressing the negative or positive value of an advantage or disadvantage in terms of money. Chance of occurrence is expressed as 1.0 for something that is certain to occur, 0.5 for something that has a fifty-fifty chance of occurring, 0.1 if the chance of occurrence is one out of ten. As can be seen from Table 3.2, the alternative advantages and disadvantages are arranged in terms of dollar value and summated to give a total value. Table 3.2 is based on complex problem-solving procedures but is an analysis of only *one* alternative in career selection. In actual practice, several alternatives ought to be evaluated and compared. By using step-method models such as this, it is possible to approach problems logically and to consider relevant alternatives. It is not mandatory that an alternative with the greatest positive money value be selected. What is important is that all aspects of a problem be thought out and evaluated. How well the goal path determination procedure is followed depends largely on the breadth of consideration given to each detail and how realistically the planner models the problem and makes value assignments for various outcomes (11).

Creativity

Innovative salespersons must be able to use their creative abilities to the fullest to come up with new ideas and strategies. An understanding of the creative process aids inventiveness. Creativity involves four separate stages: the *preparatory stage,* the *digestive stage,* the *incubation stage,* and the *illumination stage* (12).

The Preparatory Stage. Creativity is built on a good general store of knowledge and sensitivity to the needs of others. In addition, it is important to accumulate facts and data concerning a specific problem while keeping an

Personal Preparation

open mind. At this point there should be no attempt to put information into neat categories, make judgments, or think too deeply about the data collected. Creativity in making a sales proposal is enhanced by knowledge of a prospect's business problems and operations and by knowledge of product features and benefits. Following top sales trainer and consultant Carl Stevens's admonition "If I am to sell what my prospect buys, then I must sell through my prospects' eyes" is the necessary first step in creative selling (13).

The Digestive Stage.   The next step is to work over information and material gathered and to sort it into as many kinds of meaningful combinations as can be thought of. Attempting to uncover relationships among facts is helpful at this stage. Let your mind suggest different choices without passing any judgments. Consider *all* possibilities and combinations no matter how unreasonable any one may seem. In a word, *meditate* on the knowledge available.

The Incubation Stage.   This stage involves giving the subconscious a chance. Put the problem out of your mind; do something else; rest on it. The subconscious organizes and suggests solutions to data input, even during sleep or while the conscious mind is engaged in other tasks.

The Illumination Stage.   Suddenly the right idea will hit—the solution will present itself! Maybe this will happen while eating a meal or while mowing the lawn. Insight comes when all the mentally stored elements come together into a recognizable whole that transfers from the subconscious into the conscious (14). This stage is dependent on the other stages, however. It is the preparatory input stage that is perhaps the most important. (See Photos 3.1a–d.)

Learning Methods

Many students who are not of superior intelligence excel because they understand how to learn. Others break learning rules and fail to realize their potential. Sales representatives must be learners to succeed. They must be aware of techniques that help to save time in acquiring knowledge. To spend time looking over study material while the mind is far away is pretending, not learning. Learning is *the art of asking oneself questions and providing the answers*. If the questions are comprehensive and realistic, thought about the materials is forced. Some forms of "motorization," such as writing, organizing, or saying the material to be learned aloud, aid retention. Repetition is important for remembering answers to questions asked. It also helps to construct a logical framework on which all the elements to be learned can be hung, so that all the parts can be seen in their correct relationships with each other.

For greater learning efficiency, periods of rest must be alternated with pe-

Photos 3.1a–d   The Creative Process

a. Preparatory intake of information

b. Digestion of the information

c. Incubation of the information

d. Illumination—write it down and act on it

riods of concentration. The subconscious, which works during rest, must be allowed to work. Learners who work hour after hour or all night without rest are not using their time to best advantage. A tired mind loses much of its ability to recall and organize. A reward after each thirty- or forty-minute period of study may help. A positive attitude is essential. Attitude is perhaps the most important factor in learning besides intelligence. Many learners are mentally blocked from understanding material simply because they suggest to themselves that they are unable to master it. Of course, a quiet atmosphere with few distractions, good lighting, and firm study furniture is helpful. Organizing and summarizing materials at the end of each study period initiate review and force a repetition of answers and more thought about material. Finally, goal setting and planning on index cards, including time scheduling, are relevant to productive learning. Allow at least 10 percent reserve time, since learning projects frequently take longer than expected (see Figure 3.2).

Systems Thinking

A system is a group of parts (like an automobile engine) combined to accomplish a certain purpose. A systems thinker reasons in terms of the total relationships among the parts of the system and considers the effects of any introduced change on all elements in the system. Champion chess players *systematize* their strategies and visualize their many possible moves to comprise a game plan. The amateur pool player shoots one shot at a time without regard to the next shot, while the professional looks ahead strategically and makes sure the cue ball winds up in place for succeeding shots. Systems-thinking physicians foresee the effects of the medicines given to cure one body system on all body systems. The excellent thinker in every situation thinks in terms of the total effect of any planned action. Innovative salespersons must accordingly think beyond the direct effects of actions and contemplate secondary and long-range effects. They must view the prospective buyer in the buyer's operating system, which is usually the buyer's home or company. The market must be viewed as a related group of prospects. Sales representatives must realize that selling key people in a community will influence their ability to sell to other prospects and possibly start a bandwagon effect. Sales reps must view their product lines as systems of products and determine how these systems might be sold to fill corresponding systems of buyer needs. Representatives, like chess masters, must anticipate competitive moves and counter those moves strategically. Representatives must also be aware that their firm is a system operating toward the common goal of profits. They must realize that all sales actions affect this overall system and their positions in it. Systems thinking, then, involves taking a total view of problems and opportunities and thinking beyond them, through evaluation of the effects of a series of planned moves on every component of the system.

Using Models. A great aid to systems thinking is the model. Just as models can be used in career planning, so can they be used by salespeople to highlight important buyer benefits. Through systematic thinking, sales representatives can construct models that clarify how the features of their offering will solve their prospects' problems. For example, a graph is a model that an insurance sales agent can use to clarify the relationships between Social Security and insurance needed to produce a given retirement income for an elderly widow. A securities sales representative may dramatize the long-run up-

Figure 3.2　Index-Card Planning

STEP 1:
List activities. Then number each according to order.

```
 _____
|            Things to do Monday                  |
|_____|
| 1    Get brakes fixed on car                     |
| 7    Call John Davis (real estate broker)        |
| 4    Mail package to California                  |
| 5    Mail film to Chicago                        |
| 8    Return books to library                     |
| 10   Study for product exam                      |
| 6    Call on scheduled accounts                  |
| 3    Proposal for Callis Company                 |
| 2    Check air accommodations to Florida         |
| 9    Get secretary's birthday present            |
|                                                  |
|                                                  |
|_____|
```

STEP 2:
List in order. Then check off when completed.

```
 _____
|            Things to do Monday                    |
|_____|
| ✓   1. Leave car at garage - ride with Bill        |
| ✓   2. Call airlines office (Florida)              |
| ✓   3. Write proposal letter - Callis Company      |
| ✓   4. Put California package in office mail        |
| ✓   5. Put Chicago film in office mail              |
| ✓   6. Call on scheduled accounts                  |
| **  7. Call John Davis from office (OUT-CALL TOMORROW)|
| ✓   8. Drop by library on way home                 |
| ✓   9. Drop by gift shop on way home               |
| ✓   10. Study for exam.                            |
|                                                    |
|_____|
```

Personal Preparation

ward trend in stock values by a model showing the overall rise in the Dow Jones Index over the past several decades. The sales representative assumes the role of teacher in communicating complex information. Simple models resulting from systems analysis that outline important relationships can facilitate these explanations.

FORMING APPROPRIATE ATTITUDES

An attitude is a tendency to respond in a certain way. Attitudes grouped together in consistent patterns make up traits. Traits are a major part of total personality. While attitudes will be treated again in the next chapter and throughout this book, an overview is necessary here because of the special emphasis placed on attitudes by those who have achieved great success. Napoleon Hill and W. Clement Stone's book *Success Through a Positive Mental Attitude* is indicative of the importance placed on attitudes (15). Many attitudes are treated, but five stand out in their analysis of success:

- An attitude of confidence
- A service attitude
- A team attitude
- A self-improvement attitude
- An efficiency-improvement attitude

An Attitude of Confidence

An attitude of confidence is primary. A rep must believe in the product to be sold, believe in the company offering it, and believe in personal capacity to make a sale. Faith in oneself is promoted by constantly suggesting success to the subconscious mind (16). From faith in oneself comes a salesperson's ability to inspire confidence in prospects. Salespersons entering an interview with a defeatist attitude convey to prospects the idea that something is wrong with a proposal to buy or with the value of a product. The cowardly, under-confident sales representative, in fact, is a stereotype of many comedy characterizations in books, plays, movies, and on television. A prospect approached by a rep without self-confidence becomes infected with pessimism and embarrassment instead of excitement about the product and doesn't buy. A rep with confidence has product and market knowledge, particularly knowledge of the customer's product line and its market applications. Realistic optimism based on such knowledge often fulfills its own prophecy in selling and belief is one of the strongest motivational forces.

Salespeople must think positively to succeed.

A Service Attitude

Frank Bettger, the internationally known insurance salesman and writer, states that a service attitude is the most important secret of selling. He advises: "Find out what the other fellow wants and then help him find the best way to get it" (17). Marketing writers call this same idea the marketing concept. It may be defined as consumer orientation. It is based on serving consumers' needs and wants as the best way to profits. A retail druggist in Tuscaloosa, Alabama, who would go out of his way to help any customer is an example. Sometimes he would deliver prescriptions ten miles away at no charge. He was always cheerful, but more than that, he was always interested in his customers' problems. He was very successful. Although he took a great deal of personal time with his customers, he was able to manage three drug stores in Tuscaloosa. A flour sales representative told his customers that the price of flour would probably be lower in a few days, that they should hold off buying in quantity until then. Who wouldn't buy flour from a rep so truthful, so helpful? The personal touch of being a prospect's friend reveals the salesperson's sincerity and supplies a competitive edge to many transactions. In selling, building long-term relationships carries high payoffs.

A Team Attitude

Good sales representatives must have a team attitude. They must work well with others to advance company interests if they are to achieve their own goals. Sales representatives can expect failure when their company and their

Personal Preparation

customers sense that they are only out for themselves. The player on a basketball team may score more points playing as an individual, but five players working together smoothly and assisting each other are necessary for championship. Cheerfully carrying out what management asks, coordinating customer service with repair people and other members of the corporate team, and working well with buyer personnel are all part of a rep's role as a team player. Good relationships with other sales representatives in prospecting, making proposals, and team calling assure a salesperson of being able to get help when it's needed. "Badmouthing" other corporate members may get back to them. And even if it does not, the fear that it has may affect relationships with them.

The proper team attitude of a successful sales rep extends to customer relations as well. It is, after all, the ongoing mutuality of buyer-seller benefits from exchange that gives personal selling its value in contemporary American business life. Prospects sense a salesperson's team attitude toward them. Industrial purchasing agents ranked "willingness to go to bat for the buyer within supplier firm" as the third most important quality of outstanding salespersons in 1981 (18).

A Self-Improvement Attitude

Sales representatives should develop a positive and persistent self-improvement attitude. Jack Lacy, a top sales trainer, tells the story of a man who completely reshaped his personality within a few years. He rose from complete failure in selling to outstanding success. Lacy has known thousands who have successfully remade their personalities (19). Certainly, the person with a poor personality and poor selling habits has a distinct handicap in sales work. There must be a change before full selling potential is realized. While experience in selling leads a rep to improve, sales representatives with planned programs of self-improvement move faster and enjoy the benefits of improvement sooner. Some specific self-improvement methods are discussed in Chapter 4.

An Efficiency-Improvement Attitude

In business there are four attitudinal "sets" (preparations) that improve efficiency and promote profits: (1) a consciousness of wasted capacity, (2) expectations of simplifying transactions, (3) application of the "principle of postponement," (20), and (4) acquisition of additional products in the mix. Awareness of and attempts to use these efficiency-promoting concepts are keys to work improvement.

Wasted Capacity. In every sales operation, time is wasted. Equipment and spatial capacities go underutilized. The waiting time that salespersons spend before seeing a prospect, for example, can be used to learn new product features, to plan strategy, or to do other necessary work. Sales representatives who fail to show buyers how to get maximum use out of their products may well cause prospect dissatisfaction, losing future sales. Many salespersons, with additional space in their cars or open space in their stores, promote new products with little additional cost, increasing profits. Whenever there is additional, unutilized potential, an opportunity knocks. Every sales representative should be prepared to look for such opportunities. Using existing assets more efficiently is an important step toward increased profits and leads to personal recognition and reward.

Simplifying Transactions. Sales representatives are in business to get orders. Transactions that require many hours of negotiation are not simple and may prevent a sales representative from closing other deals in territory. Anything that makes transactions simpler and cuts down on negotiating, or bargaining, time makes selling more efficient.

Consider the modern supermarket, where people can buy enough groceries to feed a family for a week in less than thirty minutes because of routinization factors—self-opening doors, shopping carts, wide aisles, traffic patterns, displays, point-of-purchase advertising, self-service, branding, and fast checkout. Vending machines, mechanical coin changers, speaker systems in drive-ins, price tags, prepackaged foods, charge plates, installment credit, and guarantees are all designed to make the transaction more routine or easier. Many of these simplifying devices have resulted in marketing fortunes. Together they allow the American retailing system to be the most effective in the world.

Simplifying transactions is not only an opportunity for those in business for themselves, but it is an attitudinal "set" a salesperson should adopt to facilitate territorial operations. Sales proposals, establishing friendships with prospects, providing avenues for prospect contact when services are needed, visual aids, advertising pieces, checklists for making surveys of prospects' problems, and dozens of other methods reduce negotiations and save selling time (which to a rep is money). Looking for ways to save negotiating time while not lessening effectiveness is a "quick fix" for improved sales performance.

Principle of Postponement. Product adjustments for customers should occur as late as possible in the marketing process. They should be postponed to allow for reduction of marketing risks. Every change that makes a product more suitable for one group of customers carries the probability of making it less suitable for other customers. Initialed water glasses are not etched until a customer buys them. Inventory problems are reduced by not having to carry thousands of different glasses. Automobiles can be mass-produced, yet have custom features that many different buyers want, as long as dealers can make changes at the dealership after customers express exact desires. Alterations at the retail level have simplified clothes marketing. Mixing paint to customer specifications has enabled paint retailers to carry a much smaller primary stock, for color pigments can be mixed in at the point of purchase. Sales representatives should be aware of the principle of postponement and prepare to customize products for each buyer or to modify sales presentations, or adjust it to the particular needs of their prospects.

Expanding the Line Offered.   Sales representatives who have many products to offer during a call can meet many needs. They have a better chance of making a sale and selling more per successful interview than do reps with only one product to sell. Since a salesperson must travel to see prospects anyway, why not have a broad assortment of products to offer to optimize valuable selling time? While it may be efficient to have a number of products, there are limiting factors. Too many choices may confuse a prospect. During interviews, sales representatives may not be able to focus attention properly on all products carried. Product knowledge may also be spread too thin if products are complex or creative selling demands are involved. Salespersons should be set to see the opportunities and limitations of expanded-line possibilities.

In summary, Charles Roth, a well-known sales author, comments that the main attitudes necessary for success are a genuine love of other people, optimism, and enthusiasm—attitudes that can be learned (21). When sales representatives use positive attitudes to solve prospect problems, they promote harmony and create a buying atmosphere.

AWARENESS OF DYNAMICS

Prediction of and adjustment to changing environmental conditions are essential to success in selling. Successful people study trends and plan ahead to meet opening opportunities. Those who fail tend to view their environments as unchanging, aiming their efforts where the targets *were* rather where they will be. By determining the patterns of change, salespersons who would succeed can redirect their efforts in the field to newly emerging targets. Change opens up new opportunities for selling and closes down old ones.

Product Life Cycle and Patterned Market Change

While individual sales reps succeed or fail in the short term, their efforts take place against the background of the longer-term growth and maturity of market opportunities and products. What shall be talked up with prospects, which prospects will be called on and how often, the degree of enterprise support for field sales efforts, product pricing, and availability to meet prospect needs—all depend on the period of time during which a sales offering earns a payout sufficient to keep it on the market. After products are developed, or born, they live for a time and then they die. They go through a life cycle of development, introduction, growth, maturity, decline, and market withdrawal. Only successful products go through all these stages. Many fail early. Nearly a third of all new products fail (22).

Sales volume, profits, advertising, competition, production costs, product availability, market exposure, and so forth, vary by the stage in a product's life cycle. Figure 3.3 shows the generalized life cycle of a consumer product and the kinds of promotional activity appropriate at each stage.

More important to sales representatives are the differences among prospects most likely to buy a product as it matures in the marketplace (see Figure 3.4). New products spread into markets in the manner of a bell-shaped curve—slowly at first, then at an increasingly rapid rate, up to a peak rate when a majority of the market has accepted them, then at a decreasing rate. The speed with which new products spread into the markets depends on the nature of the market, the kinds of prospective buyers, and the product's characteristics. Products are accepted faster in "modern" areas like New York than they are in "traditional" places like small, rural, conservative towns. Products that have a strong relative advantage, that are culturally compatible, that can be tried without much money outlay or risk, and that are simple and easy to understand speed over the diffusion curve faster than those without these characteristics (23).

As shown in Figure 3.4, innovators are the first group to accept and buy. Innovators are likely to be wealthier, have higher incomes, and be younger, more educated, more socially active, more cosmopolitan—more oriented to the world at large than to a local social system—and more willing to take risks than later buyers. The second group of buyers, the early adopters, consists of local community leaders who are not quite so wealthy, educated, or young as the innovators but who are far more influential in determining a new product's success or failure. The early majority, who accept soon after the early adopters, and the late majority represent 68 percent of total market opportunity. These groups exhibit fewer innovator characteristics. Finally, laggards are those who hold out longest and may not even accept (buy) a new product, even when it has strong relative advantages. This group is composed of poorer, less educated, older, and socially more isolated individuals than the previous groups. The dynamics described by this model alert reps to possible changes in customer composition and opportunity for sales. They also explain why many people wait until they see others buy. The hesitant hope to reduce risk and to feel more assured about the worth of a new product.

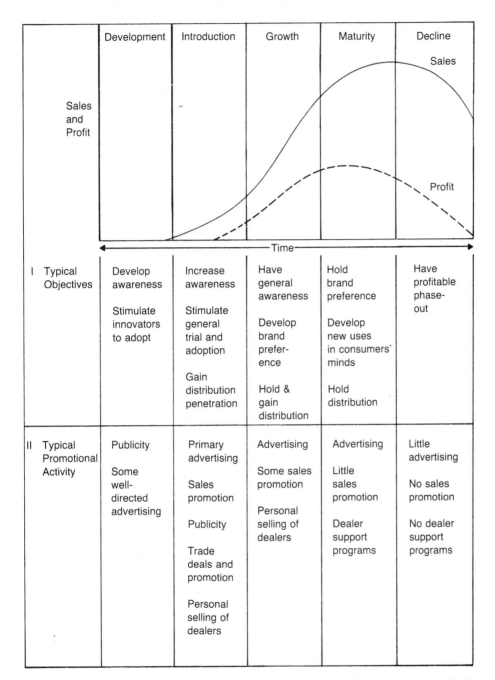

		Development	Introduction	Growth	Maturity	Decline
	Sales and Profit					Sales / Profit
		◄─────────────── Time ───────────────►				
I	Typical Objectives	Develop awareness Stimulate innovators to adopt	Increase awareness Stimulate general trial and adoption Gain distribution penetration	Have general awareness Develop brand prefer-ence Hold & gain distribution	Hold brand preference Develop new uses in consumers' minds Hold distribution	Have profitable phase-out
II	Typical Promotional Activity	Publicity Some well-directed advertising	Primary advertising Sales promotion Publicity Trade deals and promotion Personal selling of dealers	Advertising Some sales promotion Personal selling of dealers	Advertising Little sales promotion Dealer support programs	Little advertising No sales promotion No dealer support programs

Figure 3.3 The Generalized Product Life Cycle and Typical Promotional Activity

Source: James F. Engel, Martin R. Warshaw, and Thomas C. Kinnear, *Promotional Strategy: Managing the Marketing Communications Process*, 4th ed. (Homewood. Ill.: Irwin, 1979), p. 649.

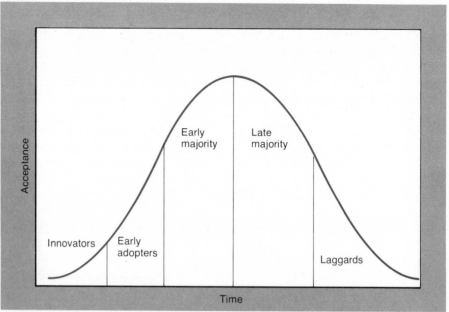

Source: Everett M. Rogers, *Diffusion of Innovations* (New York: Free Press, 1962), p. 162.

Figure 3.4   Diffusion-of-Innovations Curve

Trend Analysis

An eye for dynamics requires awareness and understanding of important trends affecting possible sales of a product. The population of the United States is constantly increasing. But the increase is anything but uniform among age groups. A declining birthrate over the past two decades means that there were fewer people graduating from high school in 1982 than in the late 1970s. Consumers born during the baby boom following World War II are currently in the market for houses and other nest-building products. Shifts in population from the Northeast to Florida, California, and Texas affect markets. Movement of industry toward pockets of cheaper labor in the South affects sales of many products. Inflation rates influence buyer behavior. Great cyclical swings result from government entry into or exit from markets (24). Women's liberation, consumerism, and raw material shortages are other examples of trends that affect markets and selling opportunity. Reps should study trends affecting company products so that future opportunities are not missed through making calls on prospects whose potential for purchase has, for all promotional purposes, died.

Opportunity Analysis

A useful concept is opportunity analysis, or looking at cycles to see changes in terms of opportunity for individuals. This concept stresses the need for good timing in discerning favorable circumstances. Opportunity for sales representatives is based on the industry cycle and on a selected firm's position in its industry. If a firm or product headed for prosperity is selected, a sales representative has every chance to be swept along toward success with the current. On the other hand, if opportunity is diminishing because of unfavorable environmental changes, reps can fail in spite of intelligent effort. People have made millions promoting trading stamps and certain fast-food franchises when they were on the "up" side of an opportunity cycle. Now the main current of opportunity has slackened, and it is more difficult to promote new businesses in these fields. Fortunes are being lost by promoters entering markets that are already saturated. This does not mean that salespersons should change their jobs after establishing themselves in a firm whose cycle is declining slightly. To salespersons already committed to an enterprise, this concept should be translated into taking advantage of trends within their territories and within the range of their product offerings. The student of selling should view the prospective job market in light of a firm's ability to provide opportunity in the present and in the future. It is an era of change, which requires constant adjustment to new circumstances.

BUILDING MOTIVATION AND SELF-IMAGE

Sales representatives should possess confidence and quiet dominance. Expecting success in closing sales promotes enthusiasm, persuasiveness, and, consequently, signed orders. Salespersons can increase motivation levels and build self-image by: (1) increasing product knowledge, practicing effective selling techniques, and understanding prospect behavior; (2) using self-suggestion and positive thinking; (3) visualizing objectives. Napoleon Hill, after studying the lives of hundreds of successful persons, concluded that confidence building through positive self-suggestion and visualization of goals is very important for success (25). Health improvement through exercise and sensible living, careful dressing, and grooming enhance self-image. Overmotivation (overdrive), however, can destroy health and undermine poise. The power within an individual to move other people to action is promoted by a confident self-image. A tactful, self-assured personality inspires positive prospect response.

QUESTIONING AND LISTENING

The successful all agree that proper questioning and listening techniques are important in being well received by customers and in learning about their particular problems. Sales representatives can ingratiate themselves with prospects by asking intelligent questions, listening attentively, and adjusting their responses to prospect personality and needs. Questions should be used in every phase of prospect contact. Good persuaders do not argue with prospects. They attempt to reduce the natural conflict-of-interest situation that exists, by listening. In persuasion, the idea is to adjust to the prospect rather than requiring the prospect to make any adjustment other than agreeing to a sales proposal. Prospects will usually listen to a salesperson if they are listened to first.

Ralph Nichols explains that listening principles are neglected in the educational process and has several suggestions for developing the art of listening (26). Nichols identifies as bad listening practices branding subjects as uninteresting, criticizing the talkers, allowing the mind to wander, pretending attention, avoiding the difficult, and reacting to emotional words. Guessing what the speaker will say next, determining supporting ideas, and mentally summarizing what has been said are his suggested practices for improving listening and learning capacity. Listening can be the strongest type of persuasive activity. The patience to remain silent and receive feedback often separates the professional from the amateur salesperson.

FOCUSING ON A DOMINANT THEME

Jack Lacy calls it "hot button" selling, Frank Bettger calls it the "key issue" selling, and Denby Brandon calls it the "law of attention and focus." No matter what sales experts call it, all advise salespeople to use the strategy of determining and focusing on the most important buying motive as the strategy of success. This gives the sales representative's efforts the unity and direction that come from simplicity. Persuaders should emphasize key selling benefits in such a dramatic way that prospects can visualize themselves enjoying a product. Many feel that success is dependent on stressing the important determinants without getting enmeshed in unimportant details. When focusing on a dominant theme to drive toward a goal, the important concept is to alternate periods of effort with periods of rest. In a sales presentation, this alternation allows response to and reflection on prospect ideas. In most work, progress is fostered by laying aside a project and approaching it later, refreshed and with increased determination. Denby Brandon calls this work-rest-work idea the "law of alternation" (27).

EVIDENCING ENTHUSIASM

Enthusiasm aids persuasion because it commands attention, creates interest, stimulates motivation, stirs emotion, and promotes action. Few people buy anything unless their emotions are aroused, and few are aroused emotionally about a product unless a sales representative shows *eager interest* in an offering. To generate enthusiasm, success theorist Norman Vincent Peale advises that one key is to begin deliberately behaving in a confident manner, as if you are able to meet situations and personal confrontations easily (28). He also recommends that sales representatives believe in the importance of their work to the economy and take pride in their vocation. While enthusiasm can be generated by just deciding to be enthusiastic, it is also promoted by belief in and knowledge about a product, by personal health, by a positive self-image, by increasing speech tempo, dramatic gestures, and the introduction of other exciting actions into presentations. Enthusiasm must be mixed with sincerity for maximum effect. Overdone, enthusiasm can easily lead to offensive, high-pressured presentations.

DEVELOPING PERSONALITY

When competing deals are otherwise balanced in a prospect's mind, the personalities of competing salespeople usually make the difference. Personality factors, in fact, are primary in affecting job tenure, promotion, and other important areas of human acceptance. Most prospects, depending on their self-images, prefer extroverted, happy, intelligent-sounding salespeople who have personal warmth, remember names, and appear genuinely interested in the prospect's conversation and problems. Perhaps foremost in the long list of mental, physical, and emotional virtues affecting persuasion is the commu-

© King Features Syndicate, Inc., 1976.

nication of genuine concern for other people. Personality development will be treated in detail in the following chapter. It must be realized that the impression made on others is more than half of the success equation. Personality modification is both possible and practical. Some academically weak students who have good personalities are more successful salespeople than academically talented graduates who nurse self-centered tendencies.

LEARNING PERSUASIVENESS

Persuasion and salesmanship are almost synonymous. Persuasion is the opposite of coercion. Selling goods, ideas, or oneself is critical to success. Persuasion theory will be treated in detail in Chapter 5, but no complete presentation of success elements can be advanced without consideration of this vital component.

SUMMARY

Success is characterized by emphasis on goal-directed planning, development of positive personality attributes, and principles of interpersonal communication. Specific goal definitions guide and motivate. Good methodology combines with intelligence to produce superior performance. Systems thinking adds a new dimension to problem consideration by stressing the interrelationship of all parts of a problem. Positive attitudes help to assure readiness to respond correctly when occasions demand action. Recognizing dynamics and trends allows prediction and encourages the formulation of strategy to hit moving markets. Motivation furnishes the power to accomplish. A confident self-image sets a proper interview tone. Questioning and listening methods promote two-way communication between seller and prospect, reducing conflict of interest between them. Dominant-theme emphasis keeps a rep on a straight track toward goals. Enthusiasm stirs prospects to buy. Personality development improves the receptivity of customers. Knowledge of persuasion oils the sales-closing machinery. Analysis of success patterns is a foundation for good selling. It is a foundation built by practitioner experience.

REVIEW QUESTIONS

1. Identify the ten key success elements.

2. What do you understand by "success"?

3. What is meant by planning?

4. Suggest rules for proper goal definition.

5. Contrast the "traditional" career with the "protean" career on the following dimensions:
   a. Who's in charge?
   b. What do I value most?
   c. How do I measure success?
   d. What is my attitude toward work?
   e. What is my basis for self-esteem?
   f. What does my future success depend on?
   What is the basic difference between these two views?

6. Discuss model building as a form of complex problem solving. In what ways is it relevant to the sales representative?

7. Outline the steps in the problem-solving process.

8. Explain the creative process. What four steps are involved?

9. What is meant by "systems thinking"?

10. Name the five attitudes suggested as major factors in success.

11. Explain each of the four suggested attitudinal "sets" that are helpful in improving efficiency. Give an example of a situation in which each set might be applicable.

12. Outline the product life cycle. In what way(s) is this concept of value to the salesperson?

13. Of what value is trend analysis?

14. List the ways in which salespersons can increase their motivation levels and build their self-image.

15. List ways that you can develop motivation and enthusiasm.

APPLICATION QUESTIONS

1. Many of you had more than one place where you could have gone to school and therefore had to make a decision for a fairly complex problem. In making the decision about which school to go to:

   a. What were your objectives?

   b. How did you make your decision? Would you say that to a large degree you followed the complex problem-solving process as described in this chapter?

   c. If you didn't, structure this decision using the complex problem-solving process, stating the problem, the facts, alternative courses of action, and so on.

2. As the section on opportunity analysis stressed, your chances of being successful will be increased if you work for a firm that is growing and that develops good new products—products that will move quickly into the rapid growth stage of the product life cycle.

    a. Which industries and products do you think will be among the *most* rapidly growing in the future?

    b. Which of these would you most prefer to work in?

    c. Which industries and products do you think would offer the poorest opportunities, with declining sales now and in the future?

INCIDENTS

3–1

Wayne Spenser, age twenty-four, is talking to Mary Kraft, age forty-three. Both sell real estate for the Golden Key Agency.

Mary: Hi, Wayne, what's the matter?

Wayne: Mary, I'm thinking about getting out of this business. My sales have been poor lately, and I guess I'm a failure at selling real estate. Prices are so high nobody can afford it.

Mary: You shouldn't think about quitting, Wayne. Sure we've had a slump during the recession, but all those young nest builders are out there, and they need homes. Stick with it. You have what it takes.

Wayne: I don't think so anymore. Mr. Keyes called me in and wanted me to set a goal of selling two houses a month. You know that in this business there just isn't any way to know what you can do. He wanted me to break down how many showings I plan to do each week and organize my prospecting. I've never done that before, and I don't intend to start now. I've always played it by ear.

Mary: Wayne, let me show you what I do. See? I make it a point to show at least five houses a day, and I call my prospects a day ahead to arrange my appointments.

Wayne: Where do you get all those prospects?

Mary: Well, besides the ones assigned to me by Mr. Keyes, I advertise in the newspaper myself, and I have about a dozen friends who keep their ears open for me. One of them works for Welcome Wagon, and several live in big apartment complexes.

Wayne: That's too much organization for me. Besides, I'm tired of Old Man Keyes always pushing . . .

Mary: He's not so bad, Wayne. He's been under a lot of pressure lately because sales have been down for the agency.

Wayne: Aw, Mary, real estate isn't any good. I've never fit into this agency. Anyway, the other salespeople aren't friendly. Say, let's go down to the coffee shop and have a cup. There's nothing else to do.

Mary: I'd like to, but Mrs. Rachels wants me to show her a house and there she is now. You'd better stay with it, Wayne. Great days are coming . . .

Wayne: You can say that because you sold three houses last month. I guess I'm just not cut out to be a salesperson.

QUESTIONS

1. What problems do you see in Wayne's success philosophy?

2. Analyze this conversation in terms of success theory.

3–2

Carl Delman has just taken over his father's prosperous tennis shop and sporting-goods store. He had to leave college with only six credit hours lacking because the senior Delman died suddenly of a heart attack, and Carl's mother and younger sister felt incapable of running the operation. The store has two employees, one who meets the customers and another who strings the rackets and repairs golfing equipment. The store has enjoyed a 20 percent increase in sales in the last two years, and Carl's father was in the process of building a new display room, 20×20 feet, when he died. The room is now finished. Carl wants to dismiss the salesman and has told the racket stringer that he wants to run the business "just like his father." Carl has brought in his best friend from school to help him meet the public. Sales have dropped within the last month, and some of Carl's father's customers have been hesitant to accept him. He has learned that some of them have even taken their business elsewhere. He doesn't know what to do with the spare room, since the racket repairman knew only that his father planned to put in a line of bicycles. Carl plans to leave it vacant for a while, except for minor storage.

Using Schnelle's Complex Problem-Solving Method, analyze this case. What would you advise Carl to do to make a continuing success of his father's business?

1. Napoleon Hill, *Think and Grow Rich* (New York: Hawthorn, 1967), p. 31.

2. *Ibid.,* pp. 77–78.

3. Norman Vincent Peale, *Enthusiasm Makes the Difference* (Englewood Cliffs, N.J.: Prentice-Hall, 1967), pp. 60–83.

4. W. Clement Stone, *The Success System That Never Fails* (Englewood Cliffs, N.J.: Prentice-Hall, 1962), p. 117.

5. Vince Lombardi, in "The Invincible Vince," *Sales Manual: 1980* (Nashville, Tenn.: Southwestern, 1980), p. 65.

6. Peter Brill and Mark Twain, in Darrell Sifford, "The Corporate Ladder Teeters: Rung by Crowded Rung Disenchantment Rises," *Knight-Ridder Newspapers,* June 19, 1981.

7. *Sales Manual: 1980,* p. 62.

8. Ivy Lee, in Alfred Armand Montapert, *Success Planning Manual* (Englewood Cliffs, N.J.: Prentice-Hall, 1967), p. 5.

9. John H. Veiga, "Do Managers on the Move Get Anywhere?" *Harvard Business Review,* vol. 59, no. 26 (February–March, 1981), pp. 20–38.

10. The material in this section is adapted from Wroe Alderson and Paul E. Green, *Planning and Problem Solving in Marketing* (Homewood, Ill.: Irwin, 1964), pp. 72–76.

11. Kenneth E. Schnelle, *Case Analysis and Business Problem Solving* (New York: McGraw-Hill, 1967), p. 125.

12. C. H. Sandage and Vernon Fryburger, *Advertising: Theory and Practice* (Homewood, Ill.: Irwin, 1975), pp. 289–291.

13. James F. Robeson, H. Lee Matthews, and Carl G. Stevens, *Selling* (Homewood, Ill.: Irwin, 1978), p. 135.

14. Sandage and Fryburger, *Advertising,* p. 291.

15. Napoleon Hill and W. Clement Stone, *Success Through a Positive Mental Attitude* (Englewood Cliffs, N.J.: Prentice-Hall, 1960), pp. 17–20.

16. Hill, *Think and Grow Rich,* p. 71.

17. Frank Bettger, *How I Raised Myself from Failure to Success in Selling* (Englewood Cliffs, N.J.: Prentice-Hall, 1949), p. 53.

18. Somerby Dowst, "How Top Industrial Salespeople Serve Customers," *Industrial Marketing,* (November, 1981), p. 95.

19. Jack Lacy, "Secrets of a Winning Personality," recording (Chicago: Businessmen's Record Club, 1961).

20. Wroe Alderson, *Marketing Behavior and Executive Action* (Homewood, Ill.: Irwin, 1957), pp. 296–304, 423–425.

21. Charles B. Roth, *The Secrets of Success Encyclopedia* (New York: McGraw-Hill, 1965), pp. 5–34.

22. Sandra Salmans, "New Products as Risky as Ever," *New York Times,* October 20, 1981, p. D2.

23. Everett M. Rogers, *Diffusion of Innovations* (New York: Free Press, 1962), pp. 1 ff.

24. Jesse Levin, "Budget Deficits and Inflation," *Financial Analyst Journal,* vol. 30, no. 4 (July–August 1974), pp. 44–46.

25. Hill, *Think and Grow Rich,* pp. 52–77.

26. Ralph G. Nichols, "Listening Is Good Business," *Management of Personnel Quarterly,* vol. 1, no. 2 (Winter 1962), pp. 2–9.

27. Denby Brandon, "Power for Your Purpose," recording (Memphis: private label, 1964).

28. Peale, *Enthusiasm,* p. 20.

Personality Development

Personality, a key success element in selling, is the mirror that reflects people's attitudes and attributes and helps to determine how prospects will respond to their persuasive appeals. A good personality affects people's ability to sell by *positively* influencing prospect responses. Chances of achieving personal goals are enhanced or diminished by differences in personality. Understanding the personalities of others, to adjust to their needs, is a must for sales success. An improved personality can be translated into more positive reactions from customers, increased earnings, and happier work experience. Salespeople with good personalities enjoy greater promotion opportunities, have firmer holds on their jobs, and have better working relationships with others.

Many writers indicate that personality can be changed to great advantage. Jack Lacy, the famous sales trainer, records that personality can be improved dramatically through persistent effort. He claims to know thousands of salespeople who have increased their abilities to project a favorable image to others (1). Frank Bettger reviews his own successful transformation, which involved a deliberate plan to strengthen his weaker attributes (2). Dale Carnegie's *How to Win Friends and Influence People* (3) has sold millions of copies. And Dr. Maxwell Maltz, a plastic surgeon, has provided a clear explanation of a relatively new approach to help you realize your personality potential in his book *Psycho-Cybernetics* (4). Ideas from these and many other sources will be examined in this chapter.

What has personality development to do with personal selling? John Molloy, best-selling author, syndicated newspaper columnist, and management consultant,

"...and give me good abstract-reasoning ability, interpersonal skills, cultural perspective, linguistic comprehension, and a high sociodynamic potential."

Drawing by Ed Fisher; © 1981 *The New Yorker Magazine, Inc.*

asked the wives, husbands, and associates of some of the most successful men and women in America to describe them. The word they used most often was supersalesman. In spite of the fact that more than 85 percent of the people being described never held a job in direct sales, they sold all the time ... most of those around them responded to their charismatic personalities rather than their power. (5)

A practical approach to personality understanding and development requires a look at:

- A self-image approach to change
- A trait-development plan
- Observing and remembering

A SELF-IMAGE APPROACH TO CHANGE

The Cybernetic Model

People like Maxwell Maltz and Ben B. Smith (6) have popularized a concept of personality change that can be valuable in selling, public-relations work, and in everyday life. Human cybernetics is an important key to personality change. It furnishes a positive model, is optimistic about the chances for improving ability to relate to others, and is a logical method backed by evidence. According to cyberneticists, the mind is like an amazingly efficient computer that is instructed or "programmed" in accordance with an individual's conscious thoughts (see Figure 4.1).

Each time we solve a problem, we "write" a program. That is, we instruct our minds with a particular solution pattern. This pattern will be used time and time again to meet similar circumstances. Through reuse, what was once a new program becomes an old one—part of a repertoire of filed behavior patterns. We draw up an old "program" from our subconscious and use it when we come in contact with a "new" but similar circumstance. We may modify old programs as new behaviors are tried and found to work. We learn from experience to change, but sometimes experience is a bitter teacher. Experiential learning not only takes time, but punishment for failure is unpleasant and sometimes painful. Lost sales, for example, are expensive. Maltz contends that "synthetic experience" or imagined experience is almost as effec-

Figure 4.1 Cybernetics = Pilotage Model
The term cybernetics was coined by Dr. Robert Weiner in 1948 from the Greek. It signifies the art of pilotage. The type of thinking visualized is intended to chart a course through complex processes and systems to achieve a desired goal.

tive a teacher as real experience. The mind and body respond just as if the experience were real (7). It is basically through synthetic or imagined experience that we can reprogram our mental machinery without the cost of actual trial and error better adapting our personality to our needs.

A Goal-Directed Mechanism

Human mental equipment is marvelous. It is a goal-directed mechanism. If a mind is programmed with thoughts of failure, the whole mechanism is instructed to produce failure. Individual mental resources will bring this about. If instructed with a belief in success, all faculties will respond accordingly to produce success. These notions reinforce the *power of positive thinking* espoused by Norman Vincent Peale (8). It is compatible with the Judeo-Christian teachings on the power of faith. The mind as a goal-directed apparatus works in efficient but mysterious ways to fulfill instructions. *Visualizing goals in detail,* verbalizing them, writing them down, and continually reviewing them are essential. This kind of emphasis gives clear instructions to the mental "computer," which takes a visualized goal, such as making 125 percent of quota, and produces real results.

Self-confidence is an important element in personal success.

Reprinted from *The Saturday Evening Post* © 1974 The Curtis Publishing Company.

"Inferior people have inferiority complexes, superior people have superiority complexes. It's as simple as that."

Problems with the Old Self-Image

Because old programs are recalled for use when meeting new situations, capabilities for adjustment to the new can be limited. Sometimes parents have unintentionally programmed their children with negative thoughts. A mother or father may have continually reminded a child of a lack of some specific ability. In the process, the child may have become convinced of this inability and lost self-confidence. To overcome conviction of inability, it is necessary to reprogram that inhibition. There is no hindrance to personality development in admitting to failure on a test or in a specific selling circumstance. But continual self-suggestion of being a failure, or the conviction of certain failure at certain kinds of tasks, is a hindrance. Some students freeze when any kind of mathematical model is shown on a blackboard. They tell themselves that "math is not their bag" thus inhibiting their minds from accomplishing a solution simply and logically. Similarly, salespeople can program themselves negatively, concluding that they are not cut out for selling. The truth is that a person would not be able to lift a hand off a desk if the person's mind had accepted the suggestion that it was an impossible task. Maltz reports that while persons practicing basketball free throws from the line physically improved their ability to make shots by 24 percent, persons who went through the motions mentally only (imagining that they were shooting the ball) were able to improve 23 percent. A third group, which practiced neither physically nor mentally, showed no improvement (9).

One of the most debilitating problems of salespeople is lack of confidence—just plain fear. "Hot doorknobs," or fear of being rejected, can keep a rep from visiting the best prospects available. Cybernetics has an answer for this too. Negative feedback, which can be so useful in getting a person on course to his or her goals, can also stop that person altogether. The problem is that the person is dwelling on possibilities of failure instead of on possibilities of success. Self-fulfilling prophecies are issued to the mind. Finally, a self-generated judgment of inability to sell can result in a self-labeling of failure. The concept of "purpose tremor" shows how and why people "lock up" in certain situations—such as when attempting to thread a needle, the thread gets close to the eye of the needle and the hand shakes, or when an attempt is made to pour liquid into a small test-tube opening and the same thing happens. The hand shakes because of trying too hard and overreacting by being too careful. Many students experience this on important tests. Salespeople who are overly concerned about making a good impression usually make a poor one; they act self-consciously and nervously. Overconcern can jam the mechanism. If the stress can be transformed and used positively, it can work *for* rather than against a person. Turning slight tensions during an interview into enthusiasms may create excitement, arouse emotions, and promote a proper buying atmosphere. Much worse than the salesperson with "purpose tremor" is the salesperson who projects a lack of enthusiasm.

Reprogramming

The answer to the problems of fear, anxiety, and stress is *reprogramming*. The main keys to reprogramming are belief, vicarious experience, and goal visualization.

Belief. People have been known to accomplish amazing feats under stress or hypnosis. All of us have heard of people who could lift objects several times heavier than they normally could during a fire, a wreck, or some other traumatic event that immediately reprogrammed belief out of necessity. We have also heard of people under hypnosis who imagine pain to such an extent that their bodies react exactly as if the pain were real. The four-minute mile was once a mental barrier to athletes, who believed that running a mile in under four minutes was impossible. There is a story about a man who was locked in a refrigerated railroad car in Russia. He kept a log of his experiences, writing on the car wall with a piece of chalk. He described, legibly at first, the decreasing temperature in the car as the trip wore on. Finally, in an almost unintelligible scribbling at the base of the wall, he wrote of the terrible sensations of freezing to death. His body was removed, but the amazing thing was that the refrigeration in the car was off. It was only slightly cool. The man's body had responded to his mental suggestion and died.

Imagined Experience. Imagined experience became reality for the man locked in the railroad car. When salespersons reprogram their minds with positive beliefs to free themselves from inhibiting fears of failure, their potential for success is amazing. Athletes released under hypnosis from inhibiting negative beliefs have been known to be 25 percent stronger.

Synthetic experience (sometimes expressed in other words) is advocated by many successful people. Jack Lacy stresses the importance of imagining an interview. Salespersons visualizing an interview in their minds can positively suggest to themselves mental pictures of overcoming objections, making effective demonstrations, and closing sales successfully. This kind of mental practice can pay big dividends. Individual "servomechanism" can be programmed to project an interview without the penalty of losing an order to gain experience. This imaginative planning can be applied to job interviews as well as to public speaking and to many other selling-related activities.

Goal Visualization. To perform well in a crisis, each person, sales rep or not, should have practice under less stressful conditions. Stress should be translated into assertive rather than defensive attitudes. Crises should be evaluated in their true perspective (11). Often, people blow potential consequences out of proportion. If a sale is lost, there will be other sales. Dwell on successes and glance back at failures only long enough to learn what went wrong. This is using informational feedback positively. Focusing on the present, practicing gradualism by building slowly up to a hard job, and attempting to postpone angry reflexes until they blow over are practical behavioral guides to better results. Living up to a revitalized self-image pays big dividends in career performance and contentment.

A Spiritual Dimension

Many success writers emphasize that there is a spiritual-moral dimension of personality development. Norman Vincent Peale contended that a deep faith in God is the primary factor behind sustained enthusiasm (12).

W. Clement Stone, Chairman of the Board of the Combined Insurance Company, built a fortune from persuasion. He sees prayer as a success aid in all fields and has written: "Regardless of one's beliefs, prayer from a psychological viewpoint is beneficial in crystallizing one's ideas toward an objective and developing a stimulating internal force" (13). Cybernetically, people who believe in a personal, all-powerful God with whom they can communicate have a self-image of being supported by this power, and they often have a special approach to success and personality development.

THE TRAIT-DEVELOPMENT PLAN

Frank Bettger credits much of his personality development and success in sales to Benjamin Franklin. It was Franklin who inspired him to change by selecting a trait he wished to improve, writing it on a card with instructions on how to put the desired change into practice, keeping the card in his pocket for quick and easy reference, and practicing the trait for several days (14). Frank Bettger reprogrammed himself. Many students have tried this method out. They each selected those personality elements they felt needed improvement and gave a rationale for each personality element selected. They recorded and analyzed their impressions of the responses of other people as each trait was practiced. Most reported that this project gave them greater sensitivity to weaknesses in their personality programming, and many admitted that it helped them improve their relationships with others. An important consideration of this simple method is that it is available for use at any time. When used, only one or two personality factors should be practiced at a time. Before long, application of the new traits will no longer be conscious. When application has become automatic, these modified behaviors become new assets of the personality.

There are dozens of behaviors or personality protocols recommended for analysis and practice in every book discussing the qualities of a good salesperson. The truth is that almost any salesperson can benefit from almost every positive attribute in the dictionary. Enthusiasm, attitude, good listening habits, and other personality-related success elements together with behavioral trait modification are primary to any personality self-improvement project. Other elements are also very important. Dale Carnegie, who wrote the simplest and most successful book on personality development, emphasized just a few key elements in his advice (15). Jack Lacy mentions a limited group of attributes that give a sales representative an "engaging, assuring, compelling, and dynamic" personality needed for success in selling (16). The following short list of self-improvement objectives has been selected from many sources:

- Calling people by their names
- Smiling and being pleasant
- Praising and complimenting other people
- Talking in terms of others' interests
- Being socially sensitive
- Refraining from criticism
- Monitoring voice and appearance
- Using humor carefully
- Being sincere
- Keeping healthy

Calling People by Their Names

A prospect's name, correctly pronounced, is to the prospect among the most magic sounds in any language. Dr. Archie Dykes was promoted from Chancellor of the University of Tennessee at Martin to Chancellor at Knoxville, and within a few years, he became Chancellor at the University of Kansas at Lawrence. While at Martin, Dykes made it a practice to know not only all of his faculty and staff by name but also hundreds of students. He realized that knowing people by name expressed interest, reflected personal concern, and constituted the substance of courtesy. Customers like personal touches. If sales representatives can remember the names of their prospects, their secretaries, and others to whom they have been introduced, can pronounce them correctly and say them in a friendly tone, those reps will find quicker personal and product acceptance. Requesting a repeat of a name not clearly heard during an introduction, pronouncing it several times mentally, using it in conversation as soon as it fits, and using association to aid recall show courtesy in viewing prospects as people. Not using a customer's name in a sales interview depersonalizes a presentation and creates an awkward atmosphere. Students who practice learning names find it a fast way to initiate new friendships. A prospect's name is a vital key to a sale. It should not be forgotten.

Smiling and Being Pleasant

An honest smile, used appropriately, helps prospects to identify with a salesperson, generates a pleasanter atmosphere, and sets the stage for promoting positive buying emotions. A fake smile not supported by mood or other actions tends to convey insecurity, insincerity, nervousness, sarcasm, ridicule, and other negative attitudes. Compare the unnatural facial gestures made by a child told to smile for a camera with the smile that results from inner happiness. Prospects should be able to infer from a smile that a rep identified with them, is happy and relaxed in their presence, and is honestly glad to be talking with them. Positive preinterview expectations can put sincerity into a smile or greeting. The rest of an interview's tone should be pleasant to support that initial smile. A genuine smile opens doors and closes sales. When smiling and being pleasant become a natural habit, people feel happier through the smile's self-suggestion. A pleasant person radiates a contagious optimism attractive to everyone met.

Praising and Complimenting Other People

People like to receive recognition for the things they do well. Even more, they appreciate encouragement for things they are not sure they do well. A football player is confident about skill on the field, but may be uncertain about acting ability. A student may be sure of personal ability in school but long for some indication of being a good dancer. Complimenting people on qualities they are uncertain about and prefacing critical suggestions with a little praise work wonders in getting messages heard (17). Flattery is an insincere compliment. Look for something that can be complimented sincerely before offering praise to anyone. Speak well of other people in a prospect's presence. Everyone feels more comfortable talking to a person who sees the good in others rather than the bad. A safe practice is not to join a prospect in criticism of a competitor. Prospect criticism may be a test to find out what kind of person a rep really is.

Talking in Terms of Others' Interests

Thinking in terms of others' interests has to take place before *talking* in terms of those interests can occur. A salesperson has to use imagination to mentally occupy a prospect's place. Sales representatives who see the needs of others learn to anticipate the wants of others. They develop the ability to focus on main buying motives. They receive a positive response to their presentations. Salespersons tell prospects they will get the proper service, but do they indicate concern by anticipating a prospect's need for a match, a pencil, or a writing pad? Does the salesperson realize a prospect's need for position in the firm, for esteem, for economy of operation? To practice thinking in terms of prospects' interests, their situations must be thought through thoroughly. A salesperson should ask, "What would I want?" and offer a best solution to projected prospect needs. Smart salespeople look and listen for signs and words indicating prospect desires.

Being Socially Sensitive

It is practical to learn to show social sensitivity. Increasing social sensitivity requires practicing manners, improving conversational ability, and learning to respect the resources of others as if they were one's own. Some may regard manners as superficial, but prospects see good manners as a sign of professionalism. All prospects appreciate salespeople with knowledge of the social graces. Smoking without permission, discussing politics or other emotionally charged issues with prospects whose positions are unknown, interrupting conversations, telling dirty stories, using profanity, or calling attention, even indirectly, to any personal deficiency in the other is bad manners. A significant part of social sensitivity is respect for another person's resources. For example, when writing an order while using the prospect's unprotected desk for support, a writing pad should be used instead of a thin piece of paper. Keeping feet off furniture is another example. Respect for another's time is essential. Purchasing agents frequently complain that salespeople take up too much executive time. Salespeople who will not end an interview when the business ot it is accomplished are less welcome than a party guest who will not take hints to go home. Another thing to be watched is interrupting before another person has finished talking. Writing letters of congratulation and gratitude is a good practice.

Refraining from Criticism

Most people criticize others a lot more than they realize. Trying for one day not to say anything critical about anyone would be a challenge to most. Both being critical and not being critical are habits. Criticism is necessary for correction of society's ills and for reform. It gives a common ground for conversation. The habit of not being critical, however, enables prospects to feel more secure in a sales representative's presence. Trust and confidentiality—rapport between rep and prospect—can be built through restraining criticism. Criticism is negative. In most instances, it is unprofessional. It does nothing to promote proper buying atmosphere.

Monitoring Voice and Appearance

Often as much is communicated by tone of voice, gestures, and appearance as by words. Tone of voice and inflections radiate cues about attitudes and motives. A confident voice inspires trust. A weak, faltering voice inspires doubt. An angry or loud voice increases interview conflict. Voice is the rifle that fires a salesperson's ammunition—words. Variation in voice and rapidity of speech spark enthusiasm and excitement. Monotonous presentations generate little feeling or emotion. Reps must make sure prospects can hear them. Words must be pronounced distinctly. Speech mannerisms such as "you know" and "would you believe," should be avoided. Speaking into a tape recorder and listening to the replay can help a rep improve speaking ability. Speech courses and practice in front of a mirror or a group hone communication skills.

Gestures can reveal more about a person than words. A smile, hand movements, posture, walk, and facial expression combine to give a continual picture of moods and thoughts. People who use gestures well are expressive. Salespeople are really actors. Their performances affect their paychecks. Salespeople show "stagefright" by such behavior as fumbling with their hands, smoothing their hair, and staring at the floor. Sitting with feet flat on the floor, but not stiff, with an alert posture, not a slouch, conveys a rep's vitality during a sales call. A friend who will tell a salesperson about distracting mannerisms or imitate them can help a rep to see what prospects see.

John T. Molloy, wardrobe consultant to many of America's top corporate executives, advises that selling to businesspeople means wearing clothes that are conservative but that do not place the sales rep above the prospect (18). Small men and women should wear attention-getting devices such as stickpins or handkerchiefs. Larger salespeople should not call attention to their size but should wear nonauthoritarian clothes of soft colors and textures. Reps should dress as well as those called on and should carry a good pen and pencil. Avoid the cheap kind. Clean fingernails are especially important. Being clean and well groomed has an effect on self-image. They give poise. Remember, prospects who do not know a sales representative respond to clues in an effort to evaluate both the rep and the offering. Clothes and appearance should make a prospect feel comfortable. Overdressing or underdressing is a mistake.

Using Humor Carefully

Good, clean humor can relax interview tension and create a friendly atmosphere. Humor misused can be destructive. Usually, a rep can be the object of a joke but never prospects, not even indirectly. Good-humored fault-finding

"I'll take it."

The salesperson's appearance can affect selling success.

The Saturday Evening Post, © Vahan Shirvanian.

even with old friends is hazardous. Can a rep know for sure that a prospect does not have relatives who are alcoholics, in mental hospitals, or in the ethnic groups ridiculed in a joke? Dirty and sacrilegious stories are the mark of the unprofessional salesperson. They are very offensive to many people. Knowing when to laugh and smile in an interview is important. Never laugh *at* prospects—laugh with them. A good stock of inoffensive jokes is good practice *if they are well told.* If friends will not laugh at a story, chances are prospects will not either.

Being Sincere

Prospects like to buy from sales representatives who are honest and genuinely committed to serving them. Companies also promote salespeople who are committed to their work and to the company. Customers buy thousands of dollars' worth of merchandise on the sincerity of a salesperson's word. Evidence of hypocrisy increases a prospect's sense of risk. Can a buyer be expected to trust a rep who lacks loyalty to the company represented? If a customer were to admit to damaging a product in such a way as to void its guarantee, should a rep advise that customer to lie about the damage, or say that it'll be taken care of? If a customer knows a rep is not going to tell company headquarters the truth, the rep may well lose the customer. Being out of a job could result as well for the rep, for a company *must* be able to trust its representatives. Lying to customers and prospects rarely, if ever, pays. Truth with prospects nearly always pays, even if it makes them temporarily angry. In the long run, truthful dealings build respect. Salespersons often purposely point out certain minor deficiencies in their products to establish sincerity. Often, sales reps refuse to sell products that they feel will not meet a customer's needs. A reputation for sincerity and truthfulness in dealing with prospects makes it easier to close sales. Good word about a salesperson gets around. Some reps may manage to fool a few people in the beginning, but in the long run, a bad reputation closes the door of opportunity for them permanently.

Keeping Healthy

Health maintenance is essential to the salesperson desiring to stay on the job, to endure travel, to lift products, and to project a confident voice and image. *Nation's Business* has reported that more than 50,000 United States businesses have physical fitness facilities for employees. By the mid-seventies, the total cost of employee fitness facilities amounted to more than $2 billion a year. Over 300 of the facilities had employed full-time recreational directors (19). Mental and physical health depend on attitude, knowledge, and a willingness to maintain good health habits. There is little question that despair, guilt, frustration, and anger can destroy personality and body and retard healing. Dr. Maxwell Maltz contends that rapid healers have one thing in common—they are all cheerful, optimistic, positive thinkers with a zest for life (20).

Health is affected by diet, rest, and exercise. Many salespeople eat too much sugar, fat, salt, and starchy foods and not enough fruits, vegetables, and other fiber foods. Some, instead of trying to lose weight by eating smaller servings, try harmful crash diets.

Being well rested enhances ability to think, to remain calm, and refreshment of body systems. Research at Harvard University indicates that people are overweight because of lack of exercise. Exercise converts fatty tissue into beneficial muscle, strengthens the heart's collateral circulation, and reduces cholesterol levels in the blood (21). Kenneth Cooper, author of *The New Aerobics,* advocates running, walking, cycling, and swimming on a regular basis (22). A salesperson can walk briskly, do push-ups, bent-leg sit-ups, and chair hangs even when on the road. Parking just a little further away from prospect locations is an easy way to exercise. Health is a personal thing. Developing a good diet and an exercise program to reach and maintain correct weight determined by medical examination pays big dividends. Doing an enthusiastic sales job requires good physical and mental health.

OBSERVING AND REMEMBERING

The ability to notice important details, recall them, and use them strategically is a necessary part of persuasive selling. A salesperson's observations affect the quality of information stored. Memory influences ability to recall and use strategic information. Sales representatives usually have little time with a prospect or in a prospect's office before beginning a presentation. But an observant salesperson can notice many important clues that can be used to customize each presentation. Remembering names and recalling vitial personal information are the essence of social sensitivity. They indicate the personal interest the prospects expect of professional sales reps.

Ideas for Observing

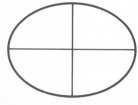

Figure 4.2
Basinger's Scene
Scanning Model

The mind screens and filters information taken from the environment. In a book written for police officers and lawyers, Louis Basinger contends that careful observers should know what to look for before experiencing a scene (23). The search for specific material should be systematic. What is intended for observation should be verified. Immediate overlearning (see p. 118) should be pursued to mentally fix pertinent information. Most people spend too much time looking at the bottom right of a scene or at the middle. First, the total scene should be scanned. Then an observer should divide the scene into four quadrants and note the elements in each quadrant (see Figure 4.2). The light should be behind the observer if possible.

Matthew J. Culligan, who has been a master salesman as well as chief executive officer of several major corporations, writes:

> Observation is . . . the conscious process of seeking out significant details of the environment, sorting through them, connecting one with another, re-

Photo 4.1
After scanning the whole scene, divide it into four parts and examine each part in detail. You can tell a great deal from this executive's office. The pictures of his family, the football, the Alabama elephant, and the degrees and pictures on the wall offer hints about some of his interests.

lating them to our perceptions, and attempting to arrive at conclusions about what they mean, what they tell us, or where we should look for more information.

What are the kinds of clues that Culligan looks for while scanning the environment of a new prospect?

The decor and furnishings of the outer office.
The demeanor and professionalism of the secretary.
The neatness or messiness of the office, particularly the secretary's desk and adjacent areas.
The manner in which the secretary handles calls, greets guests, and interacts with the person for whom he or she works.
The decor and furnishings of the inner office.
The demeanor of the prospect.

The way in which the prospect interacts with the secretary.

The personal items found in the office—family pictures, awards, trophies, desk paraphernalia, and so on.

The way the prospect is dressed.

The indications of good or bad grooming and of the habits of personal hygiene.

The physical fitness and posture of the prospect.

The state of the prospect's desk, and the room in general—neat, messy, cluttered, chaotic, etc. (24)

It is very important for a salesperson to predetermine what to look for during exposure to a prospect and the prospect's place of business. As Culligan noted, look for pictures on the office wall, trophies, or desk furnishings that might indicate interests, accomplishments, or affiliations of the prospect (see Photo 4.1). Social and professional associations can be determined from framed membership certificates, recreational interests from trophies or pictures, artistic taste from other room furnishings. Dress, cleanliness, and greeting manner also give clues to a prospect's nature and inclination. Salespeople must learn to be detectives in picking up clues from prospective buyers and their work environments.

It is a good practice not to rely too much on memory. The ability to recall is affected by future information intake. New information can decrease the amount of older stored material that can be brought back into the conscious mind. New salespeople or salespeople who have been moved to a new residence can become quite frustrated trying to remember where everything is. Writing down (do not abbreviate) all nonroutine activities and information and keeping that information in a customary place relieves the burden on memory. All people have experienced losing memorandums written to themselves or forgetting the meaning of abbreviations used when making notes. It is good discipline to keep everything in a particular place. Things left out of a customary location are lost. Doing these two things, careful recording and equally careful storage, frees the mind for absorbing other, more important data (25).

Practice shows little evidence of permanently strengthening memory. It is better to concentrate on *methods* of storing and maintaining information. It helps to "get into" a subject (focus the mind) for a few minutes before attempting to memorize, particularly in the morning shortly after arising. Fatigue, alcohol, insufficient sleep, and old age are enemies of recall ability. Vitamin B may help the memory of people who are deficient in this vitamin. Stimulants like tea and coffee may keep alertness high in the short run. However, the best aids are not vitamins, stimulants, or other physical aids, but good methods of storing and refreshing the memory.

Four Essentials for Improved Recall

Four basic suggestions are made to salespeople wishing to improve their ability to remember:

- Be motivated and have the right attitudinal set to master the material.
- Respond and react fully to the material.
- Concentrate and give meaning to the material.
- Review the material at proper intervals.

Be Motivated and Have the Right Attitudinal Set to Master the Material. Approach matters to be remembered by setting your mind to learning the material and suggesting to yourself the importance of retaining it. Set definite learning goals. Goals set by someone else are rarely effective. Intend to store the material in the memory instead of cramming and forgetting it soon after it is learned. Impress yourself with the benefits of storing the material. Quick learning is a joy. Quickly learned information is assimilated more easily and retained longer.

Respond and React Fully to the Material. Getting stimulated about material to be learned impresses it on the mind more successfully. Material seen is retained better than material heard. The best retention comes when as many of the senses are involved as possible. Saying aloud information to be memorized involves your facial muscles and hearing. Writing it down brings muscular activity into play. Repetition implants it in the mind. Speaking the words into a tape recorder and playing back the tape allows two hearings. Putting information on memory cards is another kind of double exposure. Reacting to information emotionally and enthusiastically helps to fix it in memory.

Concentrate and Give Meaning to the Material. Fixing the mind on material by (1) classifying or grouping it, (2) visualizing it, and (3) associating it gives more meaning to it (26). Grouping and regrouping information reinforce its acquisition. This gives meaning to information and will help you to associate newly received information with your current store of experience. Complex material and long numbers should be divided into groups. Objects or materials should be examined for similarities in space, time, or distance. Incorporating new information into a framework gives it meaning and significance. Information that is stored *with existing knowledge* is better retained.

Trying to visualize everything stored in the memory is like actually seeing the information. Making up stories about the material, no matter how nonsensical or fictitious, is a good way to incorporate details. Exaggerate the object to be learned visually, and put it into action or motion (27). The story-visualization method is especially effective for disconnected words and numbers.

Associating (relating) materials to be memorized in every possible way strengthens impressions. Harry Lorayne and Jerry Lucas contend that all memory is based on association (28). Relating new information to something already known makes for more effective assimilation. Association is particularly recommended for remembering names and faces. Names are like nonsense symbols because they rarely have any connections with past experiences. That is, names are hard to remember because they cannot be associated with anything familiar. When meeting new people, it is important to make sure their names and your own have been heard correctly. By carefully saying one's own name, with a pause for a count of three between given and surnames, prospect filing and recall are eased. "Ms. Peyton? How do you do? I'm Charlie (count of three) Margolis of (another pause) Kanda Corporation." It is perfectly permissible to ask for a name to be repeated if it was not understood the first time. Immediate association of a name with characteristics of the person—physical, mental, and emotional—aids in remembering both person and name (29). Mr. Fox may have a long nose. Mr. Woodman may have a lumberjack build. Mr. Waverly may have curly hair. Mr. Strongham may be skinny and weak. Names like Gillette and Ford can be associated with advertised products. The names of some people can be associated with the name of a town. Visualize that person in the town. If you meet a Virginia Griffin, and you know people named Virginia and Griffin, form a mental picture of all three persons doing something together. Some names are particularly challenging. Mr. Kamzelski might be pictured as a can of Kam dog food skiing "zealously" down a mountain. Even foreign languages can be learned by this mental picturing and associational technique. Double associating a name by writing it down and saying it over and over again to yourself—visualizing the silly associational picture you built in the imagination—overcomes trouble with names and faces. Using association to remember positions and occupations of your prospects also works. Picturing a person actively working at a particular job brings more of the memory into play. Imagination is the key to memory. It's fun and creative to use your imagination.

Reviewing Material at Proper Intervals. Forgetting occurs at a rapid rate, especially just after material is learned. Overlearning retards the pace of forgetting. Overlearning is the practicing of memorizing material beyond the point where you are first able to recall it correctly (30). It is good practice to recall material soon after it has been placed in storage for the first time. Waiting too long to touch up a fading impression may allow it to disappear for good. It is good to brush up soon after first storage at bedtime that same day, and about a week later (31). Correct brushing up is assured by checking the original source, if possible. Distortion can be reduced by careful observation, by noticing gaps, and by frequent review and recitation (32). When recently committed information proves difficult to recall, assuming the same posture and mood and otherwise reliving the situation at the time of first learning the material are effective memory joggers. Thinking about lost information intensely for a while, resting, and returning to it later with a renewed focus is a much commended approach (33). Your ability to recall vital names and information will directly affect your selling success.

SUMMARY

Although personality is strongly influenced during early childhood years, a widespread belief exists among psychologists that personality can be improved by adults who are motivated to do so and have the techniques at hand. Self-image theory explains the importance of a healthy belief in oneself, and cybernetics encourages salespeople who want to improve their capabilities, and personalities, by furnishing them with an important model. In cybernetics, the mind is compared to a computer with a programming unit. Negative goals programmed into that human computer will coordinate all a person's efforts to produce *negative* results. Positive goals programmed into the control unit will coordinate all mental machinery to produce *positive* results. Since the mind is a goal-seeking mechanism, it is extremely important to set definite goals and to review them often. Synthetic experience, such as imagining (mentally picturing) active participation in an interview situation or some other selling activity, can give some of the benefits of field experience without its penalties. The "hot doorknobs" (purpose tremor) syndrome can be avoided by knowing products well and practicing sales calls ahead of time.

Another approach to personality development is to work on one trait at a time. An honest self-analysis should reveal a person's weaker personality traits. Acceptability can be improved by focusing attention on each weak attribute for a period of several days. Health maintenance is an extremely important personality asset. Good health is a must in personal selling, for it is physically and psychologically difficult work. A positive mental attitude, a balanced diet, proper rest, and sensible exercise are ways to maintain good health. A good memory is important to selling. In attempting to improve ability to recall, approaching material to be learned with a proper attitude, responding and reacting fully, concentrating and giving meaning to material, and reviewing it at proper intervals can make all the difference. Mental visualization, association, and imagination play important roles in remembering information.

REVIEW QUESTIONS

1. What is meant by personality? In what ways can personality improvement affect a salesperson's performance?

2. Personality understanding and development are of considerable importance to the salesperson. What are the three elements of this process?

3. Explain all the elements of the cybernetic model. How can it be used to improve personality and goal accomplishments?

4. What are the essential elements of the trait-development plan?

5. List self-improvement objectives that have proved valuable to salespeople.

6. Why is recalling the names of prospects of value to the salesperson? How might the sales representative accomplish this recall?

7. What are the elements of social sensitivity?

8. Why is the choice of clothing important to the sales representative? What are some "rules of thumb" concerning the choice of clothing?

9. Under what circumstances is it appropriate for sales representatives to lie to prospects? To their own companies?

10. What are the key elements in successful observation? What are some of the elements that the salesperson should look for in a prospect's office?

11. What are the four basic suggestions for salespeople who wish to improve their ability to remember?

APPLICATION QUESTIONS

You will benefit the most from the material in this chapter and learn the material better if you attempt to apply these ideas to yourself. Try, in particular, to apply these concepts to areas where you may be having a problem. For example:

1. The cybernetic model is a method that is useful in reprogramming your brain for success rather than failure. Most people are nervous when they have to speak in front of others. Picture yourself in front of your personal selling class, making a sales presentation. Your goal is to convince members of the class to purchase a product. Believe that you can do it, and visualize yourself going through the presentation.

2. Think about a situation where, in the next couple of days, you want to persuade someone to do something. Picture the situation in your mind. What is your objec-

tive? What points will you make to convince the other person? In what order will you mention them? Now, several times, picture yourself going through this situation. Go through the entire situation and visualize a successful ending.

3. The text provides a list of self-improvement objectives including calling people by their names and smiling and being pleasant. Select the objectives that you would most like to work on. Write each one down on an index card. For three days try to improve in one of these areas, referring to the card several times during the day.

4. Go to the door of the room you are in now. Enter the room as if you were a stranger. Follow the observation techniques mentioned in this chapter.

5. How would you apply the suggestions for a better memory and recall to the material you are learning in this course?

INCIDENTS

4–1

Vice president James Davenport and sales manager Tom Powell are discussing promoting either sales representative Saul Abraham or Mike Kolb to zone sales manager.

James: Tom, Saul and Mike both have excellent sales records, but tell me how you see each of them and which one you recommend.

Tom: Well, Mike was outstanding in college. He knows the technical side of the products better than Saul. Both of them have essentially the same selling records after six years with the company. Mike learns faster than Saul. I vote for Saul.

James: Why? I thought you just said that Mike was better . . .

Tom: I said he is better technically and can learn faster and that *is* important in our business. But Saul is a good listener, and he's good enough technically. I believe I can work better with Saul, and the other salespeople like him. We'll have less turnover of junior salespeople with Saul.

James: Well, I like them both, and they both seem to have good personalities. Mike had a 3.3 grade average in college, and Saul had a 3.0. Mike has outsold Saul by about 5 percent of quota. Are you saying that Saul is more cooperative?

Tom: Saul always thinks of the other fellow first and never says anything bad about anyone. He's better liked by the sales force, but they respect him, too. While he may not be quite as aggressive as Mike, I've never had a customer complaint on Saul. I've had four customers say they felt that Mike was a bit high pressure and arrogant. Mike is polite to us and respectful, I know, but he is *so* out for Mike. He's critical, too. I don't think he has the leadership qualities Saul has.

James: How do you think Mike would take it if we promote Saul over him?

Tom: Jim, he's ultra-ambitious and won't like it, but he'll mend. Saul is more level-tempered and just . . . well, more mature.

James: I can see what you're trying to say. I must confess I've always felt Saul was more of a team player—a company man. Mike is a driver and an excellently motivated individualist . . . I agree, in the zone position, it would be easier to teach Saul the technical side than it would be to try to change Mike's personality. Let's give Mike some additional territory, but let's give Saul the zone.

Tom: Right.

QUESTIONS

1. What do you think is more important for management, personality or high technical competence? Why?

2. Which man, Mike or Saul, is more achievement-motivated? Why?

3. Do you think Powell and Davenport looked at this situation logically?

4–2

Bill Mullins has worked for the Gulfside Chemical Company for twelve years. Until the last three years, he had always made over quota and was considered one of the best senior salespersons. Although his sales performance seems to slip a little more each year, he sold 90 percent of his quota last year. Everyone likes Bill. He's an extrovert with an excellent sense of humor, although sometimes his stories are a little off-color, and he uses profanity occasionally in talking to some customers. He has been depressed lately, because his wife left two months ago after eighteen years of marriage. The word is that Bill has been drinking heavily and that is why his wife left him. He was arrested for drunken driving last Tuesday at 4 p.m. and lost his license for at least a month. This morning he missed the eight o'clock sales meeting at the branch and came in at nine o'clock, looking a little "smashed." He was not quite drunk, but he was not quite sober either.

If you were the sales manager, how would you handle this situation?
What would you say to Bill?
Do you think this is a common managerial and personal problem in personal selling?
If Bill keeps going in the same direction, what will be the eventual outcome?

4–3

Professor Daniel Reinhold has just assigned a personality project to his sales class. It requires a preliminary self-evaluation by the student of his or her weak and strong attributes. Louise Garraway has her hand raised . . .

Dr. R: Yes, Louise?

Louise: Dr. Reinhold, isn't there a test of some kind that each of us could take to assess whether or not we're introverts, extroverts, or in between? Knowing ourselves better would seem like a good idea for a starting point for the project.

Dr. R.:   I think you're right, Louise. That's why I've brought in this Temperament Checklist for each of you to fill out. It was developed by a friend of mine at the University of Rhode Island, Dr. Eugene Johnson. He's used it in personal selling and sales management development seminars all over the country. After you fill it out, I'll tell you how to interpret your answers. But this is not a test—it's just an exercise that only you will see the results of.

TEMPERAMENT CHECKLIST

This checklist will indicate certain of your temperament qualities and how they affect your adjustment to your associates and activities, both business and social. There is no such thing as a good or bad mark on this form. A mark of 70% is no better than 30%—it simply means the individuals differ in terms of human qualities.

Instructions: For each question circle "YES" if this would be your answer all or nearly all the time, "NO" if that would be your answer all or nearly all the time, and "S" if your answer to the question would be "Sometimes."

1. Would you rather stay home and read a good book than go out with a group of friends?_____ YES   S   NO

2. Do you like to do jobs carefully and thoroughly, even when a less perfect job would be all right?_____ YES   S   NO

3. When you are going to buy something fairly expensive, do you look around carefully before buying?_____ YES   S   NO

4. Do you like to do arithmetic problems?_____ YES   S   NO

5. Have you lost out in something you wanted to do by not making up your mind quickly enough? YES   S   NO

6. Do your friends think you are particular about details?_____ YES   S   NO

Source: Larry J. Leitner & Assocs.

7. Would you like to have things more settled and safe in your life—with nothing to worry about as you look ahead?_____   YES S NO

8. Do you like to make minor repairs or adjustments on autos, appliances, or about the house?   YES S NO

9. Does your mind frequently dwell on things you would like to see, do, or have?_____   YES S NO

10. Are you in the clouds one day and "down in the depths" another day?_____   YES S NO

11. Do you blush easily?_____   YES S NO

12. Are you careful not to lend money to acquaintances unless you are sure of their honesty?_____   YES S NO

13. Do you allow people to crowd ahead of you in line?_____   YES S NO

14. Have you ever been afraid of losing a job because your work went badly?_____   YES S NO

15. Does it annoy you to have someone watch you at work?_____   YES S NO

16. Can you keep on doing tiresome, routine work over a long period of time?_____   YES S NO

17. Are you inclined to keep quiet when out with people you do not know well?_____   YES S NO

18. Does it annoy you to have people talk about you?_____   YES S NO

19. Do you like to read serious books or attend lectures?_____   YES S NO

20. Do you have strong religious or political convictions?_____   YES S NO

21. Do you have a strong desire to feel more certain of yourself and to be more self-confident?_____   YES S NO

22. Do you question the wisdom of your decisions after you have made them?_____   YES S NO

23. Do you like to take care of the details of your work?_____   YES S NO

24. Do you come right to the point with what you have to say regardless of the consequences?_____   YES S NO

25. Do you find people so opinionated that it is hard to reason with them?_____   YES S NO

26. In the organizations to which you belong, are you usually satisfied to be a member rather than a leader?_____   YES S NO

27. Do even the most dramatic of your experiences generally leave your personality much the same?_____   YES S NO

28. Can you express yourself orally more easily than in writing?_____   YES S NO

29. Do you remember people well?_____ YES S NO

30. Are you inclined to exaggerate about your experiences or about what you can do?_____ YES S NO

31. Are you usually late for an appointment?_____ YES S NO

32. Is it easy for you to change an opinion or belief?_____ YES S NO

33. Do you like to be busy with several things at the same time?____ YES S NO

34. Do you find it easy to get started with new projects?_____ YES S NO

35. Are most people willing to cooperate with you and your plans?__ YES S NO

36. Do you accept people's mistakes and little annoying actions good-naturedly?_____ YES S NO

37. When you are out with two or three friends, are you usually the one who decides where to go and what to do?_____ YES S NO

38. Do you like to have power or influence over people, so you can make them do as you wish?_____ YES S NO

39. Are you quick to say what you feel like saying as compared to other people?_____ YES S NO

40. Are you inclined to go ahead and do things without thinking much about the outcome?_____ YES S NO

41. After you have done the big and difficult parts of a job, do you dislike finishing up the odds and ends?_____ YES S NO

42. Have other people told you that you are a proud, stuck-up, or egotistical person?_____ YES S NO

43. Do you laugh readily?_____ YES S NO

44. Do you care what other people think about you? YES S NO

45. Do you like to gamble?_____ YES S NO

46. Do you feel at ease upon entering a room where there are several strange people?_____ YES S NO

47. Do people say you are a person who will have his/her own way? _____ YES S NO

48. Do you prefer jobs where you work with other people?_____ YES S NO

49. Do you speak to people first on meeting them? YES S NO

50. Are you answering these questions quickly, without much thought or deliberation?_____ YES S NO

Your instructor will give you insight into what your responses mean in this exercise.

For the scoring of questions 1–27, give two points for all "yes" answers; for questions 28–50, give two points for all "no" answers; give one point for each "sometimes". Add the three part score. The final score is the percent of introvert in the person's temperament. Scores are classified as follows: 64–100 = introvert; 36–0 = extrovert; 37–63 = ambivert (a mixture of the two). The introvert temperament is precise, meticulous, what one would call the results-oriented person—good in selling where a scientific or engineering background is required. The extrovert is the action-oriented person, more interested in people and activity than in details and procedures—good in selling where cold calls, personal contact, canvassing, high participation, and public relations services are required.

NOTES

1. Jack Lacy, "Secrets of a Winning Sales Personality," recording (Chicago: Businessmen's Record Club, 1961).

2. Frank Bettger, *How I Multiplied My Income and Happiness in Selling* (Englewood Cliffs, N.J.: Prentice-Hall, 1954).

3. Dale Carnegie, *How to Win Friends and Influence People* (New York: Simon and Schuster, 1964).

4. Maxwell Maltz, *Psycho-Cybernetics* (Englewood Cliffs, N.J.: Prentice-Hall, 1960), p. 1 ff.

5. John T. Molloy, *Live for Success* (New York: Morrow, 1981), p. 84.

6. Ben B. Smith, *The Magic of Self-Cybernetics* (New York: Frederick Fell, 1971).

7. Maltz, *Psycho-Cybernetics,* p. xi.

8. Norman Vincent Peale, *The Power of Positive Thinking* (Englewood Cliffs, N.J.: Prentice-Hall, 1964).

9. Maltz, *Psycho-Cybernetics,* p. 32.

10. Jack Lacy, "Secrets."

11. Maltz, *Psycho-Cybernetics,* pp. 187–204.

12. Norman Vincent Peale, *Enthusiasm Makes the Difference* (Englewood Cliffs, N.J.: Prentice-Hall, 1967), p. 35.

13. W. Clement Stone, *The Success System That Never Fails* (Englewood Cliffs, N.J.: Prentice-Hall, 1962), p. 117.

14. Frank Bettger, "How I Raised Myself from Failure to Success in Selling," recording (Waco, Texas: Success Motivation Institute, 1962).

15. Carnegie, *How to Win Friends.*

16. Jack Lacy, "Secrets."

17. Paul P. Parker, "How to Use Tact and Skill in Handling People," recording (Waco, Texas: Success Motivation Institute, 1964).

18. John T. Molloy, "Clothes Make the Salesman—Never Wear Green," *Sales and Marketing Management,* vol. 115, no. 10 (December 8, 1975), pp. 58–62.

19. "Staying Trim, Productive, and Alive," *Nation's Business,* vol. 62 (December 1974), pp. 26–28.

20. Maltz, *Psycho-Cybernetics,* pp. 225–245.

21. "Personal Business," *Business Week,* January 5, 1974, p. 70.

22. Kenneth M. Cooper, *The New Aerobics* (New York: Evans, 1970).

23. Louis F. Basinger, *The Techniques of Observation and Learning Retention* (Springfield, Ill.: Thomas, 1973), pp. 7–33.

24. Matthew J. Culligan, *Getting Back to the Basics of Selling* (New York: Crown, 1981), pp. 22–23.

25. Donald A. Laird and Eleanor C. Laird, *Techniques for Efficient Remembering* (New York: McGraw-Hill, 1960), pp. 10–17.

26. Basinger, *Techniques of Observation,* pp. 36–43.

27. Victor Werner, "How to Remember Everything," *Retirement Living,* February 1973, pp. 44–45.

28. Harry Lorayne and Jerry Lucas, *The Memory Book* (New York: Stein and Day, 1974), p. 21.

29. Werner, *How to Remember,* p. 44.

30. Basinger, *Techniques of Observation,* p. 45.

31. Laird and Laird, *Techniques for Efficient Remembering,* pp. 197–215.

32. Basinger, *Techniques of Observation,* p. 50.

33. Laird and Laird, *Techniques for Efficient Remembering,* pp. 137–147.

Communications and Persuasion

Every good sales representative must be able to communicate effectively. This involves much more than the competent use of words. Understanding theories of communication gives sales reps access to new areas of thinking and practitioner experience. Communication entails nonverbal as well as verbal ways to put across a total sales message. It includes formulating persuasive strategy based on past experiences of successful communicators. To provide an understanding of a sales representative's role in persuasion, the following topics will be treated in this chapter:

- Communication ideas
- Nonverbal communication
- Persuasive strategies

COMMUNICATION IDEAS

Communications Involve a Common Basis

"Communications" comes from the Latin word *communis*, meaning common. The more a communicator has in common with other people, the better he or she can communicate with them. A child may try to talk to a butterfly, but there are no common denominators for communication. Communicating with persons from a country with a different language and culture is also very difficult. People communicate best with others like themselves who share common experiences. To the salesperson, this means that it is important to strive for maximum identification through emotional ties with prospects, weaving conversation around agreeable, mutual interests. The communications model (see Figure 5.1) shows that communications take place only within shared fields (areas) of experience (1). If there is little overlap, the transmission of exact meanings becomes a difficult challenge, for meanings are in people, not in messages.

Communication Elements

The model shows the elements of communication: "source, encoder, signal or message channel, decoder, and destination" (2). In the armed forces, it is necessary to encode and decode messages formally to keep the contents secret. In ordinary conversation, we encode and decode through words and nonverbal signals, although the sender and the encoder are usually the same person. When people say, "Good morning," they are encoding. They do not really mean to comment on the quality of the day. They are saying, "I recognize you as a person, and I am acknowledging you pleasantly." The person decoding the message will determine accordingly that the sender is simply attempting to be polite. Sales representatives must be particularly certain that

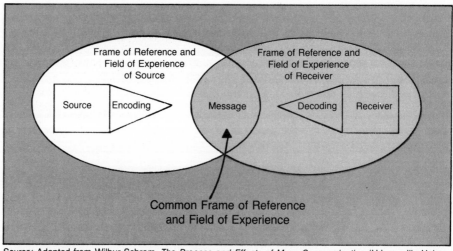

Source: Adapted from Wilbur Schram, *The Process and Effects of Mass Communication* (Urbana, Ill.: University of Illinois Press, 1960), p. 6.

Figure 5.1   Schramm's Communication Diagram

their messages are interpreted correctly. Many English words have dozens of meanings. Potential exists for misunderstanding the exact intent of messages. The salesperson's choice of words, phrasing, how the words are said, and gestures used must all be "in tune" with one another.

Receivers consider the source of messages in determining how much attention to give to a message and its content. Messages believed to be from reliable and competent sources are persuasive (3). This is why a prospect's impression of a sales representative is so important. Receivers always attempt to read the attitudes and motivations of senders. The appearance of a salesperson as sender and the way in which words are presented may convey more meaning to the receiver (the prospect) than words do. One reason why testimonials of satisfied customers are so effective is that prospects believe that such seemingly unbiased sources have no monetary stake in an outcome. While prospects expect sales representatives to use every known device to influence sales, they usually believe that another customer is sincere in evaluating a product.

The *signal* concerns the way the message is transmitted and the clarity of a communication. Face-to-face communications, which allow interpretation of nonverbal signals and more complete feedback, are usually persuasively superior to written messages or telephone conversations. Personal interviews allow more shared ideas and joint interpretations and reduce the chances of *noise*. *Noise* is any audible or other distraction that distorts message quality. A distraction can be so great that a message may not even be received. Salespersons should minimize distractions during interviews by attempting to select times and places as free as possible from interference. For example, it is bad practice to talk to a prospect in an atmosphere of distraction such as in a busy passageway. *Feedback,* or the response of a receiver to a message, is necessary to judge the effect of a message and to determine whether the communication has been decoded properly. A more elaborate communications model showing the mechanics of feedback is shown in Figure 5.2. Salespersons must be better listeners than talkers. Listening and careful observation are necessary for adjusting to feedback.

Four Rules for Communicating Effectively

There are four especially important rules for good communication (4). First, messages must be planned and delivered in such a way as to attract a receiver's attention. Not only should messages be loud or visible enough to be noticed, but they should contain some cue to grab a receiver's interest. A message should also reach a receiver when he or she is apt to be tuned in. Second, a message should incorporate words and other symbols that relate to common experiences of the sender and the receiver. A well-planned message harmonizes with a receiver's point of view to avoid rejection or meaning dis-

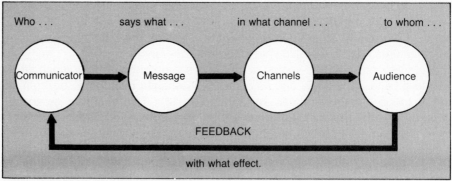

Source: Philip Kotler, *Marketing Management: Analysis, Planning and Control*, 3rd ed. (Englewood Cliffs, N.J.: Prentice-Hall, 1978), p. 456.

Figure 5.2   Communications Model

tortion. Third, a message should be designed to appeal to or arouse the personal needs of a receiver while suggesting a way to meet those needs. Prospects require action to fulfill their needs. The action a rep desires a prospect to take should be *specifically* suggested. The last rule is that the method suggested for meeting needs should relate to group influences affecting a prospect at the time of the suggested action.

Communication May Have a Two-Step Flow Effect

Communication often flows from a source, through media, and to opinion leaders, who influence mass accepters of an idea (5)—see Figure 5.3. Opinion leaders may be different for different products. Usually, people are leaders because they know the most about a product, are socially well located, and/or are distinguished in a certain area. This suggests that salespersons should concentrate on opinion leaders and use their testimony to influence later buyers. Many prospects are much easier to sell if they are assured that respected

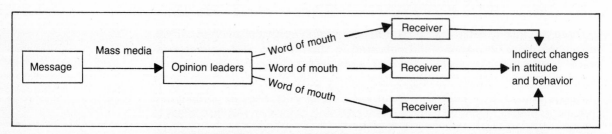

Figure 5.3   Two-Step Flow of Communication

Personal Preparation

leaders have endorsed a product. Positive word-of-mouth product evaluations are often the best promotion.

Two-Way Communication

Two-way communication promotes prospect participation and encourages adequate feedback. To promote persuasive two-way communication, easily understood words should be used and probing questions asked frequently. Careful listening, not merely to what a prospect says, but also to what the prospect means, is necessary. Inexperienced salespersons have a tendency to monopolize an interview and not to give prospects a chance to react. Questions should require more than just a simple yes or no answer. They should cause the prospect to think deeply about needs. Examples of such questions are: "If you could have an automobile custom-made for you, what kind of features would you like to see included?" or "How long does it take to do your entire payroll operation by hand?" Questions like these stimulate a prospect to review needs and give a sales representative a useful response. Don't be tempted to plan strategy while a prospect is speaking; careful listening and observation will provide you with valuable feedback and important clues as to how to proceed. Everything a prospect says should be analyzed and considered as a basis of response.

Words Have Different Meanings

Words are symbols into which messages are encoded. Because words have different meanings to different people, and suggest different mental images, it is almost impossible to transmit exact meanings by words alone. There are dozens of meanings for the word "round," and there are at least eight meanings for the word "frog," depending on the context in which the word is used (6). Eskimos have three words for "snow." The Greeks have three words for "love." And some tribes distinguish between all the different varieties of rice, with a different word for each (7). Children relive movies as they describe vivid scenes, but their words mean little to a receiver who has not experienced the picture or the music. Even small children have surprisingly large vocabularies. The reason they are not able to communicate as well as adults is that they are self-centered senders who expect listeners to understand without sharing their experience (frames of reference). Sales representatives need to be sensitive about using words within the experience of their prospects. Words also mean different things in different cultures. In England, the hood of an automobile is a "bonnet." In the Navy, the ceiling is the "overhead." To sailors, there is a difference between ships and boats. Some cultures have private meanings for hundreds of words. Such private meanings serve almost as passwords for acceptance into a culture or group and distinguish group members from outsiders. Scientific fields also have words forming private vocabularies. Persons who have experienced similar educations and events can shorten conversations by using common terms well understood by their colleagues. But sales representatives must use concrete terms to establish commonalities by using the vocabulary of the field. In industrial or medical sales, professional salespersons must establish themselves through the use of an appropriate vocabulary.

Denotation and Connotation. Words have both denotative and connotative meanings. *Denotation* indicates associations the word has for most people. *Connotation* refers to secondary associations that may differ among members of a language group. The word "cat," for example, usually denotes a four-footed domestic animal of rather mild disposition. To someone who has been bitten by a cat or to an animal trainer, the word has different secondary associations. Words that may have powerful connotations interfere with effective communication. People are tempted to categorize and prejudge all "sailors," "salespeople," and "politicians." That is, they tend to stereotype all members of certain groups. There is a tendency to evaluate on one-word cues. Furnishing more information in place of a word that might be misleading because it has a stereotyped image to a prospect enhances communication effectiveness.

Word Attributes. Word attributes may be concrete or abstract, active or passive, emotional or neutral, and holy or profane. Words may have racial or political overtones. Concrete words convey more accurate meanings than abstract words like "beautiful" or flexible." It is better to say, "This unit types 300 words per minute" than to say, "This unit types quickly." It is also better to use active verbs rather than passive verbs. "She bought that machine without seeing it" is better than "That machine was bought by someone who had not seen it." Some words, like "communism," "death," and "home," have emotional content. A sign saying "Home for Sale" is better than a sign saying "House for Sale." The word "home" stirs positive emotions in most people, while the word "house" is more neutral. The use of profanity reflects on the sincerity and credibility of a source and is offensive to most prospects. Sexual profanity will lower a salesperson's credibility even more than religious profanity (8). Words like "Democrat" or "Republican" may be emotionally charged to many buyers. Slurs against a buyer's political party, however indirect, may promote an atmosphere of conflict. The political scene, in fact, shows how essential words can be. It is hard for politicians to be against bills entitled "Truth in Packaging," "Fair Employment," and "The Right to Work." Jimmy Carter created an uproar by his expression "ethnic purity," and other politicians have been career-damaged by using words carelessly.

Use Understandable Words. Signals sent must be, above all, understandable and prospect-oriented. Short sentences and short words are usually preferred in sales presentations. Ability to use multisyllabic words may impress prospects, but such words may either fail to communicate a basic selling message or make a prospect feel uneducated for want of comprehension. Easily understood words in messages make for more effective communication.

Use "You" Not "I."   In selling, it is far better to overuse the words "you" and "we" than it is to use pronouns like "I," "me," and "mine." Salespersons who overuse references to themselves indicate their self-centeredness rather than an orientation to the personality needs of others.

NONVERBAL COMMUNICATION

The potential for reading and sending nonverbal signals in the sales interview situation is exciting. More than two-thirds of communication between a sales representative and a prospect can be nonverbal (9). While prospects may hide truth and inner feelings with words, they reveal intent, attitudes, and emotions through body language. Sales reps also send out nonverbal signals that prospects receive subconsciously. These "body language" messages form the basis of prospects' impressions of a rep's intentions. All salespersons must learn to read and respond to customers' nonword signals and to increase their effectiveness through properly expressing this silent language.

One pioneering application of anthropologist Edward T. Hall's method of analysis of nonverbal communication—proxemics—focused exclusively on salespersons' silent language. Action, gestures, and dress were observed in order to predict whether or not a sale would take place at the end of encounters between retail salespeople and their customers. The probability of a correct prediction being due to chance alone—that is, forecasting a sale when one did later take place, and forecasting a no-sale when none later occurred—was 25 percent. By scoring only nonverbal cues, sale/no-sale outcomes were correctly predicted 74 percent of the time (10).

Scientific stress on nonverbal communication is new. Because it is largely an unconscious language, which varies from culture to culture, great care must be taken in interpreting signals. Nonverbal cues are indications that should be read only in conjunction with other evidence. People may cross their arms and still be interested and receptive. Noses may be rubbed because they itch rather than as an expression of prospect doubt. Usually, nonverbal clues support a speaker's words, and when they do, they tend to verify what is said. When nonverbal and verbal messages conflict, it indicates that the whole truth is not being told. A woman prospect, for example, may say she is not interested because she wants to bargain. However, her expression and the way she handles the product may show that she is interested, indeed.

Full coverage of nonverbal communication is beyond the scope of this text. This section is designed to increase awareness of this iceberg existing below the surface of word communication, to give some sources for further study (in the Notes at the end of the chapter), and to highlight certain signals for use in selling prospects.

The elements of nonverbal communication are:

- Space
- Body messages
- Touching
- Timing and voice characteristics

Space

The distances preferred by people who are communicating yield important clues to their personalities, purposes, and the formality with which they plan to converse. While lovers may be less than a foot apart when talking to each other, impersonal business is usually conducted from a distance of between four and seven feet (11). A sales interview should be conducted as close as four or five feet from a prospect, and even closer if the prospect is an extrovert or well known to the salesperson. Close distance promotes a more friendly and less formal interview climate. When too much distance separates a prospect and a salesperson, the salesperson may wonder why the prospect seems so psychologically distant and why good two-way communication is not forthcoming.

The average American has an imaginary *privacy bubble* that surrounds the body and extends out about two feet in every direction (12). If this personal space is invaded, the person will normally move back, stiffen, or become defensive in some other way. Introverts have a larger privacy bubble than extroverts. Mexicans demand less space and like to converse at closer intervals. Blacks have a larger personal space zone than whites (13). Violent prisoners in jail for assault often have a personal space bubble many times larger than normal, and invading their personal spaces could be fatal. Interrogators for the police are advised to interview suspects at close range with nothing between questioner and suspect. The recommended procedure is to move even closer as the questioning progresses in order to break down suspects' defenses by violating their personal space (14). Many excellent sales representatives enter the personal space of indecisive and extroverted prospects by getting very close and maintaining good eye contact. *If handled correctly,* the silent pressure of being near is permissible with most prospects, improves attention and communication, and indicates friendliness and sincerity. Attempts to move closer to prospects depend on prospects' sensitivity to pressure and the selling situation. If a prospect indicates annoyance, a salesperson can move back a little. Introverts and prospects who wish to maintain a formal interview may resent attempts to move nearer as being "pushy," while others may interpret it as a sign that the salesperson is confident about a product. Certainly, if nothing else has worked with a prospect, this is a strategy that might be tried.

Space also indicates dominance. Persons of high rank or status tend to relax in close contact with subordinates, while lower-ranked persons tend to stiffen. Sales representatives who are ill at ease in close proximity to an important customer are conveying, "I haven't much confidence in myself or my product." The way a salesperson enters a prospect's office also indicates confidence and self-image. The quicker the entry, the greater your status will appear. Salespersons who lack confident self-images may stop at the door and talk to the seated executive from across the room. Stopping halfway to the desk indicates more confidence. Stopping in front of the desk indicates a feeling of equal conversational status with the executive. A failure to approach a prospect sets an improper interview tone—one of subordination on the part of the sales representative—unless a prospect is of extremely high rank. The layout shown in Figure 5.4 shows application of space use by rank that can act as a cue to knowing "who's who" in an office.

"Come all the way in, Ferguson. I want to have a little talk with you about self-confidence."

THE SATURDAY EVENING POST

Salespersons indicate much about their personalities by the way they enter an office.

Reprinted from *The Saturday Evening Post* © 1961 The Curtis Publishing Company.

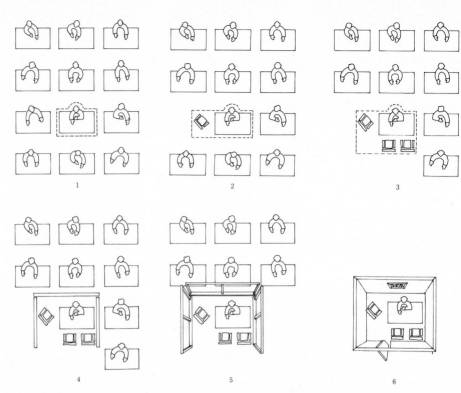

Source: Henry E. Kates and Karen W. Crane, *Body Language in Sales* (Indianapolis: Market Builder Library, 1980), p. 57.

Figure 5.4   The Progression of Earned Space Ownership in a Large, Corporate Office

Prospects, like other individuals, assume "ownership" of customary places in conference rooms, restaurants, and parking lots, just as a student feels a priority over a customary classroom seat (15). Moreover, if a prospect is sharing a table with a rep, he or she will unconsciously subdivide the table into two equal parts and assume ownership of the nearest half (16). People can be made quite uncomfortable by another person's putting something on "their" side of a table. Sales representatives should respect these imaginary territorial boundaries. (See Figure 5.5.)

Liking for people is expressed by drawing closer to them, looking into their eyes, and taking a position near them. People are said to be "distant" when they attempt to avoid being close. When prospects try to avoid direct communication through a more impersonal method than face-to-face interviews, they may be signaling refusal attitudes instead of giving a flat "no." People don't like to break bad news to those in their presence. They seek a more impersonal way to refuse requests. Special actions of avoidance signal negative attitudes before a prospect makes verbal a rejection of an offer. This gives a sales representative a chance to try a new tack before closing to a committed "no."

Body Messages

Messages are sent by means of body postures and positions, body movements, the face, and the hands. Representatives receive conscious and subconscious messages from prospective customers in the same way. While it is dangerous to be "clued in" to any one signal and to react to it, signals in conjunction with words and a succession of consistent signals give good indications about prospect thinking.

Postures and Positions. See Figure 5.6. Tense and rigid postures indicate anxiety, defensiveness, and/or unreceptivity. Perhaps a prospect is concerned that the interview is too long or that the product does not meet his or her needs. Perhaps the prospect feels too much pressure. On the other hand, relaxing too much can show boredom and inattentiveness. A receptive prospect exhibits a semirelaxed posture, a slightly tilted head, and an open-armed, open-legged position (17). Women unconsciously indicate receptivity and sincerity through the display of their open palms (18). When prospects cross their legs with their knee pointing toward a speaker they are indicating receptivity. If the knee points away, this implies orientation in another direc-

Figure 5.5
The natural tendency is to stake out the space each of you will call your own.

Source: Henry E. Kates and Karen W. Crane, *Body Language in Sales* (Indianapolis: Market Builder Library, 1980), p. 55.

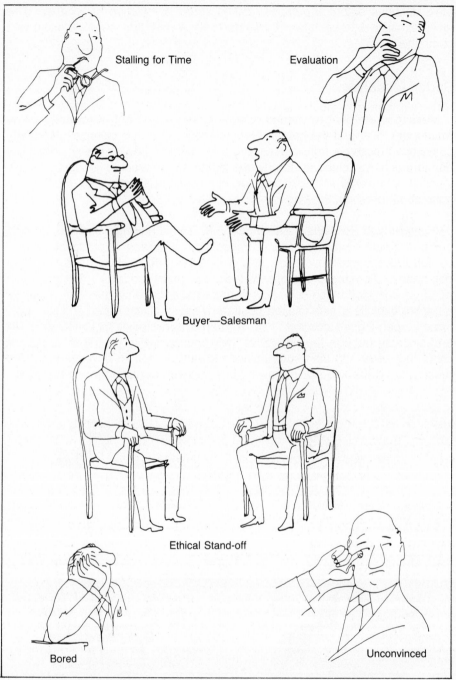

Stalling for Time

Evaluation

Buyer—Salesman

Ethical Stand-off

Bored

Unconvinced

Source: Matthew J. Culligan, *Getting Back to the Basics of Selling* (New York: Crown, 1981).

Figure 5.6

tion. Locked ankles and clenched hands reveal holding back of strong feelings or emotions (19). In tense interviews, as in a dentist's chair, people tend to sit with their ankles locked. The crossed-arm position, while sitting or standing, shows defensiveness and a lack of receptivity to a presentation. Handing a cross-armed prospect something, requiring the prospect to shift position, may regain attention and receptivity. When people lean back in chairs using both hands to support the head from behind, they may be showing feelings of superiority. Complimenting the customer or showing respect caters to these feelings. Prospects who put their hands on their hips may be "telegraphing" that they have reached a decision and are ready for a trial close. (20). Any change of position indicates a change of mind. A prospect may be trying to end an interview, may have reacted to something just said, or may have decided to accept if asked for an order. Interestingly enough, people of the same opinion in a group tend unconsciously to assume the same body postures. This is especially the case when reacting to a speaker who has just expressed their point of view. If prospects agree with a rep, they may imitate the rep's body position. This is a definite closing signal. Such opportunities should be met with at least a trial close.

Body Movements. Body movements send messages. There is an unconcious tendency to get into the same rhythm as that of people talked with. Gestures tend to move in similar patterns, as in music. This is part of the "commonness" that harmonizes face-to-face communications. Some sales representatives are better persuaders because of their basic body rhythms. Their individual movements aid their expression (21). Their head moves upward when they ask questions. They tilt their head slightly, moving closer to prospects to show that they are listening with more interest. Posture, rhythm, and tempo—all convey alertness and enthusiasm.

As important as it is to send correct messages through actions, it is also necessary to interpret prospect motions accurately. For example, a male customer may want to hint that he is out of time or for some other reason wishes to end an interview. He may shift forward in his chair, move backward, or get up and walk around (22). If standing, he may walk away. He may start cleaning off his desk to say—without causing embarrassment—that time is up, he has other things to do. A perceptive rep should try to reinterest the prospect, conclude by closing, verbally acknowledging the realization of the value of the prospect's time. In a group-selling situation, the person who deliberately moves to a position different from the rest of the group may be attempting to assert superiority. A prospect whose body motions are imitated by others in the group is likely to be the dominant person of that group. That prospect should be the focus of special selling efforts (23). Variations in body movement and messages are almost endless. Many movements are not universal in meaning. The burden of learning regional variations is up to each sales representative. Like the poker player, the salesperson must be adept at noticing every detailed movement that might reveal the intentions of the other "player" in the "game."

The Face.   The face, particularly the area around the eyes, is a complex of small muscles capable of communicating hundreds of messages. Prospects use their faces to indicate approval, expectation, happiness, concern, or a state of relaxation. The prospect may even try to use facial expression to prove disinterest in order to bargain. However, timing can indicate whether the prospect is sincere or not. Fortunately, fairly accurate face reading is a skill possessed by everyone. Reading prospect emotions by observing facial expressions is an important sales tool. The eye area is the most important. Magicians depend on the eyes of a subject to select the "right" card. Eye expressions change when the right card (the card selected by the subject) appears. The pupils enlarge with excitement. Similarly, salespersons can tell at what point their words have made an impression on a prospect. Good eye contact conveys interest and sincerity, while eye avoidance in our culture is associated with dishonesty and insincerity. Eyes can smile, and many emotions are conveyed by the positioning of eyebrows. Catching the eye of a

"Come now, where's that infectious little smile?"

THE SATURDAY EVENING POST

Everyone appreciates a sincere smile!

Reprinted from *The Saturday Evening Post* © 1957 The Curtis Publishing Company.

prospect gets attention, just as catching the eye of a waiter can get service in a busy restaurant. While stares and glares are considered threatening, longer contact usually indicates interest. Contact that is too long invades the prospect's privacy and is considered bad manners in our culture (24). Remember, the deadpan look is for comics and poker players, not for salespersons showing enthusiasm and attempting to generate interest.

Hands.   Our hands help us to communicate by allowing us to draw pictures in the air; to express size, shape, or direction; to command attention; and to convey dominance or acceptance. (See Figure 5.7.) Prospects with tightly clasped or fidgeting hands reveal tension. Hands tapping the desk indicate impatience or restlessness, signaling a loss of attention or too long a call (25). Prospects may cover their eyes to indicate embarrassment, cover their mouths to say something they don't want you to repeat, or hit their foreheads to show forgetfulness. They may touch their noses to indicate that they don't fully believe what you are saying (26). If they "steeple" their fingers (touch fingertip to fingertip), they may be signaling dominance, superiority, or weighing up of alternatives. Fist clenching, on the other hand, may be strongly defensive or indicate mental disagreement with what is being said. Message evaluation is shown by chin stroking. Interpretations of hand movements must be done with care since any one of these signs can also mean something else. Signals must be interpreted in the context in which they are expressed.

For all its value in aiding a sales rep to "read" prospect reactions, understanding nonverbal communication's real value to those making sales presentations is to make their own meanings clear. As John T. Molloy has noted, "Although you cannot control other people, particularly strangers, by reading their body signals, you can control the way other people will react to you if you control your own [body signals]" (27).

Dress

"FACT: People who look successful and well educated receive preferential treatment in almost all their social or business encounters" (28). It is an old maxim of personal selling that you only get one chance to make a good first impression! Recently, behavioral scientists have confirmed this widely held belief. As Dr. Ellen Berscheid of the University of Minnesota put it after fifteen years of research, "It is a myth that 'beauty is only skin deep!' " (29). One of the most obvious ways salespersons communicate with prospects is through their appearance. While not everyone can be an Adonis or a Venus, all sales representatives can look well managed. A well-managed appearance communicates subliminally to a prospect that a rep is a creditable source. While there are many sources of advice on appearance, each with several sets of rules, good sense and good taste are really what are required. Sales reps

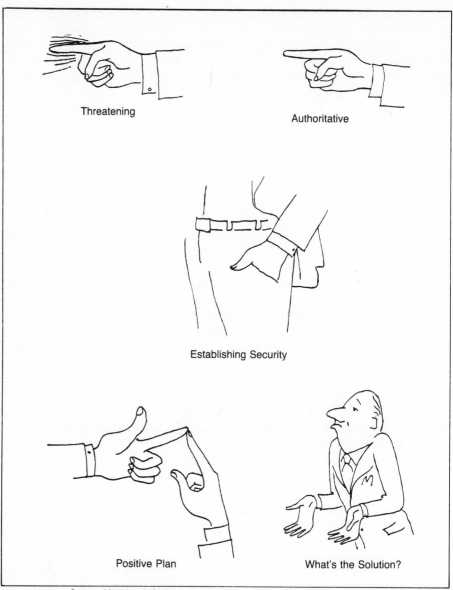

Threatening

Authoritative

Establishing Security

Positive Plan

What's the Solution?

Source: Matthew J. Culligan, *Getting Back to the Basics of Selling* (New York: Crown, 1981).

Figure 5.7 Hands as Communicators

should dress in a manner that causes prospects to focus on their clothes rather than on the content of their presentation. This means that dress that is conservative and calls attention not to the rep but to the message will gener- ally be more successful in communicating positively with prospects than will clothes that are the ultimate in current fashion and color and attract attention to themselves.

Touching

Touching indicates intimacy and should be done with sincerity. The handshake is of particular significance. A firm handshake indicates liking and friendliness, but the prolonged handshake (like prolonged eye contact) is too intimate for most sales situations. A limp, loose, or cold handshake shows a tendency toward uninvolvement, unfriendliness, and aloofness (30). The first physical contact with a prospect is critical. Remember, closeness means liking, but too much or inappropriate closeness indicates insincerity. Touching is as close as one person can get to another. While touching (putting the hand on a shoulder or back) may cause some prospects to drop their defensiveness, it will embarrass and offend others. Touching to get a prospect's attention is rude. The best rule is to confine touching to the handshake, except under unusual circumstances with special friends or with those who need consolation.

When prospects touch or handle a product, they may be signaling an intent to possess it. Prospects usually convey true feelings about products by the ways they handle or try them. If a product is handled carefully, it may be that a prospect sees it as valuable. If it is handled roughly, it may be that a prospect feels it is of little worth or durability. To a degree, prospects form opinions about products by the ways salespersons handle them. Aluminum-cookware salespersons carefully pull their wares of of velveteen sacks to suggest that their quality is like that of fine silver.

Timing and Voice Characteristics

Timing and how things are said, like body language, give clues to attitudes, emotions, and thoughtfulness. Late appearances for engagements, neglect through inattention, and wasting prospects' time indicate that a sales representative is unreliable and discourteous. Needless to say, being late does not set a harmonious interview atmosphere. Timing during conversations may be just as critical. Interrupting indicates an attempt to dominate. Few prospects appreciate being interrupted, especially when they have just begun speaking. Long pauses before answering a question reveal the answer is not natural and may be false (31). Long pauses in the middle of expressing an idea are especially bad in persuasive communications, because the prospect's mind is distracted from *what* is being said to *how* it is being said.

A good presentation voice should have proper tone, appropriate volume, and pleasing pitch (32). Tone of voice shows positive or negative attitudes toward a listener. It can reflect joy, sadness, apprehension, and fear. Apprehension may be interpreted by prospects as dishonesty. Speakers who increase their pitch and speak faster than the normal 125 words per minute tend to seem more alive and dynamic. Sales representatives who talk too softly may lose listeners and may be thought of as shy or inhibited (33). Talking too loud is also offensive and indicates a lack of manners and refinement as well as an attempt to be domineering. Pitch should be varied to produce interest. A monotone voice is boring to everyone. Lower pitch levels are more pleasing. While pitch level does not seem to affect the amount of information a prospect comprehends, it influences a prospect's attitude toward sales representatives and their messages. Voices differ, but through practice and interest, voice quality can be improved and acceptability enhanced.

PERSUASIVE STRATEGIES

The knowledge of general persuasive strategies that should guide selection and direction of specific selling methods is the substance of Chapters 8 through 14.

Successful persuasive strategies follow the train of thought of prospects and neither challenge nor argue with them. Prospects cannot be expected to buy anything that is completely incompatible with their beliefs and attitudes. Prospects won't buy unless they believe that by buying they will accomplish one or more specific goals. The more goals prospects see themselves accomplishing through product purchase, the more likely they are to buy. This is why all a product's benefits and uses are explained in a complete presentation. The more clearly a prospect sees buying as accomplishing multiple goals, the more likely a rep's recommendations are to be accepted. If recommendations do not fit in with a prospect's thinking, a proposal will be rejected or altered, or the very structure of a prospect's thinking will be changed (34). A good presentation adjusts to prospect concepts of how a product fits in with the prospect's attitudes, needs, and motives *without* rearranging basic thought patterns. *The power of suggestion, selected strategic ideas,* and *propaganda techniques* as applied to persuasion should help in building sales representative–prospect rapport and in forming prospect conviction.

The Power of Suggestion

Under hypnosis, people will do things they would not ordinarily do. As the chapter on personality mentioned, hypnotized people are able to do even more than they ordinarily can, because they are free from inhibiting restraints. Conscious suggestion has proven to be the basic tool in the salesperson's magic kit. Even hardened attitudes can be changed over time through repeated conscious suggestion. Hitler, who misguided millions of people, said that people would believe a lie if you told it often enough. Conscious suggestion is used in brainwashing. Yet it can also be used for good persuasive purposes. Repeated conscious suggestion is the basis for successful advertising campaigns and personal selling. Vividly suggesting the benefits of using a product increases its acceptability and desirability. Appeals to what is felt to be a prospect's dominant buying motive are the basis of sales and advertising success. Positive and precise suggestions clarify benefits to use. In closing, a prospect should be asked to take a specific action. Many a sale has been lost because no order was ever asked for. Sometimes, persuasive appeals have a delayed effect. Using variations in appealing to prospects' main motives can relax resistance and persuade prospects to definite courses of action—buying products to fulfill need goals. If ideas leading to a purchase are not sown, it is unlikely that many sales will be reaped.

Ten Strategic Ideas

Many studies have been made to find out what general types of persuasive strategy are most useful, with whom, and under what circumstances. The following ten suggestions were formulated from basic persuasion generalizations on opinion and attitude change, found in *Persuasion* by Marvin Karlins and Herbert Ableson, but paraphrased to fit the selling situation (35).

1. *Attempt to promote harmony early in an interview by initially expressing views held by the prospect.* This is part of establishing rapport. Coming on strong with anything that might promote conflict reduces rapport. Later, on, closing will be easier if *agreement* on minor points and features has come first.

2. *Put the best selling points at the beginning or at the end of a presentation.* Those points made in the middle of a presentation stand the least chance of influencing a prospect or being remembered. When organizing a sales-presentation strategy, use some of the best selling points or features to gain attention at the very beginning. Be aware that the very first words are especially important. Prospects use them in deciding whether or not to give time and attention to a presentation. Make a positive impact just before asking for an order. Save a climactic closing feature for closing sales presentations.

3. *Appeal to as many of the prospect's senses as possible.* People understand products better if they can see them, touch them, hear them, taste them, or smell them. Sales representatives should carry the actual product, samples, or pictures of a product into meetings with prospects for demonstration. The impression on a prospect's mind will be stronger because of appeals to more senses. Few things are as persuasive as actually experiencing a product. New cars shine, smell clean and new, sound efficient, and respond easily to prospect steering commands. As prospects "experience a product" with their senses, phrases like "Shines like glass, doesn't it?" are useful in stimulating perception.

4. *Enlist the active participation of prospects in discussion or demonstration.* Several studies have shown that active participants are more persuadable than passive listeners. Getting prospects to participate is part of leading them to believe that they are making up their own minds rather than being sold. If a prospect can drive a car, operate a machine, or try on clothes while the benefits of buying are suggested, attention and interest will be maintained. Ask questions to bring potential buyers into the discussion. One of the most important persuasion strategies is letting prospects think they made up their minds themselves. No one likes to appear so weak-willed as to be "sold." Few ever say, "I was sold a new car." No. People say, "I bought a new car today." Even if prospects do not buy on a particular sales call in which they participated, they remember participation interviews the most clearly. It doesn't take long for the effects of persuasive communication to wear off, unless the sales points are ingrained through participation.

5. *Balance appeals in some cases by admitting to prospects one or more minor shortcomings in offerings.* To admit that a product is not perfect may enhance your believability. It may also be good strategy if your prospects are intelligent, not initially in agreement, or when competitors will tell them anyway before the sale is closed. Highly intelligent prospects like to hear both sides of an argument and are less susceptible to the "card-stacking" propaganda technique of citing a long string of plus features. If prospects don't know a salesperson well, one of the most important things for them is to determine whether or not the salesperson is telling the truth about a product. Less intelligent individuals are more easily persuaded if limiting features of a product are not brought up. The decision to admit minor deficiencies depends on the situation. Any weakness in a product should be overbalanced with the weight of a product virtue. "Yes, this typing unit is louder than we would like it to be, but having a removable typing unit will give you much more flexibil-

ity, and it will be easier to clean the typeface. The number printout is quieter than the competition's, and the numbers are what you'll use most, aren't they?"

6. *Use both emotional and factual appeals to change attitudes.* Studies show that information alone seldom changes attitudes, especially attitudes that are shared by a prospect's reference group. Prospects need factual appeals to *justify* mentally the changes proposed, and they need emotional appeals to *want* to change. A fear appeal is a negative appeal and should be used with care. Studies indicate that a mild fear appeal is better than a strong one in persuasive situations where people will hear communications from the other side of the same issue. On the other hand, a strong fear appeal may be more persuasive in situations involving a threat to a prospect's family or when such a strong appeal is backed by a highly respected source or when immediate action should be taken. Sales representatives often appeal to prospects' fears of losing a buying opportunity through failure to act quickly. Stronger fear appeals are used effectively by insurance company representatives and sales reps for safety equipment. Humor is seldom an effective persuasive technique.

7. *In situations in which a group of prospects is being sold, such as in a partnership, concentration on extroverts, women, or highly intelligent persons is the most effective tactic.* Evidence suggests that these people are more persuadable and often may help to persuade others. Introverts and the less intelligent are more difficult to persuade and are usually less influential. The highly intelligent are more susceptible to logical, balanced arguments and usually will listen to reasonable arguments with open minds. However, they are influenced by authoritative sources. Use of high-powered testimonials from competent authorities sways such prospects.

8. *Persuade, if possible, without directly opposing a prospect's reference-group standards.* Whenever possible, make messages reinforce group influences. Every individual relates to a group of people when decisions are made. The average person does not like to make decisions that are incompatible with peer-group thinking and values. A member of a very conservative club, for example, would hesitate to buy loud, gaudy clothes or a flashy automobile for fear of losing status and commonality with club members. Persons who identify strongly with particular groups resist the influence of appeals that conflict with group thinking. In this regard, opinions that prospects share with others are more difficult to change than those that they hold privately. It strength-

ens a prospect's loyalty to your product if you can get him or her to write a letter of endorsement or to openly promote your product to others.

9. *Don't expect prospects to draw their own conclusions from the evidence given. Conclude by giving a product-favoring interpretation of the facts and evidence.* Even intelligent persons may not interpret favorable facts about an offering favorably, and few people are insulted by a simple concluding statement, even when the interpretation is fairly obvious. If prospects are very suspicious or unreceptive, however, it is possible that such a conclusion could be interpreted as a propaganda ploy or as an insult to their intelligence. Such interpretations are rare.

10. *Sales reps regarded as highly creditable sources can ask for bigger orders or higher prices than are likely to be received.* Part of the bargaining process is to take a position beyond what is expected. Politicians do it. Labor unions do it. Real-estate salespersons do it. Real-estate sales representatives may ask $59,500 for a house that they would be willing to sell for $57,000. Prospects feel that they are getting a bargain when the lower price is paid. If a position is too extreme, however, the house will not be considered, and it may acquire the image of a house nobody wants. Studies on attitude change indicate that *polar position taking* by a persuader has more change effect than taking positions closer to those of a persuadee. It depends on the competitive situation. Polar position taking in a tightly competitive deal would probably be unwise.

Propaganda Techniques

To most people, the word "propaganda" has a negative connotation of unfair competitive influence or manipulation. Some propaganda techniques, however, are persuasive, usable, and acceptable in particular selling situations (36).

Testimonials involve open endorsement of a product by those who are respected by prospects in the target market. It is one of the most persuasive techniques and should be considered in all selling efforts. A looseleaf-type binder with many testimonial letters from satisfied buyers is an impressive sales tool.

Name calling is associating a competitive product with something undesirable by giving it a bad label. A salesperson may say in referring to a competitive machine that has a noise problem: "Make sure you don't get an accounting machine that sounds like a threshing machine. Noise is an important factor in an office." This technique should be used indirectly, if at all. A competitor should not be mentioned by name.

Card stacking is giving one-sided arguments for a product. Most prospects expect salespersons to be biased in favor of their products, so they are seldom offended if a salesperson tells them only good things about an offering. Card stacking is especially effective with less sophisticated prospects who will not hear other presentations from competitors.

The *bandwagon* technique is the suggestion that everybody's doing it (buying the product), so the prospect should too. This is a technique that is particularly useful in selling clothes and automobiles. It can also be used for products that are not quite as style-oriented. Persons who are strongly influenced by reference groups are more susceptible to the bandwagon technique than are those who pride themselves on being individualistic. Individualistic prospects may be "turned off" by such an appeal. Most prospects do not want to be out of style or the last to adopt a better product. The bandwagon is a good appeal for most prospects.

Association is an effective propaganda technique that is usable in persuasive situations. The salesperson should always associate a product with pleasant scenes or events to promote positive emotional images. For instance, automobiles should be demonstrated and shown in conjunction with pleasant surroundings. Word pictures can be painted that encourage prospects to associate products with favorable settings. "You would feel comfortable in this suit in any luxury hotel," or "This car would be comfortable on a long-distance vacation." Positive mental images of products are built by association.

SUMMARY

Effective communication requires a common field of experience between message sender and message receiver, transmission of the intended message to the receiver's senses, and proper encoding and decoding. Messages should attract attention, create interest, harmonize with a receiver's point of view, and relate to reference-group influences. Good questions, careful listening, and adequate feedback enhance two-way communication. Words are encoding symbols and affect the reception of messages. Specific, understandable words with good connotation for the receiver are the building blocks of good sales presentations. Nonverbal communications include the use of space, body movement, body contact, physical appearance and arrangements, and vocal variations and silences. These convey intent, emotions, and attitudes. It is essential that the sales representative learn to read and use nonverbal language. Persuasive strategy features the use of the power of suggestion, ideas giving insight to interview planning, and propaganda techniques.

REVIEW QUESTIONS

1. What are the factors that facilitate communication? What are the implications for the salesperson?

2. What are the elements of the communications model? Briefly describe each one.

3. How buyers judge the salesperson's image affects how they accept the salesperson as a source of information. Discuss.

4. Briefly outline the four important rules for effective communication.

5. What is meant by the two-step flow of communications? What is its value to the sales representative?

6. Why is two-way communication advantageous to the salesperson?

7. "The range of word meanings is a potential minefield for the salesperson." Comment.

8. Distinguish between connotation and denotation. How is this distinction important to the sales representative?

9. What kinds of words should you avoid in a sales presentation?

10. Why is nonverbal communication (body language) important to the salesperson? What are the elements of nonverbal communication?

11. In what ways does the distance between a salesperson and a prospect affect the communication process?

12. In what ways do salespersons and prospects use "body messages" to communicate?

13. Which of the facial elements is the foremost in nonverbal communication?

14. Outline some of the ways that people communicate with their hands.

15. Why is dress important to the salesperson?

16. What do the voice elements of tone, volume, and pitch convey?

17. What are the ten basic rules of persuasive strategy?

18. Name and briefly describe the five propaganda techniques that are considered valuable in selling situations.

Personal Preparation

1. Go back and read the first sentence in this chapter. If someone asked you what this sentence meant after you had *first* read it, what would you have said? How would you answer this question now, taking into consideration the material that you have read in this chapter? Does this sentence communicate more to you now than it did before? If it does, this is evidence that communication depends on the knowledge of the receiver.

2. The first of four rules for communicating effectively is to attract the receiver's attention. Before you can sell something, you must have the attention of the person with whom you are speaking. What would be a good method of getting attention in the following situations:

   a. You find yourself sitting next to a person you have never met but whom you think you would like to know.
   b. You are entering a home where you will attempt to sell life insurance to a family.
   c. You are entering a professor's office where you will attempt to convince her to adopt this personal selling book for her classes.

   In each of these situations what types of verbal and nonverbal behavior would you look for to determine whether you are being succesful?

3. Whenever you have to make a sales presentation, there are certain parts of this text that you should review. The ten strategic ideas listed in the chapter is one of these parts. Former students who are now very successful salespeople attribute their success to a periodic review of concepts such as these. Years from now, you are likely to find yourself in a situation where you will be more successful if you use these ideas. You will use these ideas more if you review them. For this reason, it is a good idea to keep this book. Although you will forget some of the main points, you will know where you can go to retrieve this information and refresh your memory.

   Think about some product you are interested in and that you know something about. You have graduated, and you are now selling this product. In selling this product how would you:

   a. Promote harmony early in the interview?
   b. Decide which selling points should be at the beginning or at the end of the presentation?
   c. Appeal to as many of the prospect's senses as you can?
   d. Get the prospect actively involved?
   e. Balance the appeal by admitting minor shortcomings?
   f. Use emotional and factual appeals?

5–1

Roger Willis of Highlift Equipment Corporation sells industrial elevators. He is calling on Mike Polski, vice president of Dutton Warehouses.

Roger: Mr. Polski, I'm Roger Willis of Highlift Equipment Corporation. I would like to discuss with you incorporating vertical elevators in your next warehouse expansion.

Mike: *(Putting newspaper down on desk in front of him and offering hand):* Sit down, Roger. I was just reading about the campaign for the next congressional election. What do you think of Reagan and Reaganomics?

Roger: I haven't had a chance to study it yet, Mr. Polski. I'm optimistic that the economy will pick up, however, no matter who wins. We seem to be in a time when business is beginning to think expansion. Is your company planning any new warehouses in the future?

Mike: Well, we may build a two-story in about a year, but that's so far off . . . We're just in the thinking-about-it stage. I'm not sure if Mr. Dutton is planning to go one-story or two. It does depend on just how much space we think we will need six months from now. *(Still looking at morning newspaper)* Say, look at these women at that Women's Conference. How do you feel about women in politics?

Roger: It depends on who the woman is, I guess. Some have made a very positive contribution, while others seem to have taken a short-range viewpoint. Mr. Polski *(pulls plans out of briefcase),* here are some warehouse plans that offer twice the storage capabilities of one story on the same amount of land with negligible loss in stock-movement efficiency. These buildings cost much less per square foot to build, even equipped with four vertical elevators. That would make a nice building, wouldn't it?

Mike: Yes. I would be glad to see what you have. *(Puts paper on a side table so he can look at the plans)* Land space is expensive today, and I plan to recommend that we go two-story on this one.

QUESTIONS

1. What was Roger's major communication problem in getting started on this interview?

2. Did he handle the politically charged questions correctly? Should he have been more open and stated his real views?

3. How did he regain attention and establish favorable two-way communication?

5–2

James Appleton, vacuum cleaner sales representative, is calling on Jane and Robert Smythe in their suburban home.

Robert Smythe: Yes?

James Appleton: Hello, I'm James Appleton, and I'm conducting a survey. May I come in?

Robert: Sure, what do you want to know?

James: We're interested in how many square feet of carpet you have in your house. Can you give me an estimate?

Robert: Say, are you a salesman? Wasn't that a vacuum cleaner you left on the porch?

James: Can I show you how it works? *(Sprinkles a bag of dirt on the rug.)*

Robert: What are you doing?

James: Don't worry, our vacuum cleaners are wonderful. I'll have it up in a jiffy.

Jane Smythe: What's going on in here? What is all that dirt doing on the carpet? I just shampooed it, and it is still damp.

Robert: You had better get that up, or I'm going to call a cop.

James: I'm trying. Something's wrong. It usually works.

Robert: Why didn't you ask me before you did that?

James: Have you got any shampoo?

Jane: Yes, here it is, and here's a brush. Get every bit of that up.

Robert: I see you have a Supervac. You know our vacuum played out on us last week.

James: There, it's almost clean. Can I show you how my great Supervac works?

Robert: I'd wash the whole thing with a toothbrush before I'd buy anything from you or your company. Get out of here fast before I change my mind and call the police. *(Reading Robert's body language, James makes a hasty exit.)*

Jane: Why did you tell him we needed a vacuum cleaner?

Robert: That's the only way I knew to get his goat since I couldn't hit him. Maybe he will think twice before he tries to con someone else.

James: *(outside to himself)* There must be a better way.

QUESTIONS

1. Tell James a better way to establish rapport and gain the prospect's attention.

2. In regard to communication theory, what do you think Jane and Robert think of the source of the communication and the pretense of conducting a survey to get in?

5–3

John Merino sells agricultural chemicals to farmers. His main line consists of herbicides (weed- and grass-killing chemicals) and insecticides. The herbicides are mostly premerge (mixed with the soil during planting to prevent weed and grass growth), and the insecticides are sold later in the growing season after the crop comes up and is threatened with insect infestation. John has an excellent education and has a tendency to express himself in big words. He feels that this gives him a professional image. He also likes to wear fashionable suits when calling on customers.

John's sales manager went with him on a call because John is behind on quota. John was dressed in a fashionable three-piece suit and wore highly polished black shoes. The sales manager heard John use these two sentences during the course of the conversation with a farmer:

"With this particular premerge compound, photodecomposition will occur unless incorporated."

"This compound is subject to microbial breakdown when applied to the soil and may be antagonistic with preapplied compounds."

The farmer replied at the end of John's presentation that he would consider the chemicals and would call if he needed any of John's products. John's sales manager reviewed the interview with John and told him that the farmer probably didn't understand all of the interview. She also suggested that John wear clothes more suitable to field interviews. John agreed that perhaps farmers would not identify with him unless he spoke in simpler terms. He also decided that he should dress in more appropriate clothing.

John didn't shave the next morning and wore some faded jeans and a tattered jacket. He left his sports car at home and borrowed an older compact model. This time John talked in as simple words as he could and even tried to imitate the particular dialect that was used in that part of the state. He tried to talk "country." When he finished, the farmer spoke to him with perfect diction and without the slightest trace of a country accent (the farmer knew he was being talked "down to"):

"Mr. Merino, I'm going to be honest with you. If your chemicals are so good, why haven't your sales been good enough to keep you in clothes and a good truck? I need another hand here on the farm, and it doesn't matter whether you can talk well or not. Would you be interested in a steady-paying job?"

What communication mistakes did John make with the first farmer? With the second farmer?

If John's sales manager had been present for the second interview, what do you think she would have said to John?

Why is it important to establish identification (a commonness) with your prospects?

5–4

The Hampton Corporation makes a full line of aquatic equipment for divers and wants to expand its operations by going international and selling to aquatic interests in Spain. Several alternatives have been suggested as to how to do this. One corporate vice president recommended that American sales representatives, who already know the product, be taught Spanish and transferred to Spain under a bonus agreement. A member of the board of directors recommended hiring Puerto Rican or Mexican American citizens and training them in product knowledge for the job. The corporation president wants to hire Spanish nationals and train them in the United States.

In terms of what you know about communications theory, make your recommendations as to which of the three alternatives you would select and fully support your decision.

NOTES

1. Wilbur Schramm, *The Process and Effects of Mass Communications* (Urbana: University of Illinois Press, 1954), pp. 3–26.

2. *Ibid.*

3. Wilbur Schramm, "Information Theory and Mass Communication," *Journalism Quarterly* (Spring 1955), pp. 13–146.

4. Wilbur Schramm, *The Process and Effects of Mass Communication.*

5. Elihu Katz, "The Two-Step Flow of Communication: An Up-to-Date Report on an Hypothesis," *Public Opinion Quarterly,* vol. 21 (Spring 1957), pp. 61–78.

6. S. I. Hayakawa, "How Words Change Our Lives," *Saturday Evening Post,* December 27, 1958, p. 72.

7. Stewart L. Tubbs and Sylvia Moss, *Human Communication* (New York: Random House, 1974), pp. 111–140.

8. *Ibid.,* p. 133.

9. William G. Savage, "Sure Listen; But Watch Their Gestures, Too," *Administrative Management,* vol. 33, no. 8 (August 1972), p. 33.

10. Richard F. Wendel and James Hulbert, "Hidden Dimensions of Retailing," *Business Viewpoints,* May 1969, pp. 57–76.

11. Edward T. Hall, *The Hidden Dimension* (New York: Doubleday, 1966), pp. 107–122.

12. Julius Fast, *Body Language* (New York: Evans, 1970), pp. 28–63.

13. Tubbs and Moss, *Human Communication,* p. 146.

14. Fast, *Body Language.*

15. Albert Mehrabian, *Silent Messages* (Belmont, Calif.: Wadsworth, 1971), pp. 24–39.

16. Fast, *Body Language,* pp. 25–33.

17. Mehrabian, *Silent Messages,* p. 11.

18. Gerard I. Nierenberg and Henry H. Calero, *How to Read a Person Like a Book* (New York: Pocket Books, 1973), pp. 1 ff.

19. Flora Davis, *Inside Intuition: What We Know About Nonverbal Communication* (New York: McGraw-Hill, 1973), p. 16.

20. Nierenberg and Calero, *How to Read a Person,* p. 1.

21. Fast, *Body Language,* pp. 132–134.

22. Davis, *Inside Intuition,* pp. 128–142.

23. Mehrabian, *Silent Messages,* p. 3.

24. Davis, *Inside Intuition,* p. 80.

25. Tubbs and Moss, *Human Communication,* pp. 151–152.

26. Nierenberg and Calero, *How to Read a Person,* pp. 1 ff.

27. John T. Molloy, *Live For Success* (New York: Morrow, 1981), p. 39.

28. John T. Molloy, *Dress For Success* (New York: Warner Books, 1976), p. 12.

29. Ellen Berscheid, in Jane E. Brody, "Surprising Effects of Attractiveness," *New York Times,* September 1, 1981, p. C1.

30. Molloy, *Live for Success,* p. 132.

31. Mehrabian, *Silent Messages,* pp. 7–8.

32. Davis, *Inside Intuition,* p. 210.

33. Tubbs and Moss, *Human Communication,* pp. 155–161.

34. Dorwin Cartwright, "Some Principles of Mass Persuasion," *Human Relations* (London: Plenum, 1949), pp. 253–263.

35. Marvin Karlins and Herbert I. Ableson, *Persuasion,* 2nd ed. (New York: Springer, 1970), pp. 1 ff.

36. Propaganda techniques are from Alfred McClung Lee and Elizabeth Briant Lee, *The Fine Art of Propaganda* (New York: Harcourt, Brace, 1939), as treated in Steuart Henderson Britt, *Consumer Behavior and the Behavioral Sciences* (New York: Wiley, 1966), pp. 454–455.

Understanding the Buyer

Before selling strategy can be properly devised, sellers must know *how* to identify and classify prospects, *why* prospects might want to buy a product, *how* prospects make their decisions, and *who* and *what* influence them. Thus it is important to know how to measure a market and how to identify personality differences among prospective buyers. *Why* a prospect wants to buy a product is the cornerstone of strategy. If a salesperson wants to use a customized appeal during a sales call, some premise (estimate) of buyer motivation must be made. Sales experts stress the idea of focusing an interview on *one* dominant buying motive. This requires being able to identify dominant buying motives first. Identification is made easier by learning to recognize the motives that usually prompt people to purchase. The quality of persuasive appeals and strategic timing depend on *how* buyers make their decisions. In order to make the best possible estimate of how prospects think, a sales rep must understand buyer decision theory. Accordingly, this chapter is offered to give you a better understanding of the basic areas essential to selling strategy. They are:

- Buyer identification
- Buyer motivation
- Buyer decision theories and models

BUYER IDENTIFICATION

Who is the Prospect?

A key task facing every sales representative is determining who is the prospect for a product or service. For many goods, the answer is relatively simple. Few men buy pantyhose; few women smoke cigars. Identifying the proper prospect for home purchases, major appliances, or vacations among consumers, or for a new company headquarters, manufacturing capital goods, or pension plans for industrial buyers is complex. Obviously, for many goods there is not a single prospect, but a group of prospects acting as a decision unit. Figure 6.1 describes the different decision-making units.

Buying decisions vary enormously. Every sales representative must meet the challenge of carefully assessing the roles played and the influence wielded by each of the several participants involved in a particular buying decision. When several persons influence a purchase decision, it would be naive not consider the influence that each party to a purchase wields.

Market Identification

The sales representative identifies markets in terms of certain buyer characteristics. Prospects may be described in terms of income, geographic location, education, occupation, age, sex, race, and many other easily determined attributes. U.S. censuses give this kind of socioeconomic information about most localities. A salesperson's company should also be able to furnish profiles (identifying characteristics) of the kinds of customers who have traditionally bought the products it sells. Sometimes, however, distinguishing characteristics are not easily measurable or noticeable. In these cases behavioral characteristics such as club memberships, hobbies, interests, life-styles, and philosophies that distinguish prospects from nonprospects must be searched out. For industrial products, characteristics of the *firms* that might use a product are the keys to more profitable prospecting.

Buyers Are Different

Although the best prospects for a product will have much in common in terms of age, income, education, and other measurable characteristics, there will be many different personality types among customers. The strategies that might work for an extroverted prospect may be completely wrong for an introvert. Even more challenging is the prospect who seems to change moods

Figure 6.1 Who Participates in the Buying Decision?

Consumer Decision-Making Units

Initiator. The initiator is the person who first suggests or thinks of the idea of buying the particular product.

Influencer. An influencer is a person who explicitly or implicitly carries some influence on the decision.

Decider. The decider is a person who ultimately determines any part or the whole of the buying decision: whether to buy, what to buy, how to buy, when to buy, or where to buy.

Buyer. The buyer is the person who makes the actual purchase.

User. The user is the person(s) who consumes or uses the product or service.

Producer Decision-Making Units

Influencers. Influencers are those members of the organization who directly or indirectly influence the buying decision. They often help define specifications and also provide information for evaluating alternatives. Technical personnel are particularly important as influencers.

Deciders. Deciders are organizational members who have either formal or informal power to select the final suppliers. In the routine buying of standard items, the buyers are often the deciders. In more complex buying, the officers of the company are often the deciders.

Buyers. Buyers are organizational members with formal authority for selecting the supplier and arranging the terms of purchase. Buyers may help shape specifications, but they play their major role in selecting vendors and negotiating with the purchase constraints. In more complex purchases, high-level officers of the company might participate in negotiations.

Users. Users are members of the organization who will use the product or service. In many cases, the users initiate the buying project and play an important role in defining the purchase specifications.

Gatekeepers. Gatekeepers are members of the organization who control the flow of information to others. For example, purchasing agents often have authority to prevent salespersons from seeing users or deciders. Other gatekeepers include technical personnel and even switchboard operators. The main impact of gatekeepers comes from their ability to control the inflow of information on buying alternatives.

Source: Philip Kotler, *Marketing Management: Analysis, Planning, and Control,* 4th ed. (Englewood Cliffs, N.J.: Prentice-Hall, 1980), pp. 134, 174–175.

from visit to visit. Some personality differences typically encountered among prospects are discussed below.

The many notions presented in this chapter for identifying and classifying prospects are under the constant scrutiny of the behavioral scientists who developed them. Each represents a falsifiable hypothesis about how and why prospective customers behave as they do. Each has been subjected to testing by scientific method. "The scientific method has been well defined as the method of tested, and therefore testable, hypotheses; and testable in this context means falsifiable by comparison with empirical evidence. The method never has proved any statement about the objective world to be true. It has proved that some very important statements are false" (1). The extent to which any salesperson finds any of these notions appropriate or useful depends on the salesperson, the product, and the market served.

Introverts and Extroverts

Introverts are usually rather quiet, studious people who may be suspicious of salespersons. Usually, they are very analytical and want complete information about an offering, but if they think a representative is wasting their time, they may terminate the interview without notice. They often prefer rational appeals over emotional appeals and are not heavily influenced by the salesperson's personality. They listen well, but it is difficult to elicit feedback from them. They are sensitive buyers and easily take offense at statements that conflict with their basic attitudes and beliefs. It is hard to establish two-way communication with introverts, since they pride themselves on their independence of thought and their individuality (2). Most introverts are formal and like to talk to a salesperson at a comfortable distance. The imaginary personal space bubble of an introvert must not be violated. Personal "territories" must be respected (see Chapter 5). They prefer not to be "sold" but to feel they have made up their own minds about purchasing a product. Introverts prefer a formal, businesslike interview.

Extroverts, on the other hand, like to talk, care little for formality, and react to a sales representative's personality when considering a buying proposal. They are people-oriented and will avoid causing unpleasantness or hurting a salesperson's feelings. Like the introvert, they like to be listened to when talking, but they may get off the subject of the business at hand (3). Extroverts are more socially minded and less analytical than introverts. They tend to be interested in testimonials and appeals that emphasize that others are buying a product. They like to laugh and joke. With extroverted prospects, a sales representative may move in closer and be more animated in nonverbal communication. Susceptible to emotional appeals, extroverts tend to be impulsive deciders. Most people are combinations of the two types, but a rep must decide in *which ways* each prospect is introverted or extroverted.

Other Prospect Profiles

Joseph W. Thompson classifies prospects into ten different types and suggests a strategy for handling each type (see Figure 6.2). Knowing how to vary selling strategy to fit the prospect is one of the basic differences between the experienced salesperson and the rookie. Experience can be gained more rapidly if a salesperson considers types and matches strategy to the type perceived.

Transactional Analysis

Transactional analysis is one of the newer and more sophisticated guides that can be used for typing prospects and devising selling strategy. Its basic concept is simple enough to understand and to use as a model for improving communications. An *ego state* is a condition of mind, a consistent mental reference state, that influences the behavior of both prospect and salesperson. An ego state is a set or system of feelings that prompts certain consistent patterns of behavior (4). Each person has three ego states that determine that person's mental attitudes, communications, and actions. They are the *parent*, the *child*, and the *adult*. One ego state is dominant at any particular time and influences a person's words and actions. Prospects may change from one ego state to another during the course of an interview. Since each person is a combination of the three ego states, six ego states are represented when two people communicate. Many combinations can take place (5). Transactional analysis (TA) is a conscious attempt to identify the ego state of another person in order to formulate a suitable strategy for more effective communication. Voice tones, gestures, vocabulary, speech rates, and facial expressions all can give clues to the ego state prompting them.

The Parent Ego State. When people are acting in the parent ego state, they behave the way their parents seemed to act toward them when they were children. Behavior in the parent ego state is judgmental, authoritative, dominant, arbitrary, and demonstrates a superior attitude. Frequently, someone in the parent ego state communicates closed-mindedness, criticality, and outmodedness in views and thoughts. Accusing voice tones and dominant types of body language (the pointing finger) are typical parent ego state behaviors. A prospect who won't listen, attempts to dominate a sales interview, and is highly critical is probably acting from the parent ego state. High-pressure, unyielding salespersons are also acting from this state. The parent ego state reflects the idea that the *parent* is right, and the person to whom the parent talks is the *child*, who must "shape up" and yield to superior authority.

Figure 6.2 Prospect Classes and Strategy

Classification:	General Strategy:
1. The silent prospect	1. To get a response, ask questions and be more personal than usual.
2. The procrastinator	2. Summarize benefits he will lose if he doesn't act. Be positive, self-assured and dramatic but not overpowering. Suggest that he has the power and ability to make decisions. Use showmanship to overcome indecision.
3. The "glad hander," talkative or over-enthusiastic type	3. Salesman must lead prospect back into the sale. This person sells you, but doesn't seem to buy. Say, "By the way, that reminds me, etc." Keep on the track—be brief.
4. Slow or methodical type	4. He appears to weigh every word, so slow down and amplify on details. Adjust your tempo to his.
5. Pugilistic, chip-on-shoulder or argumentative type	5. Usually insincere and tries salesman's patience. He is a difficult type to deal with but sincerity and respect on the salesman's part create respect.
6. Over-cautious or timid type	6. Take it slow and easy. Reassure on every point. Use logic, but make it simple.
7. Ego-involved or opinionated type	7. Give him rope by flattering his ego and catering to his whims. Listen attentively. Take the cash and let the credit go.
8. Skeptical or suspicious type	8. Acknowledge his background, stay with facts, be conservative in statements.
9. The grouch	9. Ask questions to ascertain real problems. Listen and let him tell his story.
10. Impulsive, changeable, fast type	10. Be rapid, speed up, concentrate only on important points, omit details when possible.

Source: Joseph W. Thompson, "A Strategy of Selling," in Steven J. Shaw and Joseph W. Thompson (eds.) *Salesmanship* (New York: Holt, Rinehart and Winston, 1966), pp. 13–25.

Personal Preparation

The Child Ego State. The child ego state is not related to age. It is reflected in defensive and in emotional reactions. Every person has a *child* somewhere within who responds and acts out behavior patterns learned in the preschool years. Eric Berne, leading advocate of transactional analysis, believed, as do many, that the child ego state is the most valuable one (6). A person in the child ego state is both creative and innovative. Because children are more submissive and humble (at times children can also be rebellious), they are more adjusting and better liked. A person may, however, communicate and act out of childlike emotions and fantasies (7). A child feels disappointments, joy, love, and triumphs more keenly than does an adult. People avoiding problems and attempting to escape reality are usually acting in the child ego state. They are receptive, apologetic, and malleable. Persuasive service representatives often are dominated by their child ego states and project a friendly, helpful attitude that allows their prospects to enjoy the dominant role.

The Adult Ego State. Persons acting out of the adult ego state are realistic and rational. Problems are faced squarely. People function much like computers using mathematics and probability in decision making. All alternatives are considered in an orderly, unemotional manner. Emphasis is on the present. Approaches to situations are scientific and thorough. Indicative of this ego state are nods, open-minded listening, and a willingness to exchange information without emotional involvement. A fair, businesslike attitude indicates the adult ego state. The highly professional innovative sales representative acts out of this reference. The sales representative is friendly but realistic and "fact-minded." Customers accept this kind of salesperson as a great source of help (see Figure 6.3).

Life Positions. A person in the dominant parent ego state transacts from an "I'm O.K.—you're not O.K." life position. One in the child ego state assumes a yielding nature and transacts from a "You're O.K.—I'm not O.K." position. The adult ego state transacts from an "I'm O.K.—you're O.K." position. This last combination of life positions is the most desirable for effective communication (8). A feeling of not being O.K. retards an individual's development because this feeling does not enhance a person's self-image when dealing with others. The "I'm O.K.—you're not O.K." position is both futile and dangerous. People with such a perspective on the worth of others are liable to ride roughshod over them in ways that can become criminal. When superiors convey a "You're not O.K." attitude to subordinates, resentment and possibly a poor self-concept result. Such a negative self-concept is unproductive in selling. Salespersons who must put up with this attitude from prospects feel its psychological pressures. Prospects who sense a "You're not O.K." judgment by sales reps do not buy from them and often will refuse to see them when they call. A sales rep must convey through dress and body language an "O.K.-ness" to forestall negative prospect reactions.

Figure 6.3 Transactional Analysis, Ego States, and Situations

When people are acting out of this ego state, they talk and behave in reference to their concept of parental behavior, formed when they were children. Persons acting out of this state tend to be authoritative, dominant, judgmental, arbitrary, protective, critical, rule abiding, outmoded in thinking, and superior in attitude.

Persons acting out of the adult ego state tend to be realistic, scientific, unemotional, rational, fact-minded, and they emphasize the present. Such people are likely to have fair, businesslike attitudes and a willingness to exchange information without emotional involvement.

When persons act out of this ego state they imitate patterns of behavior learned in preschool years. The *"child"* is creative, imaginative, submissive, humble, emotional, sometimes unrealistic, and sometimes rebellious.

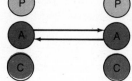

In this exchange, a critical, authoritative supervisor or prospect may converse with a submissive and humble employee or salesperson. The *child* may resent the superiority exhibited by the *superior*. The *child* will probably reserve hostility and withhold information from such a supervisor or prospect that would indicate his or her true feelings. Such conversations rarely uncover the real facts.

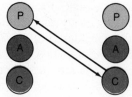

In this exchange, two rational persons are talking productively, unemotionally, and realistically. They are likely to transmit accurate information and get to the root of a problem. This is a desirable transaction from both sides.

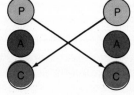

This exchange is likely to wind up in heated words or a fight. Both authoritative ego states are clashing and neither is submissive or yielding. Such cross communications can be highly unproductive.

Sources: Based on information from Dudley Bennett, "Transactional Analysis in Management," *Personnel,* 52, no. 1 (January/February 1975), 34–36; and Heinz Weihrich, "MBO Appraisal with Transactional Analysis," *Personnel Journal,* 55, no. 4 (April 1976), 173–175.

Strokes.   Just as infants need stroking by physical means, so adults need stroking through signals of support and acceptance. If a person does not get positive recognition, negative attention through reprimand or correction may be sought to replace it. Negative strokes are better than no strokes at all. Strokes are an important part of interpersonal communication: People seek strokes from others. Sales representatives must communicate positive strokes to prospects to satisfy this need. Positive strokes can be based on prospect performance in, say, accepting a proposal, demanding greater information, or placing an order. Sales reps have many opportunities to deliver positive strokes to prospects in the ways they encourage prospects to outline their needs and in the manner in which prospect objections are handled.

Games.   Instead of waiting for strokes that produce good, positive feelings from others, some people seek to create positive stroking situations through games. Since prospects, like everyone else, often play such games, those who sell must be aware of common patterns of proper reaction. Proper reactions allow salespersons to avoid losing situations. Prospects acting from an "I'm O.K.—you're not O.K." (parent) position sometimes play "Now, I've got you" in an attempt to get positive strokes by putting down a seller. This game is best played with subordinates seeking negative strokes in the child ego state of "Kick me." Either participant in such a transaction can initiate the game. Both can get strokes from playing it. Neither role is very productive for sellers or buyers. Another parent ego state game is "Blemish," looking for and emphasizing faults in others. Still another is "Critique," enjoying the power to review and evaluate another's performance. Sometimes, "You're not good enough" is played by prospects through maneuvers shaped to let a rep know that the prospect can only feel better by putting someone else down. Negative strokes desired by any salesperson can be found with ease. Selling is a tough business psychologically and physically. "Look how hard I tried" and "Why does this always happen to me?" are games sales reps sometimes play. But not for long. Field sales representation demands cultivation and assumption of the adult role in both salespeople and prospects. To attempt the parent role with a dominating prospect can only result in "Uproar." Adult-adult transactions avoid games. Sometimes game playing is the only way a prospect can be sold. When that is the case, it is hard to fault a rep who is willing to assume a role desired by a prospect and to become a "Rescuer."

Viewed in 1972 as just one more trendy fad, transactional analysis has stood the test of time (9). It has proven flexible enough to be used in conjunction with skills and techniques from many other areas of the behavioral sciences. Its promise is that it builds and sustains a relationship between a prospect and a sales rep for the long run rather than emphasizing the short-run objective of making a sale.

BUYER MOTIVATION

To direct persuasive appeals, some premise, scientific or intuitive, must be used to identify buyer motivation. Familiarization with ideas of how motivation works should result in more realistic assessment of dominant prospect-activating forces. A motive is an inner tension that causes a prospect to act. If there is no problem (or disequilibrium), there is no motive. Often, a prospect is unaware of a problem or need. Salespersons should be able to translate unrecognized needs into an action-producing want. First, a sales representative must estimate potential buying motives and identify the most dominant one. Motives are based on needs. Salespersons must question, observe, and recognize what needs prospects are likely to have, based on their circumstances. Salespeople must form an initial premise and then try to get prospects to reveal their specific motives. Often, the situation is complicated because prospects may have several motives. Buyers are sometimes hesitant to reveal real motives. This is particularly true if revelation will affect how they feel others will see them. Sometimes buyers are unaware of their drives. If salespersons are unable to uncover much about a buyer's motives or about the selling situation, they must rely on past experience and standard appeals. The usual motives for wanting to buy must be assumed. Such salespersons are at a disadvantage in meeting customer needs and satisfying wants. Sales representatives can learn to assess motivation better by learning more about:

- The kinds of motives
- Maslow's dynamic theory
- Sociological influences

The Kinds of Motives

Freud was a pioneer in motivational theory. To Freud, the *id* is the originator of strong drives and urges. Sex or the wish to return to the security of the prenatal state are the underlying drives. Advertising strategists and occasionally salespersons are accused of overstressing the sex motive. Freud's explanation proved to be too simple, and later writers recognized the urge for power and the need to be accepted by others as being just as important. Today, scores of motives are recognized and classified. Classifications that are particularly useful for sellers are: emotional, rational, and patronage motives. Some motives may fit into more than one classification, and in such cases the motive is included where it is most likely to occur.

Emotional Buying Motives. Buyers prefer to appear rational and scientific in their decisions. People hesitate to admit that they bought an expensive car to be envied. Nevertheless, most buyers are persuaded through direct or indirect appeals to their emotions. A manager may buy a computer out of a desire to point with *pride* to the fact that the company now has a data-processing system. Love, hate, fear, the urge to be esteemed, the need for power, the need to accepted and liked, the desire for achievement, the need for recreation and pleasure, and the need for bodily comfort create strong tensions and disequilibriums that ultimately move consumers and business prospects to action. Most people are not highly rational computers when it comes to buying decisions. Most people recognize this but still feel they must *justify* purchases to themselves or to others on rational grounds.

Rational Buying Motives. Rational or economic buying motives include such reasons as resale potential, dependability, flexibility, durability, efficiency, reciprocity (you buy from me; I'll buy from you; we'll both profit), cost savings or earning potentials, economy in use, or uniformity of finished product. A main motive for industrial buyers may be to advance in the firm. Many industrial buyers who can fully justify a purchase for the firm's benefit will not buy unless a purchase is beneficial to themselves or without career risk. A manager of an office for a chain of theaters may not buy a bookkeeping machine because of fears that it will replace some of his or her employees. With fewer people to supervise, "office manager" would be a title with less prestige. While economic buying motives are widely accepted as the force behind purchases of industrial goods, there are usually emotional motives somewhere behind the economic ones. For example, a retailer may want to make more money in order to take a trip to California. Emotional motives are more direct and usually stronger than economic motives.

Patronage Motives. A special set of motives explains why people buy from one source instead of from its competitor. People like *variety and selection* and patronize stores and salespersons affording more ample choice. *Price* is one of the strongest of patronage motives. If prospects are convinced that a price is lower for the same quality, they will usually buy. A reputation for *quality* helps reduce a buyer's risks. *Service* given with a product is another patronage motive. With some products such as computers, software (service) is as important as the hardware (the machinery). *Location and convenience* are also important. People do not like to be inconvenienced. Many would rather pay $10 more per night to stay in a motel on the beach than walk across the street to a motel 300 feet from the water. *Personality of a salesperson* is stressed throughout this book as a very important reason for buying from a particular firm. A firm's *reputation* is another strong patronage motive. What other people think about a firm matters a great deal in their selection of a buying source.

Maslow's Dynamic Theory

A. H. Maslow's *Dynamic Theory* not only classifies motives (see Figure 6.4) but also explains their interactions. Maslow recognizes five motive levels. He writes that satisfying needs at one level frees a person to recognize other needs. In other words, a person is released from a lower level of need to satisfy a higher level of need (10). Maslow's basic level of need comprises the *physiological needs* or body needs (for food, water, and so on). These needs cease to exist as active determinants of behavior once they have been satisfied. After the basic level of need has been satisfied, *safety and security needs* emerge. When a person's security is threatened, tensions develop and threats to security become motivators. Compared with people who lived in earlier times or people who live in less civilized cultures, most American safety needs are met through law. There is little daily threat to citizens in this country. Safety needs do become important, however, in times of emergency.

Maslow stated that there were five levels of need from basic needs to more social needs. Self-actualization needs may be hard to define and are never really satisfied. When a person satisfies lower-level needs, he or she is released to recognize higher-level needs.

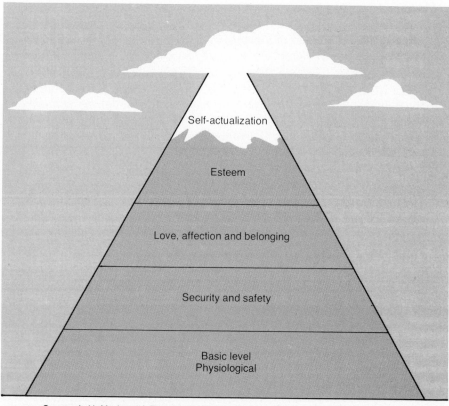

Source: A. H. Maslow, "A Theory of Human Motivation," *Psychological Review*, 50(1943), 370–396.

Figure 6.4 Maslow's Motivational Theory

When *physiological* and *safety* needs are met, *love, affection, and belonging needs* emerge. The satisfaction-release-motivation cycle repeats itself. People feel the absence of sweethearts, spouses, children, or friends. This level of need in our society is strong and is often at the root of severe psychological maladjustments and pathologies. The love need is both a giving and receiving need. All people have a need for a good self-image and want to feel strong, adequate, and confident. The *esteem need* is a desire for prestige and reputation. Satisfying this need leads to feelings of self-confidence, worthiness, and a stable, high-level self-image. Not being able to satisfy this need leads to inferiority complexes and damages self-image. Many things people buy are related to needs for esteem—new and expensive cars, showy houses, and fashions. With the other levels satisfied, the esteem need level can lead to strong buying motivations.

If all of the other need levels are satisfied, the need for *self-actualization* will surface. This is the need to reach one's full potential—physically, mentally, or spiritually. Alexander the Great is reported to have cried when he had no more worlds to conquer. When people extend their horizons, they always find new potentials for personal development. Television advertisements for food are more often aimed at self-fulfillment of women as creative homemakers than at basic hunger. Magazine advertising frequently appeals to self-actualization needs.

The five motivation levels do not appear in the same order for all people. Most religions urge, in fact, that believers reverse the natural order and put spiritual self-actualization first. Sales representatives should recognize that in our wealthy society, they must appeal to the three higher levels of need in most cases. In less developed societies, safety and physiological needs might gain more response, but in America the more social needs (love, esteem, self-actualization) will probably continue to receive major emphasis.

Sociological Influences

Many motives stem from a person's relationships with groups. People are gregarious beings. Their needs to belong and to be esteemed can be met only through membership in groups. Cultural membership is the most fundamental influence on buyer motivations. From cultural membership, a buyer learns a basic set of values, attitudes, beliefs, and techniques for dealing with the environment. To a considerable extent, these influences determine an individual's wants and shape the ways that wants will be satisfied.

Within each culture, a variety of subcultures exist. Formerly, much use was made in American schools and by American political, business, and religious leaders of a cultural concept called "the American Way of Life." Today, Americans are wiser. The Civil Rights, Youth, and Women's Movements have forced the recognition that there are many "American Ways of Life." These movements are evidence of variations within the basic American value structure; other evidence of such variations are the differences among religious groups, people from different regions, ethnic backgrounds, and races. Each group subscribes, in the main, to dominant values, but each possesses distinctive taboos and preferences. These differences result in life-styles that are roughly similar yet culturally distinct. These distinctions lead group members to have different wants and needs and to seek satisfaction in distinctive ways. Members of groups tend to look at the groups they belong to in relation to those they do not belong to. It is from this tendency to place a membership group as either subordinate or superordinate to others that leads to social stratification.

Social stratification can take many forms. One is the caste system. In a caste system, the social position of members of a caste is fixed at birth. It cannot be changed up or down. Should a member of a higher caste marry a peson of a lower caste, both take on the rank of the lower caste. Another form of social stratification is the estate system. In estate systems, social position was originally determined by land tenure or the holding of an estate. Hence the name. Under the estate system, social position at birth did not foreclose opportunity for advancement. Seizing and holding land, receiving landholdings through merit in battle, or marrying up the social hierarchy were all possible. Vestiges of the European estate system still exist. In England, major royal ceremonies have elaborate protocols regulating the dress and participation of those attending by rank. A more familiar reminder of estate systems can be found in civilian and military uniforms. Still another, comparatively close to the original, is to be found in participant dress and roles played at most college and university graduation ceremonies.

Social class systems differ from caste and estate systems in being more open—people can move up or down—and in being more informal. All are equal under law in a class system. Simply put, a social class is made up of people who tend to share similar values and to be similar in behavior. Members of a given social class have jobs that strike most of a society's members as of about equal worth, which means that incomes are similar. Educational backgrounds do not vary much among members of a social class. Since to a considerable extent, educational opportunity in the United States is a function of the incomes of previous generations, disparities of wealth among members of a particular social class are rare. Figure 6.5 shows both the traditional view of American social classes and more recent views. Although the value of social class as a tool in understanding differences in buyer behavior was called into question early in the 1970s, recent studies have tended to reestablish it as a useful tool (11).

The importance of social class to salespersons is that social classes act as reference groups for their members. People are influenced by their reference groups in several ways. First, reference groups expose people to new behaviors. Second, reference groups shape people's behavior because of the peo-

Figure 6.5 Characteristics of Six Major American Social Classes

1. *Upper uppers* (less than 1 percent). Upper uppers are the social elite who live on inherited wealth and have a well-known family background. They give large sums to charity, run the debutante balls, maintain more than one home, and send their children to the finest schools. They are a market for expensive jewelry, antiques, homes, and vacations. While small as a group, they serve as a reference group for others to the extent that their consumption decisions trickle down and are imitated by the other social classes.

2. *Lower uppers* (about 2 percent). Lower uppers are persons who have earned high income or wealth through exceptional ability in the professions or business. They usually come from the middle class. They tend to be active in social and civic affairs and seek to buy the symbols of status for themselves and their children, such as expensive homes, schools, yachts, swimming pools, and automobiles. They include the *nouveaux riches*, whose pattern of conspicuous consumption is designed to impress those below them. The ambition of lower uppers is to be accepted in the upper-upper stratum, which is more likely to be achieved by their children than themselves.

3. *Upper middles* (12 percent). Upper middles are concerned with "career." They have attained positions as lawyers, physicians, scientists, and college professors. They believe in education and want their children to develop professional or administrative skills so that they do not drop into a lower stratum. This class likes to deal in ideas and "high culture." They are the quality market for good homes, clothes, furniture, and appliances. They seek to run a gracious home, entertaining friends and clients.

4. *Lower middles* (30 percent). Lower middles are concerned with "respectability." They exhibit conscientious work habits and adhere to culturally defined norms and standards, including going to church and obeying the law. The home is important, and lower middles like to keep it neat and "pretty." They buy conventional home furnishings and do a lot of their own work around the home. The lower-middle-class wife spends a lot of time shopping for the family looking for buys. Although "white collars" make up a large part of this group, so do "gray collars" (mailmen, fire fighters) and "aristocrat blue collars" (plumbers, factory foremen).

5. *Upper lowers* (35 percent). Upper lowers lead a day-to-day existence of unchanging activities. They live in small houses and apartments in dull areas of the city. The men work at manual jobs and have only a moderate education. The working-class wife spends most of her time in the house cooking, cleaning, and caring for her children. She sees being the mother of her children as her main vocation, and she has little time for organizations and social activity.

6. *Lower lowers* (20 percent). Lower lowers are at the bottom of society and considered by the other classes as slum dwellers or "riffraff." Some lower lowers try to rise above their class but often fall back and ultimately stop trying. They tend to be poorly educated. They often reject middle-class standards of morality and behavior. They buy more impulsively. They often do not evaluate quality, and they pay too much for products and buy on credit. They are a large market for food, television sets, and used automobiles.

Source: James F. Engel, Roger D. Blackwell, and David T. Kollat, *Consumer Behavior,* 3rd ed. (New York: The Dryden Press, 1978).

ple's desire to "fit in" with the group. A shriner, for example, might be motivated to buy a motorcycle or an antique car to fit in better with his group. The desire to be recognized as numbering among a community's business leaders can motivate a business owner to purchase safety equipment or to provide a new fringe benefit—say, dental insurance. The need to belong, to be accepted, and to be esteemed by one's reference groups—groups to which one belongs or aspires to belong—explains many purchase decisions. Awareness of human needs for belonging and self-esteem, approval and recognition, can help a sales representative not only to sell more but to aid prospects in buying the things that meet these needs.

DECISION THEORIES AND MODELS

Knowing *why* prospects buy is not enough. An understanding of theories about *how* people buy is needed. Learning theory and self-image matching through purchases must be examined to explain the influences, timing, and processes of prospect decision making.

Howard's Learning Model

John Howard sees customers as *learning* to buy products. As Figure 6.6 shows, prospect decision making is divided into three stages: extensive problem solving, limited problem solving, and automatic response behavior. *Extensive problem solving* is the most important stage, because buyers recognize problems at this stage and search for solutions. Personality traits, prices, time pressures, financial status, social and organizational setting, social class, and cultural membership influence prospects' searching behavior. Internal, or personality, variables influence actions of buyers. Internal variables might be attitudes (predispositions) or motivations. How a product is seen and understood is influenced by differences in individual prospects' attitudes and motives (12). A salesperson's job is to furnish information and assurances that influence prospects' perceptions of an offer. External variables, such as time pressure and reference-group influences, should be identified and taken into account in selling strategy. It is during the stage of *extensive problem-solving behavior* that buyers seek information to solve problems and are most receptive to selling appeals. Salespersons may place buyers in this receptive stage by highlighting problems with present purchases.

Each time a purchase is made and a product yields satisfaction, a buyer learns that the product satisfies needs. The tendency to buy that product again is reinforced. After a few purchases, less search and mental activity will be deemed necessary. The buyer will have entered the *limited problem-solving stage*. Buyers still consider purchases briefly and are still open to consid-

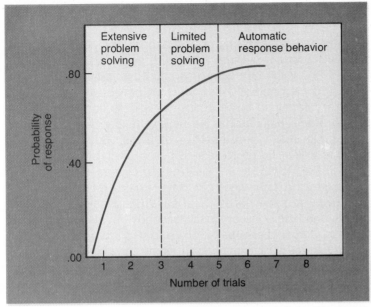

Source: John A. Howard, *Marketing Management,*
rev. ed. (Homewood, Ill.: Irwin, 1963), p. 36.

Figure 6.6   John Howard's Learning Model

eration of alternative products, but a purchasing habit has begun to take shape. When this happens, sales reps must show buyers clear and definite relative advantages to get a change in product choice. In the final stage, *automatic response behavior*, habit formation is complete. The probability of repeat purchase is very high, for buyers believe that a problem has been solved. It takes strong sales appeals to make loyal customers switch. During this stage, buyers do not consider alternatives unless forced to do so.

Howard's learning model explains why new products without a definite relative advantage over existing products have such a difficult time in the market. It also explains why a salesperson who encounters a consumer in ARB (automatic response behavior) for a competitive product must use strong persuasive methods to change a buyer's mind. The model underscores the importance of establishing habitual buying behavior in prospects for both product and company. It suggests that a full-line strategy is helpful in serving all a prospect's needs. It shows the need for customer cultivation. It indicates the need for a more informative risk-reducing strategy if prospects are "open" in the *extensive problem-solving stage*. A harder-impact strategy, perhaps with more emotional appeal, will be necessary to help buyers change from a competitive product when in the *automatic response behavior stage*. New products without strong or relative advantage are likely to fail because purchasing habits are so ingrained.

Kotler's Explanations and Models

Philip Kotler reviews five explanations of why people buy: *Marshall's Economic Model, Pavlov's Learning Model, Freud's Theory, Veblen's Concept* and *Hobbes' Model* (13). Each offers insights into buyer decision behavior. Famed turn-of-the-century economist Alfred Marshall saw buyers as rational, calculating individuals determined to get maximum satisfaction from money. *Marshall's Economic Model* emphasizes the buyer's tendencies to compare your products' prices with those of competitive offerings. Buyers attempt to select the offering that yields the greatest satisfaction (utility) for the money. The *Pavlovian Model*, like Howard's, emphasizes the customer as a learner. This explanation stresses the importance of strong reinforcement (satisfaction from use), strong drives, and the necessity of cues (the weaker stimuli that influence how, when, and where the prospect responds). It also stresses the tendency for buyers to "forget" because of failure to use a product for a long period of time. *Freudian theory* indicates that people buy things because of subconscious influences. Many research approaches attempt to probe deep into the subconscious and determine subconscious motives, to obtain direction for selling appeals. However, it is unwise for salespeople without adequate psychological training to attempt to determine unconscious motives.

Thorstein Veblen wrote that most consumption is motivated by prestige seeking. Buyers decide to consume conspicuously with reference to their social classes, reference groups, and family pressures. Thomas Hobbes postulated that buyers are guided by group and individual goals. For example, industrial purchasing agents consider both what a purchase means for their company and how it affects their personal goals.

Kotler offers a model (Figure 6.7) of buyer decision-making processes. The model is oversimplified, since it does not explain what goes on inside the buyer's psyche. But sales representatives can take their pick from the theories about motivation discussed earlier. The model organizes and shows as a process the working together of influences, information channels, mental digestion, and buying responses. The model also gives sales representatives some ideas about the sequence and various factors involved in buying decisions. Prospect decision making is complex. It involves many influences that must be considered when devising effective selling strategies.

Alderson's Assortment Theory

Wroe Alderson, marketing's most prominent theorist, saw buyers as engaged in a process he called assorting. As *assortment* is a system of goods used for a particular purpose. For example, to play golf, a person needs a golf course, golf clubs, and golf balls. An assortment without the golf balls would be useless. It could not be labeled as *closed*. Closure results from acquiring

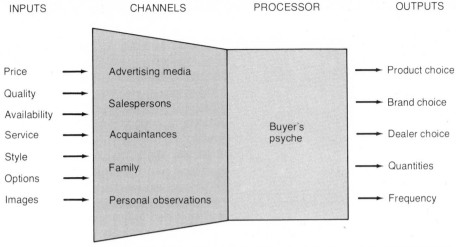

INPUTS	CHANNELS	PROCESSOR	OUTPUTS

Price → Advertising media

Quality →

Availability → Salespersons

Service → Acquaintances | Buyer's psyche

Style →

Options → Family

Images → Personal observations

→ Product choice

→ Brand choice

→ Dealer choice

→ Quantities

→ Frequency

Source: Philip Kotler, "Behavioral Models for Analyzing Buyers," *Journal of Marketing*, vol. 29, no. 4 (October 1965), pp. 37–45.

Figure 6.7 Kotler's Model of Buyer Decision Making

the needed golf balls. The assortment would then have *potency*, or the power to satisfy (14). Alderson explained that buyers are seeking closure and potency of assortments. Complete systems of goods are accumulated to accomplish a task or satisfy a need. An *out* condition—being out of a good—opens up an assortment and provides motives for buying. A sense of incompleteness may develop when a new good comes into the market and buyers recognize that without the new good, their assortments are incomplete. According to the assortment notion, a salesperson should make buyers aware of the incompleteness of assortments and offer products to complete, or close, an assortment. "You have everything you need for an efficient and confidential office, Mr. Bennington, *except* an Acme paper shredder." The drive to close a product group can be a dominant buying motive.

Self-Perception and Image

There are four components to self-image. The *real self* is what people are. The *reference-group self* is how people think others see them. The *ideal self* is how people would like to be viewed by others. The *apparent self* is how others actually view them (15)—see Figure 6.8. People constantly try to reach the ideal self. Appeals directed toward achievement of the ideal self always command interest. Who and what people are, are projected by the clothes they wear, the automobiles they drive, the houses they live in and the ways they are decorated, the ornaments and implements they use. Nearly every

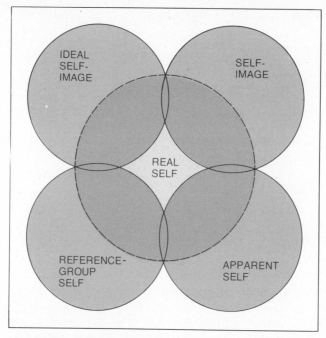

Figure 6.8 **Buyer Images**

Source: C. Glen Walters, *Consumer Behavior: Theory and Practice,* rev. ed. (Homewood, Ill.: Irwin, 1974), p. 87.

purchase that is visible affects perceptions of personal status. Through careful buying, a prospect tries to bring the real self closer to the ideal self. Under this concept, a prospect buys to project an image. People who see themselves as "the life of the party" or as "VIP on campus" buy a red sports car to buttress their extrovert image. People who see themselves as sophisticates would never shop at a bargain clothing store. They buy stylish goods even if they are unable to afford them. Couples who want to establish themselves in an upper-middle-class neighborhood buy a station wagon instead of the pickup truck they really need.

Suits or cars or houses incompatible with prospects' self-images go unbought. The risk of losing image can be a strong and real objection. What many prospects do is generalize about products—to them each one has a definite image (as do firms). Buyers examine a product's image and compare it to the ideal self-image they seek to achieve. If a product reflects qualities a prospect desires to project, strong purchase drives may result. Through suggestion, a salesperson can influence the delicate mental processes of product-image formation. "That sweater really brings out your eyes," or "This car is perfect for the traveling executive." Some products have little image dimension, but most visible products, consumer and industrial, may be viewed at

Personal Preparation

least partially as extensions of personality. Salespersons project product image in the ways they handle and show their wares. They must be aware that prospects are constantly asking themselves if a product being shown "is really me."

SUMMARY

In professional selling, it is important to be aware of the socioeconomic and behavioral dimensions of target customers. Salespersons should know that customers differ widely in characteristics and temperament. Thus selling strategy must be directed toward meeting specific prospect needs. Extroverts may be outgoing and friendly, while introverts may be cold and rational. Transactional analysis concerns conversational reference states of bargainers and suggests interview strategies. Customer motivation is complex, but classifications of motives and theories based on research give important clues as to which motives to expect in particular situations. People are highly influenced by other people and refer to reference group and social class norms in deciding on products and sources of goods. John Howard has shown how customers "learn to buy." Philip Kotler's model shows the many influences involved in buying decisions. Alderson explained that people buy to complete useful *assortments* of goods, which they "close" for maximum use potential. People buy in reference to their ideal self-image and the image they would like others to have of them.

REVIEW QUESTIONS

1. What characteristics of prospects must be understood before an effective selling strategy can be devised?

2. Distinguish between extroverted and introverted prospects. What is the impact of these personality types on the salesperson?

3. List and describe the prospects types suggested by Thompson.

4. What is transactional analysis? How is TA relevant to the sales representative?

5. What are the three types of buying motives? Give examples of each type.

6. What are the basic premises of Maslow's theory? What are the five levels of motivation? Describe these levels.

7. What is meant by social class? What are the six recognized social classes? How is social class relevant to the sales representative?

8. What are Howard's three stages of prospect decision making? Briefly describe each of these stages. What is the value of this theory to the salesperson?

9. Outline the five theories of buyer behavior reviewed by Philip Kotler and described in the text. Of what value are they to the salesperson?

10. What are the components of self-image? Of what value is self-image theory to the salesperson?

APPLICATION QUESTIONS

1. List each of the emotional, rational, and patronage motives presented in this chapter. (For example, emotional buying motives include love, hate, and fear.) Suppose you did not yet own the car you are currently driving but were thinking about buying it:

   a. Which of the listed buying motives would be important to you? Which is the most important? Are your motives mostly emotional, rational, or patronage motives?

   b. Which of the product features of the car would satisfy these motives?

   c. How do you think the salesperson could best describe these product features in order to motivate you to buy the car?

2. There is probably some product you are thinking about buying or you may have a friend who is buying a product. It should be a product that is purchased from a salesperson. Even if you (or your friend) do not want to spend the money now, you could learn something by going out and talking to various salespeople about this product. While you are doing this, consider the following:

   a. Are you, or is your friend, an introvert or an extrovert? Do you act as the text indicates an introvert or an extrovert would act when purchasing a product?

   b. Did the salesperson act in a parent, child, or adult ego state? How about you or your friend?

   c. Did the salesperson do any stroking?

   d. What were your, or your friend's, buying motives? Did the salesperson determine what they were?

   e. What problem-solving state were you, or your friend, in—extensive problem solving, limited problem solving, or automatic response behavior?

   f. How did the components of self-image enter into the process?

6–1

Ted Carr, who had just completed his training program with the Alk Manufacturing Company—marketers of packaging supplies for the baking industry—was making his first out-of-town field trip. One of the accounts that Ted's district sales manager told him to be sure to call on in Beloit, Wisconsin, was the Meilee Supply Company. Meilee appeared to have a lot more potential than Ted's predecessor had realized. According to the call reports Ted inherited with the territory, his contact at Meilee was Sara Winsted. Ted decided that Sara was a good prospect for a new promotion designed to make plastic bags more adaptable to the needs of bakers who wanted their breads to have a home-baked appearance but who did not want to sacrifice productivity. The promotion included a free mandrel through which fresh-baked loaves could be quickly loaded into the plastic bags and sealed semiautomatically with a twist-tie. Ted has just been shown into Sara's office. . .

> *Ted:* Ms. Winsted? I'm Ted (Ted pauses slightly after his first name to let it sink in) Carr from the Alk Company. (*Ted extends his hand.*) I'm here to show you a new pro—
>
> *Sara:* It's about time somebody showed up from your company. The last clown that represented Alk in this territory really did a number on us. Everyone in southern Wisconsin and northern Illinois has got your line. And what we've got is a large unsalable inventory! You know why? I'll tell you why—that guy gave everybody else a better price than he gave us. If he came in here, I'd kick him right out the door.
>
> *Ted:* You say you've got a large unsold inventory?
>
> *Sara:* Boy, have we ever. (*Consulting her files*) It's too bad you guys don't stand back of your distributors. Your competition takes back unsalable stuff. Not only is the stock we've got on hand old, but it's overpriced as well. I was told there'd be price protection when I took in that big order.
>
> *Ted:* (*Uneasily*) That big order? Nothing in my records—
>
> *Sara:* So they sent you out here without telling you how you'd been treating us, huh? Or didn't you think we were important enough to check out?
>
> *Ted:* (*Increasingly uneasy*) My records do show that you're a steady customer, Ms. Winsted, but not any big order. Perhaps our new promotion could help to move some of that unsold stock. It's des—
>
> *Sara:* (*Interrupting*) Here it is. My order record for Alk. Just take a look at that sad story. A lot of garbage cluttering up my warehouse!
>
> *Ted:* (*Taking the file card from Sara*) Maybe, if we had a training session with your sales representatives, we could get them to use the new promotion to use up some of your stock. In addition, I'd be glad to schedule some calls on your key accounts and—

Sara: And turn 'em over to Rogers out in Dubuque? What kind of jerk do you think I am? I'm not letting you get next to any of my good accounts.

Ted: (*Consulting the file card to look at Winsted's inventory record while searching desperately in his mind for something to say*) I really don't know what to say, I—

Sara: Oh, I know you aren't responsible, it's the rinky-dink company you work for.

Ted: (*Brightening*) Why, Ms. Winsted, this record card shows that you're out of stock on several items. They're the very ones included in our new promotion. It looks to me like you should be placing a fairly large stocking order and are in good shape to realize the full benefits that'll come with using our new loaf loader.

Sara: What? Let me see that card. A greenhorn like you probably can't even figure out what it says. (*Sara starts reading the card and starts making surprised noises under her breath.*) Well, I'll be damned. That sure doesn't look the way I thought it did. You know you may be right about a new stocking order. You'd better check the warehouse on your way out—I'll sign a blank order, but, remember, none of your underhanded tricks—I'm wise to you guys from Alk.

Ted: Before I leave, Ms. Winsted, I want to show you our new loaf loader promotion. It's bound to be a moneymaker for you. Charley Olson in Green Bay said it increased his business by over 20 percent in one- and two-pound loaf bags. (*Placing the loaf loader on Sara's desk to begin the demonstration*) As you can see—

Sara: I got to hand it to you kid, you've got guts. The last ninny that Alk sent out here couldn't take it. What'd you say your name was? Fred? Mine's Sara (*extending her hand*).

Ted: (*Grasping Sara's extended hand*) Mine's Ted. Glad to meet you, Sara. This loaf loader promotion is really something, why. . .

QUESTIONS

1. In terms of transactional analysis, from what ego state was Sara acting? Ted?

2. What are the probable life positions of Ted and Sara?

3. Did Ted handle the situation correctly? Explain.

6–2

Greg Lynnson sells raw material steel in various shapes and qualities to manufacturers. He is calling on a new purchasing agent, Paul Mason, whose company manufactures tools of many kinds. Greg has been kept waiting for twenty minutes, although he was on time for the appointment.

> *Greg:* How do you do, Mr. Mason I'm Greg Lynnson, with Durable Steel Corporation. I'd like to review your steel needs with you.

> *Mason:* (*Does not extend his hand, nor does he return Greg's warm smile. He replies coldly . . .*) You may sit over there if you wish. This the flu season, you know. We already have a two-month supply of steel on hand, and we're likely to use the same supplier again.

> *Greg:* (*Taking the appointed seat about six feet away from Mason*) Thank you, sir. As you know, we are a leader in raw steel because of our service and our prices. We will even ship steel by air to customers in a tight situation and pay half the freight. Our prices are competitive, even though our delivery service is faster. We have warehouses within 50 miles of your plant. Our competition can't match that, can they? We feel that our tonnage is of better quality and our stock is easier to handle. It comes in more shapes and sizes than other suppliers' in this area. For how long a period do you usually order?

> *Mason:* It varies.

> *Greg:* We've found that a six-month supply is good for customers who use average amounts. May I ask how much steel you usually use during a six-month period?

> *Mason:* You may ask, but our production output is not common knowledge, and I intend to keep it that way. I'm sure your prices and service are no better than our supplier's.

> *Greg:* Yes, sir, it's true that prices are similar in this industry, but steel, especially alloy steel, may become scarce again. Many companies are buying from more than one source to assure themselves an alternate source should steel suddenly become scarce. We'd like to prove ourselves to you by being one of your suppliers.

> *Mason:* I could care less what other buyers are doing, Mr. Lynnson. I feel that we can get better discounts by dealing with one supplier. That is sound logic.

> *Greg:* Have you ever considered staggering your orders? If you order from one supplier for one order and another the next time, you would be buying in the same quantities and getting your full discount. You'd have the healthy situation of two suppliers: should either one not be able to fill your needs at any time the other probably could.

> *Mason:* Well . . . that sounds plausible. Leave your price list here, Mr. Lynnson, and I'll think it over.

Understanding the Buyer

QUESTIONS

1. Would you classify Mason as an introvert or an extrovert based on the answers he gave Greg?

2. Do you think that Greg handled the situation correctly?

3. What is the best way to handle customers who give you a cold reception?

6–3

Raymond Perry, sales manager for Welting Company, and Neil Randall, product manager, are discussing the plans for marketing Bright Star Heaters, a portable fuel-saving kerosene heater that uses less than a gallon of fuel in a 24-hour operating period and does not require a vent of any kind. Although this is a new addition to the Welting line, competitive heaters have been on the market for several years. Bright Star has almost identical features with other quality models. Neil wants a low-key marketing approach, contending that as much money as possible should go into manufacturing materials to assure quality. Ray contends that a large marketing outlay will be required to change consumers from existing fuel economy alternatives such as wood stoves and from competitors' brands. He proposes a price-cut introduction to get "pioneer" users, and a huge and bold advertising campaign to attract much attention to the new product. Neil feels that if dealers carry it, no advertising will be necessary to get consumers to try it beyond co-op advertising with them.

Analyze the two different points of view in light of Howard's Learning Theory and other motivational ideas.
Which point of view is given most support by Howard's theory?

NOTES

1. Reavis Cox, Thomas C. Fichandler, and Charles S. Goodman, *Distribution in a High-Level Economy* (Englewood Cliffs, N.J.: Prentice-Hall, 1967), p. 3.

2. Carlton A. Pederson and Milburn D. Wright, *Selling Principles and Methods*, 6th ed. (Homewood, Ill.: Irwin, 1976), pp. 84–85.

3. *Ibid*.

4. Eric Berne, *Transactional Analysis in Psychotherapy* (New York: Grove Press, 1961), pp. 17–22.

5. Dudley Bennett, "Transactional Analysis in Management," *Personnel*, Vol. 52, no. 1 (January–February 1975), pp. 34–36.

6. Eric Berne, *What Do You Say After You Say Hello?* (New York: Grove Press, 1971), pp. 12–20.

7. Bennett, "Transactional Analysis in Management."

8. Heinz Weihrich, "MBO: Appraisal with Transactional Analysis," *Personnel Journal*, vol. 55, no. 4 (April 1976), pp. 173–175.

9. Thomas C. Clary, "Transactional Analysis: An Update," *Training and Development Journal*, June 1980, p. 54.

10. A. H. Maslow, "A Theory of Human Motivation," *Psychological Review*, vol. 50 (1943), pp. 370–376.

11. Charles M. Schaninger, "Social Class Versus Income Revisited: An Empirical Investigation," *Journal of Marketing Research*, vol. 18 (May 1981), pp. 192–208.

12. John A. Howard, *Marketing Management*, rev. ed. (Homewood, Ill.: Irwin, 1963), pp. 33–113.

13. Philip Kotler, "Behavioral Models For Analyzing Buyers," *Journal of Marketing*, vol. 29, no. 4 (October 1965), pp. 37–45.

14. Wroe Alderson, *Marketing Behavior and Executive Action* (Homewood, Ill.: Irwin, 1957), pp. 195–214.

15. C. Glen Walters, *Consumer Behavior, 3rd ed.* (Homewood, Ill.: Irwin, 1978), pp. 181–188.

Selling Environments

To meet selling opportunities fully, sales representatives must understand, estimate, and be responsive to many changing environmental influences that affect sales opportunities and selling situations. Company salespeople and sales managers need to know how their companies work as systems, what can go wrong with them, and how they can be kept healthy. Your customers' firm environment influences motivations and purchasing behavior. The firm system for which you work *is* your *internal environment.* It requires personal adjustments and sets restrictions on individual sales operations.

Other environments are usually less controllable than a company environment. Normally, the *competitive-environmental* pressures that affect the chances of making sales change as time passes. Continued sales representative attention is required to keep up with competitive changes. Customers revise their attitudes toward products. Rapid changes in the American *culture* may open and close doors to selling opportunities. *Economic fluctuations,* too, greatly influence the demand for products. Awareness of how income changes, price changes, and advertising changes affect sales is part of every successful seller's sales kit. A sales representative's actions can keep a company out of *legal* trouble or ensnare it in legal tangles. In this chapter, environmental situations that influence the opportunity to sell will be examined. They are:

- The firm-system environment
- The competitive environment
- The business environment
- The sociocultural environment
- The legal environment

THE FIRM-SYSTEM ENVIRONMENT

A company is a behavior system—a group of people working together toward a common goal (1). Such a group can be thought of as a complete team unit with characteristics, tendencies, and illnesses similar to those of an individual. Just as a football or a basketball team must behave as a coordinated unit to win, so must a firm system. To make good decisions, a salesperson must understand the nature of the firm-system team.

System Characteristics

According to Wroe Alderson, every economic behavior system (whether the enterprise is a corporation, a partnership, or a not-for-profit endeavor) has four dominant characteristics (see Figure 7.1). They are:

- A power unit
- A communications structure
- A system of inputs and outputs
- A system of internal and external adjustments

A *power unit* is composed of one or more persons who form a system's brains and who direct and coordinate all operations. The board of directors, president, and managers are parts of this power unit. They plan, direct personnel, and see that plans to meet enterprise objectives are carried out. The power unit may be thought of as a team's "coaching staff." It is expected to see to the overall situation, to make sure that everyone is working together to win. The power unit sets territories, quotas, and rules of operation for each salesperson. Every undertaking also has *communications structures* through which all system members receive plans and instructions from the power unit and through which feedback on how goals are being met is transmitted back to the power unit. Whenever a group works together toward a common goal, there is a need for coordination. Coordination, in turn, is accomplished through good communication. On a good selling team, everyone knows "the signals." Each salesperson on a selling team should be set to receive and interpret signals from management as well as to transmit information from the field to supervisors.

The firm is a *system of inputs and outputs*. Just as fuel input for an engine yields the power to move as output, so personnel, money, materials, machinery, and methods become an enterprise's input. Its outputs are products, services, sales, and profits or accomplishment of other human goals. The quality and availability of inputs vitally affect results. Organizations are also characterized by a *system of internal and external adjustments*. To survive and to grow, an enterprise must adjust internally to changes in its environ-

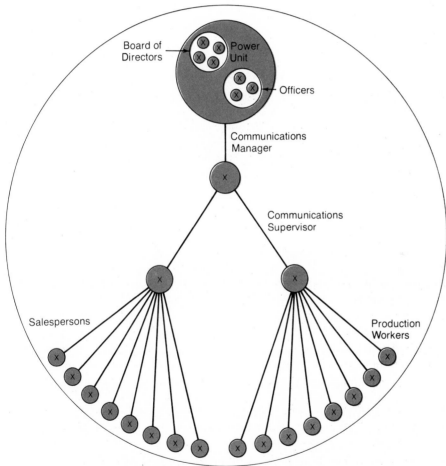

Source: Based on Wroe Alderson's behavioral system in Wroe Alderson, *Marketing Behavior and Executive Action* (Homewood, Ill.: Irwin, 1957), pp. 35–97.

Figure 7.1 Model of the Aldersonian Behavioral System

ment. If a competitor, for example, offers a product at a lower price with a strong relative advantage over your organization's product, important adjustments must be made in your market offering, or your firm will eventually lose customers. Government regulations, consumer attitudes, and business conditions change quickly. There are dozens of rapidly changing factors in selling environments to which enterprises and representatives must adjust. The ability to adjust, or "plasticity," as Alderson calls it, is essential to a healthy system. When a system (or salesperson) becomes unyielding, inflexible, or unresponsive, adjustment to changing situations cannot take place. Just as the home team must adjust when an opposing football team changes its defensive tactics, a salesperson must adjust or suffer competitive disadvantage.

System Tendencies

Successful organizations are able to attract and retain quality members. Each member of a successful system has an expectation of gain from belonging. A newcomer may enter a system as a salesperson because of a feeling that joining a team is more beneficial than working alone. This expectation of gain from belonging is an organization's "structural glue," because it holds the organization together. Nearly every decision made by the power unit strengthens or weakens the "glue" or unity of the system. This is why managers must consider the secondary effects of every directive on the cohesiveness of a firm team. Going with XYZ Company because the opportunity to advance and make a better living will be increased is a common motive for joining an organization. Should it later be discovered that the XYZ Company managers promote only fellow lodge members, a nonmember's expectation of gain is weakened. Loyalty to the enterprise may be shattered, and resignation may result. An entire system can become more vulnerable because of managerial decisions that block paths of advancement for members. Such blockages diminish the opportunities to be gained from belonging. Firms tend to stay in business and persist even after their original goals are achieved. The March of Dimes retained its organization after polio was conquered, redirecting its efforts toward fighting birth defects. A carriage company going into the manufacture of automobile bodies illustrates this tendency to shift purposes to survive after an original purpose is no longer relevant in light of a changing environment.

Organizations also tend to develop pathologies or sicknesses just as a person develops illnesses. Some typical corporate illnesses will be analyzed in another section of this chapter. Nearly everyone must live in a system to achieve need and want satisfaction. As a salesperson, you must be aware of maladjustments in your firm's system. A weakness in a customer's firm may point to problems that can be solved by buying your product. Selling the right product may affect the health of both the seller's work environment system and the customer's.

System Functions

A system working as a team performs certain functions that enhance gains from belonging. The system is expected to create a *surplus*, or an excess for reserve, to assure its survival and growth. In a corporation, this is known as *earned surplus* and can be used to take advantage of special opportunities or to provide security for team members. A system's power unit is responsible for *rationing*, or dividing the gain of a system among system members. If a surplus is not divided fairly, members' expectations of gain from belonging will diminish. Many are likely to drop out to seek a fairer system. A system can provide security for members by protecting them against competition and loss of market. This defensive function can be supported by financial strength and aggressive selling.

System Power and Communications Operational Structures

Two structural operations—the power group and the communications network—are critical to system accomplishments. But, according to Alderson, the power group has a tendency to behave in such a way as to promote its power to act. Managers constantly strive to maintain themselves and their advancement. Such desires are common. They explain many actions. Most managers, in fact, are concerned about their positions in the organization and seek to advance themselves within it. Some firm members will even attempt to weaken the position of other members in order to promote themselves. They are engaging in positional behavior. *Positional behavior* explains why system members must behave with discretion. Don't criticize people in the power structure, for example, or tell a fellow sales representative about a selling mistake you just made—unless you want it to be passed along to your supervisor. People in competition with you in the firm have a motive for making you look bad so they may advance. Positional behavior explains why a group of firm members at the same level may promote the weakest and not the strongest member in selections or evaluations. It explains why sales managers may resent and suppress "star" salespersons whom they view as threats to their personal security. Office managers' opposing the purchase of a computer that they feel may lead to the loss of their jobs is another example of positional behavior. Positional motivation is an element in nearly every industrial selling situation.

In a free-enterprise system, power is maintained through persuasive communication rather than through coercion. The same persuasive techniques learned as a sales representative serve managers well. The power unit members use *power symbols* to maintain the image of power. Special dress, bigger offices, perhaps diamond tie tacks, or titles are designed to emphasize high position and to remind subordinate members of the necessity to conform to directives and instructions. Trademarks, buildings, and image personnel are symbols that reflect an enterprise's market power. Such symbols are highly valued.

System Pathologies

Human undertakings, like humans themselves, can have pathologies or illnesses that come about because of weaknesses in the power unit, the communications structure, the inputs, or because of a lack of adjustment to internal and external environmental changes. Power unit leaders sometimes become obsessed with personal power and may begin to disregard the needs of other system members. Often, leaders neglect to listen to information coming up from lower organizational levels. Sometimes leaders are over- or under-confident. Occasionally, they expect too much or too little of subordinates. Members of the power unit may be torn between conflicting loyalties: to the enterprise and to themselves and others. Sometimes there are simply too many members in the power unit, resulting in indecision, conflict, and wasted executive resources. The communications structure may contain both authorized and unauthorized systems. The unauthorized system, or grapevine, may distort reality or leak confidential information. Bad news, even bad news that requires action, sometimes fails to flow up the channel. Often power unit members substitute idealism for information and formulate unrealistic plans and orders based on wishes instead of analyzed information. Because of the lack of feedback, power unit members may be cut off from reality.

A potentially serious sickness exists for many enterprises in the 1980s. Input resources, particularly energy, have become increasingly scarce. High energy costs and high labor costs can drive up prices. Sales representatives may find their products overpriced in comparison with the prices of those of foreign or domestic competitors. Scarcity of input may reduce supplies to the point where decisions to ration output among customers, at least temporarily, may become necessary. Input changes, therefore, also affect sales situations.

System Remedies

Understanding how a system works is the first step toward *preventive maintenance* for preservation of a healthy system. Preventive maintenance involves the practice of anticipating and correcting potential problems before they develop. *Maintaining growth* promotes system health by providing advancement opportunities for members, strengthening its "structural glue." Good *feedback mechanisms* (communication systems and listening managers) built into a system help in detecting problems at early stages. *Realism* instead of idealism for power structure members fosters system health. The *power principle* itself, or "acting in such a way as to promote the power to act," encourages the capacity to adjust to changing conditions. Other remedies are suggested by the nature of the individual organization's pathology.

Application of the Model

The Aldersonian behavioral system model can be used to understand your company and your customers' companies. The model not only specifies system parts that must be kept healthy (communications, power, inputs, and adjustments) but also provides insight into the motivations involved in corporate buying situations. Each firm operates the four subsystems differently. In some firms, communications are formal. In others, salespersons must be careful observers to receive needed information. In some firms, communications are implied. In this case, management expectations must be anticipated, since they may never be communicated verbally. The concept of *positional behavior* that reveals purchasing motivations and team member rivalries can aid a new salesperson in adjusting to the corporate world. Many times reps are not in a position to correct pathologies or system deficiencies, but understanding them helps reps in predicting and reacting to company environments.

THE COMPETITIVE ENVIRONMENT

In 1980, imports rose some 16 percent over 1979 (see Figure 7.2), increasing the foreign share of the United States domestic market considerably. Automobiles, electronics, toys, sporting goods, clothing, shoes, office machines, cameras, tape recorders, sewing machines, and a host of other consumer products from abroad seriously threaten the sales of American industries (2). Since much foreign competition is based on lower labor costs, domestic salespersons find it increasingly hard to justify the prices of their products against those of competing foreign products. As more and more *American* products pour into the marketplace, competition among American manufacturers is also increasing. Customers have a greater variety from which to select. Customers will have more exposure to competitive sales representatives. Increasing competition can be expected in the last part of the growth stage of a product's life cycle. At that stage, many new firms enter the market to take advantage of profit opportunities created by successful innovators. Few salesper-

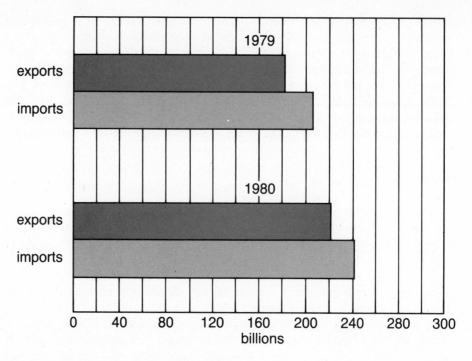

Source: The World Almanac and Book of Facts, 1982

Figure 7.2 Competition from Imports

sons sell products that are so advantageous, different, or protected by patents or trade secrets that competition fails to be a major environmental consideration. In normal selling situations, there are changes in product lines each year, designed to keep a company up with or ahead of rivals. It is a lucky sales representative who doesn't feel the pressure of increased competition.

Competition is generally greatest in highly populated city areas. Sales personnel in competitive companies may change, making a great difference in the selling potential of a product. If a rep suddenly finds a "star" salesperson competing for business, improvement of selling methods or personality may be necessary just to stay even.

Sales representatives must look to future as well as present competitors and develop specific strategies to outwit rivals. If a company emphasizes research and stays one step ahead of other firms in developing new products and features, its chances of sales success are greater. In selling, as in most sports, relative strength determines who wins in close rivalries.

Personal Preparation

Product Sales' Sensitivity to Business Conditions

Most products are affected by business cycles and economic conditions. The sale of automobiles, appliances, and other durables is highly responsive to changes in the personal incomes of consumers. Purchase of durable goods can generally be put off when consumer discretionary incomes are low. When real personal income is rising and discretionary income (income that does not have to be spent on necessities) rises with it, consumers usually buy more new cars and other types of durables.

Security sales are dependent on the outlook for economic prosperity and on speculation about interest rates. Money is often taken out of the stock market and invested in bonds and mortgages when interest rates are high. The housing market and the myriad dependent industries associated with it suffer when interest rates rise to high levels. High interest rates increase consumer monthly house payments significantly.

Durable industrial equipment is even more sensitive to cycles. It may be very responsive to changes in consumer demand for the buying industry's products. Suppose a firm needs ten minicomputers to operate, and suppose the firm normally replaces a depreciated machine each year. If this firm has a 10 percent increase in business, it will buy two more machines—one as a replacement and one to take care of additional business. The equipment sales representative, therefore, has twice the sales potential that he or she had the previous year. Suppose, on the other hand, that business decreases 10 percent. The company would then put aside the depreciated machine and would not need to replace it. The other nine machines would be sufficient for operations. The equipment salesperson would have zero potential with this company for that year. If that condition were multiplied throughout the market, a bad selling year—irrespective of effort—would result.

During a recession, companies have a tendency to repair existing equipment or to rent equipment rather than to commit additional capital to investment in new equipment. Fortunately, most products are not as sensitive as industrial equipment to the business cycle. However, most products are affected to some extent. Used equipment, repair services, and cheaper consumer goods that can substitute for higher-priced goods may even enjoy increased sales during recessionary periods.

Inflationary Influences

A high rate of inflation also influences buying decisions. The cost of holding big inventories is high. When the price level is increasing rapidly, it pays to buy more stock for inventory and to hold it rather than to buy it later at much higher prices. Buying in anticipation of a price increase is always an important closing appeal. Sales representatives often use inflation to load customers with larger inventories. Once inventory levels are high, however, replacement sales again depend on customer purchases. Purchases may decline during inflation because of a loss in real spending power. If inflation and taxes rise faster than income, consumers have proportionately less to spend for items other than necessities. Expenditures for necessities are less responsive to income changes than are discretionary goods—durables and luxuries. So, while inflation may create an opportunity to sell more in the short run because of buyer desires to hold goods instead of money, it decreases selling opportunity in the long run because commercial customers may sell off stocks when faced with uncertainty.

The Effects of Economic Fluctuations on Sales Opportunity

Every salesperson should have at least an elementary understanding of how changing economic conditions affect selling opportunities. In the past, fluctuations in economic conditions were called business cycles. The evidence of truly cyclical movements in American economic history is slight, particularly if the term "business cycle" is taken to mean that there is a rhythmic pattern of inevitable, uncontrollable ups and downs in economic activity.

Whatever value may be attached to the works of Lord Keynes, publication of his *General Theory of Employment, Interest, and Money* in 1936 changed the way economic fluctuations were perceived. After Keynes, economic fluctuations were no longer seen as inevitable or uncontrollable. Panics, depressions, and recessions came to be understood as resulting from complex movements among consumers, financial institutions, and investors as they viewed future opportunities (3). Even earlier, the presidential election of 1932 "marked a convulsive reaction against the idea that government should ever again adopt a posture of detached helplessness in the face of substantial deflation" (4). It was four years before Keynes provided a theoretical basis for understanding economic fluctuations and ten years before that theory had been accepted sufficiently for a consistent policy for management of the economy to evolve.

While the old-fashioned notion of uncontrollable economic cycles has been discredited, there are "wavelike motions in aggregate economic activity" (5). Most economists see four phases to economic fluctuations: (1) *revival* from a low point moving upward to (2) *expansion* to (3) *recession* as an upper turning point is passed, followed by (4) *contraction* until a new, lower turning point is reached. Before the Great Depression of the 1930s, the dominant view among economists and businesspeople was that government intervention into business activities was more likely to do harm than to do good. Economic fluctuations were seen as self-correcting. This is still the most conservative view. The consensual view that emerged from the Rooseveltian New Deal was that intervention on the demand side—tax breaks to consumers, transfer payments such as Social Security, unemployment compensation, and other income payments—would stimulate buying, which would, in turn, stimulate investment and employment. This is the most liberal of contemporary views.

The programs put together by the Reagan administration, and passed by the Congress in 1981, have been labeled as "supply-side stimulators." Their avowed purpose is to stimulate investment and saving through raising possible returns. However, the demand side was also served by these tax cuts, the most massive in U.S. history. Further, through indexing of tax brackets in the years after the series of tax cuts is complete, the role of future government participation in the economy will be limited. In many ways, by operating on both the supply side and the demand side, plus limiting government's economic role, "Reagonomics" is more comprehensive than the policies of the New Deal.

While the traditional "business cycle" is no longer a dominant view among economists, there are those who believe that there are long-run (or kondratieff) economic movements that indicate serious contractions are likely to take place every fifty years or so. Usually these contractions are severe enough to be called depressions; less severe movements are usually called recessions:

Franklin Roosevelt introduced the word "recession" in 1937 when a slight recovery foundered and he sought to soften the blow semantically. Now, a recession is popularly defined as two consecutive quarters of decline in the gross national product. A depression is generally defined as a recession in which unemployment exceeds 10 percent. (6)

It is interesting to note that the term depression was itself a euphemism, coined to replace the more severe term "panic." There have been three recessions since 1975. Many believe a fourth will arrive in late 1983 or early 1984 (7).

Some believe that economic contractions occur because of an overexpansion of debt. Others think they may be related to sunspots, banking system failures, changing expectations of the future, over- or under-consumption, over- or under-investment, overproduction, the length of women's skirts, and so forth. Today, most people realize that economic fluctuations are complex phenomena. Overexpansion of debt is a "monistic" explanation, that is, a single cause of contractions. Using it as an explainer, boom times take place when credit is rapidly expanded. As the burden of carrying the burgeoning debt increases, incomes are no longer adequate to service it. When this happens, the economic structure built by overexpansion of debt collapses. Debt holders demand payment; debtors cannot pay. Forced sales to meet debt payments ensue. Debt holders become concerned with liquidity of funds. Repossessions take place. Pessimism replaces optimism. Many existing goods offered for sale compete with new items, forcing prices down. Unsalable goods mean that employers let workers go. With lessened incomes—for even unemployment compensation is but partial protection and for but a limited time—families cut down on spending. Fewer goods are sold. More workers are let go. And on and on. Albert Summers contends that the U.S. economy is heading for the end of a fifty-year, kondratieff, cycle. As in 1929, debt is enormous. Unlike 1929, today's debt is mostly governmental. Under these circumstances, debt may produce inflation rather than depression (8).

Inflation can be caused by excessive government spending, public expenditure deficits, high labor costs (the wage-price spiral), falling productivity, managerial ineptitude, or even increasing raw material costs. The recession of 1974 was accompanied by increasing energy costs. Recession and inflation took place simultaneously. A certain amount of inflation is built into cost-of-living wage increases if productivity increases do not match them. With higher wage costs, sellers will seek higher prices. The higher prices sought act as a stimulus to workers to seek higher wages. Such is the form of the wage-price spiral.

Deficit spending by government may supply increased purchasing power without increasing the amount of goods available. Consumers and businesses then drive prices higher by chasing after the same amount of goods with more money. Higher energy prices based on raw material imports from exporting countries with near monopoly market control increase prices and decrease real incomes of consumers in importing countries. Inflation always gives buyers a reason for buying now—prices are likely to be higher in the future.

The causes of economic fluctuations are obscure. Surely, some of the explanations shed light on the complex mosaic that makes them up. But as one study of economic cycles concluded some years ago, "The *average* cycle is one that never happened. . . . Each is of different wave length and amplitude. . . . the forecaster can never assume that the past will repeat itself" (9). Each phase of contraction and expansion changes the opportunities and challenges that sales representatives face in the marketplace.

Technological Changes

Technological changes also change sales opportunity. For example, computerization, transportation, and communication advances may promote or retard the market climate for an offering. Transistorization and the resulting inexpensive pocket calculator have profoundly affected the office-machines industry. Consider the effects of the home computer that can be bought for less than $1,000. Every technological innovation has repercussions through-out the economy. Important innovations stimulate prosperity while causing readjustments in product offerings.

Selling in Scarcity

In the early seventies, many petroleum-based products became scare. So did certain other critical raw materials for hundreds of American industries. As during World War II, some sales representatives had to face the unusual sit-uation of not being able to supply the needs of even their best customers. They were required to institute and coordinate elaborate allocation programs. Steel, aluminum, plastics, and synthetic fibers used by so many firms in fab-ricating hundreds of industrial and consumer products were suddenly in short supply. Salespersons found themselves working just as hard during these temporary shortages, attempting to allocate (ration) fairly, discourage bribery, ignore threats, and maintain goodwill by steering customers to surpluses in other firms' stocks and sometimes even to those of competitors (10). Special care was taken to keep purchasing agents informed of any changes in allo-cation procedures. Many salespersons used the situation as an opportunity to extract more information about customers' future plans and programs. Given the scarcity of certain raw materials and the political instability and monopolis-tic tendencies of some foreign suppliers, the situation may reoccur. Salesper-sons will have to be prepared to switch their thinking to accommodate tem-porary shortages that may occur more frequently in the future than they have in the past.

THE SOCIOCULTURAL ENVIRONMENT

Because markets are composed of people with money (or credit) and incli-nations toward certain products, the trends of the sociocultural environment have considerable effect on selling opportunities. Population and income trends, education and occupational changes, spending behavior develop-ments, fashion cycles, and myriad cultural influences constantly modify selling situations. An analysis of these cultural changes provides a basis for estimat-ing selling opportunity and buying motivations.

Population Trends

The rate of population growth in the United States has slowed considerably because of a declining birthrate (see Figure 7.3). More people are living alone than ever before. There is even discussion of future stationary population or

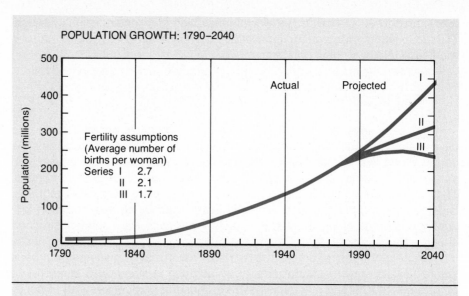

POPULATION GROWTH: 1790–2040

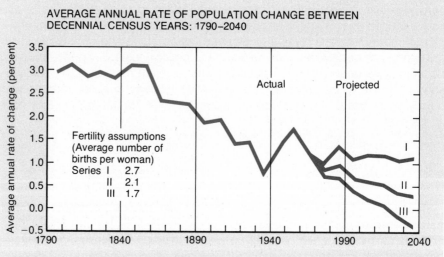

AVERAGE ANNUAL RATE OF POPULATION CHANGE BETWEEN
DECENNIAL CENSUS YEARS: 1790–2040

Source: *Social Indicators 1976,* U.S. Government Printing Office (U.S. Department of
Commerce), Office of Federal Statistical Policy and Standards, Bureau of Census, p. 4.

Figure 7.3   Population Estimates

zero-growth situation. While lives have been extended because of medical
advances, the low birthrate trend could diminish the market for children's
products.

Even though the birthrate was low during the Depression, it was high just
after World War II. Babies born in the late forties and through the fifties

Personal Preparation

formed a "baby boom," creating markets and crowding school facilities. Those postwar children are now swelling the labor force, and the women in this group are in their childbearing years.

Although the birthrate is now low, and may remain so, a greater number of children should be born during the next few years. Large numbers of women of childbearing age, many of whom have delayed having children because of career commitments, are beginning to start families. While families may be smaller, there will be more "higher order" births (first and second children). Since last children in large families get hand-me-downs that have already been purchased, the market for children's and infant's products should continue to grow with the prospect of more "higher order" births. The demand for houses, apartments, and associated products—furniture, textiles, lawn mowers, do-it-yourself home improvements, paint, construction materials, construction equipment, house trailers, land, and air conditioners—should begin to gain strength in the eighties. The mid-seventies recession with high prices and high interest rates and the even higher interest rates of 1980 and 1981 may simply have temporarily suppressed the pent-up demand for living space. With about 20 percent of the population moving each year, affluent home owners will continue remodeling houses to meet their new self-images. This will support the home decorating market (11). The suburban movement, with its emphasis on backyard living, the countermovement to the central-city high rises, and the population shift from the Northeast to the South and West will continue to influence the types of products purchased. Shifts to sunshine areas stimulate the purchase of sportswear, recreational equipment, and air conditioners.

Income Trends

With the recession of the mid-seventies over, and the crunch of 1980-81 relieved by the Reagan administration's massive tax cuts, the long-run trend toward increased real family incomes may resume. By 1980, more than half, or 30 million, U.S. families made over $20,000 per year (12)—see Figure 7.4.

Baby-boom young adults are now productive in the labor force. There are more working women increasing the output of the nation's goods and services. Productivity should begin to rise again with better technology (13). Increasing energy costs and raw material costs (from monopolies in supplying countries) could dampen prospects of increased discretionary income (income left after buying necessities like food, clothing, and shelter). Better technology and the discovery of new, less expensive energy sources, on the other hand, could accelerate income growth. Greater discretionary income allows people to spend more for luxuries, services, durables, and investments. Ethnic groups, particularly blacks and Spanish-speaking Americans now, to a limited extent, are beginning to share in increased affluence and are buying more

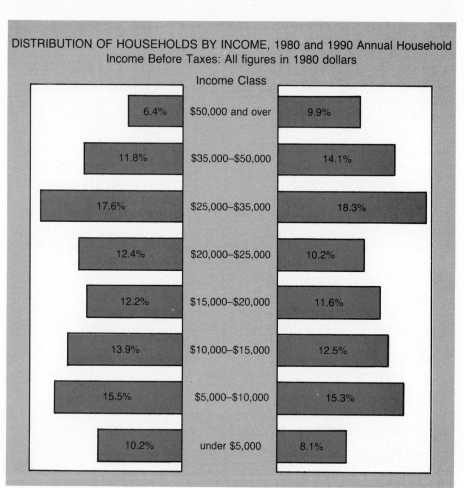

DISTRIBUTION OF HOUSEHOLDS BY INCOME, 1980 and 1990 Annual Household
Income Before Taxes: All figures in 1980 dollars

Income Class

1980	Income Class	1990
6.4%	$50,000 and over	9.9%
11.8%	$35,000–$50,000	14.1%
17.6%	$25,000–$35,000	18.3%
12.4%	$20,000–$25,000	10.2%
12.2%	$15,000–$20,000	11.6%
13.9%	$10,000–$15,000	12.5%
15.5%	$5,000–$10,000	15.3%
10.2%	under $5,000	8.1%

Source: The Conference Board, Inc. Fabian Linden, "At the end of the Eighties—what will be the single most important segment of the marketplace?" *Across the Board,* Vol. XVIII No. 3, March 1981. Based on Bureau of the Census Projections.

Figure 7.4 The Changing Income Pyramid

middle-class products. If incomes do become much higher—as many fore-casters predict—better markets for the discretionary goods will follow.

Spending Trends

The purchase of durable goods, particularly cars, has significantly fallen since 1978. The shift to services (intangibles, such as haircuts, rentals, and repairs), which spurted during the fifties, has slowed down (14). Moreover, this shift should continue in the 1980s, if affluence increases. Sporting equipment, home appliances, health foods, pets and pet care, accessories, do-it-yourself products, and leisure-recreational offerings show continuing promise if present spending trends continue. People will also be able to afford better medical care.

Education Trends

Most people today go to school for more years than their parents did. A larger percentage of young people finish high school and college. By 1980, more than 25 percent of the population 17 and older had some college training (15). Educated buyers buy a different mix of products. They are more thoughtful and deliberate in their purchases than are the uneducated. Increasing educational levels suggest that sales reps must become more professional in their approaches, presentations, and closings.

Style and Fashion

The normal fashion cycle is composed of the following stages: *distinctiveness*—when only a few distinguished people know of and use a product; *emulation*—when a product is popular with middle socioeconomic groups; and *economic emulation*—when all economic groups accept an innovation and it appears in bargain basements (16). The fashion cycle accelerated during the sixties. Wardrobes became rapidly style-obsolete. Style obsolescence stimulates buying. When people become dissatisfied with serviceable but out-of-style items, they buy new ones. Many have become disenchanted with playing the fashion game. Today, many middle- and lower-class people are still wearing old styles and are no longer accepting new styles as quickly. Not conforming to style pressures has become increasingly acceptable. Nevertheless, when old clothes *wear out*, new purchases do reflect existing fashions.

Cultural Changes

Cultural changes include many trends, but *other-directedness*, consumerism, feminism, life simplification, youth orientation, leisure spending, reference-group influences, self-service acceptances, security consciousness, and changing moral and work attitudes are among the most important. David Riesman contends that society has become more *other-directed*. Once people were tradition-directed and followed traditional ways of doing things and buying products. People next became *inner-directed* or independent in their decisions. Now, people are other-directed and prone to consider the reactions of their reference groups (17). People are deeply concerned about what their peer groups think of them. The value of testimonials in selling is greater today, as buyers become more other-directed.

Consumerism reflects the increasing tendency of consumers to question sellers. Pressures for restrictions on sales of specific items and regulation of the ways many goods are sold reflect growing consumer questioning. Books such as Rachel Carson's *Silent Spring,* Ralph Nader's *Unsafe at Any Speed,* and Vance Packard's *Hidden Persuaders* have encouraged the consumer movement. Although waning in influence, the consumer movement has succeeded in obtaining a hearing of its case by the legislature and executive branches of government (18). Automobile safety legislation, labeling acts, packaging legislation, and a host of other laws and regulations have been the result. Sales representatives should realize that new activism by consumers will continue to influence market decision making and selling methods.

Much of the new legislation has helped ethical salespeople and companies to provide safer and more acceptable products. Technological advances, more educated consumers, and a growing distrust of corporate motives could exacerbate a trend toward more active consumerism unless sellers adopt the marketing concept in greater numbers.

Feminism has fostered products associated with the feminist image, such as certain cigarettes, emancipated clothes, little cigars, and certain perfumes. As the labor force participation of women increases, a greater number of products are being designed to release housewives from household chores. Blenders, disposals, dryers, compactors, dishwashers, and self-cleaning ovens are part of a trend toward simplified housekeeping that enables more women to work outside the home.

More and more food is being prepared outside the home. People in today's markets are demanding instant satisfaction by purchasing such products as Polaroid cameras and fast-food services. Even older people want to be included in buying products catering to a *youth image,* especially with regard to clothes. More leisure time has encouraged booms in motel rooms, campers, tennis rackets, bicycles, health club memberships, boats, and a host of other leisure-recreational products and services. With the prospect of a decreased work week and earlier retirements for some, the trend should continue and bolster the sales of recreational products.

THE LEGAL ENVIRONMENT

Trends point to even more laws restricting the operation and decisions of salespersons. Both Carter and Reagan dedicated themselves to lessening business regulation, but history is against them. As population grows and improved transportation and communications facilities develop, people will interact more and tend to get in each other's way to a certain degree, providing cause for more regulation. In addition, social and legal trends, such as more liberal legislative bodies, consumerism, environmentalism, and feminism, will promote new laws affecting sales. This section is not designed to afford sales representatives proficiency in any legal area but rather to make them aware of legal pitfalls and complexities. If a sales representative is unaware of important restrictions, the rep and the company represented can get into serious trouble. This section offers an overview of:

- The law of contract and agency
- The law of warranty
- Fraud
- Laws affecting pricing decisions
- Green River Ordinances

The Law of Contract and Agency

A contract (see Figure 7.5) is an agreement that binds a sales representative and the company to perform what a customer was promised. A valid contract involves an offer, an acceptance of the offer, *consideration* (money, written promises, or goods given to show intent to enter the contract), parties with the capacity to contract, and a legal objective (19). If a salesperson can legally obligate a company, care in entering legal contracts must be exercised.

An offer does not become a contract until the opposite party accepts the terms of the offer. An offer can generally be withdrawn at any time before acceptance (20).

A request for bids is simply an invitation to make an offer (21). If buyers propose terms different from those stated in the offer, they are making a counteroffer. A valid offer must state what the person making the offer promises and asks in return. Once a valid offer is accepted, the contract must be performed or the buyer (offeree) can sue for damages. It is important that contract data be correct and that a proposal offer be profitable for a company before an offer is tendered to a buyer.

Acceptance must be made freely and not under threat or duress—undue influence (22). The giving of money or products is substantial evidence of intent to enter a contract. Evidence of unfair dealing may be cause for the courts to set aside a contract or render it unenforceable. A buyer must have the capacity to contract. Under most circumstances, a buyer must be legally qualified to contract, either personally or as a bona fide agent of a corporation. Infants, insane persons, drunks, aliens, and corporations may not have full capacity to contract in certain circumstances (23). Many kinds of contracts with minors

PURCHASE ORDER — FOR JOHN DEERE AGRICULTURAL EQUIPMENT

C18986

☐ NEW ☐ USED ☐ DEMONSTRATOR ☐ TIME SALE ☐ CASH SALE

PURCHASER'S NAME AND ADDRESS (First Signer)

		INITIALS
Last Name, then initials		
Street or R F D		
Town, State and Zip	STATE	ZIP CODE

DATE OF ORDER

ORDER NO

BRANCH | DEALER ACCT NO | TO BE DELIVERED ON OR ABOUT

DEALER NAME AND ADDRESS

PURCHASER'S NAME AND ADDRESS (Second Signer)

		INITIALS
Last Name, then initials		
Street or R F D		
Town, State and Zip	STATE	ZIP CODE

PURCHASER'S SOCIAL SEC. NO. (First Signer)

COUNTY OF FIRST SIGNER

I (we), the undersigned, hereby order from you the Equipment described below, to be delivered as shown above. This order is subject to your ability to obtain such Equipment from the manufacturer and you shall be under no liability if delivery of the Equipment is delayed or prevented due to labor disturbances, transportation difficulties, or for any reason beyond your control. The price shown below is subject to your receipt of the Equipment prior to any change in price by the manufacturer. It is also subject to any new or increased taxes imposed upon the sale of the Equipment after the date of this order.

INVOICE No.	INVOICE DATE	INVOICE AMOUNT	QTY	EQUIPMENT (Give Model, Size & Description)	SERIAL No.	DEL'D CASH PRICE

I (we), offer to sell, transfer, and convey the following item(s) at or prior to the time of delivery of the above Equipment, as a trade-in to be applied against the cash price. Such item(s) shall be free and clear of all security agreements, liens, and encumbrances at the time of transfer to you. The following is a description and the price to be allowed for each item

		SALES TAX	
		1. TOT. CASH PRICE	

A TOTAL AMOUNT OWED

	QTY	DESCRIPTION OF TRADE-IN	SERIAL No.	AMOUNT
B OUT OF POCKET EXPENSE				
C TOTAL (A plus B)				
D NOTE AND CASH RECEIVED				
E MAX FLOOR PLAN ALLOWABLE (C less D)				

2. TOT. TRADE-IN ALLOWANCE	
3. CASH WITH ORDER	
4. TOTAL (ITEMS 2 & 3)	
5. BALANCE DUE (ITEM 1 LESS ITEM 4)	

The Warranty on the reverse side is a part of this contract and the following applies where permitted by law: Neither seller, John Deere Company, nor the manufacturer makes any other representations or warranties, express or implied (AND EXPRESSLY DISCLAIMS THE IMPLIED WARRANTIES OF MERCHANTABILITY AND FITNESS) or has any obligations to the Purchaser except as provided on the reverse side.

I (we), promise to pay the balance due (line 5) shown above in cash, or to execute a Time Sale Agreement (Retail Installment Contract) for the purchase price of the Equipment, plus additional charges shown thereon, on or before delivery of the Equipment ordered herein. Despite physical delivery of the Equipment, title shall remain in the seller until one of the foregoing is accomplished.

Purchaser's Signature _____

Accepted by _____
Authorized Signature for Seller)

Purchaser's Signature _____

Date Accepted _____ Salesman _____

DC-770-STOCK 9-77 PRINTED IN U.S.A

DEALER'S COPY

Source: John Deere Company, Moline, Illinois.

Figure 7.5 The Sales Contract

can be voided at the minor's election, although adults are fully bound. Most sales representatives are not agents and have the power to solicit only written offers (called orders) from customers. Written orders must be signed by a branch manager or some other authority before they become obligatory (24). Such *orders* may contain a clause stating that the salesperson cannot make statements that are binding and point to the terms of the written agreement as the legal obligation of both parties. Branch managers, for example, can look at the terms of an agreement and determine before they sign it whether, say, a proposed trade-in would be profitable or not. By handling the offer and accepting in this way, a company is not bound by the statements (promises) a salesperson made while soliciting an order. The written contract itself becomes the binding document. If a salesperson has made false and misleading statements, however, a buyer can usually have the contract declared void by legal authority.

Salespersons owe certain obligations to their companies. They are legally bound to be loyal. They should never reveal confidential information that might hurt the company. They should not sell to themselves (buy their company's goods) without making full disclosure of all the facts. They must always represent sellers in transactions, since it is illegal to represent both buyer and seller. They must not mix the company property with their own without a strict accounting (25).

The Law of Warranty

Sellers must use "due care" in designing, manufacturing, preparing, inspecting, or selling goods. A buyer can sue for damages due to negligence if a buyer is injured because of a defective product. Unless effectively disclaimed, every product has an implied warranty for merchantability and, sometimes, an implied warranty of fitness for a particular purpose (26). If a buyer inspects merchandise or is asked to inspect merchandise and declines to do so, the implied warranty does not pertain to defects an inspection would reveal. Statements in a contract like "as is" or "with all faults" may exempt the seller from implied warranties (27). A product must be adequately packaged and conform to its label—statements in the label are express warranties. False or misleading statements, beyond the normal exaggeration of benefits, or puffing of wares, to induce buyers to purchase usually mean that buyers can void a contract if they desire to do so.

Fraud

Fraud is the misrepresentation of an important fact that is knowingly and deceitfully made to induce a buyer to rely and act on that misrepresented fact to the buyer's personal detriment. A person who relies on a wrong statement must be harmed in some way (usually economically). Merely stating an opinion about a product is not fraud. But making positive statements, without a basis of information and knowing that the statements made are probably wrong, *is* fraud (28). Salespersons must be sure to have a good basis for product claims and should not make careless statements about what the product can accomplish if they are uncertain about a promised capability. Because salespersons are also subject to a buyer's fraudulent statements and can be defrauded themselves, salespersons should get promises to buy (contracts) in writing.

Laws Affecting Pricing Decisions

The Sherman Antitrust Act of 1890 was passed to protect the public from monopoly practices that would hinder competition. The courts soon determined that a combination of sellers that sought to fix prices affected competition adversely. The Clayton Act, a 1914 amendment to the Sherman Act, contained provisions that were intended to restrain businesspeople from circumventing the Sherman Act by engaging in such practices as exclusive dealing contracts and tying agreements that substantially affected competitor opportunity. Section 2 of the Clayton Act made price discrimination illegal under certain conditions. Price discrimination is a monopolistic practice that entails supplying certain buyers at one price and other buyers at another price.

The Robinson-Patman Act, like the Clayton Act, was an amendment to the Sherman Act designed to close loopholes in the law. The Act specifically forbids price discrimination in interstate commerce where the effect of such discrimination may tend to lessen competition or to create a monopoly in any line of commerce. It does allow differentials or quantity discounts based on differences in manufacturing or marketing costs for selling in larger quantity. However, the burden of proving cost savings is on the seller. It allows differences in prices for different-quality goods. Prices may be legally lowered in a market to meet competition in good faith. Other provisions of the law call for advertising allowances and services to be made on a proportionately equal basis to all customers. It outlaws dummy brokerage houses set up by buyers to disguise actual price concessions. The Federal Trade Commission, set up in 1914 as a companion law to the Clayton Act, is responsible for enforcing the Robinson-Patman Act. Violators are subject to triple damages from successful private damage suits. The actual enforcement of the Sherman Act has varied, but in 1962 corporate executives of several electrical equipment manufacturers went to jail for conspiring to fix prices. Since that time, more sales representatives have been trained in this legal area.

Laws Relating to Competition

The Federal Trade Commission, under Section 5 of the FTC Act, is given broad powers to oppose unfair methods of competition in commerce and unfair or deceptive acts and practices. Usually, the Commission holds trade practice conferences by inviting firms in a particular industry to Washington, D.C., where leaders in that industry decide which practices should be disallowed. The FTC usually orders an offending company to "cease and desist" its malpractice. If the company persists despite an FTC order, cases can go to the court system. If a competitor is injured because a corporation or its sales representatives acting as its agents act wrongfully against a firm or issue misleading statements hurting another firm's business, an affected firm can sue (see Figure 7.6).

Green River Ordinances

Municipal ordinances have been passed in some urbanized areas restricting salespersons from calling on customers door to door. Such restrictions usually result from resistance to door-to-door solicitors by local merchants and some consumers. The first legislation of this kind, stipulating that door-to-door solicitation without prior permission of householders was illegal, was passed in Green River, Wyoming, in 1933 (29). The laws are not so widespread in the United States as to pose a serious threat to national distribution of products and selling efforts by this method, but salespersons should investigate any restrictions in their areas.

SUMMARY

The internal working environment for the salesperson is the firm, which can be viewed as an organized team or system. Belonging to a system affects the motivations and decisions of people in the system. System members are usually motivated to maintain or better their positions in an organization. This desire for betterment may conflict with deciding what is best for the organization itself. Systems can have illnesses, especially in communications or power structures, that need to be anticipated and corrected.

Competition, foreign and domestic, is increasingly affecting selling situations. Some products are especially sensitive to economic conditions and business cycles. Salespeople should use knowledge about economic conditions in strategic planning and in personal appraisal of selling opportunities.

Figure 7.6   Procter & Gamble's Personnel Guidelines for Legal Constraints/Antitrust Laws*

Procter & Gamble's business is conducted throughout the world under conditions of intense competition. The Company has always been and remains committed to the concept of fair and vigorous competition as the mechanism most conducive to economic and social progress. Our performance demonstrates that, as a company, we thrive on such competition. In general, the laws of antitrust and trade regulation codify a philosophy to which the Company fully subscribes.

We try at all times to conduct our business in accordance with the letter and the spirit of the law of each of the nations in which we operate. It is each manager's duty to conduct the business falling within his or her area of responsibility in a lawful manner, and each is held accountable for doing so. This specifically includes the laws of antitrust and trade regulation.

While generally these laws are not extensive, their meaning is not always clear. In addition, several sets of antitrust laws may have applicability to the same transaction. Accordingly, while the legal principles of antitrust reflect Procter & Gamble's philosophy of full and fair competition, it is recommended and expected that each manager make full use of Procter & Gamble legal advisers with regard to the interpretation and application of these laws.

In applying these principles, the following should guide your actions in the United States and abroad:

1. The Company's basic policy is for its employees to have no contacts with our competitors. This enables us to maintain our full independence and freedom to act. Any business activity on your part which puts you into contact with competitors, whether at meetings, in telephone calls or by correspondence must be an authorized exception to the Company policy concurred in by your manager and the Legal Division.

2. The Company offers its products for sale to its customers at a price which it unilaterally determines to be appropriate. All competing customers are offered our products on the same price basis. Plans concerning prices and the terms or conditions of sale of our goods may never be discussed with competitors.

3. Accurate information about conditions in the market is essential to effective competition. The Company obtains available information about the market, including the activities of competitors, from trade and other public sources. The Company will not permit competitive information to be obtained through bribery, fraud, theft or coercion.

Government personnel, particularly in foreign countries, may ask or require your discussion or meeting with representatives of competitors. Before undertaking such discussions or meetings, you should secure concurrence of your manager and the Legal Division.

Source: *Procter & Gamble—Your Personal Responsibility.* Courtesy of The Procter & Gamble Company.

* This brief summary statement is intended to synthesize much more detailed guidelines, which exist throughout the company.

Great changes are also occurring in the sociocultural environment. The increases anticipated in real personal incomes, spending behavior shifts, population changes, consumer education, consumerism, and attendant trends continually shift selling opportunities.

The legal environment always conditions a salesperson's decisions and opportunities. Sales representatives should be aware of all actions that might jeopardize employing firms. All sales reps need to know the legal obligations of a company for products sold under warranty. They also need to know the laws regarding prices, fraud, and advertising and what constitutes violation of them. The law is complex and requires study. A lawyer's services are valuable. Knowledge of selling's interaction with its environments permits more realistic strategic planning.

REVIEW QUESTIONS

1. What are the environmental situations that influence the opportunity for selling?

2. What are the four dominant characteristics of an economic behavior system? Describe these characteristics.

3. What is the "structural glue" that holds a firm together?

4. What is positional behavior, and how might it affect the salesperson?

5. What is a power symbol? Give some examples. What is the relevance of power symbols to the salesperson?

6. What are some system pathologies, and how can they be prevented?

7. Briefly delineate the characteristics of the competitive environment.

8. Explain why consumer durables are highly sensitive to economic conditions.

9. What impact does inflation have on a salesperson's prospects of selling success?

10. What are the stages of the business cycle? What impact does the business cycle have on the sales representative?

11. What impact does technological change have on the salesperson?

12. What are the elements of the sociocultural environment?

13. List the important population trends that affect the sales environment.

14. What are the elements of the fashion cycle? Describe them.

15. What dimensions of the American culture are changing? How will this affect demand patterns?

16. What are the legal areas of particular interest to the salesperson?

17. What are the elements of a valid contract?

18. Briefly outline the essentials of the law of warranty.

19. What is meant by a "Green River Ordinance"?

APPLICATION QUESTIONS

1. Each of you belongs to some groups, such as clubs, school organizations, athletic teams, or businesses. Take one of these groups and answer the following questions:

    a. Which members represent the power unit?

    b. What is the communication structure?

    c. Is there any earned surplus? How is it allocated?

    d. How do members engage in positional behavior?

    e. What are the power symbols?

    f. What other environmental factors mentioned in the chapter affect the organization? How?

2. This chapter discusses several of the most important environmental trends and specifies some products affected by these trends. Prepare a table that lists each trend and the affected products.

    a. Can you see any pattern in the types of products affected?

    b. What other products that are not mentioned would probably be affected?

    c. Why do you need to be aware of these trends?

INCIDENTS

7–1

Ralph Hudgins sells steel cable, but he has only one roll left that is marked 12,000 pounds strength. His sales manager has told him that this particular roll was rejected by another customer because it had a defective section. Hudgins had been led to believe that the cable is weaker because of the defective section. He is calling on John Kilgore, a cable prospect.

Ralph: Mr. Kilgore, I'm Ralph Hudgins with the Atlas Cable Company. I noticed that the cable you have on your cranes looks rusty. Have you considered replacing it to ensure the safety of your workers?

John: The cable we are now using *is* a few years old, but I believe it's still strong enough for our purposes.

Ralph: Yes, sir, it *may* be, but then it *may not* be. With our cable you would be sure, because it tests 12,000 pounds tensile strength. It would be fine for lifting the scrap vehicles you have to lift.

John: Well, we've been lifting some heavy scrap lately. Some of those trucks weigh 8,000 pounds. Do you have any of that strong cable in stock now?

Ralph: You're in luck. We have a roll in stock that is 12,000-pound test. It should be enough for several of your cranes, and it's only $435.

John: That sounds O.K., and you're probably right, Ralph, you can't be too safe. Can you deliver it tomorrow?

(A week later on the telephone)

John: Mr. Hudgins, I have bad news We rerigged our cranes with your cable, and it broke this morning, crushing an operating vehicle. The cable failed to hold a 7,000-pound scrap truck, and the load narrowly missed killing our foreman. You told me that it was guaranteed to hoist 12,000 pounds. I'm afraid your company will have to pay for the truck cab and engine that are almost a total loss.

Ralph: That's terrible. I don't have any idea what could have gone wrong. The cable spool said 12,000 pounds, didn't it?

John: Well, our lawyer will be over to call on your manager shortly.

QUESTION

1. Evaluate this conversation in regard to the laws of warranty, fraud, and agency. From what you know, do you think Ralph is in trouble?

7–2

Donna Pelligrini is a sales representative for Monroe Corporation. Monroe produces polyethylene pellets, which are sold to converters who produce extruded plastic products like dish drainers and toys and to others who convert the pellets into plastic packaging film. Polyethylene is a by-product of petroleum refining. The slowdowns in gasoline consumption and in oil used for home heating have created several temporary shortages of the by-product pellets. Because Monroe is a division of a major oil company, its sales representatives have had less of a problem with out-of-stocks than have many of their competitors. Nearly every Monroe rep has had to allocate the pellets among the many prospects who are seeking them.

Donna has one prime prospect she has been trying to sell for two years: Bergdorf Plastics. Bergdorf is headed by Hans Gluckmeister. Hans holds less than progressive views about what roles are appropriate for women. He believes women should tend to children, and the home, and support their husbands in their careers. Women sales reps are not made to feel welcome at Bergdorf. They rarely come away with orders. Hans' antifeminist stand together with Bergdorf's very large potential have made Bergdorf an account Donna especially wants to sell.

After Bergdorf, the next biggest prospect in Donna's territory is the Foote Toy Company. Gerald Foote's volume is about half of Hans'. Unlike Hans, Gerry has long been a customer of Monroe. Over time, Monroe's product quality, service, and prices and Donna's work on the account have given her and Monroe the bulk of Gerry's business. Foote is such an important part of Donna's overall sales that the amount of polyethylene she has available to sell to others is largely determined by Foote's requirements.

This month, for the second time this year, Monroe has had to cut back on the quantity of pellets it can supply. It cannot possibly increase its output for the next three months. The quantities for sale are adequate to cover existing accounts during that period. Monroe's reps have been told to allocate the amounts available among their best accounts. Difficult as Monroe's situation is, it is less difficult than that of its competitors.

Donna saw in this situation her opportunity to sell Bergdorf. She was convinced that once Hans saw Monroe's quality and service, he would convert to Monroe. On her next call, she took an order from Hans for roughly a quarter of his needs for the whole year. A quarter of Hans' needs just about equals half of Gerry Foote's needs. Consequently, Donna had to cut back on Foote's order.

At a trade association meeting, Foote heard Hans bragging to everyone that he was in good shape because he had managed to get Foote's raw materials. Foote was not pleased. When Hans saw Foote's reaction, he stopped talking of his coup. Each of Donna's customers is unhappy. Each feels that Donna and Monroe failed to act according to the long-run interest of either.

Should Donna have sold Hans?
What should she do now to restore the situation with Foote? With Hans?
What other kinds of dilemmas besides the one Donna now finds herself in can a sales rep get into during a time of shortage?

7–3

Martin Laughton has been with Armstrong Chemical Company ever since graduating from college three years ago. Martin had interrupted his college career after completing two and a half years to go into the service. He had messed himself up with drugs and alcohol and thought the service would give him a chance to straighten himself out. He had been quite surprised by the amount of drug use in the military and by how little attention was paid to drug use that was for "recreational purposes" and did not appear to interfere with reporting for duty. Fearful of his own reactions, Martin had avoided using any new drugs but smoked marijuana once in a while. After getting out of the service, Martin finished college while holding a full-time job—the midnight shift—with Amtrak. He didn't have the time, the money, or the inclination to use drugs and was pleased with himself for having stayed "clean" since leaving the service.

Martin's sales record at Armstrong has been good. Even in his first year he exceeded his quota by 17 percent, and his record has continued to show improvement. He is being considered for promotion to district sales manager. He is enough older than the newer sales reps to appear authoritative but young enough to relate to them. This combination has made him a particularly effective field trainer of newly hired reps. His record as a trainer is another reason he is being considered for early promotion to district manager. According to usual company policy, five years is the minimum between hiring and eligibility for promotion.

Currently, Paul Rogers is one of Martin's field trainees. Paul is outgoing, intelligent, and personable. He is a graduate of a prestigious school and was at the top of his group in Armstrong's centralized basic training program. Unfortunately, a good share of the time, mostly after working hours, Paul is "stoned out of his mind." So far, his use of "grass" has not seriously affected his job performance, but he has been late for appointments and sloppy in some preparations for prospect presentation. And now it appears that Paul has added excessive drinking to his smoking habits. He has shown up at sales calls with bloodshot eyes and physical unsteadiness that hardly reflects well on Armstrong. Martin feels that if Paul weren't required to meet him as part of the training program he might well not work at all on some days. Martin hesitates to "blow the whistle" on Paul because he has had other trainees so much less talented than Paul who did not do nearly as well as Paul does despite his use of drugs. Furthermore, Martin recognizes that drug use—including heavy use of alcohol—is increasingly common. He knows many people who use marijuana frequently. Some are daily drinkers. Others sniff cocaine. Martin knows times have changed, but he still feels troubled. He wonders if times have changed enough that Paul's behavior is now acceptable. He also wonders how his own promotion would be affected if he discussed his concerns about Paul with his manager, John Sullivan, who uses marijuana.

By appearing to "rat" on Paul, will Martin hurt himself with John?
Should Martin be promoted?
What should Martin's concern for Paul be?

NOTES

1. Discussion of firms as organized behavior systems is adapted from: Wroe Alderson, *Marketing Behavior and Executive Action* (Homewood, Ill.: Irwin, 1957), pp. 35–97.

2. U.S. Department of Commerce, "International Commerce Report," *Commerce America,* October 21, 1981, pp. 18–21.

3. John Maynard Keynes, *The General Theory of Employment, Interest, and Money* (London: Macmillan, 1936), p. 313.

4. John P. Lewis, *Business Conditions Analysis* (New York: McGraw-Hill, 1959), p. 295.

5. David H. McKinley, Murray G. Lee, Helene Duffy, and L. Randolph McGee, *Forecasting Business Conditions* (New York: American Bankers Association, 1969), p. 5.

6. Benjamin J. Stein, "A Scenario for a Depression," *New York Times Magazine,* February 28, 1982, p. 16.

7. Leonard Silk, "The Great Repression," *New York Times,* March 14, 1982, p. C1.

8. Albert Summers, "Cycles for All Occasions," *Conference Board Review,* April 1976, pp. 8–12.

9. First National City Bank, New York, *Monthly Economic Letter,* April 1963, p. 38.

10. Michael P. Rothfield, "A New Kind of Challenge for Salesmen," *Fortune,* April 1974, pp. 156–162.

11. *Wall Street Journal,* March 13, 1973, p. 20.

12. Walter Kiechel, "Two-Income Families Will Reshape the Consumer Markets," in Richard F. Wendel (ed.), *Marketing 81/82* (Guilford, Conn.: Annual Editions, Dushkin, 1981), pp. 100–105.

13. Fabian Linden, "The Arithmetic of Affluence," *Conference Board Record,* September 1975, pp. 13–16.

14. Fabian Linden, "The Business of Consumer Services," *Conference Board Record,* 12 (April 1975), p. 13.

15. U. S. Bureau of the Census, "Current Population Reports," Series P. 20, No. 356, *Educational Attainment in the United States* (Washington: U. S. Government Printing Office, 1980), p. 8.

16. E. Jerome McCarthy, *Basic Marketing,* 7th ed. (Homewood, Ill.: Irwin), p. 246.

17. David Riesman, *The Lonely Crowd* (New Haven, Conn.: Yale University Press, 1961), p. 1 ff.

18. Phillip Kotler, "What Consumerism Means for Marketers," *Harvard Business Review,* May–June 1972, pp. 48–57.

19. John W. Wyatt and Madie B. Wyatt, *Business Law,* 5th ed. (New York: McGraw-Hill, 1975), p. 36.

20. *Ibid.,* p. 43.

21. Michael P. Litka, *Business Law* (Harcourt, Brace & World, 1970), p. 86.

22. *Ibid.,* p. 153.

23. Ronald A. Anderson and Walter A. Kumpf, *Business Law,* 6th ed. (Cincinnati: Southwestern, 1975), pp. 199–207.

Personal Preparation

24. *Ibid.,* pp. 842–843.

25. *Ibid.,* pp. 817–819.

26. Wyatt and Wyatt, *Business Law,* pp. 198–208.

27. *Ibid.*

28. Anderson and Kumpf, *Business Law,* pp. 220–224.

29. Theodore N. Beckman, William R. Davidson, and W. Wayne Talarzyk, *Marketing,* 9th ed. (New York: Ronald Press, 1973), p. 247.

SELLING TECHNIQUES

Part I emphasized personal preparation of sales representatives and the areas of development and understanding basic to success in selling. Part II examines specific practical procedures and focuses on the interaction of salespersons with prospective buyers—the interview. Successful sales representatives build on the experiences of others. In doing so, they can select from a broad range of tested methods and techniques to reach personal goals. Consider the competitive advantage of the sales representative who understands the better procedures used by professionals in the field over representatives who insist on learning by trial and error alone. There are many psychologically sound ways to meet the challenges of recurring selling situations. This part is designed to broaden your consideration of methods and techniques for use in tactical situations, by offering you proven and effective alternatives for accomplishing prospecting, planning, and interviewing.

8

Prospecting and Preapproaching

Sales are the objectives of all personal selling activities. Sales are made to prospects; after buying, these prospects become customers. The prospect is the target of all personal selling efforts. Careless prospecting and using poor techniques are like fishing in a well. Yet thousands of salespersons start each workday without any idea of whom they are going to call on. Prospect selection is critical to sales success. Poor prospecting is responsible for a large portion of sales failures. Knowledge of techniques and information sources for more prosperous prospecting is a necessary first step in building sales plans. Enough calls on the right type of prospects, each asked to buy, will produce orders even if your presentations are deficient, your product knowledge scanty, and your level of market knowledge low. On the other hand, the best personality, presentation, product, and market knowledge are wasted on nonprospects—those unable to pay or unwilling, ineligible, or unauthorized to buy. Finding a "live" prospect—someone you feel is willing, able, eligible, and authorized to say "yes"—is only part of a sales rep's precall preparation. Each prospect must be thoroughly investigated and analyzed in order to customize an approach. In this chapter prospecting and preapproach activities leading up to planning and routing are looked into; these include:

- Understanding prospecting terms
- Qualifying prospects
- When prospecting is especially important

- Prospecting methods and techniques
- Additional prospect sources
- Ideas for better prospecting
- Preapproach investigation and analysis

UNDERSTANDING PROSPECTING TERMS

A *prospect* is a person or firm who needs or wants a product and has the ability to buy. A *lead* is a person or firm that has not yet been qualified and put into the prospect category. A *referral* is a lead that has been given to a rep by someone else—usually another customer. A *hot prospect* is someone who is considered ready to buy and deserving of immediate attention.

Qualifying Prospects

Examining leads and possible leads to determine if they might be potential buyers is known as *qualifying*. A lead or a referral becomes a prospect if the individual (1) has a need or desire for the product, (2) has the financial ability to buy, (3) is eligible to buy, and (4) has the authority to buy (1). Sales representative experience shows that people sometimes buy when there is little apparent need for a product but *want* it anyway. For example, a man bought a multithousand-dollar payroll accounting machine, although he only had two people on his payroll. Another, who wanted fancier, more expensive equipment for an accounts receivable service, insisted that if the salesperson did not show him a more elaborate posting machine, he would call a competitor. He bought the machine but failed to pay for it. After he tried the machine, he found it had *too much capacity* and was *too expensive* to operate. The key to looking for and qualifying prospects is finding need.

Some people buy unneeded things simply because they want them and have the money. Such people are rare. Individual buyers or firms must have the ability to pay—the enabling factors of money, credit, or assets that can be turned into money. Usually people or firms without ready cash or its equivalent can buy on credit, can rent, or are able to make other financial arrangements if a product is truly needed. Lack of funds to buy is more often an excuse than a real objection. If products are forced on a prospect who *really* lacks the ability to pay, a lot of time is wasted. Goods may have to be repossessed, with unhappiness resulting for everyone.

A prospect may not be eligible to buy or possess the authority to say "yes." Life insurance salespersons know that many unhealthy people who would like to buy life insurance at regular rates cannot pass the required medical examination and are, therefore, ineligible. Some drug items are only avail-

Learning how to "peck" on the right doors is the theme of this chapter.

able to physicians and pharmacists. The sale of explosives, chemicals, and guns is restricted. Sometimes only specific groups of individuals, such as students in university apartments, are eligible to rent particular real estate.

In dealing with corporate executives or employees, a sales representative must be sure that the person contacted has the *authority* to buy. Purchasing agents usually have this authority. A production worker may give an "O.K." but may not be authorized to buy. Most industrial sales representatives have experienced wasting hours talking to some official-looking corporate executive who lacks authority to buy and who has but moderate influence on a particular purchasing decision. When a lead meets all four criteria: (1) need, (2) ability, (3) eligibility, and (4) authority, that lead is *qualified* and becomes a prospect.

Qualifying Questions

Asking the right questions can tell a rep quickly if a lead is a true prospect. Potential customers can be asked directly or indirectly if they are in the market.

- If you could see that this machine would save you money, would you buy it?
- If you could make $100 per month on this merchandise rack, would you let us put one in your store?
- Would you be able to own a home in the $50,000 to $60,000 range?
- What features would you want on a boat that you would buy?

Qualifying questions save prospect and salesperson time and set a business-like tone to interviews.

WHEN PROSPECTING IS ESPECIALLY IMPORTANT

The importance of prospecting varies widely from firm to firm. Some individual sales representatives have markets so limited that there is little question of the identity of their prospects. Some salespersons, in fact, have fewer than ten special accounts and are precluded from selling to anyone else. If you were selling a product that could be used only by battery-making firms, all other firms could be eliminated. Your prospects would be easy to identify. On the other hand, when there are numerous customer types and characteristics of typical customers are not easily obtainable—no obvious, identifying characteristics—prospecting may be critical to your success. Prospecting for life insurance, investments, and office equipment is complex and involves the expenditure of a great deal of time and effort. Most firms have ideas from experience in the market as to who will buy their products. From analysis of past sales records, they can give their sales representatives rough profiles of the kinds of people who normally buy. Even if a product is new, the firm should have built it to fit specific target markets. Consequently, it should be able to describe the characteristics of individuals in those markets. Prospecting is likely to be of special importance (1) if many firms or most people can use a product; (2) if there are broad target market definitions; (3) if market identifying buyer characteristics are not readily apparent; or (4) if you sell long-lasting products to former customers. Under these conditions the potential from good prospecting methods is high and success may be determined by prospecting skill.

PROSPECTING METHODS AND TECHNIQUES

There are several systematic ways to locate and qualify prospects. The plan or combination of plans that should be followed depends on the territory, sales representative, and product. Most sales reps use all the techniques over time, unless they find that one certain method is so productive that the others are not necessary. The prospecting methods are:

- The center-of-influence method
- The spotter method
- The endless-chain method
- The observation method
- The advertising- or telephone-lead method
- The cold-canvass method

The Center-of-Influence Method

Sales representatives who have influential people—accountants, lawyers, doctors, teachers, city officials—helping them find prospects have a better chance of locating buyers. Some sales representatives make it a point to look up influential acquaintances and use them as *centers* of prospect information. Such people often belong to several clubs or organizations and come into daily contact with many people. A young woman enrolled and took courses in medical school simply to gain centers of influence for her insurance business. Denby Brandon, general agent for Pan American Insurance Company in Memphis, Tennessee, hosted a local television show that helped him gain contacts for his insurance business. Salespersons join country clubs, civic organizations, fraternal orders, and other groups to become closely acquainted with influential people. Prominent socialites, ministers, businessmen, and businesswomen who interact with many people, supervisors, coaches, and noncompetitive sales representatives are among those with respected occupations who know many people. Satisfied customers can act as centers of influence: "One sales executive described the customers of his firm as the unpaid sales force" (2). All of these people can be used as *centers of influence.*

There is almost no marketable product that cannot be sold more easily by the center-of-influence method. Referrals are among the most valuable tools available to a sales representative. As a prospecting method, the center-of-influence can be quick, inexpensive, and a formidable aid in securing interviews with prospects. Few things can assist a rep as well as satisfied customers and others who know the value of what that rep has done.

The best approach to a center of influence is low-key but honest. The sales representative can explain the product without pressure and assure the center of its quality and benefits. If the center buys from the low-key sales presentation and the product genuinely fits the buyer's needs, it is an ideal situation. If the product does not fit, the center can still recommend the rep or the product. Because of their interactions with others and their knowledge about the needs of others, centers can furnish valuable leads. They may even be persuaded to go on a sales call and introduce you. Long-term cultivation of centers is important. Sales representatives should thank these unpaid business partners and treat them as valuable. When centers give leads in *confidence,* this confidence must be respected. The center's name should not be used.

The Spotter Method

Spotters, bird dogs, or *sales associates* are different terms for people who look out for prospects for salespersons (see Photo 8.1). Spotters are sometimes paid directly for leads or prospects that result in a sale. They are gen-

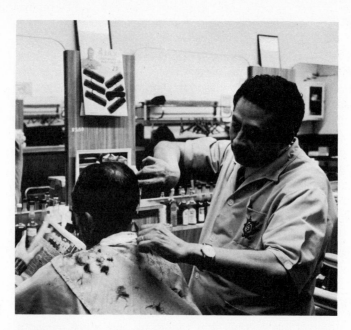

Photo 8.1

Barbers and others who come in contact with many people
are good spotters and can help the sales representative
find prospects.

erally used for information and are not expected to be important centers of
influence. Route drivers, gossips, repair people, police officers, taxi drivers,
salespersons for other products, bookkeepers, meter readers, retail clerks, in-
spectors, managers, barbers, bus drivers, secretaries, junior sales representatives, customers—people who get around and hear information about other
people—make good spotters. As mentioned in Chapter 1, Joe Girard, report-
edly the most successful automobile sales representative in the country for
years, promises his customers money for bringing in other prospects who
buy. This not only furnishes Girard with a steady stream of prospects, but it
also gives prospects another important reason for buying (3). People can earn
a little by referring qualified prospects to you, and you can earn a lot more by
selling to those prospects. Everyone gains but your competitors. But in some
places, paying spotters is illegal, so state and local laws should be checked.
Junior sales representatives are special types of spotters. They can use various prospecting methods to identify good prospects and allow senior sales
representatives to close sales. This is a productive way for new sales representatives to learn this basic step, and it allows the more experienced sales
representatives to come in and to close the sale, which reduces the risk of lost
sales.

The Endless-Chain Method

Referred prospects from satisfied buyers are often *hot leads,* especially if you have a note of introduction from the buyer or, better still, a signed letter praising your product. (See Figure 8.1.) Buyers are thought of by prospects as impartial sources of information. Actually, a new buyer has a psychological stake in praising your product. The sales manager of the Quality Stamp Com-

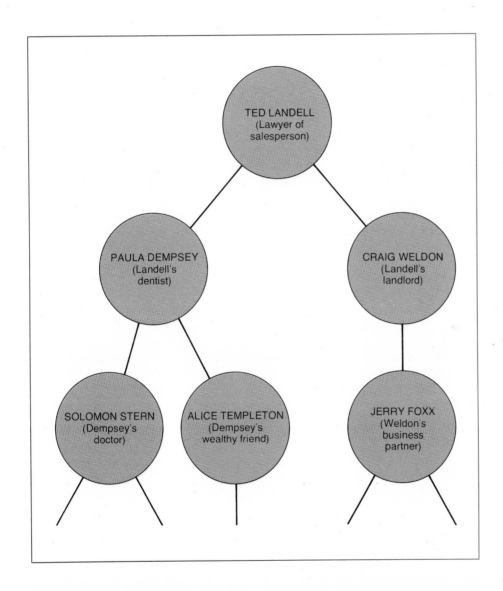

pany (trading stamps) equipped each sales representative with a notebook filled with copies of letters from satisfied customers. New accounts were hard to get, but these letters of testimony from leaders in such retail operations as gasoline service stations, dry cleaners, and clothing shops created immediate interest among prospects and helped close many deals. Using successful, well-known merchants as buyer examples, even without testimonial letters, is like magic in interesting others. Most merchants cannot afford to dismiss an offer, without consideration, that has already been accepted by successful business acquaintances. Intangibles, encyclopedias, pots and pans, and books are also sold by referrals and name dropping.

If buyers refuse to give you a letter of testimony at the time of sale, perhaps they will after using your product successfully. The chances are when you are given the names of prospects by a buyer, other needed prospect information, such as income, personal characteristics, and motivation for buying will be forthcoming. A special advantage of this method is that you not only have names, but you also have qualified prospects to see. Word-of-mouth will soon get around however, if a salesperson fails to satisfy referral customers. One disgruntled customer can negate endless-chain efforts in a small community by promoting counterinformation that embarrasses contacts and centers of influence.

The Observation Method

Salespeople can find prospects through organized observation. Insurance sales representatives look through local newspapers for marriage, birth, and death notices that signal an opportunity to sell. Marriages and births indicate an acceptance of more financial responsibility. Death reminds people that life insurance is necessary. Automobiles sales representatives may notice accident reports. Since automobile insurance pays for damaged vehicles, prospects with heavily damaged automobiles have both the need and the ability to pay. Office equipment salespersons look for new construction and fire damage in their territories (see Photo 8.2). Machines are durable, but they seldom survive fires. Again, the insurance may enable the prospect to buy. Sometimes overheard conversations furnish leads. Salespersons should always listen for leads in clubrooms, trade fairs, and other places where prospects may gather.

The Advertising- or Telephone-Lead Method

Direct mail campaigns, newspapers, magazines, and bulletin boards may create enough interest that certain prospects will contact a company either to buy a product or to find out more about it. Such advertisements can be indi-

rect, as when readers are promised a free memo book or some other type of premium for responding. One company has found it highly profitable to sell health insurance through newspaper advertisements. Real-estate brokers make heavy use of the classified sections of newspapers. Calls to all kinds of businesses are prompted by ads in the Yellow Pages. Direct mail with return postage guaranteed works for products that are bought fairly often. Trade magazines are also a good way to reach prospects in a particular industry or market segment. Interested purchasing agents may respond. When prospects return an inquiry from any advertising source, they have qualified themselves by showing a genuine interest. Most inquirers know they are extending an open invitation for a salesperson to call on them promptly. Some sales representatives even use plastic signs on their cars to invite inquiries.

The telephone is a more direct and personal method of securing leads and qualifying prospects. Telephone calls require little time and little expense. They are particularly appropriate when there are too many leads to qualify through personal visits. Securing an appointment by telephone is one way to qualify prospects, because leads who grant appointments are either interested in an offering or have little sales resistance. (See Figure 8.2 for procedures.)

Figure 8.2 Precall Planning for Telephone Prospecting

I. Establish criteria for qualifying prospects
- A. size of prospect's business
- B. type of business
- C. financial condition
- D. facilities

II. Develop a list of prospects
- A. use the criteria established above to develop the list

III. Prepare an opening statement
- A. identify yourself and your firm
- B. establish rapport to reduce negative reaction to the call
- C. make an interest-creating statement or comment that will focus the prospect's attention on your product or service
- D. example:

  "Good morning, Mr. Banning. I'm Paul Rafferty of Handy Household Products. I just heard that Banning Housewares has added another branch in Center City. Congratulations. I'm calling because I know you'll want to see a demonstration of the fantastic new floor finish we've developed that's actually tougher than wax."

- E. to establish rapport
  1. make a friendly remark
  2. mention something you and the prospect have in common
  3. tactfully acknowledge that he or she is probably busy
  4. say something to stimulate pride
- F. put yourself in your prospect's shoes in creating the interest-creating comment

IV. Prepare fact-finding questions
- A. searching questions that demand a detailed response
- B. questions that begin with *who, what, where, why,* and *how*.
- C. fact-finding questions to help you determine if the potential customer is a valid prospect
- D. example:

  "What type of truck tires do you stock?"

V. Prepare a sales message
- A. stress benefits over features
- B. use a sales vocabulary

VI. Prepare your request for an appointment
- A. the request should include a lead-in

  "I would like to meet with you to show you in detail how our Model X-5 can increase your sales volume."

- B. the request for an appointment should be based on several product benefits, not just one
- C. in requesting the appointment with an actual question, give your prospect a choice:

  "Would ten o'clock Wednesday morning or three o'clock Friday afternoon be better for you?"

Source: Phone-Power Self-Instruction Kit, Courtesy of Bell Telephone Company, Memphis, Tennessee.

Another advantage to the telephone is that a sales representative's secretary or spouse can make the calls to assure that valuable personal interview time is spent with genuine prospects. What a difference this makes in sales volume!

Telephone prospecting has proved to be particularly effective for locating prospects for automobiles, investments, and other intangibles: "Records show that from five to eight good prospects may be secured out of each 100 telephone calls made when prospecting for life insurance and health-and-accident customers. Good salespeople have closed between 40 and 50 percent of the prospects secured in this manner" (4).

With rising fuel and other sales call costs, the use of the telephone as a prospecting tool seems likely to grow. As a 1982 Bell System ad advises, the Yellow Pages is a "Who's Who in Business" that tell "who's where and what's what" (5). It is an old technique of industrial sales reps to check the ads in the Yellow Pages and to "qualify" potential prospects by ad size and placement. The new Business to Business Yellow Pages available in many metropolitan areas increase the possibilities for use of the telephone book as a prospect list. Todd Chemical Company, a marketer of floor cleaners and waxes, has gained as many as 700 new accounts a month through nine telephone sales reps who make eighteen to twenty-four calls a day (6).

The Cold-Canvass Method

The cold-canvass method can be productive and is helpful if no other method proves fruitful. It involves calling on every door that might have a use for a product. It works best with products that nearly everyone needs—encyclopedias, Bibles, automobiles, typewriters, pocket calculators, vacuum cleaners, home appliances, and other tangibles. Calling cold for insurance and investments works less well. These products require a more professional approach in order to maintain image.

Sometimes, instead of calling at every door, sales representatives pattern their canvassing. An office equipment sales representative might select particular professional people from the phone book. An air-conditioning salesperson may call only on homes without central air conditioning—suspects who by observation should be the best prospects. Door-to-door salesworkers frequently ask about prospects in a neighborhood. Aluminum cookware sales representatives, for example, might ask where single young working women under the age of thirty-five live, since they are more likely to buy expensive sets of cooking utensils. After finding primary prospects, a sales representative may go into an endless-chain plan.

For some products, cold canvassing is best. It covers all bases and depends on selling percentages. There may be less competition with prospects identified by this method. Only a few seconds need be spent at places that

Cold canvassing may not be the best way to prospect, but it frequently uncovers a potential customer with a need.

obviously do not have potential. A cold canvasser who visits and tarries too long with nonprospects is violating the very spirit of cold canvassing. If places canvassed contain no prospects and the occupants do not recommend any, a rep should leave gracefully but quickly.

ADDITIONAL PROSPECT SOURCES

Internal Records

In addition to regular prospecting techniques, there are many specific sources of names and information that can yield good returns. A fruitful and inexpensive source of prospects is internal records kept by a sales representative's company. Credit departments keep customer and purchase records, which can furnish vital qualifying information.

Service Personnel

Coordination with service department repair personnel is important for industrial equipment, automobiles, office equipment, and other products that require servicing. Service personnel either visit customer facilities or repair equipment in branch service centers. In either case, they are in an excellent position to recommend new equipment to prospects and to inform salespeople when products need replacing. Often, service personnel sell operating supplies. A sales representative can help them in return for vital information concerning major replacements. A close rapport with repair personnel can be like having a business partner.

No rep should depend on the firm to keep all the records. Each sales representative needs to keep individual, territory records. This is especially true if you sell durables to a limited number of customers. You should have a file for each customer, and if your products are big and expensive, a file for each product. Files should give an idea of when equipment will need replacing. Other important internal sources are managers and fellow sales representatives. A company sales force should be a team where everyone works to win sales.

Use of Directories or Lists

Again, the Yellow Pages telephone directory is a good source for prospects. It classifies business firms and professional persons (listing them in alphabetical order and furnishing addresses and phone numbers). Other important directories are the Thomas Register, Dun and Bradstreet directories, College Placement *Annual,* and *Fortune* directories. Trade associations representing target customers are a good source of information. Chambers of commerce and Welcome Wagon personnel can supply lists of old and new firms to help qualify prospects. Care must be taken to maintain good relations with such sources. List brokers and others sell lists for a living. Here, cost must be balanced against possible gains.

Group or Party Plans

Some products are sold by party plans. Women's clubs anxious to raise money for various projects may agree to listen to a sales presentation for a reasonable "donation." Demonstrations of products before large groups of prospects are ideal because they are economical in time and word-of-mouth interaction generates interest. Almost everyone is familiar with plasticware parties, where hostesses are rewarded for letting sales representatives demonstrate products' uses to friends and acquaintances in the hostess's home. Salespersons for some soaps and other home products operate in the same way. A salesperson who can arrange to show products before large groups of prospects should do well.

Fairs, Shows, and Exhibits

Sales representatives often consider exhibiting at fairs or trade shows as a public relations duty done for the firm rather than as an opportunity to make sales. Initial contacts with important prospects and unexpected sales can be made this way. One office-machine corporation demonstrates equipment at business schools of universities to reach future executives before they are in any position to buy. A wise salesperson talks to students (many of whom have parents in business) to secure present and future leads by asking careful questions. Some office-machine companies have schools to train machine operators. Not only can they supply trained personnel for firms that might hesitate to buy the equipment without operators, but these graduates are important prospect-generating sources who influence future purchases.

Contests

Contests can be another angle in prospecting strategy. Those registering for prizes at least show interest in a product. This is especially true if the product itself is the prize. Contest rules usually require contestants to make a statement about a product or to consider product benefits in some way. Contestants become prospects who have to sell themselves to make a good entry. Sampling a product to be able to turn in labels to qualify entry is another contest technique that generates prospects.

Other Sales Representatives

Fellow sales representatives and competitive salespersons can help you find prospects. In the search for prospects, every sales representative will uncover potential customers who are in fellow salespersons' territories. Colleagues also uncover leads. Cooperation means more sales for everyone. Sometimes, competitive sales representatives cannot supply a customer with a needed product. If you have good relations with competitors and help them in similar situations, they may refer that customer to you. All kinds of salespersons make good spotters because they know the value of good spotters. Some sales representatives even hire full-time employees whose sole responsibility is to spot prospects.

IDEAS FOR BETTER PROSPECTING

Although these are the main methods and sources of prospects, there are several ideas or principles that can make for better prospecting.

Classify Prospects

An important concept is to group potential buyers. New business can come from present customers, old customers who have not bought lately, lost customers, and new prospects. *Old Customers* who haven't bought lately certainly deserve attention. Every effort should be made to discern their reasons for not ordering recently. Are they buying from a competitor? Is there something new to offer them that was not available at the time of the last call? Or have they just been neglected? *Present customers* are even more important. They are probably the best prospects for new business. The easiest way to increase sales is by selling more to current customers. Do they know about the whole line? *Lost customers* need to be found. The fact that a prospect now buys from a competitor is no reason to write that prospect off. The competitive substitute may be giving so much trouble that the lost customer may acknowledge a mistake and start buying from you again. Prospects prejudiced against a company because of misunderstandings with an earlier sales rep can be brought back to company products by attention and diplomacy. *New prospects,* however, are the building blocks of business. This means no rep should ever be satisfied by just calling on present customers. Sales representatives who cut their lunch hour short to do a little canvassing or make a few extra calls at the end of a selling day usually get more orders than those who do not. The number of prospects must always be kept up, for to run out of prospects is to run out of opportunity (see Figure 8.3).

Be Mentally Set

Cybernetics also works in prospecting. Sales representatives should program themselves to be continually alert and to listen for prospect information. You should be actively discovering new ways to find new prospects all the time. Prospects for most products can be anywhere. This mental set should motivate you to ask many people many questions and may lead to more sales.

Know Whom You Are Going to Call On
Before You Leave the Office

It is a good idea to make a prospect list for each week, subject to change, before going to work on Monday. This gives both purpose and motivation. Each night, territorial possibilities should be reviewed and the next morning's calls planned. Reconsideration and revision ought to take place the next morning before the first call.

Figure 8.3   Prospecting Methods and Source Summary Table

METHODS	STRATEGIES
Center of Influence	Persuade influential and/or important people (those who interact often with prospects and customers) to help you prospect.
Spotters	Persuade people who are not centers of influence, but who are in a position to gain information about other people, to help you prospect.
Endless Chain	Ask everyone you interview for the names of potential buyers.
Observation	Be alert for various changes and events in your territory that might affect your sales, by watching, reading, or listening.
Advertising or Telephone	Use these communication aids to prospect directly and inexpensively.
Cold Canvass	Knock on every door in a prospecting area to uncover potential buyers.
Internal Records	Gather information from company records that may point you to prospects.
Service Personnel	Work closely with repair persons and other personnel who visit customers and who may tell you when customers need to buy again.
Directories or Lists	Gather information from these sources that may help you contact prospects.
Group or Party Plans	Use this plan to allow many types of people to witness the product at once, saving time and causing word-of-mouth interaction.
Fairs and Exhibits	Demonstrate the product when interested people gather and get names and addresses for interviews.
Contests	Use contests to find out who is interested in your product.
Other Sales Representatives	Swap information with other sales representatives (colleagues and competitors) who can find prospects for you.

Keep a Customer Record Book

Remember that everyone forgets. You will forget important facts about a prospect unless you keep a book with the names and pertinent information about all your better customers. Jot down in a *prospect book* everything about customers that might help you sell them on future calls (see Figure 8.4).

Set Up Customers for the Next Sale When an Order Is Signed

While installing bookkeeping machines, successful office-machines sales representatives remind new buyers that the machine should be traded in at a

> *Walker Mfg. Co. - Leeds Street*
> Silas Walker (5 minutes) Interview on June 6 at 10 a.m. Good prospect! Has need with 500 employees. Manual system with little proof - could justify equipment on proof and time savings of payroll alone. Possible payback period in 2 years. *Note:* Walker is 44, extrovert, tends to talk off the subject, very pleasant personality. (Do survey)
>
> *Bentco Wholesale Co. - Leeds Street*
> Not a prospect at present. Has competitive equipment, so recheck periodically - might have to go to larger system in 2 years and trade in. Mr. Todd is new man.
>
> *Meltone Acceptance Corp. - Dale Street*
> James Elrod, President. Interview on June 8 at 9:45 a.m. Key Prospect!! Probably needs the E-1900 to computerize workload, present system is cumbersome. Work up sketch for Elrod. Sell complete survey of present operations. Note: Elrod is 54, very temperamental, very egotistical. (Could be a gold mine here.)

Figure 8.4   Prospect Book Scratch Notes

specific time. The rep would suggest that if business increased at its present rate, there would be a need for a new posting machine in so many months, or that with the present rate of tax credit for new investments, the customer's corporation should keep equipment as modern as possible and trade it in every three years. Prospects primed during a previous sale are set up for the next closing effort.

Do Not Prejudge Prospects

There is a difference between qualifying and prejudging prospects. Sometimes a prospect's appearance might indicate poverty when the exact opposite is true. Qualifying should be based as much as possible on facts and not on responses to sketchy information or personal bias. The person who is a prospect but does not appear to be may well not have been pressured by competitors and may be much more approachable than the obvious prospect. Some of the best fruit is hidden under the leaves.

PREAPPROACHING

After a prospect has been qualified as a potential buyer, it still may not be time to make a sales presentation. The preapproach involves all the necessary preparations that must be completed before a target prospect is called on. To call on a prospect "cold," with no knowledge of needs, problems, personality, or peculiarities indicates intent to treat all potential buyers alike. To treat all prospects alike shows an unwillingness to make adjustments to individual personalities and needs. Such an unwillingness is inconsistent with the basic ideas of marketing. When sales representatives approach prospects with vital information about specific prospect problems, they flatter the prospect by their interest. Prospects are likely to respond favorably to such a "professional." Preknowledge of buyers allows customization of strategy. Thus preapproaching involves:

- Strategic information about the buyer and firm
- Obtaining preapproach information from competent sources
- Ensuring a good reception

Strategic Information About the Buyer and Firm

The critical phase of a successful sales call is preapproaching. Sales reps must know that their prospects—whether current buyers or not—will benefit from what will be offered. To assure that prospects have the information needed to make a "buy" or "no-buy" decision, reps must know their prospects almost better than the prospects know themselves. Each prospect's lacks, wants, needs, and desires contribute to favorable or unfavorable decisions about presentations. The process is called *preapproaching* to emphasize the kinds of information that are necessary *before* a sales call is made or an appointment sought. The most important bit of information a salesperson needs to be effective with prospects is the answer to the question each prospect asks when a sales presentation is made: "What is in it for me?" Lower costs, higher profits, enhanced chances for personal recognition and promotion are all among the reasons prospects buy. By taking time to prepare carefully necessary information about prospect needs, reps can save considerable time in presentations and even reduce the number of presentations that must be made (7).

Personal Information. Practically everything that can be found out about a prospect can be used strategically. This type of information is so important in some industries that sales managers urge their sales representatives to make fact-finding calls on buyers before attempting any persuasive calls. You should know a potential buyer's full name, whether he or she wishes to be addressed formally or informally, and the person's position and authority in the company in regard to buying your product. The person's educational background and technical competence, interests and hobbies, and even social affiliations are all important data to reps who would succeed. Figures 8.5 and 8.6 present two preapproach sales call planning forms. Each has much to offer, but the more detailed format of Figure 8.6 digs deeper into possible answers to the eternal prospect question of what are the personal benefits of accepting a particular offering. Knowing a prospect's interests and hobbies helps establish commonness and rapport. Knowing a prospect's politics and philosophies makes it possible to avoid saying something offensive. All people are interested in their families. Buying behavior often reflects this interest. Specifically knowing what people do during the workday makes it possible to approach them under the best of circumstances and at the right time. Certainly, individual needs for a product and ability to pay for it are essential preapproach information. How each individual prospect treats sales representatives, how each likes to be approached, how each likes to buy, what times each likes to be visited, how each usually pays for purchases, and who else influences decisions are must information for salespeople who would succeed at meeting wants and needs through selling.

Personality Traits. Prospect personality traits are important to strategy. Is the person an introvert or an extrovert? Are there personality needs, such as a need to dominate or a need to feed the ego? Is there susceptibility to flattery? Does the prospect drive a hard bargain? Is the prospect truthful? Does

Figure 8.5 SALES CALL PLANNER

Account _____

Person to See _____

OBJECTIVE of this call (What do you want *HIM* to do?)

_____

_____

1. OPENER (Attention and interest into your story)

_____

_____

2. QUALIFYING QUESTIONS (What additional information do you need?)

_____

_____

_____

3. FEATURES	4. BENEFITS	5. PROOF

6. OBJECTIONS you can anticipate:

The Objection:	Your Answer:

7. THE CLOSE: List three preplanned closing questions to determine whether you have achieved your call objective:

Source: "Pre Call Planning," *Principles of Professional Salesmanship* (New York: American Management Associations, 1977), p. 82. (Italics added).

this prospect have any peculiarities in dealing with sales representatives? A prospect with a reputation for being argumentative and overbearing with sales representatives interpreted the salesperson's arguing back as "believing in the product." Armed with this information, the sales representative made an exception to the rule of never arguing with a prospect and answered him forcefully. The prospect bought.

The Total Buying Situation. When sales representatives consider a corporation or a business firm as a potential buyer, they must gather information about the total buying situation or corporate decision unit. Company name and location are essential for research and routing and must be determined. The purpose of the business and the product assortment it sells give clues to needs. Usually, the volume of business also affects a firm's purchasing potential. The way the firm is organized indicates approach strategy. Who in the firm initiates purchases for a particular type of product? Who uses the product? Who else influences the purchase? Does the purchasing agent have sole authority? Or does the decision to buy rest with engineering or accounting? A firm's financial capabilities should be determined relative to financing purchases. The credit position and liquidity of a firm determine its ability to pay and indicate whether or not a sales representative should press for rental or extended terms for high-dollar items. The vocabulary used in the trade should be known to give salespersons insight and to create an impression of being "insiders."

The Firm's Problems. The firm's problems are the focal point of selling strategy. Problems that can be alleviated or solved by your products constitute selling opportunities. Sometimes a question session is necessary before real problems are uncovered. It is helpful to review all previous contacts with a prospect firm if you have them in your internal records.

Obtaining Preapproach Information from Competent Sources

General Sources. The sources of preapproach information are for the most part the same as the sources already mentioned for identifying and qualifying prospects. Preapproaching, however, involves deeper research and indicates more detailed questioning of sources who know more than just names and possible needs. *Chambers of commerce personnel* usually have detailed knowledge about operations of important area businesses. *Trade association secretaries* often keep clippings with details about successes and problems of industry firms. Certainly, *employees of a prospect firm* are in a position to tell a great deal about who really makes buying decisions and about how they are made. *Secretaries of prospective buyers* may be open in revealing strategic facts. They are also in an excellent position to know about buyer problems and competitive activity.

Analysis of *credit ratings* and annual reports reveals financial strengths, weaknesses, and buying-power information. A *diary* of past dealings with specific prospects can prove an invaluable aid in gathering and interpreting preapproach data. Government records and publications—especially *The Census of Manufacturers* and *The Census of Business* should not be overlooked.

The Preliminary Call. System sales representatives may call on prospects to gain preapproach information for proposals before making sales calls aimed at signed orders. Prospects themselves are usually the best sources of information about themselves. In such cases, sales representatives must first sell

Figure 8.6 BLUEPRINT: PREPARATION

My prospect's name is (I'm sure how it is spelled and pronounced) _____
Prospect's exact title is _____
The complete name of prospect's company is _____
Business address _____
Business phone _____
Home address _____
What are prospect's duties? _____
How long in this business? _____
Marital and/or family status _____
Outside interests, hobbies, sports, etc. _____
_____

What industries does prospect's business serve? _____
_____

Can this person say "yes" to my proposal? _____
Who are the major buying influentials? Rank them in order of importance. _____
_____
_____

What distribution channels does the company use? _____
_____

What are the primary market areas served?
   National _____
   Regional _____
   Local _____
   State (list) _____

Company credit rating _____
What information do I need from my prospect? _____
_____

From other sources? _____
Prospect's problem is _____
Is prospect aware of this problem? _____
How I plan to make prospect aware of problem _____
_____

My recommendation to answer prospect's problem _____
_____

Exactly how it will benefit prospect? _____

_____

What does prospect want from me? _____

Why does prospect want it? The "real reason," prospect's personal buying motives _____

_____

What prospect lacks or needs _____

_____

_____

My most important authentic preapproach information is _____

_____

From conversation with:

   Other customers _____

   Prospect's accountant _____

   Prospect's banker _____

   Prospect's attorney _____

From observation:

   Pictures in office _____

   Awards in office _____

   Literature in office _____

   General environment _____

Do I know anyone whose opinion prospect values, who can lay some groundwork, get information, or get an appointment for me? _____

_____

Present source prospect buys from _____

_____

Competitor's financial strength _____

Present price _____

Our price _____

Is prospect a previous customer? _____ Satisfied customer? _____

_____

Why or why not? _____

Best sales contact time _____

Any extra costs to acquire and maintain this business? _____

_____

Account potential:

   Revenue _____

   Quantity _____

Source: James F. Robeson, H. Lee Matthews, and Carl G. Stevens, *Selling* (Homewood, Ill.: Irwin, 1978), pp. 88–89.

Prospecting and Preapproaching

the operations survey or fact-finding interview. Asking for executive time is like asking for money. Some executive prospects resist such surveys, feeling that they disrupt normal activities, constitute a threat to a firm's right to privacy, or create obligations to purchase. Most potential buyers, however, realize that a sales representative selling industrial systems or accounting equipment or even raw material or ancillary supplies is unable to analyze problems and serve needs without detailed operational information. If prospective buying executives decide that a sales representative is a professional who may be able to suggest possible improvements without threatening the executive's position in the firm, they normally will permit the necessary information gathering. It is best to get permission from an authoritative executive to make needs surveys, if contact with the right employees is desired and suspicion is to be avoided.

Ensuring a Good Reception

Preapproach activity includes mentally preparing a prospect for a call. The more positive information prospects have about a represented company and its products before a call, the more receptive they will be to a sales presentation. Direct mail advertising explaining product benefits, or even a personal letter, may be sent ahead to pave the way for an interview appointment request. Buyers often need time to consider the merits of offerings and may resist the closing appeals of sales representatives who call without sending information ahead to start the deliberating process. Thorough planning of the time and setting of the call are relevant to receptivity.

SUMMARY

This chapter has introduced specific techniques for selling. Prospecting is a vital early step in the selling process. For many sales representatives, separating good prospects from poor ones through determining needs and the ability to buy is critical to effective and efficient selling strategy. Salespersons with products whose prospective buyers are hardest to identify have the greatest need to use tested prospecting methods.

Prospects can be found by using the center-of-influence method, the spotter method, the endless-chain method, the observation method, the advertising- or telephone-lead method, and/or the cold-canvass method. Other sources of names and information about prospects include internal company records, sales representatives' prospect records, lists and directories, fairs and exhibits, party plans, contests, and other salespersons. Sales representatives should remember that they can sell more by reactivating old customers, selling more products to current customers, affording tactful attention to lost customers, and actively searching for new buyers. Good prospecting also involves being mentally set to look for prospects, planning calls from prospect lists, keeping a diary about customers' habits and purchases, preparing buyers for becoming prospects again, asking questions frequently, and not prejudging whether or not a prospect is qualified.

Preapproach information is necessary before detailed plans for visiting a prospect can be formulated. Such knowledge permits the customization of selling strategy. It is important to know about a prospect's personality, interests, and special needs. Often it is good strategy to make a special visit to a prospect's place of business to survey problems in detail before attempting to make a selling approach. Preapproach information can be obtained from chambers of commerce, trade associations, employees of a prospect's firm, credit ratings, financial statements, and other sales representatives. Advertising or personal letters should be sent ahead to prepare a prospect for an actual approach.

REVIEW QUESTIONS

1. What do you understand by the following terms?
   a. prospect
   b. hot prospect
   c. lead
   d. referral

2. What is required for a lead to become a prospect?

3. In what ways can a prospect with no cash resources still be a viable prospect?

4. Under what circumstances is prospecting of particular importance to the sales representative?

5. Outline the various prospecting methods and techniques.

6. Outline the precall planning process for telephone prospecting.

7. What are some in-firm prospect sources?

8. Name some directories or lists that are good prospect sources.

9. Briefly describe group or party plans as a prospecting and selling technique.

10. Discuss the advantages and disadvantages of contests as a method of generating prospects.

11. What are the four categories of prospect types?

12. Suggest seven ideas for more effective prospecting.

13. What is involved in the preapproach process?

14. What are the major items of personal information about the prospect that the salesperson should determine prior to the sales call?

15. What should be known about the firm prior to the sales call?

16. How does preapproach information compare with information obtained in identifying and qualifying prospects?

17. What are some sources of preapproach information?

APPLICATION QUESTIONS

You have just started working for Sears, Roebuck, selling IBM personal computers. This morning, your sales manager met with you and the other salespeople. During this meeting she said, "In order to be successful, we need to identify the best prospects and determine ways to reach these people. Please give me your ideas about how you intend to locate and qualify prospects."

a. How would you suggest using each of the six prospecting methods mentioned in the text?

b. Which of the six methods would probably yield the most prospects?

c. IBM has been advertising this new product in the *Wall Street Journal, Fortune,* and other publications. Find one of these ads. How could you make use of this ad to develop prospects?

INCIDENTS

8–1

Wilsher Corporation is a large, nationally known company in the office equipment and supplies field. The most recent addition to the Wilsher line is a new copier. Like the copiers of Xerox and IBM, Wilsher's new copier makes dry, electrostatic copies. Ken Adams and Bill Renner, sales reps for Wilsher, were hired as part of Wilsher's program to introduce its new copier. Each has been with Wilsher about six months. The new division in which they work was organized after Wilsher's management decided that its existing sales force could not handle the aggressive sales effort needed to introduce its new copier and still continue to meet its obligations to customers for its other products. After attending a weekly sales meeting at Wilsher's branch office in Detroit, Ken and Bill have gone for coffee together.

Ken: Boy, Gaffney was really after me today, wasn't he? All that stuff about prospecting. Hell, what I need isn't more prospecting, what I need is a bigger territory. Everybody I meet already has an IBM or a Xerox. I just wish Gaffney would say something specific about where I ought to go to find more prospects. All he does is criticize. What's your schedule like today? You seem to have a really good territory with lots of possibles.

Bill: Well, here's my list for this week. First stop, Troutbrook Community College to demonstrate how our new machine makes transparencies as easily as regular copies and at less cost than on a Thermofax. Then, during lunch, I'm driving over to the Central Library.

They may be putting in several machines in their periodicals department. After that, I'm scheduled to see a couple of accountants in the same neighborhood. After that, I'm going to do some phoning to try to line up some appointments for Friday afternoon. My vet told me about two friends who are opening new offices. I hope to give them our billing and records presentation.

Ken: Friday afternoon? It's only Monday morning. You sure are lucky to have a growth territory. I've hit my schools, banks, everybody. It's all over among the accounts I've been assigned.

Bill: What about your insurance agents? Our new copier seems ideal for them. I got a big order from Builders' Materials last week—for billing applications. It made me start thinking about architects and licensed engineers—I'm seeing my first architect on Thursday. And that order I got from that small CPA outfit last September was worth an extra 5 percent in my bonus. That's what got me started looking up accountants in the Yellow Pages. The Yellow Pages are also good for finding those doctors and dentists that operate out of offices in their homes.

Ken: I've been working the referral approach myself. You know, getting physicians to give me names of friends. I haven't tried the phone book yet. I guess it'd be better than driving around looking for them.

Bill: Didn't you sell a machine to Leitner Electric a couple of months ago? I noticed driving home the other night that they're building a new office way out on Woodward in your territory. They must be expanding. Why not try them? Joe Leitner is happy with his machine, isn't he?

Ken: How should I know? Love 'em and leave 'em, that's me. But thanks for the tip. I'll hightail it right out there from here. Hope Joe's in. I guess Gaffney's not all wrong—I may just need to do a little more planning. I just don't like his constant Monday morning probings about what I've got on for the week. Hey, it's a quarter after ten!

Bill: Yeah, time to hit the trail. It'll take me about five minutes to get over to Troutbrook and my appointment's at ten-thirty. I like to make sure I'm always a little early. Take care, Ken.

QUESTIONS

1. Who is the more likely to succeed in the long run as a sales rep for Wilsher, Ken or Bill?

2. If you were Mort Gaffney, how would you approach Ken to increase his prospecting effectiveness? Are probes at the Wilsher branch office's Monday morning sales meetings enough?

8–2

Susan White sells securities for a national brokerage firm. One of Susan's biggest assets in the business is Dr. Edwin Basalt, a general practitioner, who has recommended Susan's services to over twenty-five other doctors. Susan has even been able to establish other centers of influence in the medical community as a result of Dr. Basalt's support. Just a week ago, Susan heard something that greatly upset her. She heard from Dr. Blanton, another customer, that Dr. Basalt had told him that he was going to use another broker. Susan knew that the stock market as a whole had gone down in the last few weeks, but she had told Dr. Basalt that she expected it to go down and had advised him to sell some of his more speculative issues. Then she remembered that Basalt had bought a stock against her recommendation. She looked it up to make sure and there it was. Basalt had purchased 1,000 shares of Alacon at $79.50 a share, and it had gone down to $33. Susan remembered cautioning him against buying the stock but wrote it up anyway when Basalt insisted.

Dr. Basalt was pretty cold over the phone but agreed to see Susan for just a minute or two. Susan was very polite as usual but asked Dr. Basalt directly about the Alacon deal. Basalt answered that the loss on the Alacon deal was only part of it. He said that there were two other stocks that he wanted to buy that went up even in the face of the bearish market, and he would have made $20,000 on those two stocks if he had trusted his own inclinations and bought them when he wanted to. He finished his explanation with this sentence: "I don't know, Susan; I like you, but you don't seem to give good advice anymore."

How should Susan handle this situation?

8–3

Jack Schindler, a new representative for Schindler Supply Co., of Parkersville, Wisconsin, has a territory that extends from Green Bay in the north down through Port Edwards and Madison into Parkersville. When his uncle hired him, he told Jack that he'd have "a tough row to hoe" in rebuilding his territory up to its real potential. The company has many accounts in the area, but most of the business has come in without active sales cultivation. Most of the largest accounts in the area—the Charmin Division of Procter & Gamble in Green Bay, Allis-Chalmers in Milwaukee, American Motors in Kenosha and Racine, and others—are in the hands of competitors. As a major mill supply house, Schindler has a complete line of materials suited to most manufacturers' needs. Historically, Schindler, which has a sales force of eight, has focused its efforts to the south and west of Parkersville toward Rockford, Illinois, and the Quad-City area, with its many farm-implement plants.

Jack realizes that getting any major business away from competitors in his territory will take time and require active solicitation. Still, Jack is anxious to get on with his life after four years at the University of Wisconsin in Madison. Rather than meet Schindler's competitors head on in major accounts, Jack decides to see if quick volume and commissions can be found among his territory's smaller accounts, where the competition might not be so strong.

While at Wisconsin, Jack had taken a course in personal selling in which several prospecting systems were discussed. One of the systems that he remembered as seeming to be a good one was that of examining present accounts and then contacting their direct competitors. For example, if Chief Oshkosh Brewery was a good account, then White Cap Brewery probably would be also. If John Deere or International Harvester bought certain items in the Quad-City area, Allis-Chalmers probably bought similar items.

Jack thinks this system might be hard to apply in his territory, where Schindler, while not unknown, is not a major supplier to any of the key accounts. Passing through Madison, on his way north, Jack decides to see if the University bookstore has any used copies of the textbook used in his personal selling course. He thinks the discussion of prospecting might give him ideas that he could apply in his territory. When he gets back to his motel room in Wisconsin Rapids that night after dinner, Jack finds a note from a Wisconsin classmate tucked in his door. The classmate, Bud Weir, had noticed Jack's name on a registration card when he checked in to the motel while Jack was out to dinner. Jack calls Bud, and the two get together. Jack asked Bud, who had gone through a sales training program at Schindler headquarters, about prospecting. The two sit down to review prospecting systems in the textbook for application to Jack's territory.

Put yourself in the place of Jack's classmate. How would you go about helping Jack to evolve a prospecting system?

What specific steps should Jack take each time he comes into a new town?

NOTES

1. Carlton A. Pederson, Milburn D. Wright, and Barton A. Weitz, *Selling: Principles and Methods,* 7th ed. (Homewood, Ill.: Irwin, 1981), pp. 186–187.

2. Gary M. Griksheit, Harold C. Cash, and W. J. E. Crissy, *Handbook of Selling: Psychological, Managerial, and Marketing Bases* (New York: Ronald Press Wiley, 1981), p. 403.

3. "Autos Joe," *Newsweek,* July 2, 1973, pp. 62–63.

4. Pederson, Wright, and Weitz, *Selling: Principles and Methods,* pp. 203–206.

5. Bell System Yellow Pages, "Who's Who in Business," advertisement, *Wall Street Journal,* May 11, 1981, p. 56.

6. Frederic A. Russell, Frank H. Beach, Richard H. Buskirk, *Selling: Principles and Practices,* 11th ed. (New York: McGraw-Hill, 1982), p. 205.

7. James F. Robeson, H. Lee Matthews, and Carl G. Stevens, *Selling* (Homewood, Ill.: Irwin, 1978), p. 85.

Planning and Approaching

Sales managers and trainers agree that sales representatives who consistently produce high sales volume are better organizers and planners than those who do not. Good planning will help you by:

- Assuring that you assign priorities to your scarce time
- Furnishing organization to coordinate your efforts
- Reminding you of what you need to do to reach your goals
- Providing you with standards to help you measure your progress

Planning is especially important after preapproach information is assembled and before prospect contact. The most productive of all nonselling time can be the time you spend organizing and interpreting prospect information and translating this into a persuasive strategy. Planning, however, must begin before this. This chapter treats planning from yearly goal setting through selection of approach methods. It will cover:

- Planning by objectives
- Planning aids
- Time and territory management
- Considerations in the approach
- Approach methods

PLANNING BY OBJECTIVES

Sales representatives should *plan by objectives* if they work independently or their firm has not adopted a *management by objectives* program. The first step in all constructive planning is to establish goals to direct efforts. Goals should be written, precisely stated, and provide obtainable targets. In many organizations, sales managers hold yearly Management by Objectives (MBO) conferences with each sales representative. At these conferences, sales quotas are determined and agreed upon. Detailed subobjectives, such as the number of calls and demonstrations necessary for that sales representative to reach an individual sales quota, are part of a territorial MBO plan (see Figure 9.1). A good plan includes a statement of the specific criteria against which performance will be reviewed and judged. Review provides feedback to a salesperson on progress in successfully accomplishing subobjectives (1). A well-thought-out review reveals whether or not sales representatives have averaged the four demonstrations daily to which they committed themselves to reach their sales goals. (MBO will be discussed further in Chapter 15.) If a salesperson's firm does not practice *management by objectives,* that salesperson would do well to set overall, detailed personal goals. Setting up a self-appraisal method to show failure or success in meeting standards can tell the rep whether the number of presentations, prospecting calls, and demonstrations planned have been made. Such a program can furnish motivation to do and sell more.

Goal setting is normally based on a review of past experiences. After sales representatives submit daily sales reports with details about calls and other activities, computers can analyze the data. Information about characteristics of better customers and the conditions under which they buy can be abstracted from these data. Such an analysis can then become a basis for setting new personal planning priorities. Typically, about 80 percent of sales come from about 20 percent of the customers in a given territory. Other past information helpful in setting new standards might be:

- The average number of sales calls made each day
- The number of calls on existing versus potential accounts
- The average time spent on each call compared with travel time to each call
- Waiting time
- Nonselling time for each day
- Number of presentations made
- Cost and profitability of the average call (2)

After past accomplishments have been examined, new goals should be specified. Goals should be translated into specific dollar, unit, and percentage increases in sales. Subgoals can take the form of increases in number of daily

Figure 9.1 MBO Planning Card

SALES YEAR <u>1983</u>

MBO CARD FOR <u>John Rankin</u>

INTERVIEW DATE <u>3</u> JANUARY <u>1983</u>

TIME AND LENGTH OF INTERVIEW <u>8:30 am</u> TO <u>9:15 am</u>

TERRITORY DESCRIPTION: Between the parkways
from the river east

PLANNED GOALS		ACTUAL	
TOTAL $ SALES	$ 240,000	$	
PRODUCT I	120,000		
PRODUCT II	70,000		
PRODUCT III	50,000		
TOTAL UNIT SALES	87		
PRODUCT I	50		
PRODUCT II	20		
PRODUCT III	17		

DEMONSTRATIONS (PER WEEK)

PRODUCT I	9		(AVG.)
PRODUCT II	3		(AVG.)
PRODUCT III	3		(AVG.)
INTERVIEWS (PER WEEK)	30		(AVG.)
COLLECTION CALLS (PER WEEK)	7		(AVG.)
INTERVIEWS PER SALE			
**PERCENT QUOTA	%		

calls, orders per call, or in average order size. An increased number of new or of cold-canvass exploratory calls each week can serve as an extension of subgoals (3). Each new plan gives a clearer idea of what can be done to reach new goals and make more profit. Records also indicate practices that should be discontinued. If analysis of past records indicates that more than two call-backs on insurance prospects are unprofitable, future call scheduling should exclude a third call-back to permit more effective use of time.

A good overall objective should be stated in monetary terms and should require action from prospects. It is important to set dates for specifically stated goal accomplishment; these are fixed only after prospect operations, prospect dissatisfactions, and competitors are understood and identified (4).

Daily planning becomes easier once general objective goals are specified. The first step in deciding on the specifics of a daily plan is a mental review of daily subgoals aimed at reaching yearly and monthly targets. A good procedure for selecting daily plan details is to write down each night all activities that should be done the next day. Priorities should be assigned to each planned activity. The selling day should start with priority one and determination to see it through to completion (5). Reviewing the next day's plan the night before programs the subconscious and promotes motivation and direction. It allows review the next morning, when the mind is fresh to reaffirm priorities. With definite goals set, there is little danger that productive selling time will be spent in a coffee shop frantically trying to decide where and how to start the day. A daily priority list should be adhered to closely unless an emergency develops or common sense dictates changes. This type of programming holds in check the human tendency to neglect important items through becoming sidetracked into spending too much time on the unimportant.

PLANNING AIDS

Certain reports, files, and schedules can make planning easier and should be used if they are practical and fit a rep's needs. *Call reports* that analyze opportunity and set new objectives, already mentioned, cannot be overemphasized. They are a valuable personal planning tool as well as a means to inform management of your activity. Almost 70 percent of firms that use call reports require salespersons to include every call made. Call reports should be filled out carefully, while details are still fresh. *Time and duty analysis forms,* which divide a salesperson's working day into half-hour periods, allow specific activities for many days to be recorded. The detail contained in these forms and their accuracy are more important than specific form design. Planning forms that help sales representatives to schedule activities vary from firm to firm. Modification of two types of planning forms (shown in Tables 9.1 and 9.2), customized to accommodate the needs of the particular sales firm, can be helpful. Note the detailed information in the major account sales plan. Specific objectives as well as date for accomplishment are stated on the completed card (6). The people who can exert major influence on the purchase and a step-by-step strategic plan to achieve desired results are also indicated. Territorial sales plans listing major accounts, their potential, calls allocated per year, and the product mix to be pushed are also included on a planning card. Each card indicates how scheduling can be made easier through the use of proper objectives specifically tailored to the needs of sales repre-

TABLE 9.1 MAJOR-ACCOUNT SALES PLAN

					XYZ Co.
					FIRM NAME
					CENTER CITY
					CITY

SALES ENGINEER   SAM DOAKS

Major Objectives	Measurable Attainable Realistic	Date to Accomplish	Persons Affecting Decision(s)	Accomplish Objective	Date to Accomplish
1. Assure continued purchase of product "B" by convincing purchasing agent of the superiority of our plant.		10/1	John Jones, Purchasing Agent	1. Convince Jones to come to our plant for a visit—make appointment.	9/15
				2. Conduct tour of plant and demonstrate paint finish.	10/1
2. Obtain an initial order for product "C" of at least $5,000.		11/15	John Smith, Plant Engineer Jim Brown, Maintenance Superintendent John Jones, Purchasing Agent	1. Make appointment with John Smith to find current supplier and find out decison maker.	9/5
				2. Determine whether moisture or aging is most important problem to Smith.	9/5
				3. Get appointment for demonstration of product "C" to Smith, Brown & Jones.	9/15
				4. Hold presentation and ask for order.	10/1

Source: Robert A. Else, "Selling by Measurable Objectives," *Sales Management,* vol. 110, no. 10 (May 14, 1973), p. 24.

TABLE 9.2 TERRITORY SALES PLAN

SALES ENGINEER <u>SAM DOAKS</u>

Account Name	SALES HISTORY ($000)			Estimates Available ($000)	Number of Sales Calls Allocated Per Year	PLANNED SALES (OR AVAILABLE SALES) BY PRODUCT LINE ($000)				
	1969	1970	1971			Prod. A	Prod. B	Prod. C	Prod. D	Prod. E
XYZ Co.	100	110	90	250	48	10	25	25	75	25
ABC Co.	75	75	90	300	48	25	50	25	10	5
EEG Co.	40	50	60	175	24	10	10	40	20	10
GFF Co.	20	30	50	150	24	10	20	—	10	30
FFH Co.	10	10	25	100	18	30	—	25	—	—
HGG Co.	0	0	30	100	18	—	10	30	—	40
JKL Co.	0	0	0	80	18	25	—	—	10	40
KGG Co.	0	10	20	75	12	—	10	10	20	30
MNO Co.	0	5	12	60	12	20	20	20	—	—
QEC Co.	0	0	10	60	12	—	10	—	40	—
ZZZ Co.	10	8	9	50	12	2	5	5	20	5

Note: Since product-line goals should have stretch, they should not be added either horizontally or vertically.
Source: Robert A. Else, "Selling by Measurable Objectives," *Sales Management,* vol. 110, no. 10 (May 14, 1973), p. 24.

sentatives of a particular company. If a rep's company is without such forms, self-designed forms for personal use in planning work just as well.

TIME AND TERRITORY MANAGEMENT

Minimizing traveling time and automobile expense must be considered in planning a sequence of calls. These must be considered together with the importance of each call and the best time to approach each prospect. Although you have an excellent idea of territorial distances, you should secure maps of your territory from service stations, chambers of commerce, or city halls to plot your route on the map with dots and numbers as a first step to more efficient territorial coverage. The first planned stop, for example, might be indicated by a "1," and "2" might designate the next planned call. (See Figure 9.2.) You might then consider the distances involved along with other reasons for call sequence and change the originally planned routing. Alternative call plans should be made in case certain stops do not require the planned amount of time.

The kind of routing plan used depends on distribution of prospects, their accessibility, how often you call on prospects, distances covered, and prospect availability (7). Several different patterns are available, depending on these factors (see Figure 9.3). A circular plan may be used when customers are distributed uniformly throughout a territory, are accessible, and call frequency is about the same for most accounts. A clover-leaf pattern is indicated when accounts are bunched up in certain parts of a coverage area. A hub point may be used for each bunch, and calls are made in loops around this hub. When call frequency is important, sales representatives may start at a far point in the territory and work their way back home. They may skip some customers along the route and call on those who should be given attention on that particular day. If business is scattered, the sales representative may make a straight reference line through each cluster of businesses, changing direction for each cluster group. The important factors to remember in routing are to use a map, to consider all elements affecting call sequence, and to consider both distance and timing. Flexibility and provisions for alternative calls are desirable, but don't go out into the territory without a plan.

Effective time management through proper routing and scheduling of prospect calls is a key element in successful sales territory management. Time is the raw material of life. It can be used wisely or it can be squandered. Many personal habits waste time. In a sense, each person is a time millionaire: "Time is our working capital. . . . Managing it is everybody's number one problem" (8). For a sales rep earning $25,000 a year, each minute is worth slightly more than 21 cents. In a year, an hour per day is worth $3,125! (See Figure 9.4.) No wonder Benjamin Franklin said in *Poor Richard's Almanac,* "Time is

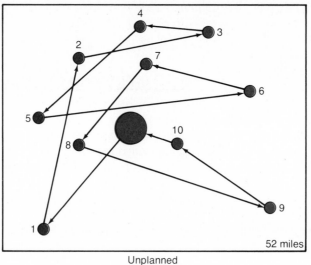

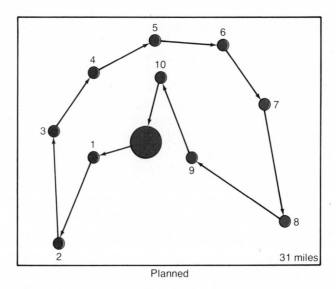

Figure 9.2 Routing, Planned Versus Unplanned

money." Efficient route planning is crucial to effective time and territory management.

After a planned route is tentatively scheduled, sales representatives should call or write for appointments. Even with careful planning, every field rep must spend time waiting in offices, get past the buffers or barriers to see the right

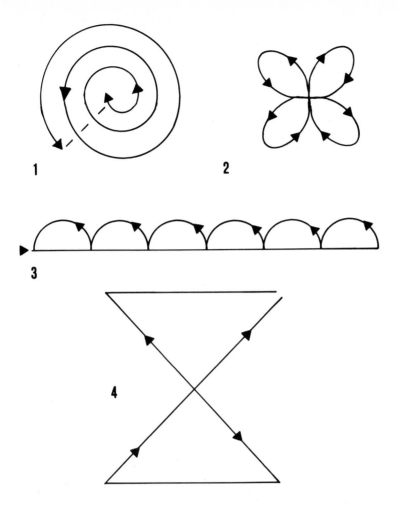

Source: Gary M. Grikscheit, Harold C. Cash, and W. J. E. Crissy, *Handbook of Selling: Psychological, Managerial, and Marketing Bases* (New York: Ronald Press/Wiley, 1981), p. 410.

Figure 9.3 Alternative Routing Patterns

persons, and follow good preinterview methods. Included in this section are the following preinterview considerations:

- The interview as a separate sale
- Cultivating assistants
- Insisting on seeing the right person
- Gracious waiting
- Knowing when 'no" means "yes"
- Remembering goals in approaching

What's Your Time Worth?

If your annual earnings are:	Every hour is worth:
$ 25,000	$12.81
30,000	15.37
35,000	17.93
40,000	20.49
50,000	25.61
60,000	30.74
75,000	38.42
100,000	51.23

Note: Hourly figures represent actual reimbursement in salary. To arrive at your time's total productive value to your company, you probably should double or triple these figures. From *Effective Time Management,* by Paul J. Meyer. As published in *Sales & Marketing Management,* March 17, 1980, p. 49.

Figure 9.4   What's Your Time Worth?

The Interview as a Separate Sale

Every sale is really two sales. First the interview must be sold to enable you to tell your sales story. If you have already called a prospect and have an interview scheduled, you will probably announce your arrival, tell the secretary of your appointment, and wait patiently until you are asked into the prospect's office. If you are calling without an appointment, the secretary or other *buffer* must first be sold on the importance of granting you an interview with the prospect. In this case, the barrier or buffer will "size you up." In this situation it is usually more important for you to sell yourself than to try to sell your product. If you are shut out at this point because of your personality, whatever great advantages the prospect might have derived from using your product will not be communicated and will not make any difference.

Cultivating Assistants

Salespeople never know who can help them to get an order. It is good to be nice to everyone from the assistant janitor on up. To make a sale, it is desirable to get as many people with access to prospects in the firm favorably disposed to both you and your product. Nearly all corporate prospects are surrounded by *barrier* or *buffer* personnel (see Photo 9.1). For all important prospects, there is at least one secretary. For most top corporate officials,

Photo 9.1
It is important to make a good impression on the buffer who protects the prospect's time by screening salespersons.

there are executive buffers. Persons with the power to say "yes" usually depend on the buffers to protect the prospect's most valuable resource—time. Buffers separate sales representatives who might have something to offer from sales representatives who probably will waste the superior's time. In dealing with buffers, there is a difference between acting professionally and acting "superior" to subordinates who can grant access to a prospect and help to get business. The buffer's concept of a salesperson's attitude is critical. Dress, body language, voice, and other clues will be read to determine whether a representative is worthy of the boss's attention. Charles Roth advises that sales representatives develop magic phrases like: "This is a courtesy call," or "I would consider it a great personal favor, if you could secure an interview with Mr. Jones for me" (9). If you can make the buffer feel important by allowing you in, you can usually get in. In making calls, a sales representative should appear patient and at ease.

If an appointment cannot be secured or time is too short to make a good presentation, it is best to reschedule the call. If the answer is no, but a "put-off" no rather than an "honest" no, you might ask the secretary for permission to speak to the prospect on the house phone and try to sell an interview that way.

Insist on Seeing the Right Person

While sales representatives should be courteous to subordinates and sell their way into seeing prospects, it is extremely important to interview the actual person with the power to make decisions. Sales representatives have a tendency to sell to employees at lower levels. They feel more comfortable with them and hope that the persuasive information will filter up to the level where decisions are made. The problem is that the employees who will be presenting the case to higher-level executives will not be as motivated or as persuasive as the rep. In addition, the product will not be presented in its best light to the decision maker; moreover, there is no chance to answer vital questions raised by the real prospective buyer. It is far better for a representative to overcome timidity and to see the right person. Key executives are people too. Often they are more understanding and considerate than lower-level employees. One of the reasons they are in a high position is the personal ability to understand and communicate better than the average person does.

THE SATURDAY EVENING POST

"Look—I said he was out!"

Try to maintain a good image while waiting.

Reprinted from *The Saturday Evening Post* © 1960 The Curtis Publishing Company.

Gracious Waiting

Waiting time should be productive time. Remember that while you are waiting, you are still selling the buffer. You might convince a secretary or receptionist that you are important if you use waiting time to review materials and plans pertinent to your product and customers. If you must read a magazine or a newspaper, be sure it's a professional journal or a financial one, not *Penthouse* or *Cosmopolitan.* If you waste time while waiting, a secretary may conclude that your time is not valuable and that you are not on a level with the boss, always a busy person. Many sales representatives have a cut-off time on waiting, like twenty-five minutes. They have found from experience that some offices will let salespeople wait as long as they will sit there and even forget them. Some prospects will let a rep wait just to convey self-importance and limited accessibility. Wait patiently until your limit, then explain to the secretary that you must go and will return at a more opportune time. It is permissible to say: "I have another appointment in a few minutes. Will you check and see if Ms. Gary will be free in a little while?" or "Could I speak to Mr. Smith on the company phone before I leave, to find out when it will be convenient for him to see me?"

Knowing When "No" May Mean "Yes"

When an interview is refused, it may be because the person is actually busy, or it may be a "no" to discourage sales representatives with little conviction about their products from taking up a prospect's time. Salespersons should have a few rebuttal phrases for the perpetual "no" of people who use "no" to shield their time. A rep should give a reason for seeing a prospect. "Tell Mr. Jordan we have a price increase that will go into effect on the first of next month, and 15 percent can be saved by ordering now, if he is interested." Or "I want to show Ms. Kane a new product that she has never seen before that can speed up her production line by 10 percent." Certainly, when a sales representative has spent a great deal of time in fruitless waiting on several occasions, it is time to try a new strategy. Trying to reach prospects on the phone or softening them up with several letters can be useful if they merit this kind of attention. When there is trouble gaining access to a prospect, it can be expected that competitors have the same problem. You may find the hard-to-see prospect to be a superior prospect, if you can make the first sale—getting in to tell your story.

Remembering Goals in Approaching

There is but a short time to gain a prospect's interest and attention. Like buffers, prospects judge your position to see if it is worth their time before listening to your entire presentation. A rep's goals should be to whet curiosity, to make prospects want to listen, to establish rapport, and to reduce any disharmony that might exist. You must quickly establish that you are there to help and not to waste time or to push unneeded products.

APPROACH METHODS

To many prospects, time seems more valuable than money. It is not surprising, therefore, that prospects concentrate maximum attention on a call's opening to determine whether or not to give the representative a full hearing. Their first mental impressions of the rep and the offering are all-important. Receptivity to the rest of the interview depends on those first few moments when they are scanning the rep's appearance, attitude, offering, and responding to important clues. If they decide, "Maybe this salesperson can benefit me, so I'll listen," the primary objective of the opening has been accomplished. If they decide, "I really don't need what this person has and my time is going to be wasted," it is difficult to get them to change their minds. The first few words from a sales representative who appears poised gain immediate interest and attention, reduce conflict, and create a first impression that leads to a better presentation. If, on the other hand, awkwardness, embarrassment, and conflict characterize the initial confrontation, reestablishing harmony and compatibility can prove difficult or impossible. Experience with more than one opening permits a salesperson to adjust remarks to fit each situation on entering a prospect's office or home. It is good practice to have several alternative openings available and to use the one that fits the circumstances best. Because every product and every prospect is different, it is difficult to devise opening words for all situations. The following methods, however, have been used to advantage by many.

The Self-Introduction Approach

Once invited, a salesperson should enter a prospect's office or home unhurriedly, but not casually, and stand facing the prospect. A genuine smile is always in order at this point to relax the atmosphere and dispel tension. A hurried entry in anticipatory fashion as if on the attack will rouse prospect anxiety. Body language should be allowed to convey a good image. Remember, while a rep is sizing up a prospect, the prospect is making many judgments about the rep from the clues signaled. Once these impressions are formed—and they are often formed in a few seconds—it is difficult to change them. Do not stop short of a prospect's immediate presence unless you have a reason for doing so. In an office, a sales representative should come to the front of the desk facing the prospect. To stop at the door or midway into the room indicates a feeling of subordination or hesitancy about the worth of an offering. It is best to establish two-way communication as equals. Staying too far away is a body language way of apologizing for being present. Having entered, a rep might say in a poised manner: "How do you do, Mr. Jones? I'm Jim Scott, representing the Acme Corporation." (Note that there should be a pause between the given name and the surname and that emphasis should be placed on the company name.) A salesperson's handshake should not be forced, since a few prospects have an aversion to shaking hands. If a prospect extends his or her hand, the shake should be brief but firm—never discomfortingly hard or "weasely" soft. It helps to look a prospect in the eyes but not to stare continually. Glance away naturally and occasionally. It is controversial at this point whether or not a prospect should be handed a business card. Giving a card at the beginning of a call assures that a prospect can call a rep by name, making conversation more cordial. Most prospects are so busy sizing up reps that they miss or forget names. Some sales representatives find it better not to use cards at all, and others extend them only at the end of interviews. In most sales situations, card or not, it is common courtesy to establish rep and company identification. Any other opening may seem evasive and unprofessional. All this is really preliminary to real opening remarks, so what is said next is especially critical to the success of an interview.

The Mutual Acquaintance or Reference Approach

Using the name of another customer or a friend is one way to start and make prospects feel obligated to listen. It also stimulates interest, especially if prospects respect the judgment of the referenced person and that person just bought under similar circumstances. A salesperson might say, "Ms. Johnson bought a copier from us this week. She indicated that you might be interested in information about copiers," or "Mr. Talbert of Artist's Piano Company in this area bought one of our payroll machines last month. Your larger payroll certainly would indicate even greater cost savings from a machine system." If a rep references the names of several customers who have bought recently, this will usually be a compelling opening, especially if those customers are a prospect's competitors. It is also possible to begin by handing a prospect testimonial letters signed by new customers in the same business or in similar circumstances, saying, "Many people in your business are switching to this promotion. Read what some of them say about what it has meant in their business." Never drop a name unless you want that person to be contacted. In many instances, prospects do contact references before buying. If you are using other people's names to gain interviews, remember that you are representing those persons as well as yourself and your firm. If they are customers, you may lose them if you stretch the truth about the depth of your relationship or their opinion of your product. If you are merely name dropping to gain a courteous reception by a prospect, the prospect may listen but resent the obligation and discredit your selling points. Persons whose letters you show or whose names you mention must be willing to back you for either to be helpful.

The Question Approach

Questions require prospect responses, indicate interest in their problems, and lead prospects to concentrate on a particular need problem rather than on the possible loss of time from an interview. Questions allow prospects to praticipate early and establish two-way communication from the very beginning. A question approach securing a hold on the prospect's mind is best. There is a habit-promoted compulsion to respond to questions. We have all been taught since childhood that it is courteous to consider a question and to answer it.

A broad range of opening questions is available in any selling situation. The challenge is to find the question that best secures attention, interest, and willingness to listen with an open mind. One kind of question that might be asked is a *qualifying or commitment-inducing question*. "If I could show you how this machine could pay for itself within two years, would you buy it?" or "If you could get 10 percent interest on a government-guaranteed certificate, would you invest $10,000 today?" or "Suppose we could find you a car that is comfortable, safe, handles well, and gives you over 40 miles to the gallon. Would you invest $6,000 in it?" This type of opening question requires thoughtful consideration on the part of prospects and usually leads them to qualify themselves. Occasionally, a prospective buyer *will* say yes, and all you need to do is prove that what has been promised can be delivered. A commitment question is excellent for separating "lookers" from "buyers." It facilitates the close.

The *benefit* question is usually a leading question designed to stimulate a mental commitment. "Mr. Smith, you would need a compact that would accommodate a tall man, wouldn't you?" "You would insist on a car that would hold up for at least 100,000 miles under normal driving conditions, wouldn't you?" "Wouldn't you want a policy that would give you cash in times of emergency?" "Do you realize that this wasted space in your store could mean $500 a year more profits for you by the end of the year?" This is a favorite approach with advertisers as well as salespersons and is a much-used headline in advertising copy.

An *image* question suggests a mental picture and is another way to make the prospect think. "How long would it take you to get out of this house in case of fire?" "If you suddenly get sick and are out for four months, what income are you and your family to live on?" "Will you have enough at retirement to maintain your standard of living in the face of 10 percent inflation?" "How are you presently planning for the expenses of Jerry's college education five years from now?" "Can you imagine how much fun it would be to own your own outboard?" Questions like these can get prospects to see themselves using the product in ideal situations. Questions can also whet *curiosity.* "Have you ever seen a television projector that can throw a picture on the wall as big as life?" "How could you cook a hamburger, in a motel, in less than two minutes, without a stove, and not upset the management?" "Can a flashlight work without batteries?" Curiosity-inducing questions grab prospect attention. If you can switch into the rest of the presentation without making this approach appear deceitful, you should have a good audience.

Devising and field testing good opening questions tailored to prospects is a good use of time. Questions that stimulate prospects to think about their needs and focus attention on your offerings are the most useful. Questions that will lead to the ending of the interview or suggest unpleasant circumstances should be avoided. "How are you doing, Mr. James?" may lead Mr. James to think that because he is not doing well, an offering should not be considered. "Do you like cars with fuel injection?" Suppose the answer is "no" and that's the only kind of car a rep can offer? Some questions stimulate thoughtful response. These should be preferred. Specific questions are usually better than general questions. Questions that suggest a positive and known response work well to advance sales calls. Just as questions in advertising copy persuade people to read the rest of the ad, they can serve the same purpose of attracting and holding attention in personal interviews.

The Statement or Benefit Approach

An opening statement is like the headline of an advertisement. It must attract attention. It can be a statement of the primary benefit gained from using the product. It should give an important reason for listening and should make the prospect's risk of *not* listening greater than the risk of listening. A statement opening ought to come as news to the prospect—something new, vital, and different, not heard before. It should pave the way for the rest of an interview and be the cornerstone of the persuasive appeal. Most prospects have a dominant buying motive. The opening statement should appeal to that motive if at all possible, and the entire presentation should be built around it.

No matter what statement is used, how it is said can make as much difference as what is said. If an opening statement sounds practiced and unnatural, it may appear to be a gimmick and lose its effect. Like every approach, the statement opening should hold the prospect's attention and stimulate thought about needs. These questions about opening statements are useful: Will it get undivided attention? Can it lead into other selling points naturally? Will it establish harmony or disharmony as the tone of the interview? Will it make the prospect think in terms of solving needs with the product to be offered? Examples of opening statements are:

- Prices on all of our models are going up next week, but you can buy at a 10 percent saving this week.
- Mr. Baker, with your present accounts-receivable load, every day you continue to use a manual system you lose another $25.
- I want to serve you by doing an analysis of your materials-handling procedure at no cost or obligation to you.
- You will get a higher return on this bond issue with less risk than on any we have had to offer in the last ten years.
- I challenge you to find any chemical that will clean your equipment better or more safely than Acme.
- Your secretary can save an hour a day with this typewriter.
- The government's new accelerated depreciation plan goes into effect on January 1, which means that they will, in effect, pay more than 40 percent of the cost of modernizing your equipment.

The Praise Approach

This approach must be done carefully, or it may be considered "flattery in bad taste" by prospects. Salespeople are expected to use flattery in persuasion. Subtle, flattering openings are acceptable in establishing communication. However, flattery often shuts off opportunity to use more effective approaches. A person may easily decide that if all the sales representative can do is offer flattery, the benefits of the offering must be weak.

On the other hand, a deserved compliment is a positive personal approach and may set a good interview tone and foster appreciation of a salesperson's sense of courtesy. Some prospects are so thirsty for a kind word that even obvious flattery is perceived as a natural attempt to be pleasant. A compliment not directed at a prospect's personal attributes is usually safer and less pointed. A pleasantly expressed appreciation of a prospect's secretary or home-office environment indirectly reflects the prospect's good judgment and taste. It does not cause embarrassment or promote a defensive attitude. Quoting a compliment that someone else has paid the prospect might please him or her. It is always gratifying to discover that other people speak well of you. Here are some examples of praise openings:

- You are certainly fortunate to have such a thoughtful secretary.
- Where did you find such a beautiful chair?
- Your company has always been the innovator in the industry. This advanced fork-lift truck should help continue that tradition of being the first to furnish your employees with the best work equipment.

- Congratulations on your promotion to branch manager, Mr. Owen. It will be a pleasure to serve you in regard to your paper supplies.
- I see that you've modernized your office beautifully. Whoever decorated it certainly did an outstanding job.
- You must be very proud of your daughter for winning that scholarship to law school for next year. I'm sure she learned a great deal by working here with you each summer.

The Free Gift or Sample Approach

Gifts or free samples may appear to prospects as attempts to buy interview time. But prospects may be willing to accept them and to listen. Many door-to-door sales representatives find greater receptivity by offering a small brush or a cosmetic sample as a goodwill gesture. A professional salesperson selling an intangible or industrial equipment can offer lunch or a golf game in the same spirit. Or a rep might offer to give advice or free consulting work that might be regarded as a "sample" of professional services. Leaving small equipment or appliances for trial might also be thought of as a method of letting prospective buyers "sample" items too expensive to give. Samples given should be in keeping with the product image and the level of selling.

Showing or giving prospects samples can quickly draw attention to offerings by bringing in senses besides hearing—sight, taste, touch, and/or smell. Something tangible is introduced into the interview and can serve as a focus for two-way conversation. Offering samples can reinforce product claims, since there is an obvious willingness to let prospects try a product before buying. In a sense, you are challenging the buyer with the implication that surely if a product is used, it will be appreciated. An immediate problem is that buyers may want to try it later and put off buying until after private trial and evaluation. Other prospects may take a sample and dismiss the salesperson before the interview really starts. For this reason, free gifts are often promised at the interview's opening but given at the end of the interview. Here are examples of this approach:

- A computer salesperson unfolds and explains a printout with a completed management report customized for a prospect.
- A candy sales representative hands a grocer a candy bar, saying, "Taste this, and you will know why this new bar is capturing the market."
- A pump salesperson hands a prospect a paperweight model of a new pump to focus discussion on an industrial need.
- Perfume salesclerks spray mist on the prospect's wrist, saying, "Doesn't it have a delightful fragrance?"

The Product or Ingredient Approach

What can be done when a product is large and indivisible and too valuable to give away or leave for trial? An office-machine salesperson might carry a hundred-pound bookkeeping machine programmed to demonstrate an accounts-receivable operation into a hardware store. "Mr. Taylor, you have a large accounts-receivable burden, and I want you to see how efficient a machine operation can be." This direct approach is honest, creates interest, and usually results in demonstration of the equipment. Not many prospects will make a rep carry a load that heavy back without at least looking at it. Most will clear off a place to put it down. A shoe salesperson uses a cut-away shoe to show premium construction. A tire sales representative shows a cross section of a tire revealing the protective steel belts. A real-estate sales representative might show an open ear of corn grown from a particular farm to show proof of high fertility.

Some salespeople like to hand products to prospects and let them open the conversation. Others hand prospects products and ask questions about them. Usually, when handed a product, prospects will ask questions that make it quite natural to start interviews. Quite often, time pressures will be forgotten, and prospects, their curiosity aroused, will allow explanation of operations or benefits. Auto sales representatives, office-equipment sales representatives, food sales representatives, clothing sales representatives, and many others agree that it is good practice to get prospect and product together from the beginning. If there *is* interest, it will soon be shown. If there is no interest, at least the prospect will have been qualified.

Special Attention-Getting Approaches

When all other approaches seem to fail, sales representatives may turn to unusual ways of getting a prospect's attention. Some salespersons have, for example, silently lighted a dollar bill with a match to dramatize how a prospect is losing money by not buying a proposed product. Other sales reps have simply walked past buffers pretending to be employees of the firm. Encyclopedia representatives have wrongfully approached prospects under the guise of "doing a marketing research survey," only to twist into full-blown sales presentations after prospects answer qualifying questions. Salespersons have even entered prospects' homes on the pretense of using the phone or needing a glass of water and worked into a sales presentation. Offers of "free" goods to be "given" to prospects for using them to "advertise the product in their area" are sometimes used to get prospects' attention and to take them unawares. A very successful shoe salesman claims he has always opened by showing a prospect an unattractive pair of shoes and then remarking, "These shoes just don't seem to fit your image." The third pair he would show would

"You're probably thinking, 'A burglar—and I have no insurance!'"

Your approach should be designed to capture the prospect's attention. Will this sales representative have trouble getting into the rest of his presentation?

© Orlando Busino 1962.

be the one he expected the prospect to buy. His rationale for this strategy was "People don't buy the first pair of shoes you show them, anyway."

As this discussion indicates, special attention-getting openings vary in their effectiveness and appropriateness. Sometimes, quite legitimate approaches—lighting the dollar bill—and quite questionable, possibly illegal, ones—spurious offers of "free" goods—can be classified together as "gimmick" approaches. An open dramatization to get the prospect's attention that links the attention-getting device to the presentation is useful. Deceptive gimmicks are a long way from the spirit of professional selling. They can create prospect anger. They can make it hard to lead into a sales pitch and promote conflict between seller and buyer when the objective ought to be harmony based on mutuality of interest. Gimmicks that take prospects unawares hurt the image of the salesperson and the firm represented. Some sales reps use gimmicks as a last resort, using anxiety to get an order as an excuse. Most should not be used at all.

Other Approaches

The shock, the service, or the opinion approach might fit a particular situation (10). In the shock approach, information can be advanced or a scene dramatized to shock prospects into seeing need. A salesperson might set a quick-burning cloth sample on fire, saying, "You wouldn't want your customers' children to wear sleepwear of this kind of material, would you? Our line of pajamas is completely flameproof."

The opinion approach is an indirect compliment that draws the prospect into conversation. "Ms. Smith, I would like you to examine this automobile and give me your honest opinion about it." The service approach simply promises a service benefit to the buyer and is, therefore, a specialized benefit approach.

Bad and Good Approaches

Bad approaches cause prospects to think negatively and make it easy for them to say no. A salesperson should never mispronounce a prospect's name, provoke an argument, talk about sex, religion, or politics, open with a dirty joke, indicate intention to waste prospect time, use vague generalizations instead of specifics, or apologize for making a sales call. It is best to use approaches that are proven, rivet attention and interest, promote identification of prospects with the salesperson, and lead easily into the rest of a presentation.

SUMMARY

Planning is necessary before approaching prospects to set up persuasive hearings for presentations. Well-defined, specific objectives should be devised ahead of time to direct planning and to provide controls for sales efforts. It is important to plan which prospects are to be visited and which route you plan to take before going out into a territory. Call reports, time and duty analyses, account sales plans, and computer-generated data on customers can greatly facilitate planning. Routing may be accomplished by a circular plan, a clover-leaf pattern, a skipping pattern, or a cluster pattern. A map with plotted call locations should be analyzed before a route is selected to evaluate time and distance considerations.

The approach should be considered a separate sales situation. Buffers protecting a prospect should be treated as important individuals. Everyone in a prospect's firm should be treated courteously. Waiting time should be used to help in building an effective image. The right person should be seen. How long to wait and how to interpret the various "no's" should be decided on in advance. The first ten seconds of exposure to a prospect are critical because in that brief time impressions are formed that are hard to change. Unhurried and poised body language and carefully selected first words are essential. Salespersons must set the tone of interviews by establishing themselves as considerate, service-oriented persons with something to offer.

A good sales representative has several methods of approach and selects the best one to fit each situation. The reference approach is excellent with prospects who are extroverts and are susceptible to strong reference-group pressures. The question approach establishes two-way conversation and involves prospects immediately. The benefit approach can hit the dominant buying motive with its very first words. The praise approach, if it avoids the appearance of flattery, can soothe the prospect's ego. The free-sample approach can buy interview time. The product approach focuses immediate attention on product offerings. Ethical gimmick approaches can be used in difficult cases. The approach selected for any situation should create immediate interest, be different, cause prospects to forget they have been interrupted, and lead smoothly into the rest of a presentation.

REVIEW QUESTIONS

1. Why should sales representatives plan? In what ways will planning enhance performance?

2. What are the essential elements of planning by objectives?

3. What is the 80/20 rule? What is its relevance to the salesperson?

4. What sorts of past information can be helpful in setting performance standards?

5. What suggestions are proposed in the text for increasing the efficiency of daily planning? Why are such activities important for the salesperson?

6. Outline the forms and reports that are useful in making planning easier.

7. What factors determine the optimum routing plan?

8. What are the basic routing plans and what conditions favor each one?

9. What are the essential elements of good preinterview planning for the salesperson?

10. Suggest some methods for getting past a prospect's buffer.

11. Why is it crucial to interview the actual person with the power to make decisions?

12. What are some of the methods suggested to minimize the negative aspects of waiting time?

13. What are the major methods of approaching a prospect?

14. What are some of the advantages of the question approach? Name some of the types of questions suggested.

15. What are some of the attributes that should characterize the opening statement in the statement or benefit approach?

16. What are some of the potential drawbacks to the praise approach? How may these drawbacks be overcome?

17. Outline some of the ways in which gifts or free samples to prospects can be incentives to provide the salesperson with interview time. What are some of the drawbacks to this approach?

18. For what product types is it particularly helpful to use the product or ingredient approach?

APPLICATION QUESTIONS

1. The planning aids discussed in this chapter can be useful to you now. Think about your past experiences and decide what you would like to accomplish in the next year.
   a. Determine what your personal goals are for the next year. What do you need to accomplish each month in order to achieve these goals?
   b. In order to achieve what you need to for the next month, what should you do each week?
   c. Now take this week, what do you need to do tomorrow and for each day in the week?
   d. Each night, review what you have done and what you need to do the next day. Rank the next day's activities in order of importance, write them down and review them as the day goes by. Try to get all of them done, and if you cannot, make sure that you get the most important activities finished. If you cannot get everything done, try to determine why this is happening. Could you be more efficient? Where are you wasting time? Could you structure your day, travel, and route more effectively? Or are your objectives unreasonable?

2. You are now a salesperson and you have successfully arranged for an interview with a prospect.
   a. Develop five good rules to follow while you are waiting for this interview.
   b. You are finished waiting and are entering the prospect's office. The first five seconds after you enter the office are very important. What should you do in terms of body language to make a favorable impression on the prospect during these first five seconds?
   c. Assume that you want to use the benefit statement approach. Give three examples other than those given in the text of a good benefit statement approach.

9–1

Bert Brewer is calling on John King, who is a prospect for a life insurance policy.

Bert: Mr. King, I'm Bert Brewer with Nordic Insurance Company. *(Hands him a calling card)* I want to congratulate you on your recent marriage. Mr. Langdon Humphries (the bride's uncle) said you might be interested in financial planning through life insurance.

John: Bert, I'm glad to meet you, but my wife and I are just getting our apartment furnished, and we can't afford an insurance policy right now.

Bert: I know how tight things are when you first get married. I've only been married for two years myself. I just wanted to meet you and Mrs. King and answer some of the questions you might have about financial planning, so when you feel able to make a move toward protection, you will consider Nordic.

John: Well, if you're sure you understand that we're not in the market for insurance just yet with all we have to buy, I guess we can talk for just a minute or two. Nancy, we have company who knows your uncle.

(Nancy enters the living room.)

Bert: Hello, Mrs. King. Your uncle, Mr. Humphries, is one of my Nordic policy holders. You must be his favorite niece; he talks about you a lot every time I see him. You know, one of the things you and Mr. King need to think about when you establish a home is financial security for the future. Might I sit down with you for a minute and simply explain some factors that might have a significant bearing on your financial future?

Nancy: Well, if you are a friend of Uncle Lang's, sure. We can talk for a minute, but we need furniture right now and not insurance.

Bert: I sure understand that. Do you *(to John)* have any life insurance protection at all?

John: Why would we need any just now? We don't have any children, and Nancy is a schoolteacher . . . but to answer your question, we don't.

Bert: Most married couples wind up with children, and if the husband is not insurable when the children are young and something happens to him, then the wife is left with a difficult burden. The monthly premiums for insurance also grow more expensive with each "insurance birthday." That is, if you take it out this year, the premiums would be less than if you waited until next year. We have plans, for example, that recognize the money needs of young marrieds and defer much of the premium cost until you get on your feet. Let me show you the details of this term policy that guarantees your future insurability for additional amounts . . .

QUESTIONS

1. What type of approach did Bert use on John? On Nancy?

2. Was it a good tactic to use Uncle Langdon's name in this situation?

3. What do you think of Bert's approach tactics?

4. How would *you* have approached John and Nancy?

9–2

The following letter was written by a "Legion of Honor" senior salesperson with the Burroughs Corporation.* Evaluate the letter with respect to planning. Write a shorter letter along the same lines, using a different product.

Mr. R. K. Weisinger, Branch Manager
Burroughs Corporation
231 Monroe Avenue
Memphis, Tennessee

Dear Keith:

As you requested, I am listing a few ideas regarding the work plan I use in working my territories.

When I first came with Burroughs several years ago, Mr. F. T. Miller was District Sales Manager. I remember two things he told me. One was that things never looked better for Burroughs men; the other was that to be successful in this business you should plan your work and work your plan. He was right about the first, because things have been getting better most of the time since then and still will, particularly if we each help a little. I know he was right about the second, too, because it has been told to me by every manager and supervisor since then.

They were all right. It is the answer to success. However, though everyone recommended it, and Burroughs gave me a territory and a quota and opportunity, no one gave me a plan. In working a territory, however, I have found that there are so many variables in the different ones, that it would be hard for the Company to devise one that would work for everyone. It is probably better, with some help, for a man to develop his own. I have talked to other salesmen about it, and many seemed to have only the plan to close a few deals for big equipment, get rid of a debit balance, and draw some big commissions. Occasionally, this works out, but most men with that plan have some lean years and many lean months and a lot of disappointments. They frequently find themselves rushing around on

*Reproduced with the permission of the Burroughs Corporation.

the last day of the month or the last week of the year trying to close something to salvage the record. And that is selling at its very toughest.

Most Burroughs men have developed their own plan of working their particular territory. Most of them are very good and well suited to the problems they face. Doing the same thing, I have found some things that work well for me in my territory, and I am giving them to you for what they may be worth.

I have found that a *Big Plan,* which is not composed of hundreds of little plans, which you carry out every day, is almost worse than no plan at all. My Big Plan is to get just as large production and commissions as I possibly can from my territory. If it goes no further than that, it is merely hoping. But I break it down to make it reasonable. If I intend to sell $100,000 a year, for instance, I figure it will take me $8,500, and then I see it will take about $2,200 per week to sell that much monthly. Then I try to sell as much of it before noon on Monday as I can. Never wait until the last of the week or the last of the month to reach your goal. To help do this, I set as a small goal to have no shut-out weeks, even if I have to work late Saturday to close the deal; but it is a lot more comforting when you start a deal on Monday. Selling is sort of like fishing; the first one is the hardest. Then they frequently come in bunches. So try to get an order as close to the first of the year as you can, and the first day of the week, and the first day of the current month. When you do, the period is generally going to be good.

The first step in planning is to analyze your territory. Work it for what is in it. If the best part of it is bank business, apply a good bit of your time proportionately to working that line. If manufacturing, or government, or retail or wholesale, figure it out and do the same thing. Work it all, but do not get so carried away on any machine, application, or business that you neglect your better prospects. It is tough to lose any business, but do not lose the easy business. That's like a pitcher walking another pitcher.

Most territories are seasonal to a degree. I know from experience that I generally get more business in my territory in January, February, and March, than any other three-month period. Be sure you build up good live prospects to the point that they are ready to close when the seasonal pickup comes. It is usually too late to start on them when buying time comes. Likewise, if we have a list of "hot prospects" when we have a price increase, which we have from time to time, it's easy to close the "hot ones" then. But, if he has not been convinced he is a prospect, it is useless to try to make a prospect of him because of a price increase. The mention of it might even serve to make him mad. Most of us are pretty happy when we have a month in which we close a lot of orders, sort of despondent when we have not; but the time to be despondent, even if we are closing some orders then, is when we are not initiating and building up a good number of live prospects; because that always means some lean times two or three months from now. If you want to keep having good months, don't get too satisfied because you are getting some orders. You must build prospects at the same time.

I find it most valuable to have a complete list of all Burroughs users in the territory and the machines they use and try to keep it up-to-date. I figure everyone with a machine three or four years old is a prospect for replacement. Be sure to give them a proposal and a chance to buy. The deals you get when the machines are this age are always easier than they would be if they were eight or ten years old, and there is very little danger of losing them to competition. I often canvass out of my users' list, and generally look it over before I make a call on any customer.

Consider the serviceman in your plan. He can be the best sales aid you have. Most servicemen know they are now in Marketing, but it is up to us to show them they are appreciated and just how valuable they are in the operation. I try to talk to the ones that work the territory I do daily when possible, look over their calls, and see that they have information and literature on any new machines we are trying to sell. I discuss the prospects I am working on with them, and the equipment we are proposing. That way they will know the situation when they call on the customer, and we can work to the same end on the deal. If they have customer trouble or any machine trouble on which I can help, through my contact or knowledge of the particular machine application, I make it a point to go with them or help in any way I can to the exclusion of anything else at that time. I have found it always pays to do this. There is no business in which cooperation between sales and service is as necessary or as effective as in ours.

Sell supplies on your calls where possible, and try to turn them over to the Service Representative. He gets a thrill out of sending in orders, too. We don't get a commission on it, but it is most valuable in promoting selling that does pay us a commission.

It does several things:

(1) Keeps us in a selling mood. Nothing helps like getting orders. After you take a supply order or two in the morning, you are in a much better frame of mind to close a machine deal later in the day. Try it.

(2) It helps the serviceman. He needs the sales for his record, and he can return the help many times over.

(3) Someone is going to get the business and our company needs it just as badly as any competition. If a competitor is in there on any basis, we are that much weaker.

(4) Better customer contact. It takes little time to ask for supply orders, and any sale you make to the customer makes the next sale that much easier no matter what it is for.

We can call on only a limited number of people daily, but we can sit down for a few minutes at night or on the weekend and drop a short note with some pertinent information to at least a half-dozen customers. They are usually prepared and softened up from this by the time you call. I have had many sales materialize a year or two later from a short note to the customer about an application. Whenever I make a bookkeeping installation in a town, I always write a few other similar businesses in that town or nearby towns, tell them of the installation, suggest they might like to visit it, and send them a picture of the machine. Enthusiasm about a new machine is usually at its peak at this time. It helps to have other people know about it. You can tell a few of them in a short time this way.

I make it a point to never call on anyone without giving them a proposal to buy something before I leave. It can be very informal, just a pencilled offer to trade on the back of a piece of literature. Be sure you let them know you are there to sell them something they need. They will appreciate your effort even if they have to say "no" that time.

We must sell large machines to build up satisfactory volume, and these should and do take time. But, if you have a full-line territory, plan to sell the full line. That is the gravy that provides the money to pay the expenses, so that all the rest of your commission is clear. The nice part about it is that it takes so little time to do it. Just remember in the back of your mind all the machines you have, look around on all calls and installations, give them proposals to trade, keep a list of people wanting used machines. If you are looking for them, you can stumble over two or three small machine prospects weekly, without canvassing for them at all. I figure that every full-line salesman should sell at least 100 units per year, and that should be a minimum goal in your planning. If you sell 150% of quota on 125 units, you and your territory are a lot better off than if you sold 150% on just 75 units. Because you have created users, users create other users for both big and little machines. If you don't sell your share in the territory, somebody is going to do it. And, when they do, your territory will be just that much weaker for you and Burroughs.

Plan to work the hot machines while they are hot. When we get something like the Microtwin was a few years ago, or our Proof Machine and "E" are now, clearly better than most competition in its range, make a point to see everyone that is a likely prospect just as quickly as you can. Tell them about it, give them a proposal, and try to close the deal. These are the easy ones. Don't wait to call until competition sells them, because they will be sure trying to beat us to it. Remember such machines won't stay hot long, because they will sure try to catch up or get an order before we do.

There are a few other general rules I have for myself. One is, if I'm trying to close a deal and think I have a chance to do so that day, I don't leave it for any reason, no matter what comes up, until I get an answer. Deals can cool off mighty fast overnight. When you get the order, they slow up thinking about objections. Since they have already bought, they start thinking how they can justify their purchase—and forget any objections they may have had to buying. But, if I am merely attending to details or looking for business or just working up a deal and hear about someone interested in buying, even if it is just an 8 07 01, across town or in the next county, I always drop whatever I'm doing and go at once to get the order. I have learned from bitter experience that whenever you hear of someone who is ready to buy, if you wait until you are working up that way the next week or even the next day, he will have just bought something else shortly before you arrive.

When you are making an installation, make it as good as if you intended to have the same territory until you were 65, but remember, this is not lost sales time, providing you use it right. I try to lay the groundwork for trading each bookkeeping machine while I am installing it, by taking time to discuss depreciation plans, cost after taxes, advantages of replacement in four or five years to stay up to date, etc. You can make the next sale easy for yourself or the salesman following you in this way. You are closer to the customer on the installation than at any other time. Use this time to build his goodwill, observe other equipment needs he has, and clinch his future business for yourself and Burroughs. Don't skimp on installation time. It is the best selling time we have.

Plan to use your time preparing layouts and proposals not as lost time, but as valuable sales time. When you draw a layout, don't just think about crossfooters, registers, carriage movement, etc., but who else in your territory can use the same or a variation of it. You can think up prospects this way, and most sales of large equipment have to be made in your mind before you can make them to the customer. You'll find some of them do not even know they are prospects until you go around and tell them. I have closed deals to customers by simply showing them a layout just completed for a similar type business. Most of them do not completely understand it, but it is impressive to them and creates respect for us and our equipment. It can help make detail time into valuable sales time.

Don't fall into the mistake of shying away from a customer because he is having a lot of trouble with his equipment, even if it is relatively new. Frequently, this is the best time to ask for an order for additional equipment. When it is down, he can easily see just how much it means to him and how necessary it is. Also he is being called on by our servicemen, zone service supervisors, and sometimes even managers. The whole magnitude of the Burroughs organization and what we are geared to do for him is spread out before him, as is the machine they are working on.

At such a time he knows what his machine means to him and what lengths we will go to in order to take care of him. He may be sort of upset sometime; but, if he needs more equipment, try to get the order at this point. At least do not be afraid to ask for it. After it is fixed, he'll just remember his trouble, and he may be looking around at something else.

There is one thing I can tell you, which I believe would be certain to increase the average sales of anyone from the top man in Burroughs to the newest junior. It is this:

Remember you are a salesman all day long. When you are going to and from work, when you are driving between calls, when you are talking to other men in the business, when you are drinking coffee or having lunch, drawing layouts, making proposals, installing equipment, you are still a salesman. Consider everything you do in relation to getting an order signed by some customer. If you spend your time this way, you will find there are plenty of potential sales you have completely overlooked. We are not technicians, systems designers, students, or goodwill men, except to the degree these things help us get orders.

Remember we are salesmen: that is what we are paid for, and it pays to remember!!!!

The above are a few of what I call my small plans or methods I use in operating my territory. For me, they have always helped in making my big plan for a good year come true. I hope some of them may help you.

Your friend,

Phil Williams
Sales Representative

Planning Letter Outline

The important ideas in Phil Williams's planning letter can be summarized as follows:

1. Planning begins with a realistic, but optimistic, attitude.

2. "Plan your work and work your plan" is a good selling motto that is endorsed by many managers.

3. Sales planning is largely an individual responsibility. It is almost impossible for a company to provide a uniform plan for all salespersons, because of the large number of variables involved.

4. Plans that are not sufficiently detailed may lead to disappointing results.

5. It is important, for motivational reasons, to start accomplishing goals as soon as possible. Break your major plan down into subobjectives and concentrate on accomplishing each of them.

6. The first step in planning is territorial analysis. Consider the actual opportunities in each separate part of your territory.

7. Plan for the element of seasonality in your territory.

8. Use price increases to sell prospects who are ready to buy.

9. Build up a good reserve of prospects. Review user records to help you develop your list.

10. Help the service representative get orders for supplies and he or she will help you find prospects.

11. Drop a short note to at least a half dozen customers each week. They will be more receptive when you call on them later.

12. Never call on anyone without giving a proposal to buy before you leave.

13. Sell the full line to make your quota.

14. Make sure all prospects know about those products with a strong advantage over the competition.

15. Give hot prospects immediate attention even if the monetary value of their order is small.

16. Give excellent customer service, and lay the groundwork for the next sale during this sale.

17. Do not shy away from customers who are having problems with the product. This is the very time you need to maintain goodwill.

18. Remember that a sales representative is a sales representative all day long.

9–3

Ronda Goumas has just arrived at Perleman Paper Company in Mc-Connellsville, Ohio. Ronda travels for Dobson Supplies, Inc., a paper and packaging supplies super-jobber out of Dayton. Perleman is one of many smaller paper houses that Dobson supplies. Dobson buys in larger quantities than the smaller jobbers are able to do, combining their smaller orders with its larger ones from industrial accounts to get the best price for themselves and the smaller jobbers. Perleman is the most important of the smaller jobbers on Dobson's books. George Swanson, who took over as owner of Perleman five years ago, has built up a considerable volume with local bakers, independent grocers and butchers, and notions, novelty, and junior department stores. He is aggressive and imaginative. Typically, George makes himself directly available to sale reps and customers who call on him. When Ronda comes behind the counter, George looks up.

Ronda: Hi, George! I'm just passing through on my way to Wheeling and thought I'd stop by. I don't suppose you want to buy anything, do you? What did you think about that Reds game last night? They're just like the weather—can't depend on 'em.

Ronda is surprised to see what is an obvious wince of disapproval pass over George's face. Ronda is puzzled. She has always thought of George as one of her friendliest customers. Now, he looks almost hostile.

QUESTIONS

1. What mistakes did Ronda make?

2. What message was Ronda really sending to George?

NOTES

1. Donald W. Jackson, Jr., and Ramon J. Aldag, "Managing the Sales Force by Objectives," *MSU Business Topics,* Spring 1974, p. 56.

2. Robert F. Vizza, "Managing Time & Territories for Maximum Success," *Sales Management,* vol. 107, no. 4 (August 1, 1971), pp. 30–32.

3. Jackson and Aldag, "Managing the Sales Force by Objectives," p. 55.

4. Robert A. Else, "Selling by Measureable Objectives," *Sales Management,* vol. 110, no. 10 (May 14, 1973), pp. 22–24.

5. Vizza, "Managing Time," p. 32.

6. Else, "Selling by Measureable Objectives," p. 24.

7. W. J. Crissy and Robert W. Kaplan, *Salesmanship* (New York: Wiley, 1969), pp. 168–169.

8. Peter Drucker, *The Effective Executive* (New York: Harper & Row, 1969), p. 312.

9. Charles B. Roth, *How to Find and Qualify Prospects and Get Interviews* (Englewood Cliffs, N.J.: Prentice-Hall, 1960), pp. 90–100.

10. Alan Reid, *Modern Applied Salesmanship,* 2nd ed. (Pacific Palisades, Calif.: Goodyear, 1975), pp. 204–208.

The Presentation

The *approach* should attract a prospect's attention and set the tone of an interview, while the *presentation* should be the main persuasive effort and must be designed to produce most of the "change of mind" that brings about a sale. Before you attempt to detail interview plans, it would be helpful for you to learn what purposes you can accomplish through the presentation, to understand the different types of presentations, to know when to use each one, and to know each presentation's strengths and weaknesses. Familiarity with techniques that can solve interview problems can make good presentations possible under adverse circumstances. A good presentation meets the main acid test: It produces orders from prospects. This chapter is designed to help you plan better presentations by giving you information on the following topics:

- Objectives of a sales presentation
- Alternative types of presentations
- Solving presentation problems

OBJECTIVES OF A SALES PRESENTATION

Every presentation is an attempt to sell an interview, a product, a service, or an idea. To do this, a complete presentation should be planned that includes both logical and emotional points. It should anticipate prospect questions, handle competition, and explain prices. The goals reflected in the definition of selling—promoting harmony, furnishing information and assurance, and leading people to buy—can be used as a basis for initiating and reviewing interview plans. In order for you to gain a full perspective of what is involved in setting interview goals, three areas need to be understood: (1) the basic strategies used in sales presentations; (2) the five important prospect decisions to be made during a presentation; (3) the ways to reduce the prospect's risk of buying and thus get an order. The methods used to customize presentations are developed throughout this chapter.

STRATEGIC INTERVIEW OBJECTIVES

Sales representatives can set strategic interview objectives by using any one or a combination of the basic selling strategies. It is important to consider the specific needs of the selling situation when planning strategies. As in all modern selling, in setting interview objectives, a would-be seller must adopt the perspective of the prospect the rep would convert into a customer. Meeting prospect needs and wants enhances prospect participation and leads the prospect to decide whether or not to order.

Five Important Prospect Decisions

A prospect must make five decisions if a presentation is to end up with an order. The seller's objectives must be: (1) to help buyers realize *needs;* (2) to help them see that the offered *product* is the best solution for those needs; (3) to help them understand that *service* will be adequate; (4) to convince them that the benefits received will outweigh the *price* paid; and (5) to help them feel that they should *buy now* (1).

When a sales representative approaches, a prospect may be completely satisfied in the *need* area. In most cases, then, the salesperson must disturb this satisfaction to get the prospect's interest. Dissatisfaction with the status quo can be brought about by communicating the benefits of having a product and/or the disadvantages of not having it. Enthusiasm is vital here. It helps the listener to visualize the use of the product or service in the best possible light.

After need is realized, a clear case must be given to satisfy it with the *product* offered rather than in some other way. The relative advantages of a proposed offering should be stressed in direct application to expressed buyer need. At this point, a prospect may want the product but not feel fully assured that the service offered will satisfy the need in the manner promised. Assurance, through risk-reducing techniques, that the product will be delivered as promised and is fully backed must be given.

Desire for a product is meaningful only if its *price* can be justified as affordable. Explanations of the various ways to buy a product (straight, installment, rental, delayed billing, and so on) or expressions of price in relation to benefits received over a product's expected life often help in clearing this hurdle. Finally, prospects must have clear reasons for buying *now* instead of later. Immediate benefit enjoyment, future price rises, and limited-time offers are ways to convince prospects that something will be lost by putting off a decision. Salespeople must always be prepared to give prospects reasons for prompt action. A buying mood lost may never be regained. A sales representative should never forget to ask for an order, since prospects can make all five decisions and still not buy because of rep reluctance to take the initiative.

Basic Strategies Used in Sales Presentations

Salespeople may select from several general persuasive strategies to serve as guides in planning an interview: *Stimulus-Response Strategy, Formula Strategy, Want-Satisfaction Strategy, Problem-Solution Strategy, Depth-Selling Strategy, Group-Selling Strategy,* and *Team-Selling Strategy* (2, 3). Each strategy suggests an overall purpose for a presentation as well as subobjectives to help accomplish that purpose. The strategy or strategies selected should depend on such factors as the selling situation, salesperson skill, the nature of the product, and prospect intelligence.

Stimulus-Response Strategy. In this method, a series of selling points (stimuli) are arranged to lead the prospect to a favorable reaction (see Figure 10.1). Stimulus-response does not necessarily demand the use of leading questions, but the strategy may take that form. For example, as particular features are demonstrated to a prospect, a rep might say: "You would want that feature on any equipment you buy, wouldn't you?" After a series of questions like this to gain agreement from a prospect, the interview might continue: "You would want this equipment delivered next week then?" The suggested answer is "yes." Stimulus-response strategy can be applied by new and inexperienced sales representatives. It relies on using tested magic phrases with customers. Prospects learn to say "yes" and a series of acceptances leads up to a sale. Except for agreement response, there is little prospect participation in this strategy. Some listeners may react negatively to not being treated as individuals with distinct needs. This kind of presentation can be memorized but may come to sound artificial. It is a strategy best used in situations in which interview time is short and salespersons confront the prospects infrequently or only once. The professional sales representative dealing with high-level prospects should use stimulus-response only as a part of an

Figure 10.1   Stimulus-Response Series

This car has beautiful lines, hasn't it?

Look at this spacious trunk. It would be nice to get all of the family suitcases and clothes back here on trips, wouldn't it?

This car has five more cubic feet of space inside, too, than most mid-sized models, plenty of leg room and extra good vision out of the front windshield. That's important for tall men like you, isn't it, Mr. Burnett?

This stainproof leatherette upholstery will keep looking like new even when the children's shoe dirt has been cleaned off. That would be nice, wouldn't it?

This is a safe car. The special power brakes stop 15 feet faster than the average car at 55 miles an hour, and there is special steel bracing in case of collision. It sure is important to be safe in an automobile, isn't it?

This car has a diesel engine with fewer moving parts, should require less repair, and is designed to last 50 percent longer than standard engines. That's important in buying an automobile, isn't it?

The diesel with fuel injection will *average* 27 miles per gallon with 32 on the road and run on less expensive fuel. That will mean big savings, won't it?

This car is equipped with air bags that could save lives. What could be more important than to walk away from a head-on collision? You'd want that kind of safety, wouldn't you, Mr. Burnett?

With this car you can have your comfort and good fuel economy, too, at a reasonable price. This is the answer for today's family, isn't it?

This beautiful gas-saving diesel is the car you want, isn't it, Mr. Burnett?

interview, usually in conjunction with an explanation of feature benefits just before closing. In this case, two-way communication interaction with the prospect should be planned earlier in the interview.

Formula Strategy. Formula strategy is associated with industrial selling, multiline selling, or complex product selling, where memorization of a sales presentation is impractical because of variation in products or in levels of sophisticated selling required (3). Formula strategy allows more customization by the sales representative and greater participation of the prospect than does stimulus-response programming. It still stresses the product features rather than customer needs. The formula approach advocated most often is based on the anticipated mental steps of prospects in making decisions: *A*ttention, *I*nterest, *D*esire, *C*onviction, and *A*ction (AIDCA). In following the formula, the salesperson can concentrate strategic efforts on one objective at a time, leading the prospect smoothly from one step to the next on through to action. That is, attention is translated into interest, interest into desire, desire into conviction, and conviction into action (4).

Attention-getting is stressed at the opening of an interview. The transition from attention to interest is critical and depends, in part, on the approach used and its relation to the rest of the presentation. For example, attention gained by blowing a trumpet on entering an office is not likely to be productive if it is unrelated to what is being sold. Interest is built when prospects can apply what is offered them to their needs and problems and can visualize using a product successfully. If a need connection is not made quickly, prospect attention may shift to finding a tactful way to get rid of the rep. Actually, interest may depend on disturbing prospect satisfaction. If a prospect feels there is no problem, there is no reason to be interested in a product. *Desire* must be built by translating product features into those benefits that meet the needs of a particular prospect. *Conviction* is reached when a buyer decides that the benefits outweigh any sacrifices that must be made in terms of money. Logic and emotional appeal may carry a prospect this far, but a mental threshold must be crossed before an order is placed, and this depends on good closing techniques (Chapter 13). Unless a salesperson is careful, attempts to close may make prospects feel that they are being controlled, producing negative reactions. Good two-way communication can be hard to establish. Formula strategy does allow the salesperson flexibility, but it requires a thinking persuader who can adjust for product and prospect differences (5).

Want-Satisfaction Strategy. Want-satisfaction interview strategy is prospect-oriented. It requires a skilled salesperson. Basically, its objectives are to find a dominant prospect need or needs and to translate need into "wants" by accentuating them, causing a prospect to visualize the want as much as possible, and finally to satisfy that want through the offering being presented. Getting prospects to talk about their needs through thoughtful questions is emphasized. Next, careful listening, suppressing all premature tendencies to talk about products is called for. Finally, the product is presented as satisfying particular wants. Questions asked are designed to cause the prospect to think analytically about personal needs. "Yes" and "no" answers reveal little. Questions that cause a listener to imagine and explain are preferred to questions that can be answered in a few words. In want-satisfaction strategy, sales representatives take on the role of the prospect's psychologist. They must be discerning, patient listeners who neither interrupt nor prevent prospects from revealing their inner personality needs and wants. This strategy fits in well with the concept of "leading" prospects to buy. When prospect needs are revealed, sales representatives must get prospects to see those revealed needs as "wants." Product features that fit a prospect's want pattern must be related to dominant buying motives by a subtle matching process. Prospects must feel in control, even though a rep may share in or actually do the controlling.

Skilled use of want-satisfaction strategy takes a great deal of time to develop. It is usually used in conjunction with important deals involving expensive merchandise or services. Attempted by an inexperienced salesperson, it may appear awkward and obvious. It requires practice and experience. Misuse can prevent promotion of important benefits and cause overstress on buying motives that are not dominant. However, it does provide good interaction between salesperson and prospect.

Problem-Solution Strategy. Problem-solution strategy goes beyond the want-satisfaction approach in professionalism and consumer orientation because it may be necessary to present each prospect with several solutions (6). Determining prospect problems can require considerable time and effort. Careful research may be required. Preparation of detailed, written proposals containing problem analysis and solution normally requires expertise. In a sense, professional salespersons sell consulting expertise in an effort to find real prospect needs. The rep must project the anticipated results of using several product solutions and let the prospect decide. This strategy is used in technical fields, where repeat sales are cultivated, and long-range goodwill is important. It is an exhaustive effort to reduce prospect risk and to instill confidence through the use of problem-solving techniques to analyze business needs. It works best with technical business products and complex intangible offerings with strong relative advantages over comparable offerings. Salespersons using this strategy can build personal reputations if they are technically competent to analyze the problem involved.

Depth-Selling Strategy. Depth selling attempts to combine the other four methods and profit from all their advantages. It is a flexible, customized approach, utilizing each of the other strategies in parts of a presentation. For example, a salesperson may begin an interview with want-satisfaction questions and listen attentively to learn about a prospect and to establish prospect confidence. She may analyze the prospect's problems in depth and propose solutions, some of which do not even mention her own product offering. She

292

Selling Techniques

may explain her own offering in terms of benefits, asking stimulus-response questions to get prospect agreement about different features of an offering. Finally, she might suggest that the prospect accept an alternative involving her product. All of these techniques are accomplished within the framework of the AIDCA formula (7). Certainly, buyers can be led to interest through careful questions and proposals and to desire and conviction through the use of stimulus-response techniques. Depth selling, therefore, presents itself as a customized strategy mix of the best of the other four plans. It requires intelligent, prospect-perceptive salespersons.

Group-Selling Strategy. Sales representatives will often find it necessary to sell to a group of individuals rather than to just one person (8)—see Photo 10.1. In this case, each member of a buying group may be interested in separate aspects of the offering and have different buying motives. Remember that "in selling to several persons at one time, it is neither possible nor desirable to be concerned with the traits and motives of each individual" (9). A machine operator may be interested in ease of operation, an engineering ex-

Photo 10.1
Often sales representatives will find it necessary to sell to a group of individuals rather than to just one person.

ecutive may be interested in machine efficiency, and the firm president may respond to profit possibilities. Proper questioning techniques are important in group buying situations to find the need as each member sees it. A complete and honest presentation of all offering benefits should characterize a group-selling meeting and cover the supposed range of prospect thinking. A sales representative should be careful to determine the effects of a product purchase on each buying team member. Logical and emotional appeals to bring out prospective benefits for each member should be based on the roles played in the group. When talking to a group, salespersons have the same problem as politicians—they must not gain the approval of some in the group at the expense of losing the support of others.

Team-Selling Strategy. In team selling, when a salesperson visits prospects with a sales manager and/or a company technician, the team leader should "carry" the interview. Other members should be passive participants reinforcing the leader in body language and affirmations but not be outspoken nor detract from the leader's role as spokesperson. It is hazardous to plan team selling where selling participants want equal time. If one team member is a technical representative or a product expert, that member's role should be to answer technical or complex questions about the product. Sometimes, if it is evident that a presentation leader has failed, it is permissible for a nonleading member to take over to attempt to close a sale. Prospects who feel outnumbered can build up sales resistance and become negative unless appropriate active-passive roles are maintained by a sales team.

Reducing Prospect Risk—A Major Strategy. Buyers who make decision mistakes have more to lose than money. Bad buying decisions not only lose time but reflect negatively on the decider. The respect of others and the prospect's self-image and even position can be damaged by poor buying decisions. Positive actions that reduce risk help to eliminate this important barrier to buying. For information to be effective, a prospect must believe. It is difficult to resist proposals logically when risk has been reduced to almost zero.

A prospect's decision to make a purchase, to modify a rep's offer, to postpone action, or to avoid commitment is influenced by that prospect's perception of risk. Prospects cannot be sure of what the outcomes of a purchase decision will be, and this uncertainty about outcomes makes for anxiety. To reduce prospect perception of risk, a sales representative often must take on the role of counselor to a prospect before deciding which basic strategy to use in making a presentation. Frequently, this means that early interviews must be devoted to fact-finding to see what, if anything, that a rep has to offer can solve prospect problems. Selling a prospect a wrong solution may result in short-run benefits for a rep, but the professionally oriented sales representative knows that it's better to lose an order now than to lose a customer over the long run. The techniques listed below focus on ways that can offer prospects assurance that giving an order will not be an uncorrectable mistake.

Sell Features and Benefits Completely. It is natural to emphasize positive benefits that seem to fit buyer needs exactly. Product attributes that establish the worth of an offering, even if not directly relevant to known needs of a particular prospect, should not be forgotten. For example, a prospect may not currently need the total capacity of a machine, but needs do change. If a prospect wants to sell or trade equipment later, its total capabilities would be meaningful in convincing a second buyer. Durability, seller reputation, and styling can slow obsolescence and allow future conversion of a product into money.

Maintain Source Confidence. The prospect must believe what a rep says. All prospects constantly judge each sales representative who calls as a source of information. If hard-to-believe product claims are made at the beginning of an interview, even if they are true, prospects may discount the rest of a presentation or become defensive. Conservative claims at the beginning of a sales call can be built up believably to stronger claims once the prospect's confidence has been gained (10). All hard-to-believe claims should be backed up with good evidence. Prospects become very suspicious of sales representatives who do not stand behind their company or their product in an effort to take sides with the listener. Such conduct by agents is unethical. Few prospects want to buy from a source who is not loyal to the firm represented.

Records and Statistics. Specific and detailed data from records and statistics can be compelling. The Environmental Protection Agency (EPA) gasoline mileage ratings may have been obtained under ideal conditions by test drivers, but the EPA's printed results usually have a convincing effect on buyers interested in fuel economy. Especially risk reducing is information obtained from supposedly unbiased sources such as governments, consumer interest magazines, and trade associations. Even sales statistics compiled by a representative's own company are convincing, though not as convincing as statistics from independent sources. Quality-control standards and product-testing results to assure that a product meets certain requirements can be cited to good advantage.

Testimonials. It is the nature of buyers to want assurances from other buyers before signing an order. If a prospect can be furnished with written or oral testimony from a satisfied user, an important assurance will have been given. Few people want to be the first buyer of a product. Most prospects welcome the testimony of reliable persons who have purchased a product under similar conditions and found it satisfactory. The findings of recognized experts may also remove risk barriers. If written testimonials are not available, a salesperson may offer to phone a satisfied customer and let the prospect talk things over with him or her. If a sales representative mentions the names of previous buyers to a prospect, care should be taken that the experiences of these previous users were good, because a prospect may accept the rep's challenge and check. A reassuring experience for a prospect is to accompany a salesperson on a visit to see a product being used by a satisfied buyer.

Factory Tours. The outward appearance of many products fails to reflect the workmanship and premium materials that constitute it in finished form. The quality of workmanship, care and orderliness in manufacture, and inclusion of high-grade materials can be witnessed by an arranged visit to a plant. Such visits are productive only when a positive quality image is projected by manufacturing conditions. Visits should be prearranged with production personnel to prevent embarrassment. After all, manufacturing operations do get out of whack, and observation by outsiders can disrupt operations.

Warranties and Guarantees. Some warranties are implied by law, but most products and services carry written guarantees that furnish full assurance that the selling company will stand behind its products and that defective products will be replaced. A warranty stated in writing and certified by a selling firm carries much more weight than a verbal promise by a salesperson (see Figure 10.2). Equipment buyers, for example, are interested in continuity of operations. The breakdown of products could stop assembly-line operations and cost important employee time. Assurance that service is quickly available to minimize downtime is particularly important in cases like this. Money-back guarantees can assure that the product has the quality to merit that kind of backing. Guarantees or "service forever" or double-your-money-back on expensive items may indicate that the price is much higher to reflect an unusual guarantee. Being able to have a selling company correct product problems encountered is usually considered fair enough by most buyers. After all, a buyer wants to buy a product, not a guarantee.

Trial. If a prospect has mental reservations about the suitability of a product and an order is difficult to close, it may be possible to offer a trial at no obligation. Many people feel morally obligated to keep a product if it is taken on trial and lives up to its stated performance. Others simply feel it is not theirs until they pay for it and may feel like they are borrowing it from the salesperson's company. If something happens to it, they feel that they must pay for it. Others may be delighted that there is an expressed understanding that a product is on trial and can be returned without question.

WARRANTY

JOHN DEERE AGRICULTURAL EQUIPMENT

EQUIPMENT WARRANTY— 12 MONTHS—HOURS UNLIMITED

All parts of John Deere equipment, except tires, tubes, radios, and batteries, will be repaired or replaced, as John Deere elects, without charge for parts or labor, if a defect appears and is reported to a John Deere dealer within 12 months from the date of delivery to the original purchaser, regardless of the number of hours of use.

*EXTENDED ENGINE WARRANTY—24 MONTHS/ 1500 HOURS

The rocker arm cover, cylinder head, engine block, crankçase pan, and timing gear cover of the engine and the parts fully enclosed within these units will be repaired or replaced, as John Deere elects, without charge for parts or labor, if a defect appears and is reported to a John Deere dealer within 24 months from the date of delivery to the original purchaser, provided that the equipment has not been used for more than a total of 1500 hours.

*This extended engine warranty applies only to John Deere-built engines.
**This extended power train warranty applies to tractors with PTO horsepower of 90 and above.

**EXTENDED POWER TRAIN WARRANTY— AGRICULTURAL TRACTORS—24 MONTHS/ 1500 HOURS

The clutch housing, transmission case, torque divider housing, differential housing, final drive housings, and parts fully enclosed within these housings, including the drive axles, will be repaired or replaced, as John Deere elects, without charge for parts or labor, if a defect appears and is reported to a John Deere dealer within 24 months after the date of delivery of the tractor to the original purchaser, provided the tractor has not been used more than a total of 1500 hours.

PARTS REPLACED DURING WARRANTY

Genuine John Deere parts or authorized remanufactured assemblies that are furnished under this Agricultural Equipment Warranty and installed by an authorized John Deere dealer or by a John Deere Service Center will be repaired or replaced, as John Deere elects, without charge for parts or labor, if a defect in materials or workmanship appears and is reported to a John Deere dealer within 90 days from the date of installation of such parts or authorized remanufactured assemblies or before the expiration of the applicable original warranty period, whichever is later.

Source: Courtesy of John Deere Company, Moline, Illinois

Figure 10.2

ALTERNATIVE PRESENTATIONS

There are five different types of selling presentations. They vary in the amount of control a selling company has over an interview and in salesperson flexibility. The *automated presentation* is essentially the company message through audio-visual equipment. A sales representative stands by to answer questions and provides a human touch in closing (11). The *memorized* (or "canned") *presentation* also rigidly reflects a company message. However, it is the way the canned presentation is given and the salesperson's nonverbal communication that make it more or less effective. The *organized presentation,* structured by the company but expressed by its salesperson, is a good marriage of salesperson and company input. The *survey-proposal presentation,* used heavily in systems selling, and the *unplanned interview,* or the completely unstructured presentation, are largely based on salesperson contributions with little company participation except backup. Each of these plans represents an important alternative that should be considered in light of the product to be sold, the customers, and the abilities of sales force members. Each will be examined to see when to use it, its advantages and disadvantages, and its capacity to achieve strategic purposes.

Automated Presentations

Automated presentations require that sales representatives make customer contact and sell an audio-visual or visual presentation to prospects. Suppose, for example, that a particular presentation is a movie showing an earth-moving machine in action, performing to the limit of its capabilities to impress prospects. The film, probably in color, with music in the background, will use a pleasing voice to explain buyer benefits. Between demonstrations, the film might show prominent buyers giving testimony about the economic savings associated with ownership of the equipment shown. Action, testimonials, and the music set a mood and maintain prospect attention. Prospects find it difficult to muster sales resistance against a film's content, since a film is not a living thing. Points are presented in a minimum amount of time clearly, concisely, and emotionally (music arouses emotions). Usually there are no interruptions. Objections are anticipated. Most prospect questions are answered in the narration. The equipment offered is shown in its best light, for films can be edited and mistakes eliminated. At the end of such a presentation, a sales representative is available to answer questions and ask for an order. The operating salesperson can ask such questions as: "That equipment can really move the earth, can't it?" or "Would you like us to demonstrate one at your location?" or "May I put your order in for delivery this coming Monday?"

There are several problems with fully automated presentations. During the

Photo 10.2

Salesperson making a memorized sales presentation.

presentation, there is little prospect-salesperson interaction. The mood of presentation is broken when the film is over. It is difficult to establish two-way communication again. Closing immediately after the presentation may seem unnatural. Another problem is customizing the applications shown in the film or flip chart to the prospect. They may coincide closely with prospect need, or the prospect may be able to say, "Well, it looked all right for them but, after all, their operation is not like mine. It might not work that well for me." If there are problems with a presentation, if the film breaks, or the electricity goes off, or there is an interruption, the mood is broken, and it may be hard to reestablish interest. Also, this type of presentation may not enhance the self-image of sales representatives. They might resent their reduced role in making sales, begin to lean on the device, and not develop the persuasive qualities that participatory presentations allow (12). It is best used in cases where applications shown coincide with prospect needs, with products that are difficult to demonstrate, when a sales force is inexperienced, or when other methods have been tried and have failed.

Memorized Presentations

Memorized or canned presentations are similar in company input to automated presentations, except that the salesperson delivers the predetermined message (see Photo 10.2). There is no real break in continuity (as when a film is over). Inexperienced sales representatives learn the right words and tested selling phrases this way. They are able to give prospects complete accounts of benefits, with high hopes that the right response chord will be struck somewhere in their recitations. This method is most popular with low-dollar items, in cases where it is important to tell a complete account in a short amount of time, and when there is little intention of revisiting prospects. This method is based mainly on a stimulus-response strategy—conditioning prospects to respond favorably through overbalancing hesitation with benefits. Again, questions and objections are anticipated in this well-ordered and well-conceived scientific "masterpiece" put together by company sales experts. An alternative to complete rote memorization is having the salesperson memorize key selling phrases and the sequence but allowing some deviation in wording. A new sales representative can learn a presentation by heart and be allowed to personalize it slightly. The NCR Corporation (formerly National Cash Register) is a classic example of the successful use of canned presentations (see Chapter 11, NCR Primer). Most door-to-door sales representatives essentially use a memorized talk.

Marvin Jolson notes that while many sales managers feel that standardization makes presentations less effective, a study he conducted indicated that the reverse may be true. In research comparing a memorized with an outlined presentation, matched groups of respondents were used. Jolson found that the group exposed to the memorized sales talk indicated more willingness to purchase, more interest in learning more about the proposal, and less expression of intention not to buy than those exposed to the outline (13). The memorized presentation was judged as a harder sell but as a more exciting one. His conclusion was that salesperson flexibility was not as necessary in persuasion as was previously supposed.

Canned presentations cannot be used in all selling situations. It would be hard for a full-line sales representative selling dozens of products to memorize verbatim so many sales presentations. It would not be feasible for repeat-call salespersons to give the same sales talk every time a prospect was visited. While inexperienced salespersons are more likely to use this kind of company-controlled presentation, they are probably less skilled in delivering the intended message. *What* is said is important, but *how* it is said is critical. It takes skill to use someone else's words and supply appropriate inflection, tonality, and gestures. A memorized speech often appears weak in sincerity and conviction. It can easily appear to be artificial and impersonal. By depriving prospects of participation and involvement, it may not seem to treat prospects as individuals at all. In contrast with strategies that call for good two-way communication or questioning and listening techniques, it limits rapport between prospect and salesperson. Prospects may, indeed, feel insulted at being treated so impersonally and may react negatively. This type of presentation tends to ignore particular prospect problems and motivation. It tries to hit on everything without emphasizing anything. It can, however, be thorough, accurate, and impressive when used correctly.

Organized Presentations

An organized, or outlined, presentation is the favorite of sales managers. In a comparative study of the major types of sales presentations, sales executives ranked organized presentations first in saving prospect time, completeness, persuasion, anticipating objections, making sales training easier, increasing sales representative confidence, and facilitating sales supervision. They reported it as the most often used of all alternative methods. In this presentation method, sales representatives follow company outlines or checklists or points that should be covered. Even the sequence of points to be made is sometimes given. The use of visuals is optional, but visuals seldom make up an entire presentation. Salespersons are free to cover features and benefits using their own words. This should make interviews less awkward and more reflective of the reps' sales personalities. The relative freedom allowed sales representatives establishes rapport and encourages more prospect interaction. Prospects can interrupt. There is less difficulty in reestablishing pattern and continuity in presentation. There is more opportunity to use problem-solution, formula, or need-satisfaction strategies in organized presentations. The method seems to have just the right blend of company control and presentation flexibility for most firms. The effectiveness of an organized presentation depends largely on the competence of the salesperson. Salespersons free to express benefits in their own words may express them awkwardly or even incorrectly. The magic words so carefully included in a canned sales talk by the company sales executives may be omitted. In any organized presentation, a salesperson may overexpand some minor or unimportant points and fail to stress benefits and information important to a prospect. Freedom to emphasize certain benefits over others means that wrong emphases may be made. With so many advantages and so few disadvantages, however, this method should be considered as a favored alternative. A salesperson who uses this method and who memorizes key selling words and phrases should be able to plan the most effective presentation of all.

Survey-Proposal Presentations

These presentations have the structure of the problem-solution strategy, require professional inquiry into prospect problems, and usually take two or more visits to implement. Accounting-systems sales representatives, industrial sales representatives, life insurance sales representatives, and others who must investigate prospect problems before proposing specific solutions must first sell the need for investigating prospect problems thoroughly. A prospect should appreciate that the solution of complex system problems involves detailed inquiry and study. After a problem is studied and analyzed, a salesperson builds a solution and shows how various hardware (products) or financial components fit together into a solution system. Such a proposal often takes many hours of study and is usually presented in writing as well as orally, complete with prices and justifications. The salesperson is implying that he or she is an expert consultant. Prospects are usually impressed by the professionalism of this approach and feel obligated to give real consideration to proposals in view of the obvious amount of time required to produce the recommended written solution. The effect of seeing a complex problem solution justified on paper lends assurance to undecided prospects. The mood at the time of presentation is usually rational. Salespersons try to establish adult-adult transactional analysis relationships. The proposal can be used by the prospect to justify and convince other members of a buying team of the merits of purchase. This option features the extreme of customization and adaptation to prospect needs. Equipment may be programmed (set) to show the exact application to the buyer's problems. Prospects usually feel obligated to justify any refusals they might make.

This option depends heavily on the professionalism and expertise of the salesperson making the problem survey and proposal. Usually, a great deal of technical knowledge is necessary. The sales representative must exude confidence through personality. The main disadvantage of the method is that it takes time to make good proposals, and if a prospect fails to buy, that time is lost. Proposal deals may be very competitive, because of the large unit prices involved and time between survey and proposal.

Unplanned Interviews

Many senior sales representatives seem to work without any planned structure. The truth is that they have made so many presentations and have so much interview experience that they unconsciously follow a pattern and use many of the same expressions in each selling situation. This kind of presentation in the hands of a skilled professional can be very successful.

In the first place, it has the unity of a particular strategy. At the same time it has the freedom for instantaneous adjustment to prospect needs. Good questions and listening can establish congenial salesperson-prospect interaction. Selling personality can be expressed without restriction.

Following an unconscious pattern takes a maximum of experience and product knowledge. Beginning salespersons should use more structure. Even senior sales representatives can and will make important omissions in unstructured presentations, leaving out benefits that stimulate prospects to buy. Unplanned calls can result in overconfidence without justification, mediocrity instead of realization of full selling potential, laxity in preapproach investigation, and, eventually, bad morale and low professional growth. An experienced professional following this nonmethod should remember to keep learning. All salespersons should pattern their minds to a general strategic approach based on personal knowledge and understanding of selling situations.

Demonstration: A Special Kind of Presentation

Nothing is likely to be more convincing to a prospect than personally inspecting, handling, or operating a product—experiencing its benefits or features firsthand. No matter how skillful a sales rep becomes in standard presentation skills, sales effectiveness increases when prospects get "hands-on" experience. Prospects may watch a camera demonstration by a sales representative and attribute the resulting clear picture to rep expertise. When prospects see the same or similar results in pictures they have taken, belief in the camera's quality results. Automobile salespersons know that prospects must feel how a car responds to personal control if a buy is to be made. They encourage prospective buyers to drive the models under consideration. When a prospect senses a product, feels the silky sheen of a material, smells a perfume or a shaving lotion, tastes a fine wine, hears a stereo, sees a color TV next to a black-and-white set, it is easier to understand product benefits and value. It is direct involvement by prospects that tells them whether or not a product is right for them.

The first dictionary definition of "demonstrate" is "to show clearly." The second is "to prove or make clear by reasoning or evidence." Nothing shows a prospect so clearly the benefits of a rep's offer as demonstration. Nothing proves so convincingly as firsthand experience.

SOLVING PRESENTATION PROBLEMS

Two interview problems—answering objections and closing—will be treated in a later chapter. However, there are other important situations that merit careful handling: interruptions, competition, prospect inattention, prospect anger, and time limitations.

Interruptions

Interruptions are any disruptions to the continuity or tone of a presentation. An excited employee may demand a buyer's immediate attention, a secretary may bring in coffee, a telephone call may take several minutes, or prospects may excuse themselves to attend to another business matter for a period of time. Disruptions can be anticipated and, often, prevented. If a meeting place is too busy to hold prospect attention, a salesperson may request a quieter meeting place, saying, "Can we talk where I might explain this to you without outside interruption, Mr. Miller? This application is vital to your business, and I know you will want to give it your undivided attention." When interruptions do occur, the main problem is regaining attention. There are several ways to do this. If an interruption occurs while a salesperson is talking, it is usually a good practice to restate the point or points made just before the interruption. If the customer was speaking, the salesperson can remind him or her of the general nature of what was being said at the time of interruption. Repetition of selling points made before an interruption reemphasizes those points and is rarely offensive in view of the distraction. In fact, all previous points might be reviewed to reestablish continuity. The prospect might be asked a question to get benefits back in mind again. The mental effort necessary to answer helps prospects to forget an interruption and to reestablish their train of thought on an offering. A rep might say, "Of the features we talked about, fast operation and improved capacity, which do you think is the more important to you?" Sometimes handing a prospect an object or brochure connected with the product will help refocus attention (14). Taking out a pencil to prepare a sketch during the interruption, moving closer after it, and going over the sketch with the prospect at a close personal distance can undo an interruption's harm. If the product is present, it might be pointed out and a particular product feature explained. If an interruption is long, communication might be reestablished through a bit of small talk before getting back to the business at hand.

It is best not to refer to breaks in a presentation as "interruptions" or "disruptions." It is usually safest to say nothing at all. Acknowledging an interruption with a smile and a statement commenting on the nature of the pleasantness of a break, such as, "Your assistant was certainly thoughtful to bring us this good coffee," or "I met Mr. Latimer earlier this morning. He really seems to be a sharp guy" (only if Mr. Latimer came in and has left). During the interruption, the rep should be careful to afford prospects the privacy they desire by directing attention to sales materials, or offering to leave the room if a conversation appears to be private. If the prospect is so disturbed by the nature of the interruption or, through body language, shows desire to end the interview, the rep may want to come back when it is easier to establish enthusiasm and mood again. Interruptions can improve buyer mood if the news is good. They can seriously disturb a buyer's receptive mood if the news is bad or if the buyer's presence is needed elsewhere. Salespersons must show evidence of understanding and sensitivity to buyer needs in these situations.

Competition

Competition affects interviews. Even if competition is not indicated, it is still the best practice to stress particular advantages of a product that competition cannot match. If competition can match all features and benefits, then prospects must be convinced by a sales representative's better service. Even when it is felt that competitive salespersons will be talking to a prospect, it is best to make comparisons without ever identifying a competitive firm by name. If a prospect brings up competitive company names and specific competitive equipment or asks point blank why your product is superior in offering, you might reply, "That is a good machine, Ms. Steele, and a good company, but our machine is constructed with a rust-resistant plating and produces 20 percent more units per hour than any other machine on the market. You want to have those advantages in the equipment you buy, don't you?" A competitor has still not been mentioned directly. All competitive claims must be true. Since competition is an ever-present threat, it is important that all of an offering's benefits be covered completely. Competitors should be treated fairly and without harsh criticism. If a competitive offering has a serious defect in terms of serving a prospect's needs, it should be pointed out indirectly by a statement like, "Be sure to check any equipment you consider for copying speed. While our machine takes only three seconds to copy, some machines take seven seconds. Our faster capability can save you hundreds of dollars in employee time over the life of the equipment."

Prospect Inattention

A sales representative should be able to tell by prospect body language if a prospect is inattentive or defensive. If prospects start to give attention to other things while a salesperson is talking, something must be done to bring them back. Smiling, drawing closer, or asking a question are among the ways that attention can be reestablished. To answer a question, prospects have to think and talk about the subject at hand. The methods mentioned for handling interruptions also apply, since this is an interruption of a prospect's train of thought. A good salesperson never lets a prospect "throw a presentation off" through inattention or any other failure to be courteous. It is a good idea to cater to ego needs and make the prospective buyer feel important and respected.

Prospect Anger

When prospects show anger toward a rep or a rep's company, the best strategy is to let them talk it out of their systems. Let the buyer confess *seller* sins. In fact, ask questions to find out exactly what is wrong and listen, listen, listen. Not every sales situation is pleasant, and you must keep in mind that the salesperson who can handle hard customers is a real professional. The person who is always angry or prejudiced may need a psychologist. So be one by being especially attentive, understanding, and quiet until the prospect or customer finishes. An angry prospect needs to explain the problem emotionally. When the verbal tirade is over, a reasonable remedy can be suggested. Prospects tend to appreciate your maturity in this and may even become ashamed at their loss of control and seek to make amends by being especially reasonable.

Time Limitations

While some prospects enjoy talking to sales representatives, for most prospects, time is money. If conserving time is not important to them, then it should be to sales representatives. A prospect's time should be respected. Tell the whole story, do a thorough job, listen carefully to what customers have to say, but don't misuse or abuse time by taking too long to "establish rapport" or by getting off on unimportant conversational topics. It is important to talk about the prospect's personal interests if the prospect wishes to, but not those of a rep. A sales representative must try to determine if time is available to make an effective presentation. Only the rep can decide whether to make an abbreviated presentation or to return at a more opportune time. If an interview can be shortened without losing its essence, it may be even more effective than a longer meeting. But the appearance of "hurry" in a call can ruin its mood. If prospects are definitely telling a sales rep through nonverbal communication that time is up, the rep might ask if they have pressing business, try to close the sale based on the points already made, or request another appointment. Purchasing agents and corporate executives report that salespeople who waste valuable time invite closed doors in the future.

PRESENTATION TECHNIQUES

Entrepreneur and showman Mike Todd once said, "You show me a showman and I'll show you a salesman. You show me a salesman and I'll show you a showman!" (15). It is natural to expect professional persuaders to be exciting to listen to, but usually they are not. Instead of presenting sales propositions in ways that get prospects into the "act," most sales representatives are stiff and mechanical. Perhaps the sensitivity that all creative people feel when presenting their own work inhibits development of presentation skills. Even such professional presenters of ideas as advertising account executives are sometimes weak in presentation skills (16).

Selling is more fun for prospect and salesperson when presentations come alive. The quickest way to make a presentation come alive for a prospect is to involve that prospect in the presentation. Handing a prospect a sample, a reminder, a personally useful item for the office that can act as a future reminder of a presentation are all ways to gain attention and generate prospect participation.

"One authority says that mental impact is 87 percent from the visual contact, 7 percent from the audio contact, 2 percent from the taste contact, 3 percent from the touch contact, and 1 percent from the smell contact" (17). Whether or not these percentages are completely accurate isn't important. What is important is that the overwhelming impression a prospect has of a sales call comes from what the prospect sees, yet sales representatives always tell but only rarely show. Most experts estimate that recall of a spoken presentation rarely exceeds 30 percent of the material presented. The problem for a sales rep is determining which 30 percent a prospect will recall.

Figure 10.3 Presentation Checklist

1. Be honest now, is there a bit of "ham" in you?
2. Is there a bit of Clarence Darrow?
3. Are you a good editor of your own material?
4. Do you get nervous?
5. Do you have a system for "psyching yourself up" before you present?
6. Do you rehearse your presentation at least ten times before you give it?
7. Do you keep your cool under fire?
8. Do you know what you really sound like—and look like—when you're making a presentation?
9. Do you have dramatic substitutes for the storyboard?
10. Are you a student of body language?
11. Do you know when to use slides and when to use cards?
12. Do you know where your hands are?
13. Do you know how to keep your audience from leaping ahead of you?
14. Do you have a system for anticipating questions?
15. Do you know how to say "I don't know" without sounding like a dummy?
16. Do you always know what the other presenters in your meeting are going to say and show?
17. Do you always have a dossier on the key people in your audience?
18. Do you know what to do when the audio-visual equipment breaks down?
19. Do you know how to avoid the "caught-in-a-coffin" look?
20. Do you make an effort to learn from actors, ministers, moderators, commentators, newsreaders—even, politicians?

Source: Ron Hoff, "What's Your Presentation Quotient?" *The Advertising Age*, January 16, 1978, pp. 93–96.

Dramatizing presentations can greatly increase overall recall and can point up a sales presentation's most important points. Wherever possible, truly professional sales presentations use drama and visual aids to gain positive reinforcement of major selling points. The presentation check list (Figure 10.3) can act as a guide to more effective presentations. Its maker, Ron Hoff, Executive Creative Director of Foote, Cone & Belding, New York, says of it, "Eighteen yes-checks and you're probably a real spellbinder of a presenter" (18). Although Hoff's list focuses on team selling situations, every salesperson can learn from it.

SUMMARY

A basic selling strategy should be reflected in the presentation, which is the main persuasive effort made to secure a sales order. Stimulus-response strategy, formula strategy, problem-solution strategy, want-satisfaction strategy, depth-selling strategy, group-selling strategy, or combinations of these are alternatives. A presentation should help the prospect realize need, see that an offered product is the best solution to that need, feel that the price is fair in relation to the benefits received, believe that service will be adequate, and understand the advantages of buying now. To reduce prospect risk, features and benefits must be sold completely, salesperson self-confidence maintained, demonstrations involve prospects, records and statistics be shown, testimonials furnished, plant tours taken, information about warranties and guarantees conveyed, and/or prospect trial without obligation offered.

The five basic presentation types differ in salesperson flexibility and company control of sales effort. Automated presentations explain product benefits completely but allow little interaction between salesperson and prospect and may not meet an individual prospect's exact needs. Memorized presentations are convenient for new sales representatives but are relatively inflexible and may seem artificial to prospects. Organized presentations are recommended by most sales managers because of their flexibility and the prospect interaction they allow. The survey-proposal type of presentation and the unplanned interview are strategically and psychologically sound for high-level systems selling. In addition, there are demonstrations, which go a long way toward convincing prospects to buy.

Four problems basic to most presentations are interruptions, the handling of competition, prospect inattention, and prospect anger. After interruptions, a rep should review previous selling points, get nearer to the prospect, hand something to the prospect, or point out a particular product feature to regain attention. Stress on a product's particular advantages is forceful, even if competitive offers are not brought up by a prospect, but, in making comparisons, competitors should not be mentioned by name nor should they be harshly criticized. The main method to diminish prospect anger is attentive listening to prospect complaints. Always respect prospect time.

1. What is the "acid test" of a good sales presentation?

2. What is meant by the stimulus-response strategy of sales presentation? Evaluate this method.

3. What conditions favor formula strategy as the method of presentation?

4. Briefly explain how each of the objectives of the common formula strategy AIDCA might be accomplished.

5. What do you understand by want-satisfaction strategy? Under what conditions is this strategy most effective?

6. In what ways does problem-solution strategy extend want-satisfaction strategy?

7. Relate depth selling to other methods of sales presentation.

8. What are some of the distinguishing aspects of selling to a group as contrasted with selling to an individual?

9. How do the various participants in team selling fulfill their specific roles?

10. What are the five decisions a prospect must make prior to placing a purchase order?

11. Buyers are exposed to certain risks when they make a purchase decision. What are these risks?

12. Suggest some of the ways in which the prospect's buying risk can be reduced.

13. What are the five types of sales presentation based on the degree of control that the selling company has over the salesperson's interview procedure?

14. What is an automated presentation? What are some of the problems associated with such a presentation? Under what conditions is it favored?

15. What are the advantages and disadvantages of the memorized presentation?

16. Why is the organized presentation popular?

17. Are unplanned interviews an effective method of presentation?

18. List the major problems that can jeopardize the effectiveness of a sales presentation.

19. What are the signs of prospect inattention?

20. Involvement of which of the senses provides the most impact in communication?

APPLICATION QUESTIONS

The cybernetic model discussed in Chapter 4 included visualizing a situation. Now that you are aware of the various approaches and sales presentation techniques, pick a product that you are interested in and know something about, list the selling points you would cover, determine the order in which you would cover them, and visualize yourself making a sales presentation.

a. How would you apply the want-satisfaction strategy in this situation?

b. How would you apply the stimulus-response strategy? What questions would you ask?

c. How do the want-satisfaction and the stimulus-response strategies fit in with the formula strategy? Can they all be used together?

INCIDENTS

10–1

Ted Darby has made calls on the mayor and three aldermen in the city of Nellburg and interested them in a copying machine for City Hall. A competitive salesperson, Barry Lindy, has also seen and made presentations to these four men. Equipment that is needed by the town is bought after these representatives of the two competitive companies make formal presentations before the whole group at a called meeting. Ted has been selected to make his presentation first.

> *Ted:* Mayor Needham, John, Bill, and Sam. It is now 8 p.m., and I know all of you have been working hard and have had a long day. The sales representative who will follow me is one of the top salespeople with the BTL Corporation, and it will probably take him at least an hour to persuade you to buy his machine. We have a copying machine like the one I am offering in Bettsburg, Leesville, and in over half the other cities this size within a hundred-mile radius of Nellburg. Our equipment is fully guaranteed to make copies like this *(shows sample)* at the rate of one every three seconds, and the price to municipalities is $4,787.50, after the 10 percent government discount. Do you have any questions about this offer? *(waits)* I sure would appreciate your business.

Mayor: Thank you, Ted, we appreciate your concern for our time. Most of us have seen the machine you have at Bettsburg. Tell Mr. Lindy to come in.

Barry: Gentlemen, I want you to see a color film of this excellent equipment that will take about an hour. After that I will explain some of the technical details of the COPIER 3000. Please hold your questions until after the film. *(Lindy shows the film and talks about the copier for twenty more minutes.)*

Mayor: I'm sorry to interrupt you, Mr. Lindy, but could you please wrap up your presentation. It's getting late. *(Lindy summarizes and leaves.)*

Mayor: Please raise your hand if you want to vote for Ted Darby's machine . . . The ayes have it. Please tell Mr. Darby he has the order, Mrs. Sedbury.

QUESTIONS

1. What was the primary need of this buying group?

2. Did they really care about the technical properties of the equipment?

3. Assuming they considered the machines equal in price and capabilities, why did they give Ted the order?

10–2

The exercise below is composed of a series of mini-incidents. These have been developed to aid practicing sales representatives in increasing their proficiency in selling. Your instructor will give you an interpretation of your response to each mini-incident.

"Those Vital Opening Seconds"

For each of the following situations, circle the letter that you feel is the best way to begin your response.

1. You're an automobile salesperson. A prospect has just walked into the showroom.
   a. Say, "I take it you're looking for a new car."
   b. "What kind of car do you want?"
   c. (Wait for the prospect to speak first.)
   d. "Shave or a haircut?"
   e. "I've got just the baby for you!"

2. You're a real-estate salesperson. You've shown a prospect three houses that seem to meet his specifications.
   a. "Which one do you like best?"
   b. "I guess none of them was that good."
   c. "If you think those houses are overpriced, let me show you mine."
   d. "Great bargains, aren't they?"
   e. "How do you feel about those houses?"

3. You're a life insurance salesperson. You talk briefly with a prospect who mailed in a "Send us your birthdate, and we'll mail you a free gift" card.

The prospect then says, "That sounds interesting, but I've got a friend who's in life insurance."
a. "Then I guess you don't want to buy anything from me."
b. "I didn't think insurance salespeople had any friends."
c. "There's no way your friend can match our benefits for the same premium."
d. "You feel loyal. I agree that it's important, if the products are identical."

4. You represent a data processing company. You call on a small-business owner, who hits you with, "Who do you think I am, General Motors? A small operation like this doesn't need fancy computers!"
a. "If you lease one of our machines, maybe you'll get bigger than GM."
b. "A small company like yours can't afford not to have data processing."
c. "Then you feel you're too small to benefit from data processing."
d. "What's your weekly payroll?"
e. "Sorry. I must be in the wrong place."

5. You sell industrial motors. You've spent a lot of time with a prospect who seems favorably impressed, but whenever you try to close, she says, "It seems OK, but I don't know. What else can you tell me about it?"
a. "I can tell you that if you don't grab it quick, your competition will."
b. "You seem very impressed with our machines, but you'd like to feel certain."
c. "What else do you want to know?"
d. "I'd be glad to answer as many questions as you have."
e. "By the time I finished telling you all about it, it might be obsolete."

6. You represent a furniture leasing company. Your prospect is a psychologist starting her own practice. She says, "Doesn't it make more sense to buy furniture than to waste money on renting?"
a. "Sounds like you're concerned about what will give you the most value for your money."
b. "How much did you intend to spend?"
c. "I guess it does, if you have enough money."
d. "If I agreed with that, I ought to come see you to have my head examined."
e. "Are you kidding? There are no advantages to buying."

7. You represent an employment agency. You call up a company that placed a help-wanted ad for a secretary to see if they'll use your service. The boss says, "Sure, sure. So you can rip us off for a month's salary."
a. "How long did it take you to fill your last opening?"
b. "Maybe you'd consider us if we only charged you two weeks' salary this time?"
c. "It beats rolling drinks."
d. "You'll never get anyone at that salary without our help."
e. "Our rates do seem high if you're not familiar with our service."

8. You sell self-improvement courses. You're telephoning people whose work promotions were announced in the newspaper. When the prospect answers the phone, you introduce yourself and say,
a. "My boss told me to call you."
b. "Have you heard the story about the two midgets?"
c. "I'm sure a comer like you knows the importance of continuing study."
d. "I'd be feeling pretty proud right now if I were in your shoes."
e. "When is the last time you were inside a classroom?"

9. You sell razor blades wholesale. You call on a retailer for the first time, and he says, "I used to order from your outfit. But the deliveries were usually fouled up."
   a. "If we foul up again, I'll use my product . . . on my wrists."
   b. "We offer the highest profit margin, so I wouldn't complain if we were late once in a while."
   c. "You're reluctant to deal with a company that messed up deliveries."
   d. "Who did you used to deal with?"
   e. "Well, shipping isn't one of our strong points."

10. You've just signed a deal with a woman to take photos at her daughter's wedding.
    a. "That's gotta be the best decision you've made since your daughter was born."
    b. "You seem to be really looking forward to the big day."
    c. "How many prints do you think the groom's family will want?"
    d. "I hope you don't regret this decision."
    e. "Just make the deposit out to cash, and I'll send you a picture from Mexico."

Adapted from Learning Dynamics, Inc., Boston, Mass., 1979.

10-3

Gary Head represents the division of Acme Abrasives Corporation that sells grinding compounds to foundries for fine finishing of graymetal, nonferrous, iron, and steel castings. Gary has been having a problem getting the attention of workers on the foundry floor so that he can sell Acme's new grinding compound "Nike" in depth to those who would work with it. Acme is the American licensee of Flaggenbauer A. G. of Germany. Flaggenbauer has convinced the sales manager that the best way to show off the features of "Nike" is to demonstrate its value on a foundry's grinding-room floor.

As anyone who has ever visited a foundry knows, it is difficult to attract attention in such a place. Most foundries are hot, noisy, and, despite advances in lighting technology, dark. Gary has had no problems in gaining access to the floors of most of the foundries in his territory. However, getting the attention of the workers in them has been something else entirely. If Gary can become the leader in his region in "Nike" sales, he will win an all-expenses-paid tour to Paris for two for two weeks. Gary really wants to win the trip. He has just the person he wants to share a two-week trip to Paris with: his wife, Marjorie.

From his sales record, it is obvious that Gary found a way to get the attention of foundry workers. He won the trip hands down.

Acme sales manager Andrew Nail has decided to travel with Gary to see how Gary is able to sell "Nike" so successfully. Their first foundry call is at Moline Iron Works in Moline, Illinois. Andrew is surprised when they pull up into Moline's parking lot. Gary gets out of the car, picks up his briefcase, but instead of starting for the Moline plant, goes to the rear of his car and opens the trunk. Inside his trunk, Gary has two piles of crisp, clean, white cotton sportscoats. He puts one on.

When Gary and Andrew enter the foundry at Moline, Andrew sees one immediate advantage of Gary's white jacket. In the gloom of the foundry, Gary's jacket stands out like a beacon. Moreover, it is soon obvious to Andrew that Gary has established a real rapport with Moline's foundry workers. Nearly every worker on the floor comes up to greet Gary. Most pat him on the back. A few use his jacket as if it were a hand towel. By the time Andrew and Gary leave the Moline foundry, Gary's sparkling white jacket is a collage of wipings, handprints, and grease marks. Andrew is a little bit unnerved to see Gary repeat his Moline performance at each of the other four foundries they call on that day. He begins to have reservations about the way Gary has achieved his "Nike" sales success.

Aloft on his return plane to Acme's headquarters in Pittsburgh, Andrew mulls over what he has seen Gary do. He wonders if Gary's methods of presentation are consistent with Acme's corporate image. At the same time, Andrew is pleased with Gary's sales success and was happy to hand him the tickets he had won for the trip to Paris.

If you were Andrew, would you advise other Acme reps to use Gary's approach to getting attention? Why? Why not?
If Gary's method of getting attention is at variance with Acme's corporate image, did he win the contest fairly?
What do you think of Gary's approach?

10–4

Sylvia Lowenstein sells name brands of women's clothing mainly to dress shops and department stores in New England. One of her best accounts is a medium-sized department store in Connecticut, and she feels she has an excellent line to offer the buyer, Mr. Haas. Mr. Haas is an introvert but has been courteous in the past. Sylvia is quite apprehensive about the interview this time, however, because of an unfortunate experience Mr. Haas had when he received part of the last order from her. It seems that the ladies' dresses reached the selling floor with a label stating: Made Especially for Morgan's Discount House. The mixup caused Mr. Haas considerable embarrassment, since his store caters to upper-middle-class trade. He, in fact, canceled part of the same order for ladies' coats that had not been shipped with the dresses. Of course, it was not Sylvia's fault that the manufacturer had shipped the dresses to the department store with the wrong label. Sylvia knows that Mr. Haas is still upset about the embarrassing dresses and has decided to visit him, leaving her samples in the car, and let him sound off at her and get it out of his system. To her surprise, Mr. Haas's secretary gives her almost immediate access to Mr. Haas. Mr. Haas simply glares at her, takes out his pocket watch, lays it on the table, and says: "Young lady, you have ten minutes to present your line." Sylvia can tell that he plans to say no more until the interview is over.

How should this interview problem be handled?

NOTES

1. Allen L. Reid, *Modern Applied Salesmanship,* 2nd ed. (Pacific Palisades, Calif.: Goodyear, 1975), pp. 220–221.

2. Joseph W. Thompson, "A Strategy of Selling," in Steven J. Shaw and Joseph W. Thompson (eds.), *Salesmanship* (Chicago: Holt, Rinehart and Winston, 1966), pp. 13–25.

3. Thomas F. Stroh, *Salesmanship* (Homewood, Ill.: Irwin, 1966), pp. 161–242.

4. Thompson, "A Strategy of Selling."

5. Stroh, *Salesmanship,* pp. 185–204.

6. *Ibid.,* pp. 228–229.

7. *Ibid.,* p. 217.

8. *Ibid,* pp. 242–255.

9. Gary M. Grirscheit, Harold C. Cash, and W. J. E. Crissy, *Handbook of Selling* (New York: Wiley, 1981), p. 229.

10. Frederic A. Russel, Frank H. Beach, and Richard H. Buskirk, *Textbook of Salesmanship,* 11th ed. (New York: McGraw-Hill, 1982), p. 231.

11. Marvin A. Jolson, "Should the Sales Presentation be 'Fresh' or 'Canned,' " *Business Horizons,* October 1973, pp. 81–87.

12. *Ibid.*

13. Marvin A. Jolson, "The Underestimated Potential of the Canned Sales Presentation," *Journal of Marketing,* vol. 39, no. 1 (January 1975), pp. 75–78.

14. Reid, op. cit.

15. Carl G. Stevens, *A Blueprint for Professional Selling* (Columbus, Ohio: Management Horizons, no date), p. 20.

16. Ron Hoff, "What's Your Presentation Quotient?" *The Advertising Age,* January 16, 1978, pp. 93–96.

17. James F. Robeson, H. Lee Matthews, and Carl G. Stevens, *Selling* (Homewood, Ill.: Irwin, 1978), p. 362.

18. Hoff, "What's Your Presentation Quotient?"

Communication Aids

The old-fashioned spellbinding sales representative is obsolete. Contemporary reps use communication tools such as visual aids, the telephone, advertising, and products themselves to increase selling potential. Every prospect, whether for a consumer or an industrial good, has been exposed to quite sophisticated presentations through watching television. A convincing proof of the ways that sight can aid sound in communication effectiveness is offered by contrasting television coverage of a sporting or news event with radio coverage of it. The television announcers talk less than their radio counterparts. Sales representatives who use communication aids can talk less, too, than their competitors who depend on spoken words alone to make sales. Moreover, they will communicate more effectively. When in doubt about which sort of communication to make, it is well to remember that in kindergarten the order was to "Show and Tell."

What can be shown? Films, portfolios, samples, models, customized presentation boards and flip charts, posters, sales manuals, tables, charts, and graphs can all be useful tools in reinforcing a sales rep's message to prospects about the benefits of buying. Through the use of visuals, reps can learn how to make telephone prospects "see" benefits at long distance. Telephone selling can speed and facilitate nearly every phase of selling, including prospecting, appointment making, and complete presentations.

Among the most useful and accessible of communication aids available to salespeople is advertising. Long ago, Bruce Barton, famed advertising innovator of the 1920s, defined advertising as "Salesmanship in print." The communications aid that advertising—product or institutional—can bring to a presentation will be gained by reps who recognize that contemporary selling can almost be defined as "advertising in person."

The communication process was covered in detail in Chapter 5. The focus of this chapter is on communication aids as a means to increase message effectiveness and retention. At the end of this chapter, you should know more about how communication devices can be used to clarify sales presentations. Some of the areas to be covered are:

- The advantages of aids and selling devices
- The effective demonstration
- The use of visual devices to sell
- Advertising as an aid to personal selling

THE ADVANTAGES OF AIDS AND SELLING DEVICES

Aids Promote Two-Way Communication

Salespersons will sell more if they know how to use selling aids and dramatization devices properly. Products or selling aids can be focal points for sales presentations, since they encourage natural discussion between salesperson and prospect. In a 1980 survey, more than three-quarters of the companies surveyed reported the use of audio-visual equipment on sales calls (1). A prospect is encouraged to ask questions about a product's features after seeing it or a visual aid. Aids provide a structure for a natural presentation. They stimulate good two-way conversation and keep interest focused on the product.

Aids Save Time

When you can show a prospect a product's features in a demonstration or visual, you can not only offer a simple and unified presentation, but you can also save time for both you and your prospect. Since the prospect can see and/or feel a model, the many descriptive words required to help a prospect visualize product features are not necessary. Valuable interview time saved by use of selling aids can be used in other important ways.

Aids Appeal to Many Senses

Perhaps the most important advantage of using communication aids (other than the telephone) is that they appeal to senses other than hearing. Seeing ordinarily makes a stronger impression than hearing. Touching, smelling, and tasting add to a total understanding of a product offering. Insurance sales representatives can introduce sight through diagrams and models. Food sales representatives can use all the senses, including taste and smell, to stimulate buying emotions and desire for purchase.

Aids Get Attention

Using a multisense approach through dramatization commands a prospect's attention and interest. A buyer feels more a participant and less a mere listener when allowed to judge the merits of an offering firsthand. While buyers may resist words and discount a rep as a prejudiced source, they are much less likely to mistrust their own personal judgment. Communication aids allow them to feel and visualize an offering. They can become a part of it. Touching a product often imparts a feeling of ownership that cannot be induced through a verbal appeal.

Aids Cause Prospects to Remember When Situations Change

Communication devices make prospects remember demonstrations. If the impressions are favorable, predispositions to buy will be strengthened. Even if a sale cannot be closed during an interview, a demonstration or dramatization may work in a prospect's mind long after a presentation is over. Demonstration aids, therefore, continue to convince and prompt buying actions in the future.

Aids Persuade the Prospect

If "seeing is believing," then "sensing is convincing." It is one thing to hear that a car responds easily to command, but it is much more impressive to feel response by taking the wheel and driving it. Prospects want to know *how* the product will work for them. While they may believe the testimony of others, they *know* when they experience it for themselves.

THE EFFECTIVE DEMONSTRATION

Most companies have detailed records proving that sales representatives who demonstrate products excel in getting orders. Words can never be as effective as seeing a product being used under favorable circumstances. Part of every salesperson's detailed goals should be to make a certain number of demonstrations every week, if the product is one that can be shown to advantage. Even life insurance, investments, and charitable contributions can be demonstrated through charts and graphs. While a good demonstration convinces a prospect, a weak or poor demonstration has the opposite effect. In a department store, a salesperson was trying to demonstrate a cookie gun that would "shoot" a shaped wad of cookie dough onto a piece of waxed paper in preparation for cooking. The dough was too thick, and after depositing three or four misshaped cookie mounds, the gun jammed. The disposition to buy was weakened by ineffective demonstration. The prospect's conclusion was "If an expert can't do it, I'll probably have trouble, too." In order to give more effective demonstrations, consider the following suggestions.

Determine If a Demonstration Is Really Necessary

If a prospect is already sold, which really was the case with the cookie gun, it is not necessary to give a demonstration. Things can go wrong even during a simple demonstration: Seeing a product malfunction leaves a lasting negative impression. Prospects draw conclusions from incomplete evidence. On the other hand, demonstrations do offer superior attention-getting benefits and can be highly convincing. They are definitely worthwhile in nearly every presentation, except in situations where the deal can obviously be closed without them. A main fault of most sales representatives is not demonstrating enough.

Plan and Organize the Demonstration

The demonstration should fit naturally into a presentation. There should be smooth transitions from interview to demonstration back to interview. The speed of a demonstration should be coordinated with the prospect's experience. If a prospect already understands a product's application, a demonstration can move more quickly. If the application is technical and new, it is better to move slowly and make sure that every feature and benefit is understood completely. The temptation of assuming that the prospect should know beforehand as much as a rep does should be avoided. Features should be explained in the best sequential order, to make the demonstration the proper length. If there is little time, those features that have a strong differential advantage over the competition should be stressed. Reps must make sure that

WATCHES

"Now you're probably asking yourself, 'Is it shockproof?'"

© Orlando Busino 1962

Demonstrations can create a big impression.

prospects understand. A few questions can gauge response. Points that may not be clearly understood should be repeated. Prospect participation requires careful planning and control. Prospects should not be allowed to attempt things they probably cannot do. Product and prospect image blend with a prospect's greater familiarity with a product.

Set the Environment

Demonstrations should be given in environments that have a minimum number of interruptions and distractions. Demonstrations of complex equipment can best be given at the branch office or at a customer's installation where there is neither traffic nor noise. A demonstration room or setting should be impressive. In some instances low background music is appropriate to help set a mood. Furniture should be arranged so that when prospects are seated, they can see the entire operation and can talk to all present without furniture blocking conversation. Everything should be in keeping with the desired image to be conveyed of a firm and of its product.

Check Out Materials

Equipment to be demonstrated should be thoroughly checked by maintenance personnel. All software such as forms, charts, and visuals should be reviewed for accuracy and completeness. Malfunctioning equipment can be the death of a sale—it is hard to overcome demonstration mistakes of any kind. All equipment should be thoroughly cleaned and operated in the demonstration room to make sure it is at optimum operational levels. It should be programmed or adjusted, if possible, to the customer's application. Demonstration materials should be in place. They should be sequenced as they will be used. Fumbling for forms and materials leaves a bad impression. Once materials are inspected and set, no one should disturb them before the demonstration. If it is planned to demonstrate equipment in a prospect's office, proper extension cords and plug-ins or other accessory items should accompany the demonstrator. If the plan is to show a prospect another customer's application at that customer's place of business, everything must be thoroughly prearranged. The demonstrating customer's best operator or the sales rep should operate the equipment. If possible, a customer's installation should be visited before a prospect is taken there.

Practice

It is necessary to master the operation of any equipment and to review exposition of any charts or software. A musical genius who could have been a concert pianist made a fortune demonstrating pianos instead. He made prospects feel that anyone could do it. A salesperson must do the same thing. The entire presentation should be gone over thoroughly before any attempt is made to show it to a prospect. Hard parts can be made to look easy through mastery of a product. Prospects should attempt only the easiest operations. Prospects do not expect to be able to master complicated parts of an operation immediately, but if it looks easy when a sales rep does it, they will believe it can be learned.

Use the Right Words

Good descriptive words and comparisons reinforce demonstrations. Consider these suggestive words to accompany a showing of the product:

- It is hard to believe that a machine could do all that in just seven seconds, isn't it?
- Did you notice how smoothly this car glided over those rough railroad tracks? It was almost as if we were on a cushion of air, wasn't it?
- Look at the clarity and detail of this instant picture—you snapped the shutter less than a minute ago.
- Have you ever tasted anything as refreshing as that?
- Look at the spaciousness of this room. You would never feel cramped in here, would you?
- It is as silent as a candle. Can you hear it?

Handle Mistakes Properly

Few demonstrations of complex operations are completed without any mistakes. Even in the simplest operations, malfunctions and errors can occur. Suppose, for example, an error is made in demonstrating a cash register. Instead of calling attention to the error, use the error to demonstrate the error-correcting procedures available with the equipment. Sometimes errors go unnoticed by prospects. Like a good entertainer, a salesperson might simply go on with the show if a mistake is small and unimportant. Sometimes demonstrators make errors purposely to illustrate points or to test for prospect attention or understanding. To be realistic, however, if a product does not work and cannot be made to work, its malfunctioning will be extremely difficult to explain away. It is necessary to know what to do when a product malfunctions and how to do it quickly for effective demonstrations. A demonstrator can suggest how easy a product is to fix when an "infrequent" malfunction does occur. Sales people need to remember that prospects are concerned that the selling company might deliver the demonstrated equipment to them, which they will regard as slightly used. It is good to explain that the product they will get is still in its package, or to offer them demonstration equipment at reduced prices.

Showmanship in Demonstrations

Showmanship, usually associated with a product demonstration, is the use of dramatic methods to impress points. A salesperson who smashes a fist down on a keyboard of an office machine, who purposely drops a watch on a concrete floor, or who jumps up and down on a suitcase is using showmanship to say that the product is durable. A sales representative who holds jewelry up against a dark background, who puts color-coordinated tie and socks against a newly purchased suit without saying a word, or who pours water in a glass while a car is going over a rough road is using showmanship—silent language to make impressive points about a product.

THE USE OF VISUAL DEVICES TO SELL

While seeing a product being used in its intended role is reassuring to prospects, there are many other visual devices that can be used to dramatize presentations and to stir buying emotions. Some of these will be examined.

Flip Charts and Felt Boards

Nothing a sales representative can do for a prospect is as powerful as a customized preparation that focuses on prospect needs. Unfortunately, the customized presentation is made less often than it ought to be. Most reps feel their general preparation for sales calls is enough. They depend on their ability to "play it by ear" once a sales interview has begun. No prospect or even long-time customer wants to feel taken for granted. A customized presentation prepared for a particular call on a flip chart or using felt boards and cutouts is an easy way to show regard for customers and prospects.

The rep who uses either a flip chart or a felt board and cutouts need not worry about a lack of artistic ability. Almost anyone can do a respectable job. Salespeople shy of their graphic arts abilities should think back to the artistic skills of their professors. The most effective of these may not have been able to draw well, but their capacities to communicate were usually enhanced through use of the blackboard.

The flip chart offers a chance for a combination presentation. Part can be done ahead of time, and part can be put in place during the interview. For example, buyer benefits in a recent ad can be written on a flip chart page in magic marker, and the salesperson can say: "These are the reasons that our customers tell us they buy from us. [The list is then gone through to reinforce the buyer benefits listed. The best order for listing of, say, five benefits would be, 1 (most important), 3, 4, 5, and 2, and the list should be gone through from top to bottom, then from bottom to top. This assures that the last listed item in each case is strong.] Which one of these do you feel is most important to you? [The flip chart can then be flipped to a blank page and the prospect's answer written. The rep can read it aloud.] I'm sure there is a very good rationale for choosing that particular reason. May I ask what it is? [This too should be recorded—perhaps, in a contrasting color. While it is entered and repeated, the sales representative has a chance to assess opportunity to meet prospect needs and to formulate tactics for the rest of the interview.]"

A felt board and cutouts offer a similar opportunity to add dynamism and prospect involvement to presentations. Materials for either—the flip chart tablet and portable easel, the feltboard, or the materials to assemble one, are readily available in most stationery stores. Use of either adds meaning to what is said; either will go far to increase prospect retention of presentation material. The big plus is the regard shown for the individual called upon.

Film

Fully programmed films with sound can cover all a product's feature benefits in vivid and convincing ways. A film can include music to set a buying mood, can offer testimonials, and can minimize distracting influences on prospects. Since visuals are carefully edited, there is no danger of product malfunction during a filmed presentation. It is embarrassing, however, when a film breaks or its start is lost because the showing equipment was not set up properly and focused. If audio-visuals are used at a sales branch, the film should be prerun in part and ready to show. If projectors are to be set up at a customer's location, it should be remembered that a salesperson's professionalism will be judged by how well the rep handles the equipment.

Easily portable equipment that is not as bulky as the big screen and projector arrangement is available. It allows more control (replays) and permits discussion by salesperson and prospect during a showing. There is less awkwardness in changing from this type of visual into the closing, since the visual does not contrast so markedly with the "straight" part of the presentation. The break from film to two-way conversation is easier with this type of visual (see Figure 11.1).

Transparency Portfolios

The inner composition of complicated products like pumps and industrial machinery can be illustrated by transparency overlays that successively reveal the interior makeup of a product. An understanding of these qualities might otherwise be impossible since disassembly might be impractical because of product size and the time required to remove outer parts.

The usual transparency portfolio for selling less complicated tangibles or intangibles consists of such items as properly sequenced feature-benefit illustrations, supporting statistical tables and charts, and testimonial letters from satisfied users. Such presentation aids may be furnished by company headquarters or constructed by salespeople.

Illustrative portfolios put together from advertisements and customer letters can be carried in loose-leaf binders. It is very effective for prospects to review buyer testimonials from sources they know and respect. Portfolio entries in loose-leaf binders are easily augmented and deleted. A salesperson also has an excuse to move closer to a prospect and converse at closer personal distance when showing the portfolio. This makes an interview seem less formal and more friendly.

Samples and Models

Products such as rugs, upholstery materials, food, heavy equipment, and pharmaceuticals can sometimes be presented through samples and models. Large lots of raw materials can be presented by small testable samples. The virtues of nonportable products can be embodied in simplified models that show the relative advantages without clouding presentations with too many complex details. Legally, samples should be taken from the lots of merchandise they represent. Prospects who hesitate to buy a rug until they see how it fits the image and decor of their home are reassured and experience temporary feelings of possession when they actually observe the texture and color of a sample in their home setting. Industrial buyers are constantly reminded of the need for a huge water pump by playing with the toy working model that serves as a paperweight on a desk. Again, it is up to sales representatives to make prospects experience the virtues of samples and models as they are shown. Salespersons who bring in heavy loads of bulky samples may put buyers on the defensive, but in most cases they are being direct in nonverbally communicating that they are there to serve and sell.

Figure 11.1

Presentation Boards and Posters

An effective way to emphasize the main points of any presentation is to use a felt board and sandpaper-backed cutouts that seem to stick to the felt as if by magic. Cutouts are easy to prepare. Different colors can be used to indicate different groups of points. Features could, for instance, be shown in orange on the right side of a board, and benefits could be shown in green on the left side. Almost any rough type of texture will stick on a felt board wherever it is placed. Cutout stick-ons can guide and furnish an outline for a sales presentation. Felt boards are usually used for group presentations, but they can be effective with individual prospects.

Posters featuring pictures of a product, successive steps of operations, or multiple uses for an offering can dramatize product worth in much the same way as carefully devised advertisement does. They reinforce a verbal presentation. Such posters show care and preparation and save time by illustrating the worth of an offering quickly. This is an inexpensive way of having prospects visualize benefits, and it brings in the sense of sight to maintain attention.

Sales Manuals

Sales manuals contain technical information about products and sometimes detailed diagrams of component parts. Seeing information about the product in authoritative print can have a reassuring effect on prospects that is much stronger than talk. People have a tendency to believe more of what they see (including printed words) than what they hear from a sales representative. Manuals also help the multiproduct and complex-product sales representatives by furnishing a quick reference for prospect questions. No one can understand all there is to know about certain products and product lines. Having information at hand to show prospects is good common sense.

Tables, Charts, Graphs, and Maps

Each of these visual devices can make it easier to explain a benefit to a prospect and save interview time (see Figure 11.2). The simpler and less complicated the device, the more effective it will probably be. Each table, chart, or graph used should have an explanatory title and be easily understood. Even if a visual is self-contained and explained in its title, a salesperson should explain it verbally to prospects and use questions to be sure of prospect understanding. Many prospects will not take the time to study data that appears complex. A visual aid that is not understood is more of a hindrance than a help. Many prospects will put away anything a sales repre-

Cost Advantage of Natural Gas

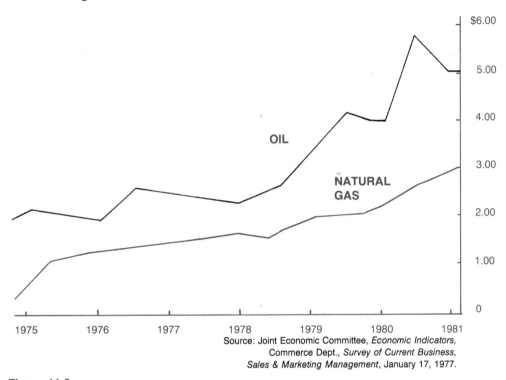

Source: Joint Economic Committee, *Economic Indicators,*
Commerce Dept., *Survey of Current Business,*
Sales & Marketing Management, January 17, 1977.

Figure 11.2

This graph could be used by a durable goods salesperson to help persuade a durable goods buyer to maintain heavier stocks of merchandise and therefore buy a larger amount.

sentative has given them and not look at it again. If a rep fails to go over materials with prospects, they may well be wasted. Nearly all visuals are expensive, and sales representatives have an ethical obligation to their companies to use them wisely.

THE TELEPHONE AS A SELLING TOOL

Demonstrations using showmanship and visual aids are usually used in presentations to dramatize selling points, but the telephone is a communications tool that can be used in every phase of the selling process. It can even take the place of an in-person sales call. If visual circuit phones come into widespread use, allowing those conversing to see each other while talking, a new era in selling will be ushered in. In the meantime, more and more firms are discovering the potential of the standard telephone. The Bell System calls it "Telemarketing." It is a fast and inexpensive method of contacting buyers and having two-way communication. A St. Louis company that sells 3,000 products (pipes, casings, and pumps for energy exploration) contacted 20,000 customers by phone, using thirty-five representatives. Sales increased from $50 million to $180 million in just three years. Instead of making eight visits per day, the sales representatives were able to interview from sixty to seventy buyers a day by telephone (2). In a program called "Tellsell," the Bell and Howell management pulled its entire sales force out of their territories two or three times a year, usually before a price increase or at the end of a promotion, and had sales reps phone dealers from their homes (3). Sales departments throughout the country are increasingly using the phone for making appointments and for follow-ups. Many are also installing inbound 800 service lines and increasing customer-service departments by adding inside salespersons who know how to make telephone inquiries. American Hospital Supply and Inland Steel are among the many firms that have successfully used WATS (Wide-Area Telephone Service) lines. Other users range from Dow, Corning, and B. F. Goodrich to the Swim Shop of Nashville—a supplier of team swim suits (4).

Advantages

The reason so many firms are discovering the telephone as a sales tool is that it has inherent advantages. The telephone reaches prospects at distant ends of a territory immediately. Busy and important buyers who would not allow a personal interview will tolerate a brief interruption to talk on the phone, long-distance or locally. (See Figure 11.3A.) Prospects who are ready to buy can be contacted immediately and asked to wait until they see *your* product. Local calls cost little. Long-distance calls are relatively inexpensive in comparison to money tied up in time and travel. (See Figure 11.3B.) Seven to eight times more prospects can be contacted by telephone than can be interviewed personally in a day, even in a city territory. Telephone selling is especially good for standard products like raw materials and intangibles that cannot be seen in any case. It is used most often for making appointments, for prospecting, and for follow-ups after delivery, but telephone selling can also be used for closing sales.

Disadvantages

On the other side, every telephone call is an interruption. Some products have to be seen to be appreciated. They do not lend themselves to telephone selling. The enthusiasm of in-person communication is missed when the tele-

Figure 11.3 A   Telephonics

GETTING BY THE SCREEN

NARRATIVE	TALK TRACK
• *Screen:* "May I ask, who is calling . . ."	• *Who's Calling?*
Response: Certainly, who am I speaking with please? . . . Mrs. Kelly, this is _____ . The spelling is S-m-i-t-h. I've got some rather important information to discuss with Jim, would you please put me through to him?	*What's your name?* *I've got important information*
• *Screen:* "What is this call in reference to . . ."	• *Reference to What?*
Response: I'm calling regarding some important business information and I should speak to Mr. Prospect directly . . . thank you.	*Important. Must speak to Mr. Prospect.*
or *Response:* I'm calling regarding some information I forwarded to Mr. Prospect . . .	*The letter I sent*
• *Screen:* "May I be of help to you . . .?"	• *May I help?*
Response: Thank you very much, but this is important enough that I must speak directly to Mr. Prospect.	*Important. Must speak directly.*
• *Screen:* "He's out of town" . . . "He's in conference" . . . "He cannot be disturbed now."	• *He's not available*
Response: I perfectly understand . . . can you tell me when would be a more appropriate time to call Jim back?	*A more appropriate time?*
or	or
Response: I perfectly understand . . . as long as I have you on the phone Mary, may I ask a few questions?	*I'll ask you then*
or	or
Response: When would be the right time to meet with Mr. Prospect?	*A good time to meet.*

331

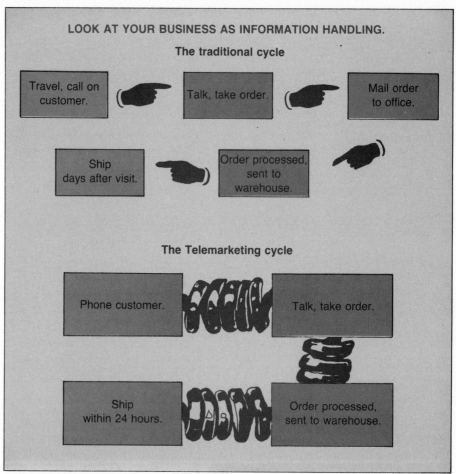

LOOK AT YOUR BUSINESS AS INFORMATION HANDLING.

The traditional cycle

Travel, call on customer.

Talk, take order.

Mail order to office.

Ship days after visit.

Order processed, sent to warehouse.

The Telemarketing cycle

Phone customer.

Talk, take order.

Ship within 24 hours.

Order processed, sent to warehouse.

Source: AT&T Long Lines

Figure 11.3B

phone is used. It is easier to say "no" over the phone than when a rep is there in person. There are more misunderstandings in phone selling and interview length is limited. Since neither sales representatives nor prospects can use gestures or other visible actions to communicate, excitement and emotion are harder to generate.

Procedures

Telephone selling is a practiced art. John Rosenheim recommends that: (1) plans be made in advance about exactly which accounts will be called and how often; (2) objectives be set for each call as well as for total effort; (3) direct mail be used to follow up and confirm what was agreed on during calls; (4) each person calling be trained in telephone technique; and (5) results be carefully evaluated and procedures redirected if necessary. He also recommends that each person's voice be audited for pitch, volume, and rate of speech (rate should be about 160 words per minute). Plans for each call should be outlined on paper with openings written down word for word. Role playing should be practiced on extension phones and, if possible, critiqued. Prices, terms, and schedules should be restated to emphasize accuracy and to avoid misunderstanding (5). Care should be taken to let phones ring for just so long, since if prospects answer a long ring, they probably have been inter-

Figure 11.4   A Step-by-Step Procedure for Opening New Accounts over the Telephone

I. Build a list of potential customers
  a. The Yellow Pages
  b. Trade journals
  c. Membership lists of trade associations
  d. The local chamber of commerce

II. Determine each prospect's ability to pay
  a. Financial condition
  b. Credit rating
    1. Dun and Bradstreet
    2. Local credit-rating bureaus
    3. Your own credit department

III. Set specific objectives for your call
  a. The clearer the target, the easier the aim
  b. Prepare fact-finding questions to ask. Do prospects currently use the product? Do they have a need for the product?
  c. Sell a limited order over the telephone. Have objective to get prospect on the books.

IV. Prepare your sales message
  a. Stress benefits over features
  b. Use a sales vocabulary
    1. Expressive adjectives
    2. Dynamic words, like rugged, power, speed
    3. Personal words, like you, me, I, we
    4. Picture phrases

V. Prepare an opening statement
  a. Identify yourself and your firm
  b. Establish rapport
  c. Make an interest-creating comment
  d. Fact-find to qualify the prospect

VI. Deliver the sales message
  a. Stress benefits over features
  b. Use a sales vocabulary

VII. Overcome objections
  a. Prepare prospect for your answer
  b. Answer the objection
  c. Stress the product benefit

VIII. Close the sale
  a. Start out with an open-ended question or a forced-choice question

IX. The sales wrap-up
  a. Confirm the order
  b. Arrange for the next call
  c. Express your thanks

Source: Phone-Power Self-Instruction Text: *Opening New Accounts,* Courtesy of Bell Telephone Company, Memphis, Tennessee.

rupted from some important business and may be unreceptive. Certainly, good telephone manners preclude calling during late-night or early-morning hours. A phone personality can be developed by evaluating others heard speaking on phones or in broadcast media. Listen to the excitement in the voices of people like Barbara Walters, Howard Cosell, Billy Graham, or other broadcast media personalities. Be aware of telephone manners. Telephone visual selling may be the wave of the future. At present, the phone must be considered a very important sales tool (see Figure 11.4).

ADVERTISING AND THE SALES REPRESENTATIVE

Advertising, like the telephone, is another valuable communications tool that can be used to create attention, interest, desire—and sometimes action. While advertising alone may inform and condition prospects for a sale, a salesperson is needed to listen, evaluate, interpret, respond to prospects, and close sales. A sales representative can ask for an order and get an immediate answer. Advertising cannot. There are many products that cannot be sold in quantity through advertising alone. However, advertising closely coordinated with personal selling can produce maximum impact and make selling easier. Every sales representative should have a good understanding of advertising as a selling aid. Reps need to know:

- How advertising can help them to present a unified message, acquire prospects, sell offerings, acquire a consulting image, and find words for presentations.
- Their responsibility in coordinating point-of-purchase materials.
- How to use direct mail and newspaper advertising.

Present a Unified Message

Advertising conditions prospects to buy by getting them to think positively about a product. Few prospects buy important items on a first call unless advertising has "softened them up" before additional appeals are made by a salesperson. A salesperson can mention the positive benefits of an offering, using the same magic words and phrases as in the advertising copy. Repetition of buying appeals used in advertising provides a unified company image and increases believability. Repeated positive suggestion is a primary persuasive strategy. Prospects may be reminded that an advertisement appeared in *Good Housekeeping* or some other medium that has a reputational stake in its featured advertisements. If reps do *not* support advertising claims in talking to prospects, questions may be raised in prospects' minds that hamper closing efforts.

Acquire Prospects

Advertising furnishes leads for sales representatives. People who send in coupons or who phone in with questions after being exposed to advertisements are usually interested prospects who should be contacted as soon as possible and given further persuasive information.

Selling the Advertising in an Offering

A wholesale dealer or a retailer may like your product but may be much more interested in whether or not *customers* know of your product and like it. A dealer sales representative does not sell tangible goods as much as ability to move stock off shelves and through cash register lanes. Dealers want profits. Dealers know that a good product advertising campaign improves their ability to sell merchandise, can increase customer flow through their stores, and can give ideas about how to talk to customers about a product (6). Through knowledge of company advertising, sales representatives can sell a campaign and its benefits just as they sell tangible product features. To be able to do this effectively, sales representatives must understand the campaign purposes and its effects on consumer sales. Samples of copy for printed media (such as magazines and newspapers) or "story boards" for television give visible assurances to dealers of support in merchandising a product. Often cooperative arrangements can be worked out with dealers whereby the product is advertised in association with a dealer's name and costs are shared. The creative work and materials for such advertisements are usually furnished by a sales representative's company.

Acquire a Consulting Image

Many professional salespeople are expected to aid dealer customers with overall advertising decisions by offering help with dealer advertising problems. Salespersons who answer dealer questions should be knowledgeable about media alternatives. They should not only study advertising from company sources, but also solicit information from experienced dealer customers. Salespersons who talk to many dealers are in a good position to accumulate and distribute operational information about advertising alternatives and their effectiveness. By aiding customers with advertising decisions, these reps enhance their professional images. To acquire a consulting image with customers, a salesperson must bear in mind that "as a general rule, consultants are expected to place the client's interest ahead of their own" (7).

Find Words for Your Presentation

Large corporations pay thousands of dollars for expertise in developing advertising appeals. Often the words and themes used in advertising appeals express product benefits clearly, concisely, and vividly. The competitive advantages of a product are brought out in positive statements whose truths are under the watchful eyes of government agencies. Such selling phrases should be considered by salespeople for use in sales presentations. Saying it face to face to a customer reinforces suggestions and words from advertisements and in selling proposals. (Selling proposals are written, and pictorial explanations show how product benefits fit a prospect's special needs and how it can be bought.) Most companies have hand-distributed folders or direct-mail pieces showing pictures of their products being used under favorable circumstances together with feature-benefit explanations. Such information left with prospects acts as a reminder between visits and is available at their convenience.

Handle Point-of-Purchase Materials

Sales representatives selling to retailers and other dealers are expected to be proficient in setting up point-of-purchase materials and other types of displays. These materials for in-store use are expensive, but if they are set up properly, more dealer sales will result, leading to bigger future orders. Dealers who associate no expense with such materials are prone to waste them or use them improperly. Salespersons should sell dealers on the importance of putting displays up and leaving them up (8). All too often, point-of-purchase materials are taken down by the next competitive salesperson visiting a dealer and thrown away. Dealer salespersons must know where products should be shelved and displayed to attract maximum customer attention. Aisle-end displays and eye-level shelving can sometimes produce over twice the sales of poorer in-store locations. Displays near cash registers or in center-of-aisle gondolas are desirable. Stocking meat, milk, bread, or whatever product category you sell at the beginning of a display—in regard to in-store normal traffic flow—may give you a decided competitive advantage. The main competition in retail stores, in fact, is the rivalry for display advantage.

Newspapers and Direct Mail

Newspapers cover all kinds of people in local geographical areas. Real estate, automobile, and other sales representatives whose products can be used by most people find classified ads important in prospecting. Direct mail can be used to find prospects, but it can also help cultivate customers. Because it can be initiated and controlled by a salesperson and because nearly every salesperson can use it advantageously, direct mail merits separate consideration. A business-machine corporation, for example, once provided a brochure explaining how physicians could use bookkeeping machine applications to solve their accounting problems. Since it was difficult to arrange personal interviews with doctors, all branch salespersons participated in a direct-mail campaign. It took only a few minutes to select a practicing physician from the Yellow Pages in each territory and to mail the advertisement with a return postcard included. The mailing was a success. Sales were made with a minimum investment of time and money. Direct mail is a rifle shot to prospects that can be used whenever you want to use it. Direct-mail sales to consumers have been "growing at an annual rate of 15%, or more than twice the pace in retail stores" (9).

Customers like attention, but personal calls are expensive. They appreciate salespersons who are interested enough to think about them between calls. Whenever a company furnishes brochures or you find any kind of information that might be of direct interest to customers, write a short note, include the new material, and put in the mail. This may take ten minutes. Sending out special mailing pieces assures that the next call made will not be completely cold. Customers may surprise reps who give such personal attention by contacting them and requesting a call.

SUMMARY

Communication aids such as the visible product, audio-visuals, the telephone, and advertising make the selling process easier and clarify sales presentations for prospects. A well-thought-out demonstration is the most effective interview tool. Thorough planning will help avoid irreversible mistakes. Good showmanship assures that an interview will maintain attention and will be long remembered. Films, transparency portfolios, samples, posters, sales manuals, charts, maps, and graphs make it easier for prospects to visualize benefits and save time in selling.

The telephone and advertising are being increasingly used to contact potential buyers rapidly and inexpensively, especially buyers who are hard to reach in any other way. Contact by telephone takes up less time and saves travel costs, but the art of telephone selling requires special techniques and practice. Advertising is especially useful in prospecting, as a selling feature of the product offering to dealers, and in paving the way for presentations. Direct mail, newspapers ads, and ads in other media can cost even less per contact than the telephone. Salespeople have an obligation to their firms to sell advertising campaigns and to coordinate advertising materials for maximum effect.

REVIEW QUESTIONS

1. What are the common communication aids?

2. What are some of the advantages of communication aids in personal selling?

3. What are some of the suggestions for making effective demonstrations?

4. Give some examples of the use of showmanship in demonstrations.

5. Evaluate film as a communication aid.

6. For what types of products are transparency portfolios particularly suited? What items does such a presentation typically contain?

7. When is the use of a presentation board recommended? What does such a presentation typically include?

8. Under what circumstances are sales manuals a valuable sales tool?

9. What are the advantages and disadvantages of telephone selling?

10. What are some of the suggestions for effective telephone selling?

11. In what ways does advertising assist the salesperson?

12. How do point-of-purchase materials play a role in the salesperson's activities?

13. How can a salesperson use direct mail as an effective selling tool?

Application Questions

1. At 2 p.m. tomorrow, you will be demonstrating a photocopy machine to a prospect.
   a. What preparations should you make before the demonstration?
   b. How would you get the prospect to participate in the demonstration? What problems should you be prepared for?

2. Find three ads in a magazine or a newspaper and underline words and expressions that might be used by a salesperson in a presentation.

Ed Ingram sells fire-alarm systems and extinguishers for the home and has decided to pick out names from the phone book at random instead of going door to door, because it's raining out. Mr. Carter answers after four rings.

Carter: Hello.

Ed: Is this Mr. Gary Carter?

Carter: Yes, who is it?

Ed: I'm Ed Ingram. Mr. Carter, if your house caught fire tonight while you were asleep, what would happen?

Carter: Are you a salesman or something?

Ed: Yes, I represent Fire Safe Alarms and Extinguishers. Would you have any warning if your house caught fire while you were asleep?

Carter: My dog would bark and wake me up, and I would either go out the door or the window, depending on where the fire was. We haven't had a fire yet. Of course, I would try to put it out if I could.

Ed: What if the fire were electrical and you couldn't put it out with water. Do you have an extinguisher?

Carter: No, I would throw soda on it or try to smother it. Look, if I wanted an extinguisher, I would have bought one from the discount store.

Ed: Our extinguishers are reliable and easy to use and can save you valuable seconds in case of a fire. Can I come by and show you one tomorrow?

Carter: Look, you woke me up . . . I'm on the night shift, and I need to get back to sleep. I've lived a long time and never needed a fire extinguisher.

Ed: I'm sorry I woke you. Sometimes fires happen while you sleep and the fumes and smoke get you before you can get out. Many lives have been saved by our smoke alarm. It warns you early— even before your dog would realize that the house was on fire. It's ionized and very sensitive and even lets you know when the batteries have to be replaced. Really, Mr. Carter, it could save your life or your family's life. Insurance companies will even give you a discount on your house insurance if you buy two, and I can show you where to put them in your home.

Carter: Look, I can get those at the discount store too, and right now I'm tired and can't afford your products. I'm sure that kind of alarm would be expensive.

Ed: Only $42.50 each and no home can afford to be without them.

Carter: I'm going back to sleep—goodbye. Don't try to call back because I'm taking the phone off the hook.

1. Evaluate Ed Ingram's telephone procedures. What did he do right, and what in your opinion could he have done better?

11–2

Marie Montesi sells real restate for the Brandon Agency. She has just learned from one of her sales associates that the Gilbert Pickards have recently moved to the city and are temporarily living at the Oak Terrace Apartments until they can find a house. Mr. Pickard is a manager for a battery manufacturing company, and they have two children, a boy twelve and a girl seven. Nancy Pickard is answering the phone . . .

Nancy: Hello.

Marie: May I speak to Mrs. Pickard, please?

Nancy: This is Nancy Pickard.

Marie: Mrs. Pickard, welcome to Centerville. I'm Marie Montesi with the Brandon Real Estate Agency. I understand from a friend of mine who lives in Oak Terrace that you and Mr. Pickard are considering a new home. We have some exciting listings now, and I want to serve you if I can by showing you some of our homes.

Nancy: Well, Mrs. Montesi, we've just come to Centerville from Chicago. Buying a home in a new city is a big step for us. We feel that we need to rent for a while and take our time and find what we really want after studying the situation for a few months.

Marie: You are very wise in being cautious about considering a new home. What generally are you looking for?

Nancy: We want a home in the $75,000–$90,000 range in the suburbs near good schools that won't be too far from Gilbert's work at the Storebest Battery factory. We want a four-bedroom with dining room and a large den, preferably on a wooded lot. It must be in a good neighborhood. But, as I say, we are not in a hurry.

Marie: We have three excellent homes that fit that description. The one on Pine Grove Road is a classic two-story that has lots of room for a family of four and beautiful trees in the yard. The other two are in Grandwood Subdivision just two blocks from the best elementary—junior high school in town! I would love to show all three of these fine homes to you. It is unusual for us to have such a good offering in executive-type homes. It would only take a few hours, and it would help give you an idea about real estate in Centerville.

Nancy: You understand that we will probably look a long time before we settle on a home. We want our children to grow up in a good environment.

Marie: Two of these homes are in Grandwood Subdivision, one of the finest subdivisions in Centerville. Could I show them to you this Saturday at one o'clock?

Nancy: Just a minute . . . *(to Gilbert)* Gilbert, there are some homes I would like to see this Saturday afternoon. Would you like to come with me or do you want to watch football? *(to Marie)* We'll go. Where can we meet you?

Marie: I'll meet you at your apartment, then, at one o'clock Saturday. I know you both will love these beautiful homes.

QUESTIONS

1. Evaluate Marie's telephone procedures. Can you find any mistakes in her methods?

2. What, in your opinion, was her best line? Why?

11–3

John H. Patterson, the founder of the National Cash Register Company, now the NCR Corporation, was one of the first, if not *the* first, industrialists in America to standardize the sales presentation and demonstrations of his sales representatives. *Every* salesperson had to learn the *Primer* and repeat it exactly as it was written. It was written by compositing the best selling procedures of the best salesperson in the company.[1] It is a historical classic and one of the first and most successful memorized sales demonstrations ever devised. Pages of the *Primer* are reproduced on pp. 342–345 for your analysis.

Identify the good selling principles used in this planned demonstration and evaluate it in the light of today's selling problems.
Could this demonstration with slight modifications to reflect new machine features be used to sell cash registers in the 1980s as it was in the 1920s?

11–4

Dick Lewis is director of bequests and trusts fund-raising for Old Ivy University. His staff includes two lawyers who have expert knowledge of the tax benefits individuals can gain through gifts to the university. Indeed, there are perfectly legal ways in which a bequest to one's heirs can be increased even if the capital is "lent" to a not-for-profit institution for a number of years. The technical details and legal intricacies of such arrangements are beyond Dick. He himself was the beneficiary of a sizable family trust that made it possible for him to work in this area of university fund-raising. As an alumnus of Old Ivy, Dick has what the lawyers on his staff lack: personal knowledge of and ease with the sorts of alumni in a position to profit personally through making contributions to Old Ivy.

[1]Samuel Crowther, *John H. Patterson* (Garden City, N.Y.: Garden City Publishing Company, 1926; Copyright 1923, Doubleday, Page and Company), pp. 103–155.

Communication Aids

Figure 11.5

The
National Cash Register
Primer

January, 1916

How to Learn the Primer.

The object of a cash register is to prevent mistakes in all transactions that occur between clerks and customers.

Mistakes occur in—
1. Cash sales.
2. Credit sales.
3. Money received on account.
4. Money paid out.
5. Making change.

Before studying this Primer, study the No. 300 with the color system and detail-strip.

The fundamental principles are the same in all registers.

While learning, never try to recite any part of the Primer without having a register before you, or a vivid image of one in your mind, so that you may describe something that you see and avoid the folly of trying to memorize lines and passages of "dead words."

Fix in mind the **idea** for which each sentence stands before attempting to speak it.

Always repeat **aloud,** and say the Primer to **somebody** (present or imagined).

3

Demonstration of the Register.

This,* Mr. Merchant, is a National Cash Register of the most approved pattern.

To appreciate what a help it would be to you, we must see what things you do in your store of which you keep a record.

I think the ordinary daily transactions with your customers may be arranged in five classes, thus:

1. You sell goods for cash.
2. You sell goods on credit.
3. You receive cash on account.
4. You pay out cash.
5. You change a coin or bill.

Am I right?

Now, sir, this register* makes the entries.

The indication* of the transaction shows through this glass.*

The amount* of the last recorded transaction is always visible, and the records are made by pressing the keys.

*Point out what is referred to.

4

When you sell for cash, these* black cash keys make the record.

 When you sell on credit, this* red "Charge" key makes the record.

When you receive cash on account, this* yellow "Received on Account" key makes the record.

When you pay out cash, this* blue "Paid Out" key makes the record.

When you change a coin or bill, this* orange "No Sale" key makes the record.

When one or more keys* are pressed, six results are accomplished at the same time:

1. The indicators* showing the last transaction disappear.
2. Indicators* appear showing a new transaction.
3. The cash drawer* is unlocked.
4. A spring throws it* open.
5. A bell* is rung to show that a registration has been made.
6. The proper entry is made inside.

---

*Point out what is referred to.

5

Cash Sales.

Cash sales are taken care of in this way:

Suppose you sell something for $1.00.*

Carry the dollar* to the register, press the "$1" key, put the dollar into the cash drawer, and shut the drawer.

You see that you have locked up the money in a safe place, and have made a record of the transaction at the same time. The indicator shows everybody in the store what has been done.

Now let us register different amounts.

Here the salesman will register various amounts, explaining to the merchant as he proceeds, about as follows:

Take 50 cents.* Press the "50-cent" key, put the cash into the drawer, and shut the drawer; 75 cents, 4 cents, 60 cents, 2 cents.

You see, Mr. Merchant, how very simple this is. Press the key, drop the cash* into the open drawer, and shut the drawer.

More than one key may be required in some cases.

You have, for example, $1.25.

---

*Show it.

6

Press the "$1" key and the "25-cent" key at the same time.

Suppose your next sale is 73 cents and the customer hands you $1.00.

Press the "70-cent" key and the "3-cent" key, put the $1.00 into the drawer, take out 27 cents change, shut the drawer, and hand the 27 cents to the customer.

You see that each cash sale is quickly registered and indicated when it occurs, with very little chance of mistake.

 Now, I will show you how the register takes care of credit sales.

Credit Sales.

One of the greatest sources of loss in retail stores is the failure to charge goods sold on credit.

Clerks put up the goods and deliver them all right, but forget to make the proper entries.

Customers, as a rule, keep no account of such purchases, and so, in nineteen cases out

7

---

of twenty, these uncharged sales are never heard of again.

I believe that you, sir, like every other merchant who uses the ordinary system, will admit that you lose considerable money in this way, won't you?

You know, of course, why these losses occur.

A customer orders a number of articles, which you put up and deliver to him.

Then you **intend** to make a memorandum of the sale, but before this is done you are interrupted, and forget one or more of the items; or it may be that the whole transaction slips your mind.

In that case the customer gets the goods and you get nothing.

The trouble is that you trust to your **memory** instead of making a **record** on the spot.

Just here the National Cash Register is a friend in need.

It stops this drain on your profits by taking as good care of your credit sales as it does of your cash.

We provide each salesman with a dupli-

8

343

cating "Charge" book like this,* which he carries in his pocket.

When a customer orders goods on credit (for example, to the amount of $5) the clerk pulls out his book, inserts name and date, and sets down the items.

Then he writes "Charge" on the slip and tears it out, like this.*

The memorandum, as you see, is in duplicate, a copy having been made by the carbon sheet.

He tears the slip in two, does up the original entry with the goods, and keeps the duplicate.

Now he is in no danger of forgetting the items, for he has a written statement of the whole transaction; and, having waited on the customer, he takes this to the register, presses the red "Charge" key and the "$5" key and puts the slip into the cash drawer where it is safe.

You readily see, Mr. Merchant, how this way of handling credit sales prevents losses.

 Two written statements of the items and prices are made in the presence of the customer before the goods are delivered—he takes one and the clerk the other.

The customer carries his home and the clerk makes a record of his in the register as soon as possible and **puts it into the cash drawer.**

Cash on Account.

If so many mistakes are made in handling credit sales in the usual way, there is also danger that cash received on account will be put into the drawer without being credited.

If a National Cash Register be used such a mistake is impossible.

When cash is received on account (say $2), fill out a "Received on Account" slip,* press the yellow "Received on Account" key and the "$2" key, put the cash and slip into the drawer, and shut the drawer.

Cash Paid Out.

 When cash (say 50 cents) is paid out for any purpose fill out a "Paid Out" slip, press the blue "Paid Out" key and the "50-cent" key, put the slip into the drawer, pay out the cash, and shut the drawer.

Money Changing.

When a coin or bill is changed press the orange "No Sale" key and make the change.

The Argument.

You remember that we divided the ordinary transactions with your customers into five classes.

Now, I have shown you that the National Cash Register takes care of each and all of them in the same way.

Whether you sell for cash, sell on credit, receive cash on account, pay out cash, or change a coin or bill, you go straight to the register and record what you have done by pressing the keys.

A clerk won't be likely to forget this, for

 in each case he has something in his hand which he must deposit in the drawer to complete the transaction.

With the cash sale, he has the cash in hand.

With a credit sale, the "Charge" slip.

With cash received on account, the "Received on Account" slip and the cash.

With the cash paid out, the "Paid Out" slip.

With a coin or bill to be changed, the coin or bill.

Every clerk must go to the **same place** to complete **every** transaction, so he forms a habit of doing this without fail.

As soon as a key is pressed a record of the transaction is made inside the register, the fact is announced by the ringing of the bell, and the kind of record is shown by the indicators.

Our system of recording transactions and taking care of receipts in a store like yours, Mr. Merchant, is simple to understand, easy to learn, quick to operate, safe from chances of mistake, and always ready for use.

Balancing the Register.

The total amount of cash registered and the number of slips of each kind deposited in the cash drawer are recorded on the adding wheels of the register.

To get a cash balance at the end of a day's business, we need not look into the drawer, but raise the lid of the register and enter in a statement book, like this,* the amount shown by the adding wheels.

Salesman then balances the register, using Statement Book, and explaining, as he goes, about as follows:

Looking here I find the amount recorded ($6.89).

This is the total amount of the cash taken in during the day.

On these adding wheels* I find recorded one "charge," one "received on account," and one "paid out" slip, which are also to be entered in their proper spaces.

Now, I have entered a record of the day's business in this Statement Book.*

*Show it.

13

In the drawer I find one "charge," one "received on account," and one "paid out" slip, corresponding to the record taken from the adding wheels.

From the total amount of cash taken in during the day ($6.89) deduct the 50 cents paid out, and the balance ($6.39) is the amount of money now in the drawer.

Let us count it.

You see there is just $6.39.

When balancing the register lay aside the "charge," "received on account," and "paid out" slips, so that a proper record may be made of them on the books.

The duplicating "charge" slip, by the way, has a special advantage which I have not explained.

The original, sent with the goods, is an itemized bill which the customer can examine at his leisure.

The amounts from the duplicate can be posted directly to the ledger, which saves bookkeeping.

Having now this written statement of the day's business which can be preserved, the last thing to do is to reset the register to zero, ready for the next day's business.

14

This is done by simply turning this key* to the right until you hear a very distinct "click," or until it stops.

On this strip of paper is printed, in the order in which it occurred, the amount and kind of each transaction made during the day, so that you can tell the amount of each transaction, as well as the total amount of all money taken in.

This is a total-adding cash register.

All the wheels of the counter now show zero.

I press the "1-cent" key* and one cent is registered.

Press the "9-cent" key* and nine cents are added to the one cent, making ten cents.

Press the "90-cent" key* and it shows a dollar.

Press the "$9" key* and the register shows ten dollars.

You see that each time a key is pressed the amount represented by that key is added

*Show it.

15

to the amount already shown on the counter, so at the close of a day's business the total amount of money taken in is shown; also printed in detail on the detail-strip, making this a perfect total-adding and detail-printing cash register.

When a color key is pressed the wheel corresponding adds one to the number previously shown by it, so that at the close of a day's business you know the number of slips of each kind that should be in the drawer.

This is an abridgment of the original primer.

16

To meld Dick's personableness with the staff's lawyers' expertise, the Development Office of Old Ivy has developed a series of automatic slide presentations that explain how various provisions of the tax code can be beneficial to both donors and Old Ivy. Each of the presentations focuses first on the university's reputation for quality, its stringent admissions policy (to demonstrate its popularity with potential students), and the success of its graduates. After use of this standardized "package," each slide presentation deals with a particular kind of trust agreement or bequest, explaining its benefits to donors.

The intended audience for the automated slide shows can vary from one or two listener/viewers—the set-up comes with a small screen for desktop presentation—to several hundred—useful for meetings of Old Ivy alumni groups in cities across the country. The presentations are clever. They have a light touch and contain new information that even tax lawyers may not be familiar with.

The intended audiences are not just Old Ivy alumni, but also their tax advisors and lawyers, and in some cases their trustees and accountants.

Dick arrived in New Orleans last night and was, thanks to the Old Ivy alumnus owner, put up cost-free at New Orleans' poshest hotel. He has a lovely suite that even has a small conference room. Three different sets of alumni prospects are scheduled to meet with him: one for a late breakfast meeting, another for a lunch meeting, and a final, really "big bucks" prospect for cocktails and dinner.

Dick has carefully rehearsed his presentation back at Old Ivy. He was well briefed on the kinds of university activities each prospect might be interested in.

For his nine a.m. breakfast presentation, he got up at six to make sure everything would go off flawlessly. A cultural anthropologist from Old Ivy had even offered advice on seating arrangements to enhance communications effectiveness. Dick carefully arranged the conference room and even discussed menus with the hotel's owner and chef. Dick arranged for room service to deliver all beverages and food prior to each prospect's arrival and made sure that waiters would not be needed. All these steps had been taken to assure prospects that the proceedings would be strictly confidential.

At last, exactly at nine, the first prospect arrives with his entourage. There is one more in the party than Dick had been told to expect, but that is handled quickly and smoothly by the hotel's staff. The breakfast goes well. The prospect obviously is very proud of being an Old Ivy alumnus and is still very fond of his *alma mater.*

After the breakfast is over, Dick, the prospect, and the prospect's lawyers and tax accountants move into the conference room. The automatic slide show tailored specifically for this prospect is in the machine. Dick starts the show. Suddenly he realizes that he is hearing Trustee Zoe Harris's voice while Head Overseer of Old Ivy Frank Wisdom is on the screen.

Dick's feeling of panic is hardly lessened when the tape begins talking of competitive admissions while cheerleaders at a football game are on the screen. Finally, when the naming of a new medical facility is screened, the cheers of the crowd at the Princeton game are on the tape. Dick's prospect begins to look agitated. Dick knows he has to do something. But what?

What was Dick's mistake?
Is there anything Dick can do to save the presentation?

1. "Highlights from S&MM's Survey of How Sales and Marketing Executives Use Audiovisual Equipment," *Sales & Marketing Management,* February 1980, p. 51.

2. "Valley: Calling by Moonlight," *Sales Management,* March 3, 1975, pp. 16, 23.

3. John H. Rosenheim, "Telephone Selling's Finest Hour," *Sales Management,* January 21, 1974, p. 30.

4. The Bell System, "Marketing in the Age of Information Is Telemarketing," advertising supplement bound in selected editions of *Time,* May 24, 1982.

5. Rosenheim, "Telephone Selling's Finest Hour," p. 23.

6. Carlton Pederson, Milburn D. Wright, and Barton A. Weitz, *Selling,* 7th ed. (Homewood, Ill.: Irwin, 1981), pp. 164–166.

7. Robert E. Kelly, *Consulting,* (New York: Scribner's, 1981), p. 28.

8. John S. Wright, Daniel S. Warner, Willis L. Winter, Jr., and Sherilyn K. Zeigler, *Advertising* (New York: McGraw-Hill, 1977), pp. 310–314.

9. "Mail-Borne Cornucopias," *Time,* December 7, 1981, p. 51.

12

Answering Objections

Two problems, which might also be regarded as opportunities, are so important to the success of the interview that they require special attention: (1) meeting the sales resistance prospective buyers express in the form of objections and (2) leading the potential buyers over the buying threshold. The first of these problem/opportunities, answering objections, is the subject of this chapter, and the second, closing a sale, will be discussed in the following chapter.

The challenges of answering objections and meeting the sales resistance of buyers can best be met by understanding the buyer-psychology involved, the sales attitude required, and the standard tested methods that have been used to advantage by practicing sales representatives. Indeed, in most instances, customer resistance denotes interest and can be read as a closing signal. Closing can seldom be accomplished before prospect questions are satisfied. Answering objections will be treated under the following headings.

- The significance and psychology of objections
- Considerations in handling objections
- Alternative ways to handle objections
- Examples of handling common objections

THE SIGNIFICANCE AND PSYCHOLOGY OF OBJECTIONS

Experienced sales representatives welcome objections. They recognize that in many instances an objecting prospect is expressing interest, participating in the interview, and furnishing valuable feedback. Disinterested prospects, prospects who are afraid of sales situations, prospects who resent a sales representative for some reason, or prospects who feel a sales presentation is an implied challenge to their personal judgment may throw up walls of resistance. However, even in these situations, prospects are throwing out leads that skillful sales representatives can grab to get prospects interested.

Objections May Be Questions in Disguise

In a selling situation, an interested prospect uses objections as a way of asking indirect questions—in effect, bargaining at the same time. Many prospects feel that asking direct questions will make them seem easy marks, weaken their bargaining positions, or encourage salespersons to shade truths about their products. On the other hand, prospects can use objections to get assurances without obligation. They feel risks are reduced by indirectly asking for information without overencouraging a sales rep. A prospect may say, for example: "They say that this model gives mechanical trouble," rather than ask, "Does this car require much maintenance?" The question form is not used, because the prospect feels that it would encourage the salesperson to respond with a biased opinion or an untruth. The salesperson would probably say that the car doesn't require much maintenance at all. By asking for information indirectly through an objection, the prospect has put the burden on the salesperson to furnish supported information to prove convincingly that the car does not require abnormal maintenance.

Answering Objections Removes Barriers to a Sale

Indeed, objections are so important to a sales call that professional sales representatives are most uneasy with quiet prospects, who hold questions in their minds and give few clues about inward resistance. Good sales representatives usually encourage prospects to air their objections in order to find out what barriers stand in the way of a sale.

Objections Are Made for Many Reasons

There are other reasons besides seeking information, attempting to bargain, and trying to terminate an interview that prompt prospects to raise objections. A prospect may not honestly have the time to hear a sales story on a particular day. A prospect may not have the money to buy a product. Rather than admitting this openly, the prospect may raise false objections with little relevance to the real reason for objecting. A prospect may be afraid to make a decision and try to hide this through resistance. This type of resistance can mislead even the most experienced salespeople. In the game of bargaining, buyers as well as sellers often unconsciously relax their standards of honesty. A prospect may feel that there is no need for the product or that there is no hurry to buy. For example, a professor has access to university libraries and may not feel the need for an encyclopedia set for her own use. A newlywed may be convinced that he should keep his old car at least until spring. If there really is an honest lack of money or need, it saves everyone's time if a prospect is qualified early. It must be remembered, however, that most buyers resist buying until convinced that the satisfactions to be gained from a product overbalance the money sacrifice necessary to obtain it. Prospects also object because of the risks involved in changing products and because it is natural to resist change. People who have found their needs satisfied for long periods of time by a comparable competitive product naturally can be expected to contest suggestions that they try an unfamiliar and unproven product even if it "may" be better than the one they habitually use. Other prospects object to defend their egos, to enhance their self-images, or just because they enjoy putting sales reps on the defensive. Some have simply developed the habit of objecting.

An Objection May Be an Excuse

Many writers explain that it is important to find out whether objections are a *real reason* or an *excuse*. Edwin Greif indicates that when prospects say they are too busy, can't afford a product, are not interested, want to think it over, or want to talk it over with someone else, they are probably making an excuse or stalling (1). The prospect with more specific objections, on the other hand, may be giving a valid reason. A real objection is a barrier to a sale and must be answered satisfactorily. An excuse should be examined to find why it was used. An excuse objection can be countered with more risk-reducing benefits. Real objections that cannot be answered satisfactorily or overbalanced may become impasses, which make it difficult to close sales.

How can a sales representative tell when an objection is really an excuse rather than a valid objection? Even when an objection appears to lack validity, the experienced rep treats it as a serious barrier to a sale. Any prospect statement is worth analysis. The real objection may have nothing to do with the salesperson's offer or the selling company. It may have much to do with the prospect's status, particularly his or her authority. However, prospects do object to individual salespersons with plain, old-fashioned dislike, and doing so may make a prospect shy of giving the real reason for not buying or for putting off a decision.

What every experienced rep has learned over time is to reexamine the apparently false objection that may be an excuse. Even the best salesperson cannot overcome a false objection. The best that can be hoped for is that in treating excuse objections a prospect's real reasons will come to light.

Noted sales trainer Carl Stevens advises that the key to spotting a false objection is to "watch the prospect intently, for he will generally drop or shift his eyes, become noticeably nervous, get angry, or try to change the subject when he voices a false objection" (2). When faced with an objection that is an excuse, the best answer is to probe the prospect as a person, asking questions in a sympathetic manner to discern what the real objection is.

CONSIDERATIONS IN HANDLING OBJECTIONS

There are several important ideas that will help sales representatives in answering objections: maintaining a proper attitude and interview tone, anticipating and forestalling objections, programming and timing objections, and clarifying objections.

Attitude

An important goal stated in the definition of selling is to reduce conflict of interest and to create harmony in a sales call. Accordingly, sales representatives must have positive service attitudes throughout presentations and especially when handling resistance and objections. They must always use tact to protect the prospect's ego and to enhance the prospect's self-image. The rep may be tempted to become a little combative when a prospect raises difficult objections that are aimed at testing the rep's temperament. Your attitude will help you to control your body language and the tone of your voice and to keep command of the interview. Objections may be designed to put a rep on the defensive. Salespeople must consider that prospects watch to see how the game of selling is played by each rep who calls. A sure-fire answer that could put prospects in their place and show them how unnecessary it was to even bring up an issue may well lose a sale. The feelings of prospects must be respected. An effective rep never says anything that would lead to contention or to a more opposing position. It is good practice to assure prospects that objections are logical and well conceived and to compliment them on their intelligence for thinking of them. Sometimes a simple pause before answering will convey to a prospect that a thoughtful consideration has been brought up, and the pause may also help you to avoid the combative position. When prospects see that a rep can take it, that the shield of goodwill will not be broken, and that a helpful rather than a superior attitude will be maintained, mutual respect will be established.

Interview Tone

Since objections are conflict points, every effort should be made to minimize their effect on interview tone. Each objection should be answered thoroughly but not dwelt on lest it be made overly important. Being concise and moving to more positive interview points, unless an objection can be converted into a big buying reason, is a bit of "best" advice. If, on the other hand, the fact that

"I warn you—I won't be back."

THE SATURDAY EVENING POST

Reprinted from *The Saturday Evening Post* © 1960 The Curtis Publishing Company.

Even when prospects object in a dramatic way, the salesperson should try to maintain interview tone.

the prospect has even made an objection is overlooked and a presentation proceeds without acknowledging it, a rep is engaging in a risky practice. Prospects may feel a rep is inattentive to their needs or that they don't have answers. They may stop listening, letting their minds dwell on unanswered obstacles. Prospects may believe that a weakness in a product offering has been found.

Anticipating and Forestalling Objections

Experience in selling a product gives a representative a good idea of the kinds of objections that will arise. If a salesperson is reasonably sure that sooner or later a prospect will raise a particular objection, it can be forestalled by answering it before it is made. The best answer available can be prepared for the objection when it *is* made. Forestalling objections prevents prospects from committing themselves in opposition. Once committed, it is human nature to defend a position. Knowing, for example, that a prospect will question the safety of a smaller car, it can be pointed out that many accidents can be avoided altogether because of the superior maneuverability. Statistics can be furnished to reduce this mental barrier before it is expressed. The objection might even be voiced for the prospect: "You may wonder about the effect of so much glass in this home on your electric bill. Be assured that all the glass you see is thermal glass designed to reduce heating and cooling expenses." Testimonials, statistics, and other forms of risk-reducing proofs should also be prepared to support answers to anticipated major objections. In this way, a salesperson shows professionalism. Even though objections are anticipated, the temptation to answer too quickly, without protecting the prospect's feelings, should be avoided.

Programming and Timing Objections

Objections can come at any time during an interview. Two-way communication can become sidetracked away from the main issue by an objection. During some presentations, it is best to use tactful ways to reduce the prospect's tendency to ask questions that ruin interview tone. Demonstrations during which most of the prospect's questions will be answered anyway go smoother with programmed participation. A prospect can be given a writing pad and pencil and be encouraged to write down any questions that might come to mind while the uninterrupted demonstration is in progress. After the demonstration is over, prospects should, as promised, be given a chance to ask their questions. The question and answer part of the interview is thereby controlled by the sales representative and conducted at an ideal time.

Clarifying Objections

Before answering an objection, a sales representative must be sure an objection is completely understood. A prospect may be asked to state it again if it is unclear. In any case, a sales representative should always restate an objection in slightly less objectionable words even if understanding has not been an issue. A prospect may say: "Why is the price for this car so unreasonable?" A salesperson might respond by saying: "The price seems a bit high to you? I suppose, if one doesn't consider the extras it includes, the price might seem high. Let me tell you what it includes . . . ," or by asking *why* the prospect regards the price as "unreasonable." Questions are sometimes a good way to find the root of sales resistance. The objection might also be rephrased: "Are you asking why this car is slightly more expensive than some models in the same size bracket? It is because of superior quality shown in the following advantageous features." The features should then be explained. In most cases it is better to listen carefully than it is to draw attention to an objection by having the prospect repeat it. If a restatement distorts a prospect's original intent, the impression of intentionally trying to change the meaning of what was said may be given.

ALTERNATIVE WAYS TO HANDLE OBJECTIONS

There are several standard ways of meeting objections that have proved effective in the field. Each method can be used to answer many different kinds of objections and to protect the prospect's ego. These methods are:

- The "yes, but" method
- The boomerang method—Selling the objection
- The counterbalance method
- The denial method
- The question method
- The failure-to-hear method

The "Yes, But" Method

The format for the "yes, but" method is to protect the prospect's feelings in the first phrase or sentence but to gently take issue with the statement in the last part of the response. This method exemplifies the right attitude to objection answering, if executed properly. It is also called the indirect denial method, the "yes, however" method, and the "yes, until" method. The opposing conjunction (but, however, until, unless) may be left out altogether without changing the basic strategy of protecting the prospect's feelings initially and then disagreeing. A prospect may say, "I've heard that the fuel injection system on these cars is a real source of trouble." A possible answer, "Yes, although it is a great fuel-saving feature, we did have some problems on our older models until our engineers corrected the defect. You can be assured that you needn't anticipate that kind of trouble with *this* model." Notice that the word "until" is softer than either "but" or "however" in this statement.

In the same spirit, the connective can be left out altogether and a new sentence started. The prospect says, "I don't like plastic grilles on cars because they have a tendency to crack with age." One reply, "I know exactly how you feel. I've had garbage cans and water buckets break on me. But this is not the cheap plastic that you and I are accustomed to. This plastic resists as much impact as certain metals even after it is ten years old. If it does break under a heavy blow, it can be replaced for one-third the cost of metal. And it stays new-looking at all times with minimal care." The prospect says, "This suit looks nice, but it is too expensive." You might answer, "Yes, this really is a quality suit, isn't it? It will outlast cheaper suits almost two to one! Considering the executive image it gives you and its longer life, you will be happy with it long after the price is forgotten."

The Boomerang Method—Selling the Objection

A sales representative using the boomerang method turns the objection into a reason for buying (see Figure 12.1). The prospect says: "We can't afford this machine right now, since we are planning to hire additional staff in the office next month." The rep might reply, "A new machinist will cost you about $890 per month, while this equipment rents for less than $600 a month. With it, your existing work force can handle all your fine parts finishing and have time to spare. In addition, the new K-7000 meets OSHA requirements." (The Occupational Safety and Health Act is federal legislation, which raised standards for working conditions in most work places.) Another prospect might say, "This house is too far from town." The rep might answer: "This house will retain its value for years to come when houses nearer town will be incorporated into the city, be subject to higher taxes, and be in deteriorating neighborhoods. The Oakwood Shopping Center, only a mile away, has an excellent assortment of stores with reasonable prices." Again, a salesperson must take care not to make a prospect appear ignorant or dense for raising a particular objection—the boomerang can wind up hitting the salesperson! Note that in each example, it was the objection itself that sold—cost in the first example, location in the second.

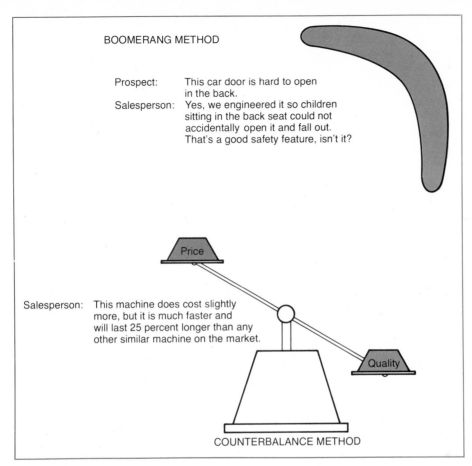

Figure 12.1

The Counterbalance Method

In some cases a prospect's objection is valid and cannot be truthfully denied. In most such cases, it can be compensated for by some other overbalancing benefit (see Figure 12.1). A small car may be harder to drive on long highway trips, but it uses less expensive gasoline. Electric ceiling heat may be more expensive to maintain, but it is cleaner and quieter than certain other kinds of heat. National brands of merchandise may have less margin of profit for a retailer, but they are nationally advertised and sales should be greater than private and regional brands. A prospect might say, "This typing unit is noisy." A possible reply is: "While it may make a little more noise, you can remove it to clean it and have much greater flexibility through its interchangeable type elements." The prospect says: "This house is too far from my work." The rep responds: "Have you considered that it is within four blocks of the finest elementary school in town? Your children could walk to school."

The Denial Method

The denial method should be used only when a prospect leaves no other choice. Even then, it should be used with respect. A prospect might say, "I heard that your company is on the verge of bankruptcy." A rep might reply, "Oh, no, sir, someone has misinformed you. I can show you our latest financial statement. It proves that our firm is in excellent condition." When prospects are requesting information or verification like this, they may regard a less direct reply as sidetracking an important point.

The Question Method

Questions can be used not only to clarify objections but also to answer them. Sometimes prospects will talk themselves out of an objection when the question method is used. Questions can be used to transfer responsibility of conversation back to a prospect and allow a sales representative more time to think. "I don't think this car is stylish-looking" might be answered with: "What specifically about it makes you say that?" The prospect says, "I can't afford it now." A possible reply is: "If it could save you money every day, could you afford to be without it?" A prospect says, "I'm not interested in offering my customers bankcard service." The salesperson might say, "If I could show you how you could save more than the service would cost, would you be interested?" A customer says, "I'm too busy to talk with you now. See the assistant manager." A reply might be: "What I have to offer you will allow you more free time every day. Could you invest just a few minutes to save hours?" A prospect who comes out with a strong remark like, "I will never buy anything from your company again," can be asked, "Why do you feel that way, Mr. Tanner?" Whenever a prospect leads with an ambiguous, judgmental statement, a question is suggested for response. Many times a prospect *expects* salespeople to request an explanation. Through asking a prospect a thoughtful question, a rep is demonstrating interest and the intention to listen carefully to what the prospect has to say.

The Failure-to-Hear Method

Sometimes prospects offer excuses under their breath or make little comments about which they are not really serious. Salespersons sometimes act

Figure 12.2   Methods of Answering Objections

METHOD	STRATEGY
"Yes, but"	Protect the prospect's feelings in the "yes," or agreement response; then gently take issue with the statement.
Boomerang	Turn the objection into a reason for buying, but be careful not to make the prospect appear ignorant for raising the objection.
Counterbalance	Overbalance an objection that cannot be denied with a more important buying benefit.
Denial	When the objection is invalid or when the prospect leaves you no other alternative, tactfully deny the objection.
Question	Use this method to clarify objections and to "answer" objections indirectly.
Failure-to-Hear	When superficial or unimportant comments are made under the prospect's breath, the salesperson may pretend not to hear. This should not be used often, and objections repeated twice should not be ignored.

as if they never heard the comment or ignore it as if it had not been said. This is a poor tactic if a prospect thinks what has been muttered is really an important point. If a prospect raises the question again, it is best to meet such an objection directly, handling it in the best way possible. Only superficial comments by prospects should be disregarded. (See Figure 12.2 for a summary of methods of answering objections.)

EXAMPLES OF HANDLING COMMON OBJECTIONS

There are almost too many kinds of objections to classify, but there are some objections that are so common that sales representatives expect to hear them on nearly every sales call. Salespeople should be prepared to handle these reoccurring objections with responses that work. Customers object to price, particular product attributes, taking time for an interview, not having a

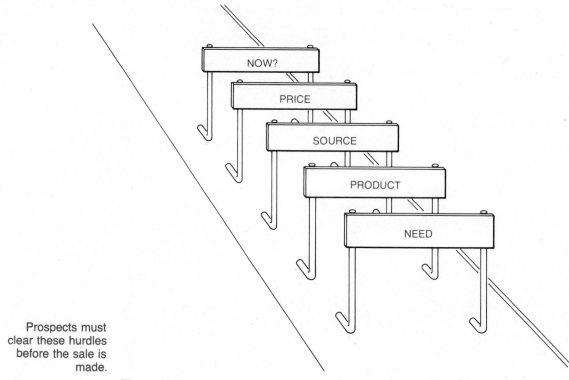

Prospects must clear these hurdles before the sale is made.

Figure 12.3

need, not having the money to buy, and to making decisions now. (Figure 12.3 shows hurdles that must be met to make the sale.)

Price

Objections to price can be expected, because to many customers this is a routine way of bargaining to get a better price. Customers expect a salesperson to justify the price. Prospects will always think a price is too high until it is overbalanced in their minds by the value to be received. This is why questions about specific prices should be postponed until the benefits are understood. Price is only relevant when compared to quality over the useful life of a product. With cost-saving devices or demand-creating programs, cost is only relevant in light of money to be saved or money to be earned.

Prospects often attempt to bargain by contending that a competitor's price is lower. In most cases, it is better to sell the quality of an offering rather than to make statements like, "Well, I guess they know what their machine is worth." Again, when price is an issue, customers should be reminded that an offering can be purchased on the installment plan or by rental and that it should be examined with respect to its durability and quality. Prospect: "We can't afford a $10,000 machine." Salesperson: "If you look at it over the life of the machine, it will cost you less than five dollars a working day; and if it can save you from hiring an extra person, it will pay for itself within two years. Isn't that a good long-term investment?"

Product

Like price objections, product objections stem from many reasons and take many forms. Retailers and wholesalers are likely to question salability of a product to customers. Final consumers are likely to question product quality and suitability to their particular needs. After all, this is part of the bargaining process. A salesperson needs to be prepared to substantiate all product claims when objections arise. Frequently, product objections come in the form of an unfavorable comparison with a competitive product or a reference to someone else's disappointing past experience. If a prospect is seeking information, a salesperson should furnish proof to reassure. If an objection is real and the product has such a deficiency, the weakness should be overbalanced by price or other offering advantages. If an objection is to suitability of use, arrangements should be made to modify the product, if possible, to fit the buyer's needs. Often prospects can be convinced that the quality they are requesting (and that a salesperson cannot offer at the buyer's price) is unnecessary for intended use. For example, extra-heavy-duty shock absorbers may not be necessary for normal city driving. Quality and performance capabilities should always be seen in light of specific applications. Examples of product objections and answers are:

Objection: My brother bought a Fastgo outboard motor last summer and has had to have it repaired six times since he bought it.

Answer: Can we phone him? Repair frequently varies with conditions of use and running time. But this (hands prospect repair-frequency table) shows that our repair frequency is 20 percent less than our nearest competitor and repairs are rare within the first 500 hours of running time. Your brother's motor is under a two-year guarantee, and we are quite interested if he has had a problem.

Objection: I don't like that color car.

Answer: Come look at our color chart. This model comes in twenty-one different colors and you can select just the color you want.

Objection:	Our customers don't ask for your product, and our present brand is moving quite well. Why should I try something new that might not sell?
Answer:	Read this letter from Mr. Jacob Goldsmith. He put our product side by side with the brand you now carry and reports ours outsold the old type by a 20 percent margin. Will you try the same experiment with no risk to your profits?

Taking Time for the Interview

Since time is money to a busy prospect, a salesperson should be prepared to answer the standard objection, "I just don't have time to see you today," or "I'm too busy." This may be a "put-off" in the form of an excuse, or it may be the truth. If it is the truth, the salesperson usually should respond, "I certainly understand. Would next Friday afternoon at two o'clock be a more suitable time?" or " When would be the best time to see you, Ms. Hanley? It will only take a few minutes to show you how installation would save you $25 a month on your natural gas bill." After replies like this, a prospect usually reveals whether the first answer was an excuse or not. If it was an excuse, it will likely be followed by another objection like, "To tell the truth, I'm really not interested." In which case a salesperson had better have a good approach answer ready, like, "Would you be interested if I could prove that fifty merchants in this area alone have averaged a $100 a month net with only the investment of some previously wasted store space?" Remember, the rep who always respects a prospect's time is the rep most likely to be given a hearing on the next visit.

Not Having a Need

What should be done when a prospect meets a salesperson at the door with, "Sorry, we don't need any," or "We are overstocked now"? Again, the best answer may be an attention-getting opening or a question that forces a review of need. Perhaps the following responses will give you some ideas:

- Did you know that customers will double their purchases from you the first really warm month of summer?
- How many hammers do you have in stock, Mr. Smith?
- Last week, Mr. John Patterson of Maury City lost his whole house to fire because his fire extinguisher gave out before the fire did. Are you sure the one you have is the right capacity to put out more than a superficial fire?

- This chart shows the recommended inventory stock according to weekly store volume. Is your present stock adequate according to this?

Not Having the Money to Buy

When the prospect says, "I can't afford it," this usually means, "I don't believe that your product is worth the money you are asking me for it." Even businesspeople will plead lack of money to buy an industrial product that can be justified on the basis of paying for itself in two years in cost savings or extra sales. There are ways to buy products other than immediate pay-out of current cash. Products can be rented. Products can be bought on an installment plan. This objection immediately suggests that a prospect is not yet sold and needs to be persuaded that a product is worth its cost. For example, if a prospect said, "I don't have the money to buy it now," the salesperson replies, "For just 10 percent down, we can arrange for you not to have to make a payment until two months from now. Would that help?" or "You can see that this

"I'll be brief. . . ."

THE SATURDAY EVENING POST

Reprinted by permission of the artist, Joseph Zeis.

Sometimes you can anticipate objections and forestall them before they arise.

equipment will save you $200 a month. Did you know that you can rent it for only $85 a month?" If a product can be justified in a consumer's mind as being worth more than its price, a way can usually be found to buy it.

Making a Decision Right Away

Buying emotion and desire can fade if a sales representative fails to close a sale during an interview. It is natural for a prospect to say, "I'd like to think about it," or "I'd like to wait until next week to decide." A prospect then has time to think of all the other things that can be done with the money. Moreover, a competitor may sell him or her before "next week." A salesperson must always be armed with some reason why prospects should buy now instead of later—price increases, product availability, a special available if the product is bought now, or a start on saving (or making) money right now. This is one objection that can be expected with every interview. In selling a one-of-a-kind product, like a particular home or plot of land, a standard answer is, "Someone else may buy it before you have another chance." Even with products that are standard, a salesperson can always answer, "I know we have some available today, but we may not tomorrow. If you like it, get it while we have it!" In giving a reason for buying now, the temptation to misrepresent or fabricate a reason when none exists to get a quick decision should be resisted.

SUMMARY

Skill in meeting sales resistance and answering objections is vital in selling. Objections from prospects are natural in the selling process and should be expected and welcomed. A salesperson should, in fact, try to draw out hidden objections so that any barrier to a sale may be dealt with openly. Two main reasons why objections occur are: (1) Prospects wish to find out more information without asking questions that might weaken their bargaining positions, and (2) prospects wish to end an interview if they are not interested. A salesperson should try to determine whether objections are real or are excuses. All real objections must be overcome or they remain barriers to the close. Excuses, on the other hand, can be passed over with less attention.

Salespersons should convey a helpful attitude, protect a prospect's feelings, anticipate objections, and determine the real nature of an objection before answering it. Every effort should be made to promote a harmonious interview tone. Sales representatives should not lose control of an interview by showing anger or resentment, even if a prospect exhibits a combative attitude. If objections can be anticipated before they arise and be answered satisfactorily, it prevents prospects from committing themselves to opposition and defending their negative positions.

There are six standard techniques for answering objections. The "yes, but" method uses the strategy of agreeing with prospects initially to protect their feelings and then taking issue gently without antagonism. The boomerang method turns an objection into a reason to buy. The counterbalance method overbalances an objection with a stronger benefit. The denial method meets an objection head on and is used only in certain circumstances. The question method can be used to find out the motive behind an objection. The failure-to-hear method should be used only in cases where objections are just excuses or are superficial.

Objections to price, product features, buying now, paying for a product, and taking time for an interview are common. Prospects will also tell a salesperson that a product is unneeded. An innovative sales representative should have several good answers for each of these objections and never be caught off guard when they come up in an interview.

REVIEW QUESTIONS

1. What are some of the positive aspects of customer resistance (objections)?

2. What are some of the factors that aid in the handling of objections?

3. List the standard ways of responding to objections that have proved effective.

4. What is meant by the "yes, but" method of answering objections? Give an example of this method.

5. Describe the boomerang method of answering objectives. Give an example.

6. Describe the counterbalance method of answering objections. Give an example.

7. Briefly outline the denial method of answering objections. Show the method in operation with the aid of an example.

8. Outline the question method of answering objectives. Give an example.

9. When is the "failure-to-hear" method of answering questions appropriate?

10. List a simple classification scheme for objections.

APPLICATION QUESTIONS

Cut out a total of three advertisements for the same kind of product, such as automobiles, articles of clothing, houses, or another product.

a. Identify three objections that you could expect in almost any interview for any one of these products. How would you answer these objections?

b. List two objections that might be raised for the specific product you selected. Supply a good answer to each objection or let another student supply the answers.

c. Provide several answers to an objection to buying now.

d. What types of excuses could be raised that are not real reasons for refusing to buy?

INCIDENTS

12–1

Harriet Belfiore is with HomeGuard, a marketer of security systems for safeguarding people's houses and apartments. Harriet's product line varies from simple doormat or weight-actuated systems that set off a siren to sophisticated systems that not only sound alarms but even video-tape intruders once a peripheral warning system is activated. Harriet is scouting southern New England for distributors for Home-Guard's line. Harriet's prospect is Martin Gilbaine a building materials dealer. As Harriet enters, Gilbaine rises:

Harriet: Mr. Gilbaine, I'm Harriet Belfiore with HomeGuard Systems, Inc., out of Hartford. I've come out to see you to show you the profit opportunities in our home securities systems distributorships.

Martin: I'm very busy today, Harriet, but I don't want to appear rude when you've come all the way to Framingham to see me. I guess you didn't get my letter saying I had no interest in home security systems.

Harriet: No, I didn't get your letter, Mr. Gilbaine. It may be a good thing that I didn't because in twenty minutes I can show you how you can add another $60,000 to your bottom line this year!

Martin:	Okay, but home security systems are new and expensive, and we don't really have too many break-ins out this way.
Harriet:	Our system is particularly new, Mr. Gilbaine, and by using state-of-the-art technology, we've been able to bring the price way down.
Martin:	Even if the price is down, I don't think many people around here even lock their doors. Why, at night, any movement on the streets would be sure to attract attention—it's so quiet.
Harriet:	Mr. Gilbaine, did you know that the majority of break-ins now take place in the daytime?
Martin:	The daytime?
Harriet:	Yes, the daytime. Now that more than half of all married women in this country work, burglars know that they've a 50-50 chance of finding a house with no one at home. Compared to the losses that a working couple can suffer with just one robbery, the price of our new HomeGuard System is low.
Martin:	Well, I've got an ADT system in my home—same as here at the yard.
Harriet:	Our system has all the features of the ADT system, plus one extra that's really important. We've got a panic button!
Martin:	A panic button, what's that?
Harriet:	The HomeGuard panic button allows a homeowner to signal a central switchboard of trouble in case an intruder breaks in when a family member is at home.
Martin:	Gee, that's something. My system doesn't have one. Bet it costs a bundle.
Harriet:	Not in a HomeGuard System—it comes as part of any of the security packages in our line.
Martin:	That's sure a plus. I wish I had the dough to invest in your line. But my cash is short, and interest rates are murder right now.
Harriet:	Our HomeGuard plan requires an investment of only $5,000 and requires only minimal stocking. Last year our distributor in Farmington made over $70,000 net with minimum stocking.
Martin:	But Farmington is only minutes from Hartford, and it's easy for a distributor so close to you to hold a minimum inventory.
Harriet:	That's true, we guarantee delivery anywhere in New England the next day on orders received before 4 p.m.
Martin:	Well, leave your literature and an estimate of a minimum stocking order, and I'll think about it.
Harriet:	Mr. Gilbaine, HomeGuard thinks you're the best candidate for one of our distributorships in this area. It's important for us to get distribution in this area as soon as possible. I'd like you to call Mark Cetipane in Providence. He can tell you about how hot the

security system market is and how profitable the HomeGuard System is. I don't want to have to approach your competitors, but I do need an answer soon. What day next week can I see you to get your decision? I won't offer the distributorship to anyone else in the area in the meantime. We really want you to represent HomeGuard in this area.

Martin: Well . . . does Cetipane have a system set up? When can we go to Providence and see a system in operation?

QUESTIONS

1. How well did Harriet do in overcoming Mr. Gilbaine's objections?

2. How many methods did Harriet use? What others might have been more effective?

12–2

Sandy Johnson has just completed the management training program at Isaac & Aronson, one of New York's largest retailers. Sandy, who comes from Moline, Illinois, graduated from Beloit College and has started on her MBA in NYU's night program. At Isaac & Aronson, management trainees are expected to rotate through all the departments to get a better understanding of the managerial tasks involved in running a big city department store. To get the exposure desired by Isaac & Aronson's management, Sandy is now working in the major appliance department of I & A's Manhasset branch. A customer is looking at a medium-size freezer.

Sandy: Hello, I'm Sandy Johnson. That's really a nice freezer isn't it?

Customer: It does look like what I'm looking for, but $600 is a lot of money.

Sandy: I know the price does seem high, but this is our energy-saving model. Compared with other freezers of the same size, it costs almost $15 a year less to run. In ten years that's a savings of over $150! And it's frost-free.

Customer: Oh? I wondered about that. My neighbor got one of these last year and has had nothing but trouble with it. She says the frost-free feature doesn't work at all.

Sandy: Really? I'm surprised to hear that. It's the first time I've heard of that happening. I hope she's contacted our service department. These freezers are all guaranteed. Have you noticed the textured steel on the door? It helps hide smudges and fingerprints and wipes clean with a damp cloth.

Customer: My, that is nice. Whenever my children are home . . . I don't know how they do it, but they manage to get smudges and fingerprints all over the refrigerator. But, still, I don't know . . . it's a lot of money.

Sandy: There's no question that $600 does seem like a lot, but think of the savings you'll realize by being able to take advantage of supermarket specials. [Nineteen point eight cubic feet] can hold a lot of savings.

Customer: Well, both my husband and I do work.

Sandy: Think of the time savings of being able to prepare meals in advance and keep them frozen until you need them. So this freezer offers convenience, fewer supermarket trips, and savings from storing foods when prices are low. And to make sure your food dollars are protected, this model offers a power-interruption warning light and has a key eject lock that makes it almost impossible to accidentally leave the door open!

Customer: It's nice all right, but the money . . .

Sandy: Do you have an I & A charge account? With our easy payment plan, you can start realizing the savings this freezer offers right away! Think of its energy efficiency—up to $15 a year saved in energy costs—plus the chance to make your food dollars go farther. That's important to all of us today, isn't it?

Customer: It certainly is. Goodness, you really do come on strong, don't you? I just came in thinking about a freezer. Now, I feel like I'm being railroaded into buying one. I'm not at all sure about it. In fact, I wonder if I'm not being sold a bill of goods. With my children away at school and all, I'm not at all sure I need a freezer. I've gotten along without one so far. *(Customer leaves.)*

QUESTIONS

1. Where did Sandy go wrong? Or did she?

2. What advice would you have given her if you had been observing this customer contact?

12–3

Lee Summers is a native of St. Louis, Missouri. His family owns and operates a small-business-forms company for which Lee acts as a combination sales rep and sales manager. Competitive activity by such big firms as Moore Business Forms has made the St. Louis market particularly tight. Lee is the

Summers Business Supply Company's only rep in St. Louis. The other reps are in Memphis, Kansas City, Omaha, and Des Moines. All are doing pretty well, but none has the competitive activity that Lee has faced in St. Louis. Fortunately, Summers had built up strong relationships with many local businesses, some of which have become headquarters of national companies over time. Lee has made it a special point to try to get Summers established as a source for such firms as McDonnell-Douglas, Monsanto, and General Dynamics. He's been reasonably successful. Lee took special pride in landing the Futronics account when it relocated its headquarters from northern New Jersey to St. Louis. For more than eight years, Summers has had an exclusive with Futronics.

When Mel Kuzlow, Futronics' chief purchasing agent retired, he was replaced by Ron Williams, who switched all of Lee's business to another supplier. Lee was dumbfounded. Futronics had never complained to him or his office about any problems. They'd been regular customers since 1974. Suddenly, Lee couldn't seem to offer anything right. The new supplier was no cheaper. Service was not as good as it had been with Summers. Lee began to feel there was just something about him Williams disliked. Lee felt he had always behaved in a businesslike way with Futronics personnel; he had always checked their stock to make sure there would be no interruptions by Futronics being out of stock. Now Lee was thinking of having Carl Richards, Summers' Kansas City rep take over the account, if only to find out what had gone wrong.

Before discussing the account change with Richards, Lee decided to make one last call on Futronics. When he called to make an appointment with Williams, he was told that Williams had left Futronics. Lee asked to see his successor. Williams' successor turned out to be Shirley Maguire. When he called on her, she greeted him warmly and placed a sizable order. Lee was pleased to be back as a supplier to Futronics. He thanked Shirley for the order. Since Shirley had worked in the purchasing office for some time, Lee felt he knew her well enough to ask how he had messed up with Williams.

Shirley: Oh, Lee, you didn't. Ron sort of left under a cloud.

Lee: Under a cloud? I don't understand?

Shirley: Well, I don't know if I should tell you this or not, but Ron only dealt with suppliers who offered him a kickback. He knew you weren't the type, so he never proposed such a deal to you. Or did he?

Lee: No, he didn't. I'm glad he didn't, because I don't know how I'd have reacted. Futronics is an important account to us, but no account is that important. I thought he just didn't like me.

QUESTIONS

1. Did Lee handle the situation correctly?

2. Should Williams' kickback scheme have come as a surprise to him?

3. Should he have asked Williams what was wrong?

4. What would you have done in Lee's place?

1. Edwin C. Greif, *Personal Salesmanship* (Reston, Va.: Reston, 1974), pp. 245–249.

2. Carl G. Stevens, in James F. Robeson, H. Lee Matthews, and Carl G. Stevens, *Selling* (Homewood, Ill.: Irwin, 1978), p. 211.

Closing the Sale

Closing is the climax of a sale. It is the part of the selling process that directly affects the outcome. All other efforts can be carefully accomplished, the prospect mentally prepared to accept an offer, but the opportunity to sell can be lost by failing to close or by a weak closing effort. It is a maxim in selling that successful salespeople close early and often. What this maxim means is that successful closes are based not on what a salesperson does at the end of a sales call but on careful assurance of prospect agreement point by point throughout each call.

Only missionary salespersons get paid for merely making calls. All others are paid to make sales. Closing is a matter of leading a prospect to the point of decision. The processes of leading a prospect to the point of saying "yes" or "no" include all the topics covered so far in this second part. They also include a series of intermediate or "trial" closes to assess opportunity to ask a prospect for an order. A trial close is a question that seeks to find out how effective a presentation has been up to that point. "This software pack will really work for you, won't it?" If the answer is yes—the rep should ask for the order. If the answer is no, it is time to probe for remaining barriers to a decision. The discussion has not been closed, as it might have been had an order been asked for at that point.

The trial close has particular application in industrial marketing. All too often, industrial sales are of such magnitude that many calls and proposals are made and negotiations conducted before a final decision to buy or not to buy is reached. A series of trial closes helps to keep reps on track toward the eventual goal of offering and delivering value to prospects. Often the first sale or trial close an industrial sales rep must make is getting the prospect's agreement that there is a need to consider a change.

If you are a good prospector, some customers will recognize a need and consider your product. If you are a good approacher, prospects will listen to your presentation. If you make a good presentation, you will create a desire for your product. But only a good closer sells. No one can expect an order every time a prospect is visited, but a good closer gives a prospect a real opportunity to buy whenever an appropriate buying circumstance is recognized. The essentials of becoming a professional closer are:

- Developing a good closing attitude
- Timing the close
- Having command of many closing techniques
- Learning to handle recurring closing problems
- Customizing the close
- Knowing what to do after the close

DEVELOPING A GOOD CLOSING ATTITUDE

The sales representative should be confident, enthusiastic, and sensitive at the time of the close. Whether aware of it or not, every salesperson projects an attitude to a prospect. Attitude can lose a sale. Attitude can be improved.

Attitudes Are Projected

Salespersons project an attitude by what they do and what they say. If you are confident of receiving an order, that confidence will be conveyed to a prospect by your tone of voice, the words you choose, and your nonverbal communication. Buyers will feel that a fair offer is being made and that they are expected to buy. Attitude alone conveys that buying is the reasonable thing to do. On the other hand, if you begin to perspire from fear as you approach the big moment, and if your voice cracks and your hands tremble, a prospect will receive negative signals. Prospects may think: "You are about to ask me for an order and you're afried. Perhaps you are not accustomed to getting orders because your product is so bad." At best, a prospect's buying mood and enthusiasm are diverted to concern over what is wrong with the sales representative. The prospect may be embarrassed for the rep because of the rep's lack of sales experience. It *is* hard for a rep to avoid showing concern, particularly when a single sale can mean over a thousand dollars in commissions. Nevertheless, a professional learns to expect positive results and channels emotions into optimism instead of fear.

A salesperson may be loaded with confidence and enthusiasm but still turn a prospect off by being insensitive. A prospect may have been sending verbal and nonverbal signals, but the rep unsure in call preparation has been dominating the conversation without sensing that something is wrong. Perhaps it is an unanswered question. Perhaps such a grand finale is being made of the close that the prospect has become apprehensive and resistant. Perhaps the prospect thinks the rep is presenting a routine without any concern for the prospect's feelings. Closing a sale is the time when a salesperson should be the most sensitive to feedback cues.

Attitude Can Lose Sales

A salesperson's attitude not only affects prospects, it also affects the salesperson's actions. A rep's attitude may be so bad that he or she may fail to ask for an order until the prospect has already been sold by a competitor. Sales representatives fail to ask for orders because they are afraid of being rejected or disappointed. They may be afraid that if prospects say "no," they will be committed to maintaining a negative position. Some salespersons even have guilt feelings about asking others to make decisions. Remember that an interview left unfinished because of a failure to close is unfair to the prospect and unfair to yourself. Opportunity has been taken away from the prospect. A potential buyer has lost the buying mood. Such an unhappy customer may fall prey to a competitor selling an inferior product for more money. A salesperson who fails to ask for an order has also taken opportunity away for personal achievement, for there is risk of losing a sale, thereby wasting all previous selling efforts. The employing company is certainly a loser. Suppose the salesperson goes back to sell the same prospect and invests $400 more in effort—that effort could have been used to call on other prospects. Few sales representatives make the mistake of closing too soon or too often. Most make the mistake of closing too late and not often enough.

Ways to Improve Personal Attitude

Sales representatives can improve their closing attitude through belief in themselves and their products. Through thorough knowledge of products, prospects, and selling techniques, and through preinterview practice, a sales rep can gain the self-confidence needed to close successfully. If a rep really believes a prospect is being helped by buying a product, confidence and enthusiasm will develop and be communicated. A rep who does not believe this must be an excellent actor to hide personal feelings verbally and nonverbally.

To increase personal belief in a product, a salesperson can imagine how satisfied a prospect will be using it. Belief in oneself also can be increased through self-suggestion and through the kinds of personal reprogramming suggested in Chapter 4. A thorough study of product benefits and selling techniques (especially closing techniques) enables salespersons to go into a sales interview with confidence in their capacity to close successfully. Preplanning and preexperiencing an interview mentally before going into it and reviewing the types of closes appropriate under the circumstances will give more self-assurance. It allows the salesperson to be sensitive to the prospect's needs. It is normal for even experienced sales representatives to feel pressure in closing, but good ones have learned to look forward to this exciting point in a sale and to channel their emotions into enthusiasm.

TIMING THE CLOSE

When to ask for an order is just as important as *how* to ask for it. A good salesperson has to know how to tell closing time (see the closing clock, Figure 13.1). While there may be one best time to close during every sales call, there are usually several times when closing would be appropriate. The keys to sensing closing times are trial closes, verbal closing signals, and nonverbal closing signals.

Trial Closes

Good closers have been said to close early and often in a single sales call. How soon and how often to close depends on what is being sold and the prospect's receptivity. If a product is easily understood by prospective customers and they look receptive, it may be appropriate to try an early close. If, on the other hand, a complex and expensive product is being sold that prospects have difficulty understanding, buyer questions must be resolved before a final close is attempted. If a salesperson feels that all important buyer questions—need, product, source, price, and the "time to buy" are resolved, the time has come for a trial close, even if definite closing signals have not been received.

A trial close is an attempt to find out if a prospect is ready to buy without actually insisting on a final decision on a total offer. A prospect might be asked about color or some other minor point. A salesperson might say, "Do you like this beige or the blue carpeting better?" If a prospect shows real interest, even on this minor point, an order-clinching close should be the next step. "Could we deliver the blue to you next Wednesday?" If a trial close fails to get even a partial commitment from a prospect, the seller must continue to

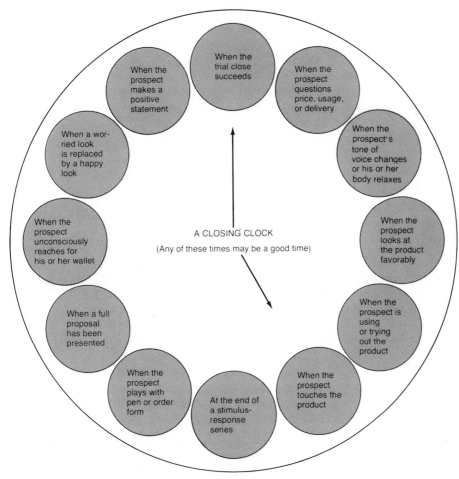

Figure 13.1   A Closing Clock

sell benefits and attempt another trial close after more reasons to buy have been given.

It may not be necessary to say anything to attempt a trial close. A nonverbal action may be taken that induces a prospect to volunteer an opinion. Carpet salespersons might run their fingers back and forth over carpet samples, watching the prospect's expression or waiting for verbal comments. The trial close is a method of preserving options, of easily and harmoniously continuing interviews. If there is any barrier in a prospect's mind, the trial close may bring it out. If a customer should say, as the salesperson runs her hands over a carpet sample, "I'll bet that would feel good on my bare feet," a closing signal has been announced. If the response is: "That would probably show dirt," another barrier to the sale has to be overcome before another trial close is attempted, but at least the barrier has been identified.

Verbal Closing Signals

Every good salesperson learns to recognize both verbal and nonverbal closing signals. If prospects ask questions that indicate interest, such as inquiries about price, delivery, or care of a product, they are sending positive closing signals. When use, warranty, or storage (placement) of a product are asked about, a trial close is indicated. Any compliment to a product, the selling or producing company, or the sales representative may signal a closing opportunity. Objections to product features that are really questions can be turned into positive feature benefits and may also merit an attempt to close. For example, a prospect may say, "I'll bet that wouldn't last me five years." Reassurance that it will last much longer can be followed by a close.

Nonverbal Closing Signals

Nonverbal signals can include practically any changes in voice, posture, or expression that indicate changes in attitude. A prospect may simply raise or lower her voice, or lean forward or backward in her chair to indicate a change of mind. Suppose a prospect who has been crossing his arms or legs uncrosses them and opens his hands. In body language, he is indicating a more receptive frame of mind. Some sales representatives pay particular attention to the face. When the prospect's face relaxes, they try a trial close. Smiling, affirmative nods, looking admiringly at a product, indicate a ready-to-buy attitude, especially if these gestures have been absent before. Attempts to use or operate a product are positive signals. Touching or handling a product with respect nearly always indicates interest. A prospect's resistance to the rep's efforts to leave or to collect sales materials may be a signal. Picking up a pen or reading a sales contract usually has significance. Again, any change that could mean a prospect is becoming more receptive or less defensive is worth noting. When prospects change their minds, they usually change their verbal and nonverbal signals (see Photo 13.1).

It must be understood that there are times when it is not good to try a close. It may show insensitivity to ask for an order when the prospect has practically no information about a technical product, has indicated great disinterest or hostility that can't be interpreted as an attempt to bargain, or has major questions unresolved. To close on a negative indication without resolving problems is to be unresponsive to the prospect's need for information. If a prospect looks worried and says: "I don't understand how to change discs on this word processor," how easy it is should be shown and a close *then*

Photo 13.1
Is this prospect ready
for you to ask him for
the order?

made. Sales representatives seldom have problems in recognizing wrong times to close, but often fail to recognize real closing opportunities (see Figure 13.2).

HAVING COMMAND OF MANY CLOSING TECHNIQUES

Buying involves risk and few prospects like to take risks. Usually a prospect has more to lose from buying than a sales representative has to lose if an order is not signed. Good closing techniques are designed to make it easier for buyers to decide. Closing methods are seldom powerful enough to sway unconvinced or resistant prospects who have been subjected to incomplete or weak sales presentations. While trial closes should be attempted early and often in an interview (for most products) and repeated even after a prospect says "no," closes work better when a prospect begins to send closing signals and understands an offering's benefits. The tested methods included in this section can all be used to make it easier for the prospect to come to a buying decision.

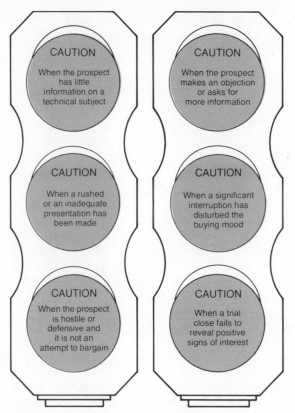

In these instances something more should be added before you attempt to close again.

Figure 13.2   Closing Caution Lights

Choice Close

The choice close is a favorite method because it leads a prospect to say "yes" without heavy pressure. Making choices is reasonable, everyday behavior. People have a natural inclination to express personal preferences. "Which machine would you prefer, the one with a tape recorder or the one without the tape recorder?" A prospect might say, "The one with the tape." The prospect has been led right into a buy. An offered choice must always be between one available offering and another to be effective. A prospect should never be given a choice between buying or not buying or between buying an offered product and a substitute from another source. Choices among different styles, colors, features, models, or amounts might be given. Choices can be narrowed by recommending that selection be made from among two or three products. Some ice cream parlors offer two dozen flavors. Patrons are

"Oh, I think one will be enough."

THE SATURDAY EVENING POST

Reprinted by permission of the artist, Joseph Zeis

Choice closes often bring positive results.

sometimes confused by the decision range. Such confusion is increased when complex, high-value, or highly styled products are involved; so choice must be restricted to a few *desirable* products. If a prospect has trouble deciding, a salesperson may be asked to recommend a "best" choice. "Why don't you take this one? I honestly believe it's best for you," is one way to guide an undecided prospect. A series of choices by a customer about colors, features, and amounts leads to a specific product choice and a sale.

Minor-Points Close

No one likes to make big decisions. Sales representatives who can get prospects to make decisions on minor points can effectively lead up to acceptance of a total offer. This is a natural method to use with the choice method in getting a decision. Once prospects have committed themselves on one or a number of minor points, it becomes harder for them to back out of making a major choice. A sales representative might ask in the course of the discussion, "If you were to buy a car, what color would you want? Would you want tinted or regular glass? Do you want bucket seats or standard? Vinyl or plush interior?" The prospect, after expressing preference on all these points, will find it easier to accept the whole car described by previous choices. A salesperson wants a prospect to establish a mental pattern of making selections and commitments.

The Assumptive Close

A sales representative assumes that a prospect is going to buy. A prospect must consciously resist in order not to buy. A rep may get out an order blank or point to the signature line or start processing the sale. If a prospect doesn't stop the rep, the decision to buy has been made. A salesperson may say, "Our truckload discount is a real savings, isn't it?" If the prospect agrees, preparation of the papers for signature can begin as if the sale were made. The assumptive close works best if a salesperson really does have the attitude that a prospect will buy and expresses this in nonverbal communications and words. For example, "When you use this new overwrap sealer, the quality of your bread will show to everyone." While it may be unwise to be too presumptuous at the start of an interview, a prospect will gradually accept as more and more benefits are agreed to.

Summary Close

When a presentation is nearing its high point, it is good to summarize all of the benefits a prospect will enjoy from accepting an offering. Repetition is allowable and prepares prospects to make decisions. This is particularly true if there are many benefits and the ones that mean the most have been emphasized. "This tree is hardy in this climate. Its roots go far below the surface and won't bother you on top of the ground. The leaves do not have to be raked but will rot and make your soil rich, and it is not susceptible to most tree diseases. This tree will furnish you with shade and maintain a symmetrical shape. Can we plant it in your yard this afternoon?" Sometimes with sophisticated prospects a more balanced summary containing a few disadvantages in what is called a "T"-account or balance-sheet close is a good choice (see Figure 13.3). The benefits are listed on one side of a sheet of paper and the disadvantages on the other, showing that the advantages outweigh the disadvantages. A prospect, seeing the logic and fairness of this method, can mentally justify signing the order.

Standing-Room-Only Close

One of the biggest barriers to buying is the option of putting off the decision until later. Perhaps the strongest support for buying is the knowledge that a product is so good that it is scarce and that opportunity to buy can be lost because "everybody wants it and is buying it up." The Standing-Room-Only close (SRO) not only gives a strong reason for buying now, but it supports a prospect's decision by indicating that if everybody else is buying, the product must be good. This close works especially well on one-of-a-kind items like

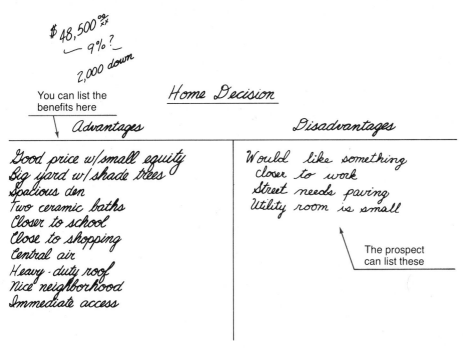

$48,500 ⁰⁰/ₓₓ
— 9%?
2,000 down

You can list the
benefits here

Home Decision

Advantages

Good price w/small equity
Big yard w/shade trees
Spacious den
Two ceramic baths
Closer to school
Close to shopping
Central air
Heavy-duty roof
Nice neighborhood
Immediate access

Disadvantages

Would like something
closer to work
Street needs paving
Utility room is small

The prospect
can list these

Figure 13.3 "T"-Account Close

houses, farms, and antiques. It should be indicated to prospects that it may not be possible to get the same offer later. A realtor might say, "Another couple was looking at this antique desk, and they said they were coming back this afternoon to let me know what they decided. It is an excellent buy, so I'd advise you to take it now. It may not be here tomorrow." A car salesperson might say, "We have one demonstrator left in this model at 20 percent off. If you like it, buy it," or "You won't be able to find a lot like this ever again. There are only three on the waterfront, and should you decide to sell it, the price could double in two years."

Special-Deal Close

Perhaps a presentation has been good, but the prospect is still undecided after closing has been attempted several times. The prospect wants to wait and decide later. If a special offer can be made, it will often tip the scales. "If you will order this color TV today, we will sell you an aerial at wholesale price and install it free. This is in addition to giving you the break in price we've already discussed," or "This week only our company is giving a $200 rebate on compact cars. Won't you let us order the model you like for you now to take advantage of this saving?"

Closing on Resistance

If a prospect's objection can be turned into a reason for buying, it can be closed on. Suppose a prospect says, "I'm too busy to change over my dryers to an automatic system." A close can be made after assuring the prospect that even while the system is being changed, dry-cleaning loads will go out faster. Suppose a prospect says, "I don't have the money to buy." A possible reply is: "Your labor savings of $60 each month will more than cover the payments of $50 a month. Give us your order today, and you can start enjoying this extra profit next month." Suppose a prospect says, "I like it, but I want a compact with automatic transmission." The car salesperson's reply, "We can get you this model with automatic transmission. Which color would you like?" is a close.

Stimulus-Response Close

Stimulus-response tactics have already been treated in an earlier chapter. In this close, a salesperson asks a series of leading questions or gets agreement on several minor points before closing. If the prospect is programmed to say "yes," to say "no" to the close would require willful prospect resistance to the pattern of saying "yes."

Success-Story Close

Salespersons can tell prospects about customers who had the same or similar problems and solved them by buying the product. By giving specific details such as names and events in the narrative, a salesperson enables prospects to put themselves in the place of the satisfied customer who bought. It seems natural to follow the example and buy. "Sam Allison thought the same as you do about plastic shirt bags but bought them to judge customer reaction. It was so strongly favorable that he's converting from poly-white kraft to all plastic. They cost less and Sam's complaints on quality have gone way down. Why not order 25,000 and see what they'll do for you?"

The Contingent Close

In a presentation, a sales representative makes a sale dependent on proving some point to a prospect. A rep might say, "If I can show you how this equipment can pay for itself in two years, will you buy it?" Then the rep proceeds to outline proof based on the cost and productivity of the machine. An aluminum-siding sales representative might say, "If I can prove to your satisfaction that this siding will save you enough in paint and electricity to pay for itself three times over in the next ten years, will you order it?" Or a copier sales representative might ask, "If I can get you $1,000 for your present copier, will you invest in this new model?" Such contingent statements set up easy closes if prospects agree with them.

The Turnover Close

Sometimes when a salesperson and the salesperson's manager visit a prospect together (or a junior salesperson and a senior salesperson), a prospect may not respond to the closing efforts of one of the team. The junior sales rep, for example, may turn a prospect over to a senior by saying something like, "Mr. Robbins is more familiar with that application than I am." Under usual circumstances, however, it is best for the team leader who has presented most of the selling points—even if this person is a very junior rep—to close. There is often an interruption in interview mood during a turnover.

Ask for an Order

Asking for an order is the simplest and most natural of all closing methods. This should not be done in such a blunt manner as, "Sign the order." The word "sign" can frighten prospects, making a decision seem so legally binding. Of course, no salesperson ever orders a prospect to do anything. It is better to be a bit indirect, like, "Is there any reason why you shouldn't affirm this order and allow us to get this to you as soon as possible?" or "If you will write your name here, you will start realizing these savings right away," or "Since this will pay for itself within three years, will you authorize us to deliver it to you immediately?" Remember, prospects *expect* to be asked for an order from salespeople. (For a summary of closing techniques, see Figure 13.4.)

LEARNING TO HANDLE CLOSING PROBLEMS

Common closing problems confronting a sales representative include: (1) leading up to the close in a presentation; (2) handling uninvited guests; (3) getting around "no's", and (4) introducing order forms and getting signatures.

Leading Up to the Close in a Presentation

Everything done during a presentation should lead up to the close. The entire tone of an interview should promote harmony and lessen feelings of pres-

Figure 13.4 Summary of Closing Techniques

TECHNIQUE	EXPLANATION
Choice Close	Give customers a limited choice and lead them into the sale
Minor-Points Close	Decisions on minor points are easier to obtain and lead to the acceptance of the total package
Assumptive Close	Actions assuming the sale is made downplay the significance of making a buying decision
Stimulus-Response Close	A series of leading questions makes it easier for the prospect to say yes when asked for the order
Summary Close	Summarize benefits before asking for the order
"T"-Account Close	A summary close on paper, arranged in balance-sheet fashion
Standing-Room-Only Close	A statement suggesting that the opportunity to buy is limited because demand is great and few are left
Special-Deal Close	A "special" offer is made to get prospect to buy now
Success-Story Close	Prospect is told of a buyer who had a similar need or problem who solved it happily by buying the product
Closing on Resistance	Answer the objection or turn the problem into a benefit and then ask for the order or close using any of the closing methods
Contingent Close	Get an agreement by the prospect to buy if the salesperson can substantiate the benefits promised or the contingency happens as predicted
Turnover Close	Turn the closing over to another person present, who has a better chance to make the sale
Ask for the Order	Simply ask for the order directly or indirectly; this can be straightforward and honest
Trial Close	This is usually a question or a nonverbal action designed to elicit some commitment on the part of the buyer without harming the chances of continuing with the interview
Pretend-to-Leave Close	The salesperson pretends to leave but "just happens to remember" another benefit or special offer after the prospect has relaxed sales resistance

sure and tension. Even if a stimulus-response strategy is not consciously used, verbal agreements and affirmative nods from a prospect should be encouraged by leading questions. Objections should be answered and barriers to buying such as inadequate information should be overcome. The prospect's risk in buying should be minimized through assurances. A salesperson may get a prospect to agree that if a barrier to a sale is removed, the prospect will buy. Representatives should remove barriers or answer objections and ask for orders. Hasty presentations are to be avoided.

Handling Uninvited Guests

Sales interviews should be held in as private a place as possible. If another person comes in and interrupts a presentation just before the close, the mood of a presentation may be lost. Worse than that, the third party not having been present to learn benefits of an offering may say something to make a "ready-to-buy" prospect reconsider and cool off. A couple had almost decided to buy a dining room set when a friend interrupted and said she thought the set selected would look out of place between two existing carpeting colors. The

Photo 13.2
If necessary, direct a little of your selling effort to the third party, and use a summary close.

couple didn't buy. If there is no way to keep a third party from taking part, salespersons can direct a little of their selling effort to him or her and use a summary close. If everyone is not on a seller's side when the seller asks for an order, a sale can easily be lost (see Photo 13.2).

Getting Around "No's"

Prospects know they can say "no" many times and change their minds and say "yes." After saying "yes" once, they are committed. So "no" is the most flexible and safe position for a prospect who wishes to preserve bargaining potential. Prospects understand that a few "no's" may soften up a salesperson and get a better trade-in or a better price. Prospects actually *expect* a presentation to continue after the first "no." Good sales representatives pretend that a prospect's "no" has not been heard and continue with other positive selling benefits. This is why some selling benefits should be kept in reserve to use if a first attempt to close fails. Going beyond each "no" is easier if a salesperson still has something else to say. One tactic after a particularly meaningful "no" is to pretend to leave, saying something like, "Oh, yes, I forgot to tell you, this equipment is subject to a 10 percent price increase next week. You could save $100 by buying today. You can't buy a finer desk computer for the money!"

Introducing Order Forms and Getting Signatures

It is a good practice to introduce the order form early in a presentation, so the customer can get used to it. It does not weaken a close. Making decisions is hard, but "signing" a legal contract is a real commitment. A prospect can easily back out later if a salesperson says, "You can cancel if you change your mind." A relaxed closing atmosphere in which a buyer does not feel pressured into signing is desirable. An "X" near the signature line and pointing to it is good, suggestive psychology. As mentioned earlier, using a statement such as "Just put your name here, and we can have it in the hands of your secretary next week" may be better than using the more legal term "sign here" or "put your signature here," each of which sounds more formal and binding.

CUSTOMIZING A CLOSE

A decided competitive advantage over the average salesperson can be obtained if you have the right closing attitudes, if you know when to close, if you understand several good closing techniques, and if you can handle closing problems properly. Expert closers select the most appropriate closing method to use in each selling situation. While the application of closing methods is learned largely through selling experience, some writers have contributed insights into matching closing methods with the following situations:

- Closing by type of prospect
- Closing purchasing agents
- Closing in systems and industrial selling
- Closing when not in the presence of the prospect

Closing by Type of Prospect

Prospects are different. What may be perfect for one may not work well for another. Alan Schoonmaker and Douglas Lind contend that prospects can be divided into "dominant people," "dependent people," and "detached people" (1). Dominant people are identified by their attempts to assert themselves over others and by their desire for esteem. The walls of their offices are crowded with diplomas, awards, and trophies to show accomplishment. They would prefer to be looked up to than to be accepted as friends. They continually try to see if a sales representative is "good." If their attempt to "test" a rep by interrupting and controlling a sales situation succeeds in revealing a lack of professionalism, they will write that sales representative off as a weakling. Dominant people expect good salespeople to be seasoned and firm. They expect to be asked for an order often and may not buy until the rep's selling maturity is proved by closing a sale several times. A direct close or a pretend-to-be-leaving-and-then-return-with-another-point close is useful with dominant types, but assumptive or minor-points closes are not.

Dependent people are friendly, and they try to identify with others and to be nice. They are warm and thoughtful. Their offices convey a relaxed informal atmosphere, often abound in pictures of family or acquaintances, and are rarely neat or cold. Such prospects are gracious and hospitable. They expect others to be friendly and to exhibit the social graces in return. The strategy with such prospects is to minimize closing decisions as much as possible. Choice, minor-points, and assumptive closes work best with dependent people. Statements like "Shall we order five boxes then?" work well.

Detached people, according to Schoonmaker and Lind, are very cold, businesslike, and unfriendly. They do not care for others to be overly friendly or domineering. They are interested in facts and logic. They are not interested in small talk or attempts to establish rapport. Like most introverts, they like to position themselves at a comfortable distance from others. Their offices are neat but cold, with very little on the walls. They don't like emotions and prefer rational arguments. Pressure selling with this type will almost certainly fail. All product claims should be backed by evidence. Reasons for acting now must be given. The "T"-account or balance-sheet close is ideal to use with such prospects.

Charles Roth in *Secrets of Closing Sales* writes that it is important to set your talking pace to correspond with that of a prospect. He advises that indecisive buyers and silent prospects be pushed a little harder than others, that egotists be complimented, and that gripers be listened to in setting up for the close (2). The important thing for a salesperson is to be conscious of using different closes appropriately.

Closing Purchasing Agents

Most purchasing agents are seasoned buyers. Many who see sales representatives day in and day out have been subject to good closing techniques by many professionals. While purchasing agents may not always be high-ranking executives, they are nearly always experienced. Barry Hersker and Thomas Stroh write that these expert buyers put sales representatives into three classes—"the top closers, the mediocrats, and the bottom rung" (3). Top closers give good service to purchasing agents. They know their product applications and their competition. Top closers see nearly all buying contacts in a company with the knowledge of its purchasing agent and bend over backwards to fill every request and need of a buying company. They are eager for business and close more sales. The "mediocrats" give ample service, but the prospect has to be the creative one, shoulder the hard work, and not expect too much. The "bottom rung" consists of those salespeople who do not study prospective firms before calling, make excessive promises in order to close, waste time, are unfair to competition, and will not listen to find out buyer problems before recommending solutions. Professional buyers get rid of such reps quickly and do not grant reinterviews. With professional buyers, the close is not as important as the selling-service style.

Purchasing agents are trained not to overbuy or to purchase higher-quality goods than their companies need. Many industrial sales representatives tend to oversell quality. It would be better for them to listen and then close by recommending quality just good enough to meet the purposes of the buying firm. Since purchasing agents are more educated and sophisticated than ever before, they expect to be asked for orders but also to be led up to a close by the rep in a professional way that builds a good case for buying.

Closing in Systems and Industrial Selling

Systems and industrial salespersons often sell complicated, high–unit-value products to buying teams made up of many people. Negotiations for a period of many months frequently precede a close or loss of a sale. Selling strategies may entail making contact with and persuading several persons in a prospective firm who have influence on buying decisions. Frank Burge advises that the top executive is the place to start, because the top person can get representatives in to see everyone who can help with the study of present operations necessary to assess needs (4). Systems sales representatives who are busy working within a firm's operating structure to lay the groundwork for a proposal and a close usually win out over less aggressive competitors who are unwilling to work within a firm's structure.

In industrial selling, a salesperson does not concentrate on the close. On expensive and complex items, the primary focus is on a mutual understanding that a product is right for a particular application. According to Charles Bergman, the industrial buyer feels a great weight of uncertainty and risk when deciding to commit capital funds. He advises sales representatives to root out hidden objections and concerns and to deal with them (5). The close for industrial products should come as a matter of course after a series of low-risk, "trial" closes diminishes and the apparent uncertainties of a final decision. Bergman maintains that some good industrial salespersons never ask for the order at all. The order is implied after all sales barriers are removed. The NCR Corporation has found an innovative way to shorten negotiation time, to reduce risks for industrial prospects, and to facilitate sales closes for systems equipment (6). NCR sales representatives carry a portable computer terminal into a prospect's office and attach it to the telephone line. The prospect and the sales representative can then communicate with NCR's main computer in Dayton, Ohio. During the first call, the computer can ask prospects important questions about present operating procedures and equipment and analyze need. During later calls, the computer can answer technical questions with authority and even communicate all the alternative ways proposed systems equipment may be obtained. Prospects get customized answers and can make more assured decisions with less negotiation. Sales representatives' statements are backed by competent authority. This is a computerized version of a systems presentation.

Closing When Not in the Presence of the Prospect

Buying decisions in corporations today are being made by people who never see sales representatives. Jim Rapp calls closing procedures designed to face this situation "closing by remote control" (7). He recommends the following for reorder buyers and other buyers you can't face directly in asking for orders: (1) influence someone inside the organization to represent your cause; (2) write out a proposal with a cover letter specifying the time and date you will call for the order, and have your advocate present this to the decision maker; (3) in this proposal establish that a decision must be made by a certain date; (4) give evidence that you have good product knowledge by furnishing credentials or references; (5) work out a complete package offering including all details about price, delivery, warranties, etc., in advance; (6) try to communicate with the decision maker by telephone or in some other way in addition to the message proposal; and (7) follow up by finding out if everything is going according to your plan. Accounts can be closed in this way without seeing inaccessible prospects.

AFTER THE CLOSE

A sales representative's postclosing emotions must be controlled. A professional attitude is called for whether a sale is won or lost. If after getting an order, a rep appears too elated, buyers may feel they have lost a contest. Exhibiting the letdown (relaxation) that often comes from goal accomplishment may prompt a buyer to wonder why a rep is not more pleased to have the business. Sales representatives cannot let strong victory emotions cause an image loss or detract from the customer's satisfaction from having decided to buy the rep's product. Enthusiasm generated by a successful close can be directed toward interviewing and closing other prospects.

After prospects have committed themselves and signed orders, they should be reassured that they did the right thing and be thanked. "Ms. Chapman, you couldn't have gotten a better deal for the money. You'll always be glad you made this investment." Prospects who have committed themselves usually lose their resistive attitude and are eager to prove that they have made a right decision in buying. If an order is signed, it might be suggested that a buyer purchase additional products needed to go with the primary product (like service policies). Even if suggestion selling is practiced at this point, another lengthy presentation is not called for. If a sale *is* lost, a rep should shake the prospect's hand and say thanks for listening to the presentation. A refusing prospect may well be one of a salesperson's best customers in the future when the prospect's needs change. Above all, a rep should not stay around and fail to end an interview after a sale is made. Prospects do not need an opportunity to reconsider while a rep is present. It is possible to talk buyers out of a sale. A rep can only lose by remaining too long. GOQ—Get Out Quickly! Or, in the words of a Woody Allen movie title, "Take the Money and Run!"

SUMMARY

For most salespeople, closing is the most important skill required during an interview. If a prospect is expected to buy and this is conveyed by verbal and nonverbal communications, the chances of making the sale increase. A good time to close is when prospects understand an offer and when they give you signs that indicate interest in a product. If a prospective buyer relaxes, regards a product favorably, touches it, or asks questions that reveal intent to own it, a trial close to gauge the extent of interest is worth a try. There are many different closing situations, but a closing technique exists for every closing circumstances. *Choice closes, minor-points closes, assumptive closes, stimulus-response closes, summary closes, "T"-account closes, standing-room-only closes, special-deal closes, success-story closes, closings on resistance, contingent closes, turnover closes,* and *directly-asking-for-the-order closes* are field-tested ways to make sales.

Leading up to the close in a presentation, handling third parties, getting around "no's," and introducing order forms are common problems in closing. Standard strategies for handling these problems should be thoroughly understood. Salespersons should also be aware of specific closing methods and strategies to use in dealing with dominant prospects, dependent prospects, and detached prospects. Closing purchasing agents and industrial buyers and closing when not in the presence of the prospect require tailored techniques. After a successful close, reassure and thank the buyer, possibly suggest additional products, and leave quickly.

REVIEW QUESTIONS

1. What are the essential requirements for expertise in closing the sale?

2. What are the characteristics of a good closing attitude?

3. What are some of the characteristics of a poor closing attitude?

4. What are some of the ways to cultivate a good closing attitude?

5. What are the keys to the appropriate timing of attempts to close?

6. What is meant by a trial close? Give an example.

7. What are some verbal closing signals?

8. What are some nonverbal closing signals?

9. What are some indications that closing is not appropriate?

10. What closing methods are available to the sales representative? Briefly describe each method.

11. Give an example of:
    a. a choice close
    b. an assumptive close
    c. an ask-for-the-order close
    d. a standing-room-only close
    e. a success-story close

12. What factors in the presentation create a positive atmosphere for closing?

13. What may a prospect mean by the word "no"?

14. Schoonmaker and Lind identify three types of prospects. Briefly describe each type and suggest how closing methods should vary for each one.

15. Hersker and Stroh suggest that purchasing agents, as expert buyers, place sales representatives into three classes. What are these three classes, and what are the characteristics of the salespeople falling into each of them?

16. What are Jim Rapp's seven suggestions for closing when the salesperson cannot close in the presence of the prospect?

APPLICATION QUESTIONS

1. When you began the course, you had some idea of what personal selling and persuasion were. You also had some idea of what salespersons did and what they were like.
   a. Have your ideas changed at all?
   b. Would you be more willing now to have a job as a salesperson than when you started the course? Why or why not?

2. Refer to the second application question at the end of Chapter 6. Instead of the questions given, answer the following ones after talking to salespeople about some product you (or a friend) are interested in buying:
   a. Did the salesperson determine your motives?
   b. How were you approached?
   c. How well were objections handled?
   d. How did the salesperson attempt to close the sale? Which closing methods did the salesperson use? How successful would you say the closing methods were?

3. Using some of the closing methods you have learned, try to persuade a friend to go somewhere with you or help you to do something. Describe this experiment. Did the closing methods work?

13–1

Cloris Knight works in the Melko Gallery on Chicago's Michigan Avenue. The Melko Gallery sells both paintings and sculpture. Some of the paintings are by world-famous artists, such as Pissarro, Picasso, Sisley, and Miró. Others are by lesser-known contemporary artists. The sculpture line is equally varied. In addition to working in the gallery, Cloris represents Melko in its sales to businesses that want to enhance their corporate images by having fine works of art in their offices. Most of the prospects that Cloris sees fall into one of three categories: connoisseurs and collectors who know just what they want and for whom price is secondary, corporate interior designers who want large, quality modern works at prices that are impressive, but not too high—say, $1,200 to $3,500, and people buying art for the first time to display in their homes.

Cloris is showing a painting by Herman Melko, the gallery's artist-owner, to a prospect from Lake Forest. The prospect's husband has just been transferred to the corporate headquarters of Mid-Central Industries in Chicago from Kansas City. He has just been named executive vice president at Mid-Central. Cloris has learned these things from her prospect, Mrs. Forbes. Mrs. Forbes seems much attracted to the Melko painting. It is a post-impressionist canvas of the Chicago skyline seen from Lake Michigan.

> *Mrs. Forbes:* I just don't know—$3,500 does seem a lot for a picture to me.
>
> *Cloris:* Mr. Melko's work has been appreciating for some time, Mrs. Forbes. The Art Institute has recently purchased two of his canvases for over $5,000 apiece. Neither of them has the charm of this one.
>
> *Mrs. Forbes:* Well, Jeffrey did tell me he liked it when he was here last week. I told him I wanted to decorate the room around the picture not plug a picture into an already finished room.
>
> *Cloris:* That's exactly the way I think room decoration should be done, Mrs. Forbes. One of the nicest features of this particular work is that the variety of colors will permit any color scheme for the room. It really is a unique picture in its colors, isn't it?
>
> *Mrs. Forbes:* Yes, that's what first attracted me to it. I particularly like the greens and blues. I like the frame too.

Cloris:	Yes, its very simplicity focuses attention on the picture, but at the same time, it will go with any room decor.
Mrs. Forbes:	It's even the right size for hanging over the fireplace in our new living room.
Cloris:	Let's see, the colors, size, and frame are right for your room, aren't they, Mrs. Forbes?
Mrs. Forbes:	Yes.
Cloris:	Because Mr. Melko's show has just ended, I can have this canvas delivered to you by tomorrow afternoon. Will that be soon enough for you? After all, you and your decorator will want it there when you start planning the room, won't you?
Mrs. Forbes:	Yes . . . it would be helpful to have it there as soon as possible.
Cloris:	Will this be cash or charge, Mrs. Forbes?

QUESTIONS

1. Did Cloris work her close in the most effective way?

2. How might she have helped Mrs. Forbes to make up her mind sooner? Should she have done so?

13–2

Kermit Brothers is a real-estate agent who is showing a house to Janet Stokeley. Janet has told Kermit that she wants a house with at least three bedrooms, a library or den, a modern kitchen, and two and a half baths. Shade trees in a larger-than-average yard are among Janet's other requirements. Kermit has found a house that meets all of Janet's requirements.

Kermit:	This house has everything you asked for, Mrs. Stokeley, plus a good deal more. The owner is willing to let you assume his mortgage, and if the Florissant Savings and Loan objects, he's willing to finance it himself until conditions change. The interest rate will be far below the market. The rooms have the right dimensions for the kind of furniture you've told me you have.
Janet:	Well, it certainly comes close. The laundry room could be bigger and more modern. That's the first gas ring I've seen in a laundry room since I was a child. The price seems high compared with Philadelphia.
Kermit:	The price is a reasonable one for this neighborhood. Brent Park School is just across the park. There's an excellent shopping

center on Kingsley Avenue. The willingness of the present owner to finance the deal himself if Florissant doesn't allow you to assume his mortgage will keep your payment—including taxes and insurance—to under $500 a month. That's a real value for a house like this. It was built in 1938 for the daughter of the Malek Pencil people. She never lived in it. Dr. Reventlow is selling only because he wants to take advantage of the opportunity he's been offered at Sloan-Kettering in New York. The laundry room can be added onto later without any real problems. Let's go outside, there's something I want to show you.

Janet: Well, this yard has certainly been neglected. The lawn really needs cutting.

Kermit: Yes, the grass really is healthy, isn't it? That's because Dr. Reventlow had it all professionally landscaped only three years ago. Look at this sunken patio, all herringbone brickwork, and private as can be. Isn't it nice to think of being able to sit out here in the evening with a cool breeze and complete privacy? Your boys will love playing out here. The swing set and the sandbox over there are added pluses. I wish I had trees like these. You might find another house you like as well, but I doubt there's one around with trees like these and such a lovely patio.

Janet: Well, it is nice. But my husband is an avid gardener—it's his big relaxation. Where could he put in a garden with all this shade?

Kermit: Back beyond that hedge, there's an open sunny place with rich loamy soil perfect for a garden. Dr. Reventlow and his wife are avid organic gardeners and had it all worked over to make it the best around. You know, Mrs. Stokeley, this house seems to be exactly what you asked to see. It's near the best grade school in the area, has convenient shopping, is walking distance to your husband's office, and has this beautiful yard. I can't imagine you'll find anything more suitable than this.

Janet: Well, I do like it, Mr. Brothers, but Tom has set a pretty strict limit on price. He did like it when we drove by the other day. I have to discuss it further with him.

Kermit: The only problem is that a house like this—with so much going for it—isn't likely to stay on the market long, even with a market as sluggish as this one is. It could be gone tomorrow. We don't have an exclusive on it. I know that others are showing it this afternoon. Let's put a "sold" sign on it now, before it gets away from us. I'm sure you'd hate to lose it. If you gave me a check for $800 as earnest money (a monetary pledge given to a seller by a buyer to bind a bargain), you could reserve it and work out the details of your offer to Dr. Reventlow with your husband later.

Janet: Well, I'd sure hate to lose it . . . that garden tract is something my husband will love . . .

1. Did Kermit use a sufficient number of trial closes in this conversation?

2. Was Kermit more proactive than he should have been with Janet? Was he too pushy?

3. What signals did Janet give to Kermit that enabled him to push for a close?

13–3

John Travis represents a line of catalytic crackers for use in petroleum refining. At Delta Refining he has been having a difficult time getting through to the key gatekeeper in the decision process, Dr. Irvin Masterson. Dr. Masterson does not sign orders, but he is the real power behind the throne. He has more technical expertise than anyone else at Delta. John knows that his new cracker—with its low energy input requirement—is just what Delta needs. He has carefully planned his presentation to convince Dr. Masterson to sponsor a seminar on the new cracker for Delta's engineering staff. With Dr. Masterson's co-sponsorship, John feels that an order for several crackers in each of Delta's twenty-eight refineries would be assured. John carefully shows Dr. Masterson all the features of the new cracker, traces the cost-savings elements to Delta, particularly emphasizing how his crackers' costs are negligible compared with Delta's present thermal crackers, added to the company's gain from conversion, and on and on.

The technical detail and the flip chart presentations, the engineering estimates, and the trial balance sheets John has worked on for weeks have taken all his time. So important did they loom in John's mind that he was determined not to omit any item Finally, John has gone through all his exhibits and has run out of words. An awkward silence follows.

Dr. Masterson: All very interesting, Mr. Travis. Now, you've told me all about your cracker, but you've not said what it is you want me to do.

John suddenly realizes that he never told Dr. Masterson why he went to all the trouble of making his detailed presentation. Quickly, he goes over in his mind several ideas to sell Masterson on the idea of the seminar, but realizes he has no set plan—he has been selling the cracker not the seminar.

Is it too late for John to bring up the seminar?

What does John's experience offer other sales reps as an object lesson about sales presentations?

13–4

George Galloway sells new cars for Columbia Motors. He sees a man looking at the new Z cars and in particular a green four-door model.

George: That's a beauty isn't it? I'm George Galloway . . . here are the keys. Drive it around the block and you'll fall in love with it. May I ask your name sir?

Howard: I'm Howard Barron, but I'm not that interested; I just want to look around.

George: Is that your car, Mr. Barron? *(pointing to a 1978 gas guzzler)*

Howard: Yes, it's still in good shape, isn't it?

George: You've taken real good care of it, but it probably doesn't give you better than 10 miles per gallon in town and about 16 on the road, and that's not ideal the way gas costs today. That green four-door Z will give you almost as much room and way over twice the gas mileage. It's as modern as tomorrow. Can I put you in that one for less than $9,000?

Howard: No, I just came to look, thank you.

George: *(Opening front door, adjusting seat, and motioning for Howard to get in)* Get in, Mr. Barron, and feel the front-wheel drive as well as look at it. *(With Howard driving)* Drives like a dream for an ultra mileage car, doesn't it? It has special springs and suspension that give it that floating feeling. I told you you'd love it. We can have it ready for you in just 15 minutes.

Howard: No . . . my wife always has a part in the car decision.

George: Can we drive by and show it to her now? I'll bet she would like to see it, too!

Howard: Our house is about three miles from here.

George: Great, let's go . . . see how it handles in traffic . . . and it's super both in town and on the highway. How do you like the computerized engine controls that save you the gas and still give you all the power you need? If your wife likes it, will you trade for it if we give you $300 over book for your present car?

Howard: Not today, Mr. Galloway. Today I'm just finding out about it. *(Stops in front of home, introduces George to his wife, and explains that he's come to show the car to her)* I told Mr. Galloway we were just curious about the Z car, honey.

Kay: I see you found a green four-door, but you know I need a small wagon to haul the kids and things.

George: The back seat folds down, giving you all this room, Mrs. Barron. That's something special isn't it? Here, try it and see how easy it is! This car is just right for both of you, isn't it? Why not let it start saving you gas money today?

Howard: No, we're waiting for interest rates to come down a bit before we seriously consider a car.

George: Is that what's holding you two up? We guarantee interest rates for a year. If the rates come down, we apply the lower rate to the rest of your principal. Even if they go up after they come down in the first year, we will apply the lowest rate during the first year to your payments. With this consideration and giving you $300 above Bluebook value for your present car, I know you can't beat that deal. It's also guaranteed for maintenance for two full years. You should save enough in gasoline each month to help you considerably on the payments. The car should cost you less than $8,000 with your car in on it. If you'll buy it today, I'll have them swap this radio for a stereo. You couldn't have a nicer car for these times. Talk it over . . . is it a deal?

Howard: You've been very helpful, Mr. Galloway, but, no, we've decided to shop around before we invest that much money in an automobile.

George: Look at *Consumer Research Advice Monthly,* Mr. Barron. Do you see the ratings of the Z car in comparison with the competition? See where it says "best for price"? You could waste valuable time, and this car has exactly what you want with the stereo, doesn't it? Is there any reason why you two should wait any longer to have what you want?

Howard: *(After another conference with Kay)* No, we're going to be brash and take up your deal.

George: Now that's a "no" I love to hear. You've made a wise decision.

QUESTIONS

1. What kind of closes did George use?

2. Did he close too soon and too often? Explain.

3. How did he overcome each "no"?

NOTES

1. Alan N. Schoonmaker and Douglas B. Lind, "One Custom-Made Close Coming Up," in *Closing the Sale* (special report), *Sales & Marketing Management,* vol. 118, no. 8 (June 13, 1977).

2. Charles B. Roth, *Secrets of Closing Sales* (Englewood Cliffs, N.J.: Prentice-Hall, 1953), pp. 57–63.

3. Barry J. Hersker and Thomas F. Stroh, "The Purchasing Agent Is No Patsy," in *Closing the Sale* (special report), *Sales & Marketing Management,* vol. 118, no. 8 (June 13, 1977).

4. Frank Burge, "In Systems Selling, the Close Is Systematic," in *Closing the Sale* (special report), *Sales & Marketing Management,* vol. 118, no. 8 (June 13, 1977).

5. Charles Bergman, "Secrets of the Industrial Close," in *Closing the Sale* (special report), *Sales & Marketing Management,* vol. 118, no. 8 (June 13, 1977).

6. Thayer C. Taylor, "Closing by Computer," in *Closing the Sale* (special report), *Sales & Marketing Management,* vol. 118, no. 8 (June 13, 1977).

7. Jim Rapp, "The Remote-Control Close," in *Closing the Sale* (special report), *Sales & Marketing Management,* vol. 118, no. 8 (June 13, 1977).

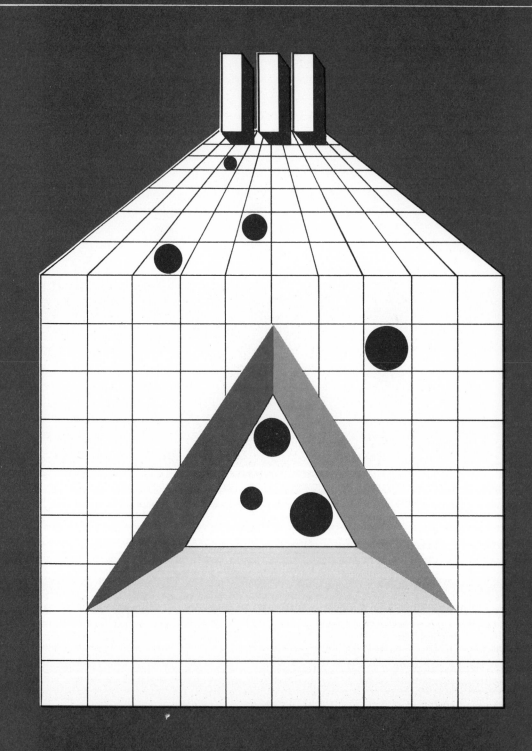

INSURING FUTURE OPPORTUNITIES

Part three examines the long-range aspects of successful careers in selling. To succeed in sales, career representatives must deal ethically with their customers and the companies they represent, build reputations for service in their territories, and gain insights into the processes of sales management. The chapter on ethics and goodwill concerns your interpersonal dealings inside and outside the firm you represent. The chapter on sales management is designed to help you understand the thinking of your superiors and to prepare you to take the first steps toward eligibility for managerial roles. To prepare for that first step up the promotional ladder, ways to approach the job market and to sell your professional abilities to corporate recruiters are discussed in the last chapter of the section.

Ethics and Goodwill

Salespeople who promote fairly and give service win long-term patronage by customers. Gaining a favorable reputation through ethical dealing builds for the future. A satisfied customer is a triple asset, because a satisfied customer (1) becomes a preferred prospect for future business; (2) will often furnish referral leads and preapproach information; and (3) often promotes the reputation both of a sales representative and of a product to other potential buyers. Ethical procedures of customer cultivation lead to customer satisfaction.

ETHICS

Basically, ethics is the study of the rightness and wrongness of human behavior. Everyone has ideas of what is right and what is wrong. Most people prefer to act in ways they feel are right rather than in ways they feel are wrong. Ethics is studied in an attempt to make accepted standards of behavior clear, to see how and why accepted standards have come about, and to show how to go about living up to accepted standards in everyday life.

Everyone lives up to some standard of behavior. For most, personal standards of conduct for everyday life are as natural as breathing. Only those faced with difficult decisions become conscious of their individual ethical codes. A code of ethics is not something a person is born with; usually, it is something

Selecting a company with compatible ethical standards enhances a selling career.

"To close on an upbeat note, I'm happy to report we received twenty-two per cent more in kickbacks than we paid out in bribes."

Drawing by Dana Fradon; © 1976 *The New Yorker Magazine,* Inc.

a person is born into. While growing up, everyone is subject to lists of "dos" and "don'ts." Some "oughts" and "ought nots" act as guides to surviving childhood. Others deal with social rather than physical survival. To survive in a society, each member must learn to consider how his or her behavior affects the interests of others. Through learning to consider the interests of others, each person learns what is expected in the way of moral behavior.

For salespersons, ethical behavior promotes customer goodwill. It fosters profitable relationships between members of a sales force and those they work for. For sales representatives, the payoff of ethical behavior is that it *pays*! Such an attitude finds support in the work of the Greek philosopher Aristotle. Artistotle, the pupil of Plato and the tutor of Alexander the Great, laid the foundation on which the structure of ethics for Western civilization was built. In his *Nichomachean Ethics* he wrote: "Every art and every inquiry, and similarly every action and pursuit, is thought to aim at some good. . . . But a certain difference is found among ends. . . . The end of medical art is health, that of shipbuilding a vessel, that of strategy victory, that of *business* wealth." (1) Wealth to Aristotle was not the enrichment of an individual, but the bettering of living standards for all. He saw an increase in wealth as promoting harmony among individuals in families, enterprises, and society. Further, Aristotle noted that ethical behavior stems not from the choice of goals, but rather from the means chosen to achieve those goals. Ethical conduct proceeds from attitudes of honesty, loyalty, fairness, and consideration of others. These dispositions are *perfected* in few if any individuals. Nevertheless, individuals should aspire to perfect these dispositions. The study of ethical problems in selling acts as a reminder to salespersons of the qualities they should exhibit in their dealings with customers and the members of their firms.

Ethical problems rarely have easy solutions. Ethical behavior begins where written rules and laws leave off. Many practices, while legal, promote distrust, anger, and suspicion in interpersonal dealings and in transactions between enterprises and their customers and employees. Ethical practices, on the other hand, promote harmony and trust in transactions, shorten bargaining time, and strengthen customer disposition to buy through reduction of perceived risk.

Today, there is public suspicion of the business community. Many see a lack of ethical behavior in business dealings. Public suspicion and the perception of a decline in standards of conduct have led corporations and buyers to seek out salespersons of good moral character and ethical attitudes. Thus, in order for the markeplace to be a healthy one, businesspeople "must be under steady pressure to adapt to public values. When they escape this imperative, the public loses" (2). Every sales representative must understand the major areas of ethical problems in selling. Through such an understanding, those who sell can build reputations for high standards of personal integrity. The major ethical problem areas may be classified as follows:

- Ethical duty to self
- Ethical responsibility to employers
- Ethical dealings with customers
- Ethics and conscience

Ethical Duty to Self

Sales persons' perceptions of right and wrong are well-established before they ever go to work. Each person may embrace a differing view, but there do seem to be some universals. No matter how well established their personal perceptions of right and wrong are in family and other personal relationships, there are those who think that different standards apply once they enter the business world.

"It is common to hear people say that ethics is of little concern to business persons. It is said that ethics is ethics and business is business. . . . The practice of business depends for its very existence on the moral behavior of the vast majority of citizens. Imagine trying to practice business in a society where lying, stealing, and other immoral actions were permitted. . . . At a minimum, business requires a society where contracts are honored and where private property is respected. Bribes, kickbacks, fraud, and monopolistic activities in the restraint of trade have all been judged inappropriate, because they are immoral practices. (3)

Each person who sells has a responsibility to maintain an ethical self-image and a moral belief in the products and practices of the enterprise represented. Self-image theory emphasizes that personal views of oneself are critical to relationships with others and to ultimate selling success. There are many occasions in a selling career when there is a temptation to act against one's personal standards of conduct. In such cases, "Conventional morality can provide a simple and workable approach to solving ethical problems. . . ." Reps "need only ask questions such as 'How would it look in tomorrow's newspaper?' or 'Would I want my family, friends, and employer to know about this decision?'" (4). If compromise with your ethical standards for short-run gain causes you to begin to view yourself as a dishonest person, your damaged self-image can lead you to even lower levels of practice, and the ensuing guilt can erode your personality. A few theorists feel that the answer to guilt feelings is to eliminate conscience, rationalizing that "everybody's doing it" rather than to suffer the frustrations of denying self when tempted. However, such an approach can lead to long-run failure for a salesperson trying to build a reputation in a territory. One misrepresentation can undermine a salesperson's ability to sell in an area. Hundreds of legitimate transactions may not restore the confidence of prospects. A self-image of honesty is not only useful in projecting sincerity but is necessary for personal satisfaction.

Ethical responsibility to self in selling begins with the selection of a company. (See Figure 14.1 for a company's ethical policy statement.) If selling a firm's product would be against personal moral scruples, a rep should not sell for that firm. Making decisions about what appear to be conflicting loyalties between a personal code of ethics and corporate policy should be avoided. For example, when questioning *over time* "presents real problems," then "you have begun a [deciphering] of signals from your conscience that can only enhance corporate responsibility" (5).

Investigate the operating procedures and selling techniques of a prospective employer to avoid future compromising situations. Personal self-respect (which is a valuable personal asset in self-image theory) will suffer if a person attempts to please an employer who expects that person to misrepresent, trick, or otherwise deceive prospects to get orders. While it is true that it is possible to make money by selling socially questionable products in a deceitful way, consider the nonmonetary advantages of selling one of the thousands of beneficial lines that a rep can promote with full confidence. Even in the most respected of companies, enough situations arise to test character, but ethical problems can be minimized by careful selection of a work environment.

Figure 14.1   An Ethical Policy Statement by Johnson & Johnson

JOHNSON & JOHNSON POLICY STATEMENT

1   No corporate or subsidiary funds or assets shall be used for any unlawful purpose. Nor shall any Johnson & Johnson company engage in the practice of purchasing privileges or special benefits through payment of bribes, illegal political contributions, or other forms of payoff.

2   No undisclosed or unrecorded fund or asset of the corporation or any subsidiary shall be established for any purpose.

3   No false or artificial entries shall be made in the books and records of the corporation or its subsidiaries for any reason, and no employee shall engage in any arrangement that results in such prohibited act.

4   No payment on behalf of the corporation or any of its subsidiaries shall be approved or made with the agreement that any part of such payment is to be used for any purpose other than that described by the documents supporting the payment.

5   Any employee having information or knowledge of any unrecorded fund or asset or any prohibited act shall promptly report such matter to the general counsel of Johnson & Johnson.

6   All managers shall be responsible for the enforcement of and compliance with this policy, including necessary distribution to ensure employee knowledge and compliance.

7   Appropriate employees will periodically be required to certify compliance with this policy.

8   This policy is applicable to Johnson & Johnson and all its domestic and foreign subsidiaries.

Source: *Sales & Marketing Management,* vol. 116, no. 7 (May 10, 1976), p. 38.

Ethical Responsibilities to Employers

Since close supervision of personal selling is impractical, every sales representative is placed in a position of trust. However, there are many situations in personal selling in which loyalty to an employer will be tested. Ethical problems commonly arise in these areas:

- The use of assets and expense accounts
- Time accountability and reporting
- Defending and promoting a firm's image
- Loyalty to firm personnel
- Job switching
- Gifts or bribes
- Contests

The Use of Assets and Expense Accounts. A good test to apply when using the firm's money or materials is, "If it were mine, would I use it or spend it that way?" If the stationery, the car, the visual aids, the advertising materials, the electricity, the paper, the packaging, or the telephone belonged to you, would you tolerate the same degree of waste? If the company were yours, would employee appropriation of office supplies for personal use be desirable? A careful use of seemingly inconsequential company assets communicates that you are loyal to the firm and interested in its profitability.

Expense accounts present special temptations. It is almost impossible for managerial accountants to devise "unpaddable" expense accounts that still allow the salesperson flexibility. A sales representative must be trusted to make correct odometer readings and to deduct miles driven on personal business. Meals, tips, and taxi fares are often misrepresented, because receipts are not always required for these minor items. The temptation to eat hamburgers and falsely claim an entire meal allowance presents itself daily "on the road." When motel accommodations exceed company limits in large metropolitan or resort areas, some sales representatives add more to mileage turned in or add the difference to lower-cost rooms elsewhere. Sometimes other salespersons show fellow sales representatives ways to get by company accountants. Falsifications, whether advised by other persons or not, are outright expense-account cheating—they violate the spirit of trust as well as the actual rules. While an employer probably does not want a rep to go hungry or to stay in a dirty motel, neither is a waste of money highly thought of. More than likely, your expenses will be compared to those of other sales representatives to determine your honesty, loyalty, and profitability.

Time Accountability and Reporting. Salespersons who work on straight salary and waste time are in a sense stealing profits from an employing company. They fail to sustain sales support personnel such as clerks and mechanics whose jobs depend on sales made. Even if representatives work on a commission basis, a company still loses if too much time is spent over coffee, extra-long lunches are taken, or the territory is left early. Another, more conscientious sales representative could be taking advantage of the lost sales opportunities. Sales representatives dissatisfied with their salary should talk with superiors rather than purposely waste time in retaliation. Salespersons who handle another line of products other than those known to their employers are engaging in the unethical practice of "kiting." Employers have a right to expect full-time work from salespersons hired to sell their products. If an employer *agrees* that the line of another company can be handled, then a rep's obligations have been fulfilled through disclosure.

Reporting is a clerical task that many salespersons dislike. Some sales representatives pad daily reports with fictitious calls. The temptation exists to overstate the number of real calls made in a territory. A real call has not been made if the salesperson was refused an interview. A full demonstration is not a brief glimpse of the product by a prospect. A sales report can be distorted easily by sales representatives who don't write down events when they take place or who "fudge a little" in an effort to justify time expenditures when time has been wasted.

There is an ethical responsibility for off-time if it affects job performance. Some salespersons work a second job. Without proper rest, they fail to do either job well. Salespersons who party too much or drink too much or report to work tired are not giving their employers full measure.

Defending and Promoting a Firm's Image. Some customers will speak out against the firm a salesperson represents. In an effort to be agreeable and win their confidence, reps will be tempted to side with them. While it is permissible to admit errors and mistakes made by your company, it is disloyal to speak against your superiors' motives and attitudes. The customer's respect rises when you support your employer. If what a customer says disparages your manager, you might reply, "I'm sorry you feel that way about Mr. Connors. I've worked for him for years, and he has always been fair to me." Sometimes it is wiser just to listen and not respond to the prospect's negative comment. Even if accusations appear just and you agree with them, reinforcing them with a statement like, "You're right, we do have inept repair personnel, but good help is hard to get" is unwise. Such an agreement is unlikely to bode well for future sales. A better reply would be, "We didn't repair your equipment properly last time, Ms. Anderson. I will inspect it personally next time before it leaves our shop if you will let me know when it is sent in again. Our service personnel are human and occasionally make a mistake like this, but we always make it right."

Loyalty to Firm Personnel. In nearly all large organizations there are cliques or informal groups of employees who seem to agree on certain issues. Often such groups become "politically" active, seeking to promote the good of the clique members above that of the organization. Clique members and certain independent persons may attempt to tear down the reputations of other members of the firm to gain advantage. It is unethical to join in character assassination of others. This is especially true when evidence is skimpy. Efforts to tear others down to increase your own position can win you many enemies, while justifiable support in defense of criticized supervisors, peers, and subordinates can gain you respect and trust.

Sales representatives are sometimes tempted to sell to prospects who are outside their territorial boundaries. The representative may know these prospects personally, run across them accidentally, or actually make an effort to find them. Territory jumping, when it becomes known, like claiming credit for others' ideas or efforts, lessens respect and support by other members of the selling team.

Job Switching. While it is usually considered acceptable for a salesperson to advance by taking a better job with a competing firm, active efforts by sales managers to attract (proselytize) sales reps from competitors is often seen as unethical. For a small firm without resources for a strong training program, the only way that qualified salespersons can be found may be through recruiting from competitors. Such "raiding" is, naturally enough, resented by managers whose organizations are weakened by competitive hiring. It is not surprising that the injured managers conclude that the practice is unethical. Job switching to a competitor does raise ethical questions for the switcher. Switchers have had access to confidential information and competitive secrets in their former jobs. Under strict ethical standards, it is unprofessional to take advantage of a former employer by trying to switch old customers right away to the new one. To use a former employer's secrets competitively is equally improper. Certainly, it is wrong to destroy the image of a previous employer with customers you used to cultivate for that employer. Another consideration in job switching is adequate notice of intention to leave. An old firm can be left with undeserved problems, unless time is given to recruit a replacement without damaging customer relations. A good reference from every firm ever represented is a long-run asset for any career salesperson.

Gifts or Bribes. Occasionally, buyers will attempt to bribe sales representatives to obtain special bargaining concessions such as lower prices, higher trade-in allowances, or larger allocations of products in short supply. Such gifts should be refused tactfully, allowing the sales representative to act in the best interests of an employer and in fairness to all customers. This kind of artificial inducement in the marketplace distorts the operation of fair bargaining. Any kind of preferential treatment in response to bribes endangers goodwill with all customers—even those who make the bribe successfully.

Contests. Contests are designed to motivate sales representatives to make more sales of all products or to make more sales of specific products in a line. The pressures to win tempt some sales representatives to sell the wrong products to customers—products that yield points in the contest but are not a good match for customer needs. Sometimes order dates are falsified to fall within a contest period, or pressure tactics and trickery endangering goodwill are initiated as part of an extra effort to win. Cheating in contests is unfair to the company and unfair to other salespersons participating in the contest.

Ethical Dealings with Your Customers

Considerable pressure exists for sales representatives to lower their ethical standards when dealing with customers, because sometimes there is a large, short-run monetary gain from making small moral compromises and because a few customers and competitors are sometimes unethical in their strategies. Often a small bribe to a purchasing agent or a half-truth representation of a product can mean gaining rather than losing a large order. Representatives see some competitors resort to unethical tricks in selling and are tempted to retaliate in kind. Prospects who seem otherwise upright may relax standards of moral integrity in a bargaining situation. Some may even misrepresent competitive offers in an effort to get special prices and delivery concessions. Even purchasing agents for reputable companies may drop hints that personal gifts will influence their partronage. Strong moral character is required to play by the rules when the opposition is cheating. Long-run gains from ethical dealings in terms of goodwill, reputation, projected self-image, and personal satisfaction outweigh short-run temporary advantages. Areas for ethical concern in dealing with customers include:

- Misrepresentation of products
- Gifts and entertainment
- Special treatment
- Keeping secrets confidential
- Competitive fairness

Misrepresentation of Products. Intentional misrepresentation of important facts about products to induce buyers to purchase is fraud, but misleading half-truths and withholding certain kinds of information are a question of ethics. Prospects expect sales representatives to emphasize the strong points of their offerings. They do not expect salespeople to stress product weaknesses. Many salespersons feel that it is up to the prospect to find the disadvantages of buying. While they will answer questions truthfully, they do not volunteer negative information hurting their bargaining positions. Pointing out a few minor weak features of the product offering in an attempt to promote a balanced argument is good selling strategy. It is not productive to emphasize deficiencies of an offering. Words or actions intentionally designed to deceive the prospect are unethical, even if true on the surface. Suppose, for example, that a sales representative says that a copying machine will easily make transparencies from printed copies but knows that the special materials necessary for this process are so expensive as to make it impractical. The truth has been told, but the buyer has been deceived. A car sales representative may declare that the compact automobile will pull a heavy trailer, failing to add that such pulling will wear out the motor on a short trip. Few buyers forget much less harmful deception, and most who have suffered the consequences of having been "told the truth" in misleading words will spread the word to other buyers not to patronize the products of companies employing such sales representatives.

Salespersons who take advantage of customer trust and ignorance to overload inventories, sell more expensive products than are necessary, or recommend repair items when the original equipment parts are not worn are acting in bad faith. The more a customer trusts and the less a customer knows, the greater the responsibility of the seller to be fair. The building-materials dealer who purposely overestimates the number of bricks needed for a house, knowing that they are not returnable, and the mechanic who installs unnecessary parts in an automobile just to sell them, are examples of sellers violating prospect trust. On the other hand, if a customer insists on buying a product with greater capabilities than are apparently needed, against the salesperson's recommendations, the responsibility for consequences rests with the buyer.

Gifts and Entertainment. Buying decisions should be based on the worth of an offering, not on the efforts to buy customer patronage. Small gifts in appreciation for business are legitimate promotion. Gifts and bribes to corporate buyers to induce them to act in their own interests rather than in the interests of the firm they represent are competitively unfair. It is hard for legitimate sellers to compete for business when decisions are based on the personal gain for a buying agent and not on the value of the products to a buyer's company. Many purchasing agents resent any attempts to influence them unduly. Many find efforts to obligate them to buy from a particular supplier equally offensive. Even the few that are "on the take" respect salespersons who tactfully decline to participate in wrongdoing to get business. Lavish entertainment can become unethical if sales representatives substitute it for good selling techniques. If representatives are spending their firms' money primarily because they can participate along with prospects in enjoying entertainment, a serious question of ethical responsibility arises.

Special Treatment. Affording some customers special treatment can generate ill will with customers who do not get extra concessions. Many customers try to take advantage of their customer status to make excessive demands on the sales representative's time. Suppose a customer requests that an equipment salesperson stay on long after equipment is working properly and operators are trained. The salesperson should diplomatically decline, if possible. The first priority of a sales representative should be to spend time productively. It is possible to become so service-oriented that other ethical obligations are forgotten.

Keeping Secrets Confidential. Telling customer's and employer's secrets is a fast way to ruin a selling career. It helps sell few products. Leaking strategic information to competitors or betraying confidences is a serious selling "sin." It is an unfortunate personality habit with some sales representatives. Customers know that if a rep tells them things that are confidential, that rep is likely to tell their confidences to others. A professional image requires respect for confidentiality.

Competitive Fairness. Salespeople should be familiar with unfair competitive tactics to be on guard against inadvertent use of them. Unethical salespersons may bribe secretaries to learn the amounts in secret bids. They may schedule their sales calls behind the calls of a competing salesperson, "rearrange" competitive displays or even sabotage competitive products. They have been known to pay confederates to pose as customers to complain about competitive products. Most often they name a competitive product and put it down viciously and unfairly to prospects. This type of activity reflects on their professionalism. Oddly enough, though, it can help "advertise" positively the very product they seek to damage. Wise prospects know that products pointed out by competitors and given attention must be good. Often stirred by "bad-mouthing," they investigate to find out the truth for themselves. In the last analysis, ethical selling is fair to everyone. It promotes long-run business over short-run temporary gains.

Ethics and Conscience

Is there a guide for salespeople in tight ethical situations? Popular belief holds to the slogan: "Let your conscience be your guide." Webster's dictionary defines conscience as "consciousness of the moral right and wrong of one's own acts or motives." Is not the conscientious sales representative, then, likely to behave with scruple and honor? Not necessarily:

Conscience often . . . is not a good guide in moral matters. Not all consciences are the consciences of a Schweitzer or Martin Luther King. The political terrorist and assassin, for example, appeal to conscience as a source of justification for their actions. But many of their acts remain morally heinous nonetheless. A criterion is thus needed that enables us to distinguish a good conscience from a bad one. (6)

Is there such a criterion, or standard, in the kinds of shifting environments that sales representatives find themselves in as they make their daily calls? Obviously, conscience is important, but by itself conscience is insufficient. After all, consciences vary from person to person. Eighteenth-century philosopher Immanuel Kant offered a way to put the individual conscience into the perspective of the "universality" of the obligations of the individual to self and society. Although Kant never traveled more than sixty miles from his birthplace in Konigsberg, Prussia, his work has traveled far and influenced Western thought in the two hundred years since the publication of his *Critique of Pure Reason* in 1781. The final formulation of Kant's "categorical imperative" (an act that is of itself objectively necessary) offers the criterion by which many modern moral dilemmas can be resolved, not only in personal selling, but in other areas as well. This formulation reads: "Act so that you treat humanity, whether in your own person or in that of another, always as an end and never as a means only" (7). People, then, are ends in themselves and can never ethically be used as a means to the ends of other people, enterprises, or societies.

GOODWILL

Goodwill is an intangible asset. It is an attitude that customers and prospects have about you and your company that assures favorable consideration of your offering in the future. It occurs when you have established good public relations with your customers and the general public because you have shown positive service attitudes in your business dealings. There are many practices that build goodwill; some of the more important ones will be treated in this section.

Sell the Right Product in the Right Amounts

It is better to lose a sale than to lose a customer. Customer orientation means having the customers' best interests in mind in recommending products. In the short-run, more commission may be made by selling a customer a model with too much capacity or a higher price, or by overstocking a dealer with slow-moving products that stay in inventory. Temporarily, a rep may profit by selling something that fails to meet buyer needs. But in the long-run more will be sold and the confidence of customers kept by selling products that meet customer needs.

Overstocking a customer (selling a dealer too much of an item) means a long wait before a reorder can be placed. Overstocking may mean a short-run gain, winning a sales contest, say, or moving a "dog," but in the long-run customers may be lost. Overstocking customers in a territory may limit realization of future sales potential. Underselling (selling less than is needed), on the other hand, can be worse than overselling. Retailers or wholesalers who don't have enough stock because too small an order is recommended lose sales and customers by being out of an item in demand. The underselling rep also loses out by missing the larger commission on the order that should have been recommended. Insurance customers with inadequate coverage suffer loss when their houses burn down. Materials shortages in factories can stop assembly lines and embarrass purchasing agents. A sales representative must see the world through the customer's eyes when recommending specific models, qualities, and quantities. Every prospect must be thought of as a long-term customer.

Assure Maximum Customer Benefits from Product Use

Seeing that a customer gets maximum satisfaction from owning and using your products and services is an important sales representative responsibility. It begins with the presentation made and the product recommended. Do not yield to the temptation of giving a prospect unrealistic expectations of product performance when emphasizing the benefits of buying. Inform the buyer of the total uses or applications of a product, the best procedures for operation, and the proper care and maintenance. It is important for the new car salesperson, for example, to explain to a purchaser where the hood-release lever is or how to refill a windshield washer solvent container. The operator of the new typewriter reasonably expects to be told by a seller the easiest way to take the typing unit out for cleaning and how to change ribbons without getting dirty. Consider the operator of a copy machine untold of the meltdown and fire danger certain plastics or paper present if used in the machine. A salesperson who doesn't explain safety precautions is negligent and may face legal involvement if someone is injured.

It is good practice for a rep to watch a customer using a newly purchased product. Optimal use is what a prospect buys and expects to be delivered. Doing a good job training customers in the use of a product will keep salespersons from losing goodwill. No conscientious rep wants a customer to have cause to ask, "Why didn't the sales representative tell me about that?"

Maintain Open Communication Channels with Customers

Customers feel more assured when they have an open line of communication for contact with the reps who call on them. Questions about products that go unanswered build barriers of ill will. The salesperson who thoughtfully takes the time to call customers to inform them of specific delivery times gives those customers a chance to prepare to receive their orders smoothly. Customers may need to make special physical arrangements, such as moving furniture or otherwise preparing to absorb a new product into work routines. If an order cannot be delivered as scheduled, it is best to notify its buyer of the de-

Figure 14.2   Sample Questionnaire for Feedback

Dear Customer:

YOUR OPINIONS ARE VALUABLE TO US. Would you mind taking time to fill out this brief questionnaire so that we might serve you better in the future? Our customers mean a great deal to us, and we want you to keep coming back.

Were all Travel Ways Inn personnel courteous to you?
Courteous _____ Fairly courteous _____ Discourteous _____

Did you find your room clean and well supplied?
Yes _____ No _____ (If no, please tell us what was wrong) _____
_____

Did all lamps and appliances operate properly?
Yes _____ No _____ (If no, please explain) _____
_____

Were you bothered by noise of any kind?
Yes _____ No _____ . . . . _____

Was your bed comfortable?
Yes _____ No _____ . . . . _____

Was the pool and playground area clean and properly maintained?
Yes _____ No _____ . . . . _____

Please rate our restaurant facilities.
Excellent _____ Good _____ Poor _____ (If poor, please tell us why)
_____

Additional Comments _____
_____
_____

                              Thank you,
                              Travel Ways Inn

Insuring Future Opportunities

lay and the reasons for it. Customers who eagerly anticipate the delivery of a product and who are not notified that a delivery promise has to be broken may feel that the salesperson didn't care enough to call to explain why the product would not arrive as expected.

It is not enough to expect a customer to call the sales representative if something is wrong. An important device that allows buyers to express attitudes about their experience with a product or service is the questionnaire. Some motels, for example, leave questionnaires and self-addressed, stamped envelopes in rooms inviting customers to evaluate the accommodations. Few customers take the time to complete the questionnaire, but all customers know that the motel ownership cares and wants to provide good service. (See Figure 14.2 for a sample questionnaire.)

Give Customers Attention

Customers appreciate any kind of thoughtful attention. Follow-up calls after a sale is made show that a rep is interested in more than just getting orders. A follow-up call gives a customer an opportunity to ask questions or express needs. Some sales representatives make it a practice to be present when a product is delivered. They help to place it in use and stand by to explain care and operating specifics. A buyer might see a need for additional units or other products at this time while the enthusiasm of physically possessing a new product is high. An installation follow-up call can be a good opportunity for setting up a future sale by reminding buyers about replacement or replenishment times. If at delivery a rep discovers that a product is not suitable for a buyer's operation or setting, a lost commission or order may be prevented through exchange of the product delivered for a more suitable model. Products are not really sold until a customer is satisfied and pays for an order.

Using the telephone and direct mail are inexpensive ways to assure customers that they are remembered between calls. Using these communication devices requires a minimum investment of time and money. Both make it easy to inform customers of new products, to keep the company name in customers' minds, and to make sure customers feel remembered. Many salespeople acknowledge birthdays, special holidays, and business expansion occasions by personal cards or phone calls (see Figure 14.3 for an example of a goodwill contact letter.)

Give Good Service

Retailers buy more than inventory from you. They buy prompt delivery, display arrangement, return privileges, advertising, and a whole package of serv-

March 17, 1982

Mr. Fred Latham
173 Larkspur Drive
Travathan, Oklahoma 33908

Dear Mr. Latham:

Thank you for purchasing your Wellbuilt tractor from us. This garden tractor is every bit as durable and versatile as our larger models, and it comes with a full range of auxiliary attachments that are available at our South Elm Dealership.

When you bought the Wellbuilt, you also bought a year's free maintenance service with it. It is very important to us that you are satisfied in every way, so please call us if you have any problems at all. You may reach me at 275–4871.

Thank you again for becoming our customer. We are grateful for the privilege of serving you, and we hope that you enjoy your Wellbuilt tractor so much that you will tell your friends about it.

Sincerely,

Walter James

Walter James
Wellbuilt, Sales

Enclosure

Figure 14.3   Goodwill Letter

ices. Insurance companies and their beneficiaries expect prompt and courteous payment of claims with a minimum amount of red tape and a maximum amount of attention. Machine and equipment customers expect products to operate without frequent breakdowns. Everything possible to keep equipment running through preventive maintenance, proper servicing, and prompt repair is the reasonable expectation of any industrial equipment buyer. An insurance company that "drags its feet" in settling legitimate claims loses its policy holders. Tractor repair personnel who are slow to respond to service calls and who seem not to care that a farmer's harvest is disrupted because of malfunctioning equipment rarely get asked back the next growing season. Seeing that the customer gets satisfactory service over the life of the product *is* the responsibility of sales representatives as well as company service personnel.

Help Buyers by Offering Advice

Salespersons are in a unique position to furnish consulting advice to customers. Since they visit hundreds of customers each year and are familiar with solutions to common problems, sales reps have a broader view than many customers. Because of their wide exposure to many different kinds of operations, salespeople often know the best way to accomplish business goals. While it is risky to advise in areas where you are inexperienced, you are obligated to suggest ideas to customers that will help gain business, cut costs, or enhance enjoyment of products in areas where you are competent. Selling companies usually furnish brochures that deal with operating problems that customers might face. Learning the solutions to common problems from as many sources as possible and tactfully advising customers of solutions observed help to build the goodwill that strengthens long-term customer–sales representative relationships. Advice should be given only as suggestions or on the request of a customer. If a customer is cool to a rep's ideas, it is a mistake to insist that a suggestion be implemented.

Handle Customer Complaints Fairly

Customers are not always satisfied with products or services as received. Sometimes products are deficient on delivery, have latent defects, are damaged in shipment, or for some other reasons are unsuitable for their intended use. Customers should know how to get in touch with the salesperson who took the order in cases like these. Dissatisfied customers do not reorder, and they damage a salesperson's reputation in a territory. The firm may be liberal in accepting a customer's word in exchanging merchandise, or it may insist that each claim be clearly substantiated. Regardless of the position of a firm's management on returns, it is best to listen to and to communicate with all disgruntled customers.

A customer's claim can usually be investigated through company records, product inspection, and questioning and listening. Listen attentively and quietly to the customer's side, even if the customer is excited and angry. Frequently, after customers explain a complaint, their initial anger and emotionalism are diminished and they are able to talk of their problems calmly.

Being able to explain a problem to a receptive listener seems to help customers to see all sides of a situation. It promotes a feeling that a sales rep is interested in a fair settlement. Mistakes like billing errors, incomplete contents, defective merchandise, wrong sizes, wrong colors, and wrong mechanical adjustments of equipment usually can be corrected quickly. Problems that stem from improper customer care and usage, on the other hand, are harder to adjust. Few firms are willing to subsidize customer abuse of products. This

Sometimes products do not perform as customers expect. Listen carefully to the complaint and, if possible, see that the customer goes away satisfied.

"Hi, Mr. Shultz! How did that plant vitamin work on your garden?"

THE SATURDAY EVENING POST

Reprinted from *The Saturday Evening Post* © 1957 by Al Johns.

is especially true if a customer was given proper instruction on operational maintenance.

The main objective in handling claims is to make a customer feel satisfied that all has been done that can be done to be fair. Even if a problem arises from customer negligence, it is best to take some good-faith action to restore lost confidence. Suppose, for example, that minor damage is done to the fender paint of a new car. It is simpler to have it touched up than to argue about whether or not the scratch occurred before or after the car was driven out of the lot. One practice customers especially dislike is being referred from one person to another when they come to settle a claim. It is better for the first person who hears a complaint or problem to stay with the customer until the matter is resolved. If a salesperson needs help from someone else in the organization when handling a customer claim, it should be done without completely turning over the customer to someone else. A responsible rep remains until customer satisfaction is achieved and the matter is closed.

It is important to reach a mutually acceptable solution to a customer complaint in the first interview. All particulars of an agreement should be made clear to a complainant. Any promised follow-up action should be taken as soon as possible. Delays in problem solutions and claims adjustments are disturbing to customers. Delays in doing what was promised make salespersons appear insincere. Following up at the earliest possible moment shows a customer your dedication to correcting mistakes. Quick resolution of problems makes customers feel important, aware of your eagerness to serve, and leads to repeat sales.

SUMMARY

Ethical conduct proceeds naturally from attitudes of honesty and fairness. It is a prime factor in long-run customer relationships. High ethical standards promote a professional self-image that is projected in dealings with prospects. A salesperson's first duty to self is to select a firm with a product and standards in marketing that are compatible with the salesperson's ideals. A salesperson can gain respect in a company by using assets and expense accounts fairly, by spending time efficiently, by accurately reporting selling activities, by creating harmony in the firm through loyalty to fellow employees, and by following the rules in sales contests. Proper notice should be given before leaving a company, and secrets learned in that employment should remain secret. Sales representatives who use deceptive methods to produce sales in the short run ruin their reputations and lose customers in the long run. The more a customer trusts, the more obligation there is to deal ethically. Special treatment in the form of large gifts, lavish entertainment, bribes, and unwarranted service is a substitute for good selling methods and good product offerings and is competitively unfair. While the bargaining situation produces temptations on both sides, the buyer's decision should be based on the worth of an offering instead of personal gain. Confidence-keeping and competitive fairness are essential to a professional selling image.

Goodwill is a long-term asset to sales representatives and their companies. Goodwill must be earned through careful customer cultivation. It is important to sell the right product in the right amounts, to make sure that customers know how to use and care for a product, to give customers attention and to see that products are giving the satisfaction intended, and to see that customers get every purchased service due and expected. Repair service is a very important part of a product offering to customers of mechanical products. Fair and rapid claims adjustments are important in the insurance industry. Sales representatives are expected to act as consultants to help customers with problems of product offerings.

1. Why is a satisfied customer a triple asset to the sales representative?

2. Why study ethics? In what ways is ethical behavior of specific value to the salesperson?

3. What is the relationship between legal and ethical issues in selling?

4. What are the salesperson's few major ethical problem areas?

5. From an ethical perspective, what are some of the issues that should be examined before a sales position is accepted?

6. List the ethical responsibilities that the sales representative owes his or her employer.

7. What expense account items are most likely to be falsified? Why?

8. In what ways can salespeople "steal" time from their employers?

9. What are some of the ethical issues involved in switching sales jobs to a competing employer?

10. In what ways can sales representatives "cheat" in sales contests?

11. What are the areas of ethical concern in dealing with customers?

12. What is the legitimate role of gifts and entertainment in personal selling? In what ways can such efforts break ethical standards?

13. What are some examples of unfair competitive tactics in selling?

14. What is meant by goodwill?

15. Name some of the more important ways of building customer goodwill.

16. How does the salesperson lose from overselling a customer? From underselling a customer?

17. How can the salesperson ensure that the customer will derive maximum satisfaction from the product?

18. In what ways should the salesperson maintain communications with the customer after the sale? Why is this important?

APPLICATION QUESTIONS

1. Assume that you now are married and have two children. While you are attempting to sell a product, the following situations happen. What would *you* do?

   a. You have to stay in a hotel costing $60 a night and the company will only pay

$40. You can make up the difference by saying that you paid more for meals and taxi fare than you actually did.

b. A prospect asks you to spend a whole day playing golf.

c. You will make a $10,000 commission if a computer system is purchased. The prospect has the contract, the pen is in his hand, and he says, "You will be making a good commission if I sign this order, how about sharing a little?"

d. The prospect is ready to sign the order for a $20,000 piece of office equipment. You are in the prospect's office, and your manager has come with you to help you close the sale. Although the prospect needs the equipment, you know that the company has limited resources, which should be spent in building up their inventory. The prospect turns to you and says, "I'm convinced that you are an honest person. Do you really believe that I should spend the money on this now?"

2. Explain how you can tell the truth and misrepresent a product to the customer. Give an example.

INCIDENTS

14-1

Steve Hall is returning a gasoline-powered lawnmower to the Grass Master Lawncare Center. Finally, he gains the attention of Fred Hearn, the salesperson.

Steve: I'm returning this excuse for a lawnmower. The darn thing quit on me five times before I got halfway through with my front yard. I don't know what's wrong with it, but I don't want it.

Fred: Well, maybe it's your fault. What kind of oil did you put in it?

Steve: (Angrily) The blasted oil they sold me for it here, that's what. I wasn't shown anything about it, but I followed the directions they told to me, and it won't work. So here it is. Give me my money back.

Fred: Well, it wasn't my fault it didn't work. Why don't you bring it back this afternoon when Mr. Beecham is here? It's a used mower now with all those grass stains on it!

Steve: I want my money back now, and I haven't got time to come back this afternoon. If you don't give it back to me, I'm going to call the Better Business Bureau.

Fred: Go ahead, I don't care. I just work here. Say, there's Mr. Beecham coming in now. Why don't you tell *him* your troubles. Maybe he can do something about it. Hey, Mr. Beecham, this man is mad about his mower and wants to get his money back.

Beecham:	What seems to be the matter, Mr. Hall?
Steve:	This mower doesn't work properly, and I want to return it.
Beecham:	We certainly want you to bring it back if it is not satisfactory. But tell me everything you did before it acted up on you.
Steve:	Well, I filled it with the oil you sold me, and I put in some gasoline I had kept through the winter for my old mower.
Beecham:	That might be what's wrong. Sometimes water gets in those cans. If you can leave it here for about two hours, I'll have it working perfectly for you or give you a brand new mower. You've always been one of our good customers, and we want to keep it that way.
Steve:	Sure . . . I have to have a mower, and I have to get the grass cut. Will you show me how to take care of it? I didn't even get a book of instructions with it when I bought it.
Beecham:	I apologize that no one showed you how to maintain it, but you can rest assured I can show you how to get maximum service from it. Thank you for giving us a chance to satisfy you with it.
Steve:	Thank you, I'll be back in a couple of hours.

QUESTIONS

1. Contrast the way Mr. Beecham handled Steve with the way Fred handled Steve.

2. Since it was probably Steve's fault that the mower didn't work, should Mr. Beecham have insisted that Steve pay for servicing the mower?

3. What violations of maintaining goodwill were shown?

4. What principles for maintaining goodwill were shown?

14–2 Here is an excerpt from *The Grapes of Wrath** by Nobel prize-winning author John Steinbeck. The novel tells of the dislocation of tenant farmers from their homes in Oklahoma during the dustbowl days of the 1930s. The fierce erosion of the land from overfarming combined with the economic distress of the Great Depression forced hundreds of thousands of tenant farmers to leave the lands they had farmed for as many as three generations. Most migrated to California. The best way to get to California from Oklahoma was by car. This excerpt focuses on the selling practices of used-car dealers during the time of the migration nearly fifty years ago as seen by Steinbeck and, undoubtedly, by many of the migrants.

In the towns, on the edges of the towns, in fields, in vacant lots, the used-car yards, the wreckers' yards, the garages with blazoned signs—Used Cars, Good Used Cars.

*John Steinbeck, *The Grapes of Wrath* (New York: Viking Press, 1939), pp. 83–89.

Cheap transportation, three trailers. '27 Ford, clean. Checked cars, guaranteed cars. Free radio. Car with 100 gallons of gas free. Come in and look. Used Cars. No overhead.

A lot and a house large enough for a desk and chair and a blue book. Sheaf of contracts, dog-eared, held with paper clips, and a neat pile of unused contracts. Pen—keep it full, keep it working. A sale's been lost 'cause a pen didn't work.

. . .

Owners with rolled-up sleeves. Salesmen, neat, deadly, small intent eyes watching for weaknesses.

Watch the woman's face. If the woman likes it we can screw the old man. Start 'em on that Cad'. Then you can work 'em down to that '26 Buick. 'F you start on the Buick, they'll go for a Ford. Roll up your sleeves an' get to work. This ain't gonna last forever. Show 'em that Nash while I get the slow leak pumped up on that '25 Dodge. I'll give you a Hymie when I'm ready.

What you want is transportation, ain't it? No baloney for you. Sure the upholstery is shot. Seat cushions ain't turning no wheels over.

Cars lined up, noses forward, rusty noses, flat tires. Parked close together.

Like to get in to see that one? Sure, no trouble. I'll pull her out of the line.

Get 'em under obligation. Make 'em take up your time. Don't let 'em forget they're takin' your time. People are nice, mostly. They hate to put you out. Make 'em put you out, an' then, sock it to 'em.

Cars lined up, Model T's, high and snotty, creaking wheel, worn bands. Buicks, Nashes, De Sotos.

. . .

Goddamn it, I got to get jalopies. I don't want nothing for more'n twenty-five, thirty bucks. Sell 'em for fifty, seventy-five. That's a good profit. Christ, what cut do you make on a new car? Get jalopies. I can sell 'em fast as I get 'em. Nothing over two hundred fifty.

. . .

Flags, red and white, white and blue—all along the curb. Used Cars. Good Used Cars.

Today's bargain—up on the platform. Never sell it. Makes folks come in, though. If we sold that bargain at that price we'd hardly make a dime. Tell 'em it's jus' sold. Take out that yard battery before you make delivery. Put in that dumb cell. Christ, what they want for six bits? Roll up your sleeves—pitch in. This ain't gonna last. If I had enough jalopies I'd retire in six months.

Listen, Jim, I heard that Chevvy's rear end. Sounds like bustin' bottles. Squirt in a couple quarts of sawdust. Put some in the gears, too. We got to move that lemon for thirty-five dollars. Bastard cheated me on that one. I offer ten an' he jerks me to fifteen, an' then the son-of-a-bitch took the tools out.

. . .

Lookin' for a car? What did you have in mind? See anything attracts you? I'm dry. How about a little snort a good stuff? Come on, while your wife's lookin' at that La Salle. You don't want no La Salle. Bearings shot. Uses too much oil. Got a Lincoln '24. There's a car. Run forever. Make her into a truck.

Hot sun on rusted metal. Oil on the ground. People are wandering in, bewildered, needing a car.

. . .

All right, Joe. You soften 'em up an' shoot 'em in here. I'll close 'em, I'll deal 'em or I'll kill 'em. Don't send in no bums. I want deals.

Yes, sir, step in. You got a buy there. Yes, sir! At eighty bucks you got a buy.

I can't go no higher than fifty. The fella outside says fifty.

Fifty. Fifty? He's nuts. Paid seventy-eight fifty for that little number. Joe, you crazy fool, you tryin' to bust us? Have to can that guy. I might take sixty. Now look here, mister, I ain't got all day. I'm a business man but I ain't out to stick nobody. Got anything to trade?

Got a pair of mules I'll trade.

Mules! Hey, Joe, hear this? This guy wants to trade mules. Didn't nobody tell you this is the machine age? They don't use mules for nothing but glue no more.

Fine big mules—five and seven years old. Maybe we better look around.

Look around! You come in when we're busy, an' take up our time an' then walk out! Joe, did you know you was talkin' to pikers?

I ain't a piker. I got to get a car. We're goin' to California. I got to get a car.

Well, I'm a sucker. Joe says I'm a sucker. Says if I don't quit givin' my shirt away I'll starve to death. Tell you what I'll do—I can get five bucks apiece for them mules for dog feed.

I wouldn't want them to go for dog feed.

Well, maybe I can get ten or seven maybe. Tell you what we'll do. We'll take your mules for twenty. Wagon goes with 'em, don't it? An' you put up fifty, an' you can sign a contract to send the rest at ten dollars a month.

But you said eighty.

Didn't you never hear about carrying charges and insurance? That just boosts her a little. You'll get her all paid up in four-five months. Sign your name right here. We'll take care of ever'thing.

Well, I don't know——

Now, look here. I'm givin' you my shirt, an' you took all this time. I might a made three sales while I been talkin' to you. I'm disgusted. Yeah, sign right there. All right, sir. Joe, fill up the tank for this gentleman. We'll give him gas.

Jesus, Joe, that was a hot one! What'd we give for that jalopy? Thirty bucks—thirty-five wasn't it? I got that team, an' if I can't get seventy-five for that team, I ain't a business man. An' I got fifty cash an' a contract for forty more. Oh, I know they're not all honest, but it'll surprise you how many kick through with the rest. One guy come through with a hundred two years after I wrote him off. I bet you this guy sends the money. Christ, if I could only get five hundred jalopies! Roll up your sleeves, Joe. Go out an' soften 'em, an' send 'em in to me. You get twenty on that last deal. You ain't doing bad.

Limp flags in the afternoon sun. Today's Bargain. '29 Ford pickup, runs good.

. . .

Spattering roar of ancient engines.

. . .

Sure, we sold it. Guarantee? We guaranteed it to be an automobile. We didn't guarantee to wet-nurse it. Now listen here, you—you bought a car, an' now you're squawkin'. I don't give a damn if you don't make payments. We ain't got your pa-

Insuring Future Opportunities

per. We turn that over to the finance company. They'll get after you, not us. We don't hold no paper. Yeah? Well you jus' get tough an' I'll call a cop. No, we did not switch the tires. Run 'im outa here, Joe. He bought a car, an' now he ain't satisfied. How'd you think if I bought a steak an' et half an' try to bring it back? We're runnin' a business, not a charity ward. Can ya imagine that guy, Joe? Say—looka there! Got a Elk's tooth! Run over there. Let 'em glance over that '36 Pontiac. Yeah.

. . .

Cadillacs, La Salles, Buicks, Plymouths, Packards, Chevvies, Fords, Pontiacs. Row on row, headlights glinting in the afternoon sun. Good Used Cars.

. . .

Goin' to California? Here's jus' what you need. Looks shot, but they's thousan's of miles in her.
Lined up side by side. Good Used Cars. Bargains. Clean, runs good.

QUESTIONS

1. Could Steinbeck's indictment of the morality of used-car dealers of the 1930s be repeated today? How accurate do you think Steinbeck's description of the business practices of used-car salespeople is today?

2. How widely held do you think Steinbeck's views of business ethics are? What can business do to undo harmful impressions?

14–3

Roberta Ransom sells for General Distributors, which offers a full line of plumbing and electrical supplies to contractors, builders, and the ultimate consumer. She is on the road three days each week and in the office on Tuesdays, Thursdays, and Saturday mornings. Six months ago Roberta had an especially pleasant interview with a Mr. Merlin Cochran, who was interested in two fiberglass tub-shower combinations for the upstairs addition that he planned to make. Roberta quoted a price for the two fiberglass units, and Cochran seemed pleased and promised to call her when his construction progressed to the point that the units could be installed. There was no commitment made to buy the units. Sure enough, five months later, Cochran called and told Roberta to deliver the two units. By this time, however, there had been a price increase of 5 percent. The units were delivered to the site and partially installed in the upstairs addition. Cochran received a copy of the bill a few days later reflecting the price change. Roberta had never experienced a customer reaction any more heated than Cochran's—he had changed from "Dr. Jekyll" to "Mr. Hyde!" Roberta just listened as Cochran swore at her and General Distributors over the phone, but Roberta kept her composure. After Cochran had steamed for about five minutes, Roberta tried to explain to him that price increases during the last few months were not unusual and that she was certainly sorry that there had been any misunderstanding. Cochran's last words were, "Come get these two units and if you scratch anything getting them out, you're responsible." Roberta talked the whole thing over with her sales manager, Mr. Taylor, who agreed that Roberta could offer the units at the first price quotation, although that price had been out of the catalogue for four months.

Roberta went to the construction site and found the two tub-shower units walled in. She explained to Mr. Cochran that General Distributors would sell him the units for the old price and that she was sorry for the misunderstanding. Cochran's answer was, "I'm too angry now. Come get these units and you had better not harm anything. Within two more days they are going to get the staircase up, so you had better get them today!" Roberta could see that it would be impossible to remove the units without tearing out part of the already constructed wall and possibly marring the subfloor. Cochran had specifically said that the subfloor had better not be scratched, but Roberta could not understand why that would hurt anything. Roberta tried again to get Cochran to accept the order at the lower price and finally had to leave with the issue still unresolved. There was no way to get the units out without hurting the units or disturbing the already completed construction.

What would be the best way to handle this customer grievance?
Do you think Roberta and General Distributors did the right thing in permitting the customer to pay the old price?
Have negotiations reached the point where General Distributors should take legal action against Cochran, irrespective of the possible loss of goodwill, or should they simply absorb the $400 cost?

14–4

Charles Mulder has been a salesperson for the Easy-Plane Boat Company for two weeks, since leaving Aqua-Queen, a competitor that also sells a line of speedboats to dealers. He is calling on Lois Werne, an account he had formerly cultivated for Aqua-Queen.

Lois: Come in, Charles. I guess you want to talk about your new boats for the spring, don't you?

Charles: Yes! But I'm with a new company, Ms. Werne. I'm now with Easy-Plane. These are better boats than the ones you handle now. Believe me, I know both lines very well. Easy-Plane is rapidly taking the market from Aqua-Queen. I want to show you why it would be good strategy for you to switch. You've been a good customer, and I know you can gain profits from handling this more popular line.

Lois: Wow! This is a surprise! What about those new Aqua-Queen models for the coming season, which you were talking about just two months ago?

Charles: Have you seen Easy-Plane's new model? Confidentially, before I left, I found out from the sales manager that Aqua-Queen has been losing its market position for several years now and is presently in a very weak financial state. But Easy-Plane is increasing its market share every year. The boats have a stronger hull, look better, and will move faster with the same power. When five of my best accounts switched, I got wise and changed companies. You have to believe in the products you sell, don't you?

Lois: But I built up the Aqua-Queen name with my customers. What will I tell them if I switch lines? Besides, I understand that Tyson, your new credit manager at Easy-Plane, is hard to deal with.

Charles: I'll admit he's a pain, but I'll handle him for you. Say, I found out something before I left "Queen." I saw a memo on Ned Dunstan's desk—he's the "Queen" dealer nearest you. It indicated that he planned to spend over ten thousand dollars on an advertising campaign this spring. Easy-Plane has a plan whereby they would pay for half of your advertising. That would help you ward off Dunstan's challenge in this area without costing you nearly as much. I'll tell you what . . . if we can do business, we will take a weekend in the Bahamas together with our families to celebrate. I'll see that it won't cost you a thing. I'll just leave this material with you. Think about it!

Lois: I'll consider it, Charles. But it would be a big step for me to change lines.

QUESTIONS

1. What are the ethical and goodwill issues involved in this incident?

2. Which of Charles's actions, if any, would you consider to be unethical?

NOTES

1. Aristotle, "Nichomachean Ethics," in Saxe Commins and Robert N. Linscott (eds.), *The World's Great Thinkers* (New York: Random House, 1947), pp. 3, 51–52.

2. Mel S. Moyer, "Marketing Policies and Public Values," *The Business Quarterly* (Canada), Winter 1980, pp. 50–51.

3. Tom L. Beauchamp and Norman E. Bowie (eds.), *Ethical Theory and Business* (Englewood Cliffs, N.J.: Prentice-Hall, 1979) p. 2.

4. Douglas Dalrymple, *Sales Management: Concepts and Cases* (New York: Wiley, 1982), pp. 457–458.

5. Laura L. Nash, "Ethics Without the Sermon," *Harvard Business Review*, November–December 1981, p. 84.

6. Beauchamp and Bowie, *Ethical Theory*, p. 18.

7. Vernon J. Bourke, *History of Ethics* (Garden City, N.Y.: Doubleday, 1968), p. 169.

Sales Management

Promotion to the job of sales manager is a logical step up the corporate ladder for most sales personnel. The representative who becomes an assistant or zone sales manager may later advance to higher-paying positions such as branch sales manager, district sales manager, and vice president in charge of sales. Many corporate presidents are selected from sales managers because they have been trained through sales experience to project good images. They are able to persuade people. They can promote good public relations within and outside the organization. Even if a rep does not aspire to be a manager, understanding the responsibilities of a sales team "captain" is good preparation for a sales team member. Understanding the tasks of sales management facilitates communication between reps and their immediate supervisors. It also gives salespersons greater knowledge of their work environment.

Sales managers must plan, organize, lead, control, and secure personnel for the activities of the selling team. Managers set selling objectives and devise selling strategies. They are responsible for salesforce results. They research the market, forecast sales, set territorial boundaries, fix quotas, help salespersons with problems, and select, train, and motivate sales force members. They take part in product planning, market expansions, sales-policy formulations, and the development of selling control and evaluation methods. Most managers are expected to help in selling important prospects. Persuading problem accounts that sales representatives find difficult to close is another sales management task. Sales managers are well paid for all of these responsibilities. Their salaries, including bonuses, are on the average about 40 percent higher than the salaries received by the sales force (1). In addition, they receive many indirect rewards, such as opportunities for personal growth and overall job prestige. Sales managers are selected from individuals with proven sales ability, communication skills, product knowledge, organizational loyalty, and leadership personality. Managers must, after all, set an example for sales personnel. Projecting a positive image inspires greater selling effort. The manager's responsibilities will be examined in detail under the following headings:

- Approaching the leadership challenge
- Planning
- Recruiting and selecting
- Training
- Motivating
- Evaluating, compensating, and controlling

APPROACHING THE LEADERSHIP CHALLENGE

A fundamental decision area for new sales managers is determining how to establish leadership through image and example. The respect of the sales force can be won by showing competence, fairness, positiveness, decisiveness, and acceptable supervisory style.

Competence

To appear competent, a manager must exhibit superior knowledge of products, policies, and selling techniques. Many sales-management development programs are designed to meet this competency requirement by having potential managers make example demonstrations at sales meetings and introduce new products at company branches. Aspiring managers must study new products and applications thoroughly to be able to sell in problem situations. They must learn to convey the competency image that salespersons expect of their leaders.

Fairness

To show fairness, a manager must be careful in deciding which representatives get the largest salary increases, the promotions, the praise, and the prizes. The manager who plays favorites by giving greater increases to cronies or selecting certain persons over others for superficial reasons dissolves the glue that holds the selling team together. That glue is the expectation, of gain from belonging. Every decision, in fact, should take into consideration firm members' expectations of gain (2). Young firm members who find no chance for advancement quit. Old firm members become demotivated when hope of promotion is lost. Fairness can be initiated by establishing definite standards of evaluation for greater compensation—standards such as quota attainment or profitability—and using them in rewarding personnel. The sales force must realize that intangible factors such as leadership qualities enter into promotion decisions, but other rewards should be based almost entirely on merit and experience. Patterns of bias and favoritism are quickly noticed and resented.

Positiveness

A positive, enthusiastic atmosphere inspired by the sales manager must prevail for maximum results. A primary responsibility of every manager is maintaining a working environment that inspires productivity. Negative attitudes have no place in motivating salespersons who must face many disappointments in selling situations. While it is foolish to be overoptimistic or unrealistic, a "can-do" attitude must dominate. Uncertainty, pessimism, or setting goals too high can infect the sales force with feelings of inadequacy and undermine confidence. Positive, realistic goal setting and approaches apply the principles of cybernetics and contagiously stimulate sales force self-images. This primes each individual's mental capabilities for success.

Supervisory Style

Supervisory style concerns the assumptions managers make about salespeople and the basic approaches they take to motivate them. One manager may assume, for example, that sales personnel are basically lazy, irresponsible, and incapable of good work unless closely supervised or threatened with dismissal. This kind of manager is likely to set rigid work policies. Generally, rigid managers are very restrictive about giving information to the selling team. The opposite of this supervisory style is the manager who assumes that personnel are responsible, creative, and capable individuals desiring to participate in decisions and working best when fully informed. This type of manager promotes full communication with team members. Motivation comes not through fear but through positive incentives (3). A manager with this style trusts members of the sales force with responsibility and creates an environment with few restrictions. It is generally conceded that with today's shortage of qualified sales applicants, together with the inclination of sales representatives to resent close supervision, the dictatorial, threatening, overly restrictive, noncommunicative style is "out." The participative, trusting, and positive incentive style is "in." Most salespersons consider being their own boss and working their territories with relative freedom as part of their job benefits. The greater the intelligence, education, resourcefulness, and selling experience of the persons manage, the less restrictive their work environments should be. While part-time, lower-level salespersons might need tight supervision and restrictive policies, professional industrial sales representatives require more freedom.

The benevolent good-friend style of leadership can be taken too far, however. It is almost a proverb that super salespersons who have risen from the ranks fail as managers. Too often, these new managers are overconcerned with popularity. They bend the rules for too many individuals, exhibit indecisiveness, and show irresponsibility by putting the firm's welfare in second place (4). The friendly manager often fails to delegate. The hard decisions that need to be made are dodged. Managers should recognize the aspirations of subordinates, but they must also apply a reasonable amount of discipline and put the good of the firm first.

The Leadership Model. Leadership is the impression leaders make on their followers. It involves providing good examples to inspire willing sales force compliance with supervisory requests. Managers must be aware that they are continually under close observation by sales personnel. If a manager wears certain clothes, handles a demonstration in a certain way, or shows particular ethical standards, sales representatives are likely to take note and copy.

A primary principle of leadership is to give subordinates the *authority* needed to carry out their responsibilities. This means that managers who expect results from territorial operations should see to it that salespersons have flexible expense accounts, latitude to make sensible decisions, and general resources necessary to carry out assigned responsibilities.

Management by Objectives. Management by objectives (MBO) is a particular way of ensuring that sales personnel participate in decisions. MBO entails joint determination of goals by the manager and the salesperson. In situations where conflicting goals occur, managers are expected to apply some pressure. For example, if salespersons purposely set low yearly goals in order to look good at the end of the year, it is up to managers to pressure for higher goals. MBO also requires setting up definite times to compare progress with goals. If salespersons can be persuaded to set realistic goals, they will have fewer excuses for not attaining them. Detailed objectives set through MBO act as guides to field activities. MBO is particularly popular as a leadership device in selling because of the ease in measuring sales results—sales made, demonstrations given, interviews accomplished, expenses entailed, and profits generated (5).

Managerial Expectations. Managerial expectations are a powerful force in meeting the leadership challenge. This does not mean setting unattainable goals, but it does suggest that sales managers should communicate a high opinion of their sales force's capabilities. If a manager indicates the feeling that each member of a sales team has high potential, each will be motivated to live up to that potential. Managerial expectations build up self-images, and improved self-images focus the mental resources of sales personnel on the path to success.

PLANNING

Since sales managers are responsible for their sales force's success or failure, they must make organizational decisions, forecast sales, plan products, establish territories, set quotas, and submit budgets. Each of these planning functions will be discussed below.

Planning Organizational Relationships

Organization is essential to coordinate effort. Every person on a sales team should know his or her responsibilities. Work loads should be allocated appropriately. And authority should be defined. The steps involved in organizing are: reviewing objectives; determining activities necessary to accomplish these objectives; grouping activities into job designations; assigning the right person to each job designation; and providing for easy control (6).

Job descriptions are detailed listings of all the activities, responsibilities, and authorities associated with each job position. They should be written. The total work load of a sales force can be divided by separating groups of job positions by product, geographical area, customers, or combinations of these. When grouping activities, it is important to have the right number of subordinates reporting to each superior. If a manager or supervisor controls too few people, expensive executive time is wasted. Too many personnel put under one manager may spread that manager too thin. A manager can supervise more salespersons if they are intelligent, well trained, have fewer selling problems, and/or sell uncomplicated products.

Organizations may be centralized or decentralized. Centralized organizations, like the Armed Forces, have a few people at the top making most of the decisions. Subordinates operate under strict policies or rules. This promotes coordination and tight control and assures uniformity of procedures. It discourages individual freedom in accomplishing results. Under decentralization, field personnel are made responsible for results, but they have more freedom in achieving those results and in meeting selling problems on their own initiative. While most firms set down important policy guidelines for such matters as meeting legal requirements, they usually allow considerable freedom in selling practices.

As firms grow larger, it usually becomes necessary to create "staff" or advisory positions. Lawyers, product specialists, and research experts are examples of staff people who gather information and give advice to sales force personnel. Staff members have little authority but great influence over those in the field. Specialized advisers free managers and salespersons from research, technical aspects, and other nonselling assignments, allowing them to spend more time on planning and making sales calls. *Too many* staff personnel tend to generate unnecessary reports, increasing the nonselling time of sales force members.

Sales managers can use organizational planning to keep work environments healthy. A top-heavy organization with too many supervisors and too few workers can be prevented by including fewer top-level positions in organizational charts. Cliques or informal groups can develop that spread rumors, cause dissension, and damage morale. Cliques can be discouraged by having fewer persons under one supervisor and by improving information flow in an organization. The better an organization is managed and the more highly motivated its members, the less important these informal groups will be. When cliques do develop, they should be influenced by the manager to work for organizational purposes, instead of against the formal structure. (See Figure 15.1 for a sales organization chart.)

Territorial Estimates and Sales Forecasting

Sales and territorial estimates are the basis for most of a firm's budgeting and planning. There are two basic methods for estimating territorial potential: The build-up method and the buying-power method (7). The build-up method is useful when there is a list of potential buyers and accurate estimates of what each will buy. This method entails identifying possible customers, finding out how many are in the territory, and determining the average amount each can be expected to purchase. If the firm is selling to manufacturers, for example, managers can use the U.S. Government Census of Manufacturers to find the number of particular establishments in a certain geographical area, annual sales figures, and net worth data—all of which help make good estimates. In the index-of-buying-power method, purchasing power and credit availability are put together in an index and used to estimate potential. Consumer companies have too many customers to use the build-up method, so most use the index method. Since markets are people with the ability and will-

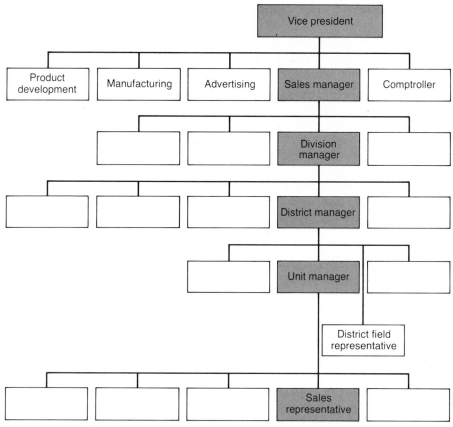

Source: *The Challenge of Sales Management at Procter & Gamble,* Procter & Gamble, Cincinnati, Ohio.

Figure 15.1   Procter & Gamble Sales Structure for a Typical Product Line

ingness to buy a product, buying power and number of people are important measurable factors in forecasting sales. *Sales & Marketing Management* magazine's "Annual Survey of Buying Power" gives an estimate of buying power in different countries and cities. But for the individual firm, competitive factors and target-market differences must be used to adjust such gross estimates (8).

Nearly all company plans depend on estimates of total sales. Sales managers are usually involved in making aggregate sales forecasts. There are several methods of forecasting sales of present products. *Customers* may be questioned about their buying intentions if a few prospects comprise the market for a product. *Company officials,* including sales managers, may estimate sales by using an averaging method. All the estimates are added together and divided by the number of executives making the estimates. *Sales representatives* can also give their opinions about how much can be sold at certain prices. However, salespersons are not always aware of the influences affecting sales and have a tendency to underestimate deliberately to encourage assignment of lower quotas. Sometimes recent sales are plotted on a graph and the *trend line extended* (see Figure 15.2). If sales have gone up at a rate of about 6 percent in each of the previous four years, it may be assumed that sales will rise again at 6 percent in the coming year. This is rarely a safe assumption. Factors that affect sales can change drastically from one year to the next. A better approach is to find out which factors influence sales, to estimate how these factors are likely to change in the forecast year, and to derive a sales forecast based on the strength and direction of changes in *influencing factors.* If the demand for a certain automobile, for example, is influenced by the amount of income consumers have, the price of gasoline, and the relative increase in the price of competitive cars, these three factors could be estimated and the forecast based on them. Sometimes statistical experts examine past years to determine the relative influence of various factors on sales. They then express the relationship in a mathematical *formula* that is used to predict sales for the next year. Some product sales are easily forecast when sales follow some leading factor. If sale of lumber follows construction permits issued, then the number of construction permits would indicate demand (sales) for lumber.

New product sales are more difficult to forecast. Sales depend on how fast new products will be substituted for the old products they were designed to replace. Such estimates involve educated guessing. Usually, new products gain acceptance slowly at first. At a certain point, sales begin to climb at a rapidly increasing rate until the market is nearly saturated and the growth rate falls. Forecasters look at the experience of similar products introduced earlier to estimate how well a new product should sell in the coming year. An expensive method of getting a data base for forecasting is setting up test markets in selected cities to find out how rapidly customers will accept a new product before estimating total market sales. While sales forecasts for old or new products are not always accurate, they are made to plan production schedules, to gauge raw materials purchases, and to determine future personnel needs.

Product Planning

Sales managers usually do not have direct responsibility for product planning. Increasingly, they are deeply involved in it (9). Product planning concerns developing new products and modifying or deleting old products to meet the firm's changing marketing opportunities. The greatest return on investment in a new product usually comes during the market-growth stage in the

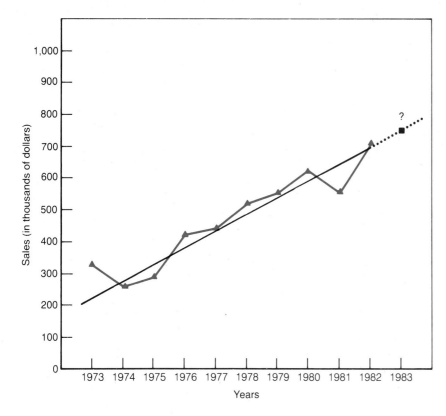

Figure 15.2   Trend Projection

product's life cycle. Many executives feel that they must have products in this stage to maintain market share and to maximize profits. The push for new products and for improvements in existing products is vital to the firm's prosperity and growth. New products must be created that have strong, built-in advantages over existing products. People's buying habits do not change without vigorous promotion of new products. New products that can be produced with existing equipment and sold without changing the basic sales organization involve less expense and offer fewer risks. Sales managers, aware of these considerations, can furnish timely advice in helping to plan new product strategies. Feedback information from the sales force can be translated into workable suggestions for modifying product lines to fit target markets better. Insights gained through field sales experience make sales managers valued members of product planning teams.

Territorial Planning

Territorial potential is measured in terms of people and purchasing power. Sales managers must divide and assign territories fairly on the basis of their potential. Customers who constitute a territory should be located in the same geographical area to make coverage by salespersons easier. Geographical boundary lines can be drawn to make identification and control by management less complex, but a sales territory is and must be a group of present and potential customers rather than a unit of area. If areas are too large, unnecessary traveling expenses are incurred. If the sales potential is too great, salespersons will tend to call only on the best accounts, leaving much potential business unsolicited. If territories are too small, sales calls wasted on poor prospects will discourage salespersons. Although senior sales reps may be assigned to the best territories, territories and quotas must be assigned on an equitable basis. Otherwise, negative morale develops and potentially good representatives quit. Territories are established to motivate sellers, to permit the evaluation and control of selling efforts, and to cultivate customers properly. In some businesses, such as life insurance—where personal friendships and contacts are important—territories may not be assigned. The product, the customers, the competition, the geographical lay of the area, and the type of salesperson affect territorial divisions (10). Territorial assignments require frequent review to take into consideration changes in selling conditions.

Setting Quotas

Quotas are set to motivate sales representatives, to appraise selling effectiveness, to form a basis for sales contests and compensation, and to budget marketing expenditures. Quotas should not be set only in terms of sales goals. Interview, demonstration, profit, and expense quotas should also be established to give salespersons a set of guiding standards (11). Each of these quotas can be determined at yearly management-by-objective conferences with field sales representatives. Quotas should never be impossible to attain. Negative morale is immense when compensation plans, contests, and honors are based on unrealistically high quotas. Quotas set too low are an equal psychological hindrance.

Budgeting

Budgets provide monetary standards for control and coordination. The sales budget divides sales expectations into categories by customer, product, and territory. Expense budgets are set to reveal cost problems and to identify resource waste. When actual figures are different from budgeted figures, managers must reconcile actual sales performance with planned performance. The sales budget is based on the sales forecast and territorial potential estimates. The expense budget is determined by estimating the costs required to reach sales goals.

RECRUITING AND SELECTING

Sales managers often have complete responsibility for selection of sales force members. At a minimum, they have an important influence in screening applicants. It would be against good management principles to make sales managers responsible for sales results without having them participate in critical staffing decisions. There is probably no managerial activity more determinative of success or failure than picking the members of the selling team. No amount of training or motivation can overcome bad selection decisions. A team of well-selected sales representatives can cover a multitude of managerial mistakes. Recruiting and selection are interrelated and entail the following steps:

■ Determining the quantity and kind of personnel needed
■ Assessing sources of applicants
■ Screening applicants
■ Selecting the right people

Determining the Quantity and Kind of Personnel Needed

It is hard to determine the quantity of salespersons needed, for a good rep may outperform two, or even three, weak ones. Good methods produce the best estimates. If too many representatives are hired, selling expenses will go up in relation to sales produced, increased personnel turnover is likely, and profits may decline. It is bad practice to hire more sales representatives than are needed, with the expectation that many will quit, leaving only successful producers. If too few representatives are hired, they will tend to "skim the cream" in their territories, calling on only the best accounts, neglecting customers, and losing many opportunities for sales to competitors. Some considerations involved in determining how many salespersons to hire are sales force turnover, territorial expansion plans, increases or decreases in competitive activity, changes in products, and economic conditions. Many companies simply rely on intuition and past experience to estimate the number of salespersons needed. It is far better, however, to have a more scientific approach because of the importance of the decision.

Still, Cundiff, and Govoni identify three rational methods for approaching quantity determination: *the work-load method, the sales-potential method, and the incremental method* (12). The first step in the *work-load method* is to classify customers into categories by their contributions to sales volume. They determine how long interviews should be for each class of customer and how many calls should be made for each class. The total interview time necessary to do a good selling job can be found by adding together the total time that should be spent with all classes. The interview time each salesperson can spend with a customer each year is estimated by subtracting nonselling time (utilizing the number of hours in a typical workday) from the total time. The final step involves dividing the yearly interview time available to each sales representative into the total interview hours necessary in the firm's total territory. The result is the number of sales personnel needed.

The *sales-potential method* entails dividing the yearly dollar sales volume each salesperson can be expected to accomplish into the total forecasted sales volume, making allowances for personnel turnover. This method is too simple since the forecasted sales volume *depends* on how many salespersons are selling for the firm.

The incremental method involves hiring additional salespersons as long as the estimated sales generated by that additional person, less costs, yield a profit. This method does take into consideration that as salespersons are added to territories, other factors being equal, sales per salesperson will decrease because about the same amount of prospects will be shared by more representatives. All three methods give a rationale for the quantity decision and are better than intuitive guessing.

Written job descriptions and analyses of past experience are very useful in determining the kind of personnel needed. A complete, written job description should be prepared for each sales position. This involves a job analysis to determine the qualifications necessary to do the job. The wide variety of selling situations requires sales representatives with varying backgrounds. A sales applicant who might do very well in one job might fail in another. Selling accounting-system equipment, for example, requires a technically competent, highly intelligent sales representative who is proficient in detail (an introvert characteristic) and yet able to relate well to customers (an extrovert characteristic). A salesperson with these qualifications would probably be unhappy and ineffective as a door-to-door sales representative for aluminum cookware. Some salespersons are good closers but deficient in service-attitude requirements. They would not do well selling a wholesaler's line to retailers. An important device used by many sales managers involves carefully reviewing the characteristics of the firm's best sales representatives. It is fairly easy to analyze personnel profiles to determine age, marital status, education, and work-experience factors that characterize the best sales personnel. It is harder to determine attitudes and other personality factors that characterize "stars" and harder still to measure these qualities in applicants. It is in this area that managerial skill in selection really counts. Usually it is assumed that

Insuring Future Opportunities

sales representatives with whom customers can identify (relate) because of their attractive personality have a persuasive advantage. Intelligence, communications ability, appearance, health, drive, a positive self-image, money motivation, enthusiasm, competitiveness, and determination are important qualities of most successful salespersons.

Sources of Applicants

Having several good sources for applicants increases the chances of finding outstanding salespersons and reduces screening costs. The sources to be used depend on the specific qualifications needed for each job, current availability of applicants from each source, and the time available to screen and hire new personnel. Some companies fill sales positions from current employees, selecting production workers or others who have had a chance to learn the company's products, traditions, and policies. Company officials have had a chance to observe the personalities of such individuals, but success in other departments does not always transfer to personal selling. An excellent source of talent is *"walk-ins"* who study the company, match their talents with company requirements, and show personal persuasiveness through selling themselves to management officials. Unfortunately, there are usually not enough of these qualified aggressive individuals to fill all needs.

Colleges and universities provide applicants with proven intelligence, problem-solving ability, good health, and ability to communicate well. Education can provide technical competence, a confident self-image, and the projected image that many company recruiters seek.

Many college seniors reject sales, however, because they fail to consider its opportunities and requirements. Many feel that sales won't give them a professional image. Some feel that they do not fit the erroneous picture of sales representatives and their work that they have in their minds. Companies recruiting in college markets must show the challenges selling provides, its proper image, and its compensation potential to attract highly qualified college graduates.

Many companies give special consideration to hiring *salespersons who have experience with other companies* in the same industry. Managers can reduce training costs, gain an internal source of competitive information, and perhaps enlarge the market by letting a new representative bring old accounts into the fold. Active solicitation of competitive sales team members is considered unethical. Usually these experienced sales reps require higher compensation to make a change.

Employment agencies, private and government, can furnish applicants quickly and help in the screening process. Private agencies often charge a fee. Both government and private agencies are sometimes more concerned with opportunity for applicants than with the needs of a requesting company. Agencies are often used when other sources are exhausted. Blind and full-disclosure *newspaper ads* provide a large number of individuals with widely varying qualifications. Because many applicants apply, screening and selection costs will be high. Blind ads (ads that do not reveal a company's name) give recruiters a chance to sell a company before an applicant rejects an employment possibility. Sales managers and the entire selling team can also look for prospective salespersons in their many contacts outside the firm.

Screening Applicants

The five major tools used in the selection process are the application form, the personal interview, references, tests, and physical examinations. Government restrictions forbid using discriminatory hiring practices in regard to race, sex, religion, or age. Screening devices must be justified as important to the selection process and must not be designed to screen out qualified members of minority groups.

Application Forms. A properly designed application form (Figure 15.3) can gather a wealth of valuable information about a person. Particularly important are work experience, educational attainment, health, personal interests, special achievements, reasons for wanting to work for a company, reasons for leaving past positions, geographical background, and special abilities. Experience in sales or sales-related activities reveals that an applicant has had to learn to adjust to others and has tried and liked sales. Military experience indicates maturity and the experience of having to adjust. Athletic experience indicates the desire to compete and win in addition to health, enthusiasm, and self-confidence. Unaccounted-for time, too many jobs in too short a period, a criminal record, or failure to have work experience in school are negative factors. Questions on many application blanks indicate the applicant's willingness to travel, relocate, work unusual hours, or otherwise accept any undesirable working conditions associated with an opening. Questions relating to personal habits (drinking or smoking) may be asked as well as questions about an applicant's spouse. Most firms require a great deal of information in attempting to match the profile of an applicant to profiles of successful sales representatives already employed. The work and educational history sections of the application provide sources of references who may be less biased than the references an applicant suggests.

Interviews. Interviews allow assessment of an applicant's appearance, personality, attitudes, interests, sociability, intelligence, and communications skills. Some firms conduct several interviews before hiring. Most firms pattern their interviews for maximum effectiveness. Nearly all interviewers look for nonverbal indications and realize that they must judge on incomplete evi-

Figure 15.3

DATE OF APPLICATION _____

RANDOM HOUSE INC.

EMPLOYMENT APPLICATION

AN EQUAL OPPORTUNITY EMPLOYER

INSTRUCTIONS

1. Type or print in ink.
2. Answer each question fully and accurately. Use additional sheet, if necessary.
3. Do not include information regarding race, color, religion, age or national origin.
4. Read declaration carefully — then sign and date form.

Name	Last	First	Middle	Area Code Telephone ( )
Address	Number Street	City	State Zip	Social Security No.

EXPERIENCE
List All Employment - Including Previous RANDOM HOUSE, INC. Employment and U.S. Military Service - Start with Present Employer.

Dates Employed	Employer's Name and Address	Major Duties Performed	
From To			
Starting Position			Starting Salary (Base) $ Per
Terminal Position	Supervisor's Name and Title	Reason For Leaving	Last Salary (Base) $ Per
Dates Employed From To	Employer's Name and Address	Major Duties Performed	
Starting Position			
Terminal Position	Supervisor's Name and Title	Reason For Leaving	Base Salary $ Per
Dates Employed From To	Employer's Name and Address	Major Duties Performed	
Starting Position			
Terminal Position	Supervisor's Name and Title	Reason For Leaving	Base Salary $ Per
Dates Employed From To	Employer's Name and Address	Major Duties Performed	
Starting Position			
Terminal Position	Supervisor's Name and Title	Reason For Leaving	Base Salary $ Per

EDUCATION
Show All Formal Education Including U.S. Military Schools.

Institution and Location	Dates Attended		Graduated		Degree Received	Major and Minor Fields of Study
	From	To	Yes	No		
High School (Last Attended)						
College or University						
Other						
Other						
Other						

1185 10/77

447 (cont. on p. 448)

Figure 15.3
(cont.)

EMPLOYMENT INTERESTS

Describe Type of Position Desired

Date available for employment	Salary expected
	$ Per
Will you travel?	**Will you work nights?**
☐ None ☐ Occasional ☐ Frequent	☐ Yes ☐ No

MISCELLANEOUS

Reason for applying at Random House, Inc. - Referred by a Random House, Inc. employee, private employment agency, newspaper advertising, etc.	Are there any types of jobs you are not able to fully perform because of physical or mental injury, disability or disease? ☐ Yes ☐ No. If Yes, explain. Yes *will not* disqualify you from consideration for employment.

| If employed, can you submit proof of U.S. Citizenship?
 ☐ Yes   ☐ No | If employed, can you submit proof of age?
 ☐ Yes   ☐ No | |

Have you ever previously applied for employment at Random House, Inc. or other subsidiary companies or locations of RCA? If yes, give place and date. ☐ Yes ☐ No	Are you in the U.S. on a visa which prohibits you from working here? ☐ Yes ☐ No
Have you ever previously been employed at Random House, Inc. or other subsidiary companies or locations of RCA? If yes, give place and dates. ☐ Yes ☐ No	Have you ever pleaded guilty or been found guilty of a crime, civilian or military? (Do not include minor traffic violations.) ☐ Yes ☐ No If yes, explain. Yes *will not* disqualify you from consideration.

Note clerical skills and office machine or technical equipment.

Describe your hobbies or other avocational interests.

Professional Attainments.

Do you have a currently effective agreement with employers or others concerning inventions you have made or may make?
☐ Yes   ☐ No   If Yes, please furnish copy of agreement and indicate the number of months the agreement remains effective after termination.

_____ Months

REFERENCES
List Former Supervisors Not Previously Shown or Others Familiar With Your Work - Exclude Relatives.

Name	Occupation	Address	Telephone
Name	Occupation	Address	Telephone
Name	Occupation	Address	Telephone

dence. The idea is to give applicants a chance to express personality variables and the recruiter a chance to see if qualifications match the position. Applicants are appraised through careful questioning. Interviewers attempt to provide an atmosphere in which applicants can relax and be natural. Applicants who show nervousness are at least indicating that they care about the interview and should not be judged too harshly for not being perfectly poised (see Figure 15.4). Employment interviews are treated in the next chapter, and additional interview techniques and responses are discussed.

References. References are more realistic if they are not suggested by the applicants. It is better to question persons not listed by the applicant as references. Few former employers or professors want to give applicants bad references. References that are not confidential are almost worthless. Interpreting references takes a special talent. They must be "decoded" for inferences, indications, and for what is not said. The reference may read: "John Jones will make you a good employee, if you can get him to work for you," or "Sam Smith was not late for work too often." Others condemn by leaving unsaid the comments recruiters expect to read or hear about outstanding talents. When studying the real meaning of a reference, managers must learn to read between the lines and take into consideration tendencies to rate applicants too high or too low.

Tests. Tests can be obtained that are designed to measure an applicant's intelligence, personality, interests, and aptitudes. Intelligence tests indicate verbal and mathematical reasoning capabilities. They are useful for qualifying sales representatives for high-level jobs. While very high intelligence is not required for all selling situations, a good intelligence test can gauge an applicant's ability to solve problems and indicate the applicant's trainability. Personality tests are questionable. Personal qualities and attitudes are difficult to measure on paper. Answers to many questions can be "faked." Personality tests do not always measure what they are supposed to measure. Conclusions depend to an extent on the psychologist who interprets the responses. While a test interpreter may conclude that a person is "aggressive" because he or she walks fast, talks fast, and eats fast, this may not always translate into selling "aggressiveness."

Interest tests can also be faked by intelligent applicants who can guess the best answers. However, just because personality and interest tests are imperfect measures does not mean careful use cannot provide insights into an applicant's attitudes. Mechanical, clerical, and mathematical aptitudes may be important in selling complex products such as major equipment or accounting systems. Firms often require that a minimum score be attained on tests like these to judge an applicant's ability to learn and demonstrate a product line.

It is best to use tests to substantiate judgments determined from other selection tools and to eliminate untrainable applicants. It is illegal to use tests to discriminate against minorities.

Figure 15.4 Interview Guide

Name of applicant_____

*REMEMBER . . . .

Establish rapport and try to put applicant at ease.
Sell Taylor Company to the applicant.
Get answers but try not to let the applicant feel pressured.
Encourage the applicant to talk by keeping your responses short.

Invite the applicant to sit in a chair facing your desk.
Express appreciation for the interviewee's interest in the company. Ask:

Who told you about Taylor Company? How did you become interested in us?

Why do you feel that you want a career in selling?

Where do you expect to be in your career seven years from now?

I've asked you some hard questions. Now I just want you to relax and tell me about yourself. What do you like and dislike; what are your strengths and weaknesses; and what are some of your important past experiences?

Now tell me why we should hire you as a salesperson.

What kind of a person was your last boss?

If we hired you, when could you go to work, and what kind of money would you expect?

Promise the applicant the company's thoughtful consideration and an early decision on further processing.

RATE THE APPLICANT:

APPEARANCE	Excellent	Poor
POISE	Excellent	Poor
VOICE	Excellent	Poor
COMMUNICATION	Excellent	Poor
LIKABLENESS	Excellent	Poor
OVERALL	Excellent	Poor

RECOMMENDATION:

Physical Examinations. Selling is a rigorous activity. It sometimes requires extensive travel, lifting of heavy products, and enthusiastic presentations. Physical examinations can reveal health deficiencies that preclude investing in an applicant who has or probably will have serious physical problems. Some corporations are too quick to eliminate otherwise qualified persons who have physical stamina but minor health defects. If a prospective sales representative is able to show vitality and enthusiasm during an interview, and the defect is not major, it should be weighed against other qualifications that are more significant.

Selecting the Right Person for the Selling Job

Selection tools can furnish only information about an applicant—a manager must balance all factors to make a final decision. For selling situations involving complex products, high-level intelligence and mathematical abilities are required. For most selling jobs average intelligence, good general knowledge, acceptable appearance, and reasonable health are sufficient. The variables that really matter are those that are the hardest to measure—attitude and character. A few questions every sales manager should ask before adding a new member to a sales team are:

- As a salesperson, will the applicant work hard, relate well to customers, and present a good image?
- Does the potential rep indicate adaptability by having work, military, and/ or athletic experience?
- Do tests and educational attainment reflect that the applicant is intelligent and trainable?
- Does the applicant's personality give an impression of social sensitivity?
- Is the applicant likely to enjoy working for the firm?
- Is the person likely to quit before making a profit for the company?

Every new salesperson is a big investment in training and development costs. If the wrong individual is trained and quits, the person who should have been hired and developed may be working for a competitor. Hiring the right person is the most important sales management function. Adequate information before making a decision is a must.

TRAINING

Training should be planned for new representatives soon after they report for work. Too many companies put new salespersons in out-of-the-way corners of sales offices, expecting automatic orientation because of the sales-office atmosphere. In a few days, the new member may be assigned errands in and near the office. Recruits will have a higher image of a company if definite training periods that provide real orientation and a sense of belonging are scheduled during the first week. Sales managers must take differences in experience into consideration in training both new and experienced members of a sales force. Separate plans should be devised for new representatives without previous experience, new representatives, senior representatives, and supervisory sales personnel. Good training programs involve four major planning areas:

- Goals of the training program
- Content of the training program
- Methods and personnel to be used
- Evaluation of the program

Goals of the Training Program

A good training program increases profits by increasing sales volume, decreasing selling costs, smoothing introduction of new products into the market, boosting salesforce confidence, improving individual self-image, generating enthusiasm, fostering goodwill, and lowering sales force turnover. Knowledge gives both confidence and enthusiasm in selling. When sales representatives learn answers to customer problems through good training, their selling time will be used more effectively. Specific goals should be detailed in writing before the program is planned.

Content of the Training Program

The content of the program should be spelled out separately from its goals. Program content depends on the type of product, the experience and knowledge of the trainees, and the nature of the selling situation. Sales managers responsible for moving complex product lines that frequently include new offerings or new applications of product systems emphasize product knowledge in their program. Managers responsible for consumer products that are easily understood tend to stress selling techniques and merchandising principles. New salespersons have to learn everything—company policies and history, product features and benefits, methods of operation, personnel and their place in the organization, selling techniques, and work-planning methods. More experienced sales representatives must master new products, new product applications, new markets, and new communications techniques (such as transactional analysis and nonverbal language). Markets can change dynamically. Selling environments can also change. Changes in either necessitate continual updating of information. Self-analysis and confidence-building together with attempts to restructure attitudes are included in many corporate training sessions to boost confidence and self-image. To many sales managers, training is part of their motivational efforts. It is an attention-giving device that lets trainees know a firm expects continued learning. Learning is growth. It promotes self-esteem and production and prevents stagnation. While training periods are shorter for the more experienced, sometimes experienced reps must unlearn bad selling habits before such habits can be replaced with effective techniques.

Sometimes the nature of a selling situation indicates special program content. Missionary sales representatives must learn to be good instructors and teachers to train dealer salespersons. Sales managers who train intangible or system representatives to sell life insurance, securities, franchises, and accounting systems must prepare their selling forces to offer customers consultation in business and legal matters associated with the offerings. A certified life underwriter (CLU) insurance representative may study for years to meet the knowledge requirements to qualify as a top consultant salesperson.

Methods and Personnel to Be Used

New personnel can be trained in formal sessions where sales supervisors demonstrate products, simulate interviews, or direct discussion participation and role playing. Some trainees may take formal correspondence courses or attend company-paid college classes or university-sponsored management development programs. Many trainees are given personal training sessions with immediate sales supervisors (zone sales manager or senior sales rep) in which they are asked to give complete demonstrations of products in a line. Some are assigned to read policy manuals to understand company standards. Few methods are more exciting than calling on prospects in the field with experienced seniors. A total view of a coordinated sales effort yields insights that can never be explained in a branch office—a holistic combination of personality variables, body language, sales points, and persuasion techniques unified to convince a real buyer cannot be duplicated in artificial situations. Even more instructive is a new representative's first attempt to persuade a prospect under a senior's watchful eye. Good training programs must include field observation and direct participation. Selling is an art that requires practice, as well as a science that must be applied.

Companies vary in respect to when they send trainees to the "home office" for formal instruction and to see production lines in operation (for tangible products). Some companies with less complex product offerings omit home office instruction from their programs. Other companies have products of such a complex technical nature that a sales trainee is required to work in production for months before graduating to selling. Still others may allow trainees to sell less consequential products before working into consultative sales—selling aluminum cookware to ultimate consumers before selling bulk aluminum to industrial accounts. Although staff instructors are used at the home office, senior representatives and junior sales managers do most of the training of new salespersons.

Experienced successful sales representatives with well-developed (and sensitive) egos who need training must be approached cautiously to protect their self-images. Sales meetings and yearly conferences that feature their participation refresh their knowledge. Some managers feel that this mature group should be separated and recognized at conferences rather than being included on the same level as more junior sales representatives. This group learns from sharing sessions where new selling tactics are discussed. Often, these seniors are asked to make demonstrations for which they must prepare.

Visual aids are being increasingly used in training for all levels of salespersons. Films, specially prepared training folders, and programmed instructional materials can be edited and designed to assure that trainees are learning correct techniques. A sample demonstration may turn into a bad example, but training films can be carefully edited.

Evaluation of the Program

All methods should be reviewed for effectiveness and matched with stated objectives to determine whether the training program is living up to expectations. Effectiveness can be determined by the time and expense required to raise a trainee to some measurable level of performance or accomplishment. How much have sales increased since the installation of the program? How much are sales expenses down in relation to the volume of sales produced? Have customer complaints diminished? Is morale noticeably better? Has sales force turnover declined? There is no such thing as a perfect program. Constant improvement based on good feedback can lead to a more effective training operation.

MOTIVATING

Sales managers can substantially affect company profits by motivating a sales force. Good motivational practices are almost as important as selecting high-potential sales personnel. Leadership through example, sales training, sales meetings, conferences, contests, and compensation plans either stimulate sales force members to greater effort or have negative effects at high expense. Motivating will be considered under the following headings:

- The motivational problem
- Usable theory in motivating sales personnel
- Motivational style
- Compensation plans
- Sales contests
- Sales meetings and conferences

The Motivational Problem

Although sales force members are basically motivated by the same drives as customers, there are some notable differences. Sales personnel are more money-motivated than most individuals. The selling job subjects them to emotional highs and lows not experienced in many other occupations. Travel and after-hours work may deprive them of spending as much time as they would like with their families. They work most of the time without supervision and have a special need for managerial attention. Senior sales representatives may fall into unproductive routines and find it hard to maintain enthusiasm in territories and with customers that are too familiar.

Motivational profiles point out another basic problem—each sales rep must be approached with different motivational techniques. An ideal salesperson would be a blend of achievement-oriented and affiliation-oriented profiles. Most individuals lean in one direction or the other. The achievement-oriented salesperson has strong needs to complete unfinished work, to excel, and to be given specific feedback. This competitive individual works hard alone. Less group involvement is needed by achievers than by affiliative types. Those with high achievement orientation often lack the social sensitivity to win complete customer approval (13).

Affiliative types, on the other hand, need to be with other people. They can be told in general terms how they are doing, and have a higher tolerance for unfinished work than do the achievement-oriented. While affiliative types may be as competitive, they usually possess the social skills that earn acceptance by both customers and supervisors (14). The needs of various sales force members are different and require tailored motivational approaches gained from a never-ending learning process.

Usable Theory in Motivating Sales Personnel

The challenge of leadership is important in motivating sales personnel. In addition, work motivational theory indicates that because of independent working conditions, sales force members need more individual supervisory attention, more group participation meetings, and more training opportunities than do less independent workers. Supervisory and group support are needed to recharge self-images assaulted by refusals and the self-subjection that is a part of selling. Sales managers should provide an encouraging work environment that includes such basics as good products, good prices, realistic territories, competitive compensation levels, realistic training opportunities, and suitable training aids. Sales personnel who are well compensated and have their basic and safety needs met are released, according to Maslow's theory, to pursue fulfillment of social, esteem, and self-actualization needs. Accordingly, praise and supervisory approval, special recognition, and promotional progress can mean more than money in stimulating greater production (15). A letter from the president of the company, a commendation certificate, a quota-maker pin are the kinds of incentives that satisfy higher-level needs.

Motivational Style

The full information management approach is a motivational style compatible with today's sales force and selling environments. It features consultations with sales personnel before changes are made, reprimands that are made in person to maintain good communication with the salesperson, and communications involving adult-adult ego states. Managers should always praise good work either in person or through a personal letter. Appropriate disciplinary actions should be taken when necessary or sales personnel will lose respect for their managers.

Compensation Plans

Trends are away from straight-salary and straight-commission compensation plans. Today, most compensation plans feature salary plus incentive in the form of a commission or a bonus. Table 15.1 indicates the types of plans commonly used and the direction of change from 1980 to 1981. Public-relations positions are more likely to be compensated by straight salary. Insurance and other intangible selling are more likely to have higher commission elements in their pay packages. In straight-salary plans, there is little incentive for a salesperson to push harder, and straight-commission sales representatives become so intent on orders or volume that they tend to forget goodwill, service, the firm's image, and the profitability of transactions for the company. In most sales situations, there should be a floor under the representative's income to assure that the grocery bills and other necessities will be paid. The more significant the salesperson's skills are in creative selling, the higher the incentive part of the pay package should be. Incentive pay should be made frequently (monthly or weekly) for best results. It should be based on a salesperson's individual accomplishments.

Smaller firms that do not have good training programs for inexperienced salespersons may pay high salaries or commissions to attract more experienced sales personnel. Larger firms, which may offer more opportunities for advancement, may pay less in actual money but may have better fringe benefits. When firms heavily overpay salespersons, they may have difficulty in persuading good persons to leave the field to take managerial positions. When salespersons are underpaid, the best ones may quit to take more attractive opportunities elsewhere—sometimes with a direct competitor—leaving only low producers in the sales force. High turnover is a waste of resources and is upsetting to customers. A pay level slightly above the competitive level is just a little more expensive to the company in terms of pay rates, but it attracts and retains better personnel, paying dividends in the long-run.

Sales Contests

Sales contests offer special rewards for special selling efforts. Contests can lift slumping sales. They can generate new enthusiasm in a sales force. However, contest themes must be mature to be effective, internal promotion of a contest must be correctly timed, rules should be clear and fair to all, prizes

TABLE 15.1 ALTERNATIVE SALES COMPENSATION AND INCENTIVE PLANS 1981

	PERCENT OF COMPANIES USING PLANS				
	ALL INDUSTRIES		CONSUMER PRODUCTS	INDUSTRIAL PRODUCTS	OTHER COMMERCE/ INDUSTRY
METHOD	1981	1980	1981	1981	1981
Straight salary	18.9%	20.4%	12.5%	18.3%	29.3%
Draw against commission	6.3	7.2	7.3	5.0	11.0
Salary plus commission	29.9	28.6	27.1	31.6	25.6
Salary plus individual bonus	33.2	27.9	39.6	33.2	"
Salary plus group bonus	2.5	5.6	4.1	2.6	8.5
Salary plus commission plus individual or group bonus	9.2	10.3	9.4	9.3	—
Total	**100.0%**	**100.0%**	**100.0%**	**100.0%**	**100.0%**

Note: Some year-to-year differences reflect changes in the organizations reporting data.

Source: American Management Associations, *Executive Compensation Service,* in *Sales & Marketing Management,* February 22, 1982, p. 78.

should be desirable, and there must be many winners. Contests can generate bad morale when themes are embarrassingly childish, when rules encourage cheating, when competition among salespeople becomes cutthroat, when prizes are undesirable, or when certain sales personnel are unduly handicapped by territorial or product restrictions. Prizes include such incentives as products, cash, travel opportunities, or special recognition symbols such as certificates of commendation from top management. If prizes are too significant, salespersons may be tempted to overstock customers or cheat. A contest may be too expensive for a company if its prizes are too costly. If prizes are of little worth, there may be little incentive to participate.

Sales Meetings and Conferences

Local sales meetings should take place several times a month to promote better training, motivation, and communication. New product knowledge, analysis of recently experienced selling successes and failures, recognition of achievements, review of future plans, review of market and business conditions, and discussion of special problems are sample topics. Sales managers should avoid the temptation to dominate meetings and should encourage participation and communication of ideas. All meetings should be positive and encouraging, even when it is necessary to point out mistakes and problems. Managers should not appear to be critical parent-bosses. They should hold meetings on an adult-adult basis with the "I'm O.K.; you're O.K." position prevailing. Salespersons should be allowed to discuss mutual problems with each other. Special training for new products, new product applications, and new selling ideas motivates salespersons by arming them with knowledge about offerings.

Yearly national conferences assemble salespersons at a central place and often feature prominent speakers, top company personnel, and entertainment personalities. Such large group meetings promote contagious enthusiasm and interaction among salespersons from all parts of the country. Local salespersons are given a chance to meet company officers and top sales "stars." Such meetings are costly in terms of travel expense, facilities, and territorial neglect and may even be regarded by personnel as an opportunity to have a good time rather than to learn (16). Regional meetings are apt to be taken more seriously as work meetings, but they require a company's top executives to travel more and usually fail to engender the same enthusiasm as do national meetings. Aggregate travel costs are less because sales personnel travel shorter distances, but it is often impractical to have well-known sales trainers or motivational speakers at each of several regional meetings.

Speeches by very successful sales personalities and audio-visuals featuring success can be inspirational at meetings. Salespersons have an opportunity to evaluate the mannerisms, the tones of voice, and the personalities of successful persons. This is stimulating. Testimony from a star sales representative is worth much more than reading words in a sales manual. Records featuring the ideas and voices of America's top sales personalities are available for local meetings. The personalities themselves are often available for big national get-togethers.

EVALUATION AND CONTROL

The sales manager must check, by means of feedback information, to see if planned goals are being achieved. It is not hard to determine if sales representatives are reaching their quotas, if territories are yielding expected potentials, if expenses are being kept within limits, or if total sales are reaching forecast levels. Computers can be programmed to analyze reported sales and sales yield results. They can analyze results by sales representative, by product, by geographic area, by customer, and in relation to other factors. Such analyses can quickly reveal which products and which salespersons are living up to expectations and which are not. Further analysis can sometimes indicate why. Daily call reports, turned in by field sales personnel, show how many calls, interviews, demonstrations, prospecting attempts, collection attempts, and other activities were undertaken. These, in turn, can be compared to subgoals and provide indications of effort to produce sales. Sales dollars generated per interview show how effective a salesperson has been in getting results. Actual expenses can also be compared with planned expenses to determine in part costs of supporting sales.

When salespersons are evaluated solely on the basis of sales, problems can arise. Salespersons may be so intent on making short-run sales that they neglect other important matters such as prospecting, reporting, introducing new products, selling the full line, learning, and account profitability. Many companies have therefore devised more elaborate evaluation techniques, including subjective (opinion) evaluation scales to judge sales reps. Subjective forms are especially useful for new salespersons and for those being primed for managerial positions. Sales managers are often given the responsibility for making such judgments. Salespersons should not feel that they are under continual scrutiny for the minutest details. All evaluation criteria should be selected carefully. Salespersons should be informed about the criteria used to evaluate. The evaluation points used channel sales force efforts. Areas that are not evaluated are likely to be neglected. Overevaluation can hinder field sales efforts by restricting freedom, and too much subjective evaluation encourages bias and hypocrisy.

SUMMARY

It is important to understand the functions of the sales manager because it helps new salespersons to understand supervisors, their working environment, and the next possible step in promotion. Sales managers are responsible for providing a productive work environment and for maintaining a leadership image. They should be competent, fair, informative, and encouraging. They should bolster the self-images of their sales personnel by expecting them to do well. Sales managers set up organizational relationships, estimate territorial potential, and forecast sales. They help with product planning by crystallizing information from the field into suggestions for new products and product features.

Selecting salespersons is the most important responsibility of most sales managers. The work-load method, the sales-potential method, and the incremental method are three ways to determine how many new salespersons should be hired. Important from the very beginning, too, is the writing out of detailed job descriptions for all sales force positions. Careful job descriptions indicate the types of sales recruits needed. Applicants can be found from "walk-ins," at colleges and universities, in other companies, through newspaper ads, through recommendations of personnel, and through employment agencies. Sales hopefuls can be screened by effective use of employment application forms, personal interviews, references, tests, and physical examinations. Application forms can yield socioeconomic characteristics of an applicant, past work experience, education, and interests, and are useful in initial screening. Personal interviews can reveal an applicant's personality attributes, poise, image, and sincerity. References, even from supposedly unbiased sources, must be carefully interpreted to discern the true opinion of the person giving the reference. Tests, especially intelligence tests and aptitude tests, can be valuable selection tools. But care must be used in testing, so that minorities are not subject to unfair discrimination. Physical examinations should be used to screen out persons with physical handicaps that would hinder performance in strenuous selling work but should not eliminate those with physical defects that would not hamper their job performance. Final selection rests on the judgment of the sales manager or top corporate official responsible for hiring applicants.

Training should be segmented to fit the experience of new and experienced sales personnel. The amount and types of training needed depend primarily on the nature of the product and the professionalism required in selling situations. Most firms use home-office training for beginning salespersons and on-the-job training under senior supervision. Experienced salespersons and seniors learn about new products and developments in sales meetings and at conferences. It is important to let senior salespersons participate in training sessions.

Motivating salespersons is important because selling is emotionally demanding. Sales managers should set a good leadership example, treat salespersons like responsible professionals, and appeal to belongingness, esteem, and self-actualization needs. A salary plus commission or bonus, if well-devised, can help ensure sales and service. Sales contests, meetings, and conferences are widely used motivational tools. A sensible mixture of comparing sales work methods with planned objectives and a minimum of subjective evaluation can provide valuable bench marks that let managers know how well a sales force is doing. Managers have a great deal of influence on the success of a sales force. They are the ones who must initiate new directions when problems arise.

REVIEW QUESTIONS

1. What functions and activities are the responsibility of the sales manager?

2. What are the skills that lead to selection as a sales manager?

3. What are some of the attributes that contribute to a sales manager's gaining the respect of the sales force?

4. What is meant by supervisory style? Briefly describe and evaluate the two extreme styles?

5. What is meant by leadership? What are some of the basic principles of leadership?

6. What steps are involved in effective organizing?

7. How may the total work load be divided?

8. Contrast the centralized and decentralized approaches to sales force management.

9. What are the two basic methods for estimating territorial potential? Briefly describe each.

10. What are the methods of forecasting sales for existing products and new products?

11. What are the elements of product planning? What role does the sales manager play in this process?

12. Why is the setting of territories so important? The setting of quotas?

13. A major function of the sales manager is the recruiting and selection of salespeople. What specific activities are involved in this process?

14. What are the factors involved in determining the number of sales force members to be hired? Name the specific methods that may be used to determine this number.

15. What are some of the sources of applicants for selling positions?

16. Name the five major tools used in the sales force selection process.

17. What are some of the key questions that a sales manager should ask before adding a new member to the sales team?

18. What are the factors that determine a training program's content? What does a new salesperson need to learn?

19. On what basis can training programs be evaluated?

20. What are some of the specific motivational problems faced by salespeople?

21. Briefly compare straight-salary and straight-commission compensation plans for salespeople.

22. What precautions should be taken in devising sales contests?

23. How can a sales manager control and evaluate the sales force?

APPLICATION QUESTIONS

1. What supervisory style would you expect your sales manager to have if you were selling encyclopedias? What would you expect if you were selling computer systems? Should you expect any differences in supervisory styles in these two situations?

2. You are participating in a management-by-objectives session with your manager. What would be taking place? If you were trying to keep the objectives low, what would you expect the manager to do? How do you think she should do this?

3. Explain the different compensation plans and the advantages and disadvantages of each. Which would you recommend for an insurance salesperson? A public-relations representative?

15–1

Ed Kappel, a sales manager, has called Sarah Calhoun in for her first management-by-objectives conference.

Ed: Come in, Sarah, and sit down. Now that we've assigned you to a territory, it will be necessary to set some goals for next year. Ted Orniwitz sold $211,541 last year in your territory. What do you think you can do this year?

Sarah: I'm not sure, Mr. Kappel. How does the total sales forecast for this year compare with last?

Ed: We expect to sell at least 10 percent more this year. But you know one of the reasons that Ted is no longer with us is that he never cultivated his territory as he should have.

Sarah: Well, I could shoot for $250,000, but, remember, I'm a rookie.

Ed: How about putting you down for $260,000?

Sarah: I'll try.

Ed: Now, we have to set the number of calls and demonstrations you'll need to gain that volume. You've been averaging seven calls a day but just two demonstrations. Can we boost that to eight calls with four demonstrations? It'll help.

Sarah: I'd better not commit myself to make more than seven calls a day, but I will try to make four demonstrations. I like to spend selling time with my prospects.

Ed: How about seven account calls and one or two *prospecting* calls?

Sarah: Well, I'll try, Mr. Kappel.

Ed: Now that you have a territory, you realize you must make at least two collection calls a week, so I'm putting you down for that—O.K.? Now, to sell $260,000, you will have to get orders of $5,000 a week. You will have to sell the equivalent of three overwrap machines and one heat sealer each week. I think that's reasonable, don't you?

Sarah: I'll work hard to do it.

Ed: I know you will, Sarah. I'm expecting you to develop into one of our star sales reps. Remember, keep your expenses within reasonable limits. It'll help to plan your routing and avoid backtracking. Do you plan each day ahead of time?

Sarah: Oh, yes. I plot my itinerary on a map.

Ed: Well, Sarah, I guess we've got it all pretty well set. It's just a question of doing it now, isn't it?

Sarah: Yes . . . I'll do my best.

QUESTIONS

1. Who controlled this MBO conference, Ed or Sarah?

2. What other points should have been discussed?

3. Did Mr. Kappel do a good job?

15–2

Peter Daniels has been working as a sales representative for Delmar Chemical Company for nearly three years and has worked more than a year and a half under Bob Merideth. Pete has a good overall sales record; however, he failed to make quota for the last three months and has seemed a little depressed and low in morale. He has come into Bob's office with an announcement.

Pete: Bob, I know this is going to be a surprise to you, but I've talked it over with Linda and I'm giving my two weeks' notice. Things just aren't working out for me with Delmar anymore.

Bob: Pete, I *am* surprised! You made $28,000 last year and surpassed your quota. I thought you were doing well. What's wrong?

Pete: I'd rather not say. You've been very fair with me, but I feel that I may not be cut out to sell chemicals. I'm down quite a bit this year.

Bob: I've been in this business for several years, Pete, and I can tell you that everyone has ups and downs in selling. It's like football. No team does it every game. When you get discouraged, it makes it doubly hard to get orders. You're a good sales rep, Pete. You've a lot of potential. We invested over $50,000 in training you. I need to know what's wrong so I can correct it. So . . . what is it? You won't hurt my feelings!

Pete: O.K., here it is straight. I don't like my territory, and I think my quota is too high for the potential. I like to excel! I like to make quota! Competition is getting rougher every month in the city territories. Delmar makes good products, but our prices are high. If I keep on going at the rate I'm going this year, I won't make $20,000. Frankly, Bob, I can do better than that. I can make at least $30,000 selling for another supplier.

Bob: Other people have told me about the increasing competition, Pete. As a matter of fact, Joe Cook at the home office and I have talked about it. He plans to recommend several measures to counteract it—one of which will be a softening of prices on three products. The company plans to introduce two new products into the line within three months. While the details on these are secret now, Cook feels that they will more than counter our competitive problems. Keep this under your hat; I haven't told any of the others. As for the territory problem, I plan to make a thorough restudy of territorial potentials and quotas next month. As you know, more-senior salespersons with the best records are given the better territories as a reward for their achievements. That's an important reason why you should reconsider. We feel that you have potential. I'm sure you'll be reassigned in the future if you want to be.

Pete: I didn't know that the home office was trying to do something about the competition problem, Bob. I like you and the other folks here at Delmar . . . Well . . . maybe I'm just getting a bit impatient to make better money. You know how it is when you get in a sales slump at the first of the year.

Bob: Would you like to go to the home office for a week? Cook mentioned a refresher course that includes competition. I was going, but I would just as soon that you go and take notes for all the rest of us. I'll help out in your territory while you're away.

Pete: Let me talk all of this over with Linda. Do you really think those new products will push us back to where we were?

Bob: We've been in the chemical business a long time. Delmar may get behind temporarily but never permanently. Think it over, Pete. We would sure like you to stay with us.

QUESTIONS

1. Sales representative turnover is a serious problem for many firms. Do you think Bob acted wisely in trying to talk Pete into staying? Did he use the right appeals?

2. What other things can a sales manager do to assure better retention of sales-force personnel?

3. Do you think Pete was sincere in offering his resignation? Should he have discussed the problem with Bob before attempting to resign?

15–3

Richard Brighton has been zone manager for three months. One of the first changes he made was to institute a "thorough" evaluation system that involves an evaluation of field reps by each district sales manager every four months plus an evaluation by fellow salespersons. Both evaluation forms were designed entirely by Richard with no help from anyone and no input from the sales force. Each form contains more than fifteen questions. In addition to the two new evaluations, Richard has installed a one-way mirror between his office and the large sales office room where all of the sales representatives have their desks. He can watch what is going on in the sales room at any time, but his office cannot be seen from the sales room. Richard has explained to the sales-force personnel that their evaluations will be based heavily on the number of interviews and demonstrations they make. Reported interviews and demonstrations have increased considerably in the last month, but sales have declined slightly. Included below are sample entries from the sales manager's evaluation form:

The salesperson's personality is: Poor _____ Average _____ Good _____ Very Good _____ Excellent _____.

The salesperson's attitude is: Poor _____ Average _____ Good _____ Very Good _____ Excellent _____.

The salesperson's appearance is: Poor _____ Average _____ Good _____ Very Good _____ Excellent _____.

The salesperson's self-evaluation and "team-member" evaluation form contains the following sample elements:

Rank each salesperson (do not include yourself) in regard to selling effectiveness from most effective to least effective.

Rate each of the salespersons in the zone (listed below) as to company rules and regulations (A = Excellent, B = Very Good, C = Average, D = Poor).

Rate each of the salespersons below as to promotability: 1 = Very promotable, 2 = Promotable, 3 = Perhaps promotable, 4 = Not promotable.

Now rate what you consider to be your own value to the company: Very valuable _____ Valuable _____ Fairly valuable _____ Probably not very valuable _____.

Since the first evaluations were made under the new manager two months ago, a strong clique has developed among the sales-force personnel. One rep resigned, giving as the reason inability to work under Brighton. Two senior sales representatives have complained openly about the new evaluations, especially the self- and team-member evaluations.

Evaluate Richard Brighton's evaluation program from the information given. How would you improve it?

15–4

Emericon, Inc., is a relative newcomer to the office furnishings industry. Set up in 1977 as the American subsidiary of a Swedish company, Emericon has taken on such formidable office furnishings giants as Stowe-Davis, Baker, and Bernier in the high-priced end of the business. Its only near rivals are Helikon in the modern style and Kittinger in traditional styles. Sara Grovner has been with Emericon since it first started up in an old deserted mill near Rose Valley, Pennsylvania. Until 1980, Emericon had such a small sales force that there had been no sales manager. Sara took over in January 1981. She spent most of her first year as National Sales Manager recruiting, selecting, and training new sales reps. In addition to Sara, there are four other "old hands" in Emericon's sales force of sixteen. Generally, these "old hands" have gone along with Sara's ideas for reorganization—perhaps, organization—of Emericon's sales activities. Now, Sara feels Emericon is ready to have a system of quotas to serve as goals for individual rep sales efforts and as a way of evaluating performance. Sara is sold on the idea of setting quotas through a review of pertinent data about a territory with its rep and arriving at a mutually agreeable sales goal. She feels that a rep who has participated in setting a goal for the territory assigned will have little or no excuse for not meeting it.

Sara decides to start out the territorial quota review with Joe Cook. Joe worked for New Britain Hand Tools and Wallingford Silversmiths before coming to Emericon. He is a graduate of Lawrence College in Appleton, Wisconsin, and studied architecture at Sherrard in Los Angeles. He is a big-volume producer for Emericon, second only to Sara, herself. As of September 1982, in a soft market, Joe's volume looked as if it would go over $1,300,000 for the year. After the usual pleasantries, Sara decides to get down to cases with Joe.

Sara: Joe, as you know, I've long wanted to get a quota system started with our sales force. As an old-timer, I thought you'd be in the best position to help me out through setting your goal for '83. Considering this year's volume, it seems to me that a million and a half would be reasonable.

Joe: Reasonable? No way! I'll be lucky to sell a million. Don't you know there's a recession on?

Sara: What do you mean? You're going to top a million three this year.

Joe: Just because I was lucky this year is no reason to punish me next year.

Sara: Punish you? I'm not trying to punish you, Joe. Let's look at this year's figures and the potentials I've calculated for next year . . .

And so it went for more than half a day. Joe refused to agree to anything over a million; Sara would not go below a million four hundred and fifty thousand. They were factually selective in supporting their positions. Finally, Joe spoke.

Joe: Sara, you and I and the others built this company's U.S. operations without quotas. Now, I agree that we have to have some standards, but they've got to be realistic. You asked me here for my advice. I've given it. You can do what you like with it, but why ask if you're going to ignore it?

Sara felt drained. This was not at all the way the sales management books she had read on quota setting said things would work. None of them described a problem like the one she'd had with Joe. And if Joe was going to behave like this, Sara wondered what the interviews with the other "old hands" were going to be like.

QUESTIONS

1. Where did Sara go wrong? How should she have approached Joe?

2. Is there anything Sara can do now to save the situation?

NOTES

1. Richard F. Bagozzi, "Salespersons and Their Managers: An Exploratory Study of Some Similarities and Differences," *Sloan Management Review,* Winter 1980, p. 20.

2. Wroe Alderson, *Marketing Behavior and Executive Action* (Homewood, Ill.: Irwin, 1957), p. 38.

3. Douglas McGregor, *The Human Side of Enterprise* (New York: McGraw-Hill, 1960), pp. 33–38.

4. David C. McClelland and David H. Burnham, "Good Guys Make Bum Bosses," *Psychology Today,* vol. 9, no. 7 (December 1975), pp. 69–70.

5. Donald W. Jackson, Jr., and Ramon J. Aldag, "Managing the Sales Force by Objectives," MSU *Business Topics,* vol. 22, no. 2 (Spring 1974), pp. 53–58.

6. Richard R. Still, Edward W. Cundiff, and Norman A. P. Govoni, *Sales Management Decisions, Policies, and Cases,* 3rd ed. (Englewood Cliffs, N.J.: Prentice-Hall, 1976), p. 135.

7. Philip Kotler, *Marketing Management: Analysis, Planning, and Control,* 4th ed. (Englewood Cliffs, N.J.: Prentice-Hall, 1980), pp. 223–226.

8. "1981 Survey of Buying Power," *Sales & Marketing Management,* July 26, 1981.

9. Saul Sands, "Is the Product Manager Obsolete?" *The Business Quarterly,* Autumn 1979, p. 127.

10. William J. Stanton and Richard H. Buskirk, *Management of the Sales Force,* 5th ed. (Homewood, Ill.: Irwin, 1978), pp. 481–495.

11. *Ibid.,* pp. 511–525.

12. Still, Cundiff, and Govoni, *Sales Management Decisions,* pp. 63–68.

13. Saul W. Gellerman, *Motivation and Productivity* (American Management Associ-

ation, 1963), pp. 122–141, reviewing David C. McClelland, et al., *The Achievement Motive* (New York: Appleton, 1953).

14. *Ibid.,* pp. 115–141, reviewing Stanley Schacter, *The Psychology of Affiliation* (Stanford, Calif.: Stanford University Press, 1959).

15. Abraham Maslow, *Motivation and Personality* (New York: Harper & Row, 1970), pp. 35–58.

16. Still, Cundiff, and Govoni, *Sales Management Decisions,* pp. 316–317.

Starting a Selling Career

Persuasive knowledge becomes the power to achieve goals when it is used in your own business or when you are a representative of an organization. One way you can develop your persuasive potential is to initiate your own firm. This has often been a road to wealth. However, a self-owned and -managed business entails a substantial amount of risk. It usually requires a great deal of patience until the idea behind it gains momentum. If this path to success is selected, possible opportunities must be carefully researched, good books on small-business management consulted, courses taken, and experience gained by working for a similar business. Each of these minimizes the risk of failure.

Nearly everyone who has ever thought about starting a self-owned and -managed business recognizes that steps like these are likely to help that business succeed. Everyone knows the value of learning from the experience of others through careful research and building on the foundation of that research through personal experience. Yet, when it comes to gaining that first-hand experience or looking for a career, "In spite of the fact nearly every adult American man and, presently, some 45 million women have been or will be involved in the job-hunt sometime in their lives, we are condemned to go about the job-hunt as though we were the first person in this country to have to do it" (1). Unlike the would-be entrepreneur of an independent business, the job-hunting novice fails to recognize the personal need to plan for the future methodically and systematically.

Most people choose to begin careers in selling with established organizations (1) to get experience under seasoned supervision, (2) to begin making money right away, and (3) to take advantage of training programs and other available benefits. Very few people, however, know how to approach the important career step of finding the right job. Many students, in fact, work hard for years—studying diligently, making good grades, and participating in many outside activities—only to lose these advantages by taking unrealistic approaches to the job market. Others, with lesser qualifications, study the art of job finding and attain higher success by beginning with the right company. There are many ideas that can give you a distinct competitive advantage in the job market. This text would be incomplete if it failed to assist you with one of the most important *prospecting* and *sales assignments* in your career—use of sales techniques to find and land the right job. This chapter discusses:

- Selecting a good organization
- Finding an opening
- Writing résumés
- Preparing cover letters
- Selling yourself in interviews and on tests
- Selling yourself on the job
- The future of personal selling

SELECTING A GOOD ORGANIZATION

The first step in career planning is to establish definite written employment goals. It is never too early to begin research that will help you to do this. The basic idea is to determine what you really want, assess what you have to offer and are willing to sacrifice, and match your potentials realistically with the kind of job that appears likely to give you maximum satisfaction. As career planning writer Richard N. Bolles has noted, "People of every imaginable background, age, sex, race, education, and skills can deliberately set about to find a job that gives them a sense of meaning and mission in life and succeed at finding it—*provided* only that they are willing to devote a lot of hard work to the planning thereof" (2). This process does not always involve searching for sales work you think you would like regardless of its profitability; rather, it involves being open to opportunities for work that you might *learn* to like. While one approach is being willing to adjust to jobs paying the highest monetary benefits, there are some employment situations to be avoided: those that you would never be happy in no matter what the pay. Although many of the better opportunities require expertise in specific areas and entail hard work, after the expertise is gained, such jobs are usually interesting and profitable. The process of matching your employment needs to your abilities with specific organizational positions can be accomplished by:

- Self-analysis
- Deciding on a specific area of persuasion
- Writing a prospective job description
- Researching specific companies that could meet your requirements

Self-Analysis

Make a thorough list of your likes and dislikes. Make another list of your assets and liabilities. Highlight any strong relative advantages that you can offer to an employer. Decide how important money, location, travel, and working hours are to you. Review Chapter 1, which explains why some persuasive positions pay more than others. Order-makers qualify for higher-paying jobs, but such jobs entail harder work and longer hours. Try to translate your preferences into actual job features.

Deciding on a Specific Area of Persuasion

Look ahead to the job characteristics of public relations, retail selling, intangible selling, industrial selling, and real estate selling given in Chapters 17 and 18. Consider again the sacrifices you must make to be successful in higher-paying selling jobs. Consider the technical training necessary, the selling problems involved, the length of apprenticeship periods, the relocation demanded, the travel required, and the long or irregular working hours associated with each of the major types of persuasive opportunities. Consider the pay, the indirect rewards, and the promotional opportunities, and make a tentative decision on a specific area of selling.

Writing a Prospective Job Description

Now write a detailed job description that you feel would balance realistically rewards, sacrifices, and abilities and that might be available within the selling area selected. Put factors like "travel 500 miles per week" and "relocation by region" in the description if you would be willing to do these things for the probable extra compensation involved. Clearly state the features you consider absolutely necessary for your maturation and satisfaction. Rank these fea-

Figure 16.1 Future Job Description

1. Location

Strongly prefer to locate in New England-New York area for family reasons. Prefer not to locate more than 400 miles from Hartford. Will not accept overseas location for more than one year.

2. Pay and Benefits

Prefer salary plus commission or bonus. $21,000 second-year minimum with over $30,000 potential in five years. Prefer good training program and promotion potential.

3. Customer

Prefer to sell to executive business customers or professional-type customers. Prefer not to sell to ultimate consumer customers.

4. Product

Tangible or intangible product but prefer high-unit value. Must be beneficial to society. Prefer quality product even if priced above competition. Complex product or concept preferred.

5. Travel

Willing to travel but prefer not to be overnight more than once per week. Prefer auto to air.

6. Call Frequency

Prefer to make from 8–10 calls or less per day in full interview-type selling. Prefer extra compensation for irregular interval calls rather than service selling at regular intervals.

7. Type of Selling

Willing to do creative selling for possible extra compensation involved. Prefer to make programmed presentations based on researched proposals on a professional, consultative selling level. Prefer extra compensation of problem-solving selling.

8. Nonselling Duties

Willing to do extensive reports and analyses. Willing to collect accounts but prefer not to collect on a regular basis. Delivery, installation, research, and public-relations work (such as trade fairs) acceptable if compensated.

tures in the order of their importance to you (see Figure 16.1 for an example of such a job description).

Researching Specific Companies That Could Meet Your Requirements

After you have written the tentative job description reflecting your qualifications, what you want, and the features that you would accept for extra compensation, you can make a search for specific firms that might be able to supply such a selling job. At this point whether or not the firms have "openings" should not be a concern. Consider all firms that might have persons employed with job descriptions similar to your tentative description. A good place to look for companies is in the latest *College Placement Annual* at a nearby college or university placement service office. The *College Placement Annual* has firms listed under such headings as public relations, merchandising, retail management, banking, and sales that search regularly for graduates interested in persuasive careers. The *College Placement Annual* also carries detailed information on specific companies, including products, number of employees, and the kind of graduates sought (3). Trade directories, the Yellow Pages, chamber of commerce lists, and trade association lists are other valuable job information sources. When you have selected five to ten firms that appear most attractive, you can research them further in Dun and Bradstreet, Standard & Poor's, or Moody's publications. Each provides data on corporate financial conditions.

Learning how to evaluate organizations before entering the job market enables you to select the firm instead of letting the firm select you. Reflect on the products of a firm and how they will fare in the markets of tomorrow. Consider the firm's research and its ability to market new products to meet dynamically changing environments. This is an indication of its capacity to offer career opportunities. Analyze everything that will bear on long-run profit potentials. Find out the firm's reputation and standing in its industry. This information can often be gotten from trade associations or trade journals. Knowledgeable business executives are another source for checking out a business's reputation. Does the firm have significant operations in the geographical area in which you wish to locate? What are its employee policies? Does it retain its employees, or does it have considerable turnover? What are its ethical standards? Customers, suppliers, and present employees are excellent sources of qualitative information about a firm, as are former employees, particularly if they will share their reasons for leaving. Annual reports and institutional brochures put out by a firm give even more information. Check your college placement services for information packets concerning the company. After you have gathered as much information as you can find, write down the advantages and disadvantages of each company in relation to your employment needs and wants. Next, rank the companies in respect to your preferences.

FINDING AN OPENING

Several months before you plan to be available for your selling job, you should begin the second important phase of your investigations. Remind all of your relatives, friends, and acquaintances that you are in the market, and get them to help you. Tell as many people as possible of your availability. Although you may plan to approach your selected firms first, you need to have many alternatives and an open mind about changing your preferences. College placement offices can be a big help. Find out which firms are going to conduct on-campus interviews and when. Review some of the books and pamphlets at the placement office and at the library that are written expressly to give you inside information on how to approach the job market. The alumni office may give you the names of recent graduates who have found selling jobs. Professors can be a source of names of recent graduates who have found good jobs. Recent job finders can tell novices about the job market. They may give you valuable leads. Remember: Starting out with the right employer is worth the extra effort!

Newspapers

Read the many ads for selling jobs in newspapers to get some idea of salaries and the market. Some ads do not give company names, but even blind ads will help you assess the needs of employers. It is possible but unlikely that you will find a good job through the newspapers. Primary reliance on this source is the mark of an unsophisticated job seeker. Newspaper ads should be regarded as a research source. Reading ads will give a better "feeling" for opportunities.

Employment Agencies

Another natural consideration is employment agencies, both private and government. Many employment agencies represent employers rather than employees. Some charge large fees for helping you to get a job. Use agencies only after you have tried more direct approaches or if you need a job in a hurry. The best jobs are won by resourceful job seekers who take the initiative and search for opportunities. Jackson and Mayless, in *The Hidden Job Market,* estimate that about 90 percent of available jobs are never advertised and never reach employment agency files (4). Other books suggest the futility of going through long waiting lines after responding to newspaper ads or paying high fees to have access to only a small, highly competitive portion of the job market. Nearly all authorities caution that it is important to understand the fee arrangement before signing with an employment agency.

A Direct Approach

Before you respond to "openings," try this approach. Take the firms selected from your previous research and investigate them closely. Eliminate those firms that require grade-point averages, experience, or health standards that you cannot meet. Go to the library and do more extensive research on the remaining firms. Look at their advertisements and annual reports; talk to their employees, look at their trade journals, talk to chamber of commerce officials about them. After this second, more thorough research, rerank the firms in order of their attractiveness for employment. Whether or not a selected company has an opening is not a consideration at this point. Almost any large firm with an active sales force has turnover from retirements, deaths, dismissals, and resignations. Firms that are really prospering need additional personnel to expand their product lines and territories. Good sales representatives are so scarce that a good job of convincing recruiters of your "fit" with corporate needs may create an opening for you or guarantee you first consideration when an opening does occur.

Selected firms can be approached either through written résumés or by direct contacts. How to write a professional résumé and how to impress recruiters in a persuasive interview are subjects of the following sections. If you try the direct-contact method, which is probably the best method, you may want to go around the employment manager and interview the person who will make the final hiring decision. In many cases, the sales branch manager decides, with home office approval. Find out the name of the sales or branch manager and make an appointment. Or simply walk into the branch and ask to see the sales manager. Remember that sales managers are sales-oriented and interested in people with initiative and a degree of aggressiveness. Most managers will not be offended by a direct approach and may appreciate a qualified walk-in who is interested in selling. After all, if you can do a good job of selling in the future, hiring you will mean more money or a better position for them. Good managers are always looking for high-potential stars who can sell. If a manager refers you to personnel, go through channels as directed. *The biggest danger in sales-job hunting is being hired by the wrong company, not being turned down by several good ones.* It is normal to get turned down several times. By using the direct approach, you have at least proceeded in true selling fashion. Pay special attention to preferred firms that are going through expansions, are changing product lines, or have definite openings as reported by one of the many persons you have job hunting for you. If preferred firms are located at a distance, you might try the résumé approach.

WRITING RÉSUMÉS

A résumé is a concise summary of your experience and characteristics, an advertisement for your services, and—it is hoped—a ticket of admission to an interview. Big corporations get hundreds of résumés each week and discard most of them after a superficial look. Writing a good résumé and cover letter can improve your chances of surviving this initial weeding out and winning an interview.

A résumé should be short and preferably contained on one 8" × 11" sheet of white bond paper. It should never be more than two pages. It should be typed on an electric typewriter with a carbon ribbon and not contain any mistakes in spelling, grammar, or punctuation. It should contain action words and omit personal pronouns. It should be arranged attractively with neat margins and white space. There are two main styles of résumés: historical and functional. The historical résumé features a listing of work and education experiences in reverse chronological order (most recent situation first) and is the most acceptable and popular format (5). The functional résumé is arranged by listing skills the applicant possesses that are associated with the job. It is sometimes used by applicants with unexplainable gaps in their work history. The functional style is not very suitable for most selling résumés. It arouses the suspicion of many résumé reviewers. An example of a historical résumé is shown in Figure 16.2. Note the concise style and yet the quantity of detailed information.

In addition to education and work experience, a résumé should contain name, address, telephone number, academic honors, and height, weight, and age (only if you think these last three would help.) Remember, a résumé is an advertisement. Items that might hurt your chances of being considered do not belong on it unless you feel their omission would arouse suspicion. It is considered best practice *not* to include a photograph, even for a selling job. Also, leave out the names of your spouse and children, references, salary requirements, and reasons for leaving previous jobs (6). References would be overworked if you sent out several résumés. It's too public and too early to reveal salary requirements. And any reasons for leaving previous jobs would introduce a negative element. When you have finished your résumé, proofread it several times. Read it aloud to others at least once and listen to their suggestions. As you read your résumé aloud, ask yourself: "Would I hire the person who wrote this?"

It is permissible to send copies of your résumé to as many employers as

John A. Ballantine
142 Sand Road
Raging Creek, Texas 89720
(817) 527–0000

Age: 21
Ht: 6' 1"   Wt: 190 lbs.
Date available: June 1980

CAREER OBJECTIVES: To be a successful industrial salesman and to be a sales executive within reasonable time.

EDUCATION: B.S. in Business Administration from the University of Middle Texas. Courses include Sales, Advertising, Sales Management, Public Relations, Public Speaking, and Physics. Grade Average: 3.1 on a 4.0 scale.

ACTIVITIES: Debating Team. Vice President and Treasurer, Sigma Alpha Theta Fraternity. Letterman varsity basketball, two years. Sales Manager, Yearbook, Raging Creek High School.

EXPERIENCE:
Summer 1979   Sold dictionaries and children's story books for Middlewest Book Company; leading salesperson in section.

1977–78   Sold men's clothing at retail for Tamm's Men's Wear, Raging Creek, during summers and vacation periods.

1975–76   Sold ads for Raging Creek High School Yearbook. Surpassed sales of previous year by 50 percent.

1973–75   Paper route for *Daily News*; increased circulation by 20 percent.

INTERESTS: Team sports of all kinds, camping out, bronco riding, guitar, debating, and public speaking.

you wish. Some applicants send it to dozens of firms, hoping to find an opening this way. While such a "shotgun" approach is probably not necessary for selling positions, if you do send out many copies, have the résumé printed or reproduced on high-quality paper. The appearance of someone looking for just *any* job must be avoided. A basic strategy in hunting for the right employer is to appear discriminating. A future employer should feel that the company was selected because of its superiority. Sending out cheap copies of your résumé does not convey this impression.

A final note about writing résumés. As Richard N. Bolles puts it in *What Color Is Your Parachute?* "The key to an effective and useful résumé is very simple: you must know why you are writing it (to open doors for you, to help people remember you after you've interviewed them, or both) to whom you are writing it (the people who have the power to hire), what you want them to know about you, how you can help them . . ., and how you can support this claim so as to convince them to reach a favorable decision about you" (7).

PREPARING COVER LETTERS

A cover letter should accompany a résumé, typed on the same kind of paper and with the same type as the résumé (8). It should be an original, never a copy. It should not be over five paragraphs or one page long, nor should it be just one or two sentences. While a résumé is an advertisement for employment, the cover letter should be customized and directed specifically to the company to which it is addressed. Remember that the company reviewer must judge each applicant from limited evidence—only what is sent. The first paragraph of your letter should explain why you are asking that company for an interview. The middle paragraph(s) should point to your main selling features (qualifications) featured in your résumé. Your closing paragraph should suggest possible arrangements for an interview (9)—see Figure 16.3. More examples of cover letters and résumés can be found in the *College Placement Annual* or in one of the many books on the subject. If you plan to send out several résumés, keep good records, especially of the interviews you are granted. Contact the company immediately, and accept the interviews you plan to attend. This attention creates a positive impression. Regrets should be expressed if, for some reason, a scheduled appointment cannot be kept.

Like the résumé, the cover letter "should never be just a standard item. . . . It can often be the primary attention getting item that you offer. Think of it as a personal letter, a means of courting, not as a dictionary of business terms or an empty ritual such as 'Enclosed please find. . . .'" Ask yourself, 'What would I want to see in a letter if I were the prospective employer? What would make me want to meet this person?'" (10). The only thing standard in the cover letter is the standard of expression, which should be direct, grammatical, without spelling errors or awkward phrasing, and, above all, individual.

Figure 16.3   Cover Letter

142 Sand Road
Raging Creek, Tex. 89720
March 17, 1983

Mr. Robert Wellerman
Branch Manager
Duraco Oil Equipment Company
Houston, Tex. 71701

Dear Mr. Wellerman:

Oil-rig equipment is an exciting product and vital to our country's future with growing demands for energy. I am interested in becoming a part of a sales force that would see that this important equipment is put to work.

I plan to graduate in June, and as the enclosed résumé shows, my academic curriculum and my work experience have helped prepare me for sales work. The physics, sales, and management courses should be valuable in selling rig equipment. The competition of varsity athletics and debating has taught me the thrill of winning and being a team player. The sales experience in books, clothing, ads, and newspapers has taught me how to sell and convinced me that personal selling is my occupational choice.

Could I talk to you in person about employment opportunities in the oil-equipment industry? Harvey Lyles, your sales representative in this area, has me very interested in Duraco and in meeting you. I will call you next week and try to arrange an appointment at your convenience.

Yours truly,

John Ballantine

cjc

Enclosure

SELLING IN INTERVIEWS AND ON TESTS

The interview is the main event for persuasive positions. Personality is the most important factor in most selling situations. Applicants cannot expect a company to hire them without personal contact. Grades are an indication of ability to be trained and determination to excel. Some employers with technical products look carefully at grades because grades reflect self-image and intelligence. Most companies, however, are more interested in personality factors.

Prepare for the Interview

Before an interview, research the company again to find out all you can about its history, products, size, operations, and problems. You should know its credit standing, its sales record over the last ten years, its training programs, and its policies. Companies want salespeople to help solve problems. Decide what you believe the company wants in a salesperson. Companies, like customers, have dominant buying motives—a main reason for hiring new salespeople. Dress for the interview in the same kind of clothes you would expect to wear on the job. Dont wear any pins, emblems, or other indicators of political or ideological preferences that might be controversial. By dressing and wearing your hair conservatively, you allow yourself rather than what you wear to be the focus of the interviewer's attention. Men with long hair or bushy beards enter most interviews with a decided handicap. Manicure your fingernails and be as neat and clean as possible. Women should dress modestly for interviews. Applicants are asking to reflect the image of the firm—to represent the firm as a salesperson. If you are dressed and groomed properly in conservative and coordinated colors, you will enter the interview with extra poise and self-assurance. The interviewer will form an important first impression of you the second you appear.

There are other ways to prepare yourself. Be ready to answer standard interview questions and to ask intelligent questions. You should also be prepared in your attitude. Determine to be honest and consistent. Trained interviewers will test your consistency and reject you if they think you are deceptive. Figure 16.4 contains examples of questions that you might be asked. Expect these questions in one form or another and plan good answers. More will be added about key questions later. Minority members or women must never indicate the attitude that interviewers must hire them because it is the law. Interviewers are looking for applicants who want to work and gain profit for the firm. They are pleased to find qualified minority members and women who stand on their qualifications, not on their legal hiring advantages.

Enthusiasm in an interview is expected. Even a little apprehension and nervousness will hardly surprise a veteran interviewer. Sales interviewers like least of all the quiet, reserved, extra "cool" types, who seem withdrawn and answer questions too briefly. This does not mean that answers should be overdone with frantic gestures or artificial theatrics. It does mean that at-

Figure 16.4 Questions You Might Be Asked in an Interview

What made you consider us for employment?

Why did you select selling as a career?

What are your short- and long-range objectives?

Where do you expect to be in your career, and what do you expect to be earning four years from now?

Why did you leave your last job?

What do you consider to be your greatest strengths?

What do you consider to be your greatest weaknesses?

What advantages do you have to offer our company; that is, why should we select you over other applicants?

Tell me about yourself.

How would someone who knows you quite well describe you?

What makes you work your hardest—what motivates you?

What qualities do you think are important to selling success?

How would your previous work experiences help you sell?

What do you know about us?

Are you willing to relocate? Travel?

What have you learned outside of the classroom that would help you in selling?

What specific elements or features do you want in a selling job?

What college subjects did you like least? Best?

What makes you mad?

What do you dislike the most in other people?

What do you feel are the three greatest problems of the United States as a country?

If we would hire you, when could you go to work? What is the minimum we would have to offer you to hire you?

tempts to appear extra reserved will probably be misinterpreted as boredom or disinterest.

If you seem overanxious for a job and willing to take anything, it is human nature to discount your qualifications. It is far better to project to an interviewer selectivity based on your high qualifications. And because you are selective, you are interested in that particular company.

A final note on preparation is to role-play each interview before you actually experience it. Find a friend or relative who will play the part of the interviewer, or at least go over the interview in your mind and "synthetically" experience it (psychocybernetics) before it takes place. This pays big dividends in personal composure during actual interviews.

Sell Yourself from the Beginning

"Punctuality is the politeness of kings" is a saying attributed to Louis XVIII of France. Like Louis XVIII, applicants should never arrive late for an interview. Arriving two or three minutes early is a good practice. An applicant will be observed on entering the building or as soon as met by the interviewer, so be alert. A sales job is required in a screening interview to win a hiring decision interview later on with a higher company official. Some screening interviewers are unskilled and not highly paid. This does not mean that applicants should not be respectful to them, but it does mean that unless they are careful, applicants may be evaluated incorrectly and a full chance to express qualifications not given them. This is why you should see the person who can hire you in your first interview, if possible. Fortunately, the selling strategy is the same for the screening and the depth (hiring) interview—to sell yourself and to give yourself the option to accept or reject an offer. Interviewers viewing applicants for selling jobs are looking for people who are extroverted, attractive, pleasant, optimistic, and interested in others.

Practice Persuasive Principles

Greet the interviewer as you would a prospect, with a firm handshake, good eye contact, and your name. Wait for an invitation to sit down, but try to arrange it so your chair is close enough to an interviewer for good two-way communication. An open body-language position in a poised but relaxed manner—sitting straight in the chair with arms and legs not defensively crossed—conveys self-confidence. Remember that interviewers are just as much on trial as you are, and the worst thing that can happen is that you will be hired by the wrong firm. There are hundreds of firms looking for able people to hire. Public speaking courses and cybernetic practice under conditions without personal significance can help applicants learn to relax in interviews. The interviewer's job at this point is to get you relaxed—so relaxed, in fact, that you will reveal your true self.

Be Prepared to Answer Standard Questions

Interviewers usually begin with a few harmless rapport-establishing questions. "Did you have a nice trip over?" "Did you find a good place to park?" Interviewers want to get applicants talking about themselves and want to sell them on the company. Eventually, depth questions will be asked to ascertain your attitudes and motivations. Included below are questions you might expect and suggestions for replies.

"What about our company made you consider us?" This question presents an unusual opportunity to show your knowledge about the specific company that you gained from your research. This question is best answered specifically. One answer might be: "I have always wanted to sell for a firm whose products I could believe in. I am particularly impressed with your research and new products, especially the new Z copier. I believe the XYZ Company has great growth, potential, and I want to be a part of a dynamic growth company with a future."

"What are your ambitions?" "What are your long-range goals?" "Where do you want to be seven years from now?" Seven years from now, any applicant wants to be somewhere *reasonably* up the corporate ladder. An interviewer will not be impressed if you state that you expect to be president of the firm in seven years. A possible answer is: "I expect to be a high-producing, senior salesperson in the next few years and by seven years, possibly, a zone sales manager, with recognized potential for branch manager." Your response should reflect what you know about the company's promotion policies.

"What are your strengths and weaknesses?" Express your strengths in terms of the selling personality. "I have always had the ability to get along with other people and to influence them. I like to work hard, and I enjoy the challenge of competition and problem solving." Your answers to questions like this should be meaningful but concise. Answers that are too long are worse than answers that are too short. "Boomerang" your weaknesses into selling points. "I have a tendency to become overconcerned about doing a good job, but this tends to make me more careful." Admission of too many or too serious faults in an attempt to appear honest and humble is rarely effective.

"Are you a conservative or a liberal in your philosophies? Explain." Leaning slightly to the conservative side politically, morally, and socially does little harm. Questions like this can be sidestepped by answering, "I believe in the free-enterprise system, the American form of government, and high moral standards, but I think I'm tolerant of the beliefs of others."

"Why did you leave your last job?" You may have left your last job because your boss was intolerable and you felt you were treated unfairly; however, it is inappropriate to express these beliefs to the interviewer. It is best to be positive and answer, "I didn't feel that the growth opportunities were sufficient. I wanted to represent a company with greater potential for advancement" (this last may be the better of two true reasons).

"Do you like to be with people, or would you rather work alone?" As a potential salesperson, you like people—rich, poor, foreign, fat, and lean. You especially like the kinds of people who are the customers of the interviewing firm. You might answer: "Yes, I like to be with people very much; but I don't mind traveling by myself, since this is necessary in selling."

Nearly all good interviewers ask a simple and effective depth question designed to throw applicants off guard, and it usually does. "Tell me about yourself." Many people have a tendency to ramble and show disorganization when answering this question. Others relax and, in an effort to appear humble, confess too many shortcomings. David Knight, in his excellent short book, *How to Interview for That Job and Get It,* calls this the "killer question" (11). Write out your answer to this one before the interview. Portray yourself as human, with a few admitted minor weaknesses overbalanced by strengths that count in selling.

Watch for Tricks

A few interviewers will test you by purposely trying to make you angry and noting your response. This is a very negative approach for that company. It may not be a desirable place to work. Some interviewers will request a light or a pen. They want to see if you fumble around to get one or if your response is immediate. Others may tell a joke and watch for your response. Some interviewers are more interested in how long it takes you to respond. Long waits indicate deceptiveness. You must be wary of interviewers who pretend to hold views that they don't hold, or who try to get you to join in a critical attack on some person or institution. Interviewers are looking for honesty and consistency. Applicants want to cast themselves in a favorable but believable light. Smoking in an interview is only correct if an invitation to do so is issued. Use of titles shows social intelligence and courtesy.

Ask Intelligent Questions

Interviewers expect you to ask questions in an interview. Intelligent, appropriate, and prestudied questions make the most favorable impression. Questions about profits, growth potentials, policies, and opportunities show intelligent interest (12). Ask what progress you might make if you do a good job. Questions about salaries or paid vacation days should be reserved for an interview's final moments. Ask about training programs and what you would do the first year if you are hired. You want to join a company with a good training program for two reasons. You want to learn and you want the company to have a substantial investment in your success. Companies without training programs are likely to be less patient with your shortcomings because they have a smaller investment in you.

Watch for Important Decisions at the End of the Interview

Near the end of the decision interview, you may be asked questions that could be hard to answer. How would you reply if an interviewer says: "I've decided to employ you. When can you go to work?" You must either accept the job or bargain for time if you are not sure. A possible answer is: "I'm very interested, Ms. Bell, but I would like to talk it over with my family. Could you give me until Monday?" Or you might answer with a question bearing on the decision: "Could you tell me what salary or commission I might expect?" Another hard question to answer is: "What are your minimum salary requirements?" Before answering this question, you should have a very good idea about what the firm pays new salespeople from your preinterview research. To state a figure too low is to sell yourself short and lose image with the interviewer. Interviewers are also unimpressed with sky-high expectations. Ask for a salary that is slightly higher than average or respond that it depends on fringe benefits and advancement possibilities. You might turn the question around and ask for salary ranges for new recruits. If you have sold yourself well and they really want you, the firm may meet your compensation requests. Most often, however, salary and commission schedules in selling are

Watch the interviewer for nonverbal clues.

"I'd like to hear more about the retirement plan."

THE SATURDAY EVENING POST

Reprinted from *The Saturday Evening Post* © 1961 The Curtis Publishing Company.

uniform and depend on how much you produce. You might also avoid answering the minimum salary question by asking about bonuses and contests. Remember, you want to play a little bit hard to get.

Forms and Tests

Applicants should be honest, complete, and neat in filling out application blanks, but what about tests? If you know which tests will be given (and such information sometimes is obtainable by asking employees and other applicants), you can actually prepare. Mechanical, verbal, math, and intelligence tests are readily available and can be used for practice. Experience in taking such tests may give you a slight but significant edge over other applicants. Personality tests are another matter. Personality and preference (interest) tests are of questionable value and are difficult to interpret. While many such tests were designed to detect mental and emotional problems in abnormal people, they have been incorporated into the testing of job applicants. Some were designed to pry deep into your attitudes and motivations. Because these tests are often invalid, questionable, and sometimes unfair, you might attempt to avoid taking them. If you take them and are absolutely honest, you may be at a competitive disadvantage with those who deliberately fake answers. If you try to slant your answers, you may appear inconsistent. No matter what you are told about the tests beforehand, there *are* right and wrong answers to the questions. Many vocational experts feel that in this case it is not unethical for you to use your intelligence to give the "right" answer as long as it is not untrue, but be consistent.

A college professor who formerly worked for a personnel agency confided that he once advised a shy applicant who was applying for a bill collector's job to imagine himself to be a tough army general and answer all the questions from that viewpoint. The applicant scored extremely high on the personality test and was ushered into the company with great expectations. He was released later when his true, gentle nature revealed that he was unfit for the job.

The "right" answers to most sales personality tests are those that show that you are aggressive—walking, talking, eating, and working faster than most people—but not overaggressive. You are socially active and participate in group activities more than most. You are *not overly* interested in theater, music, art, or other "impractical" subjects unless they are associated with the job you are applying for (13). Generally, you are more conservative than liberal or radical. You are not overly critical or introverted. You are money- and achievement-motivated, but you are able to get along with all kinds of people. Your activity in competitive sports outranks your time spent reading. You like to socialize, but you can be alone enough to travel. Consider the job you are applying for and pursue it intelligently. A public-relations profile is different from an insurance-salesperson profile.

Don't Get Discouraged

Few applicants get the first job for which they apply. It may not be offered to you for many reasons. The organization may not be growing; there may not be any openings; the interviewer may have felt that you were over- or under-qualified; or the interviewer may not have been experienced enough to eval-uate you correctly. Most applicants can expect to participate in many inter-views before being offered a job, just as most salespersons must expect to make many calls before making an important sale. Don't lower your self-image and decide to take a situation beneath your reasonable aspirations. Relive your interviews and testing situations just long enough to profit from your mistakes and successes. Recognize your mistakes without branding yourself a failure. Regardless of the outcome, *send a letter to each interview-ing company, thanking them for the interview.* Company recruiters have been known to change their minds in response to such courtesy.

SELLING YOURSELF ON THE JOB

When you arrive at the sales office, you will probably be introduced to the office, sales, and repair personnel. Don't be surprised if the other sales rep-resentatives don't receive you with enthusiasm. After all, you are their com-petitor. Some of them may have to accept smaller territories so you can have a share. Others may have to sacrifice selling time to help train you. Some of the sales team will probably be very nice to you, and some will not. It is your place as the newcomer to be friendly and respectful toward experienced sales reps. Most salespeople are friendly by nature. When they get over resenting having to share with you and get to know you as a person, they will receive you as one of the team.

In your first days with the company, close scrutiny of you by management will continue. Dress well, be dependable, and make good use of your time—these are ways to show seriousness of purpose. Be aggressive and indicate that you want to go out and sell as soon as you are allowed and that you want to learn as much as you can about the products and the company. Ask ques-tions without being a bother, read the policy manuals, see problems, and vol-unteer to solve them. Be willing to run errands, prepare products for demon-stration, and study hard to catch up with the established sales force. Show that you are no stranger to hard work, and do everything cheerfully and enthu-siastically. Above all, never criticize or speak ill of anyone—especially your superiors. Courtesy always pays. Be your own public-relations representative and cultivate all your publics—office staff, sales force members, repair person-nel, managers. Learn everyone's name as quickly as possible. Show respect for all firm members no matter their position.

It is good to be ambitious, but don't be a threat to your immediate supervisor. Remember that everyone is vitally concerned with his or her position in the company.

Your concern about the firm's profitability can be shown through care of company property and being reasonable about expense accounts. Since managers cannot see each staff member all the time, they must judge by the actions they do see and the things they do hear. Being willing to do things other employees do not want to do, and solving problems other salespersons do not want to solve is an impressive way to take hold in a new job.

In every organization cliques or informal groups exist. Many cliques are very divisive and exclude those not in the clique while advancing the interests of clique members. Be sure you want to be identified with the clique before you "join." Joining a clique is not a formal act. It is simply conforming to clique norms, acknowledging clique leadership, and being accepted by the group. It is possible but difficult to remain neutral. To remain neutral requires acting as an individual while being friendly to people who belong to informal groups. It can be dangerous to engage in any of the "political" activities of a clique such as putting down some people and pushing up others (especially supervisors). Fortunately, many salespersons work such separate territories that cliques are seldom as active in selling as they are in situations where persons work in closer proximity.

Learning the names of organizational personnel and being friendly to everyone pays big dividends. Work hard to make your goals, especially in the beginning of your selling career, and do more listening than talking in the sales office. The same persuasive principles that count in selling and public relations can gain you the respect of your peers and your supervisors.

Sometimes, political and organizational pathologies are irreversible, and the company loses its potential for providing any promise of future opportunities. If you find yourself in a sick power structure and someone above you is really out to get you, you must have the patience to wait or the sense to find another job. Continually assess your future with the firm, and be willing to find new opportunities when the company loses its long-run potential for furnishing you a healthy working environment.

THE FUTURE OF PERSONAL SELLING

Adele Lewis, who has extensive experience in helping people find jobs, writes in her book, *How to Write Better Résumés,* that sales work is "recession proof." Openings always exceed applicants. Excellent opportunities exist in this growing occupational area (14). If the past is an indicator of the future, those who gain expertise in persuasion will be able to find lucrative employment in almost any geographic area and under almost any business conditions.

No one can really see into the future, but there appear to be many trends and innovations that will affect tomorrow's marketplace.

- Personal selling is becoming more professional and enjoying a higher image.
- Salary-plus-bonus plans and other profit-sharing plans are growing in popularity.
- Telephones that allow sales rep and prospect to see each other will have a big impact on personal selling.
- More and better visual aids, such as holographic three-dimensional projections, will improve the prospect's ability to preexperience ownership.
- Women and minorities will continue to enter the field in greater numbers and enjoy increasing acceptance.
- Salespersons may have to assume an allocation role when temporary shortages occur in product lines because of raw materials scarcities.
- America's population will become older, more affluent, and enjoy increasing leisure time.
- Appeals will increasingly be directed to higher motivational levels.
- Fewer people will actually work.
- New transportation and housing products will significantly affect lifestyles.
- Consumerism and environmentalism will produce more laws affecting selling.
- Trends toward government involvement in marketing will suffer only temporary setbacks and will continue.

Finally, opportunities in personal selling will increase because fewer applicants will have the personality, willingness, achievement motivation, and success characteristics required to fill an increasing number of selling and public-relations positions. The future holds promise for those who prepare for it.

SUMMARY

Selling yourself to an employer is one of the most important sales you will ever make in your sales career. Seek an employer who is employee-centered, who has salespeople working under job descriptions that match your aspirations, who has a good training program, and whose products promise future growth. Select an employer rather than letting an employer select you. Secure an interview with the branch or sales manager after thoroughly researching the firm and deciding that it presents an optimum long-run opportunity for you. If you sell yourself properly, there is a good chance the manager will make an opening for you, since promising sales aspirants are much in demand. Try the résumé method if employers of interest are located in other regions. A professional-looking résumé is a personal advertisement to secure an interview and should be written carefully in accordance with an acceptable format.

A successful interview is the key to obtaining an excellent sales opportunity. Before entering an interview, you should be appropriately dressed and groomed to reflect the desired image of the firm. Be thoroughly prepared to reflect your specific interests in the firm and to answer standard questions designed to help the recruiter learn about you. To justify why a firm should hire you over other applicants, you must be prepared to tell the interviewer "something special." Be prepared for acceptance, rejection, or to answer questions about what kind of compensation you expect. Be prepared to ask good questions too. If you try to supply the "right" answers to personality tests, be consistent and answer as you believe an ideal salesperson would answer.

When on the job, make good use of company assets, especially time. Learn the names of all company personnel, and speak well of everyone, never criticizing anyone.

The future is likely to be characterized by many new markets and products, but there will always be great need for professional persuaders in a free-enterprise system.

REVIEW QUESTIONS

1. What are the advantages of beginning a sales career with an established organization?

2. What are some of the sacrifices that typically accompany the successful representative in higher-paying selling jobs (as described in Chapter 1)?

3. Name the essential elements to be included in writing a prospective job description.

4. Suggest information sources that will aid the prospective salesperson to evaluate potential employers.

5. Evaluate newspapers and employment agencies as sources of selling jobs.

6. Explain the "direct approach" to gaining a sales position. Why is it important to attempt to interview the manager who will be making the actual hiring decision?

7. What is the biggest danger in sales-job hunting?

8. Briefly describe what is meant by a résumé. List the items that *should* and *should not* be included.

9. Differentiate between functional and historical résumés.

10. Why is it an acceptable procedure to send out high-quality copies of a résumé but poor practice to send good copies of the same cover letter to various potential employers?

11. What are the recommended features of a cover letter to be sent with an accompanying résumé?

12. In preparing for an interview, what are the factors that should be reviewed?

13. Suggest some of the questions an applicant might expect to be asked in an interview.

14. What characteristics do interviewers look for in applicants for selling positions?

15. Why is a company's training program of importance to the sales applicant?

16. Are there "right" and "wrong" answers to the questions on personality tests? How should an applicant respond to such questions?

17. Being rejected is discouraging. List some of the reasons that may cause an applicant to fail to secure a position.

18. Suggest the factors that will assist the novice salesperson to gain acceptance.

19. Suggest some of the trends and innovations that will affect the marketplace of tomorrow.

APPLICATION QUESTIONS

1. When you are attempting to find a job, you can consider *yourself* as the product that needs to be sold. You will have a differential advantage over other job applicants if you apply the material from this course to this job-hunting process. This chapter is designed to help you do this.

   a. Review your likes and dislikes and your assets and liabilities to an employer. Based on these factors, what features would you like to have in a job?

   b. Where could you go to get information about companies that may have positions that possess these features?

   c. One of the critical questions that interviewers often ask is: "Tell me about yourself." How would you answer this?

   d. What are five questions you might ask an interviewer?

16–1

Bob Dunning is just about to graduate from Southern Missouri State College in Cirailess, Missouri. Bob was born, grew up, and went to school in Cirailess. Now he would like to see something of the world—Los Angeles, New York, or just about anywhere but Cirailess. He had even thought of trying for pilot training in the Air Force as a way to see the world. Unfortunately, he turned out to be just color-blind enough to be rejected. The placement service at Southern has a good record in aiding its graduates in finding jobs. Most of the jobs tend to be in southern Missouri, northern Arkansas, and eastern Kansas. They all seem to be more of the same to Bob. He wants to get away. Bob has had a long-time ambition to be a sales rep because of the opportunity it gives for travel and working with new people in new places. Bob took up his problem with Dr. Hacklestack, his academic advisor. Dr. Hacklestack discussed Bob's ambitions with him, told Bob that he should consult with George West, Southern's placement director, and then called West to tell him of Bob's considerable ability as a student and of his desire to get away from Cirailess and into a selling job. Bob has followed up on Dr. Hacklestack's advice and has made an appointment with West.

Bob: (*Entering West's office*) Mr. West, I'm Bob Dunning. (*Bob offers his hand to West.*) When I called for an appointment, I told your secretary about my desire to get a sales job that'll take me away from Cirailess.

West: Oh, yes, Bob. Dr. Hacklestack called to talk to me about you. I'm glad to meet you. Won't you sit down?

Bob: Thanks.

West: Tell me about yourself.

Bob: Well, I guess there isn't too much to tell. I was born here in Cirailess. I went to McKinley Grade School and to Cirailess High before coming to Southern.

West: Surely there's more than that, Bob. Are you in a fraternity? Do you play any sports? Other extracurricular activities?

Bob: Well, I was rushing chairman of my fraternity last year and I'm social chairmain this year. I was elected co-captain of the varsity soccer squad. And I'm on the swimming team.

West: Your transcript indicates that you're also a very good student. Aren't you the Bob Dunning who wrote the second-place short story in the *Lit* the year before last?

Bob: (*Smiling*) Yeah, that's me. What really worries me, Mr. West, is that I know about going to school and about Cirailess, but I don't really have any marketable skills. I just can't see why anybody would want to hire me.

West: Well, the first thing you've got to decide before you decide no one will want you is what you want.

Bob: Well, it may sound silly, I hope you won't laugh, but all my life I've wanted to live in a big city—Chicago, L.A., New York, or somewhere like that. I've always thought that selling would be a good career for me and could get me away from Cirailess. There's nothing wrong with Cirailess, it's just that I want to see something of the world. I want to know what it's like to live in other places. I'd like to work a few years and then, maybe, if I've saved the money, get an MBA from Wharton or Harvard or Stanford. Eventually, I'd like a job in sales or marketing management—but not anything inactive like marketing research.

West: You know, Bob, it may seem to you that you're not very sure of what you want out of life, but you may be surer than you think. The way to secure your future and to get the things you want is to look carefully at the bundle of potentialities that is you and see how they work to support your goals. That way, you'll get an idea of what skills you already have and which ones you need to develop. What would you say was your strongest skill, Bob?

Bob: Skill? I'm not sure I've really got any skills. Here I am, after four years of college, and I haven't picked up any real skills. The only skill I have is that I type well enough to hold down a job at it—I got that in high school and worked at it for a year before I came to Southern.

West: Hey, hold on, Bob, you're putting yourself down too quickly. I think you don't really mean the same thing by skills as I do. You know the higher you aim occupationally, the less specific become the job descriptions. It seems to me that you must have considerable skills in communicating—witness your short-story prize. You're a quick learner, or your grades wouldn't be what they are. From the fraternity offices you've held and your election as co-captain of the soccer squad, I'd say you must have persuasive skills and maybe some supervisory ones as well.

Bob: Really?

West: Yes, really! Now, Bob, what I want you to do is: one, make another appointment with me for Friday; two, go back to your room and sit down with this copy of *The Dictionary of Occupational Titles* and assess your skills—not just those you'll discover you have, but those you'd like to have; three, I want you to write up a description of your ideal job and then prepare a résumé for that specific job. Will you do it?

Bob: I'll sure try, Mr. West. Thanks. By Friday, did you say? I don't know if . . .

West: You've got to face up to planning your life sometime, Bob. This is as good a time as any.

QUESTIONS

1. Did West really help Bob, or just push him off with an unmanageable task?

2. How would you assess your own skills?

16–2

Howard Cashdollar has an interview with Juan Rodriguez of Stable Life. Howard has two years of college. He is dressed neatly in a conservative suit, has recently had a haircut and a manicure, and has on well-shined shoes. He is clean-shaven except for a neatly trimmed moustache.

Juan: Hello, Howard, I'm Juan Rodriguez. Come in and have a seat. *(Juan shakes hands firmly with Howard.)*

Howard: Thank you, Mr. Rodriguez. I appreciate the opportunity for this interview. I've always had a great deal of respect for Stable Life Insurance Company.

Juan: Why do you say that, Howard?

Howard: Our neighbors, the Mitchells, had a policy with your company. Mr. Mitchell died five years ago, and Mrs. Mitchell was able to keep her home because of the insurance settlement. She remarked how prompt and'courteous the company was in settling the claim. I understand, too, that Stable Life has grown at a rate of about 15 percent a year over the last five years in total life underwritings. That's an excellent growth rate in today's competitive market.

Juan: I appreciate your interest in us, Howard. Our company is doing very well. Won't you have some coffee?

Howard: *(Who doesn't drink coffee ordinarily)* Thank you, sir.

Juan: We are looking for potential life-insurance agents who want a future with a growing company. Do you think you would be interested in selling insurance?

Howard: The insurance field is certainly one of my considerations. I realize that it's challenging, but I've always liked a challenge.

Juan: Good agents do very well in insurance, Howard. Those who stick with it and earn their CLU, certified life underwriter, certificate do especially well. We start trainees out at $850 per month during a four-month training and orientation period. After that period, our average salesperson earns fourteen thousand the first year with the company. I see you're a business major. Why did you select that major?

Howard: My father has a retail store in Madison, and I had a chance to talk with many of the salespeople who came in. I decided that

I wanted to be a salesperson, so I took business, with a concentration in marketing. I like to move around and meet people.

Juan: I see you're not married.

Howard: No, sir, not yet.

Juan: Howard, you make a very good first impression. I would like you to just relax now and tell me about yourself.

Howard: I grew up in Madison, where I delivered newspapers while I was in junior high school. At Madison High I concentrated in Distributive Education and lettered in baseball my last two years. I worked summers and holidays with my father, selling men's wear in his shop. I was vice president of the senior class and graduated in the top third of my class. Here at college I'm playing baseball again, I'm working in the bookstore, and I'm maintaining about a "B" average. I'm president of the Business Club and treasurer of OET, a service fraternity. Last summer I sold dictionaries door to door and made about $2,500. I like to play the guitar and sing at camp-outs, and love swimming and the outdoors. Is there anything in particular you would like to know about me, Mr. Rodriguez?

Juan: Well, I have your application and references, Howard, and they look good. Can you come down to the agency next week? I'd like to introduce you to some of our underwriters and to show you what you can really accomplish as a career underwriter. Can you come Monday about eleven o'clock? I want you to have lunch with me and some of our agents.

Howard: Yes, sir, thank you. I'll be there.

QUESTIONS

1. Which do you think were Howard's best answers in this interview?

2. Which answer would you have handled differently?

3. Evaluate his response to Juan's invitation to tell about himself.

4. Pretend you are responding to an invitation of Juan's. What would you say?

16–3

Patricia Milhouse became concerned about employment a month before she graduated college. She had a 3.0 average in marketing and was vice-president of the senior class at Woodruff Community College. The first thing Pat did in her search for a job was to go over to the employment office and find out who was going to interview during the next two months. She also read the newspaper ads every morning. She has had interviews with five national companies, three on campus and two she found in the want ads. Two of the on-campus interviewers seemed very interested until she explained that she would never consider traveling or moving more than 100 miles away from Woodruff, where her parents live and her boyfriend works. One of the two companies she interviewed from newspaper ads has a branch located in Watertown, only fifty miles from Woodruff, but the recruiter became concerned when Pat told him he needed to hire her because she was a woman applicant and his company had to hire more females or run into trouble with the law. He found an excuse to turn her down. Pat is a little discouraged at this point. She thinks that part of her lack of success is that sales managers and recruiters don't really want to hire women. The national companies that seemed interested wanted her to be willing to relocate and to do some overnight traveling. She is contemplating going to an employment agency and explaining her problem or sending out about twenty-five résumés.

Do you think Pat's approach to the job market is correct?
What mistakes has she made?
What should she do now?

NOTES

1. Richard Nelson Bolles, *What Color Is Your Parachute?* (Berkeley, Calif.: Ten Speed Press, 1981), p. 9.

2. Richard Nelson Bolles, *The Three Boxes of Life* (Berkeley Calif.: Ten Speed Press, 1981), p. 267.

3. *College Placement Annual* (Bethlehem, Pa.: College Placement Council, 1978).

4. Tom Jackson and Davidyne Mayless, *The Hidden Job Market* (New York: Quadrangle Books/New York Times, 1976), pp. 95–122.

5. Adele Lewis, *How to Write a Better Résumé* (Woodbury, N.Y.: Barron's Educational Series, 1977), pp. 6–8.

6. *Ibid.,* pp. 27–29.

7. Bolles, *What Color Is Your Parachute?* p. 157.

8. Melvin W. Donaho and John L. Meyer, *How to Get the Job You Want* (Englewood Cliffs, N.J.: Prentice-Hall, 1976), pp. 43–63.

9. Lewis, *How to Write a Better Résumé,* pp. 237–250.

10. Howard E. Figler, "Dear Howard," in Jonathan A. Eaton and Paul K. Herzan (eds.), *Career Insights: 1982–1983* (Providence, R.I.: Career Insights, 1982), p. 86.

Insuring Future Opportunities

11. David N. Knight, *How to Interview for That Job and Get It* (Connersville, Ind.: Commercial Printing Services, News-Examiner, 1976), pp. 43–44.

12. *Ibid.,* p. 113.

13. *Ibid.,* pp. 136–140.

14. Lewis, *How to Write a Better Résumé,* p. 292.

Special Selling Opportunities

Persuasive talents and techniques are required in many specialized fields of selling. While most basic strategies and methods are similar, there are important differences in approach and tactics in retail selling, industrial selling, intangible selling, and public relations. This chapter is designed to point out some of these differences and suggest customized techniques for each of these specialized selling situations.

RETAIL SELLING

In retail selling, customers usually visit stores or places of business with interest in particular products or groups of products. While route sellers, door-to-door salespersons, telephone salespersons, and home-service salespersons do contact customers, they comprise only a small part of the total retail sales force. In retailing, customers often have already decided that they have a problem or need before entering a store. This does not mean that prospects are ready to buy or that retailing is mere order taking. Since many retail salespersons cannot actively prospect, they must make the most of every potential buyer who enters the store and sell with such diplomacy that customers will keep coming back. Retail salespersons, in fact, must be expert strategists and closers. Customers, especially those desiring consumer durables and style goods, can be substantially influenced by effective selling methods. Retail management is such an important activity that it leads to positions involving six-figure salaries. Store ownership can mean even greater earning potential. It is important that the requirements for retail selling, the techniques for serving customers, and the methods for handling special retail selling problems be understood. Sometimes industrial sales representatives serve walk-in trade and should, therefore, be acquainted with in-store methods (see Photo 17.1).

Requirements

Successful retail selling requires complete stock knowledge, store policy knowledge, and a tactful, service-oriented sales personality. Salespersons should be prepared not only to present the merchandise to customers but to care for stock, watch for thefts, wrap packages, keep records, make reports, give information and directions, handle returns, and deal with customer grievances.

Floor sales personnel sometimes send customers away with "I'm sorry we don't have that in stock" or "I don't think we carry that," when the product is available in inventory. It is important to know all the benefits of all the stock and to be able to demonstrate every product whose application is not obvious. The challenge of answering customers' questions about a variety of products can be met by salespersons who study their merchandise.

Customers often complain about merchandise, return products, or ask for special favors. Salespersons must know all about lay-away, discounts, credit, check cashing, returns, delivery, exchange, and special-request handling policies of their firms. A store might, for example, have a policy of meeting prices of all competitors when proof (for example, a newspaper advertisement) is given. A salesperson must know how to handle and record these special sales and how to manage other recurring situations.

Retail sales personnel help to create the image of a store. Their dress, appearance, and behavior are always important. Customers return to friendly, helpful representatives who know their merchandise and their customers. Retail salespersons must have extra tact and patience, must be willing to listen to angry customers, and must know how to suggest merchandise without seeming to pressure customers.

The selling situation requires perception of needs and adjustment of presentations to serve widely differing personality types. An attitude of prompt service is essential.

Techniques for Serving Customers

Since most retail salespersons have little opportunity to prospect outside the store or place of business, nearly every person who enters the establishment must be regarded as a potential buyer. A salesperson should notice and eval-

uate nonverbal communications immediately—appearance (especially clothes), apparent mood, walking speed, and focus of attention. Some customers come to look and should not be approached too rapidly. Others are in a hurry and want immediate service. Some want to bargain and appear disinterested when they really are interested. Some come in to complain or to assert their egos. Many come in with the intention of getting more information and making a purchase.

The Approach. Customers who simply want to look may leave early if approached too aggressively by a salesperson. Their body language—evading eye contact and leisurely browsing without indicating any need for assistance—indicates that they want to consider the merchandise without pressure. A salesperson should be available but should not insist on dogging a browser's footsteps. Most of the time, however, it is good practice to offer service. It is important to smile. "May I help you?" is a standard approach that indicates a service attitude but is weak from overuse. The temptation for the customer is to say: "No, I'm just looking." "Is there something I can show you?" is more suggestive and may receive an answer pointing to the customer's needs. "Good afternoon, Mrs. Jones, may I help you today?" has a personal touch. Customers feel important if their names are remembered. With this approach, politeness and a service attitude are shown as well. If you know the customer well, it may be best to be less formal by calling him or her by the first name. First name use should be limited to those customers who have invited you to use their first name. A very good approach is to draw near a customer who, by body language, appears interested, and say something meaningful about the product the customer is inspecting: "Customers tell us those pants are very comfortable, and this is the first time they've been offered on special," or "This car is not only beautiful—but it has gotten over 25 miles per gallon in mileage tests," or "That blue coat certainly would look good on you. Here, let me help you slip it on." It is usually better to say something than to just follow a customer around without saying anything. Always think about your body language when approaching a customer. Convey genuine interest and pleasure at being able to be of service. When customers are in an obvious hurry, approach them promptly and respect their lack of time.

Retail Presentation. After the approach greeting, it is usually best for a retail salesperson to remain silent and listen carefully to the customer's response. If a customer indicates a desire to know more about a product, an explanation of benefits is called for. The more you can customize benefits to the customer's needs and match customer self-image with product image, the more likely you are to get a buying response. It is sometimes good strategy to admit faults in merchandise to win the prospect's confidence. This is especially true when dealing with a more intelligent clientele. If clothing does not look well on a customer—doesn't match eyes, hair, and/or complexion—or if a customer's dislike of an item is obvious, a salesperson might explain that there is something better and show that to the customer. There are two important things to remember when dealing with customers: Always attempt to get customers to try on or try out the product, and handle the product as if it were valuable (unless you are demonstrating durability). The customer who touches a product or takes part in a demonstration tends to feel possession and is usually more convinced about its worth. If a product is handled as if it were valuable, value will be conveyed to the customer. Show the product against the proper background and describe it in words that convey image. "You would be proud to get the morning paper or even welcome guests into your home, wearing this robe."

An important question in retail selling is whether a customer should be shown expensive merchandise, middle-range merchandise, or less expensive merchandise first. Nonverbal signals such as clothes and other appearance cues can indicate what level should be shown. It is best, however, to listen to customers and to bring out the quality level of merchandise expressly requested. If a prospect does not voice a preference, you can trade either up or down if you show merchandise in the middle range. Usually, it is best to start with merchandise of slightly higher than average quality. Quality merchandise is remembered after price is forgotten. More profit is gained from higher-priced merchandise.

It is important to ask questions to determine customer needs, but be careful about what you ask. Asking questions about the intended use of the product is safer than asking questions about specific styles, colors, or sizes unless an almost limitless selection is available. Recommendations of available products can come from responses to questions like these: "For what kind of occasion do you want this dress?" or "How do you intend to use your boat?" or "What kind of materials do you need to glue together?"

Good retail strategy is to allow customer choice, but *limited choice.* Help the prospect to decide by narrowing down the selection between one available item and another.

Closing. Retail salespersons should close early and often and watch for closing signals. Customers often give their intentions away by the questions they ask and the ways they look at or handle merchandise. A customer who keeps coming back to a product, who compares it with other products, or who concentrates interest on a particular product is usually ready to be asked for an order. Trial closes such as: "That looks good on you, doesn't it?" or "Isn't that a pretty color?" should also help in timing the request for an order. Choice closes, minor-points closes, and assumptive closes are especially good. "Do you prefer the four-door sedan or the elegant model with bucket

"I lose more customers that way!"

THE SATURDAY EVENING POST

It is also important for the retail salesperson to have control of a demonstration.

seats?" or "Would you like to add both the blue and the gray suits to your wardrobe?" or "Having your initials on that suitcase will help keep it from getting mixed up with someone else's. May I write it up for you?" or "May I gift wrap this for you?" The assumptive close must be done with skill and at the proper time, or customers could resent the closing effort and become resistive.

Suggestion Selling. A retail sales representative can increase sales substantially by suggesting a greater quantity of merchandise or additional merchandise that may be used with the product or products just purchased. New merchandise, items like ties and shirts that complement a new suit, merchandise on special sale, and merchandise that is obviously needed are often suggested. A service-station employee who asks: "Fill 'er up?" is practicing suggestion selling. This same alert employee may inspect the vehicle for deficiencies such as a dirty air filter, low oil, low transmission fluid, treadless tires, a weak battery, or burned-out lights and suggest that these problems be corrected. Not only will the station get more business, but the customer will travel more safely.

Salespersons should consider that most retail products suggest other products that might be needed:

- We will be glad to write up a homeowner's policy on this new house.
- A racket cover and press will protect your new racket.
- This tie is great with your new suit, isn't it?
- With this grass catcher to go with your new lawnmower, you'll have instant fertilizer available for your mulch bed.
- Why not buy a dozen golf balls, and get a 20 percent discount?
- At this sale price, would you like to take a second pair of shoes?
- How about some extra batteries? It could save you a trip back.
- If you buy two of these smoke detectors, you can get a discount on your home insurance.

Sometimes nothing need be said. To suggest purchase, a salesperson simply brings out a tie, or shirt, and puts it up against the suit the customer has just purchased—the customer will usually make a comment. While forcing unwanted merchandise on customers is wrong and may endanger future business, it is just as wrong to let customers leave without suggesting that their total needs can be fulfilled through offerings. A customer shouldn't have to go down the street to look for a blouse or other accessories to go with a new skirt because the obvious need to match it was unmet. You will nearly always sell more if you practice suggestion selling. You can also increase customer satisfaction in this way.

Postsale Courtesy. Thank customers whether they buy or not. Each customer is a walking advertisement for or against the retailing establishment you represent. In most retail situations, it is much less important for you to lose a sale than for you to lose a customer—and all the other people that customer is likely to influence. Before a customer leaves, he or she should know how to operate and use the product to get maximum satisfaction from it. Too many buyers leave a store and come back to complain that a product failed to live up to expectations, because they were never shown how to care for it and operate it properly.

Retail Selling Problems

Retail salespersons face challenges that require patience, perception, and intelligence. The following problems arise in many retail selling situations: (1) serving two or more customers at the same time; (2) serving customers who shop with friends or relatives who advise; (3) handling out-of-stocks; (4) handling returned merchandise and complaints; (5) turning over customers to more experienced salespersons.

Serving Two or More Customers at a Time. At rush times or when others are on a break, a retail salesperson may be called on to serve more than one customer at a time. The customer on whom you are waiting has first right to your time, and you should continue to serve that customer fully (in most circumstances), unless he or she indicates that it is permissible for you to give attention to a new customer. If you are convinced that your present customer needs more time to look and consider and a new customer seems impatient and neglected, you might *ask* permission: "Would you mind if I take just a moment and show him where he can find the sports coats in his size?" It is always good practice to show you are aware of a new customer you see waiting. You might say: "Someone will be with you in a little while." Never make your present customer feel rushed or pressured into leaving without deciding. If another salesperson is immediately available, the new customer should be waited on by him or her. Skilled salespersons can often handle two or more customers at a time if each is in a different phase of a purchase. This way customers feel less pressure, and all customers get enough attention. This is better than having customers leave the store because of inability to get service, even when they know what they want. When two or more customers are waiting, a salesperson should keep track of who is next, because customers can become angry if not served in turn.

Handling Customers Who Shop with Friends and Relatives. It is usually easier to talk to interested customers without the presence of third parties. While husbands or wives sometimes will not buy style goods without the opinion of the other, it is nearly always harder to sell to two people than to just one. The advice of friends is usually against buying. If a third party is steered to look at other merchandise or if another salesperson can occupy his or her interest, your chances of making a sale are usually better. If necessary, give the friend attention and watch for closing signals from both. If the friend says, "I like that on you, Susie," it is a perfect time to close. If a friend or relative sells with you rather than against you, you have an important ally in making the sale. Both customer and adviser must be catered to. Sometimes leading questions like, "Doesn't that look good on her?" get positive participation from advisers.

Handling Out-of-Stocks. Few stores can satisfy all customers' direct requests for merchandise. In most cases it is better to express regret, show a near substitute, and/or promise to order the item requested by customers if they are willing to wait for it. Some salespersons even tell customers of a competitive store (often one not in direct competition) where an out-of-stock item can be purchased. This kind of unselfish service is usually noted and wins customer confidence. If you are out of an item and the substitute available is just as good or better, you should try to persuade the customer to buy the acceptable alternative. But selling a product that will not serve the customer's purposes injures goodwill. If you are out of merchandise too often, you will lose customers permanently, since they will form the image that the store is always "out of everything." Tell the buyer who is responsible for ordering about merchandise frequently requested but not in stock. Being out of merchandise advertised on special is particularly image-destructive. An acceptable, available substitute should always be suggested. Above all, customers should never to made to feel ignorant or embarrassed for having asked for an out-of-stock item.

Handling Returned Merchandise and Complaints. Proper handling of these problems is essential to increasing business. You must first know the policy of the store—some stores will even exchange merchandise bought in another store. The main thing to be remembered is to serve the customer's needs within store policy with as much pleasantness as possible. Customers stay away from salespersons who make exchanges and returns grudgingly. If you are eager to serve return and exchange customers and treat them as courteously as you treat present prospects, they will remember and come back to you. You have successfully reduced their risks in buying. Listen to customers with a complaint. They have "honored" you by telling you what is wrong, given you an opportunity to reestablish a good relationship, and helped you correct something that might offend other customers. After all, it is the customer who never returns but complains to friends and relatives who hurts retail trade.

Turning Over Customers to More Experienced Salespersons. Retail selling is a team effort at times. Your image may clash with some prospects. They may not identify with you because of your age, sex, or size. More often, you may not have the knowledge they require about particular merchandise. You may simply not be able to make a sale with the prospect for some reason. If you realize that you can't close and you feel that another salesperson could make the sale, tactfully turn the customer over with a statement such as, "Mrs. Lacy, I would like you to speak to Mrs. James about that problem. She is our expert on antique furniture" or "I would like you to speak with our buyer [another salesperson who also buys]. I believe she can order for you exactly what you want."

Closing Comments

The key elements of success in retail selling are customer needs recognition, product knowledge, cheerfulness and enthusiasm, a genuine attitude of helpfulness, and honest service. An important test to apply is: Would you want to come back and buy again from someone who treated a customer as you did?

INDUSTRIAL SELLING

Most of the selling methods and examples covered in previous chapters apply to industrial selling. However, because industrial sales is such an important job alternative for college students and because there are some differences in emphasis and procedure, separate consideration is given here. Industrial sales representatives sell major equipment and installations, accessory equipment, services, raw materials, and operating supplies to businesses, institutions, and governments. This type of selling usually requires salespersons to go to prospects to create interest. Often, there are a limited number of important customers buying significant dollar amounts of products, after careful, rational deliberations. Quite often, too, there are several persons the salesperson has to satisfy before an important industrial sale is made. Installation, operator training, maintenance, delivery, and other services may be furnished with a tangible product and are important parts of the offering. Because of these characteristics, the market commands high-level and expensive sales personnel, requires certain customized selling techniques, and generates particular selling problems that must be solved.

Requirements

The educational and personality requirements for industrial salespersons are high because these reps are the points of contact between an important supplier and important buyers. Moreover, the product lines offered may be technical and complex. Since there are often just a few prospects, each must be carefully cultivated, and each must have a favorable image of the supplying firm. Often, many departments of the prospective corporation are involved in a purchase decision. Then, it becomes necessary for the salesperson to understand all aspects of a buying firm's operations. Because of these characteristics, the higher dollar amount involved, and the fewer orders generated, there is usually stress in each selling situation. Usually, complex proposals are necessary. Technical knowledge of a prospect's business problems and product applications to solve them can be extensive. Customers have great respect for industrial salespersons. Many consider them professional consultants, particularly when thousands of dollars of capital goods are purchased. It is not hard to understand why good industrial salespersons command high compensation. It is difficult to find people who have personalities that can project the best image for a firm and who have the educational backgrounds necessary to sell complex products.

Selling Techniques

Prospects and Preapproaching. Industrial sales representatives should know the characteristics of firms that might need their product and locate such firms in their territories. Change is often the key to need. Expansion plans, new-product promotions, operation and equipment changes, and changes in personnel may indicate new requirements for industrial products. Salespersons should cultivate people inside firms to learn when new industrial purchases are being contemplated, or call on customers often enough to be considered when the need arises. Good preapproach information about the financial, operating, and policy characteristics of prospective firms is strategic to successful approach planning. It is especially good to know the buying policies and the names of all personnel who might be brought in on a particular buying decision. Receptionists and secretaries may volunteer contact information, but if the representative goes through the purchasing agent or a top corporate official, it may be necessary to ask permission to contact certain other members of the buying team.

The Approach. Industrial sales representatives often sell prospects on doing studies of operations to see if there are problems and opportunities for new techniques and products. An approach might be: "Mr. Hartly, Alamo Corporation has a new metal-stamping machine that has increased the speed of operations like yours by as much as 30 percent. May I have your permission to meet with your engineers and study your exact procedures? This equipment could save your firm thousands of dollars each year and speed your products to your customers," or "In one minute this new chemical will clean surfaces that required thirty minutes under the old process. May I show you exactly how it works?" Industrial approaches are usually rational and to the point so that important executive time is not wasted.

The Presentation.   Presentations are seldom made without study and material preparation. Although sales are frequently made by appealing to emotional motives (especially pride), nearly every sale must be justified by practical considerations. Every industrial salesperson must remember that persons on the buying team are looking at the product in light of what it will do for them individually—will it help their positions in the company? How will it help them by helping the company? Presentations are often made before several persons with the help of prepared visual aids such as films and portfolios. All applications and benefits must be customized to fit the needs of the buying firm. Often an important part of the presentation is the explanation of a detailed problem-solution proposal well justified by cost and benefit figures.

Closing.   The standard closes all work well in industrial selling—even closing on a minor point. An excellent close for equipment and other complex products is the choice close. Prospects become absorbed in selecting between alternatives within a salesperson's line of products and may lead themselves into a purchase. "Either of these machines, Ms. Landry, will do an excellent job in all four applications. This one is capable of generating two extra reports, while this one is slightly less expensive. Which one would you prefer?" The assumptive close is also widely used: "We could deliver this model within ten days. Is that all right?" With capital and accessory equipment, stimulus-response and summary closes are also popular, because there are so many features and benefits to talk about. Because so much money is involved in many industrial deals, the special offer is often used. "We have a demonstrator model of this machine that's never been 'out of the wrapper'—it just has a lower serial number and has been declared a demonstrator on that basis. It's available for 15 percent less than the price on the proposal, but we have only one. I'm sure it won't be here long. Can I deliver it to you this week?" After a lengthy, technical presentation, the close is often assumed by a prospect. Some industrial sales representatives claim that they seldom have to ask for an order, because prospects usually comment at the end of the interview when detailed proposals are presented. A tested closing method is still the best strategy. (See Chapter 13 for more about industrial sales closings.)

Industrial Selling Problems

There are four main industrial selling problems: (1) getting in to see the right prospect, (2) selling against competition, (3) reciprocity, and (4) delivery. Getting in to see the right prospect in the beginning has already been treated. Selling against competition is critical because of the longer negotiation time and the importance of considering all alternatives on large capital or long-term purchases. The competitive effectiveness of the salesperson depends on the professional image presented, knowledge of the product, relative advantages over competitors and competitor deficiencies, and the time span between prospect problem recognition and the close. Reciprocity or the obligation to purchase from another firm must also be met with proof of the relative superiority of the salesperson's product. Delivery is a problem, because complex products that are custom-made or programmed take time to be prepared for specific prospects, and prospects want the products as soon after the orders are signed as possible. The best practice in most instances is to explain to buyers exactly why a product requires a specified delivery time and to assure that everything necessary to deliver it as soon as possible will be done. Sometimes normal delivery channels can be bypassed if a sale depends on it. Reps should know the facts and tell the truth.

International Industrial Selling: A Special Case

Like their domestic counterparts, international industrial sales representatives sell major equipment and installations, accessory equipment, services, raw materials, and operating supplies to businesses, institutions, and governments. Unlike those who call on prospects in the domestic environment, international sales reps must deal with differences in language and currency, political and legal uncertainties, and different kinds of wants and needs in addition to all the usual tasks of industrial selling.

Americans tend to forget what a cosmopolitan people they are. Yet, Americans are readily identifiable abroad by their many shared traits. Nationals of other countries see Americans as more alike than different from one another.

Most Americans do not know how powerful a seller and buyer the United States is in international markets. Americans are the world's largest international traders. No other country sells so much abroad as the United States. No other country buys so much. Unfortunately for the United States balance of trade—the difference between payments for what Americans sell abroad and what they buy there—more is bought than sold. The high level of living in the United States and the scales of business opportunity that level makes possible, together with a traditional commitment to free trade, have made the United States an attractive market for foreign companies.

Despite its preeminence as the world's largest international trader, the international marketings of the United States account for somewhat less than 7 percent of the gross national product. The American market is so vast and so rich that historically most Americans businesses have found it easier and less risky to do their selling and buying at home. The increasing integration of the world's markets has meant the U.S. market has become part of a global system where the old barriers of time, space, and technology no longer protect domestic businesses from outside competitors.

As international selling has become more competitive, American companies have found that they must look beyond domestic markets for prospects. Few products are thought of as so American as Coca Cola, yet nearly two-thirds of Coke's profits originate outside the United States. Americans sometimes speak of the mixture of their national backgrounds as "Heinz 57 Varieties." H. J. Heinz does more business outside the United States than in it. Ford Motor Company may be Coke's only true rival for the title of "The Business as American as Apple Pie." Yet, its Fiesta had its engine built in England and its transmission in France, its wheels came from Belgium, its carburetor, distributor, and plugs came from Ulster, and it was assembled variously in West Germany, Spain, and Great Britain! (Apple pie, incidentally, is a dish imported from England.)

America has always been a big seller and buyer in international markets. Without foreign sales, there would have been no Armour or Swift meatpacking giants. Without foreign sales, the American grain belt would still be home to the buffalo and might well still be labeled the "Great American Desert" on maps.

The prime American salesperson of all time may have been Frederic Tudor of Boston. Tudor turned the heavy winters of New England to profit. In 1805, when he was barely twenty-one, Tudor reacted to a whimsical suggestion of a brother that the ice on New England ponds could be easily sold in the ports of the Caribbean by developing an export ice industry. By 1833, Tudor was selling ice in Calcutta. To create a demand for cold products, Tudor sold America on the refreshing value of the iced drink.

Like Tudor, contemporary business executives have discovered that they must do it themselves if they are to succeed in selling foreign markets. The sales force makes up the bulk of people employed in foreign positions. It is international sales reps and their managers who deal most directly with overseas customers and governments.

London, Paris, Tokyo, Rio de Janeiro, have an exotic lure about them. It's fascinating to find that corn on the cob is served as an hors d'oeuvre in the United Kingdom and cornflakes as a dessert in Scandinavia and Northern Germany. It comes as something of a surprise to most Americans when they find that the average Frenchman uses twice as many cosmetics and beauty aids as his wife. Blue is a most masculine color in Sweden, but it is considered feminine in Holland. The circumlocutions of the Japanese frustrate American sales reps—it's hard to know if a Japanese prospect is tending toward yes or no. The closer physical proximity South Americans are used to in interpersonal contacts makes most Americans uncomfortable. Italians wave goodbye with the same gesture that Americans use to signal someone to come closer. In the Orient, the signal to come closer would be waving goodbye to most Americans.

The sales rep stationed abroad must possess a degree of insight to deal with the cultural differences between what took place at home and what is found in the host country. It is this insight that may be the special something that makes a successful international sales representative. In addition to this extra someting, the international sales rep must be a skilled salesperson. Foreign prospects find the quality of American goods and their prices competitive with those of the United States's major sales rivals, West Germany and Japan. Where American businesses fall down is in quality of selling effort.

There is an apocryphal tale current in international trade circles that illustrates the view foreign prospects have of American efforts to sell abroad. It concerns the Brazilian enterprise that wanted to buy a hydroelectric plant. Based on product quality desires, the Brazilians selected firms in the United States, the United Kingdom, the Federal Republic of Germany, and Japan. Inquiries were sent to each of the four firms. The Spanish-speaking export sales manager of the American firm failed to answer. The British firm sent sales literature in Spanish. (The language of Brazil is Portuguese.) The West German firm did a massive and sophisticated feasibility study and built a scale replica to demonstrate how its technology would present a near-perfect solution to the prospect's problems and on completion of both rushed a sales team to call on the prospect. The team arrived to find their Japanese rivals departing with payment for the completed project. The moral of the story is that successful international industrial sales representatives must avoid American indifference, take more care with prospect identification than the British, be as thorough in product knowledge as the Germans, and as fast as the Japanese.

Closing Comments

International industrial selling requires great effort from sales reps in every respect. The problems are more complex than in most selling jobs, but the pay is usually higher and the opportunities are increasing.

SELLING INTANGIBLES

Insurance, investments, services, ideas, and images represent intangible offerings that touch the lives of everyone. The lack of a tangible product need not handicap the creative salesperson. Actually, the opportunity to build visualizations and images in the mind of the prospect is greater, because no definite picture already exists. Because an intangible product does not command the attention of the potential buyer, the personality and communication ability of the sales representative become very important. A professional image builder who can sell an idea commands high rewards.

Selling techniques used in selling intangibles are generally like those in other selling situations. The emphasis is on making sure the prospect can visualize the offering benefits. This is even true in life insurance. When buyers purchase a policy, they are reinforcing their present self-image of providing amply for loved ones in the event of death. Visual aids that show what could happen if insurance is not purchased (fire burning up a home) or charts that illustrate the benefits from buying certain investments substitute for a tangible in a presentation. Because the salesperson can show what could happen if an intangible were bought, the prospect can imagine extremes that, while not likely to happen, could happen. This furnishes important motives for buying. Pressure to buy now instead of later should be built into presentations in some way. Generally, life insurance costs more per year as the prospect becomes older. House or health insurance when not in force leaves a prospect unprotected. Investments cannot earn interest when not possessed. Ideas do not materialize unless supported by acceptance of an offer. Elements should also be included in closing to get buyers to make decisions now instead of putting them off.

PUBLIC RELATIONS

Public relations differs from other persuasive fields in its techniques and is growing in importance and providing an increasing number of positions for educated young adults. Public relations includes those activities designed to sell corporate images and build good relationships with all organizational publics. Organizational publics include such groups as the public at large, customers, employees, stockholders, and legislators. Public relations is selling an intangible, organizational image and goodwill to everyone able to influence the success of an organization. Some representative must see to it that an organization's reputation is maintained and enhanced by interpreting feedback from publics and promoting policies and communications designed to advance organizational progress. Public relations will be discussed under the following headings:

- Gaining internal cooperation
- Communication methods in public relations
- Dealing persuasively with specific publics

Gaining Internal Cooperation

The image and reputation of an institution are influenced by every person connected with it. A basic function of a public-relations representative is to sell the importance of promoting the institution to both management and employees and to secure cooperation in protecting and projecting a good impression. This can be accomplished through good internal communications—meetings with managers and employees, house publications, posters, and other methods that might impress all personnel with the importance of promoting the enterprise's good name. A P.R. representative sometimes must make suggestions to top management personnel who may be undermining employee morale through poor policies or careless public statements. A company executive might say: "My company comes first and the country's energy problem second," damaging the firm and the industry's image. Since many executives outrank public-relations specialists, P.R. people must be diplomatic and creative. Forwarding, without comment, resulting press clippings appraising such a speech may impress an erring executive with the gravity of unguarded statements. Employees, too, should become P.R. conscious. A bulletin board slogan such as: "What people think of Dell Company affects its sales. The good impression you make for our company is important" is an example of a public-relations communication to get everyone behind the vital image-selling effort.

Communication Methods in Public Relations

Advertising, audio-visual aids, organizational publications, speeches, pre-staged events, and publicity are important communication methods associated with building an institution's reputation. Every good public-relations specialist must be skilled in using them.

Advertising.   Public-relations representatives work with advertising specialists inside and outside the firm to help in developing themes, identifying promotable organizational features, and approving ad campaign plans and copy details (see Figure 17.1). Energy companies, for example, often use the media to correct mistaken ideas about their profits and operations. Corporations frequently explain how their products benefit society, increase standards of liv-

The Electric Economy requires four vital resources. Technology's one.

America is on its way to the Electric Economy. And The Southern Company has the resources needed to get there.

The fuel. The management. The investors. And the technology.

Our technological experts are at work pioneering a process called solvent refining* — removing pollutants from coal before it's burned. This could be the best way to make full use of the country's most abundant fossil fuel.

The Southern Company has the other three resources, too.

The fuel: Coal already generates more than 80 percent of the electricity produced by the four operating companies in the Southern electric system.

The management: The system's management is continually looking for new cost- and energy-saving techniques, like introducing energy-efficient home building concepts to help customers reduce their electric costs.

The investors: The Southern Company has over 294,000 common stockholders. Investment dollars like theirs help build the facilities for the operating companies' customers.

The Southern Company: The company with the resources to meet the demands of the Electric Economy.

The Southern Company
P.O. Box 720071
Atlanta, Georgia 30346

Southern Company

the southern electric system

Alabama Power Company
Georgia Power Company
Gulf Power Company,
Mississippi Power Company
Southern Company Services, Inc.

Coal. **Management.** **Capital.**

Figure 17.1

ing, strengthen the free-enterprise system, and even help to save lives. Some advertising is public relations in nature.

Audio-Visual Aids. The P.R. representative often originates and coordinates the production of films, photographs, and records that dramatize an ideal organizational image. A university, for example, might find through research that location and size, curriculum offerings, reputation for quality, ability to help students get financial aid, favorable social climate, and physical facilities are its most important features and seek to promote these benefits in a film for high school students and their parents. Questions that might help identify P.R. "selling" points include: How does an organization benefit an area economically, culturally, and environmentally? How does it contribute to quality of life? How do its employees serve the community? Scenes and sounds that best convey these benefits must then be captured on films, tapes, and in records, with the P.R. representative planning their coordination with presentation opportunities. The representative should also suggest executive actions and institutional improvements that will enhance an organization's reputation with its publics. Many films sell the organization less directly by treating topics of public interest under firm sponsorship.

Organizational Publications. Company newspapers and magazines can reach beyond the internal organization and help in forming favorable public opinion in the community at large. Wider public readership is fostered by including content of general interest and mailing the material to such publics as legislators, who are in a position to help promote organizational interests. Articles originating in internal publications are often sent to and republished by newspapers, where they receive free favorable publicity. P.R. representatives often help to shape the image-building content of annual reports, stockholder magazines, and customer publications. People form their impressions by all contacts they have with an organization.

Speeches. Civic organizations, schools, clubs, and other groups ask for and welcome speakers recruited from organization executives, staff, and workers. Public-relations representatives may organize intrafirm conferences, speakers' bureaus, and lobbying efforts. An organization may be set up to select and train speakers, to furnish speech guidelines to ensure that good images are projected, and to coordinate speaking engagements. The public-relations staff is expected to influence and guide personnel representing an organization in public.

Prestaged Events. Public-relations staffs arrange plant tours, employee social functions, special days, awards, dedications, parade participations, and sporting events. Universities have special visitation days such as High School Seniors' Day, ROTC Day, and Band Day, when prospective students can come and form impressions of the school and its atmosphere. Manufacturers invite the public on plant tours to impress them with the care, cleanliness, and efficiency of their manufacturing methods. Whenever the public is invited, someone must make sure that property and personnel are ready to receive guests and put the institution in a good light. The coordination of such events by public-relations representatives should produce a favorable, low-key persuasive impact.

Publicity. Publicity is usually free. It can be influenced by public-relations representatives. The representative can foster "good press" by meeting with reporters, writers, and editors to assure that all favorable acts receive good coverage. Sending in photographs and edited news stories, inviting the press to special events, and seeing that expansion plans or plans involving other changes that affect the community are expressed properly are all within the functions of P.R. Releases should be newsworthy, truthful, concise, interestingly written, and timely. When reporters seek information about events that could harm institutional image, it is better to see them and to try to influence them to print the institution's side to keep damage to a minimum. Reporters seldom kill an unfavorable story but may well accept an institution's view of a situation if it is an honest one. Press conferences, press dinners, news releases, and frequent contacts with important press representatives are ways of assuring that the press is informed and image-building coverage will be received.

Dealing Persuasively with Specific Publics

Corporations and other organizations have employees, customers, stockholders (owners), suppliers, governments, universities, and the public in general to consider as their influencing publics. Public-relations representatives should be familiar with the interests of each public and the methods by which each may be persuaded that an enterprise is a valuable community member.

Employees. Employees want to feel that they are an important part of an organization and that their organization plays a valuable role in public welfare. They want to feel "included" and especially want to be informed about changes that affect them. They want to be sure that their voice is heard when complaints are justified. Denied information, employees sometimes rely on distorted sources—the grapevine or the rumor mill. Information given to employees should be truthful and clear. It can be communicated by several methods. Planned meetings, house organs, public-address systems, letters, bulletin boards, and personal visits by superiors—all are media for spreading important news. Employees' opinions should be solicited by questionnaires, suggestion boxes, editorial space in the company newspaper, committee meetings, and executive access. All of the firm's officials should be good listeners, just like public-relations representatives, and the "presentation" to sell the firm's image and team spirit should include information and assurances through the best communications media available.

Customers. Customers want good products and service and are the heartbeat of profit-making institutions. When they contact a corporation, make inquiries, or express complaints, they should be given much more than just passive consideration. Customers "spread the word" about a corporation and influence prospects for the firm's products. Nonprofit firms should be just as responsible to the publics they serve as profit enterprises. As information on new products or new safety information becomes available, customers should be informed by direct mail, advertising media, or other channels. Customers should be encouraged to visit plants. Word of mouth by satisfied customers and good reputation with the consuming public are valuable assets that should be promoted by the P.R. representative.

Stockholders. Stockholders want accurate, truthful information about their investments. Corporations want their stockholders to be convinced that the organization is doing an efficient job in maintaining investor interests. Public-relations representatives should know what kind of people own stock in a corporation and should be personally acquainted with big-block investors such as security analysts, bank-investment officers, and insurance-investment officials who require information from stock-issuing organizations. Annual reports, annual stockholders' meetings, letters, personal visits (to important investors), and tours help to keep stockholders in contact. Stockholders not only help finance an enterprise and vote on its officers and policies but are also prime customers for products.

Suppliers. Suppliers furnish raw materials and other inputs for businesses and are sometimes in a position to allocate their scarce materials in ways that affect organizational survival. Suppliers' sales representatives should be treated with respect—almost any buyers' market can turn into a sellers' market on short notice. Organizations should invite important suppliers to visit the plant and to understand operations so they can serve the organization's interests better. Communications between suppliers and firms should be made more routine. Visits to suppliers' plants also foster two-way communication and better understanding. Suppliers will give better service to and cultivate customers who do not demand excessive service, pay their bills on time, and treat their representatives well when they come to call.

Governments. Government regulations are an increasing consideration for all businesses. Public-relations representatives may advise in lobbying matters or personally participate in persuasive efforts to gain support with local, state, or national legislators. Government bureau personnel who feel that a firm is not complying with employment or reporting laws can seriously affect organizational survival. Such inspecting personnel should always be welcomed and treated cordially on visits to a company. Information should be given to them on request. One of the important functions of public relations is to maintain a good public image and so discourage efforts to pass new legislation that could be damaging.

Universities. Colleges and schools are the nesting places for the "publics" of the future. Research bureau personnel, academic consultants, and teachers are in a position to help the organization through research and suggestion. These researchers and student influencers should be received cordially by the organization's officers and given appropriate information for their research when it is requested. Corporations furnish many kinds of teaching aids to build good relations with this public. Classes can be taken through a plant on field trips, organizational speakers can serve as guest lecturers at schools, and company literature can be given for distribution to classes. Scholarships are often contributed by organizations to deserving students, to increase public and student interest in the firm.

The Public in General. Large organizations can establish favorable images with the general public by sponsoring community athletic teams, helping to build and maintain parks, and initiating cultural programs. P.R. representatives and the firm's officers should encourage employees to get involved in community affairs and organizations. Corporations should help keep the local environment healthy and clean. Open houses, plant tours, employee speeches, and other community-serving events cost time and money but pay dividends through enlarged public support. They make people feel that the organization is a contributing part of the community. P.R. representatives must be creative in devising effective ways to gain public support.

Closing Comments

Public relations requires a diplomatic persuader who influences others through an image-reflecting personality and various devices that directly or indirectly cast the organization in a favorable light. Creativity and leadership must be shown to influence employee groups to sell the institution. Selling image involves using visual aids, communicating with advertising media, and dealing carefully with several publics. While public relations does not usually require strenuous closing efforts, it does require the use of social sensitivity and tact.

SUMMARY

There are many different kinds of sales jobs open to aspirants who want to use their personalities persuasively. Four different selling fields have been treated in this chapter to give the student a better idea of how methods and requirements vary.

Retail selling can lead to lucrative positions in commission sales, store management, and store ownership. Retail salespersons should know their merchandise and present it cheerfully with a service attitude. Most retail approaches should exhibit a spirit of helpfulness and use questions and suggestions that are designed to find customer needs. Offering customers a limited choice among merchandise items and suggesting additional products are keys to increased sales. Retail selling problems include handling more than one customer at a time, handling customers' friends who advise, handling out-of-stocks, complaints, and the turnover of certain customers to more experienced salespersons.

Industrial selling requires a highly professional sales image and extensive knowledge of product applications to prospect problems. Sales often require rational justification, detailed proposals, and selling to more than one person. Gaining access to the right person, overcoming competition, selling against reciprocity arrangements, and effecting timely delivery of a product are standard problems encountered by most industrial salespersons.

Intangibles, which include insurance, investments, services, ideas, concepts, and images, provide opportunities for salespersons to build visualizations and images in the minds of prospects. Sales representatives selling intangibles must possess personal qualities and communication abilities that can make the difference since competitive offerings may be similar.

Public-relations positions require creativity in selling institutional images, but high-pressure closing is not usually necessary. Public-relations representatives should be able to write persuasive letters, press releases, and advertisements; to edit publications, films, and speeches; and to influence the many publics of the corporation diplomatically.

1. List some of the major differences between retail selling and industrial selling.

2. List the duties of the retail salesperson.

3. Into which categories can potential retail customers be placed?

4. How does closing fit into the retail sales presentation?

5. Explain the term "suggestion selling". Why is it advantageous to use this approach?

6. List some of the specific problems that often arise in retail selling situations.

7. In retail selling, out-of-stock merchandise is a problem. What are some of the suggested approaches to handling this problem?

8. What are the four main problems in industrial selling?

9. Outline the special selling ideas associated with the selling of intangibles.

10. Explain what you understand by public relations.

11. List the communication methods used in public relations.

12. List the specific publics of concern to the public relations function of a corporation.

APPLICATION QUESTIONS

1. Asking questions aids in gaining attention and in determining motives. You are a salesperson working for a car dealer and a potential prospect walks in and begins looking at the cars. What are three good questions you could ask to determine the prospect's motives and what should you emphasize?

2. A prospect has just purchased a new suit from you. Using proper suggestion-selling techniques, suggest several items to the customer that would go with the new suit.

3. Suggest a strategy to deal with each of five retail selling problems presented in the text.

INCIDENTS

17–1

Sara Morgan needs help in finding merchandise and has been waiting for ten minutes for Elaine Winter to finish her conversation with her boyfriend. Jane Bloom, who is the floor manager, usually waits on Sara but is on another floor temporarily.

Elaine: What would you like?

Sara: Could you show me where to find suits in my size?

Elaine: What size are you, about a twenty?

Sara: No, I wear a sixteen. Do you have something for about $100?

Elaine: We don't have a good slection in that price range. Try this $200 rack. These suits would do much more for you than what you have on.

Sara: They do look good, but my budget is tight, and I need the suit to work in. Do you have any on special or on sale?

Elaine: No, I don't think so.

(Jane has entered the department and overheard the last two lines.)

Jane: Elaine, we do have some on the rack by the elevator . . . some $150 suits, which have been marked off a third. I'm sure that Mrs. Morgan would want to see those.

Elaine: I forgot about those, and these $200 suits will probably be reduced in August.

Sara: This one is my size.

Elaine: Why don't you buy it?

Sara: I'd like to try it on. *(later)* How does it look?

Elaine: Try this one on. I like it better.

Sara: That's not my size.

Elaine: Well, buy the one you have on. It's O.K. It looks better than what you have . . .

Sara: I would like to take it home and show it to my husband. Can I return it if he doesn't like it?

Elaine: Sure, if you don't get it dirty.

Sara: Do you have any accessories that might go with it?

Elaine: It's my off time now. Jane will write this up for you. Nice to meet you. Jane, will you help this lady?

Jane: I'll be glad to help Mrs. Morgan, Elaine. That is a beautiful suit you have selected, Mrs. Morgan. It goes well with your hair *(puts scarf and blouse against suit)*. Aren't this blouse and scarf pretty with it?

Sara: They certainly do go well with it.

Jane: Can I show you something else before I write these up?

Sara: No, this is fine.

Jane: The store has an excellent sale on shoes in our shoe department. Thank you for shopping at the Style Center again, Mrs. Morgan. I know you'll like your new clothes. Please excuse Elaine, she's new. Come back soon.

Sara: I always like to have you wait on me, Jane.

Insuring Future Opportunities

QUESTIONS

1. What retail selling mistakes did Elaine make?

2. What did Jane do correctly?

17–2

Joe Wilson is on top of the world! Here he is living in Paris and working in various European countries as a sales representative of the Bristol Tractor and Implement Co. Joe feels he owes getting his newly rented apartment in the *rue de Seine* on Paris's Left Bank to his proficiency in foreign languages. He is fluent in both Russian and German and speaks some French. Joe's Russian father and German mother had felt it important that each of their three sons have knowledge and understanding of the countries of their forebears. As a child, Joe had resented the instruction at home in the two languages, but he certainly is pleased about it now.

As a teenager, Joe's major interest had been in cars. He became quite a good mechanic, hanging around Sorel's Garage in his home town of New Braunfels, Texas. In fact, it was his interest in and ability with engines that had made him the star of his sales training class with Bristol. They had also helped to make him an effective and popular representative in the Kansas-Colorado territory he had covered for the three years since his graduation from Texas with a degree in marketing.

Joe had been told before being transferred to Paris that his eventual "beat" would be eastern Europe. As preparation for that assignment, Joe would work out of Bristol's Paris office for several months and travel with other reps who had been working in Europe for some time. Joe was even thinking of legally changing his name back to its original Russian form as a way of being more acceptable in eastern Europe. Wilson had been the closest English equivalent of a Russian surname most Americans found all but unpronounceable. Joe's French was passable. It had improved a lot in the two weeks he had been working in Paris at Bristol's big Right Bank office.

So sure is Joe that his language proficiency is the reason he was transferred from Wichita to Paris that it came as surprise to him when Bristol's European Sales Manager, M. André Fortier, a Frenchman, told him that the reason he has been selected for the European assignment is his product knowledge and mechanical aptitude.

Fortier explained that what Bristol really wants in its international representatives is thorough product knowledge and field experience. Understanding of languages and cultures is of secondary importance in doing business abroad, he said. Joe cannot really square this with his own ideas. He thinks American businesses have done less well abroad than they might have because so few Americans bother to study foreign languages or even geography. When he brought these points up with Fortier, the sales manager admitted that knowledge of languages and cultures does not hurt a rep, but he maintained that the essential quality foreign buyers of Bristol's equipment look for is technical expertise. After all, foreign buyers can get all they want of their own language and culture from their friends and acquaintances. What they cannot get from their fellow citizens is American agricultural know-how, which is what Bristol trains its reps to have together with knowledge of Bristol's product line.

Who—Joe or M. Fortier—seems the more correct in his view of the right qualities for a foreign sales representative?
Does it seem to you that lack of knowledge of foreign languages and cultures has hurt American business abroad? Can you cite any particular examples?

17–3

Marcia Gomez graduated with an average record and a marketing concentration from a New York–area community college. She was very popular at college and well liked by everyone. Her flair for getting along with all kinds of people and her attractive looks are important in her new job, a public-relations position with the Empire Metal Products Company. Marcia's superior and the head man at Empire Metal is Barry Morris. Morris hired Marcia because he realized that Empire Metal needed a better image with all of its publics, but especially with its employees. Labor problems have plagued the company since Morris has been president. Many of the workers are relatively uneducated, and Morris thought Marcia could start a house magazine and use other public-relations devices to help. Morris simply does not understand lower-level workers. He has a tendency to remain aloof, furnish workers with little information, and never side with employees in grievances and disputes. Union officials are particularly upset with Morris's attitude, and if he appears to have little time for the lower-level workers, he is openly hostile to union officials. The corporation has a high incidence of expensive labor turnover, although it pays better-than-average rates. Morris's attitudes often show up in his nonverbal communications and in statements he makes. He is very nice to Marcia and does not seem to regard her in the same way he sees lower-level workers because of her education and personality. Nearly all of Morris's tactless statements leak into the rumor mill that thrives in the Empire corporate atmosphere. In a recent address to a Rotary Club in the area, entitled "Industrial Problems in the New York Area," Morris said that his work force was inefficient because of the "dumb hired help I'm forced to employ." The speech was also blatantly anti-union and anti-government control. Word of the speech quickly reached the workers of Empire Metal Products, and Marcia is well aware that trouble is brewing in the firm.

How can Marcia persuade her boss to improve internal public relations in Empire Metal Products?
What public-relations tools can be used?

Selling Real Estate

Real estate is an exciting field offering many opportunities and challenges to innovative salespeople, who want to work in a particular geographic area. The opportunities arise from two particularly American characteristics: the tendency to move and the desire for a free-standing, individual family dwelling. The challenges come from the buyers and sellers in real-estate transactions and from the role played by the lending institutions that are part of nearly every real property transfer.

Most of the material in this chapter centers on residential real-estate sales. The major activities of most realtors are listing and selling residential real estate. Investment real estate—rental properties, commercial and industrial sites and buildings—is an exciting and challenging field. The successful seller of investment real estate must combine the knowledge of residential real-estate selling with the skills of an industrial sales rep and a stockbroker. The planning and analysis phases of the real-estate sales job take on added importance when a realtor deals in the investment market. Investment real-estate salespersons do not make as many sales as residential real-estate salespersons, but because of price differences, the financial rewards may be greater. Because most of those who deal in investment properties have done so by expanding from residential sales, further discussion of investment real-estate sales techniques follows the discussion of selling residential real estate.

To owners of real property, a real-estate broker sells the intangible services of ability to find and persuade a qualified buyer prospect and expertise to facilitate ownership transfer. To a prospective buyer, the broker sells not only

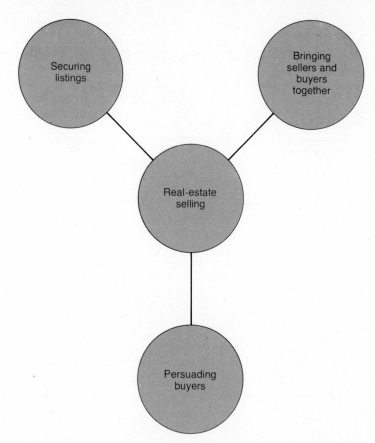

Figure 18.1

tangible, real property as an agent for the owner, but the broker also sells market knowledge that enables prospects to find the right property at the right price, advice on title transfer, and aid in arranging mortgage financing. Buyers and sellers use realtors because most feel unsure of their personal capacities to handle such a sizable and infrequent transaction as transferring property ownership.

Before any property can change hands—and a commission be earned—three separate "sales" must be made: (1) Owners must be sold on listing with a particular broker. (2) Buying prospects must be sold on making an offer. (3) A seller-owner must be sold either on accepting an offer to buy or on making a reasonable counteroffer (see Figure 18.1).

In the late 1970s and early 1980s, new challenges were added to the traditional ones of matching buyers with sellers and arranging financing. Rapidly rising interest rates and escalating prices based on land and construction-cost changes forced real-estate brokers into many new modes of behavior to survive. The shocks of these rapid changes place a new emphasis on mastery of the traditional real-estate sales skills so that real-estate sales reps can adapt to the dynamics of the changing real-estate market.

Real-estate salespersons must use diplomacy in getting sellers and buyers to compromise on any particular property. Usually, a great deal of money, sentiment, and emotion are involved in negotiations. Sellers are leaving a property that has been part of their lives and memories. Buyers are looking for a home or a working space that will serve the future. Because of the emotional involvement and risk involved, real-estate salespersons must be particularly good listeners who select words that build positive images. Salespeople must understand the legal requirements for exchanging real properly. Since real-estate agencies depend heavily on their reputations for success, salespersons must see that all transactions are ethical and fair to all parties.

Real-estate selling offers excellent financial potential for creative people willing to meet its challenges. A new salesperson usually goes to work as an apprentice to a licensed broker selling residential property. During this apprenticeship, the new agent receives valuable experience and a designated part of

The 1980s saw a dramatic shift in the long-run upward trends on which many real-estate sales careers had been based in preceding decades.

Reprinted from *The New Yorker*, January 8, 1979.

531

the broker's commission for each transaction. Some salespersons choose to stay with this arrangement and are given increasing responsibilities by brokers. Others enroll in special courses and take state examinations to become licensed brokers themselves. Only brokers are entitled to full commissions. Brokers may establish their own agencies and hire their own sales personnel. Often, because of their experience and expertise, brokers invest in real property and take title to some of the properties that they buy and sell. Small-town brokers may become auctioneers and receive commissions from estate and farm-equipment auctions. Many brokers offer insurance and other services related to property exchange. Some brokers become involved in developing and subdividing huge land tracts. Some move from selling residential to selling industrial properties. Industrial properties frequently must be justified by locational research, so many industrial brokers learn locational theory. Between the end of World War II and 1981, the United States enjoyed a rising market in real-estate values, making many brokers and investors who know what they are doing very rich. The long-run trend since the days of surveyor-developer George Washington has been upward for most U.S. real property. Successful real-estate selling requires skill in:

- Securing listings
- Prospecting and selling properties
- Negotiating and getting offers accepted
- Solving special problems in real-estate sales

SECURING LISTINGS

Securing listings involves (1) determining sources of listings; (2) precall preparations; (3) approaching and persuading owners to list their properties for sale or lease; and (4) getting signed listing agreements from owners. Buyers are more interested in contacting real-estate agencies that have a large selection of properties than in contacting those that do not. In most markets, securing listings is the most important facet of real-estate selling and requires the greatest part of a broker's time.

Sources of Listings

Approximately 20 percent of Americans move from their homes each year. Most of them list their homes with some agency. With this much turnover, a lot of business can be generated by a salesperson skilled in finding listers. The *newspaper* is a three-way source of potential listers. Owners who advertise in newspapers can be persuaded to list with an agency. Newspapers contain legal notices, estate-settlement notices, birth and death notices, news of plant closings and layoffs, and other information directly related to the transfer of real property. A real-estate salesperson can also use newspapers and other media to advertise directly for listings. In addition, owners who see agency advertisements of other properties for sale will sometimes contact that agency to list their property.

Files in the real-estate office can result in new listings. One of the best sources of listings is satisfied buyers or sellers who used the agency in the past. Satisfied buyers and sellers can advise other property owners in new or former neighborhoods to list with the agency. Both sources should be asked if they know anyone planning to move or sell property for any reason. Owners who previously listed with the agency and were not successful in selling within a contractual time frame may want to relist and try again. Perhaps the price they asked previously is more reasonable now and the house or property may sell this time.

Friends and acquaintances can help a real-estate agent with information. It is important for salespersons to let it be known that they are in the real-estate business and need information that could lead to clients. Many listing agents make it their business to join clubs and associations to interact with people who can furnish leads. An agent may have spotters who give direct leads on prospective listers who have retired, been promoted, gained inheritances, or moved into higher income brackets. They can also give information about plant closings or layoffs that may mean people will move. People who move into a higher income bracket may want to move up to a more luxurious home than the one they now own. Spotters may tell an agent about a family that has outgrown its old house because there are more children or the children are getting older. People contemplating a local move are prospects for both a listing and a new home and can provide a double benefit to real-estate salespersons.

Canvassing neighborhoods or prospecting by telephone can furnish listing leads. People can be asked not only about their own intentions but also about the intentions of neighbors and friends. Such leads can be developed long before any competitor finds out about them. It is probably best to use the telephone to *spot* listing prospects only. Attepts to *close* prospect listings over the phone often result in losing the prospect.

Precall Preparation

Once the name of a potential lister is obtained and before a prospect is visited, it is important to get as much precall information as possible. Selling strategy should be reviewed, selling goals set, and a sales kit prepared. Some people wish to move immediately and are willing to take any fair offer, while others are not really anxious to sell at all. Some owners wish to list at a price far above market only on the chance that someone might buy at that price— such listings are likely to be unprofitable. They require a diversion of selling time and attention from other listings, give the agency a reputation among buyers of listing at high prices, and hurt the broker's record for being able to move real estate within a reasonable length of time. Before a call, a preliminary evaluation of the property to determine a reasonable list price should be made.

A 6 percent broker's commission on an $80,000 home is $4,800! Many owners are tempted to advertise and to try to sell their homes themselves to save the commission. This is the major reason why a real-estate salesperson needs to devise a selling strategy before making a call. The owner must be convinced that the services to be received are worth the commission asked if a listing is to be gained. Most owners feel unsure of their asking price, their selling abilities, and their expertise in handling the legalities of a closing. They realize that they are at a disadvantage in market knowledge and in ability to bargain directly with buyers. Buyers might suspect that the owner's evaluation of the property would be too high unless the advice and reputation of reliable agency are involved. It is necessary, then, that the salesperson appear to the listing prospect as an informed professional, capable of doing a competent selling job. To further this appearance, real-estate salespeople should not drive older cars, dress too casually, or give evidence of representing an unprosperous agency.

Usually the salesperson sets as a first goal persuading owners to list exclusively with the agency. Under an *exclusive brokerage listing,* owners reserve the right to sell a property without paying a commission, but the broker gets a commission if an agency salesperson accomplishes the sale. Under an *exclusive right listing* agreement, the owner must pay an agency commission, even if the owner does the selling and the property is sold to a relative. Under an *open listing,* a property may be listed with many realtors, but the one who sells the property gets the commission. Under a *multiple listing* agreement, any realtor may sell and get a large share of the commission, but a part goes to the multiple listing service (which keeps track of multiple-listed properties and sales), and a part goes to the agency that secured the listing. Under a *net listing*, an agent gets all above a specified price (see Figure 18.2).

There are advantages to owners listing exclusively with one agency. The agency certain of getting commissions from its prospects tends to work harder to make sales than if properties were open-listed. Another advantage of an exlusive listing to an owner is that showings can be better coordinated with less inconvenience. Salespersons wishing to have an owner sign an exclusive agreement would do well to stress the advantages of listing with just one agency rather than emphasizing the contract exclusivity.

Finally, before approaching buyers and sellers, real-estate agents should

MEMBER
KNOXVILLE BOARD OF REALTORS
EXCLUSIVE LISTING AGENCY CONTRACT

Multiple Listing Uniform Sales Agency Contract

EQUAL HOUSING
OPPORTUNITIES

TO: _____, REALTORS   DATE: _____ 19____

In consideration of your agreement to use your best efforts to find a purchaser and to submit the property with the MULTIPLE LISTING SERVICE OF THE KNOXVILLE BOARD OF REALTORS. I hereby grant you sole and exclusive right to sell my property located _____

This agency is given for _____ months from date. The price is to be $_____
Upon the following terms: _____
_____

I agree that if this property is sold by myself or anyone else during the above stated period of time, I will pay _____% sales commission of the total price at the time of closing from the proceeds of the sale.

I further agree, if necessary, to pay a discount not to exceed _____%, and to furnish a letter stating the termite condition as required by the Mortgagee.

You are hereby authorized to place a "FOR SALE" sign on the property and to remove all other signs.

If a sale or exchange is made within _____ days after the expiration of this agency, or any extension thereof, to any party with whom Realtor negotiated during the agency period and Realtor notifies the undersigned in writing of such negotiations within _____ days after the termination of this agency, the undersigned agrees to pay Realtor the commission herein provided.

PRICE	ADDRESS	TYPE	ROOMS	BDRMS	BATHS	AREA	MLS NO.

Lot Size _____ Legal Descrp._____ Square Feet
Listing Realtor _____ Realtor No. _____ Phone_____ Up _____
Listing Salesperson _____ Phone_____ Dn _____
Owner's Full Name _____ Phone_____ Total _____

Type_____	Dishwasher_____	ROOM SIZES		CRPT	DRPS	Possession _____
Const._____	Range_____	Entry _____x_____				Mort. Bal. _____
Age_____	Disposal_____	Liv. _____x_____				Equity _____
Sewer_____	Compactor_____	Din. _____x_____				Payments_____Maturity_____
Driveway_____	Intercom_____	Kit. _____x_____				Int. Rate_____Type_____
Roof_____	Washer_____	Den _____x_____				Escrow _____
Garage_____	Dryer_____	Rec. _____x_____				City Tax _____
Carport_____	Walls_____	Bdrm. _____x_____				County Tax _____
Patio_____	Floors_____	Bdrm. _____x_____				Mortgagee _____
Deck_____	Frpl._____	Bdrm. _____x_____				Aug. Utility Costs _____
Windows_____	Bar_____	Bdrm. _____x_____				El. Company _____
T.V. Ant._____	Heat_____	_____x_____				Water Co. _____
Bus._____	Air Cond._____	Utility _____ Basement _____				Gas Co. _____

School: GR. _____ BUS_____ JR_____ BUS_____ HI_____ BUS_____
REMARKS: _____
_____

DIRECTIONS: _____

Owners _____ Res. Phone _____ Bus. Phone _____

Information regarding this property is from sources deemed reliable, but is not guaranteed by us and is subject to correction, prior sale, or withdrawal without notice.
It is understood that this listing is placed on the Multiple Listing Service of the Knoxville Board of Realtors.

AGENT _____   OWNER _____

Send Original to Board Office

Figure 18.2

have sales portfolios (or briefcases) complete with such items as real-estate forms, maps, charts, related real-estate newspaper and magazine articles, testimonials from satisfied customers, measuring devices such as tape measures and rulers, and photographs of houses at various selling prices currently listed with the agency. Having statistics and information in a professional-looking briefcase can help a realtor's image with buyers and sellers.

Persuading Potential Listers

While preapproach information and selling goals should give direction for specific approach tactics, flexibility should be maintained when meeting the owners. First, introduce yourself, identify your agency, and ask if the owners are planning to sell their property. A skilled salesperson learns to question, listens attentively and patiently, and bases the presentation appeal on an evaluation of communications feedback from prospects. It is important to find out who will probably make the listing decision. Usually, the owner who dominates the conversation and answers the questions is the decision maker. It is important to find out why the owners want to sell. A good agent can frequently detect the real reason why owners might agree to list a property.

Strategies and appeals center around seven benefits the realtor can offer to owners: (1) the agency's superior selling position and selling power; (2) the agency's ability to handle the "red tape" associated with financial and legal arrangements; (3) the agency's superior advertising power; (4) the knowledge and expert advice of agency personnel; (5) the agency's potential buyer file of those already looking for property; (6) the agency's ability to move property rapidly; and (7) the agency's capacity to move property confidentially.

The Selling-Power Strategy. When a salesperson talks with the owners, observing their situation might reveal a personal reluctance to show property or to persuade prospects. Such owners have a real need for sales professionals to accomplish these tasks. Potential listers can be reminded of both the negotiation position of the agency and the skilled selling effort that professional realtors are able to make. Most buyers tend to trust agents more than inexperienced owners. The salesperson might say: "Mr. Leverson, if you list with our agency, you will have seven expert sales professionals showing your home to prospects who are already interested in your house. We can get the top-market price that your property can command because we are trained in persuading people to make such big decisions. We put our reputation on the line. Buyers have confidence in us."

The Red-Tape Strategy. Most owners are awed by the legal papers and mortgage commitments associated with property transfers. Many owners who try to sell their own homes do not understand the alternative financial arrangements available to prospective buyers and fail to interest prospects by talking in terms of total selling price rather than monthly payments. Many sellers, too, have a suppressed fear that they might not be able to protect themselves legally—that some mistake might be made in drawing up legal papers. The agent can say something like the following to prospects who seem to have a fear of real estate "red tape": "Mrs. Dunstan, buyers are interested in more than just the selling price of your house. They are also interested in borrowing money and arranging for a good mortgage. Without the advice of realty experts, many won't feel that they are being offered the best possible loan for their particular situation. In addition, people who are not accustomed to handling the important legal paper work associated with property transfers sometimes make expensive errors or omissions and can even leave themselves open to lawsuits. Contracts and deeds must be carefully considered and prepared. Let us handle all this red tape for you. We will get the top-market dollar for your property and arrange all of the complicated details involved in transferring the real estate."

The Superior-Advertising-Power Strategy. Many owners realize that they are not skilled in writing ads or in painting signs for the front yard. An agency has advantages in several respects. Their yard signs are recognized, neat, and well appointed; their newspaper ads are skillfully worded; buyers are attracted by their total advertising effort and agency reputation; and prospects who call the agency about one property can be diverted to other properties. The agent might say: "We will put your house in the limelight, Ms. Statler. Not only will we place a well-worded ad in the newspaper, bringing out its best features, but we will put our well-known signs in your yard so prospects will know we are staking our reputation on treating you and them fairly. All of our salespeople will have a color picture of your attractive property to show prospects, and it will be displayed down at the realty office for all new potential buyers to see. We can give your house maximum exposure to the market."

The Expert Knowledge and Advice Strategy. If the salesperson makes a good, professional impression, the prospective lister might realize the advantages of the rep's superior experience in offering the property. Sales agents can go over some of the complications of the sale and instruct owners in real-estate procedures and terms. If potential listers are impressed by the complexity of the selling situation and the personality of the agent, they may be more willing to put the sales job into more competent hands than their own. "Mr. and Mrs. Mostello, your potential buyer may want an abstract, and expensive appraisal before buying directly from an owner, and special legal papers. Some prospective buyers want to know about such things as easements affecting the land. Sometimes owners who don't know about these things scare off the better prospects. Then, it becomes doubly hard for even a knowledgeable realtor to move a property. We can answer buyers' questions, and they usually trust our advice. Our presence in a transaction takes a great deal of the risk out of transferring real estate for both parties. Let our agency with its experience and expertise handle your sale for you."

The "We-Already-May-Know-a-Buyer" Strategy. This approach can take two forms. The salesperson can explain that the agency already has lists of prospective buyers looking for property like that of the sellers, or the salesperson can speculate on just what kind of buyer would most likely be interested in the owner's property and remark that the agency has many buyers in the classification. The sales agent can even go further and say a specific buyer is known who is looking for property such as the owner plans to sell. "This property with its built-ins and spacious yard would be ideal for a family like your own with several children. I know just such a family. I think they would be interested in seeing this house. It would be ideal for their children. If you list with us, I will try to get them to come over and look at it this week before they buy something else."

The "Move-It-Quickly" Strategy. Some sellers have a pressing need to sell their property in a hurry. Owners who are moved to another locality by their employers and owners who have found another property and need a down payment right away fit into this classification. A skillful salesperson can determine this from careful questioning and listening. Salespeople can explain why full-time salespeople or special listing services can give a property the maximum exposure to sell it quickly. "Mr. and Mrs. Whitney, it is to our advantage to sell your property as soon as we can. We may be able to sell it before you leave and provide you with an equity for your new home in South Dakota. You'll have a full sales force working every day representing your interests. We already have prospects who may want to buy your house. Prospective buyers, buying through a realtor, will be less likely to hesitate and engage in lengthy investigations after seeing your property. It would be advantageous if you could have your cash in hand and the deal legally closed before you leave, wouldn't it? Even if it takes a little longer than the three weeks you have left here, we could still handle the entire transfer without your having to be concerned about it."

The "We-Can-Keep-It-Confidential" Strategy. Sometimes sellers need to keep their move confidential until it is made. Persons who plan to quit their jobs and move, for example, may not want their superiors to learn of such plans, because it would give their superiors a chance to dismiss them prematurely. An executive may not want subordinates to know of a personal transfer until the executive's replacement arrives to take over. It is possible for realtors to sell a property before it becomes common knowledge that the owners plan to leave, but it is almost impossible for an *owner* to advertise without word getting around. Such a sale might take a little longer because the realtor cannot identify the home in newspaper advertising or use on-premises signs, but salespersons can discreetly show such property to prospects without fanfare and often without even neighbors suspecting. An agent might say: "Mr. Swain, it would be almost impossible for you to advertise in the newspaper, put a sign on your premises, or even tell your neighbors that your house is for sale without your employer's getting wind of it. We have prospects looking for homes like yours, and we can show your house without making your departure common knowledge. If you want to be especially careful, we can restrict showings to prospects coming to this locality from out of town. Won't you let us get things rolling and list with our agency now so we can handle this for you as quietly and as quickly as possible?"

Securing a Signed Listing Agreement from the Owner

A good approach strategy ends up in a close with a signed listing agreement from the owner. Usually, before owners will sign any kind of agreement, some understanding about the list price for their property is necessary. Owners who are willing to list only because they think they can get more for the property than its normal market value will quite naturally opt for an unrealistically high price. Other owners realize that they are not experts and that they might overvalue or undervalue their property. They may rely heavily on what a salesperson advises in pricing their property. For all these reasons, sales representatives must acquire experience in evaluating property. They do not want it to be valued too high and become a drag on the market or valued too low and rob the owners of potential equity.

The value of any property depends primarily on its location. Residential houses located in neighborhoods with responsible neighbors, nearby schools, parks, and shopping centers are worth more, other things being equal, than similar houses near industrial settings. Business property located at or near intersections of busy traffic thoroughfares with plenty of parking space have locational advantages. The pleasantness of the surroundings and the stability of the people in the area are important. Site characteristics such as air pollution, airport noise, access to waterfronts, dead-end streets, and traffic make a difference. Residential property located near trailer parks or near neighbors who don't keep up their yards, have vicious dogs, or have junk cars around has environmental defects. Property that is not well drained or that is subject to forest fires, mud slides, avalanches, earthquakes, or floods suffers in value. Evaluation also depends on the amount of square-foot space in the property, its quality of construction; its age, quality of built-ins, heating plant, air conditioning, and insulation, plus the attractiveness of space arrangements and landscaping. As can be seen, there are so many factors involved in making an appraisal that even very experienced realtors can make misestimations of thousands of dollars.

While real-estate salespersons must have some idea of the property's worth, it is up to its owner to decide on a list price. Property is often sold for about 5 percent less than the asking price. Since a broker usually has a percentage commission stake in each transaction, it is to a broker's advantage to list property at prices that will attract reasonable numbers of buyers. Some owners may even want a professional appraiser to set the list price, but even professional appraisers vary in their estimates. Most owners who list with a broker either already have in mind what they want or are willing ro rely to some degree on the agent's advice. This is why salespeople must have a reasonable idea about values.

It is a natural time to close once a listing price is decided. Unless the listing price is set too low, the market will determine the actual selling price. Salespersons should try to sell some type of exclusive agreement through the appeals of "concentrating marketing power" and organizing showings so that they will not disrupt household or business routines. "Ms. Higgs, you've decided that you should list your house for about $79,500. That seems a reasonable figure to me, considering all factors. If you'll sign an agency agreement with us, we'll apply a concentrated marketing effort to move your property as quickly and efficiently as possible. This agreement allows you to reserve the right to sell your own property should you find a buyer, but it will give us six weeks to move your property at its top-market value. What could be fairer than that?" Of course, any of the standard closes discussed in Chapter 13 can be applied to such situations. Bear in mind that listers are buying an intangible service. Because a property has emotional significance to people who have lived or worked in it for years, remember always to find something you can admire about it.

Before you leave the seller with the listing agreement in hand, make sure you have a clear understanding about showing the property and the date of possible occupancy by new owners. It is important to the sale of the property to be able to show it at times convenient to buyers as well as the owners. Every effort should be made to convince owners of the desirability of keeping the grass neatly cut and the house and yard in display condition. A potential buyer may receive a bad image if the property looks its worst when shown. Owners must be reminded that buyers in a market ultimately determine the fair price of the property, especially if the list price seems high. After the listing agreement is signed, an agent should GOQ (get out quickly) and not talk the owners out of the contract.

PROSPECTING AND SELLING PROPERTIES

The nature of a local real-estate market determines the relative importance of securing listings and finding buyers, but it is always important to have a good market for listed properties. The "persuading buyers" phase of the real-estate selling process consists of:

- Prospecting and selling a showing
- Showing the property
- Closing and getting signed offers

Prospecting and Selling a Showing

Prospecting involves finding potential buyers, qualifying buyers, and determining what buyers are really looking for in properties. If you are selling residential property, you should talk to buyers in terms of a "home" instead of a house. While seller-owners must break ties with their properties, buyers are buying the physical arrangements of their future homes. You are selling a tangible investment for the lister, and it is essential that you know all the selling points and match them with the dominant buying motives of prospects.

Sources of Prospects. After you secure a listing, knock on several *doors in the immediate neighborhood* and announce that the property is for sale. Residential and business tenants have an important stake in who moves in as their new neighbors and will often prospect to protect themselves. Almost everyone on *your lister file* will have to move, and some of them may want to move in the same community, especially if they are moving because they want a larger or more desirable home. There are many sources from which you can compile a list of people who need new property. *Friends and acquaintances, club members, and other spotters* can constantly be on the lookout for people planning a move or coming in from out of town. Organizations that are hiring more people or turning over employees rapidly are a prospect source. Persons who have been transferred in, have just been married, or who have suddenly come into more money are good prospects for new homes. Because people move so often, *former customers (listers and buyers)* can be contacted. They may be moving or know of someone who is moving and might recommend your agency. *Real-estate offices and on-premises signs* can attract walk-ins. Some of the best prospects, however, are the ones who see the *"for sale" sign* on a property. They show interest through their inquiry in a specific house in a specific location. Skillfully written *newspaper ads* interest many people in the agency's offerings. Planned "open houses" tend to attract many hard-to-qualify "lookers" with no intention of buying and can require a lot of selling time. If prospects are fairly scarce in a market, a salesperson can *call people* who are coming into the community or who plan to move to determine their intentions. *Direct-mail campaigns, bulletin-board advertising, special displays in heavy traffic areas* and even *billboard advertising* can uncover prospective buyers. Every realtor should have a *list of people looking for investment property* to take advantage of new listings suitable for that particular purpose. If the realtor has a good reputation, prospects from all of these sources will be easier to find.

Questioning and Qualifying Prospects. Many people look at real estate for entertainment. They may plan to buy some day, but for right now they are just educating themselves. Indulging such "lookers" can waste a lot of valuable selling time while neglected real buyers buy from someone else. Lookers should be treated courteously, for many of them will buy in the future. Not even the most experienced brokers are ever sure that lookers are not really planning to buy. Skilled salespersons can separate lookers from buyers through careful questioning, listening, and observing. Real buyers are usually less evasive, more willing to answer specific questions, and less defensive when pinned down than are lookers. Ask prospects what kind of neighborhood, landscaping, location, appliances, heating, and air conditioning they want or find out what price range they can afford, why they are looking for a new home or business property, and the type of furniture and cars they have, to separate out real prospects from lookers. Buyers will be more willing than lookers to give specific answers to questions about how long they have been looking and when they want to move. People who answer most of these questions are usually prospective buyers. When questioning buyers, remember to be a good listener. You must gain some idea of the main features buyers are searching for in property to show the most suitable property and get an offer. You must also find out about their financial positions.

Selling a Showing. Few people will buy real property without seeing it. Potential buyers must be convinced that it is worth their time to see a property. They must be sold on the possibility that it could very well fit their specific needs and is a good investment. Some realtors feel, however, that you should not show the best property for their needs first. Instead, you should show a less suitable listing to give a positive comparison. If possible, make an appointment for a specific time for more than one showing. The times chosen should be cleared with the owners to assure that the properties are ready to be shown.

Showing a Property

Everything about showing property should be planned. It is best if prospects ride with you in *your* car, for time to talk and listen on the way to showings is then available. You can take the most scenic route and show off the best environment and approach to the property. You can also park where your clients will have most the favorable first impression. Show off shopping centers, schools, fine homes, and other desirable features as much as you can on the drive to the property. Ask prospects questions and listen attentively to learn more about them and their real wants. Remember, too, that buyers need to know you are sincere and honest. For most buyers, it is a good idea to admit to some of the property's obvious negative features, but you must know all of the good features if negative aspects are to be overbalanced. Houses that have nice furniture in them are the more impressive, so it is better to show a house before the owners leave if possible. An owner should not participate very much in a showing, however. It is best if you do the showing, since owners are amateurs and may ruin a chance for a sale by what they say or show.

Ask leading questions and make positive statements woven around features for which prospective buyers have already expressed a desire. But listen carefully for the response and reaction. "You can buy anything you need at this shopping center, and they have an excellent supermarket. . . . Aren't the trees in this neighborhood beautiful, and this is one of the best elementary schools in the city for Mary. Those certainly are nice children playing on the swings, aren't they? . . . This spacious den is where you will spend many restful hours; and I want to show you the basement where you can do the woodworking you said you liked to do so much." You need to create images through what you say. People are looking for a home—a future. Place them positively in a future by helping them see themselves enjoying that future on that property.

Closing and Getting Signed Offers

Real property is unique. Most of it is one of a kind. Most can be sold. The most pressing reason for prospects to act now is to keep some other buyer from buying a desirable property first. Nearly all real-estate closes have an element of "standing room only." Buyers who know that other buyers are looking at and are interested in the same property are especially impressed with the need to make a decision. A rising market, too, continually pushes property prices higher and higher. If you have established the buyers' confidence in you, explained all financial and other contingencies of the sale, have thoroughly informed the buyers about all aspects of the property, and have built up desire by getting the buyers to see themselves enjoying the future intangible benefits of owning the property, you should ask for action. "Now, this excellent home, so well located with such nice neighbors, can be yours if you reserve it. It's very reasonably priced, isn't it? It has plenty of space, and the trees in the yard are beautiful. If you will just O.K. this deposit receipt, no one will be able to take it away from you." If you can close for the full amount required by the owner, you have a sure sale. If not, try getting the buyers to make a reasonable offer. "Remember, I showed you other houses in the neighborhood and told you their selling prices. The asking price for this home is well in line. Why don't you make the owner an offer? There's a chance that the owner would be willing to take a little less. This is a good buy and a good investment. Houses like this don't stay on the market for long. This one has only carried a sign for eight days. If you make a reasonable offer, I will see what the owner says."

When dealing with real estate, oral promises are useless. Any commitment by a buyer must be in writing, so get a signed deposit receipt (see Figure 18.3). Remind the buyer that a signed offer does not have to be accepted. Your real challenge begins with the offer. Encourage buyers to raise offers that are more than 10 percent below the asking price, but transmit every written offer to the seller.

NEGOTIATIONS AND GETTING OFFERS ACCEPTED

Every written offer should be transmitted to the owners and should be carried in person. It is best to see all the owners together when presenting the offer. Usually, this is a husband and wife for a residential property or the partners in a business property. Make sure you come at a time when there is no hurry and you can review the situation thoroughly. Owner-listers may have had many people look at a house and reject it at their asking price. You need to review a problem like this with the owners. Let them know if you think the offer is realistic under the circumstances and in line with the range of market values for the property. The offer should seldom be presented without a rational discussion of the reasons other prospects have rejected the property and of the problems of attracting prospects with the financial capacity to buy. Sometimes, describing prospective buyers and their side of a transaction helps. People are especially sentimental about their houses and about who will move into their neighborhood to take their place. They have emotional attachments and are interested in selling to people with whom they can identify. When a salesperson does get around to announcing the offer, it is extremely important to be alert for verbal and nonverbal reactions. The verbal comments may be negative because the owners are still bargaining, but the nonverbal signals may indicate relief or another positive attitude, indicating that a particular offer will be met with a reasonable counteroffer. Salespersons should suggest that a counteroffer be made if complete acceptance is not achieved for an offer.

Eventually, it may be necessary to get sellers and buyers together to talk over details, but it is usually best to compromise offers and counteroffers until the price has pretty much been settled. Getting bargainers together in the same place can result in personality clashes, emotionalism, and unyielding positions. When major issues *are* settled, a contract will be signed, and the house sold to its new owners.

SALES CONTRACT AND RECEIPT FOR DEPOSIT

1. The receipt of the sum of $_____ as earnest money
from _____
of _____,
hereinafter called "purchaser", is hereby expressly acknowledged by the undersigned Realtor and shall be held
by said Realtor in escrow pursuant to the terms hereof. Said sum is a part of the purchase price of
$_____ payable on the following terms: _____

for the purchase of the following premises, hereinafter called the "property", located in _____,
_____ County, Tennessee: House Number _____, Street _____,
Lot _____, Block _____, Unit _____, Subdivision _____

Purchaser hereby offers to purchase the property on the terms and conditions herein contained and acknowledges receipt of a copy hereof.

2. The above stated purchase price shall be paid fully in cash and this transaction shall be closed on
_____,
or, in the event a mortgage loan has been or is to be applied for and is so indicated above, then such payment
shall be made and this transaction closed on the day said mortgage loan is closed. It is agreed that the property
will be delivered to purchaser (A) on the day of the closing, or (B) within _____ days after the day of the
closing. (Strike out one.)

3. If a mortgage loan has been or is to be applied for and is so indicated above, then this contract
is conditioned upon purchaser obtaining such loan and if said loan is not approved, this contract may be
cancelled at purchaser's option and the earnest money will be refunded, provided, however, that purchaser
shall make a good faith effort to obtain said loan.

4. Seller shall convey the property to purchaser by a warranty deed free and clear of all encumbrances
except restrictive covenants, easements of record and _____
If marketable and merchantable title cannot be given, if title insurance cannot be secured, or if the improvements
are destroyed or substantially damaged by fire or other destructive force, the purchaser shall have the option of
enforcing this contract or cancelling the same by written notice to seller within thirty (30) days after the receipt
of written notice from seller of said defect or destruction. If cancelled, the earnest money will be refunded to
purchaser. The conveyance shall describe the grantee(s) as follows: _____

5. Property taxes are to be (A) pro-rated between the purchaser and seller as of the date of closing
or (B) assumed by the purchaser and paid when due. (Strike out one.) If taken over by the purchaser, insurance
(shall) (shall not) be pro-rated between the purchaser and seller as of the date of closing. (Strike out one.)

6. Upon seller's acceptance of this offer by signing the acceptance herein contained, this contract between the parties hereto shall become effective, provided ,however, that if the seller does not sign said acceptance and notify purchaser within _____ days from the date purchaser signs this offer, or if seller
for any reason declines to execute this agreement or approve the terms set out herein, then this offer is void
and any contract is terminated, in which case the earnest money shall be returned to purchaser. The date on
which seller signs the acceptance herein contained shall be the date of this contract.

Figure 18.3

(cont. on p. 546)

7. No representations or warranties about the condition of the property, title or title condition have been made unless stated herein. It is agreed that the purchaser is buying the property on an "as is" basis and has inspected said property unless otherwise stated herein: _____
_____

8. If purchaser fails to carry out and perform the terms of this contract, except for some permissible reason specified herein or other reason satisfactory and acceptable to seller, purchaser shall forfeit all amounts advanced as earnest money, together with all other amounts deposited with the undersigned Realtor or seller, provided however, that such forfeiture shall not preclude seller from pursuing any other remedy available to him including specific performance of the contract and an action for damages. If seller defaults in the performance of this contract, purchaser may reclaim his earnest money payment and pursue any remedy available at law.

9. This contract shall be binding upon the parties hereto and their respective heirs, executors, administrators or assigns, and, when approved by the seller, shall contain the final and entire agreement between the parties hereto, and they shall not be bound by any terms, conditions, statements or representations, oral or written, not herein contained.

10. Other terms and conditions: _____
_____
_____
_____
_____
_____
_____
_____
_____

REALTOR: _____   PURCHASER: _____

_____   _____

DATE EXECUTED: _____   DATE EXECUTED. _____

The undersigned seller accepts the foregoing offer and agrees to sell the property to purchaser on the terms and conditions therein set forth. Seller further acknowledges receipt of a copy hereof.

Seller agrees to pay _____,
the Realtor who negotiated this sale, a commission pursuant to the listing agreement between the seller and said Realtor. If purchaser shall default, said Realtor shall be entitled to one-half the earnest money or his full commission, whichever shall be smaller.

DATE EXECUTED: _____   SELLER: _____

_____

Figure 18.3 (cont.)

Insuring Future Opportunities

When special problems or challenges exist in any selling area, opportunity is greater for people who are willing and able to solve problems correctly. Three special problem challenges in residential real-estate selling that need more understanding are:

- Learning real-estate vocabulary and using the right words to sell
- Managing husband-wife and other group-buying situations
- Knowing real-estate law and mortgage arrangements

Learning Real-Estate Vocabulary and Using the Right Words to Sell

Real estate involves the use of many technical terms that describe the property itself or are used in connection with a legal property transfer and mortgaging. To sell homes, a salesperson should know the differences between a Georgian and a colonial-style house, a split-level and a tri-level, and an abstract and a guaranteed title. If you want a professional image, you must know what prospective buyers mean when they describe what they are looking for, using real-estate terms. While listers and buyers may not fully understand technical terms like "escrow," "easement," and "amortization," you should be able to explain all words associated with a particular sales situation. Your understanding of the vocabulary and the technicalities behind the terms is an important reason why sellers and buyers use the services of the agency.

Using the right *descriptive* words in the right situation is also critical to selling real estate. All descriptive words should suggest positive, pleasant images. A real-estate salesperson must first of all be a good listener, but when speaking, should use words that build a sale. Here are a few suggested words and phrases:

- Use "home" instead of "house" when talking to prospective buyers.
- Use "agency agreement" instead of "exclusive agreement" when talking to listers.
- Use "landscaped" rather than "planted" in referring to trees and shrubs.
- Use "young willow-oak shade tree" rather than "tree."
- Use "flowering azalea" rather than "bush."
- Use "sunroom" or "Florida room" rather than "glassed-in porch."

- Use "patio" rather than "paved area."
- Use "children" rather than "kids."

Managing Husband-Wife and Other Group-Buying Situations

Many times in selling a home, one of a group an agent has to convince is more enthusiastic or "sold" than the others. The temptation is to direct all attention to the enthusiastic person, and it is good to get them even more sold. However, the still unconvinced partner or spouse or other group member should not be neglected. Direct a fair part of your questions to the unconvinced party or parties, and include them in the communications. It is, after all, the unconvinced buyer-deciders who can cause you to lose a sale. It is good strategy to let husband-wife teams or partner-buyers have time together to "talk it over." If a wife, for example, is really sold on a property, she can do a much better job than a realtor can in convincing her husband that they ought to buy. The same is true of partners or groups of any kind. At least one enthusiastic person on a salesperson's side when the deciders go into conference is a must or the verdict will undoubtedly be "no." In negotiations between families or partnership groups, it is best to keep the groups from meeting together until most differences have been resolved. When many people who are amateurs at bargaining start negotiating directly with each other, emotions tend to get out of hand, yielding the harsh words that can raise resistance that will kill a sale. Salespersons must concentrate on maintaining an atmosphere of harmony at the critical point when bargaining parties meet face-to-face.

Knowing Real-Estate Law and Mortgage Arrangements

Keeping abreast of the law is not easy. A complete course in real-estate law is usually required before a person can obtain a brokerage license. Every real-estate salesperson who sells any property needs to realize that since the Open-Housing Law of 1968, it is illegal to refuse to sell to a potential buyer on the basis of race, color, religion, or national origin. Brokers in today's market must also know the latest developments in interest rates and mortgage arrangements. They can change daily. Many brokers call up mortgage houses every Monday to find out what the going interest rate is. Interest rates vary with the percent of down payment made by buyers and, of course, with economic conditions. One of the big advantages of having a real-estate agency handling a sale is that prospects can be told almost exactly how much a monthly payment will be. Prospects are more interested in knowing about monthly payments than in knowing the total asking price of a home.

SELLING INVESTMENT REAL ESTATE

Investment real estate is purchased by people who are seeking the financial benefits that ownership will bring. But not all buyers want the same benefits. The realtor who succeeds in investment real estate learns to assess the needs of the prospective buyer accurately. Each listing has different features that can produce income benefits. The realtor must discover what the personal objectives of the prospect are. Is the prospect looking for:

- A long-term capital gain or immediate income?
- A speculative opportunity despite the amount of risk involved?
- A secure and unencumbered property?
- An investment that can be leveraged to increase yield?
- A tax shelter?
- A property that can be improved through expenditure of personal time, money, and energy?
- A maintenance-free investment?

These are just a few of the many different ways listings can meet the needs of investment real estate prospects.

Unlike the emotional purchasers of a house for a home, investment real-estate prospects are hardheaded. There is little emotion in the decisions they make. Like the purchasing agents an industrial sales rep meets, investment real-estate prospects are interested in factual presentations. Like the stockbroker or investment counselor, realtors who deal in commercial and industrial property must focus their presentations on the investment facts of a purchase.

Investors are concerned with *liquidity, stability, appreciation,* and *yield* whether they are putting money into stocks, bonds, or real estate. Real estate is not a very liquid investment. As the recession that began in 1981 demonstrated, there can be disinflation in real estate if interest rates remain high. If anything, the investment real-estate market is more volatile than the residential market in the short run. In the longer run, investment real estate is comparatively stable. But it is not without risk. Investment real estate in dynamic growth areas will show little downside risk. This is also true of properties well located in large central cities. Investment real estate in areas with little growth, in rural areas, and in small towns is likely to be less stable than in areas that are growing, are urban, and are in medium-sized cities.

Not only do economic and population growth reduce risk of loss, they increase the chances for appreciation. Appreciation is an increase in *real* value. Real value means an increase that outpaces inflation. Appreciation is a major expectation of most investment real-estate prospects. Yield is the net return an investor realizes each year. The interest on a savings account is its yield. When savings-account interest is high, prospects for investment real estate will want a very high rate of return on their property investment. They will want this not because they will be heading for the nearest savings and loan but because if a near risk-free investment like a savings account is giving high yields so will other investments, many of which will contain less risk than real estate.

The selling of investment real estate is truly the big time in real-estate sales. It is a highly specialized field. Usually those who sell investment real estate are also involved with property management. The leasing of commercial and industrial buildings and of multimillion dollar shopping centers and industrial parks requires specific knowledge of the business operations of those sought as tenants. It also requires considerable expertise in putting together complex financing. Smaller commercial and industrial real-estate sales and leasing require less expert knowledge, but they must be viewed from the same perspective: the financial benefit that ownership will bring.

The investment real-estate prospect is interested in both the amount of income and its quality. Important as yield is, it is no more important than stability, appreciation, and liquidity. The best tool available to the realtor who would sell investment real estate is factual analysis of the opportunities that a listing has to meet prospect needs and sound investment criteria. Investment real estate presents both an opportunity and a challenge to even the most successful residential realtor.

SUMMARY

Selling real estate is a three-part challenge and involves selling an intangible and a tangible product at the same time. The salesperson must persuade owners to list, prospective buyers to buy or make offers, and then handle negotiations diplomatically. In most states, obtaining a brokerage license involves working as an apprentice to a broker and taking an examination. Brokers also sell related services and make lucrative investments in real property.

Listing prospects can be found by advertising in the media, contacting owners who have advertised properties for sale, having friends and acquaintances watch out for people who plan to move or who have recently come into more money, watching plant transfers and lay-offs, outright canvassing in neighborhoods, and using the telephone. Salespeople should try to find out why the owners wish to sell. They should review possible selling appeals and strategies. They should set goals about the exclusiveness of listing agreements. They should make up a sales briefcase before contacting potential listers. Most potential listers are unsure of their abilities to sell and of their technical knowledge about real-estate transfers and mortgage arrangements. Their impression of the professionalism of a salesperson is critical. After salespersons have asked questions about a property and listened attentively, they should decide on the right selling strategy. Suggested appeals include the selling-power strategy, the red-tape strategy, the advertising-power strategy, the expert knowledge and advice strategy, the "already-have-buyers" strategy, the move-it-quickly strategy, and the "we-can-keep-it-confidential" strategy. Before a listing can be closed, it is usually necessary to talk about the list price. An owner should decide this, but a salesperson should be expert enough in evaluating property to advise owners to secure realistic listing prices.

Buying prospects are looking for a "home" or a business property that will be instrumental in their future lives. After you get a listing, tell the neighbors that a property is for sale. They may help find a buyer. Prospective buyers can also be found through lister files, friends and acquaintances, organizations with employee turnover, old customers, signs, newspaper and other media ads, open houses, and investment-property prospect lists. Prospects should be carefully questioned to find out what they want. They must be persuaded to look at listed properties. Salespersons should not talk too much about a property before a prospect sees it and should then carefully note reactions. Well-selected words promoting positive images should be used in describing a property's assets. Real-estate prospects have two reasons for buying now—losing a desirable property to another buyer and a rising-price market. Summary and standing-room-only closes are particularly well suited if skillfully done. Realtors should get the asking price if possible or a reasonable offer.

The written offer should be transmitted to the owners in person and announced after a careful review of showing experiences and market indications. Owners and prospective buyers should be kept physically apart until major differences are resolved, for their personalities may conflict during face-to-face negotiations. The salesperson must try to maintain harmony when negotiators come together to sign the contract.

Three problems in real-estate selling are learning real-estate technical terms and using image-building words, managing group-buying situations, and knowing real-estate law and mortgage alternatives. A glossary of real-estate terms can help novices with the first problem. In selling to groups, get someone in the group on your side and then let the group "talk it over." Knowing real-estate law requires course study. Keeping up with mortage alternatives requires frequent inquiries to local lending agencies.

Investment real estate is purchased for different reasons than residential real estate. Not all buyers of investment real estate seek the same benefits. The elements of yield, stability, appreciation, and liquidity must be factually analyzed to meet individual prospect needs. Investment real estate is both an opportunity and a challenge to even the most experienced and successful residential realtor.

1. What does the real-estate salesperson sell to the owners of real property? To prospective buyers of real property?

2. What three steps must take place before real property can change hands?

3. In addition to sales commissions, what are some of the other sources of income for the real-estate salesperson?

4. What are the required activities of successful real-estate selling?

5. Outline the steps involved in the process of securing real-estate listings.

6. In what ways is a newspaper a source of listing prospects?

7. Suggest sources, other than the newspaper, of real-estate listings.

8. Why should real-estate salespeople avoid listing property that is priced significantly above its market level?

9. Give the reasons that a property owner might list with a real-estate salesperson.

10. Describe the five types of real-estate contracts.

11. What are the seven benefits that a real-estate salesperson can offer as an inducement to a property owner to secure a listing?

12. What factors determine the market value of a property?

13. Briefly describe the three "persuading buyers" phases of the real-estate selling process.

14. How may a real-estate salesperson impress a prospect while selling property?

15. Why should a prospect "buy now"?

16. List the three special problem challenges that characterize the selling of real estate.

APPLICATION QUESTIONS

1. This chapter mentioned several real-estate terms in the "Special Problems" section. Look up five of these real-estate terms in a dictionary. If a prospect asked you what these terms meant, what would you say?

2. Think about the place where you are now living. Make a list of the features that you would use to persuade a prospect to buy or rent this place from you. How would you describe these features in terms of the benefits they would provide to the prospect?

18–1

Kyle Kemp has worked as a salesperson for the Triple Star Agency for about seven months. He has noticed a "For Sale by Owner" sign in the front yard of an attractive ranch-style house and has found out that the house belongs to Mr. and Mrs. Henry Dodd. The sign has been in the yard for two weeks. Kyle is ringing the Dodd doorbell at 7:15 p.m. on Tuesday.

Kyle: Good evening, Mr. Dodd. I'm Kyle Kemp with the Triple Star Realtors, and I see you've offered your house for sale.

Henry: Yes ... You're the second real-estate salesman to come by. I'm afraid we're not interested in listing with an agency. We think we can sell it without paying a high commission.

Kyle: I can understand your thinking about that, Mr. Dodd. But tell me, have you had many people come in and look since you've had your sign up?

Henry: We have had about six or seven. I don't know. Maybe we want a little bit too much for it. I tell them the price, and they just look and leave.

Kyle: How much are you asking for it?

Henry: I'm asking $43,000. The Breedland house down the street sold for $39,500, and our house is worth at least $5,000 more.

Kyle: How much down, and how much would the monthly payments be for someone who bought your house?

Henry: I don't know. I figure that's up to them and their bank. I just need the cash to buy another house.

Kyle: I don't think your price is too high for your property, Mr. Dodd. When do you plan to vacate?

Henry: Well, we need to be gone by three weeks; but I feel like we'll get a buyer by then.

Mrs. Dodd comes to the door.

Alice: Why don't you invite the young man in, Henry?

Kyle: Thank you, Mrs. Dodd. I'm Kyle Kemp from the Triple Star Realtors. I'm glad to meet you.

Alice: I told Henry he should give up this idea of trying to sell our home by himself. Don't you think so?

Kyle: Well, I can understand how he feels, Mrs. Dodd. But I do believe you would have better results if you let us sell it for you. I believe we could get you what you want for it.

Henry: How's that, Mr. Kemp?

Kyle: A reputable realtor has many advantages over an individual, Mr. and Mrs. Dodd. Our agency has eleven experienced sales representatives, and we already know prospective buyers who would be interested in your home. We would advertise it in the paper and put an attractive sign in your front yard. We would arrange to show it at your convenience. I would recommend that we list your house for $44,500, which I feel is in range. You see, while buyers are interested in the list price, they are more interested in how much they have to pay down and how much each month. We could quote a monthly price and give the prospect alternatives in financial arrangements. You would be surprised what a difference this would make in response. We should be able to sell it before you leave. If you should be able to sell it by yourself, you won't have to pay the commission anyway. What could be fairer than that?"

Henry: We'll think about it and let you know, Mr. Kemp.

Alice: Henry, I think Mr. Kemp is right and knows what he's doing.

Kyle: Mr. and Mrs. Dodd, why don't you talk this over while I take another look at the outside of the house.

Ten minutes later.

Henry: Could I see that agreement, Mr. Kemp? Maybe Alice and I will let you try your hand at it if you think we could get $42,000 for it net.

QUESTIONS

1. Evaluate Kyle's approach tactics.

2. Did he ask the right kinds of questions?

3. Should he have tried to sell an exclusive rights agreement in this case before approaching with an exclusive brokerage listing agreement?

4. Was he wrong to suggest selling the house at about the same price the owner was asking for it before listing?

5. What did Kyle do right? What could he have done better?

18–2

The Galloway house has been a real problem for the Highland Realty Company. Several people have looked at the house, but in the last five months, no one has even made an offer. It was well built, but it is close to the expressway, and the neighborhood has deteriorated as many of the more affluent families have moved to the suburbs. The house is also large and thus more expensive than other houses in the midtown neighborhood. Mrs. Galloway's refusal to lower the asking price hasn't helped matters either. The house is worth more than the asking price structurally but less locationally.

Bob Callis showed the historic-looking house to a couple who seemed interested, John and Lynda Davidson. They were interested in a great deal of room at a bargain, and Bob could tell that both of them like the possibilities of redecorating the old home. They had inherited some antique furniture and needed a larger place. After they looked at the house, they went back to their apartment to think about it. Two days later, a middle-aged couple, Mr. and Mrs. Tom Overton, also saw the house. Bob mentioned in his closing tactics that another couple was extremely interested in the house. The next day, Mr. Overton called to say that he would buy the house at Mrs. Galloway's asking price. Bob called the Davidsons and told them that the house was sold. They were disappointed, but said that although they had decided to buy the Galloway house, there was another house that suited them almost as well that was listed with another realtor. Bob then went to Mr. Overton with a deposit receipt for him to sign. "My wife and I have changed our minds," he said. "We just don't feel we can invest that much in a midtown home." Bob immediately called the Davidsons, but they had already signed a deposit receipt for the other house that they were considering.

What was Bob's mistake?
Should any real estate be considered sold without getting a signature?
Is fostering buyer competition a good closing strategy?
When should he have informed the Davidsons that the house was sold?
Should he try to get the Davidsons to reconsider and make Mrs. Galloway an offer that reflects their loss of the earnest money? Would the above action be ethical?

Glossary

The following selected terms are commonly used in selling. The definitions are based on general acceptance and are related to selling. In some instances the definitions have been extended to include the practices connected with the terms.

Not all the terms or definitions included in the text appear in this glossary; only the most important or commonly used ones are given.

Above Market   A basic price policy of selling at a price above competitive prices and implies that more services and guarantees will be offered with the product and/or that the product itself has superior qualities.

Acceptance   The communicated agreement to the terms of a legal offer.

Adult Ego State   Behaving in a realistic and rational manner, using mathematics and probability in decision making.[1]

Advertising (or Telephone) Lead Method   Systematic way to locate and qualify prospects in which salespersons engage in direct mail campaigns, telephoning, print advertising, or bulletin boards to create interest in a product.

Amortize   Putting money aside for gradual payment of a debt (in real estate a mortgage payment that reduces the principle owed).

Apparent Self   How others actually view one, a component of self-image.[2]

Appraisal   An evaluation of the real estate's worth. An appraisal implies a certain amount of formality and expertise of the evaluator.

Appreciation   An increase in real value of property, an element to be factually analyzed to meet individual prospect needs.

Approach   The method by which a salesperson opens the avenue of communication between seller and buyer.

Association   A propaganda technique that encourages a prospect to accept an idea or item by relating it to something already accepted or to something desirable.

[1]Dudley Bennett, "Transactional Analysis in Management," *Personnel,* vol. 52, no. 1 (January–February 1975), pp. 34–36.

[2]C. Glen Walters, *Consumer Behavior,* 3rd ed. (Homewood, Ill.: Irwin, 1978), pp. 181–188.

The technique can also apply negatively by encouraging a prospect to reject an idea or item by relating it to something already rejected or to something undesirable.

Assorting   Alderson's theory that buyers are seeking closure and potency of assortments in making their choices.[3]

Attitudes   An individual's feelings or opinions that may be projected verbally or nonverbally.

Automatic Response Behavior   A stage of prospect decision making in which habit formation is complete and the probability of repeat purchase is very high.[4]

Baby Boom   A population group born right after World War II that has an overproportionate number of members. Because of its huge size, this group affects the selling of most products.

Bandwagon   A propaganda method that implies that everyone else is buying the product so the prospect should buy too.

Behavior System   A group of people working together toward a common goal, e.g., a company.[5]

Belief   The process whereby the body responds to the mental suggestion and produces an effect.

Below Market   A basic policy of selling below competitive market prices, and it implies that fewer frills and services will be offered with the good.

Bird Dogs   Persons who "point out" or designate prospects for the salesperson.

Breadth of Consideration   The range of alternatives contemplated by a person. It expands the choice of selection or the depth of inclusion.

Buffer   A person who screens salespersons to protect the time of a superior and who can be a barrier to obtaining an interview with a prospect. A buffer can also be an ally in obtaining an audience with an important prospect.

Build-up Method   A method of estimating territorial potential that entails identifying possible customers, finding out how many are in the territory, and determining the average amount each is expected to purchase. Multiplying the number of customers by the average amount each is expected to purchase gives the potential for that territory.[6]

"Business Cycle"   A rhythmic pattern of inevitable, uncontrollable ups and downs in economic activity.

Buying-Power Method   A territorial-potential-estimation method based on buying-power indices of the territory under consideration.[7]

---

[3]Wroe Alderson, *Marketing Behavior and Executive Action* (Homewood, Ill.: Irwin, 1957), pp. 195–214.

[4]John A. Howard, *Marketing Management,* rev. ed. (Homewood, Ill.: Irwin, 1963), pp. 33–113.

[5]Alderson, *op. cit.* pp. 35–97.

[6]Philip Kotler, *Marketing Management,* 2nd ed. (Englewood Cliffs, N.J.: Prentice-Hall, 1972), p. 205.

[7]*Ibid.,* p. 207–208.

Caste A social system in which the position of members is fixed at birth and cannot be changed up or down.

Canvass A method of prospecting that is not selective and involves knocking on every door to assure that every possible lead is uncovered.

Card-Stacking A propaganda method that involves getting one-sided arguments for a product; a failure to give a balanced evaluation of your product or your competitor's product.

"Categorical Imperative" An act that is, of itself, objectively necessary.

Center-of-Influence Method Systematic way to locate and qualify prospects in which salespersons use influential people to help them find prospects.

Child Ego State Behaving in a way reflecting behavior patterns learned in the pre-school years, characterized by defensive and emotional reactions.[8]

Class A social system in which individuals can move upward or downward, the class being made up of people who tend to share similar values and to be similar in behavior.

Closing A distinct verbal and/or nonverbal attempt by the salesperson to get prospects to obligate themselves to buy the product.

Closing Signals Cues given by the prospect that indicate an opportunity to close a sale.

Cold-Canvass Method Systematic way to locate and qualify prospects in which salespersons call on every prospect who might have a use for a product.

Communications An exchange of information, feelings, or emotions among individuals or groups based on common spheres of experience.

Communications Structure The means by which messages are transmitted from the power unit to the members of a behavioral system and vice versa to effect coordination of activity toward a common goal or goals.[9]

Company Knowledge Facts about the company, i.e., its history, size, place in the industry, its policies, etc.

Complex Problem Solving Encourages the use of maximum thought, concentration, and consideration of alternatives.[10]

Connotation Refers to secondary associations that a word has that may differ among members of a language group.

Consideration Money, written promises, or goods given to show intent to enter a contract.

Conspicuous Consumption A term coined by economist Thorstein Veblen, who used it to describe the tendency of people to be motivated by status; the tendency of people to buy to "show off."

---

[8]Bennett, *loc. cit.*
[9]Alderson, *op. cit.,* pp. 35–50.
[10]Based on Wroe Alderson and Paul E. Green, *Planning and Problem Solving in Marketing* (Homewood, Ill.: Irwin, 1964), pp. 72–76.

Consumerism Trend in cultural changes reflecting the tendency of consumers to question sellers.

Contract An agreement that can bind you and your company to perform that which you promised. A valid contract usually involves an offer, acceptance of an offer, consideration in the form of money or promises, parties with the capacity to contract, and a legal objective.

Contraction A phase or economic fluctuations in which a new, lower turning point is reached.

Culture The structure that results from people's interrelationships with each other and with groups.

Customer Orientation The marketing philosophy and attitude that all marketing efforts should be directed toward satisfying the customer while making a profit or satisfying the firm's goals.

Customers The people to whom sales have already been made.

Cybernetic Model A simplification comparing the mind and nervous system to the control and computing mechanisms of data-processing machines, such as computers.[11]

Decoder The person interpreting the communications message for the receiver.

Demonstration Selling technique that allows a prospect to personally inspect, handle, or operate a product, experiencing its benefits or features firsthand.

Denotation Indicates associations that a word has for most people.

Deposit Receipt A receipt for the buyer's earnest money that is given to show intent to buy the property. Signing the deposit receipt is similar to signing a purchase order for the real property.

Development The marketing arm that raises the extra monies needed to sustain the existence of not-for-profit enterprises.

Digestive Stage A stage in creativity consisting of working over information and material gathered, and sorting it into as many kinds of meaningful combinations as can be thought of.[12]

Distinctiveness The first phase of the fashion cycle, in which the product is popular with an elite, first-accepting group.[13]

Dominant Theme A main plan; a unified pattern or purpose that is recognized as more important than secondary goals.

"Due Care" Consideration sellers must use in designing, manufacturing, preparing, inspecting, or selling goods.

Durable Goods Tangibles, such as cars, etc.

---

[11]Based on Maxwell Maltz, *Psycho-Cybernetics* (Englewood Cliffs, N.J.: Prentice-Hall, 1960).

[12]C. H. Sandage and Vernon Fryburger, *Advertising: Theory and Practice* (Homewood, Ill.: Irwin, 1975), pp. 289–291.

[13]Jerome McCarthy, *Basic Marketing,* 5th ed. (Homewood, Ill.: Irwin, 1975), p. 235.

Duress Undue influence exerted over a buyer.[14]

Early Adopter A person who is not the first to accept a new product or idea but accepts it soon after the first accepters do. They are usually opinion leaders in the local social system.[15]

Early Majority (Adopter) The first half of the majority of people who accept a new idea or product.[16]

Easement A legal right or permission that one person has concerning the land of someone else (the landowner).[17]

Economic Emulation The phase of the fashion cycle in which most socioeconomic groups have accepted and can afford the style. The style may be mass-produced and lose its distinctiveness as a mode of expression.[18]

Ego State A role reference out of which a person acts and communicates to produce recognizable patterns of behavior. In transactional analysis the person acts and communicates out of the child, the parent, or the adult.[19]

Emotional Buying Motives Those that involve persuasion through direct or indirect appeals to a person's emotions.

Emulation The phase of the fashion cycle in which a style is popular in middle socioeconomic groups. They wish to copy the elite group who first accepted the style as fashionable.[20]

Encoder A person who formulates or expresses a communication message for a sender in order to promote its effectiveness.

Endless-Chain Method Systematic way to locate and qualify prospects in which salespersons use letters of testimony or notes of introduction to further prospects.

Enthusiasm Inspired zeal, interest, or conviction that is communicated to others and that may be promoted by increased knowledge, positive attitudes, health, or more noticeable nonverbal activity.

"Escrow" Putting a sum of money in the care of a third party until a contract is fulfilled.

Estate A social system in which the position of members is determined by land tenure or the holding of an estate.

Esteem Need Maslow's level of need at which a desire for prestige and reputation functions.[21]

Ethical Conduct The practice of conforming to accepted standards of conduct.

---

[14]Michael P. Litka, *Business Law* (Harcourt, Brace & World, 1970), p. 153.

[15]Everett M. Rogers, *Diffusion of Innovation* (New York: Free Press, 1962), pp. 169–171.

[16]*Ibid.*

[17]*Webster's New World Dictionary* (New York: World Publishing, 1966), p. 455.

[18]McCarthy, *loc. cit.*

[19]Eric Berne, *Transactional Analysis in Psychotherapy* (New York: Grove Press, 1961), pp. 17–22.

[20]McCarthy, *loc. cit.*

[21]A. H. Maslow, "A Theory of Human Motivation," *Psychological Review,* vol. 50 (1943), pp. 370–376.

Ethics   The study of the rightness and wrongness of human behavior.

Exclusive Brokerage Listing   A listing under which the owner reserves the right to sell the property without paying a commission, but the broker gets the commission if an agency salesperson accomplishes the sale.

Exclusive Dealing Contracts   Monopolistic practice prohibited by the Clayton Act of 1914.

Exclusive Right Agreement   An agreement for selling real estate under which the broker gets the commission regardless of who sells the property, if the sale is made within the time limits of the agreement.

Expansion   A phase of economic fluctuations, moving up from "revival."

Extensive Problem-Solving Behavior   A stage of prospect decision making in which buyers seek information to solve problems and are most receptive to selling appeals.[22]

Extroverts   People who like to talk, care little for formality, and react to a sales representative's personality when considering a proposal.

Fashion Cycle   A progression of stages concerning the knowledge and use of a product.[23]

Feedback   Indications from the receiver of a message whether or not the purpose of the message has been carried out.

Feminism   A belief that women should have rights equal to men in all respects.

Fraud   The misrepresentation of an important fact that is knowingly and deceitfully made to induce a buyer to rely and act on that misrepresented fact to the buyer's detriment.[24]

Free Gift (or Sample) Approach   The method by which gifts or free samples may be used by a salesperson in order to secure the time and interest of a prospect.

Freud's Theory   Indicates that people buy things because of subconscious influences.[25]

Games   Structuring of situations by a person in order to secure positive stroking.

Goal Definition   An expressed determination of purpose, preferably in concise writing, that can be used as a planning basis for goal achievement.

Goal Visualization   The practice of seeing yourself achieving goals in your imagination.

Goodwill   A favorable attitude customers and prospects have about you and your company that assures that your offering will be favorably considered in the future. Goodwill is worth money and is an asset to a business.

Green River Ordinances   The first legislation restricting salespersons from calling on customers door-to-door.[26]

---

[22]Howard, *loc. cit.*

[23]E. Jerome McCarthy, *Basic Marketing,* 7th ed. (Homewood, Ill.: Irwin), p. 246.

[24]Ronald A. Anderson and Walter A. Kumpf, *Business Law,* 6th ed. (Cincinnati: Southwestern, 1975), pp. 220–224.

[25]Philip Kotler, "Behavioral Models for Analyzing Buyers," *Journal of Marketing,* vol. 29, no. 4 (October 1965), pp. 37–45.

[26]Theodore N. Beckman, William R. Davidson, and W. Wayne Talarzyk, *Marketing,* 9th ed. (New York: Ronald Press, 1973), p. 247.

Hardware The physical product as opposed to the intangibles such as programming and maintenance services that are sold as part of the total offering. Services are designated as software to distinguish their importance.

Hobbes' Model Buyers are guided by group and individual goals.[27]

"Hot Doorknobs" The salesperson's fear, before approaching a prospect, of being rejected.

Hot Prospect A prospect who is ready to buy now and deserves immediate attention.

Ideal Self How a person would like to be ideally.[28]

Illumination Stage A stage in creativity when insight causes all the mentally stored elements to come together into a recognizable whole that transfers from the subconscious to the conscious mind.[29]

Imagined Experience Mental practice whereby one imagines an expected experience in a positive manner, thereby inhibiting negative beliefs.

Implied Warranty A guarantee assumed with regard to every product, unless effectively disclaimed, of fitness for a particular purpose.[30]

Incremental Method A method for determining the number of salespersons needed. This method involves hiring additional salespersons as long as the estimated sales generated by that additional person yield a profit.[31]

Incubation Stage A stage in creativity consisting of allowing the subconscious mind to organize information and data and to suggest solutions.[32]

Innovator A person who is one of the very first to accept a new product or idea. Innovators are usually wealthier, younger, and more willing to take risks than later accepters. Usually, innovators are more interested in social systems outside of their home social systems and might be characterized as being cosmopolitan or "jet set."[33]

Inputs and Outputs A dominant characteristic of every economic behavior system, according to Wroe Alderson. A firm is such a system.[34]

"Insiders" Image The view that certain people belong to a particular group because of their use of words, their knowledge, or their understanding.

Intangible Salesperson A salesperson who sells a service rather than a tangible product.

Internal Environment The political, social, or other environments within the firm or system for which you work.

---

[27]Kotler, *loc. cit.*

[28]Walters, *op. cit.,* pp. 183–185.

[29]Sandage and Fryburger, *loc. cit.*

[30]Anderson and Kumpf, *op. cit.,* pp. 198–208.

[31]Richard R. Still, Edward W. Cundiff, and Norman A. P. Govoni, *Sales Management,* 3rd ed. (Englewood Cliffs, N.J.: Prentice-Hall, 1976), pp. 63–68.

[32]Sandage and Fryburger, *loc. cit.*

[33]Rogers, *loc. cit.*

[34]Alderson, *loc. cit.*

Introverts Quiet, studious people who may be suspicious of salespersons.

Kondratiff Cycles Cycles that indicate an extreme recession or depression every fifty years because of an overburdensome debt structure.

Laggard A person who accepts a new idea only after the majority of people have accepted it or a person who will never accept the new idea or product. Laggards may be old, uneducated, poor, and socially isolated.[35]

Later Majority Adopter The last half of the majority of people to accept a new idea or product.[36]

Lead A person or firm that may be a prospect but has not yet been qualified and put into the prospect category.

Leadership Model The example set by a manager to provide a guide for subordinate personnel.

Learning A permanent change in behavior usually caused by repetitive experience or practice.

Life Positions The situations in which people "transact" from one ego state to another.[37]

Limited Problem-Solving Stage A stage of prospect decision making in which buyers consider purchases briefly, based on past experience, but are still open to consideration of alternative products.[38]

Liquidity An element to be factually analyzed to meet individual prospect needs, easily converting real estate into cash.

Listing Real property that is offered by a real-estate agency that has a signed agreement authorizing the agency to sell the property (a listing agreement with the owner).

Long-Run Economic movements that indicate serious contractions are likely to take place every fifty years or so.

Lookers People who want to look at the product but who have little intention of buying at the present time.

Love, Affection, and Belonging Need Maslow's level of need at which the satisfaction-release-motivation cycle repeats itself and an individual needs emotional satisfactions.[39]

Management by Objectives or MBO The joint determination of goals by a manager and a subordinate that usually entails subgoal setting or definite plans about how to reach the major goals.

Manufacturer's Salesperson A salesperson directly employed by a manufacturer to sell products.

[35]Rogers, *loc. cit.*
[36]*Ibid.*
[37]Heinz Weihrich, "MBO: Appraisal with Transactional Analysis," *Personnel Journal,* vol. 55, no. 4 (April 1976), pp. 173–175.
[38]Howard, *loc. cit.*
[39]Maslow, *loc. cit.*

Market People who have a need or want for a product and who can get the money to buy it.

Marketing Those activities necessary to assure that the right goods and services are moved efficiently to satisfied customers through the right channels, at the right price, and using the right promotional combinations.

Marshall's Economic Model The buyer as rational, calculating individual determined to get maximum satisfaction from money.[40]

Mediocrat A closer who has given ample but not superior service to an expert buyer.[41]

Message Channel An element of communication concerning the way a message is transmitted and the clarity of a communication.

Missionary Salesperson A salesperson who trains *dealer* sales representatives who are not employed by his or her company.

Model An ideal form of something, a simplified representation of reality, containing the essentials of a problem to be solved.

Modeling The work of a person who demonstrates a model.

Modern Selling Guides people to buy through reducing their perceptions of risk by supplying information about the product or service and assurances on the wisdom of purchasing it.

Motive An inner mental state that causes a person to act. A motive usually results from a dissatisfaction or a recognized need.

Multiple Listing Agreement A real-estate contract under which many brokers may sell the property. The realtor who sells usually gets a larger share of the commission, but a part also goes to the multiple listing service.

Name Calling A propaganda method that involves associating a competitive product with something undesirable by giving it a bad label.

Nest-Builders Recently married persons establishing their product needs for their new stage in the life cycle.

New Listing A listing agreement under which the agent gets all above a specified price.

Observation Method Systematic way to locate and qualify prospects in which salespersons gather information on prospects that will lead to sales opportunities.

Objection A communicated resistance to buying that usually consists of a specific reason for not complying with a salesperson's suggestions.

Offer A proposal to another person or group of people that constitutes a contract when accepted.

Offeree The person or persons to whom the offer is made.

Offerer The person or entity making the offer.

---

[40]Kotler, *loc. cit.*

[41]Barry J. Hersker and Thomas F. Stroh, "The Purchasing Agent is No Patsy," in *Closing the Sale* (special report), *Sales & Marketing Management,* June 13, 1977.

Open Listing A listing under which a property may be listed with many realtors, but the one who sells the property gets the commission.

Order-Getting Representative A salesperson who must frequently employ skilled persuasive efforts to convince prospects and make a sale.

Order-Making Representative A salesperson who uses imagination and creativity, interjecting new ideas into sales situations.

Orders Written offers solicited from customers by sales representatives.

Order-Taking Representative A salesperson who sells to customers without extensive persuasive efforts or creative closing techniques.

Other-Directed Prone to consider social pressures and influences or reference groups in making buying decisions.

Overlearning The practice of memorizing material beyond the point where you are able to recall it correctly.[42]

Overmotivation Motivation or ambition so strong that it causes a deterioration in effective action or health.

Parent Ego State Behaving in the way a person's parents seemed to act toward them when they were children, exhibiting judgmental, authoritative, dominant, arbitrary, and demonstrating a superior attitude.[43]

Patronage Motives Those which reflect a decision to buy from one source instead of from its competitor.

Pavlov's Learning Model The customer as a learner, sensitive to reinforcement, drives, and cues.[44]

Performance Features Features relating to a product's abilities to accomplish its purpose or capabilities.

Personality The sum total of traits, attitudes, and other attributes that characterize an individual and determine the reaction of other people toward that individual.

Personality Factor Any element that characterizes an individual (such as attitudes and traits), that is projected through verbal or nonverbal communications, and that is important in determining how others react toward that person.

Personal Selling Leading people to buy by reducing their risks through information and assurances in an atmosphere of harmony rather than conflict.

Persuasion An open appeal to reason or emotion in an effort to influence someone to do or believe something.[45]

Physiological Need Maslow's basic level of need, comprising the body needs of an individual.[46]

---

[42]Louis F. Basinger, *The Techniques of Observation and Learning Retention* (Springfield, Ill.: Thomas, 1973), p. 45.

[43]Bennett, *loc. cit.*

[44]Kotler, *loc. cit.*

[45]*Webster's New World Dictionary, op. cit.*, p. 1092, "Persuade."

[46]Maslow, *loc. cit.*

Plan   A preformulated pattern of intended actions. Planning is the act of prethinking and prescheduling activities.

Planning by Objectives   The act of preformulating activities in accordance with clear and concise objectives that are set by an individual specifically for the purpose of making effective plans.

Positional Behavior   Competitive behavior among members of a firm or behavioral system for higher positions in the firm or maintaining a position in the firm. Such rivalry can be a detriment to the firm.[47]

Power Principle   Acting in such a way as to promote the power to act.[48]

Power Symbol   A representation of status of power in a system such as the large office of a superior.[49]

Power Unit   A group of people (or a person) who make the decisions in a behavioral system and coordinate the activities of the members toward a goal.[50]

Preapproach   Involves all the necessary preparations that must be completed before a target prospect is called on.

Preparatory Stage   A stage in creativity consisting of accumulating facts and data concerning a specific problem while keeping an open mind.[51]

Presentation   The main persuasive effort of a salesperson, designed to produce most of the "change of mind" that brings about a sale.

Preventive Maintenance   Giving attention to a system on a regular basis to prevent a breakdown that might disrupt operations.

Price Discrimination   A monopolistic practice that entails supplying certain buyers at one price and other buyers at another price, prohibited by the Clayton Act of 1914.

Privacy Bubble   An imaginary space surrounding the body. A person can become uncomfortable if this space is penetrated by another person who is not a close acquaintance. The space varies with different cultures but extends about two feet for most Americans.[52]

Product   The entire unit offering to the customer that includes the services and warranties associated with the product.

Product Features   A product's or a service's characteristics and benefits to a buyer.

Product Knowledge   Information supplied by a salesperson to a buyer concerning the purchasing environment, delivery, credit, installation, training in use, warranties, advertising, maintenance, and other services relating to a product.

Prospect   A person or firm who needs or wants a product or service and has the ability to buy.

Prospect Book   A record where prospect information is recorded for future use.

[47]Alderson, *op. cit.,* p. 46.
[48]Alderson, *ibid.,* p. 51.
[49]*Ibid.,* p. 42.
[50]*Ibid.,* p. 36.
[51]Sandage and Fryburger, *loc. cit.*
[52]Julius Fast, *Body Language* (New York: M. Evans, 1970), pp. 45–49.

"Protean" A term used to describe career seekers and planners who are aware of the shape of the future and what form of activity is needed to experience goal achievement.

Psychocybernetics The application of the principles of cybernetics to the human brain. (See Cybernetic Model.)[53]

Public Relations Those activities designed to sell corporate images and build good relationships with all organizational publics.

Purpose Tremor Nervousness caused from the fear of approaching a challenging task.[54]

Quadrant One of four equal parts into which a scene may be divided for observation purposes.

Qualifying a Prospect Determining whether a prospect has a need or desire for the product, the means to buy it, and the eligibility to buy it.

Quotas Sales goals and sets of guiding standards set to motivate sales representatives.

Rapport A harmonious relationship.

Rational Buying Motives Those that reflect a rational, scientific, and economical rationale in purchasing.

Real-Estate Broker A person licensed by the state to sell and transfer real property and receive a commission.

Real Self The way people really are as opposed to what they think about themselves or what others think about them.[55]

Recession A phase of economic fluctuations, an upper turning point having been passed.

Reciprocity A mutual business exchange that usually precludes competition from influencing either of the participants. A reciprocity agreement would be one in which one firm agrees to buy the products of another firm if the second firm will, in turn, buy the products of the first firm.

Recruiting Picking the members of the selling team. (See Selecting.)

Reduced Cues Incomplete indications or cues that require the individual to fill in the gaps mentally to get the picture. If the filled-in parts are wrong, the wrong image or interpretation results.

Reference-Group Influences A trend in cultural changes, referring to the importance of the opinions of the consumer's peer groups.

Reference-Group Self How people think others see them, a component of self-image.[56]

Reprogramming A redirection of attitudes and habitual mental approaches to a problem or task to effect results that will be superior to those gained using older habitual mental sets.

[53]Maltz, *op. cit.*, p. 159.
[54]*Ibid.*, p. 17.
[55]Walters, *loc. cit.*
[56]Walters, *loc. cit.*

Résumé A concise summary of your experience and qualifications sent to a prospective employer. A résumé should also be regarded as an advertisement for your services and a possible ticket for admission to an interview.

Retail Salesperson A sales representative who customarily sells to customers who are buying goods for ultimate consumption.

Revival A phase of economic fluctuations, moving from a low point upward.

Safety and Security Need Maslow's level of need at which a person's security is threatened, tensions develop, and threats to security become motivators.[57]

Sales Management The planning, organizing, leading, controlling, and securing of personnel for the activities of the selling team.

Sales-Potential Method Method for determining the number of salespersons necessary to serve on the sales force. The method entails dividing the yearly dollar sales volume each salesperson can reasonably be expected to obtain into the forecasted sales volume, making allowances for salesperson turnover.[58]

Selecting Picking the members of the selling team. (See Recruiting.)

Self-Actualization Need Maslow's level of need at which a need to reach one's full potential functions.[59]

Self-Image The sum total of the personality traits, attitudes, and other qualities people attribute to themselves.[60]

Showing A demonstration of real property. A persuasive tour of real property given by the salesperson to the real-estate prospect.

Signal The way the message is sent and the clarity of communication.

Skimming A price policy for new products that indicates a strategy of selling the product initially at high prices to get as much as possible from those willing to pay top-dollar for the new product. Later, prices are expected to be lowered.

Social Stratification The system of social hierarchies emerging within a society.

Software A term used in the computer and complex-equipment industries to refer to the services, programming, and maintenance elements of the total offering as opposed to the physical product (the hardware or machine itself). The software is important in determining the total effectiveness of the equipment in use.

Source The originator of a communications message.

Spotter A person who "points out" or designates prospects for the salesperson.

Spotter Method Systematic way to locate and qualify prospects in which salespersons use people who look out for prospects for them.

Stability An element to be factually analyzed to meet individual prospect needs, the likelihood of a neighborhood to change and cause a change in real estate values.

---

[57]Maslow, *loc. cit.*
[58]Still, *loc. cit.*
[59]*Ibid.*
[60]Walters, *loc. cit.*

Star Salesperson An outstanding or favored salesperson in the firm, usually distinguished by a superior selling record.

Strokes Encouragement, either positive or negative, that reinforces behavior, an important part of interpersonal communication.

Style Obsolescence Stimulates buying, when people become dissatisfied with serviceable but out-of-style items.

Success Successful people exhibit a sense of commitment, striving to do the best they can, making remarkable progress, and having a need for continuing improvement.

Supervisory Style The projection of a manager's leadership qualities stemming from assumptions managers make about their subordinates and the basic approaches they take to motivate them.

Supporting Sales Representatives Salespersons who are more involved in sales-supporting activities than in actually closing sales.

Synthetic Experience Visualizing and preliving an experience through the imagination as a substitute for actual experience.[61]

System A group of parts combined to accomplish a certain purpose.

System Pathologies "Illnesses" in human undertakings that come about because of weaknesses in the power unit, the communications structure, the inputs, or because of a lack of adjustment to internal and external environmental changes.

Systems Thinking Taking a total view of problems and opportunities and thinking beyond them, through evaluation of the effects of a series of planned moves on every component of the system.

Testimonial A verbal or written endorsement of a product, service, or idea by someone other than the salesperson. Testimonials are usually solicited from satisfied and respected customers.

Title The evidence of ownership, usually a printed deed, that a buyer of property obtains upon purchasing real property.

Total Buying Situation Consists of information concerning the corporate decision unit and all pertinent facts about a corporation gathered by a salesperson prior to a potential sale.

Tradition-Directed Prone to consider long-standing and traditional influences in buying products.

Transactional Analysis The attempt to identify the ego state people are using as references when they communicate in order to formulate suitable strategy to improve communications.[62]

Trial Close An attempt to find out if the prospect is ready to buy without actually insisting on a final decision on the total offer.

[61]Maltz, *op. cit.*
[62]Berne, *loc. cit.*

Two-Step Flow Effect   The flow of communication from a source, through media and to opinion leaders, who influence mass acceptance of an idea.[63]

Tying Agreements   Monopolistic practice prohibited by the Clayton Act of 1914.

Veblen's Concept   Most consumption is motivated by prestige seeking with reference to a buyer's social class, reference groups, and family pressures.[64]

Walk-In   An applicant who applies for a sales job in person at the place of employment, without an appointment or previous communications.

Warranty   A guarantee or assurance about a product or service.

Warranty Deed   A deed to real estate containing a guarantee of title.

Wholesale Salesperson   A sales representative who works for a wholesaler. Usually such representatives sell service with the product.

Word Attributes   Overtones of words, concrete or abstract, active or passive, emotional or neutral, and holy or profane.

Work-Load Method   A method of determining the amount of salespersons needed. The method involves classifying customers into categories by importance to sales volume, determining how long interviews should be with each class customer, and determining how many calls should be made on each class. The number of salespersons needed is derived from dividing the interview hours one salesperson might be expected to spend in the field in interviews into the number of hours necessary to serve the market.[65]

Yield   Both the amount of income and its quality; in real estate, an element to be factually analyzed to meet individual prospect needs.

Youth Image   The view that a person is young because of projected appearance and actions.

---

[63]Elihu Katz, "The Two-Step Flow of Communication," *Journalism Quarterly* (Spring 1955), pp. 13–146.

[64]Kotler, *loc. cit.*

[65]Still, *loc. cit.*

Index

About The Author

Richard F. Wendel is Professor of Marketing at the University of Connecticut. In his thirteen years there, he has taught nearly every marketing course offered. He was acting Department Head from 1970 through 1974.

A former sales representative and sales manager, Wendel has published several articles on personal selling, many with Charles L. Lapp. The sixth edition of his *Marketing 83/84,* a collection of readings, appeared in 1982. He has conducted management development seminars on personal selling and its management from coast to coast.

Professor Wendel has a Ph.D. in economics from the University of Pennsylvania and an M.B.A. in marketing from its Wharton School. His undergraduate work was done at Augustana College in Rock Island, Illinois.

Dr. Wendel is a member of the American Marketing Association and was on the editorial staff of the "Marketing Abstracts" section of the *Journal of Marketing.* Currently, he is president of the Alpha of Connecticut chapter of Beta Gamma Sigma. Before returning to do doctoral work at Pennsylvania, he was a senior sales representative for Kordite Corporation and had been Assistant to the President of Flexonics Corporation of Maywood, Illinois.

Between 1951 and 1955, Dr. Wendel served with U.S. Air Force as an Aircraft Observer in the Strategic Air Command in the U.S. and Korea and was an instructor at the Senior Observer Training School at Mather Air Force Base at Sacramento, California.